COVERING CONFLICT

The making and unmaking of new militarism

Richard Lance Keeble

Published 2017 by Abramis academic publishing

www.abramis.co.uk

ISBN 978 1 84549 710 1

Printed and bound in the United Kingdom

Abramis is an imprint of arima publishing.

arima publishing
ASK House, Northgate Avenue
Bury St Edmunds, Suffolk IP32 6BB
t: (+44) 01284 700321

www.arimapublishing.com

About the author

Richard Lance Keeble is Professor of Journalism at the University of Lincoln and Visiting Professor at Liverpool Hope University. He has written and edited 36 books on a wide range of topics: including newspaper reporting skills, media ethics, peace journalism, investigative reporting, literary journalism, humour and journalism, profile writing. In 2011, he was given a National Teaching Fellowship, the highest award for teachers in higher education in the UK, and in 2014 he received a Lifetime Achievement Award from the Association for Journalism Education. He is joint editor of *Ethical Space: The International Journal of Communication Ethics* and *George Orwell Studies* and is chair of the Orwell Society.

Contents

Out of control?: The military/industrial/intelligence/media complex

By 1991, I had been seven years teaching on the International Journalism MA programme at City University London and was due a full year's sabbatical. What a privilege! But what to research? I first thought of conducting an ethnographic study of London-based defence correspondents but the MoD quickly said no to my requests for access. Earlier in the year the Gulf 'war' had exploded – so there was my topic. I had actually been profoundly shocked by the US-led attacks on a largely defenceless country leading to thousands of unnecessary deaths. I had also been shocked by the appalling coverage it had received in the corporate press. Too often the journalists reproduced the mindless rhetoric of the military – dismissing the Iraqi 'enemy' as animals to be slaughtered. Researching the conflict in depth could help provide some explanations for what I considered the unnecessary explosion of high-tech barbarism.

I was lucky in that I was living close to Cambridge and so spent hour after hour buried in books and newspapers in the wonderful university library. Every text, every academic journal I needed was close at hand. By the end of my sabbatical I had written 60,000 words. Over the next four years, while running the BA in Journalism and a Social Science at City, I completed the thesis which John Libbey, of Luton, published in 1997 as *Secret state, silent press: New militarism, the Gulf and the modern image of warfare*. I have to thank the late Manuel Alvarado, of Libbey, who took on the publishing of what was to be my first major piece of research – and to the two heads of journalism at City, Hugh Stephenson and Rod Allen who, in different ways, supported me.

This new text is, in effect, a second, updating edition of *Secret state* though, for reasons of space, it concentrates largely on the UK instead of both the UK and US. While I was researching the Gulf conflict of 1991 I was hoping it would be the last expression of US/UK militarism – at least for some time. Alas, this has not

1

proved to be the case. The major Western powers have effectively been constantly at war since then. The military/industrial/intelligence/media complex appears out of control. The US-led attacks on Afghanistan in 2001 and Iraq in 2003 were conceived in 'new militarist' terms – in that they were quickly concluded with 'victories' rapidly proclaimed against relatively puny opposition. Yet since 2001, Western military adventures wasting billions of dollars (which could so easily have been directed at socially useful projects) have turned into appalling quagmires – leading to massive civilian casualties, unprecedented refugee crises and levels of joblessness. New militarism has been transformed into disaster militarism.

SECRECY A CENTRAL THEME

Secrecy is a central theme in *Covering conflict*. The hyper-coverage of the 1991 conflict gave the appearance of transparency. Indeed, following the rapid assaults by the Western powers against puny, Third World states (Falklands 1982; Grenada 1983; Libya 1986; Panama 1989) a Big Victory needed to be *seen to be won* against a Big Enemy – if only to help 'kick the Vietnam syndrome' and (with the Soviet Union in terminal decline) provide a *raison d'être* for the rapidly expanding military/industrial/intelligence/media complex. Hence the manufacture of 'Saddam' as a global threat and credible enemy. But, in fact, the spectacle of the conflict mostly served to hide (and, effectively, keep secret) the reality in which up to 250,000 Iraqi soldiers were eliminated in a 42-day assault. One slaughter followed another. In 2016, the 25th anniversary of the conflict passed by unnoticed in the corporate media. Strange how such horrors can be quietly forgotten (Keeble 2016a).

Moreover, Fleet Street's ties to the secret state were crucial to the manufacture and representation of the conflicts from 1982 through to the assault on Libya in 2011. Hence, the chapter devoted to the ties that bind the hacks and spooks is placed prominently in *Covering conflict* to reflect its importance in providing crucial context to the overall study. An early study was published in Jeffery Klaehn's *The political economy of media and power* (New York: Peter Lang 2010 pp 87-111). The new chapter expands considerably on that work.

The focus here throughout is on the corporate media – though the critique draws on a wide range of alternative, activist, progressive sources (books, websites, journals). Throughout the stress is as much on what the media miss as what they cover: the silences as much as all the noise of the newspapers. Moreover, *Covering conflict* should be seen in conjunction with some of my other work which highlights the importance of journalism located in the alternative, international public sphere. So, for instance, there's *Peace journalism, war and conflict resolution* (edited with John Tulloch and Florian Zollmann, New York: Peter Lang 2010); Giving peace journalism a chance, in *The Routledge companion to community and alternative media* (edited by Chris Atton, London: Routledge 2015); Journalists and the secret state, in *News from somewhere: A reader in communication and challenges to globalization* (edited by Daniel Broudy, Jeffery Klaehn and James Winter,

Eugene, Oregon, USA: Wayzgoose Press 2015); and Secrets and lies: On the ethics of conflict coverage, in the *Routledge handbook, media, conflict and security* (edited by Piers Robinson, Philip Seib and Romy Frohlich, London: Routledge 2016). Plus some of the pieces I've had published on the *medialens.org* and *the-latest.com* websites.

ACKNOWLEDGEMENTS

The number of people who have helped me over the years (in the UK, Ireland, North and South America, Australia, New Zealand, throughout continental Europe and India) are too many to mention (they know who they are). Sincere thanks to you all! Thanks to Richard and Pete Franklin at Abramis who have published so efficiently many of my books (and the two journals which I co-edit) over recent years. Special thanks go to my partner Maryline Gagnère and our son, Gabriel Keeble-Gagnère, for their love and support. And this book is dedicated to Phillip Knightley (who sadly died, aged 87, in January 2017 while this book was in its production stage at the publishers) and John Pilger – for inspiring me.

Withcall,
Lincolnshire

Chapter One

The making of new militarism

RESOLVING THE DEMOCRATIC CONTRADICTIONS OF MILITARISM IN THE UK

Traditional militarism of the Second World War, in which the mass of the population participated in the war effort, either as soldiers or civilians, threw up some serious democratic dilemmas for the Western elites. Throughout the West, the old elites were discredited by appeasement and collaboration with the Nazis. Progressive movements and trade union militancy flourished in Britain (Curran and Seaton 2003 [1991]: 81-82; Lewis 1984: 221-225). The new liberal consensus backing widespread social reform and state intervention in the economy was to find expression in the Beveridge Report and the 1944 Education Act (Giddens 1985: 242). Winston Churchill was used for rhetorical, ideological purposes by Margaret Thatcher when she was Prime Minister (1979-1990) to symbolise the greatness of Britain under a Conservative leader (Barnet 1982). But Churchill, despite his virulent racist and anti-communist views (Ponting 1994), had angered many of the right by introducing Labour ministers into the national wartime government (Morgan 1990: 6-8). Then, in 1945, a Labour government was returned with a massive, unprecedented majority.

Since 1945, Britain has become, in effect, a major military base for the US (though this is little known to the electorate). In his major series of investigations for *New Statesman* in the early 1980s, Duncan Campbell (1980) discovered more than 100 US military facilities in Britain. Over 10,500 US military personnel were stationed in the UK by 2005, more than in any other European state barring Germany and Italy, both defeated in the Second World War. As Linda Colley comments (2007): 'In all, well over 1.3 million US personnel have been stationed here since 1950 without – so far as I know – any consultation of the electorate.'

Moreover, the democratic problems posed by mass conscription have been resolved in a number of ways. In the UK, wars involving mass conscription have been eliminated from military strategies. The emphasis has shifted to nuclear 'deterrence' following the secret launch of the UK nuclear weapons programme in the late 1940s. Gittings reports (2012: 205): 'Nuclear war might or might not be survivable but there was no alternative to running the risk: for some annihilation was preferable to "communist domination".'[1] Military strategy emphasised low-intensity operations away from the media glare. National service was ended, in the 1960s the war department was renamed the ministry of defence and the nuclearised army became the professional, massively resourced institution of committed volunteers constantly prepared for action and denied any trade union rights (Dockrill 1988; Wallace 1970). By 1980, as outlined in Presidential Directive 59, the 'Carter Doctrine' was promoting actual nuclear war fighting strategies and – under certain circumstances – pre-emptive use of the nuclear option. Special focus was on the Gulf and South Asia (Todd, Bloch and Fitzgerald 2009: 73).

New militarism was inherently anti-democratic. As the celebrated military historian, Michael Howard, commented on the crucial decision to wage war or not: 'Popular participation is considered neither necessary nor desirable' (Hennessy 2010: 3). And Shaw argued (1987: 153):

> The state would dispense with the people in a future nuclear war, it had largely dispensed with the pretense of involving them in preparing for war too. The secret, capital-intensive part of the state's military power was to be developed: the people were not expected to discuss or decide but merely to give their passive consent.

To a certain extent, new militarism embraced the contradictory processes of militarisation and demilitarisation. According to Shaw (1991: 14): 'Militarisation at one level has been accompanied by demilitarisation at others; for example, militarisation of elite politics or economic strategy has gone hand-in-hand with demilitarisation of mass employment, life and politics.' Moreover, new militarism did not constitute a complete break with traditional militarism since some elements of militarism (such as the emphasis on air power or the propaganda role of the media) continued in significantly modified form into the new era.

RESOLVING THE DEMOCRATIC CONTRADICTIONS OF MILITARISM IN THE US

The United States also witnessed some significant democratic advances during the Second World War. Unions gained in strength and workers struggled for higher wages. But these gains were quickly demolished. Hellinger and Judd (1991: 156-160) argue that the press's near unanimous opposition to the 1948 presidential campaign of the short-lived, anti-war Progressive Party presaged its collaboration in the hunt for internal subversive in the 1950s. When in 1952 the Progressive Party selected Charlotta Bass for Vice-President, making her the first African-American to run for national office, the media again largely ignored it.[2]

Significantly, mass conscription during the Vietnam War (though not a total war for the US) was also accompanied by substantial social dislocation – with the emergence of student radicalism, black radicalism and urban riots. Thereafter, the emphasis was on avoiding Vietnam-type confrontations. Technological development became the army's top priority. The 1970s saw the shift to an all-volunteer army. Men increasingly gave way on the battle front to the (computerised) machine. As in the UK, military strategy also shifted to stress low-intensity conflict and the deployment of relatively small, elite forces often in secret missions. Short, manufactured, spectacular, new militarist wars evolved from the early 1980s to reinforce the power of the political and economic elite and the marginalisation of the mass of the public. The shift occurred – from militarism to new militarism.

NEW MILITARISM AND THE MEDIACENTRISM: WARFARE AS FICTION

Military strategy became essentially a media event, an entertainment, a spectacle. Warfare, moreover, was transmuted into the symbolic assertion of US and to a lesser degree UK global media and military power. Media manipulation became a central military strategy. The mediacentrism was a pivotal element of new militarist societies. Significantly, James Combs identifies the emergence of a distinctly new kind of warfare with the UK's Falklands campaign of 1982 and the US invasion of Grenada the following year. He argues (1993: 277):

> It is a new kind of war, war as performance. It is a war in which the attention of its auteurs is not only the conduct of the war but also the communication of the war. With their political and military power to command, coerce and co-opt the mass media the national security elite can make the military event go according to script, omit bad scenes and discouraging words and bring about a military performance that is both spectacular and satisfying.

The shift to volunteer forces and the nuclear 'deterrent' signalled in both the UK and US a growing separation of the state and military establishment from the public. The populist press, closely allied to the state, served to create the illusion of participatory citizenship. Moreover, the media played other crucial roles in new militarist societies by engaging the public in a form of glamorised, substitute warfare. Instead of mass active participation in militarist wars, people were mobilised through their consumption of heavily censored media (much of the censorship being self-imposed by journalists) whose job was to manufacture the spectacle of warfare. People respond to the propaganda offensive with a mixture of enthusiasm, contempt, apathy and scepticism. Yet, most crucially, media consumption and public opinion polling provided the illusion of participation just as satellite technology provided the illusion of 'real live' coverage of the conflict.

MacKenzie (1984) has described the 'spectacular theatre' of 19th century British militarism when press representations of heroic imperialist adventures in distant colonies had a considerable entertainment element. Featherstone, too (1993a, 1993b) has identified the way in which the Victorian 'small' wars of imperial expansion in Africa and India were glorified for a doting public by correspondents such as William Howard Russell, G. A. Henty, Archibald Forbes and H. M. Stanley.

But Victorian newspapers and magazines did not have the social penetration of the mass media today. And Victorian militarism was reinforced through a wide range of institutions and social activities: the Salvation Army, Church Army and uniformed youth organisations, rifle clubs, ceremonial and drill units in factories. 'In these ways, a very large proportion of the population came to have some connection with military and paramilitary organisations' (MacKenzie op cit: 5-6). By the 1970s this institutional and social militarism had given way to a new mediacentric, consumerist, entertainment militarism in which the mass media, closely aligned to a strong and increasingly secretive state, had assumed a dominant ideological role.

Within this media-saturated environment, Luckham (1984: 5) has identified the potency of the 'fetishism of the weapon' within what he describes as 'the armament culture' (though he avoids adopting the notion of militarism). During the new militarist wars media consumers were encouraged to identify with weapons of mass destruction which, in turn, were constantly described as having human attributes (for instance, nuclear systems were described as 'ageing'). Moreover, Luckham argues that the modern, high-technology weapons of extraordinary destructive firepower have transmuted warfare into a form of fiction. He says:

> The limitless possibilities opened up by nuclear physics, space technology, genetic engineering and artificial intelligence have been the staple themes of science fiction. Materialised in the form of nuclear missiles, laser beams, chemical weapons, germ warfare and computers they transmute war into a new and elaborate genre of fiction (ibid: 1).

During the Second World War, weapons technology and its use, culminating in the nuclear bombings of Hiroshima and Nagasaki in August 1945, bore little relation to any strategic rationale.[3] Military strategists had become profoundly irrational and had entered the realm of fiction. As Charles Reynolds (1989: 151) argues, there is no evidence to suggest that control over weapons produced a consistent and rational relationship between the means of violence and the ends sought by its use. Since 1945 this 'fictionalisation' of military strategy has intensified with the development of weapons systems of ever-increasing firepower. Fred Halliday (1983: 545) has argued against this position, suggesting that the Cold War was essentially a rational process: '... it was not irrational in that it reflected responses by conscious political agents in the United States to what they saw as a challenge to capitalist power.' But during the 1991 massacres there was, in fact, little relationship between the massive firepower used by the US-led coalition forces and the threat posed. As Dilip Hiro reported (1992: 4):

> During the initial two weeks of their air campaign, the allies dropped more conventional explosives on Iraq and Kuwait than in the whole of the Second World War, which lasted 310 weeks. In the first 12 hours of the hostilities, the US-led coalition dropped more bombs on enemy territory than the United States had done in its 17-day air campaign, codenamed 'Linebacker-2', in Vietnam in 1972.

Militarism and, in particular, new militarism sought at the level of media-directed rhetoric to legitimise and rationalise the profound irrationality and illegitimacy of the nuclearised, over-resourced, high-technology military system.[4]

Since new militarist warfare was essentially a media spectacle, the military's main concerns were to control and manipulate the image. Unlike the militarist wars which lasted years, new militarist wars were over quickly. As Benjamin Bradlee, former executive editor of the *Washington Post*, commented bluntly on the events of January-February 1991: 'The trouble with this war was it was so fucking fast' (Macarthur 1993: 147). But the Gulf conflict of 1991, which lasted 42 days, in new militarist terms was a long 'war'. The military became, then, the primary definers of the fast-moving events while journalists, kept far from any action, were in no position to challenge their inventions.

Moreover, the strategic imperatives of new militarism meant that wars became inherently difficult to report with 'fictionalisation' further encouraged. They were fought by planes (to which journalists normally had no access) and in space and often at night. New weapons incinerate their victims making calculations of casualties even more difficult. The emphasis on computer games in military planning meant the distinctions between 'real' and Nintendo-style conflicts became blurred. In these new wars, civilians didn't die (except in 'accidents'), weapons were clean and precise, and the soldiers were all at heart pacifists. This is unreal warfare. As Phillip Knightley (1991: 5) commented: 'The Gulf war is an important one in the history of censorship. It marks a deliberate attempt by the authorities to alter public perception of the nature of war itself, particularly the fact that civilians die in war.' Yet the Gulf conflict of 1991, in fact, was not so much a unique event but the culmination of a process that began with the Falklands 'war' of 1982 and moved through the US attacks on Grenada (1983), Libya (1986) and Panama (1989).

According to the post-modernist French theorist Jean Baudrillard (1976; 1988), the contemporary post-modern culture is one of hyper-reality, of reproduction and simulation rather than production. Indeed, the mediacentric culture of new militarism was founded on imitation – with the nostalgic reinvention/reproduction of the rhetoric of classical militarism ('Hitler' Hussein, 'allies', 'heroism', 'liberation'), of Hollywood or of sport dominating media and military discourse. Michael Mann talks of 'spectator sport militarism'. He writes: (1988: 185):

> … wars like the Falklands or the Grenadan invasion are not qualitatively different from the Olympic games. Because life and death are involved the emotions stirred up are deeper and stronger. But they are not emotions backed up by committing personal resources. They do not involve real or potential sacrifice, except by professional troops. The nuclear and mass conventional confrontation involves at most 10 per cent of GNP – a tithe paid to our modern 'church', the nation. The symbolic strength of the nation can sustain popular support for adventures and arms spending.

New militarist wars ended as hyped-up media events with no more lasting effects than a popular TV series or sporting contest. Since the wars were manufactured they failed to articulate real threats, problems or conflicts that deeply affected the public and so were quickly forgotten – as in the cases of the US interventions in the Lebanon, Grenada, Libya, Panama and the Gulf.

The threat posed by the 'enemy' was greatly exaggerated. The 'enemy' is globalised and in the process fictionalised. This process was rooted in the Cold War when the Soviet threat, it has been argued, was largely imaginary – serving to legitimise the West's (and in particular the US's) military-industrial complex, global ambitions and military adventures (Kaldor 1991: 35; see also Halliday op cit: 549). Throughout the Cold War, Western intelligence services constantly exaggerated the strength of Warsaw Pact forces (Adams 1994: 255).[5] When the Soviet Union failed to intervene in Poland in 1981 following the emergence of the Solidarity movement, its military impotence could no longer be concealed. New enemies were needed if the consensus was to remain firm in the post-Cold War, new militarist era. This invention of enemies became increasingly desperate with the collapse of the Soviet Union. The manufacture of Saddam Hussein as the global threat (and later the lies over Weapons of Mass Destruction) culminated this process of enemy-invention in the 1980s.

THE MANUFACTURE OF WAR IN THE UK AND US

Moreover, the causes of the conflicts lay more in the (unspoken) dynamics of UK/US domestic and foreign politics than in any credible external threats. These threats were largely manufactured, it could be argued, to hide the reality of unnecessary offensive action. In the case of the UK and US:

- The appearance of a major 'war' was needed so that the US elite could eradicate the trauma of the Vietnam defeat from their collective memory. The first words President Bush proclaimed after the massacres were: 'By God, we've kicked the Vietnam syndrome.' Indeed, in the coverage of the crisis and massacres in the major US press, the word most commonly used was Vietnam.[6] Vietnam was a war that 'got out of control'. Desert Storm in the Gulf, in contrast, was the US military's attempt to wage the perfect 'war': to control it and give it a contrived, happy ending. As Bruce Cumings commented (1992: 104): 'Hardly a thing could be said on Saddam's behalf, he had no constituency in the US, Iraq was far more threatening than Grenada or Noriega's Panama, something truly important was at stake (hegemony in the Persian Gulf) and so the war became a surrogate for the wars the US could not win in Korea and Vietnam – a victory without cost, interrogating the past and preparing the future.'

- A major 'war' could serve to bring some sense of unity to deeply fractured societies (of mass poverty, racial and gender injustice, unemployment, recession and endemic crime) and legitimise the media/military/civilian elites in the eyes of the public. According to Jean Baudrillard (1995: 38, cited in Hammond 2007: 20), the Gulf conflict was less a battle against Saddam Hussein than a struggle to make sense of the West's role in the post-Cold War world.

- A major 'war' was needed by the US (backed up by the UK and its other allies) to assert its primacy in the 'New World Order' as proclaimed by President Bush after the Iraqi invasion of Kuwait. The US's position, basically underpinned by military power and massively burdened by debt and recession, was increasingly coming under threat from more civilian-oriented economies of Germany and Japan. War could then be seen as a symbolic assertion (though essentially defensive) of US/UK military power on the global stage.

- Even a mythical 'war' could serve to destroy the social/economic infrastructure of Iraq which, while posing no threat to the West, was seen as a threat by the Israeli elite. Israel had earlier successfully sabotaged Iraq's nuclear programme. As Dilip Hiro reports (op cit: 60), in 1979, Israeli agents destroyed two reactor cores about to be shipped to Iraq from a French warehouse; in June 1980, the head of Iraq's atomic energy programme was murdered in a hotel room in Paris; and in June 1981, Israeli jets destroyed the nuclear reactor at Tuwaitha near Baghdad. A new 'war' now on Iraq could serve as a lesson to future Middle Eastern governments who considered challenging the Western right of access to the oil reserves.

- Following the enormous expenditure on the military in the UK and US in the 1980s and the decline of the Soviet threat, armies faced a terrible problem. If they had no major enemy, how were they going to test their weapons? The Gulf 'war' provided the ideal testing ground. Afterwards, arms dealers could proudly display on their weapons 'As used in the Gulf' stickers. The massacres can then be seen as an obscenely macabre arms equipment exhibition with humans and a society's infrastructure as targets. The flights of the British Tornados, it could be argued, were not for strictly military purposes (how could they be since there was no credible fighting enemy) but to prove their value to potential buyers – in particular, Saudi Arabia.[7] Overall, the 42-day conflict was to cost a staggering $61 billion – with the allies providing $43.1 billion and America $17. 9 billion (Hiro op cit: 397).

THE MANUFACTURE OF THE WAR IN IRAQ

For the Iraq regime, too, a mythical war could also serve a number of purposes:

- It would prove the strength of the Iraqi people in facing the onslaught of a mighty, global enemy. The army didn't need to fight the 'war'. Martyrdom, in any case, was noble.

- Thus, the longer the 'war' continued the greater, more credible the 'victory' could be made to appear. In reality, one massacre followed after another.

- The 'war' could help solve some of the problems of the highly militaristic Iraqi society. Since the ceasefire in the Iran-Iraq war of 1988 thousands of men were returning to cities from the front, ending up dissatisfied and jobless (Karsh and Rautsi 1991: 18-30). Many of them were engaged in revolts against the oppressive regime, especially the Kurds and Shi'as (Pilger 1991a). A war could eliminate large groups of them. There was no record kept of them. The elites of both sides could view the Iraqi conscripts as mere non-people, animals, cannon-fodder. The brutalism of one side, it could be argued, was mirrored in the brutalism of the other.

- The Iraqi elite during the 1980s amassed a formidable arsenal.[8] But as usual with Third World militaristic states it was primarily not for use against any major foreign enemy. Instead, it was for internal security crushing domestic opposition and revolts and serving as a symbol of the power of the elite and the dominant state (Thee 1980: 23). This was the real significance of Saddam Hussein's 'Mother of Battle' rhetoric. The 'war' the Iraqi elite fought in 1991 was not against the US-led coalition – it was against the Kurds and Shi'as. As Faleh Abd al-Jabbar comments (1992: 13): 'The rout relieved Saddam of the most troublesome part of his army and preserved the most loyal divisions.' Moreover, much of Iraq's security strategy was determined by the regime's fear of a military coup. Since the regime knew it was particularly vulnerable to air attack, the air force's capabilities were deliberately held back. Norman Friedman comments (1991: 27): 'Military strategy tended toward static tactics because more mobile ones required forward commanders with greater initiative and because such men could easily turn on the regime.' Such a strategy must have been known to allied commanders before the massacres. It totally contradicts the image that dominated the press of a ruthlessly expansionist Iraqi military. This is why the 'war' was a kind of fictional, shadow contest. Neither side was really fighting the 'enemy' defined by the rhetoric. Each was rather fighting more their domestic opposition.

- The Iraqi state, supported by significant sections of the elites of the East and West for more than a decade before August 1990 was brutally authoritarian. It did not suddenly change its character with the invasion of Kuwait. National security was only maintained through the repression of all dissent, by enforced militarism and by the activities of a massive security/intelligence force. A 'war' could help alter that. Then the terror would be inflicted by the 'enemy' (until recently an ally). And that terror would be exploited to help unite the people behind the leadership.

- Iraq's claim to Kuwait dated back to the imperial carve-up after the First World War and was guaranteed to tap some considerable nationalistic fervour. Similarly, the attack on the Kuwaiti royal family had powerful symbolic significance. It highlighted the massive wealth of the Western-backed ruling elites in the Middle East, their subservience to Western financial, geostrategic interests and the exploitation and injustice on which the oil wealth was based.

- The 'war' could be used to tap the Islamic revival and help further legitimise the ruling elite. Significantly, just before the conflict, Saddam Hussein ordered the Ba'ath Party to change its slogan from 'The Ba'athists stride forward' to 'The Believers stride Forward!' and change the flag to read 'Allahu Akbar' ('God is Great'). As the conflict continued, uprisings were seen throughout the Islamic world – in Turkey, Jordan and the Yemen in the Middle East, Algeria and Egypt in Africa and in Pakistan and Indonesia in Asia (Vaux 1992: 79).

NEW MILITARISM, MEDIACENTRISM AND THE MYTH OF THE VULNERABLE STATE

The notion of vulnerability was a central element of new militarist state's dominant ideology. This is paradoxical since many theorists argue that the state in the UK and US in the 1980s became increasingly centralised, authoritarian and 'strong' (Held 1984: 349-352; Gamble 1988). As Peters (1985: 105) argues: 'In an age of vast state strength, ability to mobilise resources and possession of virtually infinite means of coercion, much of state policy has been based on the concept of extreme vulnerability to enemies, external or internal.'

The state's power grew both internally (with the increase in police powers, surveillance techniques – developed contrary to privacy laws in secret – and control of political and industrial dissent) and externally (with the global reach of its imperial, economic and military ambitions). Yet during the Cold War, the state was represented in the press as constantly vulnerable to attack from communist missiles or massed soldiers moving westwards over Europe. As the direct challenge from the Soviet Union began to wane at the beginning of the 1980s, the threat from international terrorism (still generally linked to the 'Red menace' and left wing 'extremism') was highlighted.

Following the Iranian revolution of 1979 which deposed the Shah and installed the Ayatollah Khomeini, Islamic 'fundamentalism' rapidly became the new 'global threat' to Western civilisation.[9] According to Adam Tarock (1996: 162): 'Iran's revolution, which brought with it the revival of Islam as a political ideology, fostered in the West a siege mentality which the nationalism of the previous decades had created.' Furthermore, a series of enemies was largely manufactured during the 1980s (the 'Argies', 'mad dog' Gaddafi of Libya, 'evil, drug-running, criminal' Noriega of Panama, culminating with the 'new Hitler' Hussein of Iraq) to legitimise intervention in the Third World by the US and UK.

On the home front, the state was represented as vulnerable to attack by peace campaigners (secretly working alongside their Kremlin backers), criminals (hence the emphasis on law and order), IRA terrorists and trade unionists. Significantly, Prime Minister Mrs Thatcher described the striking miners (of 1984-1985) as 'the enemy within' which had to be destroyed (Milne 1995). Moreover, the new militarist state was often represented as critically vulnerable to attack by the media – either internal or external. This is paradoxical given the enormous powers of the state to manipulate the media, to intimidate journalists (through legislation, regulation and censorship), to spread disinformation/lies and control access. It is also paradoxical given the primary role of the press in promoting and reflecting the interests (often contradictory and competing) of the dominant elites (Hallin 1986; Zollmann 2009). Yet, following the Vietnam debacle, major elements of the US civilian and military elites argued that the press had played a crucial role in fermenting opposition to the war. Since then the press has been accused, in times of alleged 'crisis' in the UK and US, of threatening the security of the state. Such accusations, it can be argued, follow on from the mediacentrism of the political culture and are part of a subtle, multi-pronged propaganda strategy to reinforce moves by the state to constrain further the media and domestic opposition and cement the dominant consensus.

For instance, following the Falklands adventure in 1982, it was argued that satellite technology beyond the control of the nation state would allow journalists editorial freedom to challenge the state. Government control of the press in the Falklands, it was claimed, was a unique event (given the remote geographical situation of the islands) never likely to be repeated. In this way, the state was seen as vulnerable to threat from technological advances within the media. In the event, the US invasions of the 1980s culminating in the attack on Iraq showed that the new media technologies were, in fact, highly vulnerable to manipulation by the state.

SECRET WARS OF NEW MILITARISM AND THE MEDIA MYTH OF DEFENCE

The dominant view reproduced in the mainstream media represents the state as having fought defensively only in exceptional cases since 1945. The Gulf 'war', accordingly, was represented as the consequence of a legitimate defensive response to an unprovoked attack by Saddam Hussein on innocent, vulnerable, tiny Kuwait (and, by implication, on vulnerable Western civilisation). But such an interpretation grossly over-simplifies a complex reality and most significantly obscures the offensive elements of the UK and US state systems and military strategies.

In fact, it is perhaps surprising to note – but since 1914, the UK has deployed troops somewhere in the globe at least once every year, usually away from the media glare. As Steve Peak pointed out (1982), the Falklands/Malvinas 'war' was the 88th deployment of British troops since 1945.[10] These deployments had taken place in 51 countries and nearly all of them in Africa, the Middle East, South-East Asia, the Far East and around the Caribbean. Newsinger (1989) describes British intervention in Indonesia as a 'forgotten war'. Britain's longest-running post-1945 campaign (leaving aside Northern Ireland) was in Malaysia from 1948-1960. But this was never described as a 'war'. It was rather known as the Malayan 'emergency'. Stephen Rose (1986) argues that British troops have been involved in more wars in more places across the globe than any other country since 1945. Ian Cobain (2016) comments:

> One reason that this is rarely acknowledged could be that in the years following the Second World War, and before the period of national self-doubt that was provoked in 1956 by the Suez crisis, Britain engaged in so many end-of-empire scraps that military activity came to be regarded by the British public as the norm, and therefore unremarkable. Another is that since 1945, British forces have engaged in a series of small wars that were under-reported and now all but forgotten, or which were obscured, even as they were being fought, by more dramatic events elsewhere.

The Borneo conflict of 1962-1966 was kept largely hidden from the British public. Valerie Adams (1986: 32) expresses some surprise at the negligible coverage. She comments: 'The whole concept of small-scale operations and ambushes, paralleling the terrorists' own tactics, should have been of immense interest at the time when the United States was taking very different measures in Vietnam, yet there was little analysis or interpretation of the British operations in Borneo.' Clearly, it was in the interests of the British elite to keep coverage of the war low-key. The British cross-border operations were of dubious legality under international law and assistance to the somewhat corrupt leaders of Brunei and Malaysia was felt to be unlikely to be enthusiastically endorsed by the British public or world community. The government wanted discreet coverage and that's exactly what the press gave it. As Bloch and Fitzgerald report (1983: 43):

> Since World War Two, the SAS have been involved in 32 theatres of war, usually in countries who do not wish the troops' presence to be known. The British government has no wish to have the foreign activities of its elite

counter-insurgency force publicised as deniability is often the only, often flimsy defence against charges of warmongering, imperialism, interference and so on.

In the case of the US, the investment in warfare and offensive military strategy is still greater than that of the UK. Cecil Currey (1991: 72-73) argues that since 1950, America has used either force or its threat about 500 times, mostly in Third World countries. Former CIA agent John Stockwell (1991: 70-73) suggests that the agency has been involved in 3,000 major operations and 10,000 minor operations which have led to the deaths of 6 million people worldwide mainly in Korea, Vietnam, Cambodia, Africa and Central and South America.[11] It has overthrown functioning democracies in more than 20 countries and manipulated dozens of elections (Blum 2004).

Pentagon adviser John M. Collins, in his seminal analysis of strategy in these largely secret wars, known as Low Intensity Conflicts (LICs), isolates just 60 examples during the 20th century. He points out: 'All LICs normally are contingencies and technically transpire in peacetime because none have yet been declared wars' (1991: 4). Similarly, Asaf Hussain (1988: 45) identifies the US's deep commitment to LIC involving both military and non-military (political, economic, cultural and social) forms of conflict. 'It means being prepared to engage in protracted struggle against various non-Western states with a minimum of US combat involvement and mobilization of indigenous forces.'

The dominant media view fails to acknowledge the inherent aggression of the state representing the short, sharp attacks (or defensive actions as argued by the administration of the day) of the US on Grenada, Libya and Panama in the 1980s as the typical forms of warfare. In fact, the reverse is nearer the truth. Some 57 per cent of Collins's sample lasted fewer than five years but 33 per cent exceeded 10 years. For instance, he pointed out that the LIC against Libya had been going on since 1970. The 11-minute attack on Libyan targets in April 1986 was just a tiny feature of this multi-pronged conflict.

WHY SECRET WARS?

Given the democratic problems posed by overt, mass participatory warfare, most conflicts of new militarist societies avoided traditional mass army battle confrontations such as occurred in the Gulf in 1991. Instead, permanent warfare is conducted through special force interventions, the support of proxy forces and leaders, through diplomatic, trade and other economic sanctions, through secret service destabilisation. Many other factors influenced the development of LIC doctrine. A feature of US/UK strategy since the start of the 20th century, it developed still further as an offshoot of the nuclear stand-off between East and West during the Cold War and in response to the US defeat in Vietnam. As Fred Halliday (1989: 72) says: 'LIC theorists insisted that US combat forces should not be involved in the long-run, Vietnam-style operations. The "lesson" drawn from Vietnam was that the US effort failed because it was too direct and too large.' Significantly, Collins's sample showed LICs mounting substantially in the post-Vietnam, new militarist era.

In addition, LIC strategy was developed in response to the perceived threats to vulnerable US strategic interests (Miles 1987). The US defense secretary reported in 1987: 'Today there seems to be no shortage of adversaries who seek to undermine our security by persistently nibbling away at our interests through these shadow wars carried out by guerrillas, assassins, terrorists and subversives in the hope that they have found a weak point in our defences' (Klare and Kornbluh 1989: 93). LIC strategies were aimed at fighting most effectively and appropriately those 'shadow wars'. During the 1980s, LIC strategist 'came out' in the US and numerous conferences were held and strategy documents compiled exploring the concepts. But the LIC debate was largely ignored by the mainstream media in both the US and UK.

Special forces, such as the UK's SAS and the American Navy Seals, which were so crucial to LIC strategies, reportedly played important roles in the build-up to the massacres and during them. They attached homing devices at or near bombing targets in Iraq, hunted for Scud missile launches and collected intelligence. They were the subject of a series of 'inordinately flattering' features in the UK and US media (Ray and Schaap 1991: 11). Yet accounts of their daring deeds of 'superhuman courage' and endurance, since they were shrouded in almost total secrecy, amount to a form of fiction (de la Billière 1995: 319-338; Brown and Shukman 1991: 81-104; Hunter 1995: 169-175; Kemp 1994: 191-197).

After the 1991 massacres in the Gulf, the SAS provided one of the dominant symbols of British heroism. Accounts of the fate of the lost SAS patrol – by 'Andy McNab' (1994) and 'Chris Ryan' (1995) – became best-sellers. As John Newsinger comments (1995: 36): '…. The image we are left with is of a lone British soldier, hungry and cold, being hunted across the most difficult terrain by hundreds of Iraqis and yet still making good his escape. … These are tales of the underdog, of British masculinity triumphing against all the odds, over the lesser masculinity of a brutal enemy. In this way is the myth of the "soldier hero", the myth of the SAS sustained.' In the end, the SAS role in the Gulf massacres was probably only minor. LIC strategy was hardly relevant against an enemy that largely refused to fight. The 1991 Gulf conflict, it could be argued, rather saw the application of LIC-type secrecy (deliberately developed during a series of invasions in the 1980s) to a spectacular, manufactured 'war' which was, in reality, a 42-day secret massacre hidden behind the media construct of heroic warfare. William Blum described the conflict as the Desert Holocaust (2004: 320-337).

THE PERMANENT WARFARE OF NEW MILITARISM MISSING FROM THE MEDIA

The arms trade, largely hidden from the glare of the media, was the archetypal 'substitute, permanent warfare' of new militarist societies. As Jane Corbin commented (1991: 4), whenever a journalist made even the most innocuous inquiry about the arms trade the phrase 'commercial confidentiality' was trotted out. 'The triumphant tone in the voice that delivers these words conveys the impression that "commercial confidentiality" is often a handy excuse for blocking the truth.'

Indeed, wars are often not fought directly; instead, the means of waging wars are sold. Moreover, arms sales to dictatorships (such as Iraq) reinforce oppressive systems and increase regional and global tensions. Following the oil price rises of 1973 and 1979, much of the revenue accumulated by Middle East governments and a large proportion of the credit distributed to Third World countries was used to buy arms. In fact, during the 1980s in the lead-up to the Gulf massacres, it has been argued that the global arms trade was exploding 'out of control' (Campaign Against the Arms Trade 1989: 21).

Of the six leading importers of major weapons systems between 1983 and 1987, five (Iraq, Egypt, Saudi Arabia, Israel and Syria in that order) were in the Middle East. Only India imported more (Stockholm International Peace Research Institute 1988). Some 40 countries sold weapons to Iraq and Iran during their war between 1980 and 1988 – some of them to both sides (Barnaby 1991: 9). The very secrecy surrounding the arms trade serves to intensify it. As a seminal work on the impact of the arms trade on the Third World argued:

> Since there is no international register of arms transfers and very few reliable published details of individual countries' arms purchases, governments can never be sure what kind or quantity of arms its rivals may be purchasing. This causes suspicion and paranoia which often sets the tone for a regional arms race (Campaign Against the Arms Trade op cit: 27).

The UK's promotion of its arms sales (particularly to Iraq) intensified during the 1980s spurred on by vigorous support from the Thatcher government (CAAT 1991). A £50 billion deal (al-Yamamah) between BAE and Saudi Arabia in 1985 amounted to Britain's biggest overseas order ever (Harkins 1995: 54-59).[12] Between 2001 and 2005, UK arms sales to Africa even reached the £1 billion mark (Barnett 2005) with global spending on arms that year topping $1 trillion (Buncombe 2005). Between 2000 and 2002, the value of UK military export licences to Israel doubled from £12.5m. to £22.5m. – though the government acknowledged that its occupation of Palestine was illegal under international law. Blair's New Labour government even supplied Israel with chemical warfare technology for creating sarin nerve gas. As Mark Phythian (2003: 234) points out: 'After nuclear weapons, it is the most feared weapon of mass destruction.'

Secrecy surrounds the activities of the Defence Export Services Organisation (launched in 1966 by the then-Labour government as the Defence Sales Organisation). Officially sanctioned leaks of sales appear in newspapers (where the social, political and moral aspects of the arms trade are rarely examined) and specialist military magazines and occasionally statements are made in parliament. Otherwise, even MPs are often not told of arms sales for reasons (yes – you guessed) of 'commercial confidentiality'.

THE IDEOLOGICAL CONSENSUS OF THE NATIONAL SECURITY STATE

The ideological consensus of the national security state served in part to undermine further the democratic dynamic accompanying mass conscription as the Cold War intensified after 1945. The security of the state was perceived to be under constant threat from communist enemies both abroad and at home. Progressive forces could easily be smeared in the press as 'communist' and physically intimidated by the state's forces. Vast areas of debate in the UK (republicanism, militarism, imperialism, Irish unity, the power of the City, state terrorism) became no-go areas. Noam Chomsky comments (1991a: 28):

> ... for the USSR the Cold War has been primarily a war against its satellites, and for the US a war against the Third World. For each it has served to entrench a system of domestic privilege and coercion. The politics pursued within the Cold War framework have been unattractive to the general population, which accepts them only under duress. Throughout history, the standard device to mobilise a reluctant population has been the fear of an evil enemy, dedicated to its destruction. The superpower conflict served the purpose admirably.

The ideological consensus which emerged around new militarism and was reproduced faithfully in all the mainstream media during the Gulf crisis sprang logically from the Cold War consensus. Such a consensus, it should be stressed, was not always monolithic. It incorporated debate and dissent – with clearly identified limits. Thus, except during short, rare periods (in the early 1960s and in the early 1980s) when the Labour Party, somewhat uncomfortably, adopted unilateral nuclear disarmament (thus marking a temporary breakdown in the consensus), the nationalistic, patriotic ideologies that underpinned the Cold War stalemate won the committed support of all major political parties and mainstream media.

Peace movement supporters tended to be labelled as 'extremist', 'unpatriotic', 'naïve', 'hysterical' or 'mad' (Sabey 1982 cited in McLaughlin 2002: 136). According to McLaughlin: 'Ministry of Defence propaganda linked the peace movement to the extreme left and claimed that CND was directly funded by the Soviet Union with the aim of undermining Western security policy' (ibid).

19

As Mary Kaldor comments (1990: 4-5), Cold War ideology both expressed and legitimised the dominant power relationships in modern society. The elite was divided over the disastrous Suez adventure of 1956 and this division was reflected in the media.[13] Following the nationalisation of the Suez canal by Egypt all the newspapers with the exception of the *Guardian* called for the use of force. But then, following the attacks, the consensus suddenly shifted and nearly all the press, including the *Daily Telegraph* and *Mail*, came out in opposition. Only the *Express*, *Sketch* and *Times* remained 'real newspaper friends' of Prime Minister Anthony Eden (Thomas 1967: 32-33).[14]

Otherwise the Cold War consensus held firm in both the media and the elite. It broke on only two occasions. In 1960, supporters of the Campaign for Nuclear Disarmament won a surprise victory at the Labour conference (Taylor 1970) and in the early 1980s massive opposition to the Thatcherite and Reaganite armaments programme and Cold War rhetoric drove thousands of peace campaigners on to the streets of Britain and the Labour Party reluctantly into the arms of unilateralists. But unilateralism was never endorsed by any Fleet Street newspaper (Aubrey 1982; Keeble 1986; McNair 1988: 176; Glasgow University Media Group 1985).

Schlesinger, Murdoch and Elliott (1983: 21) preferred to highlight the notion of the 'strong state'. The constant reaffirmation of the official perspective went hand in hand with efforts to marginalise both the impact and legitimacy of alternative viewpoints. 'Not surprisingly, alternative spokesmen and women have seen this as threatening the more general freedom to debate controversial questions in liberal democracies, and as related to the emergence of a "strong state" in such regimes' (ibid).

In the United States too, the Cold War confrontation served to reinforce the militarist consensus in the dominant financial and political elites and in the mainstream media. As Hellinger and Judd argue (op cit: 2016):

> For more than forty years there has been a remarkable degree of consensus among US elites that the nation should preserve a high level of readiness to go to war. Presidential candidates of the two major parties have tried to outdo one another in advocating military preparedness. ... For voters, the choices have been conducted within extraordinarily narrow limits. From 1945 until 1989, when the Soviet Premier Mikhail Gorbachev declared his policy of perestroika and the Eastern Bloc governments began to fall, no Democratic or Republican presidential candidate questioned the premises of the Cold War – that the national defense must be consistently strengthened to deter the communists.

SECRET STATE: SILENT PRESS

Though the dominant political ideology, reproduced in the mainstream media, stresses the myths of democratic involvement, plurality and openness, the principal characteristic of the modern state, as identified by John Keane, is 'armed secrecy' (1991: 101-103). The mainstream media are tied closely to this secret state through shared economic and political interests (Edwards and Cromwell 2009: 1). The secret state provides the essential political, social and cultural foundations for the manufacture of the Gulf war myth. Significantly, Guy Debord (1991: 3) locates his concept of the society of the spectacle in the culture of secrecy. He writes:

> The society whose modernisation has reached the stage of integrated spectacle is characterised by the combined effect of five principal features: incessant technological renewal, integration of state and economy, generalised secrecy, unanswerable lies, an eternal present.

The activities of the secret state are largely repellent, illegal, extremely costly, often in support of deeply obnoxious dictatorships – and difficult to justify in public. Hence the need of the state to maintain constant vigilance and secrecy. Yet titbits of information are supplied to friendly media, carefully orchestrated leaks, denials, lies feed the public's curiosity about the secret service, double agents and the like. Occasionally, brave whistleblowers throw some light on the operations of the secret state. Up to 1990, they included:

- 1971: Daniel Ellsberg who, in the *Pentagon Papers*, as reported in *The New York Times*, reveals the secret bombing of Cambodia and Laos (Greenberg 2012: 11-46).
- 1975: Philip Agee exposes the activities of the CIA in his book *The company* (see Campbell 2011).
- 1976: The secret signals spy base, GCHQ, revealed for the first time in *Time Out*: leading to the trial and acquittal of Crispin Aubrey, Dave Berry and Duncan Campbell (ABC).
- 1983: Sarah Tisdall jailed after releasing information on cruise missile deployment to the *Guardian*.
- 1985: Senior civil servant at the ministry of defence Clive Ponting claims 'public interest' and so the jury acquits him after he revealed secrets about the sinking of the Argentinian warship, the *General Belgrano* (with the loss of 323 lives) during the Falklands conflict of 1982 (Norton-Taylor 1985).
- 1986: Mordechai Vanunu reveals Israel's secret nuclear weapons programme in *The Sunday Times* (Quinn 2011).
- 1988: former M15 officer Peter (*Spycatcher*) Wright reveals plot to oust Prime Minister Harold Wilson in 1968.

Despite these leaks, the information we are allowed to receive hardly scratches the surface of the secret state. Nik Wright, of the security consultancy firm Mosecon (https://www.mosecon.com/about/) told the author: 'Think of a vast iceberg with just a tiny tip of ice showing on the water representing what little is known about the secret state. The rest of the iceberg submerged beneath the surface is the real secret state.' Spy sagas (le Carré, *James Bond*, Graham Greene, *Spooks*, *Kingsman*: *The Secret Service* etc) are an ever-present feature of the entertainment industry – in effect, fictionalising/depoliticisng the secret state.

Yet the real political impact of the secret state has never disturbed the dominant ideologies of the 'democratic' state. Spying, in many respects, has been transmuted from being an often reprehensible activities (dirty tricks, torture, assassination, coups) into a depoliticised entertainment spectacle. Two state systems operate in most advanced capitalist countries. There is the state of the democratic façade (elections, public opinion polls, the free press, the rule of law) and there is the secret and perhaps far more powerful state. The secret states of the UK and US operate on a global scale, as during the Gulf crisis of 1990-1991, in collusion with the secret states of more overtly authoritarian and militaristic societies.[15]

REASONS TO BE SCEPTICAL: THE DEEP THROAT MYSTERY

Yet the case of 'Deep Throat', the whistleblower at the heart of the Watergate scandal, proves how important it is for both reporters and media consumers to remain sceptical about all matters relating to secret warfare and the secret state. The source for the series of reports by the *Washington Post* duo Carl Bernstein and Bob Woodward that helped topple Richard Nixon, the US President, in 1973 – and the subject of the book and Hollywood blockbuster, *All the President's men*, featuring Robert Redford and Dustin Hoffman as the intrepid sleuths – was not (as the Great Watergate Myth suggests) a high-minded public servant appalled at White House corruption and the lies over the secret bombing of Cambodia.

Rather, it was Mark Felt, the deputy director of the FBI, angry that he had been overlooked for promotion by Richard Nixon with the top job going to L. Patrick Gray. As George Friedman commented on the intelligence website *Stratfor.com* (on 22 December 2008) in a piece titled 'The death of Deep Throat and the crisis of journalism': 'What appears to be enterprising journalism is, in fact, a symbiotic relationship between journalism and government factions. It may be the best path journalists have for acquiring secrets, but it creates a very partial record of events – especially since the origin of a leak is much more important to the public than the leak itself.'[16]

Yet mystery surrounds Felt's revelations. Why was *Vanity Fair* chosen as the outlet in which Felt revealed all in May 2005? Why were the 'Woodstein' duo not informed before publication? Was it not strange that the revelation had to be written by Felt's lawyer (Felt was seriously ill and died in December 2008).[17] And could there not, in fact, have been a number of 'Deep Throats' – as investigative reporter Russ Baker (who runs the excellent website *whowhatwhy.com*) argues in his *Family of secrets* (2008). This would suggest there were a number of other significant forces at work in the Watergate saga that now will probably remain secret forever. Moreover, does not all this suggest that the *Washington Post* duo allowed themselves to be used in an FBI plot to oust the president?

SECRET STATE AND THE MEDIA IN THE UK

The extent of official secrecy is the element missing from most histories of modern US and UK.[18] Yet many researchers have identified the UK as one of the most secretive of states. David Northmore (1990) described the UK as 'the most secretive state in the so-called developed world' with well over 100 laws prohibiting the disclosure of information. Philip Schlesinger (1991: 33) outlined in detail the significant features of the new, authoritarian, secret state in the UK. Similarly, Clive Ponting (1990: 16) argued:

> Current or recent operations of all secret services and intelligence agencies are naturally surrounded by secrecy, but in Britain a policy of maintaining total secrecy about virtually every aspect of their work was adopted at an early stage and is still taken to extraordinary lengths today. ... The experience of other Western democracies demonstrates that a doctrine of total secrecy is neither inevitable nor indispensable for the successful operation of intelligence agencies in peacetime. In Britain, however, absolute secrecy has been the policy of all post-war governments.

THE SECRET STATE AND THE MEDIA IN THE US

It is not without significance that of the two US presidents of the 1980s, one, Ronald Reagan, was a former Hollywood actor – the archetypal representative of the culture of the spectacle – with a history of collusion with the secret state (having been an informant on communist, left-wing agitators at Hollywood for the FBI during the 1940s).[19] The other, George H. W. Bush, was a former director of the CIA (1976-1977), engaged in covert activities for the agency since the early 1960s under the cloak of his oil business activities.[20] Bush's elevation to the presidency represented the actual takeover of the 'democratic' state by the secret state. The growth in the late 1950s and 1960s of social protest and the anti-Vietnam war movement resulted in a massive increase in the surveillance of the US population. The warfare state was naturally evolving into a surveillance/Big Brother state (Foster and McChesney 2014: 13). Between 1956 and 1975, the FBI, under J. Edgar Hoover, engaged in the mass surveillance of progressive, civil rights, socialist groups and journalists (ibid: 15).

By the 1980s, the growth of the power of the executive office of the president based around the National Security Council and the CIA (together with 15 other covert organisations costing an estimated $75 billion a year[21]) had created a secret state within the state. As Hellinger and Judd argue: 'There now exists a recognisable pattern of hidden powers, a covert presidency, that rests on centralising presidential direction of personnel, budgets and information; on the manipulation of the media and on the expanding use of national security to control the political agenda' (op cit: 190).

Armed secrecy remained a permanent feature of both militarist and post militarist states. Yet it could be argued that by the 1980s secrecy was 'getting out of control', thus providing one of the crucial elements of the new militarism. According to Alan Friedman (1993: xix): 'The truth is that the 1980s were a decade of deceit both at the White House and Downing Street. A period during which accountability to congress and parliament was almost completely ignored and the abuse of power became the rule rather than the exception.'

THE ROOTS OF NEW MILITARISM IN THE MEDIA-INDUSTRIAL-MILITARY COMPLEX

A number of sociologists, state theorists and arms analysts have identified the social and political significance of the military-industrial complex (Wright Mills 1956; Chomsky 1991; Barnaby 1984; Thompson 1982; Edmunds 1988; Berghahn 1981). President Dwight D. Eisenhower, on departing office in January 1961, had famously warned 'against the acquisition of unwarranted influence, whether sought or unsought by the military-industrial complex'. He went on: 'We must never let the weight of this combination endanger our liberties or democratic processes' (Stone and Kuznick 2013: 288-289). But as Todd, Bloch and Fitzgerald (2009: 77) point out on the military-industrial complex: '... unwarranted influence and misplaced power have surely proliferated in abundance, to the clear detriment of liberties and democratic process.'[22]

Shaw (1987: 150) sums up when he says: 'The military function of the state enters society through the military-economic sector, its role is determining the balance in state spending (warfare/welfare), its absorption into the political framework, its centrality to the ideological formation of the citizen.' But he adds, appropriately: 'To say that militarism has become a core, defining reality of societies in peace as well as war does not, of course, mean that peace is the same as war.' Within this context, the many secret wars of the secret state, as well as the overt wars of the new militarist states culminating in the 1991 Gulf 'war', can be seen as logical (though not inevitable) products of political cultures dominated by the military-industrial complex. In contrast, the dominant ideology articulated in the mainstream, corporate media is silent on this. It represents the state largely as being inherently peaceful though vulnerable to aggression from abnormal states outside and irrational, uncivilised enemies within.

On the military-industrial complex in the UK, Dan Smith and Ron Smith (1983: 29) comment: 'The proportion of national income spent [in the 1970s] on the military was higher than both the typical peacetime level before 1939 and the proportion devoted to the military [down from 60 per cent during the Second World War to 5 per cent] by other Western European states.' Defence spending rose by 28 per cent between 1978 and 1986 accounting for 13.2 per cent of total government expenditure. Defence was the second largest area of expenditure, after social security (Derbyshire and Derbyshire 1988: 176). By the 1990s, the military-industrial complex had grown so enormous that the defence industry accounted for 11 per cent of industrial production, defence exports were worth up to £33 billion a year (the country being the third largest exporter after the US and Russia) and defence-related jobs amounted to 600,000. In 1989, the ministry of defence was the third largest landowner in the country, the largest customer for British industry and the largest employer of bureaucrats (Paxman 1990: 237).[23]

The post-war industrial growth of the US was, to a large extent, built on the militarisation of the economy. The policy basis for the massive military expansion appeared in National Security Council memorandum 68 of 7 April 1950. The secret memo written by Paul Nitze with secretary of state Dean Acheson 'looking over his shoulder' was only released in 1975 in error (Agee 1991: 20; Henwood 1992). It suggested a huge increase in military spending to counter the Soviet Union and to support US foreign policy; a massive propaganda campaign to build and maintain confidence and sow 'mass defections' on the Soviet side; covert economic, political and psychological warfare, tighter internal security and beefed-up intelligence.

Rearmament desperately needed an international emergency – and it came with the Korean War, described by Cumings (1992) as the 'unknown war'.[24] According to Robin Andersen (2006: 37):

> The history of Korea was easily buried because, at the time, so little was known. News from the battlefield was severely restricted by the military and news organisations themselves. Military censorship blocked unwanted reporting of all kinds, such as 'any derogatory comments' about the UN. Journalists could not acknowledge 'the effects of enemy fire'.

Dean Acheson was to say later: 'Korea came along and saved us' (McCormick 1989: 98; see also Horowitz 1971 [1965]: 110-137).[25] Warfare, indeed, helped boost the global economy – and the US military budget. In 1950 it stood at $1.3 billion. Then, with the outbreak of the Korean War, an extra $16.8 billion was added to the bill, while US military forces doubled to 3.6 million. As Philip Agee (op cit: 20) comments: 'The permanent war economy became a reality and we have lived with it for forty years.' And Giovanni Arrighi argues (1994: 297) that massive rearmament during and after the Korean War solved 'once and for all' the liquidity problems of the post-war world economy and inaugurated the most sustained and profitable period in the history of global capitalism (1950-1973). By the early 1950s, even British intelligence was expressing concerns over the threat to world peace posed by the United States (Hennessy 2010: 29).

The boom in military spending continued relentlessly during the years of the Cold War. Michael T. Klare (1980: 37) identified the process in the US where the creation of large-scale military enterprises resulted in the formation of a 'self-perpetuating industrial combine' prepared to take independent measures (propaganda and 'scare' campaigns designed to create a perpetual crisis atmosphere, lobbying efforts, bribery and intrigue) to ensure a continuing demand for its products. Open warfare was mainly directed at the periphery of the imperialist world economy with the US establishing a thousand military bases abroad by the 1960s as a means of propelling US force globally (Foster and McChesney op cit: 7). By 1990, more than 30,000 US companies were engaged in military production, while roughly 3,275,000 jobs were in the defence industries. Gore Vidal (1991: 177-178) goes so far as to argue that by the early 1990s 90 per cent of the federal budget was directed towards defence. And 70 per cent of all money spent on research and development was spent on defence work (Drucker 1993: 126). As the economy fell into recession, profits from arms suppliers, in contrast, soared. Singer, IBM, Goodyear Tire, AT and T and Westinghouse all turned to military production. As Hellinger and Judd argue (op cit: 209): '... the militarisation of the economy has created a complex system of dependence on military spending that will not easily be broken.'

It can be argued that the Gulf 'war' of 1991 was manufactured in an attempt to reinforce the power of the military-industrial complex globally (in particular in the UK and US) at a critical moment when the demise of the Soviet 'enemy' seriously threatened their *raison d'être*.

THE MEDIA-INDUSTRIAL-MILITARY COMPLEX

Analyses stressing the social/political significance of the military-industrial complex often underestimate the ideological and political significance of the corporate media. For instance, in his study of the roots of the Second Cold War (1979-1982), Fred Halliday (1986: 12) highlights the 'iron triangle' which, he argues, binds 'Congress, the Pentagon and the arms industry together in an unchallenged process of military expansion'. A similar analysis of the UK would stress the links between parliament, the ministry of defence and the arms industry. Significantly, Halliday talks of the 'barrage of political propaganda promoting the idea of Soviet superiority, of declining US capabilities, of gaps in missiles, civil defence or naval strength' and thus could have gone on to mention the crucial role of the compliant media in promoting this propaganda.

Indeed, given the integration of the corporate media industries' interests with those of the military-industrial complex and the importance of the media's role in supporting and celebrating the state's militarism it is worth identifying the media-military-industrial complex as a factor behind the manufacture of the Gulf 'war' myth. Significantly, James Der Derian has highlighted the activities of what he calls the 'military-industrial-media-entertainment network' (2002: 2009). Yet the sophisticated media/ideological/propaganda system operating both in the UK and US meant that these developments (and the broader political and environmental threats posed) rarely if ever featured in the dominant political debates.

NOTES

[1] Gittings (2012: 205) adds: British willingness to contemplate nuclear war … lay at the heart of defence policy. In the view of Lord Portal of Hungerford (chief of air staff during the Second World War): 'Personally, I think it is worse for a nation to give in to evil and to betray its friends than to run the risk of annihilation…' The British government's civil defence programme, launched in 1956, was based on the proposition that while nuclear war would be a catastrophe, knowledge of 'the basic facts and of what to do … could save countless lives from otherwise certain death'. The first British atomic bomb was successfully tested on 3 October 1952 off the north west coast of Australia (in Operation Hurricane). Britain's success in the development of thermonuclear bombs, shown in four series of weapons trials (codenamed Grapple) in the Pacific in 1957 and 1958, secured an historic US/UK agreement 'for co-operation in the uses of atomic energy for mutual defence purposes'. Concluded in 1958, this agreement is still in force (see https://www.theguardian.com/science/2013/jan/16/percival-white, accessed on 8 August 2016). Significantly, Mrs Margaret Thatcher, Prime Minister from 1979 to 1990, confided to one of her foreign office colleagues that 'she was not at all sure that in the event, she could press the button'. 'I want grandchildren too,' she explained (Hennessy 2010: 314)

[2] See http://findaid.oac.cdlib.org/findaid/ark:/13030/tf6c60052d/, accessed on 6 August 2016

[3] The nuclear attacks on Japan were essentially the first moves in the confrontation with communist Soviet Union. Leader of the Manhattan project Brigadier General Leslie Groves commented: 'There was never from about two weeks from the time I took charge of this project any illusion on my part that Russia was our enemy and the project was conducted on that basis' (Stone and Kuznick 2013: 160). Telford Taylor, chief prosecutor at the Nuremberg trials, commented: 'The rights and wrongs of Hiroshima are debatable, but I have never heard a plausible justification of Nagasaki' which he considered a war crime (ibid: 173)

[4] The US even considered detonating a nuclear bomb on the moon as a show of technical and military strength after the Soviet Union launched the first satellite, Sputnik, into orbit in 1957. See Broad 2000

[5] In 1961, for instance, the US had approximately 45 ICBMs. The Soviets had four, and they were vulnerable to US attack. The US had more than 1,500 heavy bombers compared to the Soviets' 192. Overall, the US had about 25,000 nuclear weapons; the Soviets had one-tenth that number (Stone and Kuznick 2013: 302-303). Treverton, Gregory (2011) What should we expect of our spies? *Prospect*, June reported the CIA pointing to a chronic slowdown in the Soviet economy during the 1970s, while a 1981 survey stated: 'The Soviet pattern in many respects conforms to that of less developed countries and shows remarkably little progress to a more modern pattern' pp 30-36

[6] Gannett Foundation (1991) *The media at war: The press and the Persian Gulf conflict*, New York City. A database search over the period 1 August 1990 to 28 February 1991 of the mainstream US newspapers found 6,314 mentions of Vietnam (and just 985 mentions on TV). The next most common words were 'human shields' (2002 print mentions; 586 TV mentions), allied dead/casualties (1,492 print mentions; 517 TV mentions). Mentions of Iraqi casualties did not feature at all in the overview p. 42

[7] See http://www.merip.org/mer/mer112/arms-sales-militarization-middle-east, accessed on 8 August 2016

[8] SIPRI (Stockholm International Peace Research Institute annual report) shows that Iraq bought more than £431 billion worth of arms between 1970 and 1989. Supplying countries included all five permanent members of the UN Security Council. USSR £19.2 billion (61 per cent of the total); France $5.5 billion (18 per cent); China $1.6 billion (5 per cent); Brazil $1.1 billion (4 per cent); Egypt $1.1 billion (4 per cent). Others $2.8 billion (8 per cent). Out of the ten major Third World arms importers from 1971-1985, seven were from the Middle East: Iraq (8 per cent), Iran (7.7 per cent), Syria (7.2 per cent), Egypt (7.2 per cent), Libya (7.1 per cent), then – after India (6 per cent) – Israel (5.3 per cent) and Saudi Arabia (4.3 per cent). See Gresh and Vidal (1990: 14)

[9] Intriguingly, declassified files in June 2016 revealed that Khomeini had secret channels of communication with US President Jimmy Carter before and after he returned to Iran from France. Representatives of the two governments even met for talks in France. 'Through these secret meetings, Washington signalled to Khomeini on January 18 that American advisors in Tehran would not oppose a discussion about changing the Iranian constitution in order to abolish the monarchy and turn the country into a republic' (see https://intelnews.org/2016/06/06/01-1915/, accessed on 6 August 2016)

[10] He lists 1945 Java and Sumatra; 1945-48 India and Pakistan; 1945-47 Greece; 1945-54 Trieste; 1945-48 Palestine; 1945 Vietnam; 1946-54 Egypt; 1947 Aden; 1947-48 Northern Ireland; 1948 Gold Coast; 1948 Yangtze incident; 1948-60 Malaya; 1948-52 Eritrea; 1949-51 Somaliland; 1949 Aqaba; 1950-53 Korea; 1950 Singapore; 1951 Aqaba; 1952-56 Northern Ireland; 1952-56 Kenya; 1953 British Guyana; 1953-55 Persian Gulf; 1954-59 Cyprus; 1954-58 Aden; 1955-56 Singapore; 1955 seizure of Rockall; 1956 Hong Kong; 1956-57 Bahrain; 1956 Suez; 1957-59 Muscat and Oman; 1957 Belize; 1957 Togoland; 1958 Nassau; 1958 Aden; 1958 Jordan and Lebanon; 1958 Bahamas; 1959 Gan (Maldives); 1960 Cameroons; 1960 Jamaica; 1961 Kuwait, Bahamas, Zanzibar; 1962 Belize, British Guyana, Hong Kong; 1962-66 Borneo; 1963-66 Malaysia; 1963-66 Swaziland; 1963 Zanzibar; 1963 Cyprus; 1963 British Guyana; 1964 Zanzibar, Tanganyika, Uganda, Kenya; 1964-67 Aden; 1965 Mauritius, Beira blockade, Bechuanaland; 1965-77 Oman; 1966 Hong Kong, Seychelles, British Honduras; 1966-67 Libya; 1967 Hong Kong; 1968 Bermuda, Mauritius; 1969 to date Northern Ireland; 1969-71 Anguilla; 1969 Bermuda; 1969-76 Dhofar/Oman; 1972 QE2, British Honduras; 1973 QE2; 1974 Cyprus; 1976-77 British Honduras (Belize); 1977 Bermuda; 1980 New Hebrides; 1982 Falklands. In 2014, the *Guardian* published a list of British conflicts – every year since 1914. See http://www.theguardian.com/uk-news/ng-interactive/2014/feb/11/britain-100-years-of-conflict, accessed on 9 August 2016

[11] William Blum provides a list of US interventions since 1945: http://www.thirdworldtraveler.com/Blum/US_Interventions_WBlumZ.html

[12] A *Guardian* investigation revealed that more than £6 billion may well have been distributed in corrupt commissions (see https://www.theguardian.com/baefiles/page/0,,2095831,00.html). In 2008, the High Court ruled that the Tony Blair government broke the law in halting a fraud inquiry into the deal in the face of pressure from Saudi Arabia (see http://www.independent.co.uk/news/uk/politics/court-condemns-blair-for-halting-saudi-arms-inquiry-807793.html). In July 2016, it was reported that files in the National Archives relating to Mark Thatcher's likely role in the al-Yamamah deal would be held secret until 2053. Two files, one entitled 'Mark Thatcher and the Omanis; other allegations against Mark Thatcher', the former PM's son, were marked 'temporarily retained' with no date for release (Low 2016). According to John Pilger (1998: 131), Mark Thatcher was said to have received £12 million 'commission' on al-Yamamah. He denied the allegations. Margaret Thatcher was later reported to have given her consent to a failed attempt to oust the president of Equatorial Guinea in 2004, in which her son was involved. Mark Thatcher was fined $500,000 and given a four-year suspended prison sentence for having provided finance for helicopters to be used in the coup attempt (see http://www.theguardian.com/politics/2013/apr/14/thatcher-knew-of-equatorial-giunea-coup-attempt, accessed on 22 August 2016)

[13] See https://wiki.leeds.ac.uk/index.php/The_Suez_Crisis_and_the_Manipulation_of_the_Media, accessed on 9 August 2016

[14] Richard Norton-Taylor records (1990: 99): 'During the Suez crisis, the intelligence services were not content to bug the Egyptian embassy. Through GCHQ's listening post at Ayios Nikolaos in Cyprus, they picked up both Egyptian and Israeli communications. With the approval of the Prime Minister, Anthony Eden, MI6 plotted to assassinate President Nasser. But all of MI6's agents in the Egyptian army were discovered and arrested and the plot collapsed. Another plan – to place canisters of nerve gas inside the ventilation system of Nasser's headquarters – never got beyond the planning stage'

[15] Mohamed Heikal (1992: 42) says on the Gulf states: 'By 1974, every state had its secret service whose chiefs, together with the rulers, confidants and senior officials, formed an inner administrative alliance. Beyond them was an outer circle containing four elements: representatives of foreign intelligence services, confidants of sheiks and kings, oil company representatives and arms salesmen'

[16] See http://mediaethicsmagazine.com/index.php/analysis-commentary/3746656-deep-throat-and-the-ethics-of-scandal-coverage, accessed on 20 August 2016

[17] Felt's 'autobiography' *A G-Man's life: The FBI, Deep Throat and the struggle for honour in Washington*, was published in 2006. Julian Borger (2008), in Felt's obituary, comments: '… but it was clear that he had contributed little to it beyond an earlier memoir written in 1979.' See 'We got the whole truth out. Isn't that what the FBI should do?', *Guardian*, 20 December

[18] Significantly, Paxman (1990) makes no mention at all of the secret services

[19] See http://articles.chicagotribune.com/1985-08-26/news/8502250710_1_fbi-informant-hollywood-independent-citizens-committee-fbi-agent, accessed on 10 August 2016

[20] See http://www.thirdworldtraveler.com/CIA/Bush_Family_Preys_Together.html, accessed on 11 August 2016

[21] See http://www.businessinsider.com/17-agencies-of-the-us-intelligence-community-2013-5?IR=T, accessed on 11 August 2016

[22] In 1961, US defence spending accounted for 59 per cent of the almost $81bn national budget. The Pentagon also controlled $32bn worth of real estate, including air bases and weapons (Stone and Kuznick 2013: 289)

[23] By 2008, Britain had the second highest military budget in the world, in cash terms (Curtis 2010: 297)

[24] Some 749 British troops lost their lives in the three-year Korean conflict (Hennessy 2010: 3)

[25] But Edward Herman (1992: 58) commented on 'the murderous Korean War, in which the United States almost completely levelled north and central Korea, with the systematic bombing of dikes and destruction of food and water supplies, the massive use of napalm "splashed" (Winston Churchill's phrase) over houses, people, and animals and coming close to precipitating a war with China and using nuclear weapons' (see also Stone and Kuznick 2013: 245)

Chapter Two

Journalists and the secret state

THE SECRET STATE

Elements of the 'democratic' state are part of the very air we breathe in Britain: parliament, the rule of law, the 'free press', human rights, *habeas corpus* and so on. But alongside the 'democratic' state (and sometimes overlapping it) there exists a secret, massively resourced,[1] extremely powerful and highly centralised state occupied by the massively over-resourced intelligence and security services:[2]

- MI5 for domestic security – with links to intelligence services in more than 100 countries (Hennessey and Thomas 2009: 604).[3]

- MI6 – otherwise known as the Secret Intelligence Service (SIS) – supplying the government with foreign intelligence.

- GCHQ, the Cheltenham-based signals (SIGINT) spying centre. Plus the little known but 'hugely important' Her Majesty's Government Communications Centre, in Hanslope.[4] All the spy services are increasingly using new technologies to analyse social media for intelligence and surveillance use.[5]

- Secret cabinet committees set up to deal with specific emergencies – such as Margaret Thatcher's MISC 57, chaired by Peter Gregson, which planned for the miners' strike of 1984 by making sure there was a huge stockpile of coal for the power stations (Marsden 2013).

- The Metropolitan Police's special 'domestic extremism unit' monitoring the activities of protestors (Evans 2016).

- Special Branch, responsible for security in British and Commonwealth police forces.[6]

- The RAF Police – providing the policing, counter-intelligence and specialist security support to the RAF.[7]

- The National Crime Agency, set up in October 2013, to gather intelligence in the fight against serious and organised crime.[8]
- Undercover police units.[9]
- And special military forces, such as the SAS, together with mercenary groups and individuals with close ties to covert intelligence.[10]

According to Clive Bloom (2015: 191), there are also very close ties between the intelligence services and the highly secretive City of London, a massive tax haven at the heart of the British establishment.[11]

Britain is also tied closely to the massive EU intelligence system. In part, this involves the EU satellite reconnaissance programme, the Intelligence Division, and the Joint Situation Centre (SITCEN), supplying risk analyses and intelligent support for the EU's diplomatic missions, EUROPOL (the European Police Office Counterterrorism). Its remit covers most forms of organised crime including drug trafficking, illegal immigration, people-trafficking, fraud and forgery and the illegal trade in radioactive and nuclear materials (Todd, Bloch and Fitzgerald 2009: 146-153). The Five Eyes intelligence alliance also links the security services of Australia, Canada, New Zealand, the US and UK. The former NSA contractor, Edward Snowden, described Five Eyes as a 'supra –national intelligence organisation that does not answer to the known laws of its own countries'.[12] And according to Bloch and Fitzgerald (1983: 142), MI6 exchanges information on Palestinians with Mossad, the Israeli secret service. The Joint Intelligence Committee of the Cabinet Office oversees the priorities for the security services – and members of the Australian, Canadian and US intelligence communities take part on JIC discussions.[13]

As Anthony Sampson highlighted, MI5 and MI6 and their many competing factions are only part of a much wider intelligence community (2004: 151): 'This includes private companies, often employing ex-MI6 officers, which have their own interests in cultivating mystery and which rapidly expanded in the 1980s and 1990s, benefiting from the global market-place.' Such companies include Control Risks, Sandline and the Hakluyt Foundation.[14]

THE SECRET STATE AND THE LAW

The secret state is variously described and theorised: as 'shadow government', 'invisible government', 'deep state', 'security state', 'clandestine state' (Wilson 2009). It operates both within and outside the law. It is crucially protected by a raft of laws:

- The Official Secrets Acts of 1889, 1911 and 1920, revised in 1989 to remove the 'public interest' defence from whistleblowers.
- The Intelligence Services Act of 1994 which placed the intelligence services on a legal basis.

- The Regulation of Investigatory Powers Act (2000) allows the authorities to secure the phone records of journalists in cases of 'national security'. In 2015, the Interception of Communication Commissioner's Office revealed that police forces had used RIPA against 82 journalists over a three-year period to access confidential material.

- The Justice and Security Act of 2013 which allows for secret courts to consider, for instance, allegations of torture against MI5. Government ministers can apply for special courtroom measures known as 'closed material procedure' whenever the government or its secret services are being sued in UK courts. The fact that a hearing is being held in secret can itself be kept secret.

- The Data Retention and Investigatory Powers Act 2014 allows for the creation of a privatised database of everyone's communications activity. According to Joseph Cannataci, the first UN privacy chief, surveillance in the UK is 'worse than Orwell imagined' (Alexander 2015).

- The largely unnoticed re-writing of clause 10 of the Computer Misuse Act, which came into force in March 2015, effectively makes lawful GCHQ's hacking operations (Bowcott 2015).

Significantly, the Freedom of Information legislation (of 2000) fails in any way to cover the activities of the secret state (and, interestingly, the royal family, too). Members of the public can bring complaints against the security services by using the Investigatory Powers Tribunal – but in its 15-year history it has only once ruled against the intelligence services (Verkaik 2016).

The system of Defence and Security Media Advisory (DSMA) Notices (better known as D Notices) also serves to restrain the media in their coverage of sensitive security issues (Wilkinson 2009). Once a notice is issued by the secretary of the DSMA committee, editors are asked to censor reporting. The system, introduced in 1912 to prevent breaches in security by German spies, is entirely voluntary (see its website at http://www.dsma.uk/ and Keeble 2009: 272). According to John Turner, linked to the centralisation of power is the secrecy 'which pervades British politics and the patronising assumption that the government knows best. Britain's culture of secrecy is buttressed by harsh libel laws, weak rights of access to official information, the Official Secrets Act and the D Notice system' (2006: 190).

There is little democratic accountability in the secret state: the Intelligence Services Act of 1994 created the intelligence and security committee of the house of commons though this provides hardly any credible oversight. The first 'grilling' of the heads of MI5 (Andrew Parker), MI6 (Sir John Sawers) and GCHQ (Sir Iain Lobbam) in November 2013 proved an embarrassing flop. As Shami Chakrabarti, director of Liberty, commented: 'These public servants presided over blanket surveillance of the entire population without public, parliamentary or democratic mandate. Yet they faced a grilling that wouldn't have scared a puppy' (Walker 2013).

The ministry of defence and foreign and commonwealth office also keep secret, illegally, thousands of files that should have been declassified and transferred to the National Archive under the 30-year rule. As Iain Cobain reported: 'More than 66,000 separate [MoD] files are being stored at an enormous warehouse operated by TNT Archive Service at Swadlincote in southern Derbyshire, despite the department's legal obligation to assess them for declassification once they are three decades old and either hand them to the archives at Kew, south-west London, or publicly give a reason for keeping them classified' (Cobain 2013).[15] Moreover, it was also revealed that the foreign office has hoarded 1.2 million files – some of them dating back to 1840. A number of leading academics from Oxford, Cambridge and London universities were planning to take legal action to bring the archive into the public domain (Cobain 2014a).

For Richard Aldrich, historians have been slow to acknowledge the influence and power of the secret state (1998: 3): 'Unlike France, where secret service has always remained a less than respectable activity, consigned to the fringes of government, in post-war Britain it was at the very centre.' The radical historian E. P. Thompson, in an early, seminal paper on the emergence of the 'secret, unaccountable state within the state' (1980: 156-157), said it had been, paradoxically, 'aided by the unpopularity of security and policing agencies'.

> Forced by this into the lowest possible visibility, they learned to develop techniques of invisible influence and control. It was also aided by the British tradition of civil service neutrality; this sheltered senior civil servants from replacement or investigation when administrations changed, and afforded to their policies the legitimation of 'impartial, non-political' intent.[16]

Significantly, in their analysis of the contemporary secret state, Dorril and Ramsay gave the media a crucial role. The heart of the secret state they identified as the security services, the cabinet office and upper echelons of the home and commonwealth offices, the armed forces and ministry of defence, the nuclear power industry and its satellite ministries together with a network of senior civil servants. As 'satellites' of the secret state, their list included 'agents of influence in the media, ranging from actual agents of the security services, conduits of official leaks, to senior journalists merely lusting after official praise and, perhaps, a knighthood at the end of their career' (Dorril and Ramsay 1991: x-xi).[17]

Yet, examining the links between Fleet Street journalists and the intelligence services is incredibly difficult. A few researchers and journalists – such as Stephen Dorril, author of a seminal history of MI6 (2000), David Leigh and Richard Norton-Taylor of the *Guardian*, Martin Bright of the *Observer*, freelances Paul Lashmar and Duncan Campbell, investigative reporter Phillip Knightley, and Robin Ramsay, editor of the alternative journal, *Lobster* – have managed to penetrate the fog that envelops all the work of the spooks – but only slightly.

NEWSPAPERS 'PLAYTHINGS OF MI5'

While it might then be difficult to identify precisely the impact of the spooks (variously represented in the press as 'intelligence', 'security', 'Whitehall' or 'home office' sources) on mainstream politics and media, from the limited evidence it looks to be enormous.[18] As Roy Greenslade, media blogger at the *Guardian*, and editor of the *Mirror* at the time of the Gulf crisis in 1991, commented: 'Most tabloid newspapers – or even newspapers in general – are playthings of MI5' (Milne 1995: 262). Journalist (with *The Times, Observer* and *Economist*), former MI6 officer and Soviet spy Kim Philby[19] once said that MI6 had penetrated the 'English mass media on a wide scale', running agents in the *Daily Telegraph, Sunday Times, Daily Mirror, Financial Times* and the *Observer* (Davies 2008: 235). Spy novelist John le Carré, who worked for British intelligence during the 1950s and 1960s, has even claimed that the British secret service then controlled large parts of the press – just as they may do today (Dorril 1993: 281).[20] In 2015, Frederick (*Day of the jackal*) Forsythe, best-selling spy novelist and former journalist, revealed in his autobiography he had worked for British intelligence for 20 years.[21]

According to John Kampfner (2010), chief executive of *Index on Censorship*, Fleet Street editors and senior journalists are habitually invited into MI5 and MI6 for briefings.

> These are affable occasions, often over lunch. There is no harm in that. What tends to happen, however, is that journalists are tickled pink by the attention. They love being invited to the 'D-notice' committee to discuss how they can all behave 'responsibly'. It makes them feel important. Many suspend their critical faculties as a result. Far from being 'feral beasts', to use Tony Blair's phrase, the British media are overly respectful of authority (ibid).

Indeed, David Leigh (2000a and 2000b) records a series of instances in which the secret services manipulated prominent journalists. He says reporters are routinely approached by intelligence agents: 'I think the cause of honest journalism is best served by candour. We all ought to come clean about these approaches and devise some ethics to deal with them. In our vanity, we imagine that we control these sources. But the truth is that they are very deliberately seeking to control us.' Leigh identifies three ways in which the secret intelligence services manipulate journalists:

- They attempt to recruit journalists to spy on other people or to go themselves under journalistic 'cover'.

- Intelligence officers are allowed to pose as journalists 'to write tendentious articles under false names'.[22]

- And 'the most malicious form: when intelligence agency propaganda stories are planted on willing journalists who disguise their origin from readers'.

Phillip Knightley also argues that journalists have a responsibility to be more aware about the activities of the secret services:

> What's the difference between a spy and a journalist? Not much. Both are in the information business. Both go out into the world and try to find out what's really going on. They look, listen and ask people questions. They assess the reliability of what they are told. They try to decide what is likely to happen next. Then they write a report for their bosses. Only now do their paths diverge. The journalist sends his or her report off expecting it will be published for the world to read. The spy sends his report off knowing it will not be published but instead will be used for political advantage. My point is that intelligence services are well aware of the similarities between journalism and spying and take full advantage them. But journalists are not so aware (Knightley 2006).[23]

Knightley argues that journalists must cease working for intelligence agencies. 'The discovery of only one journalist so employed ... entitles hostile authorities to assume that all journalists are so employed. Any journalist identified as working for an intelligence agency should lose his international identification and any right to protection for the rest of his working life' (Knightley 1982).

According to Peter Preston, *Observer* media commentator and former editor of the *Guardian* (2016):

> MI5 has a small team of serving officers who deal with the press, or more specifically, a few 'trusties'. ... The sources either give – or give nothing away. But they don't welcome interlopers, mavericks, independents.

John Simpson, BBC world affairs editor (1998: 296-297), describes in his autobiography how he was once approached by a 'man from MI5'. 'At some point they might make me broadcast something favourable to them. Or they might just ask me to carry a message to someone. You never knew,' he says. But Simpson adds: 'It doesn't do journalists any good to play footsie with MI5 or the Secret Intelligence Service; they get a bad reputation.'

Jonathan Bloch and Patrick Fitzgerald, in their examination of covert UK warfare, report the editor of 'one of Britain's most distinguished journals' as believing that more than half its foreign correspondents were on the MI6 payroll (1983: 134-141). And in 1991, Richard Norton-Taylor revealed in the *Guardian* that 500 prominent Britons paid by the CIA and the now defunct Bank of Commerce and Credit International, included 90 journalists (Pilger 1998: 496).

In May 2015, former *News of the World* chief reporter Neville Thurlbeck, jailed for 37 days for his involvement in the Hackgate scandal, revealed that he had been an informant for both the police and MI5 (Ponsford 2015; see also Harper 2011).

Many journalists have admitted wanting actually to become spies. The BBC *Newsnight* presenter Jeremy Paxman approached an SIS recruiter at university but was turned down (Knightley 2006).[24] On the other hand, journalist and later playwright Michael Frayn was invited to join MI6 – but turned them down (Evans 2009b: 300). So too the *Observer*'s Neal Ascherson who says that, while a correspondent in Berlin and Warsaw during the 1960s and 1970s, he had to ward off approaches by spooks of both sides (Ascherson 2011): 'It wasn't just knowing that the other lot would be aware of my recruitment – in leak-riddled Berlin, within days. It was also my guess that a mere hack informant was dispensable.' He continued:

> An attempt to recruit me ended almost instantly when the recruiter tried to seize me by the penis. On another occasion, a top MI6 officer described to me in detail how he had tortured Jewish suspects in Palestine. In Germany, a drunk British diplomat suddenly disclosed to me his true profession and several names in his West Berlin network, one of whom was a colleague (ibid).

Tony Benn worked for a while at the BBC after the Second World War. The spooks offered him between £490 and £1,100 'to come on board'. 'I told them I was considering becoming an MP and they said that was perfectly all right. They had also infiltrated the Labour Party HQ and the trade union movement. Years ago we were thought to be paranoid but it turns out we were quite right' (Wynne-Jones 1996).

MI5 certainly kept a close eye on all BBC staff between 1948 and 1985 through a vigorous system of vetting. From Room 105 on the first floor of Broadcasting House, in London, the BBC employed a security liaison officer, known as 'Special Assistant to the Director of Personnel' who sent the names of all successful job applicants to MI5's C Branch who checked against the records.[25] Not even the home secretary knew of this vetting. And Lord Rees was shocked when it was revealed in the *Observer* in 1985. According to Jean Seaton, the official historian of the BBC (2015: 18):

> While the BBC and the government slugged it out in public, they also cooperated in private and in the public interest over bigger issues: planning for the threat of nuclear Armageddon or the collapse of civil order. Because of this, BBC staff were vetted. The decision by the BBC, until Alasdair Milne became director-general in 1982, not merely to accept but to argue for *greater* vetting of its staff, was partly protective: when the corporation was being routinely accused of infiltration by opponents of the state – of being full of pinkoes and traitors – the use of official clearance proved it was not.

Hollingsworth and Fielding (1999: 105) report: 'The practice was abolished soon after its public disclosure. Today only the director general and two senior executives are vetted by MI5 as they are considered key personnel in the event of a national emergency.'

Currently MI5 has 33,000 dossiers on individuals and groups considered 'security risks'; 95,000 files on people and organisations who have received 'protective security advice'.[26] But on top of these official figures, the security services have hundreds of thousands of other closed files on microfiche (ibid: 114).[27] Journalists on MI5 files have included Richard Norton-Taylor, Paul Foot and the investigative journalist Duncan Campbell. MI5 even bugged the telephone of Victoria Brittain, the *Guardian*'s deputy foreign editor, after her bank, the Abbey National, reported large sums of money had been deposited in her account (Norton-Taylor 1997).

SPLITS IN THE INTELLIGENCE COMMUNITY: AND THE IMPACT ON THE MEDIA

Yet it is wrong to see the intelligence community as unified with one single ambition. As intelligence has grown so have the competing factions within it. The media, then, become the theatre in which these various factions play out their games for supremacy. Chapman Pincher, over a very long journalistic career (he died in August 2014 aged 100), fed stories to Fleet Street from various competing factions within the intelligence services (see Andrew 2009: 627-645). As the obituary in the *Daily Telegraph* recorded:

> There were many casualties in these campaigns. Pincher revealed that 'my friend' the late Sir Maurice Oldfield, former 'C' of MI6, was a homosexual. He was one of the leading protagonists for the (discredited) theory that the late Sir Roger Hollis, former head of MI5, was a traitor. Like a number of other journalists, Pincher was aware of Sir Anthony Blunt's treachery. Curiously, it was one story he did not tell.[28]

Christopher Moran comments on Pincher's journalistic techniques, approvingly (2013: 108):

> As Pincher's fame grew, he found himself inundated with people wanting to leak him things. With seemingly little concern for the risks involved, senior figures in Whitehall often took extended lunch breaks to join the scoop-gatherer in his preferred London haunts, which included the Écu de France, the Dorchester and Kettner's Restaurant and Champagne Bar. Knowing the journalist's fondness for traditional British field sports, other officials invited him to hunts, shoots and fishing trips. ... Many went to Pincher to sell their agenda to the public, others simply to cause professional angst in their opponents.

Historian and polemist E. P. Thompson was less charitable. Pincher, he said was like an 'official urinal' at which the great and good queued up to leak. He added: 'One can only admire their resolute attention to these distasteful duties' (Thompson 1980: 116).[29] And Paul Lashmar commented (2013): 'Pincher was a primary conduit to the public sphere for intelligence officials and whether the flow was informal or formal was often obscure not least because it was not supposed to happen at all.'

Significantly, in the late 1990s, factions emerged which managed to marginalise traditional elements within both MI6 and the CIA. In the UK, the Rockingham Cell emerged triumphant; in the United States it was the Office of Special Plans (OSP), set up by the defense secretary, Donald Rumsfeld in 2002 (Borger 2003; Baker 2007: 293).

ORWELL AND THE SPOOKS

The links between the hacks and spooks are clearly well established.[30] Going as far back as 1945, George Orwell, no less, became a war correspondent for the *Observer* and *Manchester Evening News* – probably as a cover for intelligence work.[31] Significantly most of the men he met in Paris on his assignment were working for intelligences services of one kind or another. One of them was Malcolm Muggeridge who introduced him to P. G. Wodehouse (Wolfe 1995: 215; Muggeridge 1975: 256-257). Muggeridge had been assigned to keep watch on the comic novelist who was suspected of having Nazi sympathies following his broadcasts in the summer of 1941 from Berlin for the American CBS network (Donaldson 2005 [1982]: 259-260).[32] Orwell had written an article in defence of Wodehouse in February just before leaving on his assignment (though it was not published until July in the *Windmill* magazine) and may simply have wanted to express his admiration to the creator of Jeeves and Bertie Wooster (Keeble 2001a).

Malcolm Muggeridge (1903-1990) began his journalistic career as Moscow correspondent for the *Manchester Guardian* and during the Second World War served in the British Secret Intelligence Services in Brussels, Lourenço Marques in Portuguese East Africa and Paris. Later he worked closely with the CIA-funded Congress for Cultural Freedom and *Encounter* magazine (see Saunders 1999). During the late 1940s he was the *Daily Telegraph*'s Washington correspondent and became its deputy editor before a four-year stint (1953-1957) as editor of the satirical journal *Punch*.

Orwell also met the philosopher (and fellow old Etonian) A. J. 'Freddie' Ayer,[33] in Paris for the Secret Intelligence Service (MI6) who were particularly concerned about the danger of a communist coup (Ayer 1978: 286-287; Rogers 1999: 192). Another writer Orwell saw was Ernest Hemingway whom he had previously met in Barcelona during the Spanish Civil War. The American novelist, who was serving as a war correspondent and staying at the Paris Ritz, had close links with members of the Office of Strategic Services (OSS, the forerunner of the CIA) and his son, Jack, was member of the OSS (Whiting 1999: 104). Carlos Baker's account of the meeting in his biography of Hemingway (1972: 672-673), based on a letter he wrote to the critic Hervey Breit on 16 April 1952, only adds to the mystery: 'Orwell looked nervous and worried. He said he feared that the Communists were out to kill him and asked Hemingway for the loan of a pistol. Ernest lent him the

.32 Colt that Paul Willerts had given him in June. Orwell departed like a pale ghost.' Andrew Belsey raises some intriguing questions about this incident: why did Paul Willerts give a pistol to Hemingway? Where did the pistol come from? Was Willerts authorised to give away weapons that presumably belonged to the military? What happened to the pistol after it was lent to Orwell? Was it returned, or did Orwell retain it?[34] Belsey comments: 'Group-Captain Paul Willerts was Air Attaché in Paris at the time. He was the son of Sir Arthur Willerts, previously head of the press office at the FO, and before that *Times* correspondent in Washington. No doubt both were familiar with the magic circle of intelligence.'[35]

Most evenings in Paris, Orwell dined with Harold Acton, whom he had known vaguely at Eton and who was working as a press censor for SHAEF (the Supreme Headquarters Allied Expeditionary Force), currently based at the palace of Versailles (Bowker 2003: 324).

Orwell's possible links with the security service (MI5) have been explored in detail by West (1992: 162-65). West reports a 'retired CIA officer in Washington' asserting that Orwell worked for MI5 and suggests that he could have developed contacts with Maxwell Knight, head of MI5's Department B5(b) counter-subversion unit and a former pupil of Orwell's prep school, St Cyprian's in Eastbourne. Yet Anthony Masters (1984) makes no reference to Orwell in his biography of Knight. Speculation about Orwell's links with the secret services intensified after Shelden reported in his biography of Orwell (1991: 467-469) that he had drawn up a 'little list' of 38 people, briefly (and somewhat crudely) identifying their politics, religious affiliations, sexual preferences and possible communist sympathies (see also Saunders 2000: 298-301). Orwell's original list contained 130 names. The 'known' suspects include Labour MPs, the future Poet Laureate, Cecil Day-Lewis, authors J. P. Priestley and Naomi Mitchison, journalist Arthur Calder-Marshall, actors Michael Redgrave, Charlie Chaplin and the historian Isaac Deutscher (Keeble 2012). A full list of the 38 (plus the cryptic, often insulting comments about the individual) was provided by the historian Timothy Garton Ash in the *Guardian* on the 100th anniversary of his birth. He comments:

> One thing that does shock our contemporary sensibility in the notebook is his ethnic labelling of people, especially the eight variations of 'Jewish?' (Charlie Chaplin), 'Polish Jew', 'English Jew' or 'Jewess' (Marjorie Kohn). Orwell's whole life was a struggle to overcome the prejudices of his class and generation; here was one he never overcame (Garton Ash 2003a).

According to Lashmar and James (1998: 97), Orwell supplied the list to his friend, the sister-in-law of the author Arthur Koestler, Celia Kirwan (née Paget) on 2 May 1949 when she was working for the secret state's propaganda unit, the Information Research Department (IRD), recently established by the Labour government.[36] However, Newsinger notes (1999: 36-37): 'It is most unlikely that Orwell realised the real nature of IRD at the time.' Kirwan denied that the list ever reached the foreign office.[37] Lucas (2003: 110), however, is unforgiving: 'Far from being a one-off indiscretion, Orwell's list is the culmination of his response to the left from the 1930s onwards. Not only could he not co-operate with many fellow writers and activists, not only did he denigrate them publicly and privately, but he maintained a watch on them as possible subversives.'

For James Smith (2015: 145), Orwell made 'a gross miscalculation, whatever excuses are made about physical sickness clouding his judgement or the sincerity of his belief regarding the necessity of opposing totalitarian communism'. Given his wartime fears about secret files being kept by the police, 'it was hypocritical in the extreme for Orwell to then swell the secret files held by other agencies'.

Smith goes on to report that IRD later found extensive use for Orwell's overt work, becoming major facilitators of the worldwide distribution, translation and adaptation of *Animal Farm* (1945) and *Nineteen Eighty-Four* (1949). 'Some of this occurred in Orwell's lifetime and, indeed, with his knowledge.' Moreover, the 1954 animated film version of *Animal Farm*, directed by John Halas and Joy Batchelor, 'was almost entirely the child of the CIA'. 'From talking Orwell's widow Sonia Blair into signing over the rights, to funding the production, overseeing script changes, and distributing the film, the web woven around the film can all be traced back to CIA fronts and contacts' (ibid: 149).

Paradoxically, Orwell had been closely followed by the secret state since becoming a radical journalist in Paris in the late 1920s. Orwell's Special Branch file (MEPO 38/69), covering material from 1936 to 1942 and running to around 24 pages, and his MI5 file (KV 2/2699), spanning 1936 to 1951 and containing 38 pages, were released in 2005 and 2007 respectively (Keeble 2012). To what extent was Orwell aware of being followed? In Chapter 8 of *Down and Out in Paris and London* (1933), he relates a curious story concerning his brush with communist groups in Paris 'and briefly alludes to his fear that the French police were watching him during 1929'. Indeed, an SIS report dated 8 February 1929, noted that 'Blair apparently states that he is the Paris correspondent for the "Daily Herald", "Daily Express", "G. K.'s Weekly", but he makes no mention of the "Workers' Weekly"'(Smith 2015: 114).

According to Smith, the next sustained security investigation of Orwell occurred in 1936 when he travelled to the North of England for two months examining working class conditions for what was later published as *The Road to Wigan Pier*, in 1937. On 22 February 1936, a detective constable in Wigan reported his contacts with 'undesirable elements', noting that he was staying 'at an apartment house in a working class district in this Borough', that 'a member of the local Communist Party was instrumental in finding Blair accommodation' and that he 'attended a Communist meeting in this town addressed by Wal Hannington' (ibid: 115).

A four-page report filed on 11 March 1936, according to Smith, provided a 'reasonably comprehensive overview of the major periods of Orwell's life', based on 'files of security and governmental agencies, as well as possibly from a human source with access to the discussions of the "intimate friends" of Orwell' (ibid: 116). After this burst of investigation in 1936, Orwell appears to have attracted only sporadic attention from the spooks before World War Two. Just before the opening of hostilities, Orwell's house was raided by police and several books were confiscated on the basis that they came from a Parisian publisher noted for 'obscene' texts. Moreover, while he worked at the Eastern Division of the BBC from 1941-1943, he was closely watched by both Special Branch and MI5 (ibid).

Perhaps the closest clues to Orwell's possible intelligence links lie in his extremely close friendship with David Astor, the millionaire *Observer* journalist whose father owned the newspaper and who was to be its celebrated editor from 1948 to 1975 (Cockett 1991).[38] Astor's intelligence ties went back as far as 1939, when he did 'secret service stuff', according to his cousin, Joyce Grenfell (Macintyre 2014). He served in the early part of the Second World War in naval intelligence alongside Ian Fleming (later author of the James Bond spy novels) (Cabell 2008: 12) and later with the covert Special Operation Executive (SOE).[39] Thereafter, he maintained close links with intelligence.

Both Richard Crockett (1991: 94) and Bernard Crick (1982: 425-426) report that Astor had been determined to meet Orwell after reading his 'Lion and the Unicorn' (1941) and finally secured an introduction to him through Cyril Connolly, an old Etonian friend of Orwell, then editing the influential journal *Horizon* and filling in for the *Observer's* literary editor. They met in a café near the BBC off Portland Place where Orwell was working on broadcasts to India and quickly became friends. After leaving the BBC in November 1943, Orwell planned to report for the *Observer* from Algiers and Sicily following the Allied landings but the authorities turned him down on health grounds. Orwell then quickly acquired the post of literary editor at the leftist weekly *Tribune*, which he held until February 1945 when he resigned to take on the war reporting assignment.[40]

Was it a cover for an intelligence mission? Dorril (2000: 457) certainly reports that in 1944 Astor was transferred to a unit liaising between SOE and the resistance in France, helping the French underground in London spread the word to groups throughout Europe. While in Paris, perhaps inspired by Astor, Orwell attended the first conference of the Committee for European Federation, bringing together resistance groups from around Europe. The French novelist and editor of *Combat*, Albert Camus, was amongst those present. Astor was later adamant that Orwell had no intelligence links[41] and Peter Davison, editor of Orwell's twenty-volume complete works, commented: 'I doubt if Orwell would be involved with intelligence – but that by no means says he wasn't.'[42]

Adding to the extraordinary Orwell spy mystery is the evidence that he was spied on in Spain by the communists and British intelligence as he fought with the Trotskyite POUM militia against Gen. Franco's fascists! Orwell's biographer Gordon Bowker revealed that David Crook, a young communist from London, spied on Orwell, his wife Eileen, who visited him on the frontline, and other members of the contingent from the Independent Labour Party (Bowker 2003: 219). Crook had been taught the techniques of surveillance by Ramon Mercader, a communist who later murdered Trotsky in Mexico with an ice-pick. And he took his orders from the Soviet espionage agency, then known as the NKVD and later renamed the KGB. Rob Evans comments on Crook (2003):

> He insinuated himself into the ILP office in Barcelona. Soon he had the freedom of the office and, during lunch breaks, stole files and had them photographed in the Russian embassy. He was proud that within a short time, copies of all the files in the office were in the hands of his Russian handlers. Details of his activities are held in the KGB archives, although Orwell's KGB file is still under wraps.

Among his reports was an observation that he was '95 per cent certain' that Eileen Blair, who married Orwell in 1936, was having an affair with Georges Kopp, another ILP member. Crook had been instructed by the Soviets to seek out the existence of affairs, as such information could enable the communists to blackmail vulnerable targets. He passed his reports to Hugh O'Donnell, another communist from London, whose codename was O'Brien. According to Bowker (op cit: 219), Orwell was oblivious to this: '... the fact that the character in *Nineteen Eighty-Four* who first wins the confidence of Winston Smith and then betrays him is given the name O'Brien must be one of the strangest coincidences in literature.'

Adding further to the mysteries came the revelation in 2006 that Orwell's closest comrade in Spain, Georges Kopp was actually spying on him for British intelligence, in a case being run by Anthony Blunt (later to be revealed a Soviet spy). Kopp was captured in Spain and tortured but somehow managed to survive (Fenton 2006).

JAMES BOND TO THE RESCUE?

Some of the most important research into the links between hacks and spooks has been conducted by Phillip Knightley, author of *The first casualty* (2003a [1975]), a seminal history of war correspondents, and *The second oldest profession* (1986), a history of the intelligence services. He has even claimed that at least one intelligence agent is working on every Fleet Street newspaper (Keeble 2003a). Moreover, he said he was convinced 'MI5 has agents in newspapers, printers and publishing houses who tip off MI5/SIS about impending publication of material that would be of interest to the services'.[43]

In particular, Knightley has highlighted the activities, immediately after the Second World War, of the Kemsley Imperial and Foreign Service, better known by its cable address, Mercury. It was part of the Kemsley and then the Thomson chain of newspapers, which provided foreign news and features to newspapers such as *The Sunday Times* and the *Empire News*.

The head of Mercury was Ian Fleming, celebrated author of the James Bond spy novels, who had served in British naval intelligence during the war. In his official history of MI6, Keith Jeffery significantly records Fleming being chosen to communicate to the press the disinformation relating to 'Paul Lewis Claire', a French naval officer taken on by SIS, who had been suspected of defecting to the fascist Vichy regime in France, and who had been killed during a struggle in a car (2011: 406): 'The official story (as communicated by Commander Ian Fleming of Naval Intelligence to the British Red Cross in July 1942) represented Claire as "missing believed drowned", en route to Britain on the SS Empire Hurst, sunk by enemy aircraft on 11 August 1941.' It was all lies.

In 1942, Fleming created 30CU (later known as 30AU), a covert unit of soldiers expert in armed combat and intelligence gathering.[44] Charles Wheeler, who later went on to become the BBC's longest serving correspondent, and Donald McLachlan, who became editor of the *Sunday Telegraph*, were key men in the unit (Cabell op cit: 60-71). Veterans of the unit interviewed by Cabell remembered Wheeler as 'being a fierce interrogator of enemy captors' (ibid: 172).

After the war, Fleming controlled, as head of Mercury, a worldwide network of 88 journalists many of whom had wartime intelligence backgrounds (Trelford 2009). Cedric Salter, formerly of the SOE, was sent to Barcelona; Ian Colvin (who had close SIS links) to Berlin and Henry Brandon, an 'SIS asset', to Washington. Donald McCormick, formerly in naval intelligence, became Mercury's correspondent in Tangier and later foreign manager at *The Sunday Times*. He was also to write on intelligence matters under the pseudonym, Richard Deacon. Anthony Terry, *The Sunday Times*'s man in Bonn, also worked as a Mercury correspondent and as an officer of British intelligence in Berlin and Vienna. Fleming required his correspondents to write regular 'situation reports', or 'Sitreps' providing background information – not for publication – about activities in their parts of the world. Fleming's biographer Andrew Lycett (1996: 170) records McCormick saying that material from these Sitreps was 'passed on to branches of Intelligence as and when this seemed justified'. Anthony Cavendish, a former SIS officer, writes: 'At the end of the war a number of MI6 agents were sent abroad under the cover of newspapermen. Indeed, the Kemsley press allowed many of their correspondents to co-operate with MI6 and even took on MI6 operatives as foreign correspondents' (Knightley 2006: 8).

Denis Hamilton, personal assistant to the newspaper magnate Lord Kemsley (1946-1950), later editorial director of Kemsley Newspapers (1950-1958) and editor-in-chief of *The Times* and *Sunday Times* (1967-1981), was said to have 'strong intelligence connections' (Sisman 2015: 140).[45] Derek Tanye, who had served in MI5 during the war, later worked in Fleet Street as a gossip columnist on the *Daily Express* and elsewhere. Sisman (ibid: 325) reports: 'It has been alleged that he continued to work for MI5 secretly after the war, and even that he was a Soviet agent, though the case has not been proven beyond doubt.'

Eric Downton, a legendary Canadian war correspondent, who worked with Reuters and spent 24 years on the *Daily Telegraph*'s foreign staff, told Knightley (2006):

> During my time with Reuters and the *Telegraph* I was appalled by the extent to which the British news media co-operated with MI5 and MI6 and the widespread use made of British foreign correspondents by Six. Roy Pawley, foreign editor and later managing editor of the *Telegraph*, was a servile lackey of Five and Six. *Telegraph* foreign correspondents were given direct orders to work with Six. When I went to Moscow for the *Telegraph* shortly after Stalin's death, I was ordered by Pawley – who said Lord Camrose and Michael Berry were aware of these activities – to work for the Six man in the embassy who had the usual cover of press attaché. Before I left London for Moscow I was briefed by Six officials on what they wanted me to do. *The Times* and the *Telegraph*, as I observed it, were particularly close to the intelligence services but all the major British newspapers, and the BBC apparently, had degrees of symbiosis. Presumably this sort of thing still goes on.[46]

Moreover, according to Tom Bower (1995: 170), during the 1950s, SIS was at the front line of the Cold War.

> They believed themselves to be the guardians of the nation's freedom and the best judges of morality. Above all, they prospered because London's newspaper editors, respecting the government's edict not to pry too deeply into the nation's secret armoury, were still content to cultivate the popular conviction that Britain's spies were efficient, effective and invincible (ibid).

According to Richard Norton-Taylor, *Guardian* security specialist, there is a category of people who are particularly attractive to intelligence agencies: 'They may be informers, arms dealers, businessmen, even journalists. Their common value is their special access to groups or targets which the agencies have in their sights but cannot reach on their own. And if anything goes wrong, the agencies can always resort to the well-worn defence of "plausible deniability"' (see Dorril 1993: 274). Thus, during the later 1950s, MI6 began recruiting on a massive scale anyone (journalists, businessmen, academics) who might be useful on their travels to the Soviet bloc to gather intelligence – and perhaps even help with introductions to Soviet officials who might be 'turned' (ibid: 275).[47] Aldrich (2009: 18) summed up the situation this way:

> …during the Cold War, governments also launched major operations in the realm of propaganda and cultural warfare that have required close co-operation with – even co-option – of the press, academia, cultural organisations and other elements of civil society. For many years, the available forms of non-official cover for Western intelligence officers

wishing to operate in the Middle East or Asia was mostly limited to business, journalism or archaeology. Therefore, the worlds of intelligence and the media intersect at many points.[48]

Edward Crankshaw worked for the *Observer* from 1947-1968, specialising in Soviet affairs. Robert McCrum comments obliquely (2016):

> Steeped in Russia, Crankshaw seems always to have mixed reportage with espionage, attracting the attention of both the CIA and the KGB. In a world of nods and winks across Whitehall and St James's, the line between the fourth estate and the defence of the realm was indistinct. An extraordinary amount of British journalism was still conducted in London's clubland, where the spirit of John Buchan's Richard Hannay ultimately morphed into John le Carré's George Smiley.

Mark Frankland, in his fascinating autobiography *Child of my time* (1999: 92), tells of his time in the early 1950s working for SIS (he later became a distinguished foreign correspondent for the *Observer*):

> …there were few inhibitions about whom SIS could enrol as agents; certainly journalism was not the forbidden territory it became later. Journalists working abroad were natural candidates for agents, and particularly useful in places such as Africa where British intelligence was hurrying to establish itself. One of our station chiefs found an out-of-work British journalist he thought could be useful if he had cover as stringer for a London paper. P15 [the code name for the man who controlled the production of intelligence from north Africa and for whom Frankland, P15/B, worked] contacted the section that handled London operations, which sent an officer to call on co-operative newspapers, and in those days probably the only one that was not was the *Daily Worker* [organ of the Communist Party of Great Britain]. A Fleet Street daily agreed to take the man on and a new agent was born.

Frankland later served as the *Observer*'s Moscow correspondent. As Stephen Dorril records (2015: 215) 'Frankland denied being a journalist agent though he was, in 1985, singled out for expulsion by the Soviets.' Paul Lashmar also comments (2013): 'I recall at the *Observer* in the 1970s and 80s there was a back channel to MI5 via the then editor Donald Trelford to the MI5's legal adviser Bernard Sheldon. It was used rarely and only when a story did have national security implications. I have no doubt this limited channel was also available to other major national organisations.'

Sometimes journos act as 'postmen' for the intelligence services. James Mossman served in MI6 during the war and later became *Daily Telegraph* correspondent in Cairo. In the late 1950s, MI6 officer James McGlasham over a cup of coffee asked Mossman to deliver money to a man who was to assassinate President Nasser.

Richard Aldrich and Rory Cormac continue (2016: 201): 'He drove twelve miles to a location outside the city and handed over a package containing £20,000 in used banknotes, then telephoned to confirm safe delivery – but he had handed it to the wrong man. Nothing more was heard of the money.' Mossman went on to become a celebrated journalist on the BBC's *Panorama* investigative programme.

Peter Evans, home affairs correspondent of *The Times* for 17 years during the 1960s and 1970s, tells of how MI5 tried to recruit him – but he declined the offer (2009). As a result MI5 began investigating him.[49]

The mysterious and shocking assassination of David Holden, *The Sunday Times*'s chief correspondent, in Cairo in December 1977, may have been linked to his covert work for intelligence agencies. Harold Evans, his editor at the time, considers the CIA, for whom he may have been working, instigated the murder (though carried out by Egyptian police) when they discovered he was acting as a double agent for the KGB (Evans 2009a: 368-391; 2009b). Evans's revelations prompted Donald Trelford, editor of the *Observer* from 1975 to 1993, to reminisce about the activities of his 'star foreign correspondent' Gavin Young (Trelford op cit). He was once lunching in the Groucho Club when a stout figure asked him: 'Any news of Gavin?' The last he had heard Young was in the Far East. Trelford continued, somewhat nonchalantly: '"We heard," said Sir Maurice Oldfield, head of MI6 (for it was he) "that he had been swept overboard in a storm off Celebes. If you get any news, you'll know where to find me." When I got back to the office, I discovered that Gavin had survived the shipwreck. I was able to pass on the good news to the man who, I could only assume, was Gavin's joint employer.'

IRD: PROPAGANDA ARM OF THE EMPIRE

The release of Public Record Office documents in 1995 about some of the operations of the MI6-financed propaganda unit, the Information Research Department of the foreign office, threw light on this secret body – which even Orwell aided by sending them his list of 'crypto-communists'. Set up by the Labour government in 1948, it 'ran' dozens of Fleet Street journalists and a vast array of news agencies across the globe until it was closed down by foreign secretary David Owen in 1977. Such famous names as Denis Healey, Stephen Spender, Bertrand Russell and Guy Burgess helped or backed the work of IRD (Lashmar 2013). It was funded, like MI6, by the 'secret vote' and was thus beyond parliamentary scrutiny. John Rennie, its second head between 1953 and 1958, was later appointed head of MI6.

IRD distributed across the globe 'white' (true), 'grey' (partially true) and 'black' (false) propaganda, planting smears, lies, false rumours and forged official reports in the media.[50] As Phillip Deery comments: 'IRD worked hard to ensure that its propagandists – speechwriters, broadcasters, journalists and politicians – used the most effective words and phrases in their articles and speeches.'[51] And according to John Pilger (1998: 495-496):

In the anti-colonial struggles in Kenya, Malaya and Cyprus, IRD was so successful that the journalism served up as a record of those episodes was a cocktail of the distorted and false, in which the real aims and often atrocious behaviour of the British was suppressed. Thus the bloodshed in Malaya was and still is misrepresented as a 'model' of counter-insurgency; the anti-imperial uprising in Kenya was and still is distorted as a Mau Mau terror campaign against whites; and the struggle for basic human rights in Northern Ireland became and remains a noble defence of order and stability against IRA terror.[52]

Paul Lashmar and James Oliver (1998) argue:

... the vast IRD enterprise had one sole aim: to spread its ceaseless propaganda output (i.e. a mixture of outright lies and distorted facts) among top-ranking journalists who worked for major agencies, papers and magazines, including Reuters and the BBC, as well as every other available channel. It worked abroad to discredit communist parties in Western Europe which might gain a share of power by entirely democratic means, and at home to discredit the British Left.[53]

By 1960, IRD was the largest and fastest-growing department of the post-war foreign office though the official *Diplomatic List* for the year would have given no such indication (Aldrich op cit: 2-3). From 1970-1972 IRD staff were secretly drafted to serve on the European Community Information Unit: a covert propaganda operation aiming to persuade the British public to accept the Common Market (Ramsay 2003). When PM Edward Heath's files on the Common Market were released 30 years later, the ECIU's work was kept secret but some 200 files were quietly released a few months later at the National Archives, Kew. According to Ramsay (ibid), the IRD staff were used 'to soften up the public for huge price rises in basic commodities such as butter' while a government hospitality fund 'was used to entice supposedly independent-minded personalities to speak in favour of Europe'. 'Independent' people were to deluge newspapers with pro-Europe letters and to tour the country speaking on behalf of the pressure group, the British Council of the European Movement. Moreover, 'the unit persuaded Gwyn Morgan, Labour's assistant general secretary, to reveal Harold Wilson's campaign plans and to leak a copy of a report on the issue by Labour's national executive' (ibid).

But under Harold Wilson, the Labour Party cut funding to IRD when it took office in 1964, again in 1968 and 'slashed' funding in 1970 (Dorril and Ramsay op cit: 110). Col. 'Sammy' Logan, then-secretary of the D Notice committee, was actually on MI5's payroll and spent his £500 retainer spying on reporters and feeding the intelligence service 'titbits' about them (McCrystal 1999: 32). David Leigh suggests that IRD had '60 or so' newspaper, television and BBC and radio journalists on its mailing list in 1977 (Leigh 1980: 221).

The CIA's expansion in 1965 of the London-based propaganda unit, Forum World Features (FWF), with the knowledge and co-operation of British intelligence, was probably a response to the political and financial pressures on IRD (Dorril and Ramsay op cit: 110). Nick Davies suggests (op cit: 227) that FWF supplied reports to 140 newspapers around the world.

John Pilger also highlights the role of IRD in spreading propaganda during Sukarno's brutal coup in Indonesia in 1965. IRD head Norman Reddaway and his colleagues were able to manipulate the press and BBC so expertly that he was able to boast to Sir Andrew Gilchrist, British ambassador in Jakarta, in a secret message that the fake story he had promoted – that the communists were on the point of taking over in Indonesia – had 'gone all over the world and back again'.[54] Reddaway described how an experienced Sunday newspaper journalist agreed 'to give exactly your angle on events in his article … i.e., that this was a kid-glove coup without butchery'.

Then in December 2015, shadow home secretary Andy Burnham revealed during a parliamentary debate about the convictions of 24 pickets in 1972 (including the actor Ricky Tomlinson) that the Information Research Department had played a significant role in the making of the Anglia television documentary *Red under the bed*. A note from IRD to the foreign office said: 'We had a discreet but considerable hand in this programme. Mr [Woodrow] Wyatt [the leader of the investigation] was given a large dossier of our own background material. It is clear from internal evidence in the programme that he drew extensively on this' (James 2015).

CIA RECRUITS BRITISH JOURNALISTS

In the United States, as Aldrich (2009: 13) acknowledges, 'the relationship between intelligence and the media is long-standing and remarkably close'. After Frank Wisner was appointed director of the CIA's Office of Policy of Coordination in 1948, the press became a key vehicle for covert propaganda. Aldrich (ibid: 19) adds:

> Key players included Thomas Braden and Cord Meyer who in turn coopted respected members of *The New York Times*, *Newsweek*, CBS and other mainstream media outlets. Leading journalists who participated in these activities included Joseph Alsop, whose writing appeared in some two hundred different newspapers.

Following senate hearings on the CIA during 1975, the reports of the senate's Church committee and the house of representatives' Pike committee highlighted the extent of agency recruitment of both British and US journalists. Newspapers such as *The New York Times* had a secret agreement with the CIA to employ at least 10 agents as reporters or clerks in its foreign bureaux (Preston 2008). Church's report suggested that the CIA's media programme cost about $265 million a year – and that more than a thousand books were sponsored by the agency before the end of 1967 (Aldrich 2009: 20-21). The committee report said: 'The CIA currently maintains a network of several hundred foreign individuals ... who provide the CIA with direct access to a large number of newspapers and periodicals, scores of press services and news agencies, radio and television stations, commercial book publishers and other foreign media.'[55]

Publisher of *The New York Times*, Arthur Hays Sulzberger, was a good friend of Allen W. Dulles, director of the CIA 1953-61. In June 1954, for instance, the CIA asked *The Times* to keep its central American correspondent, Sydney Grayson, away from covering the coup in Guatemala (which dislodged the democratically-elected government of Jacobo Arbenz) – and Sulzberger complied (Chomsky 2005: 106). *The Times* had also significantly applauded the CIA coup in Iran in 1953. Feminist writer and journalist Gloria Steinem was revealed to be a CIA member but never apologised. She said: 'In my experience, the agency was completely different from its image; it was liberal, non-violent and honourable' (Preston 2008).

Joseph Alsop was one of 400 journalists identified as having carried out secret assignments for the CIA by Carl Bernstein (of Watergate fame) in a celebrated article in *Rolling Stone* magazine of October 1977 (Bernstein 1977).[56] Bernstein wrote:

> Some of these journalists' relationships with the Agency were tacit; some were explicit. There was cooperation, accommodation and overlap. Journalists provided a full range of clandestine services – from simple intelligence gathering to serving as go betweens with spies in Communist countries. Reporters shared their notebooks with the CIA. Editors shared their staffs. Some of the journalists were Pulitzer Prize-winners, distinguished reporters who considered themselves ambassadors without-portfolio for their country. Most were less exalted: foreign correspondents who found that their association with the Agency helped their work; stringers and freelancers who were as interested in the derring-do of the spy business as in filing articles; and, the smallest category, full-time CIA employees masquerading as journalists abroad. In many instances, CIA documents show, journalists were engaged to perform tasks for the CIA with the consent of the managements of America's leading news organisations (ibid).

The Pike committee found that 29 per cent of the CIA's covert operations were directed at 'media and propaganda' meaning that in 1978 the agency had spent at least as much as the combined budgets of the world biggest news agencies – AP, Reuters and UPI put together (Davies 2008: 226).

Hugh Wilford, in a detailed study of CIA-media links, reports (2008: 227) that 'the incidence of individual reporters performing covert tasks was less significant than the larger pattern of institutional collaboration' and he adds: 'Many of the United States' best-known newspapers co-operated with the CIA as a matter of policy.' And as Aldrich stresses (op cit: 18), during the Cold War the available forms of non-official cover for Western intelligence officers wishing to operate in the Middle East or Asia was mostly limited to business, archaeology – or journalism. The massive budgets enjoyed by the various US intelligence agencies also meant there were constant battles for supremacy amongst them. 'The press has often been the happy beneficiary of these Beltway Battles that have spilled onto the front pages of American newspapers. Inter-agency rivalry is a frequent cause of intelligence agencies briefing against each other' (ibid).

Hewitt and Lucas (2009: 115) similarly warn against over-simplifying the relations between the media and the spooks and seeing a unitary government approach. In fact, the reality is one of tensions. 'Indeed, such tensions can produce a situation when the media stands as a critic of the Executive not in opposition to but in alliance with officials from intelligence services.'

Carl Bernstein (1977), of Watergate fame, calculated that as many as 400 journalists had worked for the CIA since 1952. Phillip Knightley, in his seminal history of spying, *The second oldest profession: The spy as patriot, bureaucrat, fantasist and whore* (1986: 336), commented: 'It would be naïve to imagine that any intelligence agency does not use journalists, and the CIA was no exception. Since its founding [in 1947] it has employed up to a hundred working American newspapermen and some 12 to 15 CIA officers have used full-time journalistic cover on foreign assignments. As many as eight hundred foreign journalists have been used as "propaganda assets" by the CIA.'[57] According to David Southwell (2005: 57), a leaked internal CIA memo to a former agency director, reveals: 'We have agents and contacts with every major news wire service, newspaper, news weekly and television network in the nation.' Southwell adds: 'The CIA currently has agents working both in American news networks and key foreign broadcasters such as the BBC and al-Jazeera' (ibid).

And Nick Davies, in his remarkable study of MI6 and CIA propaganda arts, records that *The New York Times* had provided cover for at least ten CIA agents and had a general policy of co-operation with the agency (op cit: 226). He adds: 'The CIA kept no agents in Reuters, simply because it was British owned, and the CIA recognised that it was MI6 territory. However, when the need arose, the CIA used the MI6 agents in Reuters to place its own stories and Pike concluded that the agency had done this frequently.' In September 2010, it was revealed that the eminent photojournalist, Ernest Withers, who shot many of the celebrated images of Dr Martin Luther King and the civil rights movement during the 1960s, was, in fact, an FBI informer. Chris McGreal reported (2010):

> Records released under a freedom of information request show that from at least 1968, and possibly earlier, he spied on not only black civil rights activists but Catholic priests who supported a Memphis-wide strike by sanitation workers and political candidates, recording car number plates for the FBI. Withers also helped the bureau to break a militant black group called the Invaders, which had a following in Memphis in the late 1960s.

THE PRESS – AND THE EXTRAORDINARY PLOT TO OUST A PRIME MINISTER

The most famous whistleblower of all, Peter (*Spycatcher*) Wright, revealed that MI5 had agents in newspapers and publishing companies whose main role was to warn them of any forthcoming 'embarrassing publications' (1987). Wright also disclosed that the *Daily Mirror* tycoon, Cecil King, 'was a longstanding agent of ours' who 'made it clear he would publish anything MI5 might care to leak in his direction' (ibid: 369). King was also closely involved in an extraordinary plot in 1968 to oust Prime Minister Harold Wilson (suspected of radical left/communist leanings) and replace him with a coalition headed by Lord Mountbatten, Prince Charles's uncle (Marr 2007: 305-308; Cottrell 2008: 22-25, 28). Harold Evans, celebrated editor of *The Sunday Times* (1967-1981) intriguingly records in *Good times, bad times* (1983: 226) that in the late 1960s, *The Times* 'encouraged Cecil King's lunatic notion of a coup against Harold Wilson's Labour government in favour of a government of business leaders led by Lord Robens'. According to Phillip Knightley (1986: 352), MI5 did tell the home secretary, James Callaghan, about the plot – 'but Callaghan apparently decided against informing either Wilson or the Cabinet'.[58]

Wilson had taken the unprecedented step of forbidding MI5 to carry out any form of surveillance of MPs including telephone tapping, the opening of letters, examination of bank accounts. Five days later, Wilson announced the bugging ban also applied to members of the house of lords (Cobain 2014a). In 1997, with the development of email and other electronic communication, Prime Minister Tony Blair even assured the commons that the ban extended 'to all forms of warranted interception of communications' (ibid). But as Dorril and Ramsay (op cit: 65) comment: 'Unfortunately, Wilson's attempts to curtail MI5's activities did not work.' MI5 actually secretly planted bugs in 10 Downing Street despite repeated official denials, it was revealed in April 2010. This revelation was to have been included by Christopher Andrew in his best-selling history of MI5, published in 2009 but was suppressed by Whitehall officials to protect the 'public interest' (Norton-Taylor 2010a).[59] In any case, Ken Livingstone had revealed in an article in the *Independent* in November 1998 that MI5 continued to get the phone-tapping information on MPs via the CIA and GCHQ – without Wilson knowing this. Moreover, MI5 also continued to use a Tory MP, Captain Henry Kerby, who had ingratiated himself with a Labour MP, George Wigg, whom Harold Wilson made responsible for MI5 and MI6 (Livingstone 1998).[60]

The official MI5 history did, however, record that the intelligence service held a secret file on Wilson (who was given the pseudonym 'Norman John Worthington')[61] since 1947 and throughout the time he was Prime Minister. This was supposedly because of his contacts with Eastern European businessmen, KGB officers – and a belief amongst communist civil servants in Whitehall that he had similar political sympathies. Harold Wilson was, in fact, the only serving Prime Minister to have a permanent security service file (Evans, Michael 2009). Baroness Manningham-

Buller, director general of MI5 from 2002 to 2007, told *The Times* (ibid): 'You might well have a file, supposing you were a person who was a target for a terrorist attack. There was no plot, no conspiracy.'[62]

Peter Wright later confessed that just before the 1974 general election he had planned to leak a secret MI5 file on the Prime Minister to the press. 'The plan was simple. MI5 would arrange for selective details of intelligence about leading Labour Party figures, but especially Wilson, to be leaked to sympathetic pressmen' (Hollingsworth and Fielding op cit: 23). Richard Briginshaw, general secretary of the printing union, Natsopa, later claimed that his union 'had foiled attempts by the *Daily Mail* and *Daily Express* to print smear stories against Labour during the election simply by threatening to stop the presses' (Dorril and Ramsay op cit: 271).

On one occasion, Wilson confided in cabinet minister Shirley Williams (who later became one of the 'Gang of Four' founders of the Social Democratic Party in 1981) that his office in the cabinet chamber was bugged. Andy Beckett records (2010: 166): 'Williams thought at the time that Wilson was "off his trolley". But afterwards she had changed her mind: "There was a real attempt to try to undo him of a non-constitutional kind."'

David Leigh, in *The Wilson plot* (1989), his seminal study of the smearing of Harold Wilson before his sudden resignation in 1976, quotes an MI5 officer: 'We have somebody in every office in Fleet Street.' Selective details about Wilson and his alleged affair with his secretary, Marcia Falkender, were leaked by the intelligence services to sympathetic Fleet Street journalists and via the satirical journal, *Private Eye* (McConnachie and Tudge 2005: 42; Ramsay 2008: 147), and the *Spectator*. John Simpson, in his history of the reporting of the last century, *Unreliable sources* (2010: 465), records that in 1974, Patrick Marnham, of *Private Eye*, was handed a dossier on Wilson which he was told had come from MI5. Simpson adds (ibid): 'The general thrust of the documents he used in his articles was that Wilson was a Zionist-Soviet agent; not an easy double function to carry out, one would have thought.' Richard Norton-Taylor (1990: 96) also suggests that William Massie, defence correspondent of the *Sunday Express*, and Jak (Raymond Jackson), the *Evening Standard* cartoonist, had particularly close ties with intelligence.

Further false stories claimed Wilson was involved in corrupt land deals and had links with the KGB. James McConnachie and Robin Tudge report (2005: 41):

> Wilson's pedigree at Oxford University in the 1930s, when it was almost *de rigeur* to be a Marxist, aroused the conspirators' suspicions, but they were particularly interested in his trip to Moscow in 1947. As a junior minister at the Board of Trade, he was involved in selling aero-engines to the USSR; but rumour had it that he was compromised in a love tryst that kept him in hock thereafter to the KGB.

According to Wright there were also suspicions that Hugh Gaitskell, Wilson's predecessor as Labour leader, had been murdered by the KGB. Soviet defector

Anatoli Golitsin stoked these suspicions – reporting that the KGB had plotted to kill a major European leader 'to get their man in place' (ibid: 42). Edward Short, deputy leader of the Labour Party and leader of the house of commons, was also smeared: it was suggested he was involved in tax evasion, channelling secret funds via a Swiss bank account to offshore locations (Hollingsworth and Fielding 1999: 22).[63] Wright comments: 'No wonder Wilson was later to claim that he was the victim of a plot' (Wright op cit: 370).

In addition, Colin Wallace, a former army information officer during the 1970s, claimed Harold Wilson, along with other politicians, was also the target of a smear campaign, codenamed 'Clockwork Orange', waged by elements within the intelligence services during 1974-1975 in Northern Ireland (Penrose and Courtiour 1978; Thomas 1991: 148).[64] Significantly, Ken Livingstone used his maiden speech as a Labour MP in the house of commons in July 1987 to highlight Wallace's allegations.[65] Livingstone also told parliament in 1996 that seven of Wilson's cabinet and three Labour MPs were considered spies or security risks by the intelligence agencies (McConnachie and Tudge 2005: 42).

Shortly after resigning in 1976, Wilson gave his version of events to two BBC journalists, Barrie Penrose and Roger Courtiour. He even alleged that officers of BOSS, the South African intelligence service, were involved in moves to discredit his government. Penrose and Courtiour went on to publish the interviews in *The Pencourt file* (1978).

MI5 was cleared of plotting by two Prime Ministers – James Callaghan in 1977 and Margaret Thatcher in 1987. But Callaghan later said he was not confident that he had not misled the commons in his 1977 statement when he dismissed the allegations (Norton-Taylor 1990: 97). Again, in 1994, Stella Rimington, then MI5's director general, denied the existence of any anti-Wilson plot. But two years later, Lord Hunt, cabinet secretary throughout the 1974-1979 Labour government, told Channel 4's *Secret history* programme: 'There is absolutely no doubt at all that a few malcontents in MI5 who were right-wing, malicious and had serious personal grudges, were giving vent to this and spreading damaging and malicious stories about some members of the Labour government.'[66] Moreover, according to Peter Wright, MI5 always had about twenty senior journalists working for it in the national press. 'They were not employed directly by us, but we regarded them as agents because they were happy to be associated with us.'[67]

Hugh Cudlipp, editorial director of the *Mirror* from 1952 to 1974, was also closely linked to intelligence, according to Chris Horrie, in his history of the newspaper (2004: 237). And Cudlipp was closely involved in the anti-Wilson coup plot (Newton 2008/9: 7). Wright also referred to a 'senior executive' at the *Mirror* who was controlled by an MI5 Section D4 agent runner. Seamus Milne (1995: 263) reports that Cyril Morten, the *Mirror*'s managing editor, worked closely with MI6 and happily employed an MI6 agent as a *Mirror* photographer. David Walker, the *Mirror*'s foreign correspondent in the 1950s, was named as an MI6 agent following a security scandal while Stanley Bonnett, editor of the Campaign for Nuclear Disarmament's journal, *Sanity*, in the early 1980s, was exposed as an intelligence agent by whistleblower and former MI5 officer Cathy Massiter in a *20/20 Vision* programme on Channel 4 (Urban 1996: 46-47; Dorril 1993: 25-28).

According to Robin Ramsay, editor of *Lobster* magazine, Wilson had been targeted by UK/UK intelligence for refusing in 1965-1966 to send British troops to serve in the Vietnam War:

> Wilson refused for two reasons that I am aware of. The most pressing was that had he sent UK troops to Vietnam there would have been massive problems with the left-wing of the Labour Party in and outside parliament. And in those days this mattered. The second reason was suggested by the former SIS officer Anthony Cavendish, who told me twenty years ago that Maurice Oldfield, when deputy chief of SIS, had warned Wilson not to get involved in Vietnam. Oldfield had served as an SIS regional head in the Far East in the middle of the 1950s when the French were driven out of Vietnam and seems to have acquired a more rational appreciation of the situation there than the Americans did (Ramsay 2009a).

THATCHER: THE SPOOKS AND THE MEDIA

Urban (op cit) reports that during Margaret Thatcher's years at Number 10 (1979-1990) spending on the intelligence services doubled and MI5 became a key player in the government machine. Milne comments (1995: 341): 'The cosy relationship between elements of the intelligence service and the right-wing of the Tory Party proved to be a vital lubricant in smoothing Margaret Thatcher's rise to power.' Yet rivalries between the various branches of intelligence could often spill out into the pages of newspapers. For instance, soon after Thatcher became PM in 1979 she sent Sir Maurice Oldfield, head of MI6, to Belfast to co-ordinate intelligence. MI5 reacted furiously considering the appointment of an MI6 chief to oversee their officers in Northern Ireland amounted to public criticism of their work. As Hollingsworth and Fielding report (1995: 123): 'Suddenly, journalists in Belfast were receiving calls from RUC Special Branch alleging that Oldfield was a closet homosexual who combed the towns of Ulster looking to seduce young men. These malicious stories were traced back to MI5.'

Significantly, following his appointment as MI5 director general in 1985 Sir Anthony Duff and Bernard Sheldon, his legal advisor, made special efforts to cultivate close links with the press. Urban reports (1996: 54-55): 'Duff and Sheldon focused their early efforts on the editors of quality newspapers, meeting them for lunch with the aim of convincing them that the service was modern, forward-looking organisation which did not conspire against the Labour Party and was not stuffed with KGB agents.'

PROPAGANDA AND THE POPISH PLOT

One of the most controversial attempts at media manipulation by the CIA occurred following the attack on Pope John Paul II in Rome in May 1981. In September 1982, an article appeared in *Reader's Digest* by Claire Sterling, a conservative journalist, and Paul Henze, former CIA station chief in Turkey, claiming that the would-be assassin was a Turk, Mehmet Ali Agca who, they said, was working for Bulgarian intelligence, and thus ultimately for the Soviet Union. In the context of Cold War rivalries, this was an explosive story. For two years, the allegations were recycled in Britain and across the global media. Later, the story was revealed to have been fabricated (Davies op cit: 229).

MAXWELL AND MOSSAD – AND FURTHER REVELATIONS

According to Stephen Dorril (1993), intelligence gathering during the miners' strike of 1984-1985 was helped by the fact that during the 1970s MI5's F Branch had made a special effort to recruit industrial correspondents – with great success. *Guardian* journalist Seumas Milne (1995) claimed that three quarters of Fleet Street's industrial correspondents were at that time agents for MI5 or for Scotland Yard's Special Branch. MI5 was also suspected of leaking smears to the Robert Maxwell-owned *Daily Mirror* as part of an elaborate disinformation campaign against miners' leaders Arthur Scargill and Peter Heathfield in 1990. Both were accused of using Libyan funds to pay the mortgages on their homes during the earlier strike (Ramsay 2009b: 78). There was one major problem with the story: neither Scargill nor Heathfield had mortgages![68]

In 1991, just before his mysterious death, *Mirror* proprietor Robert Maxwell was accused by the US investigative journalist Seymour Hersh in his book, *The Sampson option* (1991), of acting for Mossad, the Israeli secret service, though Dorril (1993: 276) suggests his links with MI6 were equally as strong.[69] In particular, Maxwell was suspected of orchestrating the discrediting and exposure of Mordechai Vanunu after he revealed the existence of Israel's nuclear programme, in *The Sunday Times* of 5 October 1986.[70] Hersh claimed Vanunu's London address had been betrayed to Mossad on Maxwell's orders by the *Daily Mirror*'s foreign editor Nick Davies. Tom Bower (1996: 263-264), however, discounts the theory that Maxwell was a Mossad agent. Hersh's source was Ari Ben-Menasche, an Israeli who had been introduced to Maxwell in 1989. 'Since Ben-Menasche had, earlier, falsely claimed to be a former Mossad officer, Hersh's allegations were sharply devalued,' according to Bower (ibid: 264). Bloom (2015: 193) reports that in 1992 Robert Robinson, a former administrator for the joint intelligence committee, confirmed that GCHQ, which had been following Maxwell since 1989, had monitored his faxes and telephone calls from his yacht and that PM Thatcher had been informed of his activities as had representatives of the Bank of England. 'This would have shown up irregularities of enormous proportions, but also suggested perhaps that Maxwell was a lifetime "communist" with allegiance only to Israel. He would therefore have been the perfect example of an enemy within who needed to be ditched as quickly as possible.'

Further evidence of journalists' links with intelligence emerged in investigations by British Customs after the collapse of the Bank of Credit and Commerce International (BCCI) in 1991 amidst allegations of massive fraud and money laundering. The CIA, for instance, relied on the Saudi Arabian government to fund anti-communist groups such as the Contras in Nicaragua and Unita in Angola through secret BCCI accounts. Reports suggested that the CIA had paid around 500 British 'monitors' over a period of ten years – including 124 in communications and 90 in the media (Dorril 1993: 300).

Following the resignation from the *Guardian* of Richard Gott, its literary editor in December 1994 in the wake of allegations that he was a paid agent of the KGB, the role of journalists as spies suddenly came under the media spotlight – and many of the leaks were fascinating. For instance, according to *The Times* editorial of 16 December 1994: 'Many British journalists benefited from CIA or MI6 largesse during the Cold War.'

The intimate links between journalists and the secret services were highlighted in the autobiography of the eminent newscaster Sandy Gall (1994). He reports without any qualms how, after returning from one of his reporting assignments to Afghanistan, he was asked to lunch by the head of MI6. 'It was very informal, the cook was off so we had cold meat and salad with plenty of win. He wanted to hear what I had to say about the war in Afghanistan. I was flattered, of course, and anxious to pass on what I could in terms of first-hand knowledge' (ibid: 158).[71] Aldrich and Cormac (2016: 362) record how MI6 turned to Gall in 1984 to report on the 'secret' guerrilla war being fought against the Soviets in Afghanistan.

BAZOFT AMBIVALENCES

Another major controversy erupted in March 1990 following the hanging of *Observer* journalist Farzad Bazoft in Iraq on charges of spying (Keeble 1997: 62). An explosion had destroyed the Al-Iskandrai weapons complex 30 miles south of Baghdad on 17 August 1989 and Bazoft had travelled there with an English nurse, Daphne Parish,[72] taking photographs and even soil samples. After being arrested by Iraq security police he had 'confessed' (allegedly under torture) to being an Israeli spy (Timmerman 1992: 357-358). Immediately following the hanging British intelligence leaked information that Bazoft had stolen £500 from a building society ten years earlier. According to John Pilger (1992), MI5 was acting on behalf of the Thatcher government 'desperate for any excuse not to suspend its lucrative arms deals with Saddam Hussein'.

The *Sun's* 'exclusive' headline went: 'Hanged man was a robber'; the *Daily Mail's* 'Bazoft a perfect spy for Israel'; *Today's*: 'Bazoft was an Israeli agent'; a *Sunday*

Telegraph editorial condemned Bazoft as a spy, likening investigative journalism as an offence against the state. The investigative journalist Simon Henderson also argued that Bazoft was a spy for British intelligence. He had been provided with special containers for soil samples by a contact at the British embassy in Baghdad who later sent the samples to London by diplomatic bag for chemical analysis.[73] Henderson concluded: 'At no time did the British admit that Bazoft had been spying, nor did Iraq flesh out its allegations. The reason was clear: if Britain admitted to spying the two countries would have had to break off diplomatic relations.' Neither country wanted this. 'So the Bazoft incident was left to die down' (Henderson 1991: 214-216). But the veteran BBC foreign correspondent, John Simpson, argues strongly that Bazoft 'was precisely what he claimed to be – a journalist looking for a good story' (Simpson 1991a: 54-65). A few months after the execution, in August 1990, Iraqi forces invaded neighbouring Kuwait so provoking the international crisis that ultimately led to the Gulf conflict of 1991.

Yet the Bazoft mystery continued. In 2003, the *Observer* tracked down Kadem Askar, the colonel in the Iraqi intelligence service who conducted the first interrogation of Bazoft. He claimed he knew the journalist was innocent – but could not stop Saddam Hussein, the Iraqi President, in his determination to have Bazoft executed.[74]

MORE MI6 LEAKING

According to Nick Davies (op cit: 233), the reporting of the activities of the son of Col. Gaddafi, President of Libya, by the *Sunday Telegraph*, suggested involvement of MI6. On 26 November 1995, its chief foreign correspondent, Con Coughlin, described the son, Saif, as an 'untrustworthy maverick' and accused him of being involved in a plot to flood Iran with fake currency. Saif sued and documents filed to the court in April 2002 revealed that Coughlin had secured the story after three lunches and two briefings with MI6 officers. After one day's evidence, the newspaper admitted that its report was inaccurate and agreed to pay a proportion of Said's legal costs.[75]

It was Coughlin also who reported in the *Daily Telegraph*, on 14 December 2003, under the headline 'Terrorist behind September 11 strike was trained by Saddam': 'Mohammed Atta, the al-Qaeda mastermind of the September 11 attacks against the US, was trained in Baghdad by Abu Nidal, the notorious Palestinian terrorist.'[76] But in his book, *The way of the world: A story of truth and hope in an age of extremism*, Pulitzer Prize-winning reporter Ron Suskind revealed that Iraqi intelligence chief Tahir Jalil Habbush al-Tikriti, while in American custody after the fall of Saddam, was paid £2.5 million to write out a letter, backdated to July 2001, giving details of an Iraqi training programme attended by 9/11 ringleader Mohammed Atta. The moves were orchestrated by the CIA on the orders of President Bush, according to Suskind.[77]

MI6 regularly briefs favoured journalists who routinely pass on the information given as true, according to Davies (op cit: 234). In November 2006, for example, the BBC's security correspondent, Gordon Corera, reported that British intelligence had 'confirmed' they were unaware of the location of the secret prisons where Islamist suspects were being tortured – but he offered no evidence in support of the MI6 claim.

A RENEGADE SPOOK REVEALS ALL

In December 1998, Labour MP Brian Sedgemore named Dominic Lawson, editor of the *Sunday Telegraph*, in parliament as an MI6 agent after receiving information from former MI6 officer Richard Tomlinson (Machon 2005: 135). The *Guardian* also reported that Lawson had published articles in the *Spectator* while he was editor by a 'Ken Roberts', who was actually an MI6 officer, and by Alan Judd aka Alan Petty, another MI6 officer. Machon adds (ibid: 136): 'Although Lawson has denied the claims that he was a paid agent of MI6, we do know that he regularly and uncritically reproduces stories from MI6 sources in the *Sunday Telegraph*.'

Another major controversy erupted in 2001 after Tomlinson published in Russia, *Big breach: From top secret to maximum security*, in which he claimed spies posed as journalists on four out of every ten missions.[78] Tomlinson, who was assigned to Yugoslavia during the height of the Bosnian conflict, used a forged card of the National Union of Journalists to gain access to top Serbian sources.[79] Tomlinson also confirmed that MI6 still set up news agency 'fronts' to provide cover for its operations. For instance, in 1992, the Truefax agency was set up in central London by Tomlinson and a KGB defector with the aim of recruiting Russian journalists to spy for Britain.

Intriguingly, Martin Bell, the white-suited BBC correspondent in the Balkans during the civil wars of the 1990s, admitted in his personal account of those years of 'spying' for the UN and IFOR (the Nato-led peace implementation force). He said (1996: 31):

> It worked both ways. We knew things they needed to know, both for informed decision-making and for their own safety. We had been there before they arrived, and would still be there when they left. Others may see this differently, but for me it was not unprofessional behaviour or a breach of whatever codes were supposed to govern us to pass information to them. I had always wished to be declared redundant as a war correspondent and became a peace correspondent instead. And to help the UN was to serve the cause of peace.

He continued (ibid: 32): '…in all my time no intelligence service has ever asked me to work for it – except once and very briefly, and I declined. However, when my war zone wanderings are over and if I ever have grandchildren, I know how I wish the conversation to go. "Grandfather," they will ask with their eyes aglow, "were you ever a spy?" "Why yes," I shall answer, 'actually I was. Just once. I spied for peace.'"

Similarly in the reporting of Northern Ireland, there have been longstanding concerns over security service disinformation. Susan McKay, Northern editor of the Dublin-based *Sunday Tribune*, has criticised the reckless reporting of material from 'dodgy security services'. She told a conference in Belfast in January 2003 organised by the National Union of Journalists and the Northern Ireland Human Rights Commission: 'We need to be suspicious when people are so ready to provide information and that we are, in fact, not being used.'[80]

An intriguing twist to the spy saga was revealed by Yvonne Ridley, the *Sunday Express* journalist who was seized by the Taliban during her assignment as an undercover reporter at the outbreak of the assault on Afghanistan. In her account of her ordeal (2001: 202-216), she claimed that various intelligence agencies (the CIA, British intelligence, Mossad or others) had aimed to smear her as a spy so that Taliban would execute her – thus providing 'a wonderful piece of propaganda for the West'.

GROWING POWER OF SECRET STATE

Thus from this evidence alone it is clear there has been a long history of links between hacks and spooks in both the UK and US. But as the secret state grows in power, through massive resourcing, through a whole raft of legislation – such as the Official Secrets Act, the anti-terrorism legislation, the Regulation of Investigatory Powers Act and so on – and as intelligence moved into the heart of Blair and Brown's ruling clique so these links are even more significant. As Robin Ramsay comments: 'Four of the Blair cabinet are alumni of the Anglo-American elite group the British American Project; three of the Blair cabinet have passed muster at Bilderberg meetings[81]; and the entire defence team in Blair's first cabinet in 1997 were members or associates of the Trade Union Committee for European and Transatlantic Unity, created by the Americans in the 1970s – probably though not yet provably created by the CIA – and currently funded by Nato.'[82]

Mark Almond, lecturer in modern history commented: 'More than any predecessor, Blair has relied on a kitchen cabinet in Downing Street but one made up of a cabal of diplomats and intelligence officials rather than ambitious, if unelected party apparatchiks. Blair has liberated British politics from the influence of politicians' (2003).[83] Professor David Beetham has similarly highlighted the 'secret, warfare' state which has totally undermined the democratic system (2003).

Immediately after 9/11 2001, all of Fleet Street was awash in warnings by anonymous intelligence sources of terrorist threats. According to Steve Hewitt and Scott Lucas (2009: 109), the Iraqi National Congress, the opposition group with close ties to the Bush administration and US intelligence agencies, was the source for 108 English language news reports published between October 2001 and May 2002.

The former UN arms inspector, Scott Ritter, revealed in his book, *Iraq confidential*, the existence of an MI6-run psychological warfare effort, known as Operation Mass Appeal. According to Ritter: 'Mass Appeal served as a focal point for passing MI6 intelligence on Iraq to the media, both in the UK and around the world. The goal was to help shape public opinion about Iraq and the threat posed by WMD' (Davies op cit: 231; see also Meacher 2003; Thursby 2004; Woodcock 2003).[84] Ritter, for instance, described how he would be asked by MI6 agents for information on Iraq that could be planted in newspapers in India, Poland and South Africa from where it would feed back to Britain and America (Rufford 2003). He also noted that many reports had appeared in the international media about 'secret underground facilities' in Iraq and nerve-gas programmes. 'All of them were garbage,' he added (cited in Aldrich and Cormac 2016: 431). MI6 propaganda specialists, at the time, claimed they could spread the misinformation through 'editors and writers who work with us from time to time'. Thus there were constant attempts to scare people – and justify still greater powers for the national security apparatus.

For example, Michael Evans, *The Times* defence correspondent, reported on 29 November 2002: 'Saddam Hussein has ordered hundreds of his officials to conceal weapons of mass destruction components in their homes to evade the prying eyes of the United Nations inspectors.' The source of these 'revelations' was said to be 'intelligence picked up from within Iraq'. In the *Sun* of 18 March 2003, Trevor Kavanagh and Brian Flynn reported British intelligence as saying Iraqi Republican Guard units 'have been equipped with chemical warfare shells to make a desperate last stand south of Baghdad'. Next day in the same tabloid, George Pascoe-Watson and Nick Parker (under the headline 'Fiend to unleash poisons') reported: 'British soldiers stepped up chemical warfare drills on the Iraqi border yesterday – as Saddam deployed the doomsday weapons he claimed he never had.'

By 2 April, the *Sun* was reporting (citing 'Pentagon intelligence sources'): 'Saddam Hussein was last night feared to have ordered a chemical weapons attack on allied troops – as they launched the first phase of the Battle for Baghdad.' Again, on 8 April 2003, as the Baghdad was falling to the Western invaders, George Pascoe-Watson reported in the *Sun*: 'Twenty Iraqi missiles were being tested by military experts last night amid reports they were tipped with chemical warheads ... If the rockets are carrying deadly sarin and mustard gas, it will show George Bush and Tony Blair were RIGHT to claim Saddam has weapons of mass destruction.'

Early in 2004, as the battle for control of Iraq continued with mounting casualties on both sides, it was revealed that many of the lies about Saddam Hussein's supposed WMD had been fed to sympathetic journalists in the US, Britain and Australia by the exile group, the Iraqi National Congress.

In 2004 it emerged that the Iraqi defector codenamed 'Red River', who made false claims about Iraq's germ warfare programme and failed a lie-detector test, had maintained his links with British intelligence (Borger and Norton-Taylor 2004).

'Red River' was listed in a US senate report as one of four sources for claims made at the UN in February 2003 by US secretary of state Colin Powell that Iraq had developed mobile germ warfare laboratories. Trailers matching the pictures were discovered after the conflict but experts agreed they had been used to produce hydrogen for meteorological balloons used by artillery units. Another source for the mobile labs claim was an Iraqi major who had already been declared a fabricator by US defence intelligence agency.

In his evidence to a special immigration appeal commission in July 2002, the *Observer* reporter and intelligence expert, Martin Bright (2002) highlighted the way in which journalists were constantly fed unverifiable information by the intelligence services about alleged al-Qaeda threats to the UK. To illustrate his point he referred to an article in the *Independent* of 16 September headlined 'MI5 searches for terror cells based in Britain' by two journalists with 'impeccable reputations', Paul Lashmar and Chris Blackhurst.

> They report that at least three terrorist cells linked to Bin Laden are at large in Britain and that the UK has been a major base for Bin Laden's operations. They add that there are believed to be dozens of terrorists in Britain associated with Bin Laden. One 'intelligence source' is then quoted as saying: 'There is no reason why what happened in America couldn't happen in Britain or any European country. The terrorists are in place, and there is very little to stop them.' A source, this time from 'Whitehall' adds: 'The problem is, these groups are amorphous and hard to identify until the they commit a terrorist act.' This is terrifying stuff.[85]

In 2008, it was reported that the government had resurrected the Information Research Department with a new title, the Research, Information and Communication Unit, to target the BBC and other media organisations with anti-al-Qaeda propaganda (Travis 2008). A report leaked to the *Guardian*, *Challenging violent extremist ideology through communications*, said: 'We are pushing this material to UK media channels, e.g. as a BBC radio programme exposing tensions between AQ leadership and supporters. And a restricted working group will communicate niche messages through media and non-media.'

SEXED UP – AND MISSED OUT

During the controversy that erupted following the end of the 2003 'war' and the death of the arms inspector Dr David Kelly (and the ensuing Hutton inquiry) the spotlight fell on BBC reporter Andrew Gilligan and the claim by one of his sources that the government (in collusion with the intelligence services) had 'sexed up' a dossier justifying an attack on Iraq.[86] Intriguingly Dr Kelly also had close ties with intelligence. Part of his work involved liaising with the shadowy Rockingham Cell, which Scott Ritter, the maverick US arms inspector, described as a 'secretive intelligence activity buried inside the defence intelligence staff which dealt with

Iraqi WMD and the activities of the UN Special Commission' (see Baker 2007: 9; Aldrich and Cormac 2016: 430). Kelly also had a close, and somewhat mysterious relationship with the American Mai Pederson who introduced him to the Baha'i faith. She was also alleged to be a spy (Baker op cit: 257-274).

The Hutton inquiry, its every twist and turn massively covered in the mainstream media, was the archetypal media spectacle that drew attention from the broader and more significant issues – including mainstream journalists' links with the intelligence services. Moreover, Sir Kevin Tebbit, permanent secretary at the ministry of defence, did tell the inquiry that Prime Minister Tony Blair had chaired the key meeting at which a question-and-answer strategy leading to the naming Dr Kelly had been agreed (Evans 2003). But as Georgina Born commented (2005: 456):

> …Hutton's narrow remit, defined by Downing Street and backed by unprecedented and dramatic evidence of formerly hidden governmental and editorial processes, drew the public mind away from bigger questions about the legitimacy of the government's case for war. By expiating the wrongdoings of the Kelly affair, the effect of Hutton was to ward off awareness of larger possible misdemeanours.

Noam Chomsky even argues that inquiry itself was a scandal (2005: 151): 'What right does the government have to carry out an inquiry into whether the media are reporting the facts the way it wants them to be reported? The very fact that the inquiry took place is a function of the very low commitment to freedom of speech in England.'

ADMITTING (AND NOT ADMITTING) MISTAKES

Significantly, on 26 May 2004, *The New York Times* carried a 1,200-word editorial admitting it had been duped in its coverage of WMD in the lead-up to the invasion by dubious Iraqi defectors, informants and exiles. Chief among the dodgy informants to reporter Judith Miller of *The Times*, was Ahmed Chalabi, leader of the Iraqi National Congress (INC) who enjoyed a strangely mixed fate in Iraq: firstly a Pentagon favourite before his Baghdad house was raided by US forces on 20 May 2004; then becoming one of the country's three deputy prime ministers while being accused of giving US intelligence secrets to Iran (Fisk 2008: 287).[87]

Then, in the *Observer* of 30 May 2004, David Rose admitted he had been the victim of 'calculated set-up' devised to foster the propaganda case for war. 'In the 18 months before the invasion of March 2003, I dealt regularly with Chalabi and the INC and published stories based on interviews with men they said were defectors from Saddam's regime.' For instance, a report by Rose in the London *Evening Standard* of 9 December 2002 was headlined: 'Saddam and al-Qaeda – the link we've all missed.' Rose concluded: 'The information fog is thicker than in any previous war, as I know now from bitter personal experience. To any journalist being offered apparently sensational disclosures, especially from an anonymous intelligence source, I offer two words of advice: *caveat emptor*' (Rose 2004).

Rose, in an later article in the *New Statesman* (2007), reported in detail on how the 'spooks' had fed a series of lies to their media cronies: in one instance, an official insisted the preachers Abu Hamza and Abu Qatada – now said by the same agency to have been Britain's most dangerous men throughout the 1990s – were 'harmless rent-a-gobs' who might have a high public profile but had no hard links with jihadist terrorism. MI5 sources also originally claimed there was 'no connection' between the 7/7 cell behind the London bombings and the failed 21/7 cell. 'Only two years later, thanks to evidence given in criminal trials, did it become clear that both claims were false. In fact, the two leaders of the 7/7 gang, Mohammad Sidique Khan and Shazad Tanweer, had been observed by MI5 surveillance officers at least four times, and were known to be connected to another, now convicted, terrorist cell.' Rose asks why the media have been duped by the intelligence services for so long.

> One reason, aside from the lunches and the limos, is that editors are extremely reluctant to lose the access they have: the spooks' stories may be unreliable, but they often make good copy, and if everyone is peddling the same errors, it doesn't much matter if they turn out to be untrue. Another, as a seasoned BBC correspondent put it to me, may be a judgment that if MI5 and MI6 sometimes peddle disinformation, many viewers and readers may not very much care as 'we're all on the same side'.

No British mainstream newspaper has apologised for being duped over the WMD rationale for war in 2003. As the *Press Gazette* editorial of 23 November 2007 ('Manipulation: have we learned from Iraq war?') commented: 'There has been no *mea culpa* in the UK press for its failure to see through the non-existent WMDs and the bogus threats whipped up by dubious groups such as the Iraqi National Congress.'

The secret state has similarly expanded its reach in the United States since 9/11. Yet, as the journalist Ted Gup has highlighted, this growth in secrecy is hardly ever reported on by the media:

> In so doing we have tended to overlook one of the more significant stories of our lifetime – an emerging 'secretocracy' that threatens to transform American society and democratic institutions. Systematic or indiscriminate secrecy involves the calculated use of secrecy as a principal instrument of governance, a way to impede scrutiny, obscure process, avoid accountability, suppress dissent and concentrate power (cited in Aldrich 2009: 27).

THE CONSPIRACY THEORY CONUNDRUM AND THE MANUFACTURED REALITY

According to Robin Ramsay (2006 [2000]: 93): 'In a sense, the entire secret apparatus of the modern state – military, policing, intelligence and security organisation – are simply state conspiracies and, all too frequently, are conspiracies directed against the taxpayers who fund them.' Yet one of the main problems with intelligence is that anyone attempting to highlight its significance is accused of lacking academic rigour and promoting 'conspiracy theory'. As Jeffrey M. Bale comments (1995: 16): '…serious research into genuine conspiratorial networks has at worst been suppressed, as a rule been discouraged and at best looked upon with condescension by the academic community. An entire dimension of political history and contemporary politics has thus been consistently neglected.' But given the close links between politicians, journalists and the intelligence services some conspiratorial elements have to be acknowledged to be behind the mainstream media's reporting. Or as Eric Wilson (2009: 37) comments:

> Stripped of its speculative and sensationalist armature, 'conspiracy theory' stands revealed as the merely self-consciously parapolitical realisation that covert agencies and actions are an integral part of the practical exercise of governance within both national and transnational spaces.

According to Robin Ramsay, 'conspiracy theories' as a term of denigration was invented by the CIA for use against critics of the 1967 Warren commission into the Kennedy assassination 'and proved successful at scaring off the career-minded and conventional that its use spread to encompass almost any line of inquiry which strays beyond conventional narratives' (Ramsay 2016).

With the emphasis on intelligence, the focus of journalism shifts from objective, verifiable 'facts' to myth: in effect, there is a crucial epistemological shift. As general Richard Myers, chairman of the joint chiefs of staff, admitted in the lead up to the Iraq invasion of 2003: 'Intelligence doesn't mean something is true. You know, it's your best estimate of the situation. It doesn't mean it's a fact. I mean, that's not what intelligence is' (Stephen 2003; Keeble 2004: 48-49). Dorril (2003: 4) commented:

> The reality is that intelligence is the area in which ministers, and the MI6 info ops staff behind them can say anything they like and get away with it. Intelligence with its psychological invite to a secret world and with its unique avoidance of verification, is the ideal means for flattering and deceiving journalists.

The historian Timothy Garton Ash (2003b) has stressed: 'The trend in journalism as in politics, and probably now in the political use of intelligence, is away from the facts and towards a neo-Orwellian world of manufacturing reality.' With the reporting of the 'war on terror' being dominated by intelligence sources, separating the manufactured myths and the misinformation from the truth becomes all the more difficult. But it's a challenge journalists and media consumers have to take up.

NOTES

[1] Even in 1986, Phillip Knightley was able to report that 'the intelligence explosion is already out of hand' (1986: 380). Precise figures on funding of the intelligence services are difficult to identify. Hollingsworth and Fielding (1999: 48) say that with the election of the Labour Party in May 1997 they found 'new friends'. 'They persuaded the new government to increase their aggregate budget to £743.2 million for 1999-2000, £745 million for 2000-2001 and £746.9 million for 2001-2002. The amount for MI5 alone was not published until 1998 when it was announced as £140 million a year.' However, Todd, Paul and Bloch, Jonathan (2003: 106) calculate that, following leaks from the national audit office about overspends – from £140 to £250 million (MI6) and £85 to £227 million (MI5) – on high-profile city offices and a range of other scandals involving IT contract overruns, an unofficial estimate of £2.5 billion to be closer to the mark. Todd and Bloch suggest that the cost of the intelligence services is Britain's 'greatest secret'. Richard Norton-Taylor, of the *Guardian*, reported that the three intelligence services (MI5, MI6 and GCHQ) spent £2.4 billion each year (see Inside the doughnut, *Guardian*, 19 June 2010). David Leppard, in *The Sunday Times*, of 19 September 2010, reported that MI5's budget over the next four years was just £300m. According to Clive Bloom (2015: 19), the intelligence and security services were costing around £1 billion a year by mid to late 1980s. The single intelligence vote was meant to run at around £800 million 'but records of payments from the Exchequer remain secret even to this day and seem to have exceeded the billion threshold'

[2] The secret state is also theorised as the 'clandestine, parallel state' (that operates both inside and outside the law), 'shadow government', 'invisible government', 'deep state' and 'national security state'. See Tunander 2009

[3] As Hennessey and Thomas (2009: 605; 615) report, MI5 has established regional stations around Britain to work closely with police forces – with a presence in the Midlands, North East, North West, South, East and Scotland. On 10 October 2007, MI5 took over the lead role for national security in Northern Ireland (ibid: 616). In 2016, MI6 employed around 2,500, MI5 4,000 and GCHQ 'more than 6,000', according to a report in *The Times* on 22 September (MI6 hires hundreds more spies in war against terror, by Deborah Haynes). But how credible are those figures? The planned 40 per cent rise for MI6 by 2020 was said to be its biggest boost since the end of the Cold War (see https://intelnews.org/). Both MI5 and MI6 were founded in 1909. Until 1993 the identities of its director generals were state secrets. The first interview to a newspaper by a director general was by Andrew Parker, in the *Guardian*, 1 November 2016 (Johnson and MacAskill 2016). We learned for the first time Parker was born in Newcastle and went to a comprehensive school. Little else. For a critique of the *Guardian* interview see http://www.medialens.org/index.php/alerts/alert-archive/2016/831-flagship-of-fearmongering-the-guardian-mi5-and-state-propaganda.html. *The Sunday Times*'s Bryan Appleyard (2016) profiled 'Tom Marcus' who had just published his memoirs (*The soldier spy*, London: Michael Joseph 2016) and had posed as a tramp for his work. He reported that 'the pay is awful and the cost of membership can be high. Possessed of formidable expertise and very rare gifts and working absurd hours, even with enormous overtime Tom was paid less than £30,000 a year. He couldn't even afford to fit internal doors in his house until he got the advance for this book'. As in all matters relating to the spooks, the lines between fact and fiction can become very blurred…

[4] This 'designs and delivers communication systems and provides technical solutions that protect national security at home and overseas' (see http://www.hmgcc.gov.uk/about-us/ and Beaumont, Paul (2016) Whitehatters: Seeking a new generation, *Eye Spy*, No. 105, October pp 44-47)

[5] See http://motherboard.vice.com/read/your-government-wants-to-militarize-social-media-to-influence-your-beliefs, accessed on 15 November 2016

[6] Special Branch was founded in 1888. But, as John Hughes-Wilson argued in his seminal history of spying (2004) espionage dates back as far as Biblical times. For instance, he writes: 'Between 1799 and 1804, Wellington could genuinely claim that he was never surprised and that he always knew where the enemy armies were, thanks to good intelligence from either the natives or his guides' (ibid: 191). The institutionalisation of spying is a modern phenomenon

[7] As former MI5 undercover agent Gary Murray, comments (1993: 7): 'RAF "spooks" have played an integral part in numerous undercover operations, and have contributed to the detection and apprehension of a number of foreign agents, both in the United Kingdom and abroad'

[8] See http://www.nationalcrimeagency.gov.uk/

[9] See http://undercoverresearch.net/undercover-profiles/, accessed on 2 April 2016. Police informants were involved in planning and executing a sectarian attack in which six people were shot dead in a bar in Northern Ireland, according to a report by Michael Maguire, police ombudsman for Northern Ireland. The 160-page report highlighted police corruption and collusion with terrorists over many years (see O'Neill 2016)

[10] For instance, British mercenaries, the SAS and Saladin Security have fought alongside Sri Lankan forces in their war against the Tamil people (see Miller 2014)

[11] Bloom (2015: 191) also quotes the maverick intelligence officer Peter (*Spycatcher*) Wright who claimed MI5 was 'controlled by Masonic connections'. On the City of London as an offshore tax haven; see http://www.newstatesman.com/economy/2011/02/london-corporation-city, accessed on 9 May 2016

[12] See http://www.ndr.de/nachrichten/netzwelt/snowden277_page-2.html, accessed on 13 June 2016. The 'revelations' by Edward Snowden in 2013 of mass citizen surveillance by the NSA and GCHQ were hardly new. James Risen, for instance (2006: 52), in a detailed study of the work of the NSA, wrote: 'With its direct access to the US telecommunications system, there seems to be no physical or logistical obstacle to prevent the NSA from eavesdropping on anyone in the United States that it chooses'

[13] See Plesch, Dan (2004) Missing link: The role played by US intelligence has been predictably omitted from the Butler report, *Guardian*, 16 July

[14] In the US, the NSA has around 30,000 employees but it relies on a larger workforce of some 60,000 in private contractors (Foster and McChesney 2014: 26). The privatisation of US military intelligence is highlighted by Chatterjee, Pratap (2006)

[15] *Private Eye* reported (19 August-1 September 2016: 11) that the body that is meant to scrutinise and represent the public interest on disclosure of items in the National Archive, the obscure advisory council on national records and archives, is dominated by former diplomats, police officers, spooks and civil servants. It commented: 'No wonder thousands of historic files remain under lock and key in government departments or at the national archives long after the 30-year release rule should put them in the public eye'

[16] In 2016, in a release from the national archive, it was revealed (perhaps predictably) that Thompson was put under 'extensive' surveillance by MI5 for two decades as agents followed his growing disillusionment with the Soviet Union (see Sanderson, David, Spies tailed E. P. Thompson as he lost faith in communism, *Times*, 28 September p. 17). The MI5 files on two other famous historians, Eric Hobsbawm and Christopher Hill were released two years earlier

[17] Hollingsworth and Fielding (op cit: 49) report that officers of MI5's H Branch ('Corporate Affairs') interact with GCHQ, the police, customs, ports and immigration services and are responsible for liaising with the media. An earlier, excellent study of the intelligence services and their manipulation of the media appears in Leigh, David (1980) *The frontiers of secrecy: Closed*

government in Britain, London: Junction Books. Interestingly, MI5 (then known as the Secret Service Bureau) was founded on 1 October 1909 by Captain Vernon Kell – a former *Daily Telegraph* foreign correspondent

[18] The innocence of mainstream journalists over the secret state was perhaps summed up by the leftist journalist Paul Mason (2016) who wrote in his *Guardian* column: 'Today, though the secret state is large, it is under much stronger legislative control. Should a leftwing Labour party come to power, it is likely to be able to govern relatively free from a politicised sabotage from the state'

[19] In 1967, *The Sunday Times*'s Insight team revealed Philby as a Soviet agent who came close to being appointed head of MI6. During the Spanish Civil War he had reported General Franco's campaign for *The Times* – and had even won an award from the general for his sympathetic articles (Bower 1995: 53). Even after he was dismissed from the service, MI6 continued to employ him as a field agent in the Middle East under the cover of being a journalist with the *Observer* and *Economist*. Before running the revelations, Harold Evans, editor, received an injunction from the D Notice committee requesting him 'not to publish anything about identities, whereabouts, and tasks of persons of whatever status or rank who are or have been employed by either Service [MI5 or MI6]'. He ignored it – and was supported by his management (Evans 2009a: 306-310). Philby told an audience of East German spies after his defection that he had escaped being rumbled for so long because 'he had been born into the ruling class' (see http://www.theguardian.com/world/2016/apr/04/kim-philbys-stasi-tape-reveals-secrets-of-his-success-as-cold-war-spy, accessed on 4 April 2016)

[20] le Carré had previously worked for intelligence as an informant while at Oxford University (according to Roger Morris, Bill Clinton was also recruited by the CIA to spy on fellow undergraduates while at Oxford University in the late 1960s as part of Operation Chaos: see Ramsay 2008: 77 and http://www.theforbiddenknowledge.com/hardtruth/clinton_spied_students.htm and https://monolithik.wordpress.com/2011/08/16/the-real-bill-clinton-cia-agent-drug-smuggler-and-scoundrel-extraordinaire/) Interestingly, when le Carré decided to retire from MI6 following the enormous global success of his novel *The man who came in from the cold*, it was suggested he continuing spying under the cover of being either a journalist or an academic (Sisman 2015: 254-255). John le Carré admitted in an interview with the *Sunday Telegraph* (29 August 2010) that assassinations were carried out by British intelligence services during the Cold War. 'Certainly we did some very bad things. We did a lot of direct action. Assassinations, at arm's length. Although I was never involved'

[21] See http://www.independent.co.uk/arts-entertainment/books/news/frederick-forsyth-reveals-he-once-worked-for-mi6-10478684.html, accessed on 7 November 2015

[22] For instance, SIS agent Richard Tomlinson travelled around Serbia in the early 1990s carrying a press card saying he was a member of the National Union of Journalists and a British passport describing him as Ben Presley. 'Both documents were forged by MI6's Technical Services Department' (Thomas 2009: 286)

[23] On Philby's work as an *Observer* journalist, Macintyre writes (2014: 207): '…there is no better cover job for a spy than that of a journalist, a profession that enables the asking of direct, unsubtle and impertinent questions about the most sensitive subjects, without arousing suspicion. A topic of interest to the readers of the *Observer* could, when explored in greater depth, be passed on to British intelligence'

[24] But Paxman is a member of the British American Project for the successor generation set up in 1985 'to perpetuate the close relationship between the United States and Britain'. John Pilger has described BAP as a casual freemasonry' and 'by far the most influential transatlantic network of politicians, journalists and academics' (see Beckett 2004). Other BAP journalists include George Brock, Yasmin-Alibhai-Brown, James Naughtie, Isabel Hilton, Charles Moore, Rowan Pelling, Evan Davis

[25] In 1985 it was Brigadier Ronnie Stonham. Norton-Taylor (1990: 89) records: 'Stonham was replaced in 1988 by Michael Hodder, a former Royal Marines officer. Hodder was previously personnel officer for BBC radio news and current affairs, a job which gave him access to personal files.' His new title was chief assistant to the BBC's personal director, Christopher Martin, himself a former Royal Marines officer

[26] According to Phil Agee (n. d.) *Covert action: What next?* London: Agee-Hosenball defence committee p 13 in the late 1970s: 'The FBI, for example, has an index of 58 million cards of names and organisations through which it retrieves information contained in over 6.5 million files. It has compiled 480,000 files from investigations of "subversives" and 33,000 files from investigations of "extremists"'

[27] According to Hennessey and Thomas (2009: 598), in the late 1990s, MI5 held around 250,000 hard copy personal records on individuals; a further 40,000 were archived on microfiche. Not surprisingly, the two sets of figures differ considerably

[28] See http://www.telegraph.co.uk/news/obituaries/11016167/Chapman-Pincher-obituary.html, accessed on 18 June 2016

[29] See http://www.bbc.co.uk/news/uk-26781900, accessed on 18 June 2016

[30] The links with intelligence go back to the very origins of journalism. Daniel Defoe (1659-1731), considered by many the first journalist, did intelligence work for both Tory and Whig administrations in the early years of the 18th century. Arthur Ransome, who reported sympathetically on the Russian revolution for the *Daily News* and *Manchester Guardian*, was also recruited to His Majesty's Secret Service (code name S76). See Chambers 2009: 250. This was confirmed in Keith Jeffery's 800-page official history, *MI6: The history of the Secret Intelligence Service 1909-1949* (London, Bloomsbury, 2010). Phillip Knightley (2003a [1975]: 45), in his seminal history of war reporting, says of the period 1865-1914: 'The British, especially *The Times'* correspondents, were not averse to a little intelligence work for the Foreign office on the side...' During the Russo-Japanese war in 1904, for instance, *The Times'* Frank le Poer Power and George Ernest ('Chinese') Morrison acted as spies (ibid: 64). Jeffery also reports that Col. Dudley Wrangel Clarke, using the role as a correspondent for *The Times* as a cover during the Second World War, travelled to Spain where he was arrested by the authorities dressed 'down to a brassiere' as a woman (see also McCrum 2010). Jeffery also confirmed that novelists Somerset Maugham and Compton Mackenzie and philosopher A. J. Ayer worked for MI6. According to Phillip Knightley (1982): '*The Times* correspondent in Rome in the twenties was the controller of a network of spies throughout Italy working for the British Secret Intelligence Service. Dick Ellis, an Australian running a news agency in Geneva during the League of Nation's time, was also a high-ranking officer in British intelligence. David Walker and Leslie Sheridan were journalists on the *Daily Mirror* in the late thirties. They were also working for the British Secret Service. Derek Patmore, a journalist for the *News Chronicle*, was also a spy. Richard Sorge, the *Frankfurter Zeitung* correspondent in Tokyo, was a KGB agent'

[31] John Sutherland suggests that Orwell's work as imperial policeman in Burma (1922-1927) was effectively espionage. He writes: 'The Burmese police force, like its parent Indian force, was not primarily an instrument for maintaining law and order but one for gathering intelligence and nipping any possible uprising in the bud. ... [Orwell] was not moved around because he gave dissatisfaction but because he was good at his job: a competent spy in policeman's uniform' (2016: 105)

[32] MI5 files released in September 1999, revealed that Wodehouse had been on the Nazi payroll, receiving, through his wife, payments that appeared to be the equivalent of £150 a month. Wodehouse also admitted selling the rights to a novel he wrote during internment, called *How to make money*, to a German company (see Lashmar and Day 1999). Wodehouse's note to MI5 was released on 25 August 2011. He said: 'I never had any intention of assisting the enemy and I have

suffered a great deal of mental pain as the result of my action.' MI5 decided against taking any action. But in 1946, the case was re-evaluated and it was decided that if ever Wodehouse returned to the UK he would be prosecuted. Wodehouse moved to the US in 1945 and lived there until his death in 1975 (see Norton-Taylor 2011). Robert McCrum, who has written a biography of Wodehouse, commented: 'One of the murky aspects of the whole story is that the Security Services never played it straight with the Wodehouse family. They cleared him but never reported this to him' (see Malvern 2011)

[33] From October 1941 to March 1943, Ayer worked as a Special Operations Executive agent within British Security Co-ordination with cover symbol G.246, in the Political and Minorities Section. He worked on intelligence relating to Latin America, particularly Argentina and Chile. In 1950, he attended the Berlin Congress for Cultural Freedom as a member of the British delegation, which was funded by the foreign office through the Information Research Department. See http://www. spinprofiles.org/index.php/A.J._Ayer, accessed on 6 August 2009

[34] Email to author, 22 July 2011

[35] ibid

[36] Bernard Crick 'strongly suspected' that Orwell's little list of crypto-communists was compiled jointly with Arthur Koestler (Crick 1996). Lucas (2000) notes that Orwell had proposed marriage to Kirwan three years earlier

[37] In a letter to the author from Peter Davison, dated 24 February 1999 (see also http://www.mi5. gov.uk/output/former-dgs.html, accessed on 14 April 2009)

[38] Astor was named as one of the 40 Greats of the British newspaper industry by the *UK Press Gazette* on 22 November 2005 (in a glossy special supplement titled 'The newspaper hall of fame'). After he became editor of the *Observer* in 1947, he employed Terence Kilmartin (who had worked for Section D, MI6, and SOE – as did his sister – during the war and then for an MI6-backed Arab radio station) who became assistant literary editor in 1950 and literary editor in 1952 (see http:// www.wikiwand.com/en/Terence_Kilmartin; Dorril, Stephen, Spooks, *Lobster*, No. 22 p. 16). In 1956, Astor was persuaded to offer cover for the SIS agent, Kim Philby, as a journalist in Beirut. As Sebastian Faulks adds (in parenthesis) (1997: 265): 'Neither Astor nor the SIS then knew that Philby was also working for the KGB.' Ben Macintyre, in his excellent biography of Kim Philby (2014: 205), says: 'Astor later claimed, implausibly, that he had no idea Philby would be working for MI6 while reporting for his newspaper.' Astor is mentioned on a list of journalists with close MI6 connects by Robin Ramsay in a review of Anthony Cavendish's *Inside intelligence* (1967). Included were Lord Arran on the *Daily Mail*, W. I. Farr, Michael Berry (Lord Hartwell), Roy Pawley, Tom Harris, Michael Field of the *Telegraph*, Wing Commander Paul Richey at the *Daily Express*. At the *Observer*, David Astor, Mark Arnold-Foster, Wayland Young (Lord Kennet) and Edward Crankshaw. Brian Crozier at the *Economist*, Stuart McLean, vice-chairman of Associated Newspapers; John S. Whitlock, managing editor of Butterworth Publications; P. Morgan, editor British Plastic; G. Paulton, of *Arbeiter Zeitung* (Vienna), and Henry Brandon at *The Sunday Times*. See http://www.8bitmode.com/rogerdog/lobster/lobster15.pdf. Macintyre also mentions that *Sunday Express* journalist Hester Harriet Marsden-Smedley 'was said to do a little spying on the side' (op cit: 19) and that Captain Leslie Sheridan, who ran a section of MI6 known as 'D/Q' (responsible for disseminating rumours and black propaganda) was a former night editor of the *Daily Mirror* (op cit: 20)

[39] Knightley (1986: 131) records that when in July 1939 Col. Count Gerhardt von Schwerin, of the German General Staff, arrived in the UK as a spokesman for the German opposition to Hitler, he was met by David Astor. Cabell (2008: 29; 49) records that Astor and Fleming worked alongside Dennis Wheatley (specialising in deception plans), later to become the occult/adventure novelist. Cabell also reports that Fleming may well have played a central role in luring Rudolf Hess to Scotland in May 1941 (ibid: 40-52). SOE was established by PM Winston Churchill and

Hugh Dalton in July 1940 'to facilitate espionage and sabotage behind enemy lines' and serve as the nucleus of a resistance movement if Britain were invaded by the Axis Powers (ibid: 45). Other intellectuals/writers involved with intelligence during the war include A. P. Herbert, Arthur Koestler (who had previously served the Soviet Comintern while a journalist during the Spanish Civil War), David Garnett, Elizabeth Bowen, novelist Muriel Spark, Alec Waugh and his brother Evelyn Waugh, and Graham Greene (Bower 1995: 227)

[40] *Tribune* was later to be distributed to British missions abroad by the Information Research Department (Norton-Taylor and Milne 1996). '[It] combines the resolute exposure of communism and its methods with the consistent championship of those objectives which leftwing sympathisers normally support. … Many articles in it can be effectively turned to this department's purposes' (ibid)

[41] In an interview with the author, London, November 1999

[42] In a letter to the author dated 7 December 1999

[43] This quotation from an email sent by Phillip Knightley to the author on 12 May 2000. I quote it in more detail here (with permission from PK): 'It was 1973. The circulation manager of the *ST* introduced to the paper a man called Frank Donnelly or Frank Quinn – like most spies he had several names. Quinn had been running a newspaper in Belfast (a front for MI5 as it turned out) who is how the *ST* man got to know him. Quinn was annoyed with Brit intel over money and this had eroded his oath of silence. He wanted to tell his story. He had been quartermaster on the combined SIS/CIA operation to destabilise Albania in 1949 – the one Philby betrayed. So in the summer of that year we took him over the ground where the operation had been planned and executed – Malta, Corfu, London – and photographed him during the day and debriefed him at night. The story was for the *ST* magazine which had a lead print time of about six weeks. On the Tuesday of the week the story was to appear, with the presses at the contract printer (out in the provinces somewhere) about to start, I got a call from the MoD asking me to go there urgently and see the admiral who was then in charge of the D Notice committee. The admiral had a finished copy of the magazine on his desk. He made no attempt to explain how he had come by it. He said that for reasons he could not reveal, certain aspects of the Albanian operation were still "sensitive" and would have to come out. He showed me what they were. I said I'd consult the magazine editor, Magnus Linklater. It was too late to change and reprint the whole article so Linklater had the printers black out the bits the admiral said were sensitive. And we ran a paragraph on the front page of the magazine explaining why. From this and from talks with publishers who had tried to print in secrecy books that were similarly "sensitive" (kept them out of their catalogues, swore their editorial staff to secrecy) only to get a similar call from the MoD, I am convinced that MI5 has agents in newspapers and printers and publishing houses who tip off MI5/SIS about impending publication of material that would be of interest to the services. … ps: There was an interesting conclusion to the Quinn story. He was in his local on the Sunday night celebrating, revelling in being called James Bond. Next morning he was found dead in bed. His GP said he had had a heart condition for some time so there was no inquest. I went to the funeral – full of anonymous men in black coats. .. Quinn had promised me a lot more, especially about what he had been doing in Ireland. It made me think at the time. His son was briefly in touch promising more, but then failed to make further contact'

[44] See ww.30au.co.uk – a website packed with details about the assault unit

[45] See https://www.britannica.com/biography/Denis-Hamilton, accessed on 27 July 2016. Hamilton was listed among the 40 Greats of British journalism by *Press Gazette* in November 2005. 'Charles Denis Hamilton – Denis to his friends, CD to his subordinates – was a Northern radical in the historic tradition of the British Press, bent on shaking up an effete Southern establishment. That was his secret.' His secret life in intelligence was not mentioned

[46] Jeremy Wolfenden, the subject of one of the three profiles in Sebastian Faulk's *The fatal Englishman: Three short lives* (London: Vintage, 1997) worked for SIS while *Daily Telegraph* Moscow correspondent in the early 1960s. He came under pressure from both SIS and the KGB while in Moscow. He died, aged just 31, in Washington in December 1965. According to Faulks (ibid: 265): 'A whole section of SIS – the BAQ department – was given over to cultivating [journalistic] contacts, and another to giving regular off-the-record briefings to correspondents close to the front line in the Cold War. The ethics of these briefings were unclear. The journalists were free to discount what they were told, but their independence was tarnished' (see also Knightley 1986: 386-387)

[47] As Calder Walton comments (2013: xxvi): '…the Cold War was primarily an intelligence conflict in which the intelligence services of Western governments and Eastern Bloc countries were pitted against each other, and fought at the front line'

[48] Similarly Tom Bower (1995: 214) comments that during this period SIS was able to enlist 'British journalists, academics, students, industrialists, businessmen and others travelling to communist countries and the Middle East to collect intelligence or act as postmen. The organisations particularly favoured as recruiting grounds were the BBC, the British Council, the National Union of Students, the Anglo-Russian Translation Agency, national newspapers, publishing companies and Christian missionaries'

[49] For a review of Peter Evans' *Within the secret state: A disturbing study of the use and misuse of power*, 2009, see *Lobster*, Summer 2009, page 42. Tim Jones, also of *The Times*, was also approached by MI5 at a lunch at Simpsons in the Strand, London, in 1975 and he also refused to co-operate (Evans op cit: 49)

[50] According to Tom Bower (1995: 145): 'In co-operation with the Foreign Office's Information Research Department, MI5's agents were encouraged to disrupt subversive organisations, even impregnating lavatory paper with an itching substance at halls hired by communist organisations. It was often "good fun" to derail and sabotage the enemy in this way.' David Leigh (2000b) provides an example of IRD misinformation/lying from the early 1970s: a *News of the World* front page story, titled 'Russian sub in IRA plot', carried an aerial photograph of a Soviet submarine supposedly taken off the Donegal coast. It was all the work of IRD – and nonsense

[51] The terminology of terrorism: Malaya 1948-52, *Journal of South East Asian Studies*, June, 2003 Available online at http://www.accessmylibrary.com/coms2/summary_0286-4205179_ITM, accessed on 11 June 2008

[52] On this same theme, Robin Ramsay (2006 [2000]: 113) comments: 'IRD turned up in all the post war conflicts between the British colonial authorities and nationalist liberation movements in the British colonies, spreading the department "line", its very own conspiracy theory: the commies are behind it all. And if there was no evidence that the Soviets were behind the troubles in – say – Cyprus or Northern Ireland, IRD would fabricate some'

[53] See http://www.spinprofiles.org/index.php/Information_Research_Department, accessed on 14 February 2010

[54] ibid

[55] See Agee, Phil (n.d.) *Covert action: What next – CIA briefing*, London: Agee-Hosenball Defence Committee p. 7

[56] Significantly Bob Woodward, one of the *Washington Post* reporters involved in the Watergate scoop, had a background in naval intelligence while Ben Bradlee, celebrated editor at the time, had an intelligence background having worked in 1952 for the US information and educational exchange (later name the US information agency) which supplied news items to the CIA (Reed 2014). 'During this period, according to a US justice department memo, Bradlee promulgated CIA-directed European propaganda urging the controversial execution of the American spies Ethel

and Julius Rosenberg. They were electrocuted in 1953' (ibid). According to Duane R. Clarridge (1997: 217-218), who served 30 years in the CIA, Bobby Inman, deputy director of the CIA, 'was a great friend of Bob Woodward ... They'd served together in the Navy. It was an open secret in Washington that Inman had been a source for Woodward. Casey [director of the CIA 1981-1987] later told me that he suspected Inman continued to be a source for Woodward after Inman came to the CIA'

[57] Knightley (1986: 337) reports that the CIA and FBI also put several dissident publications out of business by persuading major companies to withdraw their support. Sometimes, editorial staffs were infiltrated by agents to sow disinformation and suspicion

[58] During the 1950s and 1960s, the Secret Intelligence Service had a section called Special Political Action 'which tried to influence the press' (Hennessy 2010: 43)

[59] The bugs in No 10 Downing Street were only removed by PM Jim Callaghan in 1977, the year he cleared MI5 of a plot to oust Wilson's Labour government

[60] In 2000, Northern Ireland secretary Mo Mowlam even admitted that Gerry Adams, of Sinn Fein, had been bugged. Four years later Sinn Fein's Martin McGuinness was also shown to have been bugged after a new biography carried transcripts of telephone conversations. And in 2008 it was reported in *The Sunday Times* that MP Sadiq Khan was bugged while meeting a constituent Babar Ahmad, being held at a north London prison while fighting extradition to the United States on terrorism charges (Cobain 2014b)

[61] David Leigh said wrongly in his book, *The Wilson plot*, of 1989, that his pseudonym was 'Henry Worthington'. He admitted to this error in a review of *The Defence of the realm: The authorised history of MI5*, by Christopher Andrew, London: Allen Lane, 2009 in the *Guardian*, of 10 October 2009. Andrew blames all the 'Wilson plot' theories on the 'paranoid', 'unscrupulous', 'dishonest' Wright

[62] The MI5 history also revealed that the telephone of Jack Jones, general secretary of the Transport and General Workers Union from 1969 to 1978, was also bugged by MI5. See Michael Evans: MI5 bugged Jack Jones's phone over fears he was agent of KGB, *Times*, 6 October 2009

[63] Richard Norton-Taylor (1990: 98) records how, in 1974, Chapman Pincher was given a copy of a forged Swiss account claiming Ted Short, later Lord Glenamara, was illegally investing in a foreign bank. Lord Glenamara believed it was all part of a 'dirty campaign by people in MI5'

[64] Two former colleagues of Wallace corroborated his allegations about 'Clockwork Orange': Mr Michael Taylor, a former army information officer, and Mr Peter Broderick, a former chief of Army Information Services in Northern Ireland (see Thomas 1991: 148)

[65] Andy Beckett (2010: 168-169) places the Wilson plots in the context of the 'Zinoviev letter' of 1924, the forgery that was used by intelligence to remove the first Labour government, and the 'Kinnock's Kremlin Connection' *Sunday Times* report in 1992, later exposed as having been concocted simply to discredit the Labour leader

[66] See Newton, Scott (2000/1) MI5 and the Wilson plot, *Lobster*, No. 40 Winter p 28. Significantly, the intelligence plots against Wilson occurred at roughly the same time when social democratic governments in Australia, New Zealand and West Germany were also being subjected to destabilisation campaigns. See Willy Brandt: The 'Good German', by Stephen Dorril, *Lobster*, No. 22 pp 12-15. As Dorril reports (ibid: 14): 'The run-up to the November 1972 election saw a series of scandals involving highly confidential leaks to papers and magazines in the right-wing Springer group, and allegations of bribes, which shook the Brandt government'

[67] See British intelligence and the covert propaganda front. Available online at http://nelsonmandela2.blogspot.com/, accessed on 14 June 2008

[68] Roy Greenslade, the then-editor of the *Daily Mirror*, later apologised for his role in the Scargill smears affair. See http://www.guardian.co.uk/media/2002/may/27/mondaymediasection. politicsandthemedia, accessed on 6 April 2009. During the miners' strike of 1972, the leader of the National Union of Mineworkers was Joe Gormley. Richard Vinen (2009: 39) reports that Gormley was 'conspicuously non-communist and may even have been an MI5 informant'

[69] See Dorril 1993: 276. Russell Davies, in *Foreign body: The secret life of Robert Maxwell* (London: Bloomsbury, 1995: 21-25) records how Maxwell's publishing ventures had begun in collaboration with the German company, Springer Verlag, and bankrolled by the Secret Intelligence Service. Funding was organised through Hambro's bank – and Charles Hambro had been a member of the Secret Operations Executive, the covert military organisation set up by Churchill during the Second World War. George Kennedy Young, the future deputy chief of MI6, was responsible for 'running' Maxwell while based in Vienna. Desmond Bristow, a former SIS officer, says of Maxwell: 'I know he was kept on very sort of – how would we put it? – *discreetly* by MI6 for quite a long time. Probably, in fact, till the end of his days' (see also Bower 1996: 158-160)

[70] Maxwell's *Sunday Mirror* had run a 'spoiler' on Vanunu a week before *The Sunday Times*'s exclusive, presenting him as a con man pushing false stories about Israel's nuclear secrets. See Roy Greenslade, *Maxwell's fall: The appalling legacy of a corrupt man*, London: New York: Simon and Schuster, 1992 p. 329. But Greenslade, like Tom Bower, argues that Maxwell was not a Mossad agent and that Hersh had been misled by his source, Ari Ben Menashe, a former Mossad agent and arms dealer. Vanunu spent 18 years in jail (11 of them in solitary confinement) before being released in 2004. But after speaking to the foreign media in 2007, he was re-arrested and jailed again in 2010 (though this gained little coverage in the Western media). See http://www.lobster-magazine.co.uk/free/lobster59/lobster59.pdf, p. 87, accessed on 24 November 2010

[71] Anthony Frewin, in *Lobster*, No. 30 p. 42 argues that 'the proximate cause of the attack on Gott … was his review of the memoirs of the ITN journalist, Sandy Gall, in the *Guardian* of 12 February 1994, in which he pointed out that Gall had been working with SIS in his reporting of the war in Afghanistan'

[72] Daphne Parish was sentenced to 15 years in prison but released on 16 July following the intervention by the Zambian President Kenneth Kaunda at the request of the *Observer*'s owner 'Tiny' Rowland

[73] See also Dilip Hiro, *Desert Shield to Desert Storm: The second Gulf War*, London: Paladin/ HarperCollins, 1992 pp 67-68

[74] See http://en.wikipedia.org/wiki/Farzad_Bazoft, accessed on 11 July 2008

[75] See also Hollingsworth, Mark (2000) The hidden hand, *Guardian*, 30 March and Ramsay, Robin (2000/1) A secret service? *Lobster*, Vol. 40 Winter p. 15. Ramsay says that when Coughlin was asked in the libel trial about his source, he said he was shown but not allowed to copy documents. 'This is the classic IRD disinformation technique, described in the 1960s by Charles Foley in his book, *Legacy of strife* [Penguin, 1964], and more recently by Colin Wallace working in Information Policy in Northern Ireland in the 1970s: show the dummies forgeries but don't let them take them out of the room'

[76] See http://www.telegraph.co.uk/news/worldnews/middleeast/iraq/1449442/Terrorist-behind-September-11-strike-was-trained-by-Saddam.html, accessed 1 May 2009

[77] See http://www.politico.com/news/stories/0808/12308.html

[78] Paul Lashmar, My name's James Bond: Here's my NUJ card. British spies posing as journalists make genuine foreign reporters' jobs much more difficult, *Independent*, 30 January 2001

[79] According to Gordon Thomas (2009: 286), Tomlinson's passport described him as Ben Presley – and both the passport and NUJ card had been forged by MI6's technical services department

[80] See http://www.nuj.org.uk/inner.php?docid=635, accessed 14 October 2004

[81] An annual meeting of world leaders, described as a 'powerful secret society' by Charlie Skelton in the unusual blog he wrote on his attempts to report the 2009 meeting for the *Guardian*. See http://www.guardian.co.uk/news/blog/2009/may/19/bilderberg-skelton-greece, accessed 20 May 2009

[82] See http://www.lobster-magazine.co.uk/articles/security.htm, accessed on 14 October 2008

[83] According to Anthony Seldon (2007: 57 and 83), Blair's inner circle first comprised Jonathan Powell, Sir David Manning, Alastair Campbell, Sally Morgan, Jack Straw and Richard Wilson, cabinet secretary and Britain's most senior civil servant. By 2002 Jack Straw had been edged out of the inner circle. Seldon (2005: 392) also quotes General Sir Charles Guthrie, Chief of the Defence Staff, saying 'approvingly': on the Operation Desert Fox attacks on Iraq in December 1998: 'It was clear early on that he didn't want to operate through Cabinet but through a small, tight-knit group'

[84] The government later admitted the existence of Mass Appeal. See Revealed: How MI6 sold the Iraq war, Nicholas Rufford, *Sunday Times*, 28 December 2003. Available online at: http://www.timesonline.co.uk/tol/news/uk/article839897.ece, accessed on 14 October 2006. John Pilger commented: 'We now know that the BBC and other British media were used by MI6, the secret intelligence service. In what they called Operation Mass Appeal, MI6 agents planted stories about Saddam's weapons of mass destruction, such as weapons hidden in his palaces and in secret underground bunkers. All these stories were fakes. However, this is not the point. The point is that the dark arts of MI6 were quite unnecessary, because media self-censorship produced the same result.' See http://www.coldtype.net/Assets.07/Essays/0307.Pilger.War.pdf, accessed on 21 August 2016

[85] Martin Bright, Terror, security and the media, *Observer*, 21 July 2002 http://www.guardian.co.uk/world/2002/jul/21/humanrights.comment, accessed on 14 October 2003

[86] Gilligan met Dr Kelly in the Charing Cross Hotel, London. His *Today* report, broadcast at 6.07 am on 29 May 2003, quoted his anonymous source: 'What this person says is that a week before the publication date of the dossier, it was actually rather a bland production. Downing Street … ordered it to be sexed up, to be made more exciting and ordered more facts to be "discovered"' (cited in Baker 2007: 155)

[87] The agent known as Curveball, who became one of the CIA's most valuable sources on Iraq's fictitious WMD, was later revealed to be Rafid Ahmed Alwan, who worked in Division Four of Iraq's intelligence services (see Meanwhile Curveball – the man whose lies made the case for war – looks on from afar, Martin Chulov, *Guardian*, 29 June 2009)

Chapter Three

From Hiroshima to the Falklands/Malvinas 'bizarre little war': The emergence of the new militarist consensus in the US and UK

T he origins of the new militarist consensus in the United States can be traced to America's involvement in the Second World War. Many historians now suggest that Japanese plans for the attack on Pearl Harbor in 1941 were well known to US intelligence and administration (Farago 1967; Prange 1991; Rusbridger and Nove 1991; Ahmed 2005: 282-285). For instance, Robert Stinnett (2000), following 17 years of archival research and many interviews with US Navy cryptographers, concluded that President Roosevelt deliberately steered Japan into war with the US. Gore Vidal (2003: 88) reports that 60 to 80 per cent of the American people were solidly against any European war in 1940. But then on 26 November 1941, an ultimatum from the Americans called for complete Japanese withdrawal from China and Indo-China, for Japan to support China's Nationalist government and to abandon its tri-partite agreement with the Axis powers. Of the ultimatum, Cordell Hull, secretary of state, later commented: 'We [had] no serious thought Japan would accept...' And so Pearl Harbor, when 3,000 men were killed, followed. Certainly the attack provided the opportunity for the US's fledgling permanent war economy state to join the fight against the Nazis (now that the more serious enemy, the Soviet communists, had managed to survive the German onslaught).

The 'vulnerable state' (as represented by the elite) was responding as the innocent victim of an unprovoked attack. War was waged. And journalists faced a regime of 'total censorship'. As Gary C. Woodward comments (1993: 6): 'Everything written, photographed or broadcast was scrutinised by censors. Anything that did not meet the High Command's considerations of security was deleted. In the Pacific theatre, for example, Americans were not told initially of the heavy damage to the US navy inflicted by the Japanese at Pearl Harbor.' The legendary journalist, Walter Cronkite, United Press war correspondent from 1941 through to the end

77

of the war and the Nuremberg trials, commented: 'All written copy was passed by censors. And I think this is the way it should be. We had total freedom at the front with no restrictions where we went' (Sylvester and Huffman 2005: 13).

With the nuclear bombings of Hiroshima and Nagasaki in August 1945, the first warning to the Soviet Union in the new Cold War was delivered.

GROWTH OF SECRET US STATE AND COVERT PRESIDENCY

Alongside the development of the Cold War ideological hegemony and the permanent war state was the growth of the power of the executive office of the president based around the National Security Council and the CIA (together with the many other covert organisations comprising the secret state within the state) (Moyers 1988). Secrecy and the development of a centralised, nuclear state were to become the dominant features of the domestic political scene, so covert LIC strategies, away from the glare of newspaper headlines, were favoured abroad.

Despite the enormous industrial and economic power of the American empire since 1945 (based on a massively expanding, state-backed arms economy), its overt military adventures have been disastrous. The Korean conflict (1950-1953) ended in stalemate, the Bay of Pigs invasion plan for Cuba in 1961 was a humiliating disaster (Cirino 1971: 282-284). So, too, was Vietnam. The attempt to rescue the hostages, held in the US embassy in Tehran, in 1980 crashed again – this time in a humiliating disaster in the desert (Adams 1994: 149-154). In the 1980s and early 1990s, a series of military adventures proved equally disastrous. Lebanon (1982-1983), Grenada, Libya, Panama and Iraq were all failures from a strictly military perspective – though massive propaganda campaigns were launched to portray the last four as military successes. The first followed the humiliation of Lebanon. The last three significantly followed the failures of covert action (assassination) to eliminate the heads of the 'enemy' states. It is, therefore, wrong to see the 1980s and early 1990s as a period of American supremacy. Its new militarist adventures were all based on failures rather than successes – and led inexorably to the disaster militarism of the first years of the 21st century.

SECRET WARFARE: AWAY FROM THE PROBING PRESS

But since 1945 America's main war-fighting activity was in the shady covert area – and here (through a series of managed media leaks) a number of 'successes' were claimed. The CIA's clandestine support for military coups against revolutionary or reforming regimes ranked up a number of significant 'victories': Syria 1949, Iran 1953, Guatemala 1954, Congo 1960, Iraq 1963 and 1968, Brazil 1964, Indonesia 1965, Chile 1973 (Ranelagh 1992). As Halliday points out, these successes were dependent on the relative vulnerability of the armed forces in the target country. He adds: 'When the CIA went into action against the revolutions of the 1970s this option was not available precisely because the revolutionaries had destroyed the old state machine, including its army, and replaced it with their own revolutionary armed forces. As in the case of Cuba during the period 1959-61, the CIA was thrown back on a surrogate form of covert action – aid to right-wing guerrillas' (Halliday 1989: 74-75).

The global economic recession precipitated by the oil price increases of 1973 and 1979 completely overturned the global balance of power (Baker 1991: 3-8). Initially, the Third World made extraordinary gains and 14 revolutions shook the imperial powers.[1] In response, the imperial powers, led by the United States, completely altered their economic orientation to the Third World. From being suppliers of $50 billion a year of capital to the Third World in the two decades leading up to the mid-1970s, the imperial powers moved to drawing $100 billion a year from the Third World by the 1990s. This $150 billion shift was equivalent to the entire balance of payments of the United States, 15 times the annual investment of Iraq or Egypt. The result has been a massive rise of global poverty and Third World instability (ibid).

With the advent of the Reagan administration, the US elite was determined to roll back the revolutionary successes of the previous decade. The offensive was typically multi-pronged. Under the direction of William C. Casey (1981-1986), the CIA ran a massive LIC offensive strategy – totally contradicting the media myth of defence. Counter-revolutionary movements in Cambodia, Afghanistan, Angola, Suriname and Nicaragua were backed from 1981 to 1988. And at enormous expense. In 1986 alone, the Afghanistan operation received an estimated $470 million and more than $5 billion of direct US aid to the mujahideen, over the whole period, matched 'dollar for dollar' by Saudi Arabia, with arms and equipment shipments peaking at 60,000 tonnes per day by the late 1980s (Todd, Bloch and Fitzgerald 2009: 13). The CIA and their congressional supporters maintained the flow of arms and money to the Afghan mujahideen for a further two years following the January 1989 Russian withdrawal.

> The final instalment – some $200 million in the Defense Appropriation Bill for FY 1992 – was augmented by a large segment of Soviet-era weaponry captured after the Desert Storm Iraq campaign. If many in Congress were beginning to question the wisdom of arming obvious warlords such as Hezh-i-Islami leader Gulbuddin Hekmatyar, doubts were sidelined until the end of the first Bush administration, to avoid offending Saudi Arabia (ibid: 14).

Bob Woodward's history of the CIA's covert wars of the 1980s details a complex web of clandestine activity (1987: 310-311). He also reports (ibid: 456) Ben Bradlee, *Washington Post* editor, as saying of the CIA in the 1980s: 'It's really out of control, isn't it?' At least 12 operations of security and intelligence support included those to President Hissène Habré of Chad, to Pakistan President Zia, to Liberia's Samuel Doe, to Philippine President Marcos, to Sudanese President Numeiri, to Lebanese President Amir Gemayel and to President Duarte of El Salavador (all of these dictators with appalling human rights records). Both Prades (1986: 383) and Treverton (1987: 14) suggest that by the mid-1980s the CIA was engaged in at least 40 major covert operations – but they were largely ignored by the media.

As Richard Barnet argues (1988: 218): 'The whole idea of low intensity warfare is to avoid "disturbing" – a euphemism for informing – public opinion in the United States (in the battle zone the intensity can be high indeed). The strategy depends on secrecy.' At their heart lies media propaganda through omission and mystification. Col. Oliver North, during his July 1987 testimony to the Iran-Contra select congressional committee, argued that US national security justified covert paramilitary operations and the calculated dissemination of false and misleading information to the press by (and to) US officials operating on behalf of the secret state. 'There is a great deception practised in the conduct of covert operations. They are in essence a lie,' he told the committee with graphic frankness (Keeble 1997: 41-42).

THE GREAT VIETNAM MEDIA MYTH

At the heart of LIC strategy and the Reaganite response to the Third World revolutions were American perceptions of the 'Vietnam syndrome'. For the American elite the defeat in Vietnam (in what the Vietnamese dub the 'American War') against a far less technologically sophisticated enemy – accompanied by assassinations, race and student upheavals at home – was a trauma of unprecedented proportions. Its legacy was, indeed, horrifying. Some 4 million were killed in Indochina and many millions more orphaned, maimed and made into refugees; three countries were devastated – Vietnam, Cambodia and Laos (Chomsky 2005: 125). Some 7 million tons of bombs were dropped on Vietnam (Bower 2016: 234). And it cost more than $150bn for the US alone. More than 58,000 US troops were killed and 304,000 wounded while an estimated 3 million Vietnamese and 1 million in Laos and Cambodia died (Goldenberg 2006) though the exact figures will never be known.[2] By the time Saigon fell to the North Vietnamese army in 1975, more than 70 foreign and local journalists had been killed. As Richard Pyle and Horst Fass report (2003: xiv-xv): 'An unknown number of Cambodians who had worked for the Western press and would vanish in the Killing Fields, were eventually added to an uncertain final toll.'

A scapegoat was needed and the most obvious one was the messenger of the bad tidings – the media (see Braestrup 1985). Vietnam has been described as the 'first living-room war'. Long after the end of the war, it is argued, iconic visual images still dominate our perceptions of it – a US Marine Zippo-lighting a Vietnamese village; the photograph by Associated Press's Eddie Adams of the execution of a Vietcong suspect in a Saigon street; a Vietnamese girl, Phan Thi Kim Phuc, running naked and terrified down a street after a napalm attack (see Griffin 2010: 17-18). Images such as these along with press criticism of the conduct of the war are said to have eroded public support. A series of major Hollywood movies, such as *The deer hunter* (1978), *Coming home* (1978), *Apocalypse now* (1979), *Platoon* (1986), *Full metal jacket* (1987), *Born on the fourth of July* (1989), *Rambo: First blood* (1982) and the *Rambo* sequels (1985 and 1988), helped reinforce this myth. As Griffin comments (ibid: 22):

> Intentionally or not, the corpus of post-Vietnam Hollywood films creates an image of the war in which the young American soldier was the primary victim, betrayed by his government and by the American people.

But even the US army's own official history, *The military and the media 1962-1968*, concluded that the American mainstream media was 'remarkably professional in its coverage of Vietnam' (Badsey 1995: 58). Surveys showed that media consumption, in fact, promoted support for the war (Williams 1993: 305-338).The American military, after considerable deliberations on the issue since the Korean War, opted for an entirely voluntary censorship scheme for journalists – in the main because they did not have total control over access to the front line (unlike, for instance, during the Gulf crisis of 1991 and Iraq invasion of 2003 when the military enjoyed total control). War censorship, it was felt at the time, could not be introduced since no war had been declared.

Journalists were allowed remarkable access to the frontline. Sandy Gall comments in his autobiography (1984: 230-231): 'You could go anywhere at any time to cover almost any story. If there was a battle being fought in any part of Vietnam involving American troops or South Vietnamese or both the Press could go there simply by climbing aboard a helicopter or fixed-wing aircraft.' This meant that censorship operated – but subtly. For instance, Bob Schieffer, a young reporter for *Forth Worth Star-Telegram* (later CBS news correspondent in Washington DC) commented:

> The military commanders would exert control by limiting transportation into areas where the news might be bad. If I wanted to travel to Danang, they would call flight operation and find a transport plane going there that afternoon and make a place for me. But when there was a battle where the news was not the way they wanted, it was very difficult to get transportation (Sylvester and Huffman op cit: 20).

Nor did the relative freedom enjoyed by journalists result in them flagrantly ignoring the guidelines which outlined 15 categories of information reportable only with authorisation. Between August 1964 and the end of 1968, for example, around 2,000 news media representatives reported from Vietnam[3] – yet only six committed violations so severe to warrant the military revoking their credentials (Gannett Foundation 1991: 14-15). And very few actually saw combat. 'No more than forty reporters were where the bullets were flying,' according to the *Washington Post*'s Henry Allen (cited in Rid 2007: 56). As a result, the real graphic horror of the war rarely entered the media. From 1965 to 1970, just 3 per cent of all evening visual news reports from Vietnam showed 'heavy battle' scenes (ibid: 59).

The easy access to the frontlines also, intriguingly, offered new opportunities to women reporters – even though they still suffered from acute discrimination. As Chambers, Steiner and Fleming comment (2004: 205): 'It was this feature of easy access, rather than significant changes in attitudes about women, that allowed so many women to report from Vietnam.' In all, the US military provided credentials to 467 women reporters in Vietnam.

BACKING OUR BOYS IN VIETNAM

Virtually every Vietnam reporter backed the war effort. As the Gannett Foundation report comments: 'Throughout the war, in fact, journalists who criticised the military's performance did so out of a sense of frustration that military strategy and tactics were failing to accomplish the goal of decisively defeating the North Vietnamese forces' (op cit: 15). Veteran war correspondent Peter Arnett (1993: 88) commented: 'The consensus of the American high command was that their efforts were paying off in Vietnam, but that winning would take longer than anticipated. The reporters generally concurred in that view and I heard none voice doubts that the war was worth fighting.' In 1966, he said, he was entirely caught up in the war's momentum. 'I never asked myself whether it was right or wrong and the question did not come up in conversation, not with soldiers or my colleagues because we were all of us too close to the action. Too many of our friends had died; we were unwilling to write off that sacrifice' (ibid: 193). In 1968, the *Boston Globe* surveyed the editorial positions of 39 leading US dailies with a combined circulation of 22 million and found that not one advocated withdrawal from Vietnam (Solomon 2007: 223).

The coverage of the My Lai massacre of March 1968, when hundreds of Vietnamese were slaughtered by rampaging American soldiers, highlights graphically the failures of the mainstream media in Vietnam. Evidence of the massacre (after first being covered up by the American military[4]) was presented to top national news media by Vietnam veteran Ron Ridenhour and others, but none dared to touch the story (McGregor 1998: 63-68; Neale 2001: 102-104; Andersen 2006: 56-59). It was not until November 1969, more than a year and a half after the massacre, that the small, alternative Dispatch News Service and dogged investigative reporter Seymour Hersh, who never set foot in Vietnam, published the story. It began: 'Lieutenant William L Calley Jr, twenty six, is a mild-mannered, boyish looking Vietnam combat veteran with the nickname "Rusty". The Army says he deliberately murdered at least 109 Vietnamese civilians during a search and destroy mission in March 1968 in a Viet Cong stronghold known as "Pinkville".' The report was immediately followed up by 30 newspapers nationwide. But according to Noam Chomsky (2000: 167-168), in the context of the mass slaughter of civilians in Vietnam, My Lai was a tiny footnote to one of these operations:

It gained a lot of prominence later after a lot of suppression and I think the reason is clear: it could be blamed on half-crazed uneducated GIs in the field who didn't know who was going to shoot at them next, and it deflected attention away from the commanders who were directing atrocities far from the scene – for example, the ones plotting the B52 raids on villages.

John Pilger (1986: 256) also argues that mainstream media coverage of Vietnam failed to capture the true horror. 'Atrocities were neither isolated nor aberrations. It was the nature of the war that was atrocious; this was the big story, but it was seldom judged to be "news" and therefore seldom told, except in fragment. Atrocities were reported as "mistakes" which were "blundered into".' Significantly, when *Newsweek* covered the My Lai massacre the headline ran 'An American tragedy'. But, as Pilger comments, this 'invited sympathy for the invader and deflected the truth that the atrocities were above all, a *Vietnamese* tragedy' (ibid: 259). Moreover, as Andrew Hoskins stresses (2004: 18), only a small percentage of film reports shown on television news during the conflict depicted actual fighting and graphic scenes of the dead or wounded. Nick Turse (2013) argues that My Lai was in no way exceptional:

> Until the My Lai revelations became front-page news, atrocity stories were routinely disregarded by American journalists or excised by stateside editors. The fate of civilians in rural South Vietnam did not merit much examination; even the articles that did mention the killing of noncombatants generally did so merely in passing, without any indication that the acts described might be war crimes. Vietnamese revolutionary sources, for their part, detailed hundreds of massacres and large-scale operations that resulted in thousands of civilian deaths, but those reports were dismissed out of hand as communist propaganda.[5]

Most commentators have seen a shift to more critical 'advocacy' reporting following the Vietcong Tet offensive of 1968 by which time some 20,000 Americans had been killed. But such a shift occurred among the American elite with significant sections beginning to question the cost, effectiveness and overall moral/political justification for the war. Moreover, by 1969, some 70 per cent of the general population described the war as 'fundamentally wrong and immoral' – not as a 'mistake' (Chomsky 2007: 156). But the media followed the shift in the *elite consensus* rather than created it (Hallin 1986: 21; Williams 1987: 250-254; Cumings 1992: 84). Famously, Walter Cronkite, host of *CBS Evening News*, commented after visiting post-Tet Vietnam: 'The only national way out then will be to negotiate, not as victors, but as honourable people who lived up to their pledge to defend democracy, and did the best they could' (Rid op cit: 59).

According to Spencer (2005: 58-59), television after Tet presented the war as a series of disconnected episodes of combat which reflected the disorganised pattern of the war itself. 'This fragmentation appeared to parallel a similar disjointed policy approach, which served to intensify doubts about American purpose and brought pressure to bear on an administration, increasingly concerned about growing public unease.' Two months after Tet, Johnson withdrew from the presidential race indicating 'his inability to effectively shape the news agenda and counter the growing sense that the public had been misled on questions of policy, progress and moral responsibility'.

Most significantly mass public protests against the war impacted on mainstream coverage. As Jeff Cohen commented (2006): 'It wasn't the mainstream media that turned the public against the war. Quite the contrary: it was the public – especially the ever-growing anti-war movement fortified by Vietnam veterans who spoke out against the war – that prodded mainstream media toward more sceptical coverage.' Many in the US military after 1968 were concerned to show the difficulties and daily frustrations of the war to the American public and welcomed the press as potential allies in conveying the message (Woodward, Gary C. op cit: 8). Moreover, while the mainstream media grew more sceptical about Vietnam after Tet their opposition to the peace movement persisted (Spencer 2005: 62-68). Gitlin (2003 [1980]), for instance, highlights the ways in which the corporate media trivialised the peace movement, emphasised divisions within its ranks, constantly under-estimated its support at demonstrations and represented it as an extremist part of a New Left conspiracy.

NOT TO BE MISSED: THE SIGNIFICANCE OF THE ANTI-WAR MEDIA WITHIN THE US ARMY

The significance of the anti-war movement (and its protest media) within the armed services should not be under-estimated. Jonathan Neale (op cit: 122-130), in a seminal study, identified around 300 anti-war newspapers in the armed services during the course of the war. For instance, a small group of Trotskyists were behind *Vietnam GI*, a newspaper produced in Chicago with a print run of 15,000 and a mailing list of 3,000 in Vietnam, At Fort Bragg, a chapter of GIs United Against the War put out *Bragg Briefs*. There was *Fatigue Press* at Fort Hood, Texas, the *FTA* (*Fuck the Army*) at Fort Knox, the *Last Harass* at Fort Gordon, Georgia, the *Pawn's Pawn* at Fort Leonard Wood, Missouri, the *Ultimate Weapon* at Fort Dix, New Jersey. As Neale comments (ibid: 123): 'The people who put them out were investigated, transferred, sent to Vietnam, court-martialled and given long sentences, dishonourably discharged and framed on other charges. But still the papers kept coming.'

There were at least 84 newspapers in the Air Force and Navy in the United States, including *Duck Power*, in San Diego, *Harass the Brass*, at Canute, Illinois, *All Hands Abandon Ship*, in Newport, Rhode Island, *Now Hear This*, in Long Beach, and *Fat Albert's Death Ship*, in Charlestown. From 1970 onwards, campaigning against the war moved from the campus to the barracks. According to Neale (ibid: 124): 'The anti-war movement was everywhere, on almost every base of any size.'

Not surprisingly, the desertion rate amongst US troops tripled during the course of the Vietnam War and at its height was three times the rate of desertion at any point during the Korean War.

Lauren Kessler (1984: 151) suggests the first military anti-war newspaper was the *Bond: Voice of the American Servicemen's Union*, founded in Berkeley in 1967 and published in New York from 1968. With an international circulation of more than 100,000 by 1971, it called for the withdrawal of all troops, the right of military personnel to disobey what they viewed as illegal orders and racial equality in the military.

Bob Ostertag (2006: 120), in his study of social movement media in the US, also documents the many manifestations of the GI journals as 'part of an explosion of the underground press' (which included such publications as *LA Free Press, Berkeley Barb, East Village Other* in New York).[6] By 1972, the department of defense reported 245 had been published. At Fort Leavenworth, a GI journal exposed the torture of prisoners. Legs and fingers were broken by guards. 'They put another guy's head in a cell door and slammed it, cracking his skull' (ibid: 136-137). *Vietnam GI*, launched in January 1968 by Jeff Sharlet, dared to show shocking images of a GI with a maniacal grin and holding the heads of two Vietnamese he had just decapitated. The caption began: 'The above picture shows exactly what the brass want you to do in the Nam' (ibid: 131).

In addition, the emerging Black Power movement was represented by *Black Liberator* and *Black Panther*. Ostertag argues (ibid: 151): 'The underground papers were often a bridge GIs used to cross over from private misgivings to public opposition despite their profound distrust of the student anti-war movement.' By the early 1970s, opposition to the war in the military was beginning to get out of control (though little covered in the mainstream media[7]). In May 1971, the biggest mutiny in the history of the US Air Force brought chaos for four days to Travis Air Base resulting in the arrests of 135 GIs (ibid: 154).

Many of the journalists in the alternative, anti-war media were subjected to extensive surveillance and harassment by the FBI. During 1969-1970, the editor of Miami's *Daily Planet* was arrested 29 times and acquitted 28 times (ibid: 122). In addition, the FBI launched three phoney underground newspapers on its own as well as three phoney news services. Kessler (op cit: 151) records how Cointelpro, a domestic spying programme set up by the FBI in 1956, planted scurrilous reports in the mainstream media about war dissenters, opened mail, encouraged local police to harass dissidents and infiltrated anti-war organisations.

In 1967, the Johnson administration launched Operation Chaos through the Counter-Intelligence Division of the CIA, to disrupt anti-war activities. In the following year, FBI director J. Edgar Hoover sent a memo to all local offices instructing them to 'immediately institute a detailed survey concerning New Left publications'. In 1970, the Nixon administration's Interagency Committee on Intelligence launched the Houston Plan, a programme of electronic surveillance, break-ins and infiltration of anti-war groups and publications (ibid: 152). Geoffrey Rips (1981), following a three-year study of government documents acquired through the Freedom of Information Act, concluded that the alternative press was the target of 'surveillance, harassment and unlawful search and seizure by US government agencies'.

From 1953 to 1971, I. F. Stone, in his iconoclastic *I. F. Stone's Weekly*, promoted progressive anti-war politics and criticised the mainstream press (see Middleton 1973). *Liberation*, founded in 1956 by radicals and pacifists including David Dellinger, Staughton Lynd and Paul Goodman, supported the black civil rights movement and the anti-war protests. *Win* was founded by the War Resisters League in 1965 and published anti-war features by Daniel Berrigan and poetry by Allen Ginsberg (Kessler op cit: 149).

HIDDEN FROM THE MEDIA: THE SECRET WAR AGAINST CAMBODIA

With the massive costs and casualties, the American military learned the dangers of overt warfare (Williams, Reece 1987: 7-8). The secret war waged on Cambodia for 14 months (between March 1969 and May 1970), completely hidden from the international media through a combination of lies and misinformation, showed the US government shifting back to LIC strategy. Nixon's policy of Vietnamisation, of 'peace with honour', essentially confirmed this move. Yet documents released by the Clinton administration revealed that the tonnage of bombing was almost five times as high as the very high level previously known. Noam Chomsky commented (2007: 103): 'This meant that Cambodia was the most heavily bombed country in history.' According to John Pilger (1998: 33):

> Between 1969 and 1973, American bombers killed three-quarters of a million Cambodian peasants in an attempt to destroy North Vietnamese supply bases, many of which did not exist. During one six-month period in 1973, B-52 aircraft dropped more bombs on Cambodians, living mostly in straw huts, than were dropped on Japan during the whole of the Second World War: the equivalent of five Hiroshimas.

Bill Kiernan, head of Yale University Cambodian Genocide Project, wrote about it in a small Canadian journal, *Walrus*, and it was also published on the alternative website, ZNET. The mainstream news media ignored the report entirely. Transcripts of discussions between secretary of state Henry Kissinger and President Nixon, finally released after a court ruling, revealed Nixon calling for a major attack on Cambodia under the pretense of airlifting supplies. And so Kissinger ordered the Pentagon to carry out 'a massive bombing campaign in Cambodia. Anything that flies or anything that moves'. According to Chomsky (2007: 100): 'That is the most explicit call for what we call genocide when other people do it that I've ever seen in the historical record.'[8] But it was totally ignored by the mainstream media.

By turning over the burden of the ground campaign to the Vietnamese, the US army cut casualties from more than 14,000 in 1968 to just 300 in 1972. By 1974 there were only 35 permanent correspondents left in Saigon. LIC fighting strategy predictably attracted LIC media coverage. Arnett comments (op cit: 284): 'Saigon bureaus were closed or reduced. The Vietnam story moved from the top of the network nightly news into the back pages of the papers alongside Dear Abby columns. The few reporters who remained in Saigon had to appreciate the comment made by a sardonic copy desk editor: "Gooks killing gooks don't make a story."' In fact, the secret air war intensified. One year after the Paris peace conference of 1973, the US senate refugee committee reported that 818,700 refugees had been created in Vietnam and on average 141 people were being killed every day. As John Pilger (1986: 259) comments: 'But this did not qualify as a big story.'

REAGAN AND THE JOURNALISM OF DEFERENCE

The advent of Ronald Reagan to the White House saw a massive new investment in security operations and covert action – at both home and abroad. Phillip Knightley argues (1986: 342-343) that the CIA was running so much out of control that by the time Stansfield Turner became CIA director under Carter in 1977 and tried to give orders to restrain covert operations he was simply ignored. Yet accompanying the growth of the secret state was the emergence of a supine, Reaganite media. As Douglas Kellner (1990: 227) argues: 'A combination of ignorance, servility and cowardice explains why the mainstream media have failed to fully develop, or even investigate, some of the most explosive political stories of the epoch.' He concludes: 'During the 1980s the mainstream media systematically sacrificed their journalistic integrity and became lapdogs of conservative hegemony – that is, the ideological tools of the corporate power elite.'

Press manipulation became a central strategy of the Reagan administration. Leslie Janka, a deputy White House press secretary who resigned over the exclusion of the press during the Grenada invasion of 1983, commented: 'The whole thing was PR. This was a PR outfit that became President and took over the country. And to the degree then to which the constitution forced them to do things like make a budget, run foreign policy and all that they sort of did it. But their first, last and overarching activity was public relations' (Hertsgaard 1986: 6). In the face of this PR onslaught the press offered little resistance. Hertsgaard (ibid: 9) argues: 'As much through voluntary self-censorship as through government manipulation, the press during the Reagan years abdicated its responsibility to report fully and accurately to the American people what their government was really doing.'

Reagan had placed the revitalisation of the nation's intelligence system at the heart of his 1980 manifesto. The morale of covert action warriors, badly dented by Vietnam, was quickly restored. The CIA budget was increased by 15 per cent in 1982, 25 per cent in 1983. By 1985, the agency was the fastest growing major agency in the federal government. Knightley records (op cit: 366): 'At one stage there were 20 secret operations underway in Africa alone as the agency got back into business on a scale and with an enthusiasm unmatched since its heyday of the 1960s.' Central to the LIC strategy of the secret state is a media policy of silencing, mystification and lies. Still the Vietnam syndrome persisted. Following the Vietnam trauma, the American public remained deeply divided over the wisdom and morality of interfering in the affairs of other countries. According to Richard Barnet (op cit: 217-218), no more than 40 per cent of the electorate has ever subscribed to the official worldview that underpinned the intervention strategy. Thus for the most part Reagan, for all his noisy, militaristic rhetoric, resorted to secrecy and deception to carry out policies the administration felt unable to defend in open debate.

THATCHERISM AND THE JOURNALISM OF DEFERENCE

In the face of the post-1973 global recession and extraordinary spate of 14 Third World revolutions over the decade, the Western capitalist states began an equally extraordinary counter-attack. In this context, Thatcherism, building on the inherent weaknesses of Labourism (Hutton 1996: 30), in the UK can be seen as part of a much wider, global shift to the right.

New militarism – glorified as media spectacle – lay at the root of the Thatcher offensive. In 1980, the Special Air Service Regiment (SAS), the archetypal covert paramilitary group (with the full connivance of dominant sections of the British media), set up the 'no compromise' strong state tone of the decade with their assault on 5 May 1980 on the Iranian embassy to rescue hostages seized by six terrorists demanding autonomy for the southern region of Khuzestan and the release of 91 comrades from Ayatollah Khomeini's jails (Geraghty 1980: 237-243; Kemp 1995: 149-154; Harclerode 2000: 386-408). According to Peter Harclerode (ibid: 408): 'Operation Nimrod sent a clear signal throughout the world that the authorities would deal firmly with any terrorist threat within Britain's own borders.' It was, in fact, the first time the SAS were officially deployed on the British mainland – and they became instant media heroes. As *The Sunday Times* investigative 'Insight' team commented:

> Having shunned publicity for the force for the better part of thirty years, the government seems now to have decided that the best way of making their deployment within Britain acceptable is to turn them into real-life James Bonds – objects of hero-worship. And it has to be said that the strategy has proved singularly successful ('Insight' 1980: 109).

Firmin and Pearson (2010: 214) said the siege drama made the SAS 'little known before the siege, a household name'. They add: 'And ensured that from then on, they got all the kit they needed.'

All of the six hostage-takers (members of Marxist-Leninist organisation calling itself the Democratic Revolutionary Movement for the Liberation of Arabistan) were shot except one, Fowzi Bedavi Nejad (alias Ali), who escaped after a hostage claimed he was her brother (Firmin and Pearson 2010). The *Observer*, *Sunday Times* and *Guardian* did raise questions about the circumstances in which the SAS killed the gunmen. But they generally argued that there was little else the SAS could have done – particularly since the terrorists had begun to kill hostages (Schlesinger 1991: 52). A report emerged in 2007 that Mrs Thatcher, from day three of the siege which began on 30 April, was determined on a military solution, refusing to countenance a repeat of the humiliating, botched attempt by US soldiers to rescue the hostages in the US embassy in Tehran just a week before (Milmo 2007). But, intriguingly, foreign office records released according to the 30-year rule in December 2010 revealed that Thatcher's government had originally sought to involve Arab governments in negotiating a peaceful end to the siege. Only the Palestinian Liberation Organisation volunteered to act as intermediaries. On the sixth day of the siege gunshots were heard and a body was dumped outside the embassy. The SAS was ordered in shortly afterwards (Bowcott 2010a).

The secret complicity of the BBC in the state's strategy of eliminating the hostage-takers was also a significant factor in the drama (Schlesinger 1991). Schlesinger shows that while the impression given to the public was of 'live' transmission of the SAS storming the building, in fact, ITN's report began four-and-a-half minutes afterwards and the BBC's eight minutes later (ibid: 30; see also Bazalgette and Paterson 1981). The event came at the end of a period of significant collusion between the state and the mainstream media. During two gun sieges in 1975 – at the Spaghetti House in Knightsbridge, London, and at Balcombe Street – and then later in the year during the kidnapping of a Greek Cypriot girl, Aloi Kaloghirou,[9] the police won the support of the media in their strategies to deal with the crises. Schlesinger (op cit: 49) also reports a discussion held at a closed Abingdon conference on 'Politics extremism, the media and the law' on 16-18 November 1979 which brought together top media personnel, civil servants, soldiers, policemen and politicians from Israel, West Germany, the USA and Great Britain. It was sponsored by the BBC with the International Press Institute and the Ford Foundation. Among the correspondents was the BBC correspondent Kate Adie who, intriguingly, later 'by chance' covered the Iranian embassy siege. Adie, herself, describes this as a 'surreal coincidence' in her biography, *The kindness of strangers* (2002: 107).

Yet the state's handling of the Iranian embassy siege and the media's response were to set important precedents for the decade – not least in that they showed how crucial secrecy could be maintained (enhanced even) under the glare of television cameras.

MEDIACENTRISM AND THE FALKLANDS/MALVINAS NEW MILITARIST MANUFACTURED WAR

Richard Vinen (2009: 102) says that the storming of the Iranian embassy mattered so much 'partly because it was almost the only success that the Thatcher government could claim during its first three years in office'.[10] On 14 April 1982, *The Times* featured a Gallup poll which indicated the public thought Mrs Margaret Thatcher, the grocer's daughter from Grantham, Lincolnshire, was the worst prime minister in British history (see Dillon 1989: 120). Soon afterwards, the victory of British forces in a manufactured, new militarist 'war' – after Argentine invaded a group of tiny, largely unknown islands 8,000 miles away in the South Atlantic – transformed her into a national super-hero. Just as there is considerable evidence that the American administration, through satellite, diplomatic and human intelligence, knew full well of Iraq's ambitions towards Kuwait in the build-up to August 1990 (and may well have encouraged it) and of the plans to attack the Twin Towers in New York in September 2001 so too there is evidence that Britain anticipated Argentine's invasion of the islands – and saw the opportunities for a quick and successful new militarist adventure (Morley 1991; see also Greaves 1991).

Five years before the Falklands 'war', a mini-task force was secretly despatched to the islands to deter an Argentinian attack. Official documents released for the first time in 2005 revealed that James Callaghan's Labour government ordered Operation Journeyman after 50 Argentinian 'scientists' landed on the island of South Thule, provoking fears of a larger attack. The operation was conducted in total secrecy – far away from the glare of the media. Not even the crew members knew where they were going (Travis 2005).

The press and government presented the 1982 Argentinian invasion as a 'surprise'.[11] In fact, the evidence suggests they were probably well-prepared. Many of the secret Whitehall files relating to the Falklands conflict, in any case, were deliberately destroyed in 2004 before the Freedom of Information Act came into force on 1 January 2005. In a written parliamentary reply, Ivor Caplin, a defence minister, said that the number of 'linear metres' of destroyed files had almost doubled in the years 2000-2004. In 2000-2001, 1407 linear metres of records were destroyed compared to 3,211 in 2003-04 (Woolf 2004). It is unlikely, then, that the full truth of Britain's involvement in the Falklands crisis will ever be known.

A British 'possession' since January 1833, the islands were a constant source of tension between Argentina and UK. On 12 October 1979, for instance, Lord Carrington, foreign secretary in Mrs Margaret Thatcher's government, sent a memo to the cabinet sub-committee, the overseas defence committee, warning that continuing talks with the Argentinians without making concessions on sovereignty carried a serious threat of invasion (Blakeway 1992: 13; Moore 2013: 658).[12] In 1980, Margaret Thatcher's government even offered to hand over sovereignty of the Falklands at a secret meeting with the Argentinians in Switzerland – but then opposition to the deal grew amongst both Conservative and Labour MPs after news of it leaked (*Guardian* 2005). By 1981 Argentinian impatience with lack of progress in talks on sovereignty was mounting. And British authorities were well aware this could boil over into military action (Parsons 2000: 22-23). In July 1981, the joint intelligence committee reported: 'If Argentina thought there was no prospect of eventual transfer of sovereignty, it might take military action, swiftly and without warning and this could go as far as a full-scale invasion of the Falklands Islands' (Moore 2013: 660).

There was also clear pressure in Argentina to seize islands. On 23 March 1976, General Jorge Videla[13] overthrew the Peronist government and put a military regime in place. In the battle against liberal and left-wing thought that followed, up to 20,000 people (most often university graduates) were tortured and killed. The British government made no protests. As Richard Vinen (2009: 137) comments on Leopoldo Galtieri, who became leader of the junta in December 1981:

> The government … turned away from the corporatism of the Peronist years, cut public spending and tried to revive the private sector. When these policies seemed not to work, the finance minister had attempted to revive the economy with a 'shock approach' of austerity and cuts in public spending. In purely economic terms, the junta's Argentina had much in common with Thatcher's Britain.

Moreover, in early June 1981, the defence secretary, John Nott, published a radical defence review (with the support of PM Thatcher) calling for major (non-Nato-linked) cuts – including the scrapping of HMS *Endurance* whose presence in the South Atlantic had symbolised Britain's commitment to the Falkland islands.[14] In addition, it recommended the selling off of HMS *Invincible* to the Australian navy. To many critics in the UK, these cuts seemed to send the wrong signals to Argentina. On 22 December 1981, General Leopoldo Galtieri took power at the head of a military junta. The economy was deteriorating sharply (with inflation of 600 per cent), bringing mass public protests and trade union demonstrations. Then Galtieri suffered a serious foreign policy setback when arbitration over Argentine's territorial dispute with Chile went in favour of the latter. The crusade to re-take the Malvinas, as the 150th anniversary of what Argentina considered Britain's unjust occupation of the islands significantly approached, 'was about the only policy still viable that would unite Argentine public opinion' (ibid: 26). Moreover, according to Simon Jenkins, Argentina could also expect support from the UN for any claim to the Falklands/Malvinas since it had conceded India's military seizure of Portuguese Goa in 1961 (Jenkins 2012). 'Indeed, an early plan for the Falklands invasion was dubbed Operation Goa' (ibid).

On 24 January 1982, the right-wing nationalist Iglesias Rouco revealed Argentina's plans for the Falklands which did not rule out military invasion in his column in the Buenos Aires newspaper, *La Prensa*. According to Denys Blakeway (1992: 23): 'The article was planted by the Junta, with whom Rouco had excellent relations.' On 9 February 1982, the English-language newspaper, the *Buenos Aires Herald*, published an editorial highlighting rumours of possible Argentinian military action against the Falklands.

According to Tam Dalyell, MP, Argentina's decision to invade was made on 12 January 1982 and British agents were told, on the basis that they would pass on the information to London (Murray 1993: 300). 'This they did – and the SAS were informed that they were going to the Falklands in February 1982' (ibid). Moreover, just before the invasion, intelligence on Argentina was voluminous. As Knightley records (1986: 379): 'NSA/GCHQ was reading Argentinian military and diplomatic traffic, two American reconnaissance satellites were passing over the Argentinian coast once a day ... the American navy had spy satellites reporting on Argentinian electronic emissions and an American air force spy plane, an SR 71, was making flights in the area.'[15]

On 2 March 1982, Col. Stephen Love, the British military attaché in Buenos Aires, wrote to the governor of the Falkland Islands, Rex Hunt, copied to the ministry of defence and foreign office, warning of an Argentinian invasion. Moreover, Sir Henry Leach, chief of naval staff and first sea lord (1979-1982), recalled how he had met Thatcher, the defence secretary and other top military and government officials in the house of commons on 31 March – two days before the invasion. He told the meeting: 'On the basis of the latest intelligence I think we must assume that the Falkland Islands will be invaded and that this will happen in the next few days' (Dale 2002: 58). It was also very clear to Harold Briley, BBC Latin America correspondent 1979-1983. 'Three months before the invasion I warned all BBC news editors that I expected trouble approaching the 150th anniversary of what the Argentinians say was Britain's seizure of the Falklands in January 1833. General Leopoldi Galtieri's military coup in Argentina the previous December, his ambition to create a "Greater Argentina" by winning back the Malvinas, and the appointment of Dr Costa Mendez as Foreign Secretary sent the clear signal of likely conflict' (Dale op cit: 114). Sir John Nott, defence secretary, also confirmed: 'Our intelligence services intercepted a series of signals which left little doubt that an invasion was planned for the morning of Friday 2 April' (ibid: 212).

According to William Engdahl (2004), the issue was not that Argentina's Galtieri government had, with justification, claimed sovereignty over the islands and retaken them on April 1. Nor was the issue that the surrounding area was believed by some to contain rich untapped petroleum reserves. The real aim of the Thatcher administration was to enforce the principle of the collection of Third World debts by a new form of nineteenth century 'gunboat diplomacy'. 'Argentina was the third largest debtor nation at the time with $38 billion in foreign debts and the country which appeared closest to default. The staged Malvinas conflict ... was merely the pretext to persuade other Nato members to back what was termed "out of area" military response' (ibid: 186).

But the invasion by the 'Argies' (codenamed Operation Rosario) was perfect for propaganda purposes. Britain, the vulnerable state, could present itself as the victim of sudden, unprovoked aggression. Very few people before the conflict had ever heard of the islands. A map, produced by the foreign office just months earlier, had even omitted them![16] Argentina at the time was closely allied to the United States, deeply embroiled in supporting the terrorist Contras for the Reagan administration in Nicaragua (Woodward 1987: 127-77, 187-89, 212; Andrew 1995: 465). As an official history of the conflict, published by Marshall Cavendish, records (2007: 35), under President Reagan Argentina, criticised by the Carter administration for its appalling human rights record, was 'welcomed back into the fold'. 'A two-way traffic in generals and other dignitaries began: Galtieri paid two visits to Washington; General Vernon Walters, the President's "troubleshooter", General David Meyer, army chief of staff, and Mrs Jeane Kirkpatrick, UN ambassador, went to Buenos Aires.' Perhaps even unknown to President Reagan, assistant secretary of state for Latin American affairs, Thomas Enders, travelled to Buenos Aires in March 1982 to privately assure the Galtieri government that the dispute between Argentina and Britain over the Malvinas would not draw US participation (Engdahl op cit: 187).

Moreover, despite the belligerent rhetoric of Thatcher in public, in private she and her government were keen to negotiate a settlement. On the eve of the invasion, the foreign office considered allowing Argentina a naval base on the island (Yapp 2013). Even two weeks after the invasion, the Prime Minister described 'a diplomatic solution' as being 'a considerable prize'. She was responding to a proposal that, in return for withdrawing its troops, Argentina would be represented on an interim commission and on Falklands Islands councils (Norton-Taylor and Bowcott 2013). A secret document from the National Security Council files in Washington, released in March 1992, revealed that the US sought to persuade the UK into a ceasefire before Port Stanley on the Falklands was taken. President Reagan viewed the military junta led by General Galtieri as more acceptable than any leftist Peronist who might take over (Boseley 1992). Significantly, Jeane Kirkpatrick, Reagan's ambassador to the UN, had regular contacts with members of the Galtieri government to pass on details of her government's latest diplomatic intentions (Jackson 2006). A massive propaganda campaign was, therefore, required to demonise the sudden new 'enemy' and glorify the heroic response of the British government.

THE FALKLANDS CONFLICT SETS HUGELY SIGNIFICANT PRECEDENT

The Falklands conflict was to set a hugely significant precedent repeated in Grenada, Libya, Panama and the Gulf (1990-1991) – and later on in Kosovo (1999), Afghanistan (2001) and Iraq (2003). Here was a First World country with a considerable military tradition behind it taking on a Third World country almost entirely dependent on First World countries for supplying its army. (Indeed,

Argentine's most deadly weapons had been supplied by Britain or its allies.) Crucially, Argentine was a militarist state, run by a corrupt military dictatorship and relying on a 30,000-strong army in which 12,000 were conscripts and where morale and discipline were known by British intelligence to be low (Bramley 1991; Blakeway op cit: 71). Significantly, in 2009, 120 soldiers gave testimony in a landmark court case alleging human rights abuses including murder, torture and starvation by Argentine commanding officers (Strange 2009).

Britain, on the other hand, relied on a small, professional army, strongly committed to fighting to win. Just 104 British ships and 29,000 soldiers featured in the conflict. Moreover, the British army was secretly nuclearised – just in case the Russians intervened on behalf of Argentina (Rogers 1994: 4-6).[17] One nuclear weapon was actually lost in the South Atlantic (ibid: 6). According to Tam Dalyell, MP, nuclear weapons were taken from Gibraltar and the RFA (Royal Fleet Auxiliary) Fort Austin, on carriers, destroyers and frigates and from Portsmouth – though, after a major row, some nuclear weapons were withdrawn before the fleet reached Ascension Island, in the South Atlantic (Murray 1993: 303). 'Efforts to retrieve nuclear depth bombs from the graves of *Sheffield* and *Coventry* have been only partly successful, and attempts to find nuclear bombs from the two downed Sea King helicopters have been unsuccessful' (ibid).

The government furiously denied all such claims but then in December 2003, the ministry of defence finally admitted that British ships carried nuclear weapons to the Falklands. The revelation followed a six-year campaign by the *Guardian* under the open government code. The government was also forced at the same time to publish a list of 20 accidents and mishaps involving nuclear weapons between 1960 and 1991 (Evans and Leigh 2003). Aldrich and Cormac (2016: 369) report that on 28 March, even before the formal decision to send the Task Force, Thatcher and her foreign secretary Lord Carrington, resolved to send three nuclear submarines to the crisis zone. According to Commander Robert Denton Green, intelligence staff officer to the commander-in-chief, Fleet HQ, Northwood (McManners 2008: 132):

> I was concerned about the anti-submarine nuclear weapons on board our ships; what the hell were they doing down in the South Atlantic. Some of the navy's nuclear weapons were taken off ships before they sailed south, but others remained. This led me to speculate what might Thatcher's moves had been had we lost a capital ship?

Britain's national security was hardly at stake in this little adventure for control of an unknown group of islands populated largely by penguins (Belgrano Action Group: 1988).[18] Reginald and Elliot (1985: 5) describe the 74-day conflict as a 'bizarre little war' (which, even so, took 255 British – with an additional 777 injured – and 750 Argentinian lives).[19] Some 12,978 Argentinians were taken prisoner (McGarvey 2010). The Argentinian army, composed largely of reluctant conscripts, was hardly a credible enemy.[20] As Max Hastings conceded (2000: 363): 'The Falklands War flattered the British army because the Argentinian ground force never showed the will or competence to punish mistakes, exploit vulnerabilities, seize tactical chances, in the fashion that any first-division enemy would have done.' The conflict solved nothing. Neither side ever admitted there was a war. And it was tightly limited by both sides. Though the Argentinian army withdrew from the islands, no formal ceasefire was signed (war never having been declared) and the conflict over the rights to the sovereignty over the Falklands remains to this day. Britain currently deploys 1,200 military personnel on the island to 'protect' the estimated 2,600 islanders at a cost of £110m a year (MacAskill, Goni and Balch 2006).

But the logic of the permanent war economy is to fight wars. And this the British military were all set to do. Involvement in the escapade for the British public could be realised only through their consumption of the heavily censored, patriotic media. Dillon (1987: 123) is sceptical about the impact of the media. He writes: 'There is no denying that media manipulation by the government and news manipulation by the media were features of the conflict – as they are in all conflicts. But it is difficult to determine precisely what contribution they made to public reactions already excited by Argentine's attack beyond that of conferring and reaffirming the sentiments involved.' In fact, the Falklands 'war' demonstrated the centrality of the media in new militarist societies – just as later during the 1991 massacres. As Shaw commented (1987: 154):

> While Britain in the Second World War can be seen as the archetypal 'citizen war' of total war through democratic mobilisation, the Falklands are the vindication of small professional armed forces, acting on behalf of the nation but needing no real mass participation to carry out their tasks. For the vast majority involvement was limited to utterly passive, vicarious consumption of exceptionally closely filtered news and the expression of support in opinion polls.

POOLS AND THE PROPAGANDA OF NEW MILITARISM

In 1977, a secret ministry of defence paper on 'Public relations planning in emergency operations' stated that 'for planning purposes it is anticipated that 12 places should be available to the media, divided equally between ITN, the BBC and the press. ... The press should be asked to give an undertaking that copy and photographs should be pooled' (Harris 1983: 149). But following the intervention of Mrs Thatcher's press secretary Bernard Ingham, the Falklands reporting pool was increased from 12 to just 29 British journalists.[21] Significantly there were no women reporters (though the official war artist was Linda Kitson). As Chambers, Steiner and Fleming (2004: 2008) comment: 'Women featured only as passive victims in reports on the "human interest" angle as the mothers, wives and girlfriends of the servicemen who died or survived the fighting.' According to Susan Carruthers (2000: 123):

> Few editors, or the reporters they picked, apparently anticipated a full-blown war (even if never fully declared as such) and many journalists embarked with little more than a toothbrush and change of underwear.

In the end, the reporters came to identify closely with the military (Morrison and Tumber 1988; Hooper 1982). The patriotic imperative so deeply rooted in the dominant political and media culture, together with journalistic self-censorship and the hyper-jingoism and crude 'enemy' baiting of the pops, all served to transform new militarism into spectator sport with the conflict consumed as a form of entertainment (Luckham 1983: 18). As Max Hastings, of the *Evening Standard*, wrote of his fellow correspondents in the pool in the lead-up to the assault on Port Stanley in June 1982 (2000: 348-349):

> Most of us have found great satisfaction in being able to thrust ourselves, for once in our professional lives, wholeheartedly into the service of a cause without bothering very much about moral or political dilemmas. For better or worse, we are part of British expeditionary forces 8,000 miles from home, fighting under considerable difficulties to evict Argentines from a cluster of island which feel so ridiculously British that it is hard to believe we are not on Dartmoor, or in Sutherland or Pembrokeshire.

In London and the South Atlantic, MoD media officers constantly intervened to restrict reporting of specific events. Short and formal statements from the MoD, often announced by the acting head of public relations, Ian McDonald, in a slow and halting style, combined with the D Notice system of voluntary restraint served to restrict the flow of information (Dodds 2005: 223).[22] Dodds comments (ibid: 224): 'Appropriately for a country with a highly developed culture of official secrecy, "operational security" became a catch-all term to protect a range of ills from incompetent military planning, misinformation, lack of planning, inter-service rivalry and poor organisation.' From the very start of the conflict the British media were used by the government and military for propaganda and disinformation. On 29 March 1982, ITN's defence correspondent, reported from Gibraltar that a nuclear-powered submarine, HMS *Superb*, had been seen leaving harbour and was heading for the Falklands. The next day, the *Daily Telegraph* confirmed the report, with the ministry of defence adding that it was the first of two boats to head south. But, as Blakeway (op cit: 35) comments: 'The story was bogus. *Superb* was not sailing south but heading north to return to base. British submarines did not set sail for another two days. Frank Cooper, then permanent under-secretary at the MoD, believed that the Argentines should be warned.'

Satellite facilities were denied the media – while contrived delays in the transmission of television images meant that this was largely a bloodless war (Greenberg and Smith 1982; McNair 1995: 176). The media pool included only two photographers (McLaughlin 2002: 32): the most famous war photographer of the day, Don McCullin, was blacklisted from going. In the end, only 202 photographs were transmitted, most of those contrived by the military for propaganda purposes (ibid). Harris reported (op cit: 59): 'In an age of supposedly instant communications, what were perhaps the most eagerly awaited television pictures in the world travelled homewards at a steady 25 knots.' Television reporters Brian Hanrahan (of the BBC) and Mike Nicholson (of ITN) were reduced virtually to the role of radio correspondents; footage was shot but by the time it reached London (where, like print copy, it was reviewed again by the MoD), it was almost like the 'Dead Sea scrolls', according to ITN editor David Nicholas (Carruthers 2000: 127).

But the policy was reversed when an image judged to be 'supportive' was transmitted to London at top speed. Such a photograph was that taken by Tom Smith of a soldier accepting a cup of tea from a Falklands Islands family which featured in the *Sunday Mirror* of 23 May under the headline 'Cuppa for a brave Para'. Caroline Brothers has commented (1997: 208):

> The photograph was a quintessential image of Britishness. The custom of tea drinking was projected as a hallmark of English culture, while the symbolic picket fence signalled ownership and domestication of this far-flung corner of empire, legitimising the campaign to re-establish sovereignty over it. The smiles of the village women and children expressed gratitude for a job well done, fitting effortlessly into the up-beat narrative of a conflict whose less pleasant aspects had been conscientiously expunged.

In contrast, Martin Cleaver's photograph of HMS *Antelope*'s explosion was delayed for three weeks since it was judged to be bad for morale (Dodds op cit: 225).

But not all the censorship was imposed by the state; journalists also indulged in self censorship. There were pictures of dead bodies in the Press Association library which had been released by the ministry, but newspaper editors decided not to use them (Taylor, John 1991: 15). The press were exploited not only as 'transmitters of a symbolic demonstration of military power' but also as propagandists to confuse and 'disinform' the enemy. When landings on the Falklands were being planned, disinformation was leaked to the media and, inevitably, to the Argentinians (Harris op cit: 92).

Significantly, the first operation – the retaking of South Georgia – was essentially a 'morale-boosting propaganda victory', according to Alwyn W. Turner (2010: 112) to steady the nerves of anxious politicians in London since it was a militarily insignificant target. Moreover, the Battle of Goose Green, of 28 May 1982, the first major engagement in the conflict, was more a media, spectacular event dictated by the government's need for a morale boosting 'victory' rather than military necessity, according to the official history of the conflict by Sir Lawrence Freedman (Norton-

Taylor and Evans 2005). The British commander on the islands, Brigadier Julian Thompson, did not consider the capture of Goose Green a military priority. But the Thatcher government was impatient for some kind of successful operation after a week in May 1982 when Argentinian aircraft scored several hits on UK warships. Max Hastings confirms this analysis in his account of the campaign (2000: 325): 'Although the victory at Goose Green proved of value in the end, inflicting a heavy blow on Argentinian morale, Thompson thought it a diversion from the vital drive on Stanley, and thus a battle fought to appease the politicians back at home.'

The Prime Minister's press secretary, Bernard Ingham, had briefed reporters that '...we are not going to fiddle around' while his press office had even revealed the destination of the attack which was duly reported on the BBC (Blakeway 1991: 132).

The gung-ho, belligerent response of Michael Foot, leader of the opposition Labour Party, outspoken peace campaigner and member of the Campaign for Nuclear Disarmament, to the Argentinian seizure of the Falklands took his party and even Margaret Thatcher, the 'Iron Maiden', by surprise. When parliament was recalled for an emergency session on Saturday 3 April 1982, Foot fumed: 'The Falkland Islanders have been betrayed. The responsibility for the betrayal rests with government.' He continued: '...there is the longer term interest to ensure that foul and brutal aggression does not succeed in our world. If it does, there will be a danger not merely to the Falkland Islands but to people all over this dangerous planet.' Foot's official biographer Kenneth O. Morgan (2007: 412-413) records: 'While Mrs Thatcher appeared strangely halting and subdued, Foot's fiery utterances won massive acclaim on the Conservative benches. ... The Labour benches were somewhat stunned.' The *Guardian* commented that Foot had stolen the show 'through force of oratory and command of language'. Indeed, the consensus support for the war in all the three major parties meant that any opposition, however faint, could be condemned as traitorous.[23]

The BBC, following a *Panorama* programme which dared to feature some war doubters and sceptics, was publicly attacked by ministers and Conservative MPs. For instance, the programme was denounced by Sally Oppenheim MP in the house as 'an odious subversive travesty' that 'dishonoured the right to free speech'. Margaret Thatcher did not dissent. Presenter Robert Kee, a former bomber pilot and prisoner of war in the Second World War, wrote to *The Times* dissociating himself (Dale 2002: 121-122). In their study of television coverage, the Glasgow University Media Group (1985: 127-129) showed that the controversial *Panorama* programme, 'Can we avoid war' on 10 May 1982, contained more statements in support of government policy than against. Moreover, according to John Pilger (2004a: xxii), the minutes of the BBC's weekly review board showed that its coverage was shaped to suit the 'emotional sensibilities of the public', that most of the coverage was concerned with government statements of policy and that the impartial style was felt to be 'an unnecessary irritation'.

However, following the row, the BBC developed new strategies of self censorship. For instance, the corporation decided not to publish details of the landings at San Carlos supposedly to prevent the Argentinians from gaining valuable military information in response to an MoD request (Dodds op cit: 226). Moreover, a study by Brian McNair (op cit: 177) found that coverage, in general, was deferential to and supportive of dubious official claims of military success. The war was sanitised for television viewers and the non-military possibilities of a resolution to the conflict were marginalised.

But the media 'enemy within', threatening the vulnerable state, had to be attacked. Even so there was an element of theatre here. The Conservative government was responding to the demands and prejudices of its increasingly confident right-wing. The BBC could present itself as independent of the state and the defender of journalistic freedom and integrity. As Noam Chomsky argues (1989: 48), such conflict has a 'system re-enforcing character'. He writes: 'Controversy may rage so long as it adheres to the presuppositions that define the consensus of elites and it should, furthermore, be encouraged within these bounds, thus helping to establish these doctrines as the very condition of thinkable thought while reinforcing the belief that freedom reigns.'

Military and political leaders of new militarist societies know well that long, overt wars are both costly and unpopular. The Falklands seemed to prove that a short war against a relatively weak Third World country (though its strength was generally exaggerated since victories were dependent on the existence of a credible enemy fighting force) was achievable.[24] At the same time, covert activity still remains the dominant strategy. After the Falklands, six official inquiries were held into various aspects of the government-media relations. Certainly, the clumsy bureaucracy and inter-personal rivalries within the ministry of defence (MoD) showed that 'cock-ups' (a concept much favoured in journalists' culture since it seems to embrace a healthy scepticisms towards the powerful – and, more significantly, marginalise the importance of more profound institutional and ideological factors) can co-exist with historically conditioned, long-term factors. Journalists criticised the MoD not because they opposed the absurdities and wastefulness of the imperialistic, new militarist adventure but because various manifestations of bureaucratic incompetence prevented them from getting their story.

POSTSCRIPT

Margaret Thatcher went on to win the June 1983 General Election with a whopping 140 majority. As Turner comments (2010: 118): 'The election campaign was marked by an overwhelming vote of confidence in the government from Fleet Street.' Film critic Clive James called Michael Foot, the leader of the Labour Party, 'a floppy toy on Benzedrine' while the *Sunday Telegraph* dubbed him 'an elder, ranting pamphleteer waving a stick in Hampstead' and the *Sun* 'an amiable old buffer, his jacket buttoned too tight, his collar askew, his grey hair falling lankly' (ibid). HMS *Invincible*, scheduled for sale to the Australian navy before the conflict, was saved by the government in 1983 and went on to see action in the Kosovo conflict (1999) and Iraq War (2003) before being finally decommissioned in 2005 (Shirley 2015).

NOTES

[1] Halliday, Fred (1986) *The making of the Second Cold War*, London: Verso. Lists Ethiopia 1974, Cambodia 1975, Vietnam 1975, Laos 1975, Guinea Bissau 1974, Mozambique 1975, Cape Verde 1975, Sao Tome 1975, Angola 1975, Afghanistan 1978, Iran 1979, Grenada 1979, Nicaragua 1979, Zimbabwe 1979 p. 92

[2] Noam Chomsky (2005: 126) has pointed out that the numbers of dead in Indochina are not even known within the range of millions. 'Nobody really knows the numbers, but the rough estimates are at maybe half a million or a million Vietnamese died just from chemical warfare.' See also Edward Herman (2008) They kill reporters, don't they? Available online at http://www.coldtype. net/Assets.08/pdfs/1108.Kill.pdf, accessed on 14 October 2008

[3] Some 419 international news media representatives were accredited by the Military Assistance Command, Vietnam (MACV) in 1966, including support staff. In 1968 there were 637; the following year 467; in 1970, 392; in 1971, 355; in 1972, 295; by 1974 there were just five (Rid 2007: 56)

[4] A young soldier, Tom Glen, wrote to General Creighton Abrams, commander of all US forces in Vietnam, after learning of the massacre. In December 1968, Colin Powell, later chairman of the joint chiefs of staff, was asked to check the letter. He reported that the claims were false bar 'isolated instances'. 'In direct refutation of this portrayal is the fact that relations between American soldiers and the Vietnamese people are excellent.' See Southwell, David (2005: 28) *Secrets and lies: Exposing the world of cover-ups and lies*, London: Sevenoaks

[5] See https://cross-currents.berkeley.edu/e-journal/issue-12/zinoman-and-kulik, accessed on 20 September 2016

[6] Ostertag (2006: 3) says of social movement media: 'Social movement journalism seeks to promote ideas not profits; movement journalists seek to challenge corporate control of the media, not justify it. They address readers as members of communities, not individual consumers. They cover social movements as participants, not "observers". They exist to make change, not business'

[7] John Pilger's ITV documentary, *The quiet mutiny*, of 1970, was an exception. See http:// johnpilger.com/videos/vietnam-the-quiet-mutiny

[8] The US Air Force dropped 2.7 million tons of bombs on Cambodia between 1969 and 1973. Steve Cushion comments (2015: 6): 'By the CIA's own intelligence estimates, the US bombing campaign was a key factor in the increase in support for the Khmer Rouge and the subsequent rise to power of the disastrous Pol Pot regime'

[9] See http://discovery.nationalarchives.gov.uk/details/r/C11477788, accessed on 18 November 2016

[10] Vinen (2009: 102) stresses that there had always been close links between the SAS and the Conservative Party: MPs such as Carol Mather, Stephen Hastings, Fitzroy Maclean (it was Maclean's stepson who led the assault on the Iranian embassy) and Airey Neave had served with the regiment

[11] The intelligence services also blamed cutbacks at South American stations in the years leading up to the conflict for the Argentinian invasion 'disaster'. According to Philip H. J. Davies (2004: 290): 'If anything good can be said of the war, it must be that the Falklands crisis brought badly needed Prime Ministerial attention to the intelligence community, along with badly needed additional

funding and resourcing.' According to her private secretary, Sir Charles Powell, Thatcher 'increased their funding and supported them in ways no Prime Minister since the Second World War had done'

[12] Nicholas Ridley, minister at the Foreign Office, was also a supporter of leaseback (while this was strongly opposed by Margaret Thatcher and the islanders themselves). Of Ridley, his Argentine opposite number, Commodore Cavandoli, commented: 'We had given up a third of the world's surface and found it on the whole beneficial to do so. The only claim Britain had which he felt strongly about was our long-standing claim to Bordeaux, his motive being wine. He found it hard to see the motive towards the islands where there was no wine' (Moore 2013: 659)

[13] In December 2010, Videla was sentenced for life in prison for the torture and murder of 31 prisoners, most of them shot while trying to escape after the 1976 coup. Most of the two dozen former police and military officials tried with Videla also received life sentences. Later, on 6 July 2012, on separate charges of masterminding a plan to steal the newborn babies of political opponents and hand them over to be raised by military families after killing their mothers, he was sentenced to 50 years in jail (see Goni, Uki, Former Argentinian dictator jailed for 50 years, *Guardian*, 7 July 2012)

[14] Margaret Thatcher strongly supported the withdrawal from service in the South Atlantic of the patrol ship HMS *Endurance*. When Richard Luce, of the foreign office, tried to tell her that *Endurance* mattered, 'she said that *Endurance* was no good: it just went "pop, pop, poop"' (Moore 2013: 661)

[15] Bob Woodward (1987: 212) disputes this: 'There were press reports that the British had benefited from US satellite photos. Casey [CIA chief] did not correct this misinformation. Actually, the region of the remote South Atlantic was not covered by satellite. Later, the US put up a satellite to cover the region and the Soviets followed with two of their own'

[16] During the conflict, even Margaret Thatcher was uncertain about the precise location of the islands. Charles Moore recounts in his biography of Thatcher (*Margaret Thatcher: The authorized biography, Vol. 1*, London: Allen Lane, 2013) how Michael Havers, the attorney general, had served in the RNVR and so understood maps. 'He and she would spread them on the floor and she would firmly point out the Falkland Islands in quite the wrong place. He would then find them for her' (see Watson 2013)

[17] But Moore (2013: 664) in a note, in his official biography of Thatcher, comments on the 'nuclear' submarine: 'The description is misleading. The vessel was nuclear-powered, but not carrying nuclear weapons'

[18] Richard Vinen (2009: 134) highlights the fact that there are 780 Falkland Islands of which only two are inhabited. 'In 1982 they had a population of 1,800 people, just over half of whom lived in the capital Port Stanley, on East Falkland, and 600,000 sheep'

[19] The figures for the British casualties come from *The Falklands campaign: The lessons* (presented to parliament by the secretary of state for defence, December 1982), London: Her Majesty's Stationery Office, Cmnd 8758. The figures are recorded in a note on page 27. Some 323 Argentinians died in the sinking of the *Belgrano*, 30 miles outside the exclusion zone, on 2 May 1982 (Blakeway 1991: 97). Moreover, is not the concept of 'war casualty' problematic? Casualties can be suffered long after the actual conflict is over. For instance, while 255 UK deaths were recorded during the 'war', more than 400 Falklands veterans committed suicide between 1982 and 2008. See Crampton, Robert (2008). Significantly the ministry of defence by 2008 had not released any data relating to post-Iraq/Afghanistan suicides. In March 2008, the *Independent* launched a campaign 'Fight for our veterans' for better mental health treatment for war veterans. It was backed by Robert Lawrence who won the Military Cross for bravery in the Falklands War: he was shot by a sniper just hours before the Argentinian surrender

[20] Richard Vinen (2009: 142) reports that Britain's staunchest ally was France. The French President, François Mitterrand, wanted the Western alliance to be strong in the face of the Soviet Union and he had no desire to see a member of that alliance humiliated. 'Furthermore, as a member of a resistance organisation, he had been infiltrated into France in February 1944 on board a British torpedo boat (commanded by Jane Birkin's father).' Sales of French Exocet missiles were blocked and French pilots went to Scotland to help British comrades practise dog-fights against Mirage and Super-Etenard jets with which the Argentinians were equipped (ibid: 143). But the Soviet journalist, Sergei Brilev, claimed in a book published in 2010 that the Soviet Union gave vital satellite intelligence to the Argentina Air Force. A satellite launched on 15 May was particularly useful – with Argentine missiles sinking HMS *Coventry* and the support ship *Atlantic Conveyor* on 25 May. Mr Brilev also claimed that Norway intercepted Soviet satellite photographs showing the *General Belgrano*'s position and passed them on to Britain as an ally. See Tony Halpin: Moscow 'gave junta help' in South Atlantic, *Times*, 2 April 2010. Aldrich and Cormac (2016: 372) suggest that although the *Belgrano* lay outside the exclusion zone she still clearly constituted a serious threat. 'Many asserted that Thatcher had pursued this action in order to "torpedo" an American-backed Peruvian peace plan, but now it seems clear that the *Belgrano* was sunk for operational rather than political reasons' (ibid)

[21] Bernard Ingham, a former *Guardian* journalist, claimed that he persuaded the navy to allow 29 journalists to travel with the task force. Originally they had wanted none. Ingham reports (1991: 285): 'Max Hastings, then on the *Evening Standard*, seemed near to tears at the thought of being prevented from covering a war'

[22] David Caute comments on McDonald (1986: 153): 'Instead of reality, the MoD gave us a "spokesman", a strange Dalek called McDonald, behind whose robotic communiqués lurked a fiendish joy: as if his whole upbringing and training, his deepest notions of patriotism, were at last fulfilled by *not* disclosing the truth to a huge, national audience' (italics in the original)

[23] Charles Moore records (2013: 673) that Enoch Powell's comments (rather than those of Foot) had most impact on Thatcher. She was known as the 'Iron Lady', he said. 'In the next week or two this House, the nation and the right honourable Lady herself will learn of what metal she is made'

[24] Richard Vinen (2009: 148) comments: 'Fighting the Falklands War meant throwing concern with public spending out of the window. On the advice of Harold Macmillan, Thatcher did not even invite the chancellor of the exchequer to sit in her war cabinet'

Chapter Four

From Grenada to Irangate: The manufacture of new militarist mythologies

An intriguing mythology emerged from the Falklands/Malvinas conflict – most clearly articulated by Derrick Mercer, in *Fog of war*, the result of a detailed study of the reporting conducted by the Centre for Journalism Studies, University College, Cardiff, and commissioned by the MoD (Mercer 1987: 2). While the leading media in advanced capitalist societies are best viewed as subtle propagandists for the dominant ideology, with important steering and management functions, the conflicts which emerged between government and journalists helped promote the myth of the adversary relationship. Mercer writes: 'The clash of interests between media and government has always been fundamental and frequently acrimonious. In a democracy, this is inevitable and many would say desirable' (ibid).

Accompanying the myth of the adversarial press is the myth of the unideological press concerned with theoretically unproblematic 'practicalities'. 'facts' and events (Chibnall 1977: 23). Thus, Mercer goes on: 'The media play essential roles in any democracy as channels for information, vehicles for dissent and watchdogs over authority although it should be said that journalism is more often concerned with the practicalities' (op cit: 14-15). But a significant new myth emerged following the Falklands adventure. This might be labelled the 'myth of the technological threat'. According to Mercer, the Falklands was a unique event; control of journalists was possible because of the peculiar, out-of-the-way location of the theatre of war. Such control was seen as unlikely in the future – particularly given the possibilities for instant, uncensored reporting thanks to the new satellite technology. Robert Harris came to a similar conclusion (1983: 150): 'The Falklands conflict may well prove to be the last war in which the armed forces are completely able to control the movements and communications of the journalists covering it. Technology has already overtaken the traditional concepts of war reporting.'

Ideologically this myth is a crucial element of new militarist ideology representing the strong state as, in fact, vulnerable in the face of technological advance (which, in reality, it is able to exploit to extend its power) and historical contingency. Yet the Mercer/Harris scenario completely ignores the ideological constraints of the political consensus and the patriotic imperative of the professional culture that weigh so heavily on journalists in times of war and promote the journalism of deference and conformism. Moreover, it ignores the extent to which new militarist societies demonstrated their ability to 'create enemies' and media-blitzed conflicts against relatively weak, Third World adversaries. The Falklands, Grenada, Libya, Panama and Gulf attacks were all essentially 'chosen' by the major powers. Donald A. Wells, in his seminal analysis of militarism (1967: 105), comments pointedly: 'Military men choose their wars and governments choose the conflicts in which they propose to be involved.' But the myth of technological vulnerability was to surface again during the Gulf crises of 1990-1991 and 2003 and serve to legitimise the censorship regimes then.

GRENADA: THE NEW MILITARIST MISSION TO ESCAPE MIDDLE EAST HUMILIATION

On 23 October 1983, a Mercedes containing 12,000lb of explosives was driven into the US Marine compound in Beirut by a member of a Shi'a militia, Islamic Jihad, and blew up killing 241 Americans, there to bolster the CIA-backed regime of President Gemayal, and 58 French citizens.[1] On the same day, a bomb exploded at the French military headquarters in Beirut killing 58 soldiers.[2] Another humiliating American retreat was put into motion. According to Greg Palast, Ronald Reagan was the first President of the United States to cravenly accede to the demands of terrorists when he gave in to Hezbollah's demand and ordered the Marines out of Lebanon (2006: 11).[3]

But away on the Caribbean island of Grenada, a crisis was unfolding which provided the US secret state with a perfect opportunity to assert itself and help erase the memory of the Beirut disaster. The four-and-a-half-year-old government of Maurice Bishop's People's Revolutionary Government (PRG) had been the source of constant concern to the US elite. With the Sandinistas' revolution toppling the US ally Somoza in Nicaragua in 1979 and Castro's Cuba still surviving after decades of diplomatic, economic and cultural warfare (see Freemantle 1983: 130-167), Bishop was seen as a further link in the chain of Soviet advancement in the region. As Robert Beck argued (2004: 75): 'Just like that which preceded the March 2003 attack on Iraq, the Grenada invasion was preceded by maximalist administration rhetoric about regional and strategic threat.'

After internecine strife broke out in the ruling PRG, Bishop was executed on 19 October 1983, with Bernard Coard and General Hudson Austin forming a new revolutionary military council. The US elite had clearly been long preparing for an attack on revolutionary Grenada (Corbyn 2003: 36-37): now they grasped their chance. On 21 October, the Prime Minister of Dominica, Eugenia Charles, as head of the Organisation of Eastern Caribbean States (OECS), is supposed to have requested US assistance in restoring 'order and democracy' to the island.[4] But as McMahon argues, it was not, as Reagan claimed (and the press dutifully reported), that the request dictated the US decision, rather it was the US that dictated the request – a scenario to be repeated between the US and Saudi Arabia in August 1990 (McMahon 1984: 153-165; Woodward 1987: 290-292; Mungham 1987). John Quigley also observes that OECS member countries violated their own treaty in voting for military action. The treaty allowed for military intervention only after 'external aggression' against a member country. In the case of Grenada there was no such aggressive act, nor did the OECS have the unanimous vote of all members as demanded by the treaty (Quigley 1992: 201).

THE SECRET MISSION THE MEDIA MISSED

On 22 October, the Pentagon revealed that a naval task force, comprising two aircraft carriers and around 1,900 Marines, had been diverted from its course to Lebanon and was heading for Grenada. Operation Urgent Fury (as the Pentagon was to call it in the glitzy, Hollywoody style that was to accompany all the US invasions) was launched. For the US elite it was a significant moment. It amounted to the first large-scale intervention in the hemisphere since the invasion of the Dominican Republic in 1965 and the first overt deployment of US troops since Vietnam. Moreover, it was the first time special forces were deployed on a major scale since the launch of the revitalisation programme two years earlier (Adams 1987: 221). The permanent war state was raring to go. All four US military services wanted a piece of the action – and they duly got it.

As Duane R. Clarridge comments (1997: 255): 'Although the Marines (and by extension the Navy) were circling the island … none of the other services were willing to leave all the action to them. No one wanted to be left out of the first real military action since Vietnam, but this zeal had virtually nothing to do with Grenada, and everything to do with justifying military budgets on Capitol Hill.' Robin Andersen argues that there were many cogent parallels between Grenada and Iraq, two decades later. 'Though contentious, it was the first time the formulation of "pre-emption" for security reasons was posed as a justification for military intervention. The invasion of Grenada, it was argued, was a defence against terror. But in the aftermath of both operations, flawed intelligence would be the common theme' (Andersen 2006: 120).

In all, 7,300 US military personnel and 300 police from Jamaica, Barbados and St Lucia were involved. As Jeffery Smith (1994: 64) comments: 'Virtually every element in the US military played a role: airforce, navy, army (82nd Airborne), Marines, Army Rangers, Navy Seals and Delta Force. If the Los Angeles Police Department had requested a role they would probably have gotten a piece of the action.' Above all, it was an attempt to wipe out the memory of the military humiliation in Beirut with a massive, rapid, heavily censored raid. James Combs argues that the Grenada invasion was significant in the emergence of a new kind of media spectacle warfare. He argues (1993: 27-29):

> Grenada was likely a preposterous military action producing no real results in terms of the array of power in the world, but it did help relegitimate the idea of intervention as beneficial and successful without producing a quagmire, nuclear exchange, large casualties and financial sacrifice by the citizenry. ... War was now to be conducted with not only concern with military tactics but also with how the war looked as dramatic narrative seen almost instantaneously back home.

All journalists were excluded from covering the invasion. The joint chiefs of staff imposed total operational secrecy. Even White House spokesman Larry Speakes, who had described the idea of an invasion as 'preposterous' in response to a CBS News inquiry on the eve of the operation, was excluded from National Security Council planning by White House chief of staff (and later secretary of state) James Baker and not informed until after the first landings. Admiral Wesley McDonald, in his report on the invasion to the joint chiefs of staff in 1984, commented: 'The absolute need to maintain the greatest element of surprise in executing the mission to ensure minimum danger to US hostages ... and to the servicemen involved in the initial assault dictated that the press be restricted until the initial objectives had been secured' (Braestrup 1985: 90; cited in McLaughlin 2002: 83).

A few journalists did try to reach the island by speedboat but were fired at by a US fighter and turned back. Gen. Norman Schwarzkopf, who led the military action (and later the US-led coalition forces in the Gulf in 1991), records approvingly in his autobiography how one of the military commanders, Vice-Admiral Joseph Metcalf, responded to a question by one of the reporters involved: 'Admiral, what would have happened if we hadn't turned around?' with the words: 'We would have blown you right out of the water' (Schwarzkopf 1992: 258). Two journalists did, however, manage to slip on to the island the night before the attack and were able to record the bombing of a civilian psychiatric hospital which killed 17 patients (four other journalists were captured by the military and held for two days). Without their presence that 'mistake' may never have been recorded (Rosenblum 1993: 125).

In addition, the news blackout in Grenada concealed other military blunders such as the drowning of a Seal commando team that was not even fired upon, the downing of sophisticated helicopters by World War Two surplus guns and serious logistical and intelligence gathering problems (Smith 1999: 209). There were even complaints that the military had had to use tourist maps when they went into Grenada (Clarridge 1997: 259).

Even so, the Grenada assault became a huge news story globally and hundreds of journalists flocked to the neighbouring island of Barbados. Commander Ronald Wildermuth, US Navy, with five aides, set up a joint information bureau at Grantley Adams airport and registered 369 American and international reporters on its first day of operations (Rid 2007: 68). On 27 October, the first pool of 15 reporters and photographers (12 from the major US media and three from the Caribbean media) were flown in to Grenada for a few hours accompanied by a military escort. Some 24 were taken on 28 October rising to 50 the next day. During the crucial first two days of the invasion, the media significantly ignored reporting on the media ban and the dangers it imposed. Thus journalists failed to highlight the chances it gave the US administration to manipulate public opinion. As Hertsgaard (1988: 221) comments: 'By the time the press worked up the courage to do more than clear its throat publicly about the censorship, three or four days after the invasion began, it was too late. The press had relayed enough government propaganda, sufficiently uncritically, so that the administration had successfully and irrevocably sold its version of the story to the public; the game of shaping public opinion was over and won for Reagan. In the process, the press had become, without knowing it, a passive accomplice in its own censorship.'

GRENADA: THE MEDIA SPECTACLE TEST CASE

On 27 October, the President appeared on television explaining directly to the public the rationale for the invasion. He claimed Grenada had become a Soviet-Cuban beachhead because some Cuban contractors were building an airfield there under British authorisation. Such a television appearance showed a sophisticated information policy – with the President able to present his message unfiltered by journalistic commentary or analysis. The carefully managed news conference with the American military appealing over the heads of journalists this time to the global community was to be an important feature of Gulf media strategy. Indeed, it was to prove to be a consistent element of Thatcherite and Reaganite populism – with the heads of secretive, centralised states using the mass media to articulate their views over the heads of the traditional representative institutions (parliament, congress) to the public at large. The UK government led by Mrs Margaret Thatcher was, in fact, given just 12 hours' notice of the invasion – the first of its kind by America on a former British colony – and strongly advised against it but to no effect (Booth 2013).

ADMINISTRATION LIES

Nan Levinson (1991) describes Grenada as the 'uncovered invasion'. All the major features of the operation were distorted by administration lies, misinformation, secrecy – and in the end by journalistic bickering. All the justifications provided by the administration for the attack (dutifully reported in the press) were later deemed to have been spurious (McMahon op cit: 144-167). Pentagon camera crews supplied propaganda pictures from Grenada (a device later to be used in the Gulf) of warehouses stocked with automatic weapons to 'supply thousands of terrorists' (according to Reagan). But once allowed on to the island, reporters found the warehouses were half empty, many containing cases of sardines while most of the weapons were antiquated. White House communications director David Gergen resigned afterwards in protest at the lying by his superiors (Macarthur 1993: 142).

CASUALTIES COVER-UP

The primary aim of the invasion, according to the administration, was 'to protect innocent lives' – in particular, those of American students at a medical school on the island. Yet the invasion itself cost many people their lives. For some time the administration refused to reveal any casualty figures. In the end they said 18 Americans were killed and 113 wounded. The Cubans reported 24 Cubans and 16 Grenadians killed with 57 Cubans and 280 Grenadians injured. The Grenadian High Commission later suggested 1,500 Grenadians were killed. Half the 18 US dead were said to have been from 'friendly fire'.

EXAGGERATION OF THE THREAT

On the second day of the invasion, the press reported official sources as saying that soldiers were meeting substantial resistance from 1,100 Cuban troops on the island with '4,340 more on the way' while a 'reign of terror' was endangering US medical students on the island. All of this 'information' was later found to be lies. As Garry Wills commented (1988: 356): 'The war was won because it could not be lost – the American invaders had a ten-to-one superiority over the defenders and all of the air and artillery weapons used.' On 31 October, the US state department revised its earlier figures: there were, in fact, just 678 Cubans on the island of whom only 200 were soldiers (Quigley op cit: 213-221). So much for administration claims that the island had become a massive base from which the Cubans and Soviets were planning to export terrorism. But the exaggeration of the threat and invention of an enemy was to be repeated significantly during the later Gulf crises.

Jan Servaes (1991) argues that Grenada was a test case for the 'disinformation war' later waged during the Gulf crisis of 1991. Servaes's study of six European 'quality newspapers' shows their coverage was influenced considerably by the disinformation campaign organised by the Pentagon. And as Parenti comments (1986: 51): 'Objectivity means reporting US overseas involvements from the perspectives of the multinational corporations, the Pentagon, the White House and the State Department and rarely questioning the legitimacy of the military intervention (although allowing critical remarks about its effectiveness).' Some of the most famous images to emerge from the invasion were of American students at St George's School of Medicine, who had been evacuated from Grenada, kissing the ground at Charleston Air Force Base upon their return to the United States.

These were distributed to news media around the world. But Hertsgaard (op cit: 227-228) shows how the press's uncritical coverage of this event served to reinforce administration justifications for the invasion. He writes:

> Only a handful of the students had actually kissed the ground upon returning home and subsequent reporting revealed that as a group the students were, in fact, divided on whether they had truly been in danger before the invasion. The disproportionate emphasis news accounts placed on students who did feel endangered, however, suggested that a virtual unanimity opinion existed among the students and moreover that it supported Reagan's justification for invading.

The propaganda had the desired effects in the US: an ABC/*Washington Post* poll found 71 per cent backing the invasion with just 22 per cent against (Andersen op cit: 123).[5]

THE SIDLE COMMISSION

The only formal legal challenge against media restrictions in Grenada came from the pornographer publisher, Larry Flynt (McLaughlin op cit: 85). But in 1984, the court granted the government motion to dismiss the complaint as 'moot' – relating to a unique case unlikely to recur. But in response to protests lodged by a number of news organisations over the censorship regime, the DoD set up a public inquiry into media-military relations by a 12-member panel of journalists, journalism professors and military public affairs officers. Headed by veteran US Army Major-General Winant Sidle, chief of information for US forces in Vietnam and head of Martin-Marietta corporate public affairs. The Sidle report, released on 23 August 1984, contained eight recommendations. Amongst the most important was one endorsing 'the largest pooling procedure to be put in place for the minimum time possible'; another called for voluntary compliance by the media with security guidelines. Following the report, in April 1985, the department of defense's national media pool was created by order of the secretary of defense consisting of up to 16 media representatives and three escort officers (Rid op cit: 70). Sidle proved to be another feature of the democratic façade of US politics – once the Gulf crisis exploded its most important suggestion, on the pooling arrangements, was completely ignored by the secret US state.

THE SECRET WAR IN CHAD – MISSED BY THE MEDIA.

Formerly part of French Equatorial Africa, Chad gained its independence in 1960 and since then has been gripped by civil war. In a rare instance of coverage on 21 May 1992, the London-based *Guardian* carried four short paragraphs reporting how 40,000 people were estimated to have died in detention or been executed during the tyranny of Hissène Habré (1982-1990). A justice ministry report concluded that Habré had committed genocide against the Chadian people (Keeble 2002;

2007a). In 2001, in a case inspired by the one against Chile's General Augusto Pinochet, several human rights organisations, led by Human Rights Watch, filed a suit against Habré in Senegal (his refuge since 1990). They argued that he could be tried anywhere for crimes against humanity and that former heads of state were not immune. However, on 21 March 2001, the Senegal Court of Cassation threw out the case. And so human rights campaigners turned their attention to Belgium where one of the victims of Habré's torture lived.

Following threats from the United States in June 2003 that Belgium risked losing its status as host to Nato's headquarters, the 1993 historic law, which allowed victims to file complaints in Belgium for atrocities committed abroad, was repealed. Yet a new law, adopted in August 2003, allowed for the continuation of the case against Habré – much to the delight of human rights campaigners. Finally in 2007, Senegal, where Habré has been under house arrest, arrested the former dictator to face an extradition request from Belgium over the genocide charges.

Extraordinary events but all of them hidden behind a virtual wall of silence in the West. Yet also hidden was the massive, secret war waged by the United States and Britain from bases in Chad against Libya. British involvement in a 1996 plot to assassinate the Libyan leader, Colonel Mu'ammar Gaddafi, as alleged by the maverick M15 officer David Shayler (see Machon 2005: 172), was reported in the mainstream media as an isolated event. Yet it is best seen as part of a wide-ranging and long-standing strategy of the US and UK secret states to remove Gaddafi (Keeble 2011a).

Grabbing power by ousting the eighty-year-old, pro-British King Idris in a 1969 coup, Gaddafi (who, intriguingly, had followed a military training course in Dorset, England, in 1966) became the leader of a fantastically oil-rich country.[6] Oil revenues were worth $2 billion at the time of the Gaddafi revolution – rising to $22 billion by 1980 (*Undercover* 1993: 43). And Gaddafi soon became the target of covert operations by the French, Americans, Israelis and British.[7] Stephen Dorril, in his seminal history of M16, records how in 1971 a British plan to invade the country, release political prisoners and restore the monarchy ended in an embarrassing flop (Dorril 2000: 735-738). Dorril (ibid: 735) reports: 'What became known as the "Hilton assignment" was one of MI6's last attempts at a major special operation designed to overthrow a regime opposed to British interests.' The plan to bring down Gaddafi had originally been a joint MI6/CIA operation but the CIA suddenly withdrew after they concluded that 'although Gaddafi was anti-West, he was also anti-Soviet, which meant there could be someone a lot worse running Libya. The British disagreed' (ibid: 736). Nine years later, the head of the French secret service, Alain de Gaigneronde de Marolles, resigned after a French-led plan ended in disaster when a rebellion by Libyan troops in Tobruk was quickly suppressed, according to Richard Deacon (1990: 262-264). But former French intelligence chief Pierre Lethier disputed this claim:

Mr Deacon, I am afraid, has seen fit to spread rumours fabricated by the opposition press in France. Former head of the Action Service and then deputy director for intelligence in 1978, de Marolles fell from grace in 1980 after a sinister conflict within the SDECE [France's external intelligence agency from 1944-1982] (under Count Alexandre de Marenches from 1971 to 1981) following a highly debatable counter-intelligence operation. Unfortunately, I cannot say any more about this (see Keeble 2011a: 282).

Then, in 1982, away again from the glare of the media, Hissène Habré, with the backing of the CIA and French troops, overthrew the Chadian government of Goukouni Wedeye. Bob Woodward (of Watergate fame), in his semi-official history of the CIA, reveals that the Chad covert operation was the first undertaken by the new CIA chief William Casey and that, throughout the decade, Libya ranked as high as the Soviet Union as the *bête noir* of the White House (Woodward 1987: 348, 363, 410-11).[8] A report from Amnesty International, *Chad: The Habré legacy*, of October 2001, records massive military and financial support for the dictator by the US Congress.[9] It adds: 'None of the documents presented to congress and consulted by AI covering the period 1984 to 1989 make any reference to human rights violations.'

US official records indicate that funds for the Chad-based covert war against Libya also came from Saudi Arabia, Egypt, Morocco, Israel and Iraq (Hunter 1991: 49). Prades (1986: 383) records that the Saudis, for instance, gave $7 million to an opposition group, the National Front for the Salvation of Libya (also backed by French intelligence and the CIA). However, a plan to assassinate Gaddafi and seize power on 8 May 1984 was crushed (Perry 1992: 165). In the following year, the US asked Egypt to invade Libya and overthrow Gaddafi but President Mubarak refused (Martin and Walcott 1988: 265-266). By the end of 1985, the *Washington Post* had exposed the plan after congressional leaders opposing it wrote in protest to President Reagan.

In September 1987, Chadian soldiers, supported by US and French intelligence, launched a night attack on Libya's airbase in the south, killing an estimated 1,700 troops and taking 300 prisoners.[10] Then in 1990, with the crisis in the Gulf developing, French troops helped oust Habré in a secret operation and install Idriss Déby as the new President of Chad. The French government had tired of Habré's genocidal policies while George Bush senior's administration decided not to frustrate France in exchange for co-operation in its attack on Iraq that year. Yet, even under Déby, abuses of civil rights by government forces have continued.

THRILLED TO BLITZ WITH LIBYAN BOMBINGS

Earlier, throughout the early 1980s Gaddafi was demonised in the mainstream US and UK media as a 'terrorist warlord' and prime agent of a Soviet-inspired 'terror network'. According to Chomsky, Reagan's campaign against 'international terrorism' was a natural choice for the propaganda system in furtherance of its basic agenda: 'expansion of the state sector of the economy; transfer of resources from the poor to the rich and a more "activist" (i.e. terrorist and aggressive) foreign policy' (1991b: 120). Such policies needed the public to be frightened into obedience by some 'terrible enemy'. And Libya fitted the need perfectly. As Chomsky commented: 'Gaddafi is easy to hate, particularly against the backdrop of rampant anti-Arab racism in the United States and the deep commitment of the educated classes, with only the rarest of exceptions, to US-Israeli rejectionism and violence. He has created an ugly and repressive society and is indeed guilty of retail terrorism, primarily against Libyans' (ibid).

In July 1981, a CIA plan to overthrow and possibly kill Gaddafi was leaked to the press. At roughly the same time, Libya hit squads were reported to have entered the United States, though this has since been revealed to have been a piece of Israeli secret service disinformation (Rusbridger 1989: 80). Joe Flynn, the infamous con man, was also able to exploit Fleet Street's fascination with the Gaddafi myth. In September 1981, posing as an Athens-based arms dealer he tricked almost £3,000 off the *News of the World* with his story that the Libyan leader was 'masterminding a secret plot to arm black revolutionary murder squads in Britain' (Lycett 1995).[11]

Reagan's list of terrorist states, issued in July 1985, comprised Libya, North Korea, Cuba and Nicaragua (Segaller 1986: 120). And as Segaller (ibid: 130-135) argues, Gaddafi's anti-West rhetoric played into the hands of President Reagan. 'Terrorist' outrages at Rome and Vienna airports early in 1986 were both blamed on Gaddafi and Reagan declared Libya to be a 'threat to the national security and foreign policy of the United States'.

In April 1984, the fatal shooting of WPc. Yvonne Fletcher, 25, outside the Libyan embassy in St James's Square, London, provided more ammunition for the Western elite in their anti-Gaddafi campaign. Libyan exiles in the UK were protesting at the rule of President Gaddafi when automatic gunfire from the embassy injured 11 protesters and killed WPc. Fletcher. According to leaks from the Crown Prosecution Service to the *Daily Telegraph* in 2009, the Libyan ringleaders were 'revolutionary committee' members Abdulgader Mohammed Baghdadi and Malouk Mohammed Matouk.[12] Then in November 2015, Saleh Ibrahim Mabrouk was suddenly arrested over the killing (Weaver 2015).

But earlier, in 1997, a Channel 4 *Dispatches* investigation revealed that shortly after Fletcher's killings, three Germans were arrested and charged with supplying weapons and hitmen to a US-funded anti-Gaddafi terrorist group, al Burkan (The Volcano).[13] One, Manfred Meyer, said his boss, Hilmar Hein, had claimed they were being protected by the US deputy national security adviser, John Poindexter, and that a number of Libyan diplomats in the embassy were al Burkan moles. The *Dispatches* investigation also suggested the fatal shot was fired from a handgun high up in an adjacent building. As *Private Eye* commented: 'By a spooky coincidence, one of the upper floors of that building was used by MI5.'[14]

After a six-day siege of the embassy, the Libyans were finally allowed to leave for their home country. No arrests were made. According to Gresh and Vidal (1990: 122), Gaddafi survived an attack on his barracks at Bab al-Aziziya by armed men from Tunisia in May 1984. In December 1985, following terrorist attacks at Rome and Vienna airports which resulted in 19 deaths and many casualties, President Reagan talked of 'irrefutable evidence' linking Gaddafi to the atrocities (Yallop 1994: 708).

Then, frustrated in its covert attempts to topple Gaddafi, the US government's strategy suddenly shifted. In March 1986, US planes patrolling the Gulf of Sidra were reported to have been attacked by Libyan missiles. But Chomsky (1991b: 124) suggests this incident was a provocation 'enabling US forces to sink several Libyan boats, killing more than 50 Libyans and, it was hoped, to incite Gaddafi to acts of terror against Americans, as was subsequently claimed'. In the following month, the US responded with a military strike on key Libyan targets. The attack was widely condemned. Adams (1987: 372) quotes a British intelligence source: 'Although we allowed the raid there was a general feeling that America had become uncontrollable and unless we did something Reagan would be even more violent the next time.' Hussain (1988: 45) described the raid as an act of 'imperialist aggression'. In November, the UN General Assembly passed a motion condemning the raid. Interestingly, Israel was one of the few countries to back the US. Yet when the Israeli representative came to justify his country's stance, he used evidence of Gaddafi's alleged commitment to terrorism taken from the German mass-selling newspaper *Bild am Sonntag* and the London-based *Daily Telegraph*. David Yallop (1994: 695) shows this evidence to have been 'pathetic'.

For 11 minutes in the early morning of 14 April 1986, 30 US Air Force and Navy bombers struck Tripoli and Benghazi in a raid code-named El Dorado Canyon (part of Operation Prairie Fire) that left around 100 Libyans, mainly civilians, dead.[15] Two incidents on successive days earlier in the month had provided the excuse. In the first, four Americans died when an explosion blew a hole in a TWA plane flying from Rome to Athens. In the second, a bomb explosion at la Belle disco in West Berlin, frequented by US servicemen, killed three people and injured 229. Joel Bleifuss (1990) records a report on 14 September 1990 on Radio *Deutsche Welle* suggesting that the CIA knew that a terrorist bombing of the disco was being planned but failed to maintain proper security – perhaps to give the Reagan administration a pretext to bomb Libya (see also Gearty 1991: 83-87).[16] In contrast, Laurent Guyénot (2013) highlights the report by former KGB agent Victor Ostrovsky that the Israeli intelligence agency, Mossad, had used a special operations system, labelled 'Trojan Horse' to send false transmissions to the NSA implicating Libya in the raid.

Significantly newsrooms were informed of the planned air strikes beforehand – but all held back from reporting until after the raid, thus showing the growing complicity between the media and the state over the handling of new militarist adventures (Trainor 1991: 76).

Mrs Thatcher was perhaps hoping for an action-replay of the Falklands factor when she gave the US permission to fly F111 attack jets from bases in East Anglia to bomb Libya targets. A high-level US delegation, led by Vernon Walters, had toured Europe attempting to win the support of the West Germans, the French, the Italians, the Spanish and the British for the assault. Only Thatcher obliged (Yallop 1994: 709). According to Machon (2005: 104), Mrs Thatcher was also 'anxious for revenge' after the shooting of WPc. Fletcher. It was an archetypal move of the secret state: only a select few in her cabinet were involved in the decision (Young 1989: 476). The attack on Libya was bitterly opposed by ministers John Biffen and Douglas Hurd, who 'all disagreed with Thatcher for almost the first time in open rebellion' (Bloom 2015: 161). Moreover, the attack appeared to win little support from the public (Worcester 1991: 143). Harris, Gallup and MORI all showed substantial majorities opposed. Much of the UK mainstream press, however, responded with jingoistic jubilation. The *Sun*'s front page screamed: 'Thrilled to blitz: Bombing Gaddafi was my greatest day, says US airman.' The *Mirror* concluded: 'What was the alternative? In what other way was Colonel Gaddafi to be forced to understand that he had a price to pay for his terrorism.' According to *The Times*: 'The greatest threat to Western freedoms may be the Soviet Union but does not make the USSR the only threat. The growth of terrorist states must be curbed while it can be curbed. The risks of extension of the conflict must be minimised. And in this case it would appear that it has been.' The *Star*'s front page proclaimed: 'Reagan was right.' In the *Sunday Telegraph*, of 1 June, columnist Paul Johnson denounced the 'distasteful whiff of pure cowardice in the air' as 'the wimps' raised doubts about the US bombing of 'terrorist bases' in Libya.

But there was an intriguing mediacentric dimension to the mission as the BBC, transformed into the 'enemy within' of the vulnerable state, was to come under some considerable attack from the Conservative government over its coverage of the attacks. An election was somewhere in the near future and a Thatcher government hoped a reinforcement of the Falklands factor with a Libyan factor would help her gain a hat-trick of victories. The BBC became the perfect scapegoat. Kate Adie's on-the-spot reports could not fail to mention the casualties (Sebba 1994: 266-267). Many of the main targets were missed. The French had refused to back the US attack and their embassy in Tripoli sustained virtually a direct hit (Yallop 1994: 218). Four 2,000lb bombs fell on the suburb of Bin Ghashir, causing far more devastation than any 'terrorist' bomb could ever achieve. Even so, Norman Tebbit, chairman of the Conservative Party, engaged in a highly charged attack on the BBC. (Adie was not identified by name because PM Margaret Thatcher thought it unwise to attack 'such a popular journalist' but she featured prominently in the BBC's response to the allegations: see Higgins and Smith 2011: 352.)

The Tories' backers on Fleet Street followed up the reports with predictable smears: the *Daily Mail*, of 31 October, for instance, accused the BBC of being 'a propaganda mouthpiece for Libyan dictator Colonel Gaddafi' while the *Daily*

Express suggested Adie's reporting was rewarded with favourable treatment from the Libyan authorities (ibid).[17] Yet there was an air of theatre about the whole event. Adie was one of the most trusted BBC correspondents. But both government and BBC could benefit from the Libya theatre. The Tory right, on the ascendancy at the time, and ever hasty to criticise the BBC it so desperately wanted privatised as the 'enemy within', was satisfied and the BBC, who stuck by their star reporter throughout the attacks, could appear to be courageously defending media freedom. Amidst the many contradictions and complexities of modern-day politics, mediacentric elements are put to many diverse uses by (usually competing) factions in the ruling elites.

According to Kellner, the bombing was a manufactured crisis, staged as a media event and co-ordinated to coincide with the beginning of the 7 pm news in the US (Kellner 1990: 138). Two hours later President Reagan went on network television to justify the raid. Chomsky also argues that the attack was 'the first bombing in history staged for prime-time television' (Chomsky 1991b: 127). Administration press conferences soon after the raid ensured 'total domination of the propaganda system during the crucial early hours'. Chomsky continues: 'One might argue that the administration took a gamble in this transparent public relations operation, since journalists could have asked some difficult questions. But the White House was justly confident that nothing untoward would occur and its faith in the servility of the media proved to be entirely warranted.'

Yet the main purpose of the raid was to kill the Libyan President – dubbed a 'mad dog' by Reagan.[18] CIA counter-terrorism expert Duane R. Clarridge comments diplomatically (1997: 339): 'Given the magnitude of the raid, the inescapable conclusion is that it would have been acceptable within the administration if Gaddafi had died in the bombing.' Yallop (op cit: 713) quotes 'a member of the United States Air Force intelligence unit who took part in the pre-raid briefing': 'Nine of 18 F111s that left from the UK were specifically briefed to bomb Gaddafi's residence inside the barracks where he was living with his family.'[19] In the event, the first bomb to drop on Tripoli hit Gaddafi's home killing Hana, his adopted daughter aged 15 months – while his eight other children and wife Safiya were all hospitalised, some with serious injuries.[20] According to Richard J. Aldrich (2010: 457), Gaddafi escaped only by minutes because the Prime Minister of Malta warned him by telephone of the approaching military jets. David Blundy and Andrew Lycett report (1987: 22):

> The attack on Gaddafi's Aziziya compound was a military failure. Gaddafi himself was deep underground. The administration building, where he lives, was missed by two bombs which fell thirty yards away, knocking out the windows but doing no structural damage. The tennis courts received two direct hits and a bomb fell outside the front door of the building where Gaddafi's family lives. Blasts tore through the small bedrooms to the right

of the living room, injuring two of Gaddafi's sons and killing his fifteen-month-old adopted daughter, Hana. Hana was publicly acknowledged only in death. During interviews only a month before Gaddafi had said, sadly, that he had only one daughter, eight-year-old Aisha, and wished that he had more. He did not say that his wife had adopted a baby girl ten months before.

But consider the outrage in the Western media if a relative of Reagan had been killed by a Libyan bomb. There was no such outrage over the Libyan deaths. Also hit in the raid were the Japanese, Romanian, Austrian and Swiss diplomatic residencies (*Undercover* 2014: 47).

Intriguingly, in February 2011, the German newspaper *Welt am Sonntag*, the Sunday edition of *Die Welt*, reported that Hana had actually survived, lived in London for a while, trained as a doctor and was currently holding an important position in the Libyan Ministry of Health. The information was apparently gathered from Gaddafi family documents seized in Switzerland. As the rebels advanced on Tripoli in August 2011, this news was covered prominently in most leading Western media. In the *Irish Times*, Mary Fitzgerald located what appeared to be Hana's study in the overrun Bab al-Aziziya compound. But was it all disinformation?[21]

AWAY FROM THE MEDIA GLARE, CIA AIMS TO SPARK ANTI-GADDAFI COUP

Reports of US military action against Libya disappeared from the media after the 1986 assault. But away from the glare of publicity, the CIA launched its most extensive effort yet to spark an anti-Gaddafi coup. A secret army was recruited from among the many Libyans captured in border battles with Chad during the 1980s (Perry op cit: 166). And as concerns grew in M16 that Gaddafi was aiming to develop chemical weapons, Britain funded various opposition groups in Libya. In March 1987, the Libyans were defeated at Ouadiddoum in northern Chad, in a major battle involving French and American secret services in league with a number of Arab powers – Egypt and Tunisia, Saudi Arabia, Iraq – and Israel![22] And, as concern grew in MI6 over Gaddafi's alleged plans to develop chemical weapons, Britain funded various opposition groups in Libya including the London-based Libyan National Movement.

For his part, Gaddafi continued to arm various revolutionary movements including the IRA[23]. In October 1987, French customs seized an Irish-crewed freighter, the Eksund, carrying almost 200 tonnes of arms including Kalashnikov rifles, ground-to-air SAM-7 missiles, a million rounds of ammunition and more than 2 tonnes of Semtex. This was the fifth shipment to Ireland since 1985.[24] The Libyan leader was also blamed for the bombing of the Pan Am jumbo jet on 21 December 1988 over the Scottish town of Lockerbie in which 270 people died.[25]

Attempts to oust Gaddafi continued. David Shayler, a former MI5 agent, even alleged that MI6 were involved in a plot in March 1996 to assassinate the Libyan leader as he attended the Libyan General People's Congress in his home city of Sirte (Curtis 2010: 227-229; Hunter 1991). His motorcade was attacked by dissidents with Kalashnikovs and rocket grenades but while Gaddafi escaped there were casualties on both sides. Stephen Dorril reports in his seminal history of MI6 (2000: 793): 'Three fighters were killed but the leader of the hit team, Abd al-Muhaymeen, a veteran of the Afghan resistance who was possibly trained by MI6 or the CIA, "escaped unhurt".'[26] Shayler claimed MI6 paid the al-Islamiya al-Muqatila, the Islamic Fighting Group, £100,000 to carry out the attack (Dorril 2000: 793-794).[27] It was also revealed in 1998 that a London-based exile member of the Libyan royal family, Prince Idris al-Senussi, had links both to MI6 and to the 1996 plot to blow up Gaddafi's motorcade (Leigh 1998).

THE POOL AND THE GULF 1987: THE FIRST NEWS BLACKOUT

The US attack on Libya was over far too quickly for any media pool system – as recommended by the Sidle commission – to be activated. On 7 April, it was revealed that pool reporters were kept two hours aboard the aircraft carrier *Saratoga* off Libya after Libyan missiles were fired at American planes on 24 March. The reporters were then taken from the ship without being told of the action. This sparked a strong protest to the government by the American Society of Newspaper Editors.

The pool's first real test in a war zone came in July 1987 after one powerful section of the US secret state – then backing Iraq in its war with Iran – provided naval escorts for Kuwaiti oil tankers recently registered under American flags in the Gulf. But by mid-August the military had still failed to activate the pool. Eventually, several pools were placed on navy destroyers. But according to Mark Thompson, of Knight Ridder, several reports from journalists on USS *Fox* were held up for almost two days, at least one was changed by the *Fox*'s commander before being filed and a photographer was refused permission to fly in a helicopter after the super-tanker *Bridgeton* was hit by a mine (Woodward, Gary C. 1993: 9).

THE POOL AND THE PANAMA INVASION 1989

The Sidle recommendations were again to be totally ignored during the Panama invasion launched on 20 December 1989 (codenamed Operation Just Cause) – supposedly to arrest the country's leader, General Noriega, on drug charges. Some 24,000 troops participated in the invasion making it the largest US military operation since the Vietnam War (Goldman 1991). It also constituted the twelfth US invasion of Panama since 1903 (Andersen op cit: 147). The US armed forces used the rock music of Guns N'Roses and Elvis Presley played at maximum volume to 'terrorise' Noriega into surrendering on 3 January 1990.[28] For the first two days, media reports came from journalists detained in a warehouse. Some 100 additional reporters who accompanied the troops meekly returned home when they were told by the military they had no facilities to service them (Rosenblum op cit: 126). Gary Woodward (op cit: 11) argues that the media had no choice but to work alongside the military:

> But as the Persian Gulf War loomed, members of the press would have good reason to rethink the wisdom of ceding editorial prerogative of prior restraint to Pentagon planners. A general silence on this point throughout the tanker escort operation in 1987 and the later Panama invasion meant that coveted slots in press pools would come at a very high price.

According to the International Centre on Censorship, the pool was 'activated too late to be of any help to journalists' (Philo and McLaughlin 1995, cited in McLaughlin 2002: 87).

THE CASUALTIES COVER-UP AGAIN

In many respects the Panama invasion can be seen as another testing of the media/fighting strategy that was to be repeated during the Middle East massacres of 1991. At the heart of the Pentagon strategy was the representation of the attack as swift and clean. As Patrick Sloyan, of *Newsday*, commented, the muzzling of the press in Panama created 'the illusion of bloodless battlefields' (Fund for Free Expression 1991). And, according to John R. Macarthur (1993: 16): 'What the administration prevented during the first thirty six hours of the Panama invasion were any eye-witness accounts or photographs of the shelling of El Chorrillo, the desperately poor neighbourhood in Panama City, where General Noriega's headquarters were located.'

The Pentagon was at first reluctant to provide any casualty figures. Only three weeks after the invasion did Southern Command say that 202 Panamanian civilians and 314 soldiers had died. Later it reduced the figure for military casualties down to 50 (Andersen 1991: 24). Yet the Spanish language press both within and outside the US (InterPress Service, *Echo*, of Mexico) cited more than 2,000 deaths and approximately 70,000 casualties. The National Council of Churches and the Red Cross also estimated the total civilian deaths may have numbered 2,000 at a minimum (Chomsky 1991b; see also Gellhorn 1990). A number of mass graves were discovered after the invasion.

Only 23 US soldiers were reported to have died in the operation (Herman 1992: 55). After *Newsweek* reported that as many as 60 per cent of these casualties may have resulted from US action (known in euphemistic militaryspeak, uncritically adopted by the media as 'friendly fire') the Pentagon announced for the first time that US action accounted for two of the 23 deaths and 19 of the 324 injuries (Woodward, Bob 1991: 195).

DEMONISATION OF NORIEGA

As was to be later echoed in media coverage of the Iraq and Kosovo crises, much of the media coverage of the Panama invasion focused on a demonised personality – in this case General Manuel Antonio Noriega as newly defined by the Bush administration. As Robin Andersen comments (2006: 149): 'Revelations of his perversions saturated media stories, such as his propensity to wear women's clothes. In the press, Noriega was the thug of thugs, the top narco-criminal of the hemisphere, and the perverted, depraved friend of communist regimes. He had to be deposed.'

He was accused of brutally suppressing the results of an election a few months earlier and of heading a huge drug-running operation. A leader in *The Times*, of 21 December 1989, commented: 'President Bush took a difficult, but correct decision in ordering American troops into action in Panama. The initial stated objectives, the protection of American lives, and the security of the Panama Canal – particularly following the extreme provocations offered by the regime of General Manuel Noriega in recent weeks – would in themselves have been adequate justification.' It continued: 'If the US further succeeds in extraditing General Noriega, who has been in open league with the Colombian cocaine barons, to face drug-trafficking charges in the United States, it will have won an important battle in the war against drugs.' The shooting of a US military officer by a member of Noriega's Panamanian Defence Forces was said to be the final straw for the US administration.

But such a 'human interest' focus downplayed the history of US involvement with Noriega. He was recruited by the CIA's chief of station in Lima, Peru, in 1959 to provide information on his fellow students at the Peruvian Military academy and his links with central American drug barons and US administrations were close, in particular while George Bush Snr was briefly head of the CIA during the Ford administration (1975-1976) (Perry op cit: 110-115). Noriega is said to have met Bush Snr personally twice – in 1976 and 1983 (Tisdall 2010).[29] He was involved in the CIA's Black Eagle operation, according to which Israeli stocks of captured PLO weapons were moved from Texas to the terroristic Contras fighting the leftist Sandinistas in Nicaragua by means of his network of hidden airstrips (Koster and Bourbon 1990).

In 1984, Noriega refused to accept the election victory of Arnulfo Arias and installed, to US applause, Nicolas Ardito Barletta in his place. Dan Winter, the CIA station chief in Panama, even said at Noriega's later trial for drug trafficking that he had been the agency's 'best liaison with Fidel Castro' and that his 'retainer', totalling $320,000 by the time of his capture, had been money well spent (Thomas 2009: 281). Even before the US invasion of Grenada in 1983, the CIA consulted Noriega (Clarridge 1997: 248).

But by 1989 Noriega had drawn the wrath of the Bush administration for refusing to co-operate in Col. Oliver North's plan to use a shipload of arms to accuse the Nicaraguan Sandinistas of smuggling weapons to the Salvadorean rebels.

Panama had been created in 1903 by the administration of Theodore Roosevelt and J. P. Morgan & Co. essentially to serve the interests of big banks. As Ed Vulliamy reports (2016):

> J. P. Morgan led the American banks in gradually turning Panama into a financial centre – and a haven for tax evasion and money laundering – as well as a passage for shipping, with which these practices were at first entwined when Panama began to register foreign ships to carry fuel for the Standard Oil company in order for the corporation to avoid US tax liabilities. On the slipstream of Standard Oil's wheeze, Panama began to develop its labyrinthine system of tax-free incorporation – especially with regard to the shipping register – with help and guidance from Wall Street.

When Noriega realised that his country's wealth was even better suited to an alliance with the Medellin narco-trafficking cartel of Pablo Escobar, his fate was sealed (ibid).

Then, more significantly, the administration wanted to revoke the Panama treaties of 1977 (signed by President Jimmy Carter and Panamanian strongman Omar Torrijos) according to which control of the Panama canal was to pass into Panamanian hands. In addition, US military bases were to be phased out by the year 2000 – yet the Bush administration saw them as crucial staging posts for military intervention in Latin America. On 2 January 1990, a Panamanian was due to be appointed head of the Canal Commission. These were among the major reasons for the invasion which, as Weeks and Gunson (1991) show conclusively, was in total violation of international law. It was condemned by the UN Security Council (though the vote was vetoed by the US, UK and France) while the UN General Assembly deplored the intervention and demanded the immediate withdrawal of US forces from Panama (ibid). The 'human interest' bias of the coverage served to marginalise this critical historical background to the action.

THE MYTH OF THE SUDDEN RESPONSE

The military invasion followed the failure of a CIA-backed coup attempt on Noriega months earlier (James 1990). From July 1989, US forces conducted a series of provocative manoeuvres, condemned by the Organisation of American States, clearly intended to accustom Panamanians to US troop presence. On 2 July, US troops occupied two water processing plants and set up roadblocks throughout civilian neighbourhoods. As Hellinger and Judd comment (1991: 53-54): 'These manoeuvres dramatically raised tensions between US and PDF forces, a climate that probably contributed to the death of the US officer before the invasion. None of this was reported by standard news organisations.'

After Noriega was arrested he was put on trial in Miami on 10 narrowly defined drug-related charges and sentenced to 40 years in prison. As Tisdall comments (op cit), the trial heard nothing about Noriega's contacts with CIA chief William Casey and other key figures in the Reagan and Bush administrations 'who, allegedly connived in the supply of arms to Nicaragua's Contra rebels paid for with Medellin cartel drug cash'. Tisdall continues (ibid): 'The outcome of the Miami trial, like the 1989 invasion, was never in doubt. It was a show trial, a warning to others. It was pure vengeance. It was a cover-up of decades of illicit regional meddling. But it was also a demonstration of raw American power, of which the world was soon to have more frightening examples.'[30]

THE HOFFMAN REPORT: THE PREDICTABLE RITUAL

Following the Panama invasion, the department of defense indulged in its predictable ritual of commissioning a report – this time by Fred S. Hoffman, one of its former officials. Released on 20 March 1990 and titled *Review of Panama pool deployment, December 1991*, it assigned specific responsibility for the failure of the pool system to defense secretary Dick Cheney and assistant secretary of defense for public affairs Pete Williams. The report concluded that 'excessive concern for secrecy' prevented the defense department media's pool from reporting the critical opening battles and that the pool produced 'stories and pictures essentially of secondary value'. Williams and his staff promised to handle any future military operation properly.

IRANGATE NO WATERGATE: HOW THE MEDIA COVERS COVERT MILITARY ACTION

While the US/UK new militarist states felt more confident during the 1980s and ready to indulge in military attacks on the Third World, now that a media system had been developed which meant strategic actions could be shrouded in as much secrecy as straight covert actions, LIC strategy still prioritised covert warfare throughout the decade. The most infamous instance was the Reagan/Bush secret state's illegal deals with the Iranian government to send arms shipments via Israel, the money acquired being redirected to the Contra terrorists in Nicaragua (Marshall, Scott and Hunter 1987; Simons 1992; Simpson 2013: 191-193).

The foreign editor of the Hearst newspapers, John Wallach, first reported on the contacts between the US and Iran in June 1985 and wrote about the arms sales six months later, but the story was denied by the White House and no journalist followed up the story vigorously (Pilger 1986: 570).[31] Hertsgaard comments (op cit: 302) on the early marginalisation of the Irangate stories in the press: 'And so they floated past largely unnoticed, fortifying Regan administration officials in the conviction that they could conduct whatever illegal or unpopular operations they wished without fear of detection.' The sales only hit the global headlines after an obscure Lebanese newspaper, *Al-Shiraa*, revealed them on 3 November 1986 (Nouzille 2010: 137).[33] Closely linked to this scandal was the so-called October Surprise, according to which the Reagan election team made a deal with Iran to hold the American hostages until after the 1980 election and so deny Jimmy Carter any of the benefits which would inevitably fall on the President from the release (Cohen 1991).

Kellner (1990: 88) argues that the October Surprise was 'perhaps the most explosive scandal of the Reagan years and the one most studiously avoided by the mainstream media'. Moreover, the congressional Iran/Contra hearings did more to cover-up the scandal than investigate it (Andersen 2006: 129-145). Media coverage transformed Oliver North, one of the principal organisers of the illegal shipments, into a national folk hero. As Andersen (1992: 173) argues:

> Particularly in the absence of context, the focus on a character and personality is a convenient substitution for explaining a complicated and deliberately obscure political process. News coverage of the testimony of North emphasised the military man as a personality while the most damaging and serious of his actions remain secrets kept from the American people.

Significantly, as Todd, Bloch and Fitzgerald point out (2009: 36-37), many of those indicted (and later pardoned) US officials involved in the Iran-Contra scandal would remain influential in US policy circles and resume office under George W. Bush: assistant secretary of state Eliot Abrams and former NSC consultant Michael Ledeen, who joined Douglas Feith's Office of Special Plans, teaming up with fellow Iran-Contra veteran, arms dealer and alleged Mossad agent Manucher Ghorbanifar, to direct supposed intelligence on Iran's nuclear programme to the US government and media.

NOTES

[1] Hezbollah were originally blamed for the attack. In May 2003, a US federal judge found Iran responsible for the bombing (see http://news.bbc.co.uk/1/hi/world/americas/2951938.stm, accessed on 14 October 2006). US court papers described the blast as the 'largest non-nuclear explosion that had ever been detonated on the face of the earth'. The mastermind of the bombing plot, Ali Reza Asgari, was allegedly (and somewhat sensationally) resettled in the US by the CIA in return for divulging Tehran's nuclear programme, according to Kal Bird, author of *The good spy* (see Harnden 2014)

[2] In March 1984, William Buckley, CIA Beirut station chief, was kidnapped. He died more than a year later still in captivity: see https://verbena19.wordpress.com/2007/06/26/tomgram-roger-morris-the-cia-and-the-gates-legacy/, accessed on 22 August 2016

[3] The French launched retaliatory air strikes against Hezbollah's headquarters in Baalbeck, Lebanon, on 16 November but reconnaissance photographs afterwards revealed that the HQ had been missed entirely. Twenty three US jets attacked the same target on 4 December – but they also failed to hit the target. Two planes were lost, with one pilot killed and his bombardier captured by the Syrians (Clancy 2003: 254-255). In another revenge attack, allegedly organised by the CIA and British intelligence, Islamic cleric Sayyed Mohammad Hussein Fadlallah was the target of a car bomb attack in Beirut, Lebanon, on 8 March 1985. According to Mike Davis, the CIA's operatives actually proved incapable of carrying out the bombing, so CIA director William Casey sub-contracted the operation to Lebanese agents led by a former British SAS (Special Air Service) officer

and financed by Saudi ambassador Prince Bandar bin Sultan bin Abdul Aziz. Fadlallah escaped but 80 people were killed and 200 injured, almost all of them civilians. See http://www.atimes. com/atimes/Front_Page/HD18Aa01.html# and https://verbena19.wordpress.com/2007/06/26/ tomgram-roger-morris-the-cia-and-the-gates-legacy/

[4] According to Bob Woodward (1987: 290): 'CIA records show that at one point $100,000 had been passed to her government for a secret support operation.' But Charles later denied any knowledge of any direct payment to her, her party or her government (ibid)

[5] In the aftermath of the US invasion, Bernard Coard, Hudson Austin and their associates (including Phyllis Coard, Selwyn Strachan, John Ventour, Liam James and Keith Roberts) were sentenced to death (commuted first to life imprisonment and then to 30 years' imprisonment). The US gave Grenada a grant of US$48.4m. in 1984. In 2007, the Chinese paid US$40m to Grenada towards the construction of a new stadium for the Cricket World Cup. As Goodwin argues (2008: 43): 'It is an indication that with American eyes turned increasingly to the Middle East, economic competition has replaced political confrontation in the quest for influence'

[6] David Yallop (1994: 207-208) reports that the US originally planned to send in the Marines (with British support) to remove Gaddafi shortly after the coup. But President Nixon and Henry Kissinger considered Gaddafi held two aces: Libyan oil and his intense dislike of godless communism. 'If the President sent in the Marines and the new regime were overthrown, there was no guarantee that whoever replaced it would be as hostile towards Moscow as this devote Muslim. The President decided that Libya's new leader was a man "he could do business with" and the plan to invade Libya was filed'

[7] Curtis (2010: 225) reports that the Libyan regime in 1969 'provided a quarter of Britain's oil and was home to £100 million worth of British oil investment'. The security of oil supplies 'must be our greatest concern', one foreign office official noted a year after the revolution

[8] Significantly, in October 1985 the Soviet Union refused to sign a treaty of friendship and co-operation with Libya – distrusting Gaddafi's 'violently anti-American policy' (Gresh and Vidal 1990: 122)

[9] See https://www.amnesty.org/download/Documents/120000/afr200042001fr.pdf, accessed on 9 April 2016. Habré was included on a list of leaders provided with security and intelligence aid by the CIA (see Woodward 1987: 310-311): others were Pakistani President Mohammed Zia, Liberia's leader Samuel K. Doe, Philippine President Marcos, Sudan President Nimeiri, Lebanese President Gemayel and President Duarte of El Salvador

[10] Commander of the Libyan forces, Khalifa Haftar, was captured. Disowned by Gaddafi he joined an exile brigade, the Libyan National Army. After a spell building up contacts with the CIA in the US, Haftar returned to Benghazi for the Libyan uprising of 2011. By May 2014 he was leading opposition to the government in Tripoli (Stephen and Black 2014)

[11] In 1977, *Playboy* ran a story in which convicted burglar Carmen Falzone claimed Sirhan Sirhan confessed his guilt for the murder of Robert Kennedy on 6 June 1968 and even conspired with him to smuggle plutonium to Muammar Gaddafi in Libya. As Shane O'Sullivan comments: 'This unlikely plot was used as evidence by the state in its successful attempt to rescind Sirhan's parole date in 1982' (see http://whowhatwhy.org/2016/03/14/the-tortured-logic-behind-sirhan-sirhans-parole-denial/, accessed on 23 March 2016)

[12] See MI5 in the firing line, *Private Eye*, 8-21 January 2016 p. 31

[13] On 21 January 1984, shortly before Fletcher's death, Libya's ambassador to Italy was murdered in Rome: al-Burkan claimed responsibility. As Daniel Kawczynski comments: 'It is likely that the assassination of one of Gaddafi's own intensified the pressure on the people's bureau/embassy in London, ratcheting up efforts to quell opposition there' (see *Seeking Gaddafi: Libya, the West and the Arab Spring*, Biteback, 2011. Available online at https://books.google.co.uk/books?id=O_CtAwAAQBAJ&pg=PT105&redir_esc=y#v=onepage&q&f=false, accessed on 11 January 2016)

[14] Op cit, *Private Eye*

[15] Bob Woodward reports (1987: 445-446): 'Eight, perhaps nine F111c bombers, each carrying four 2,000-pound laser-guided bombs, were to attack Qaddafi's own barracks, Splendid Gate. At least thirty-two bombs from the F111 planes were supposed to strike the compound, but at most four, perhaps as few as two, actually hit. A number of F111s had to turn back from the 14-hour, 2,800-mile flight from England; France would not permit them to overfly, making the route longer. It was a high-tech failure that was kept secret; even DIA analysts were not given the details'

[16] On 13 November 2001, four people were jailed in Berlin for the attack on la Belle disco. They were Musbah Abdulghasem Eter, a Libyan diplomat; Yassir Chraidi, a Palestinian employed by the Libyan embassy in East Berlin; Ali Channa, a Lebanese man; and Verena Channa, his German former wife, who was working for the Libyan secret agency at the time. Much of the evidence was based on files seized from the Stasi headquarters after the fall of the Berlin Wall. The documents revealed the East German secret police knew of the plot because the Channas were moonlighting for them (see Karacs, Imre (2001) Germany sentences four to jail for 1986 bombing, *Independent*, 14 November)

[17] Adie's solicitor subsequently issued libel proceedings against both the newspaper and reporter

[18] Perceptions of Gaddafi as 'eccentric' persisted even after the US and UK détente with Libya in 2003 when he reputedly renounced weapons of mass destruction and agreed to pay compensation for the Lockerbie bombing. Gene Cretz, US ambassador to Tripoli, sent a cable to Washington, in 2009 ahead of Gaddafi arriving for a UN General Assembly, entitled *A glimpse into Libyan leader Gaddafi's eccentricities*. It was revealed by the WikiLeaks whistleblowing site in January 2011. Cretz was recalled for consultations at the US state department (see Usborne 2011a). Targeted assassination of heads of countries has long been a policy of the US. For instance, Tom Bower reports on the US in 1960 (1995: 225): 'Within the new CIA headquarters in Langley, Virginia, the talk, reflecting conversations with the new president John Kennedy and his brother Robert, appointed attorney general, was about "getting rid" of presidents: Fidel Castro of Cuba, Rafael Trujillo of the Dominican Republic, Patrice Lumumba in the Congo and Achmad Sukarno of Indonesia were all at one time targeted for assassination'

[19] According to Clive Bloom (2015: 161), the F111s from Tactical Fighter Wing at Lakenheath were joined by 28 KC10 and KC135 transport and refuelling planes from Fairford and Mildenhall as well as five EF111 electronic counter-measure planes from Upper Heyford, all of which then met up with the Sixth Fleet

[20] Freelance journalist Alex Collett was murdered soon afterwards (having been taken hostage the year before at a checkpoint near Beirut manned by members of the Shi'a Muslim Amal movement) in revenge for the attacks on Libya. His body was recovered from the Lebanon's Bekaa Valley in November 2009 (Fisk 2009)

[21] See, for instance, http://www.time.com/time/world/article/0,8599,2088074,00.html, http://www.guardian.co.uk/world/2011/aug/26/hana-gaddafi-daughter-mystery and http://www.guardian.co.uk/world/middle-east-live/2011/aug/26/libya-rebels-hunt-gaddafi-live-updates, http://www.telegraph.co.uk/journalists/martin-evans/8725024/Libya-Hana-Gaddafi-alive-and-well.html, all accessed on 27 August 2011

[22] In email from Pierre Lethier to the author, 6 May 2011

[23] Secret files released to the National Archive in 2009 revealed that the Labour government of Harold Wilson in 1975 had offered to pay Gaddafi £14 million (the equivalent of £500 million today) in return for Libya ending its military support for the IRA. The offer was dropped after Gaddafi demanded £51 million (£1.5 billion today) (see Verkaik 2009)

[24] See Stephen Dorril, in *The silent conspiracy: Inside the intelligence services in the 1990s*, London: Heinemann 1993 pp 241-242. In June 1992, Libya agreed to provide information on shipments

and IRA contacts to the IRA to Edward Chapman, the British *chargé d'affaires* at the British mission to the UN in Geneva. 'This followed international pressure on Libya to "contribute to the elimination of international terrorism" following its alleged involvement in the Lockerbie bombing' (ibid)

[25] On 31 January 2001, Abdelbaset al-Megrahi, former head of security for Libyan Arab Airlines, had been controversially convicted by a panel of three Scottish judges sitting in a special court at Camp Zeist in the Netherlands, of 270 counts of murder for the bombing of Pan Am Flight 103 over Lockerbie in 1988 and demanded a payment of £51 million (£1.5 billion today). Yet evidence emerged following the trial that raised serious questions about the conviction. For instance, Tony Gauci, in whose shop in Malta al-Megrahi allegedly purchased clothes that ended up in the suitcase with the bomb, had expressed interest in receiving an award and following the conviction, Scottish police secretly sought a $2 million payment from the US department of justice. As part of the Libyan moves to rejoin the 'international community', in 2004 the government formally accepted responsibility for Lockerbie – though it stressed it was only doing so to end the UN sanctions. It also agreed to pay $2.7 billion in compensation to the 270 families of the victims. By 2008, those opposing the conviction included Dr Jim Swire and the Rev. John Mosey, each of whom lost a daughter in the bombing, Archbishop Desmond Tutu and the head of the Catholic Church in Scotland, Cardinal Keith O'Brien. Al-Megrahi was released on compassionate grounds by the Scottish government in August 2009 following doctors' reports that he had terminal prostate cancer and had only a few months to live. Immediately following the fall of Gaddafi's Tripoli compound to the rebels in August 2011, calls to re-arrest al-Megrahi were given prominent coverage in the mainstream media in the UK and US. Stephen Dorril, in *The silent conspiracy: Inside the intelligence services in the 1990s*, London: Heinemann 1993 pp 288-289 reports Brian Keenan, one of the released Beirut hostages, revealing in 1992 a 'strange story connected Lockerbie'. Following his release in the summer of 1990, he was interviewed by Syrian intelligence: 'They said the British knew all about Lockerbie. They said the British had all sorts of information prior to the event.' In May 2016, *Private Eye* (No. 1417 p. 40) claimed the conviction of al-Megrahi was 'at best, flaky and, at worst, had the whiff of cover-up'. '…most significantly, new scientific evidence – a small fragment of circuit board recovered from the debris of Pan Am 2013 – was not, as the prosecution had claimed, a match for Libyan timers.' In an earlier report (No. 1246, 2-15 October 2009), *Private Eye* had highlighted the activities of terrorist organisations, the Palestinian Popular Struggle Front and the Popular Front for the Liberation of Palestine – General Command, who 'were working together from cells operating out of Germany, Sweden, Yugoslavia, Cyprus and – as became evident during the Lockerbie investigation – also out of Malta'

[26] Anas al-Liby, a member of the group, was given political asylum in Britain and lived there until May 2000 despite suspicions that he is an important al-Qaeda figure. He is later implicated in the al-Qaeda bombing of two US embassies in Africa in 1998. See http://www.historycommons.org/searchResults.jsp?searchtext=MI5&events=on&entities=on&articles=on&topics=on&timelines=on&projects=on&titles=on&descriptions=on&dosearch=on&search=Go, accessed on 3 April 2016

[27] Machon op cit: 172; Jaber, Hala (2010) Libyans thwart Fletcher inquiry, *Sunday Times*, 19 September; Thomas, Gordon (2009) I*nside British intelligence: 100 Years of MI5 and MI6*, London: JR Books p. 23. Curtis further reports (2010: 228): 'US intelligence sources later told the *Mail on Sunday* newspaper that MI6 had indeed been behind the assassination plot and had turned to the LIFG's leader, Abu Abdullah Sadiq, who was living in London. The head of the assassination team was reported as being the Libya-based Abd al-Muhaymeen, a veteran of the Afghan resistance and thus possibly trained by MI6 or the CIA.' It was only in 2005, after the London 7/7 bombings that the British government designated the LIFG a terrorist group (ibid: 229)

[28] This was the first time music being played at maximum volume was used as a 'torture' technique by the US military. It was frequently used later at Guantanamo Bay, the detention/torture base on Cuba, and elsewhere by the CIA. Amongst the songs most used are Metallica's Enter Sandman,

Eminem's White America, AC/DC's Hell's Bells and the Sesame Street theme song. On 10 December 2008, on the 60th anniversary of the Universal Declaration of Human Rights, a group of musicians including Bruce Springsteen, Rage Against the Machine's Tom Morello and Massive Attack called on the US to stop using their music as an instrument of war. See Campbell, Duncan (2008) Musicians condemn use of their songs as instruments of war, *Guardian*, 11 December. Convicted in Miami in 1992 of trafficking, racketeering and conspiracy, Noriega eventually had his 40-year sentence reduced because of good behaviour. His period in jail ended on 9 September 2007 but then France aimed to try the 73-year-old for allegedly laundering $3m. in drug money through French banks. The offence carried a maximum ten-year sentence

[29] According to Francis Wheen (2004: 178-179): 'While awaiting trial, Noriega was approached by American prosecutors with an extraordinary plea-bargain: he could use cash from his foreign bank accounts (which had been frozen) to hire the best lawyers that dollars could buy, if in return he agreed not to mention that he had been on the payroll of the CIA since the 1970s. As they explained, rather unnecessarily, such an admission could be embarrassing, not least because the director of the CIA at the time of Noreiga's recruitment, in the days of the Ford administration, had been a certain George Bush – who, as president, was now pursuing a "war on drugs"'

[30] After completing his sentence, Noriega was extradited to France where he was jailed in 2010 for money laundering. He returned to Panama in 2011 where he was jailed for crimes committed under his rule. In June 2015, Noriega (81) apologised to his compatriots for the crimes committed by his regime (see http://www.theguardian.com/world/2015/jun/25/manuel-noriega-apologises-over-military-rule-of-panama)

[31] According to Paul Todd, Jonathan Bloch and Patrick Fitzgerald (2009: 36), the sale 'involved 1,508 TOW and 18 Hawk missiles and much ancillary equipment'

[32] Ben-Menashe, Ari (1992) Nobody wanted the scoop, *Lies of Our Time*, New York, June. Reveals the origins of the Irangate deal. Ben-Menashe was working for the external relations department of the Israel Defence Forces and a joint military intelligence-Mossad committee for Iran-Israel relations. The committee was involved in massive Israeli weapons sales to Iran – with tacit support from the Americans profits were used for Israeli intelligence activities. But then Oliver North set up his own operation in an attempt to sabotage the Israelis. 'We knew that his operation, with the assistance of the CIA, was skimming huge profits from the Iranian arms deals and channelling funds to the Contras; we also knew that this was in violation of US law at the time. I was asked to leak the story.' He discussed it with a number of leading US journalists. None could get it published. He ends rather cryptically: 'Why I still wonder, was an insider like myself unable to get either *Time* or *Newsweek* to touch the same story that the whole world ran when it appeared, unattributed, in an obscure Lebanese journal'

Chapter Five

Ending history: The press and Saddam Hussein

Following the invasion of Kuwait by Iraqi troops on 2 August 1990, the press in the UK (and US) focused primarily on the personality of Saddam Hussein, President of Iraq. A number of controversies (the supergun affair, the execution of the journalist Farzad Bazoft,[1] the interception of nuclear triggers bound for Iraq) had brought Saddam Hussein a certain amount of negative coverage in the Western media in the previous six months. Such coverage reflected the ambivalent attitude of the US/UK secret state to Saddam Hussein at this time.

Moreover, new militarism, as a system aiming to resolve the problems of militarism within advanced capitalist societies, was dependent on a public largely depoliticised and, more specifically, ignorant of the dynamics and history of the Third World. As Michael Traber and Ann Davis comment (1991: 7): 'Ignorance of the affairs of a nation's ordinary people is useful in the construction of the image of the enemy. The less we know of the enemy the easier it is to create the image that we wish. The mass media have built up or, at least, reinforced a social cosmology which divides the world into angels and devils, the good and the bad.' Premised on this ignorance and reinforcing it, a massive propaganda campaign was launched by the press and media in general to demonise this formerly unknown Iraqi leader and legitimise the response of the Western powers to the Kuwait invasion.

THE MYSTERY OF THE HALABJA ATROCITY

The representation of Saddam Hussein effectively as Iraq only emerged in the months leading up to August 1990 and then completely dominated the coverage throughout all the British media. Before the Kuwait invasion, the principal bogeyman in the Middle East for the mainstream press was Iran. Searle (1989) demonstrates how the *Sun's* racist venom was directed at this country throughout the 1980s. For instance, on 18 October 1987, after the US destroyed two Iranian ex-oil rigs in the Gulf, it commented: 'The Americans have enough firepower in the Gulf to render the country a wasteland. Maybe that would not be a bad thing for the rest of humanity.'

During the Iran-Iraq war (1980-1988) Iraq was, in general, referred to simply as 'Iraq' or 'Baghdad'. The CIA had engineered a secret 'tilt' towards Iraq in 1982 just as Iranian Revolutionary Guards were threatening to break through the country's defences. Intelligence and military links were expanded after Reagan was elected for a second term (Perry 1992: 381-383). As significant sections of the West tilted towards Iraq so the personalising of that country through Saddam Hussein declined. Robert Freedman (1991) highlights reports in the Western press which spoke approvingly of Saddam's moves to privatise the economy in the mid-1980s and he was even compared to Mrs Margaret Thatcher, the British Prime Minister, in this context. As Dilip Hiro reports (1992: 45): 'The [1980-1988 Iraq/Iran] war brought about a marked change in the Ba'ath Party itself. In the name of increasing production, the importance of Ba'athist socialism was minimized and the private sector encouraged to grow at the expense of the public sector.' The BBC's John Simpson commented (1991b: 9):

> Before the war [of 1991], it was customary for journalists and academics writing about Iraq to take some at least of the carefully marshalled demonstrations of love and support for Saddam Hussein at face value. ... Among Western academics specialising in Iraq, Peter Sluglett, of Durham University, and Marion Farouk-Sluglett, of the University College of Wales [1990], were in a minority when they questioned whether ordinary Iraqis provided Saddam with anything more than lip-service.

Even the press coverage of the chemical bombing of Kurds in Halabja on 16 March 1988 was notable for its comparative restraint (Rose and Baravi 1988; Teimourian 1988). Yet more than 5,000 civilians were slaughtered and another 7,000 maimed for life. Timmerman (1992: 293) suggests the gas was a hydrogen cyanide compound the Iraqis had developed with the help of a German company. Made in the Samarra gas works, it was similar to the poison gas the Nazis had used to exterminate the Jews more than 40 years earlier. Survivors interviewed by Human Rights Watch/Middle East confirmed that the bombs were dropped from Iraqi and not Iranian planes since they flew low enough for their markings to be legible (Human Rights Watch 1995: 70). Human Rights Watch also listed 60 Kurdish villages attacked with mustard gas, nerve gas and a combination of the two over the previous two years (ibid: 262-265).

Little blame was levelled personally at Saddam Hussein in the press for the Halabja atrocity. No Hitler/Nazi jibes emerged. The *Guardian* of 17 March 1988 was typical: 'It is hard to conceive of any explanation for the chemical bombardment of Halabja other than one which Iranians and Kurds offer – revenge.' The madness of Saddam Hussein, his lust for power were nowhere identified as the causes of the outrage. While a 24 March editorial defined the atrocity as 'Iraq's latest and greatest war crime', it mirrored the government's position on the war taking no side and calling for a ceasefire. At the same time the press gave considerable prominence to US government claims that Iranians were responsible for the chemical attacks. *The Times* carried prominently the reported headlined 'US evidence suggests Iran also use chemicals' while the *Guardian* quoted a Reuters report of US state department spokesman Charles Redman claiming: 'There are indications that Iran may have also used chemical artillery shells in the fighting.' John Pilger reports that at the time of the Halabja atrocity ('news of which the Foreign Office tried to suppress') foreign office minister David Mellor was actually being entertained by the Iraqis in Baghdad (Pilger 2002: 63).

Six weeks after the attack, a UN report, made by a Spanish military doctor, Col. Manuel Dominguez Carmona, concluded it was impossible to say whether Iraq or Iran or both were to blame (Bulloch and Morris 1992: 144). In February 1990, a US Army War College report concluded that Iraq was not responsible for the Halabja massacre and that 'it was the Iranian bombardment that actually killed the Kurds' (Pelletiere, Johnson and Rosenberger 1990; see also Yant 1991: 109 and Pelletiere 2003). Was this mere US government-inspired disinformation since Iraq was then a close ally? For example, in 1989, during an exchange in the house of lords over a decision to guarantee new credits to Iraq of up to £250 million, Lord Trefgarne, for the government, said: '…we are a major trading nation. I am afraid that we have to do business with a number of countries with whose policies we very often disagree' (Fisk 2006: 206). Certainly the media at the time raised serious questions about the supposed guilt of Iraq. These doubts were completely absent in the coverage of the 1990 crisis and the later massacres. The Halabja bombing, rather, featured prominently in all the demonisation propaganda directed at the Iraqi leader, with Hussein condemned as 'a man who would bomb his own people'.

Just four months after the atrocity, Washington stood by as the US giant Bechtel corporation won the contract to build a huge petrochemical plant that would provide Iraq the ability to generate chemical weapons (Dixon 2004). Moreover, in the year following the Halabja atrocity, Britain sold Iraq an estimated £300 million worth of military materials, including chemicals for the production of chemical weapons, while the US sold the equivalent of £1 billion worth of armaments (TUCND n.d.: 10). John Pilger reports that the UK's trade with Iraq rose from £2.9 million to £31.5 million between 1987 and 1988. 'Iraq was now Britain's third largest market for machine tools, many of which were for "dual use" – that is, they made weapons' (2002). The US also provided vast amounts of grain to Iraq with $5 billion of government loan guarantees from 1983-1990 (Herman 1992: 51). Hiro (1992: 95) sums up the US attitude to Iraq during the 1980s in this way:

> Over the years the Ba'athist regime of Saddam Hussein came to be perceived in Washington as secular and tolerable, a stabilizing influence in a region prone to volatility. Its regime came off rather well when compared

to those in such Arab countries as Syria (penniless, tied to Moscow), Lebanon (wracked by a long and bloody civil war), Libya (headed by a megalomaniac maverick), or Egypt (highly bureaucratic, debt-ridden).

Significantly, in 1992, a US congressional inquiry found that President George Bush and his top advisers had ordered a cover-up of their covert support for Saddam Hussein – with illegal arms shipments sent via third countries such as South Africa and Chile (Pilger 2002: 66).

THE END OF HISTORY? REINFORCING THE MYTHS UNDERLYING NEW MILITARISM

The ideological framework legitimising the response of the Western elites to the Kuwaiti crisis (of which hyper-personalisation was an important ingredient) had, to a considerable degree, been provided some months earlier by an obscure writer in an equally obscure American magazine. Francis Fukuyama, deputy director of the US state department's policy planning staff, in the summer 1989 edition of the *National Interest*, had contributed a 16-page essay entitled 'The end of history?' (1989).

Heralded by all the major media outlets in the West, Fukuyama was rapidly to become the intellectual guru *par excellence* of the day. The end of the Cold War, the collapse of the Soviet Union, had proved the victory of consumerist Western democracy over totalitarian Marxism. 'What we may be witnessing is not just the end of history as such; that is the end point of mankind's ideological evolution and the universalization of Western liberal democracy as the final form of human government,' he wrote (ibid: 3).

Western elites could not believe their luck. Here was a man who seemed to offer intellectual respectability to their triumphalist feelings over the collapse of the Soviet Union. The intellectual flavour of the previous year had been provided by historian Paul Kennedy whose *Decline and fall of the great powers: Economic change and military conflict from 1500 to 2000* (1988), had given much scope for the American imperial elite to indulge their fears of vulnerability. Now Fukuyama's theories could help replace Kennedy's introverted anxieties and pessimism with an unabashed optimism about the global possibilities of American-led capitalism. The ideological implications of Fukuyama's fundamentally simple theories were extremely varied. For instance, it was to articulate and in the process help justify the silencing of the history of the Middle East and of other non-capitalist/Arab/ Islamic histories which the Western elite and mainstream media sought to achieve during the Gulf crisis.

Equally, the Fukuyama theories served to legitimise the silencing of the history of Western imperialism both past and present in the region. In many ways, too, the theories articulated some of the most potent contradictions in the US/UK's elite worldview. On the one hand they sought to escape the traumas of the past (as in Vietnam) into the triumphant, ever present and mediacentric 'now'; yet on the other hand they were unable to escape the grip of the past. Moreover, central to Fukuyama's argument was the belief that liberal democracies of the US type are inherently peaceful. Most intriguingly of all, Fukuyama promoted the illusion of demilitarisation just at the moment when the US military was running 'out of control'. Thus the end of history theory articulated to a mass audience the myth of demilitarisation so crucial a component of new militarism.

IDEOLOGICAL FUNCTION OF THE HUMAN INTEREST STORY

The hyper-personalisation of the Kuwaiti crisis can be seen as an extension of the Fukuyama project. For in the process an enormously complex history was grossly over-simplified and distorted while attention was distracted from other more important social, political, geostrategic, religious and environmental factors.

The human interest angle, of which the Saddam Hussein coverage was a manifestation, is deeply embedded in the journalists' culture. As Keeble and Wheeler identify (2007c: 10-11), a fascination with 'human interest' has been at the core of the journalistic imagination since it emerged in the 17th century. Nor is it confined to the popular press. An ideological consensus informs all the mainstream media and an integral feature of it is the human interest bias (Curran, Douglas and Whannel 1980: 306; Chibnall 1977: 26). The human interest bias is built into the professional routines of journalists – the interview, the source, the profile, the human descriptive 'colour' form the essential basis of most mainstream journalism (Joseph and Keeble 2015; Joseph and Keeble 2016). Such a bias also makes financial sense: people are intrigued by other people; revelations of people's secrets form the basis for countless reports and features. As John Taylor sums up (1991: 2): 'The concept of news as human interest has remained stable because it has consistently sold newspapers. These stories are the most widely read in both tabloids and broadsheets. Their appeal carries across differences between men and women, young and old, middle class and working class.' Indeed, the human interest focus reinforces the media's function as entertainment above that of political informant, analyst or critic (Postman 1985, Thussu 2007).

The human interest bias is all the more predictable when the press deals with dictators such as Saddam Hussein. The Iraqi leader, since becoming president in 1979, had taken over full control of the state apparatus. He commanded all aspects of foreign and domestic policy and ruthlessly eliminated opponents. When dictators are 'friends' of the West the personalising of their coverage can be muted. When they become 'enemies' and the focus of assassination attempts, the size of their personal power and their 'monstrosities' provide the press with all the propaganda 'ammunition' they require.

HITLER HUSSEIN

One of the most features of the coverage of the Iraqi invasion of Kuwait was the focus on Saddam Hussein as the new Hitler. The *Telegraph*, of 3 August, wrote: 'President Hussein's decision to invade Kuwait is proof of his Hitlerian determination to get his own way.' Robert Harvey, in a leader page feature, commented: 'For once the overworked comparison with Hitler is apposite.' The *Mail* editorial of the same day commented: 'Like a rerun of Hitler's invasion of Czechoslovakia in the 1930s, the Iraqi dictatorship has flouted international opinion and grabbed a small but wealthy neighbour. Nothing justifies this outrage.' In the *Sun* of 4 August, Dr John Laffing, described as an expert on Arab affairs and author of 109 books including *The Arab mind* and *The man the Nazis couldn't catch*, wrote that 'power-crazed tyrant Saddam Hussein was exposed yesterday as a Fuhrer freak who models himself on Adolf Hitler' and had set up a shrine to the Nazi leader.

On 5 August, *The Sunday Times* said of the Iraqi invasion: 'It was a strategy on Hitlerian lines: the annexation by blitzkrieg of a weak neighbour.' The *Observer* editorial of the same day commented: 'Why this Hitler of the Gulf has to go.' 'It is going to be difficult to get out of this one without the exchange of rocket fire. If the comparison with Hitler holds good, it may prove impossible.' And the editorial went on: 'Comparing people to Hitler can be counter-productive as Sir Anthony Eden (over Nasser) and Nicholas Ridley (over Chancellor Kohl) both found to their cost. But in Saddam Hussein the world is facing another Hitler. ... He has the same kind of expansionist ambitions and brutal lack of humanity. Like the German Fuhrer he has an underlying vision of an all-powerful Iraq funded by oil and backed by force.'

The *Independent* of 3 August editorialised: 'The appetites of dictators grow with what they feed upon as Europe learnt to its cost when dealing with Hitler.' And its profile of 11 August began: 'In the overworn comparison with Hitler and Stalin there is a kernel of truth. For he shares the secret of great dictators – he understands the psychotic relationship between fear and love.' The *Mirror* intoned: 'Saddam Hussein is the Adolf Hitler[2] of the Arab world. If he isn't stopped now the West will pay a heavy price.' On 3 August, *Today* reported: 'The new Hitler of the Middle East, Saddam Hussein, held the world at bay last night after invading Kuwait.'

A similar focus was made in the American press coverage. The Gannett Foundation study found 1,035 mentions of Hitler from 1 August to 28 February 1991 in the print media (Gannett Foundation 1991: 42). On both sides of the Atlantic the analogy was reinforced in cartoon representations. Macarthur comments (1993: 72): 'Hardly any reporters were heard challenging the President in his Hitler comparisons at press conferences.'

Yet the Hitler angle did not appear to politicians and the press 'naturally' – it served a number of important ideological, propaganda purposes. With the collapse of the Soviet Union, the spectre of the 'communist threat' could no longer be raised as a justification for US/UK military action. As a propaganda tool the Hitler threat was remarkably efficient: it was simple and seemingly unproblematic. In popular rhetoric, Hitler has been transformed into an enormous symbol of evil and danger. Focusing on the enemy as a Hitler could only serve to direct massive emotional negativity to that person – and at the same time elevate the moral purity of the forces lined up against him. As the *Independent* leader of 3 August commented with commendable clarity: 'Since the changes in Russia some people have been lamenting the lack of a convincing enemy. Here he is.'

All the post-August Hitler hype sought to say implicitly: 'There have been many horrible dictators since 1945 but Saddam Hussein is the worst of all.' But by no sensible historical criteria could the validity of that assertion be assessed: it is merely serving rhetorical, ideological and ultimately political/military purposes. The *Sun* reported on 3 August: 'The beast of Baghdad inherited the title of the world's most evil dictator when Romania's President Ceaucescu was executed last Christmas day.' John Kay compiled a feature on the '10 dangerous despots that deal in death'. Predictably, top of the (somewhat eccentric) list – missing out such dictators as the US-backed Marcos, Papa Doc, Pinochet and Zia – came Saddam Hussein. Then came Gaddafi, 'the mad dog dictator who believes Shakespeare was an Arab called Sheik Spear'; 'potty' Pol Pot, Ramiz Alia and Idi Amin. Norman McCrae commented in *The Sunday Times* of 30 December: 'Saddam Hussein is an archetype of the Third World's nastiest dictators with a recently reiterated record of torture actually worse than that of the Gestapo.'

The endlessly repeated Hitler analogy represented a highly selective, ideologically motivated use of history by the US and its prominent allies. For its essential purpose was to draw on pre-Cold War rhetoric to silence many histories – in particular the imperial roles of the US and UK in the Middle East and more globally. As John Schostak (1993: 85) commented:

> By evoking the experiences now overlaid with the mythology of the Second World War, Hussein's actions and the West's counter-actions could be explained simply and simplistically to the public. The complex history of involvement by the West in Middle Eastern affairs, which had allowed tyrants to arise and be supported, was largely glossed over. The invasions and subversions carried out by Western powers all over the world could be ignored in this simplistic drama echoing the fight against good and evil.

Saddam Hussein without question was a brutal dictator. Yet for many years, the West had been happy to cultivate Iraq as a 'friend'. Significantly, the CIA was closely involved in the 1963 coup in Iraq which brought the Ba'athists to power for the first time. According to James Critchfield, then head of the CIA in the Middle East: 'We regarded it as a great victory' (cited in Pilger 2002: 65). King Hussein of Jordan, who was himself closely linked to US intelligence agencies, confirmed this in an interview with Mohamed Heikal, editor-in-chief (1957-1974) of Egypt's most influential daily, *al-Ahram* (published on 27 September 1963) (Ali 2003: 87-88).[3] Iraq, supported by the United States, invaded Iran on 17 September 1980 – and so began a terrible, eight year conflict.[4] By the end, the social infrastructures of both countries were wrecked. Some 262,000 Iranians and 105,000 Iraqis died. At least 700,000 were injured. The financial costs also were appalling: Iraq wasted US$74-US$91 billion on waging the war while Iran's defence costs amounted to US$94-US$112 billion with a further US$11.26 spent on buying more weapons (ibid: 129).

For Britain and America the confrontation against Iraq could be represented as a new struggle, a crusade even (Christian metaphors being used prominently throughout) to reverse the aggression of a brutal dictator. In this context, according to Barney Dickson (1991: 43), the post-imperial rhetoric of global responsibility could be invoked. The Hitler analogy also served a critical role in the complex, multi-faceted propaganda project to highlight the military option above the diplomatic one – after all, Hitler was removed only by force (Glasgow University Media Group 1991: 3). As Christopher Layne comments (1991): 'The 1930s analogy rests on the assumption that "aggression" must be resisted, not appeased whenever it occurs because it will snowball unless firmly stopped.' It was a sort of variant of the Cold War, old order domino theory which drove the US into the debacle of Vietnam. Those who questioned the Bush agenda were thus labelled 'appeasers' (returning again to the pre-1939 rhetoric) and thus saddled with all the negative connotations of that word. It served to highlight Saddam Hussein and the country he was supposedly running as a powerful, global threat which needed to be tamed or destroyed if President Bush's 'New World Order' was to be established.

Thus it was a crucial element of the ideological mystification that sought to represent the conflict as a legitimate war between two credible armies when in reality it was very different – an unnecessary series of slaughters of thousands of civilians and conscripts. David E. Morrison (1992: 18), in his detailed analysis of public responses to media coverage of the 'war', records how most interviewees reproduced what they both heard and saw in the media. 'He was like Hitler. He didn't care. I mean the way he treated people' is one representative view quoted.

BEHIND THE HITLER HYPE – CONTRADICTIONS

Yet there were many more ambivalences and contradictions in the Hitler angle which the press significantly avoided in their sensationalist, unproblematic coverage. Hitler, after all, had drawn considerable support from sections of the ruling elites of Europe and North America (in the City of London and Wall Street) in the six years leading up to the outbreak of hostilities (Sutton 1976, Aris and Campbell 2004). He was seen as a useful bulwark to the more serious threat of Soviet communism. And his authoritarianism and racism appealed to many in the elite. After all, Lord Rothermere, owner of the *Daily Mail*, had launched a campaign in support of the Nazi Party and backed Oswald Mosley and the National Union of Facists.[5]

Equally, Saddam Hussein was most effectively appeased from 1980 to 2 August 1990 by significant sections of the ruling elites in America, the West and East in general. This ambivalence was rarely highlighted in the media. Iraqgate/Saddamgate had to wait two years before emerging (rather tamely since this was election year, after all) in the United States and even longer in the UK. The emphasis on Second World War rhetoric (with references to 'the allies', the 'liberation of Kuwait', even the planned amphibious landing by the Marines all reinforcing its emotive power) also distanced countries such as Germany and Japan from the US/UK military adventure (Sadria 1992).

After the massacres, with Saddam Hussein still in power (and with the US maintaining its pre-invasion policy of ambivalence towards the Iraqi regime) the Hitler analogies suddenly disappeared from the media. The analogy was exposed as an ideological device to legitimise the US/allied stance. Once the complexities of the Middle East and the contradictions and hypocrisies of the US strategy emerged after the massacres, the Hitler analogy with its crude over-simplifications, faded.

MADMAN SADDAM

Along with Saddam as Hitler, the other dominant aspect of the coverage of Iraq after the Kuwait invasion was to represent him as mad. On 7 August, John Kay wrote in the *Sun*: 'Britain's elite SAS regiment could assassinate crazed Iraqi President – and defuse the growing Gulf crisis – in one blow.' The *Guardian* editorialised: 'In the two years since the Gulf war ended it has been at times hard to decide which of the two deranged regimes that staggered out of that bloody conflict was the more deranged or more dangerous.' The *Daily Mail*, of 3 August, in a centre spread headlined 'A new Hitler plots his empire', described Saddam Hussein as a megalomaniac. The *Express* headlined: 'Mad despot who wants to rule the Arab world.' The story beneath gave prominence to a piece of Mossad disinformation which was to feature regularly in the press in the lead-up to the massacres. It reported: 'This week an Israeli graphologist who examined the handwriting at the request of the secret service Mossad – without knowing the identity of the author – ruled that he is in urgent need of psychiatric treatment.'

Linked to this representation was the emphasis (and by association those who supported him) on being a barbarous, brutal beast. In effect, the press was portraying him as a monster, non-human, uncivilised and thus worthy of any treatment dealt him. The *Mirror* profiled him on 3 August: 'Already he is a mass murderer, a man guilty of genocide, a monster who has used gas and weapons on civilians and enemy troops and whose war with Iran cost half a million lives.' On 7 August, the *Sun* evoked the animal metaphor in this obscene way: 'A stone lifted at the Iraqi embassy in London yesterday and a reptile crawled out.' They were referring to ambassador Shafiq Al-Salih who supposedly shrugged when asked the fate of the British 'hostages' in Iraq. The newspaper continued: 'We hope an American B-52 wipes the crooked smile from his lips.'

In much of the coverage, Saddam is presented as the embodiment of evil. The *Mail* of 3 August: 'Hussein is known to approve 30 types of torture. They include mutilation, gorging out of eyes, cutting off the nose, sex organs and limbs, hammering nails into the body, burning with hot irons and roasting victims over flames.' What is striking about this dominant genre of Saddam profiling is the way in which he is represented as existing in a natural state of bloodthirsty anarchy in which none of the normal human factors operate. The history of British/American/ Western imperialism, political, religious, environmental dynamics play no part in this biography. It is completely untouched by history. There is little concept of Saddam Hussein as a diplomat. Thus the dominant representation remains extraordinarily one-dimensional and consistent throughout the crisis and massacres. As Prince argues on these anti-historical projections and images (1993: 244): 'Iraq was thereby exiled from the modern world and the 20th century, banished to a nameless, pre-civilised period, effectively distanced in spatial, temporal and moral terms from the West.'

The profile in the *Mirror* of 3 August is typical of press coverage. The Iraqi tyrant is said to have swept to power on a 'wave of blood – by killing and torturing his way to the top'. Then follows a list of atrocities committed by Saddam Hussein. No historical explanation or contextualisation is given. He appears to have lived in a timeless zone of barbarism. 'He ordered little children to be tortured in front of their parents. Other youngsters were buried alive. ... Now he heads an evil empire of death squads and employs 100,000 secret policemen to spy on his people.' It continues: 'Five schoolboys were publicly shot after being whipped, beaten and burned with cigarettes because their parents opposed him.' And so on. 'What he can't eat or make love to he kills.' And Margaret Thatcher's much quoted comment on 5 August: 'We can't let the law of the jungle triumph' reinforced the demonisation process.

Focusing on Hussein as an (unpredictable) animal could only serve the ideological purpose of marginalising the diplomatic track – for how could such a 'person' be expected to be trusted or engage in rational negotiations? Yet such a focus incorporated certain contradictions which the press negotiated only awkwardly. For instance, if Hussein was a madman then he was no credible threat. How could such a madman wage credible warfare? So alongside the stress on the madness was a querying of the dominant line in some of the less one-dimensional coverage. Thus Paul Johnson in the *Mail* of 3 August: 'Like Col. Nasser before him he is a boastful self-glorifying liar so easy to ridicule. But he is a more formidable strategist than Nasser and much more dangerous.' The *Mirror* quoted a 'Western diplomat' as saying: 'He is utterly ruthless. But he definitely not mad.' On 26 August, *The Sunday Times* profile of Hussein concluded: 'To psychologists the Iraqi president is clearly suffering from psychosis – a condition manifested by a detachment from reality.' But it adds, carefully: 'Psychosis or not, Saddam still remains a formidable and unpredictable opponent.'

SADDAM HUSSEIN TRAPPED WITHIN THE FRAME OF POPULAR CULTURE

The crisis, with all its immense complexities, was from the outset reported within the dominant frames of popular culture which represent reality as a simple fight between good and evil. As Gilbert Adair said: 'Saddam Hussein himself has become a concentration of pure malevolence, of a type instantly, irresistibly reminiscent of the villains in James Bond movies' (Adair 1991). And Roy Greenslade, then editor of the *Mirror*, later commented in an interview with the author: 'We covered the war in a fairly mainstream, tabloid way. Here was a recognisable enemy. Saddam was an evil man. That was the great assumption.'

According to William F. Fore (1991: 52), the mass media are the devices used by the controllers of our culture to keep it simple. In this they reproduce the rhetoric of the political elite. For instance, President Bush told congress: 'I have resolved all moral questions in my mind: this is a black versus white, good versus evil.' This moralistic, anti-historical rhetoric, reproduced in the press, helped portray the Kuwait invasion as an inexplicable and irrational undertaking. The press reinforced their anti-Iraq propaganda project by covering the developing crisis within the stereotypical frames deeply embedded in popular culture and in the journalists' dominant news value systems. As Jim Lederman, in his study of the US coverage of the Palestinian intifada, comments: 'Journalists, as professional story tellers, need sharply defined and vivid characters, preferably ones that can be identified easily by the audience as good guys and bad guys' (Lederman 1992: 18).

Edward Said and Rana Kabani have outlined the way in which orientalist myths and anti-Islamic clichés are so embedded in Western perceptions (Said 1981, Kabani 1991 and 1994 [1986]). And Stuart Hall (1995: 21) has argued that representations of the 'savage barbarian' lie at the centre of racist ideology. Moreover, in a series of Hollywood blockbusters in the years leading up to the Gulf crisis, Middle Eastern characters served as symbols for greed, primitive behaviour and violence. In films such as *The wind and the lion* (1975), *Black Sunday* (1977), *Rollover* (1981) and *The little drummer girl* (1984), the Orient was viewed as underdeveloped, inferior and the source of chaos, violence and corruption (Prince op cit: 238-248).

The demonisation of Saddam Hussein fell within these racist frames according to which 'Arabs' and 'Islamic fundamentalists' were from the late 1980s coming to replace collapsed 'communism' as the new 'enemy' for the Western elite (Power 1991). But as the veteran war correspondent Chris Hedges comments philosophically (2002: 21):

> We demonize the enemy so that our opponent is no longer human. We view ourselves, our people, as the embodiment of absolute goodness. Our enemies invert our view of the world to justify their own cruelty. In most mythic wars this is the case. Each side reduces the other to objects – eventually in the form of corpses.

Moreover, while Hollywood demonised the Arab world it also responded to the aggressive international posture of the Reagan administration by producing a series of invasion and rescue films (such as *Iron Eagle*, of 1986, *The Delta Force*, of 1986, *Death before dishonour*, of 1987 and *Navy Seals*, of 1990) that implicitly argued the need for strong US presence overseas. Prince argues: 'Films like *Top Gun* and *Rambo* dramatized the heroic ideals of empire and the aggressive heroes of these narratives functioned as personifications of a national will and warrior spirit encoded by the foreign policy rhetoric of the Reagan period' (op cit: 240). Roy Greenslade later admitted pointedly in an interview with the author: 'I can now see that our coverage in the *Mirror* was built on a lot of anti-Iraqi bias, and anti-Moslem bias and an anti-Arab bias.'

Along with the racism in the coverage went a remarkable degree of heavily loaded sexist imagery. Anthony Easthope (1986: 63-65) has highlighted the four essential ingredients of the representation of war in the popular media: defeat, combat, victory and comradeship. For the Western, predominantly male elite (indeed, the only women to feature in the story with any prominence are Margaret Thatcher, Prime Minister, and she is kicked out mid-way – and April Glaspie, the US ambassador to Iraq in July 1990 – and she ends up the principal scapegoat) defeat was to occur in the invasion of Kuwait. Significantly, this invasion was most commonly described by politicians and media as a 'rape'. (Combat and comradeship were to come with the trial of conflict, victory was to come in the end – but it was to prove only illusory.)

The sexual voraciousness of Saddam Hussein (and Iraqis/Moslems in general) was a dominant theme in the popular press coverage of the crisis and massacres. The innocence of tiny Kuwait was constantly mentioned in contrast to the brutality of Saddam who (according to the dominant frame) had personally 'systematically raped' his 'peaceful neighbour'. Under secretary of defense Paul Wolfowitz had asked whether Americans would 'let a man like that get your hands on what are essentially the world's vital organs?' Rape has, in fact, been constantly used throughout American history to legitimise military political offensives. A popular genre of colonial literature featured white women being captured and raped by native Americans while during the Spanish-American war (1898-1901), Hearst newspapers highlighted the kidnapping of a light-skinned Cuban woman to justify US intervention. More recently, President Bush used the sex attack on a US officer's wife in Panama as a pretext for invading that country in December 1989, while the rape of a white woman by a black convict was used by his election campaign team to smear the Democrats' Michael Dukakis in the presidential elections in 1988.

SADDAM HUSSEIN AS THE ARCHETYPAL BAD DAD

Anne Norton has traced a significant element of the press coverage of Saddam Hussein in the representation of the archetypal bad father (Norton 1991). 'Arab hyper masculinity,' she argues, 'is in every sense a domestic matter. Academic and popular accounts of Hafez al-Assad [President of Syria], Saddam Hussein and Gaddafi emphasise their dictatorial domestic rule, their unrestrained use of domestic violence.' Within popular culture, one of the fullest expressions of this domestic dictator appears in the film *Star Wars* (so famous President Reagan called his space militarisation programme after it) with Darth Vader, the dark father armed with an almost (but not quite) invincible war machine that must be stopped. This stereotype was most effectively deployed by the press in their coverage of the Western hostages and, in particular, the meeting between some of them and Saddam Hussein in August 1990.

According to Jean Baudrillard, the prominence given to the hostages' story in the Western media embodied his hyper-real 'non-war' (Baudrillard 1991).

> The hostage has replaced the warrior. Even by pure inactivity he [sic] takes the limelight as the main protagonist in this simulated non-war. Today's hostage is a phantom player. A walk-on who fills the impotent vacuum of modern war. So we have the hostage as the strategic site, the hostage as a Christmas present, the hostage as a bargain counter and as a liquid asset.

In reality, the public had become the real hostages – to media intoxication: 'We are all manipulated in the general indifference ... are all in place as strategic hostages' (ibid). Indeed, a survey conducted by Shaw and Carr-Hill (1991: 12) found a large percentage of newspaper readers 'not affected' at all by the massacres – 44 per cent, for instance, of *Sun* and *Star* readers. Certainly the hostages story competed with the demonisation of Saddam Hussein as the most prominent of the pre-massacres period – in both the national and local press. It is easy to understand why. Here were all the ingredients of an archetypally 'good story':

- It provided strong local/national/patriotic angles.
- And strong 'human interest' angles.
- It had strong emotional/melodramatic content with all the stereotypical good versus evil elements: innocent 'ordinary folk' surviving only at the whim of a brutal 'enemy' heavily personalised in the form of mad Saddam. As Peter Beaumont comments in his highly personal reflection on conflict and conflict reporting, *The secret life of war* (2009: 86): 'War reporting, like any other kind of journalism, requires a familiar rota of drama, the clichéd set pieces that turn history and human misery into soap opera. ... What it would rather not deal with are the grey and murky areas that have the texture of real life.'
- It provided 'ordinary' people with the rare opportunity to attain 'heroic' stature.
- 'Ordinary' people could be presented as victims of fate over which they had no control, caught up quite by chance in the brutalities and complexities of modern realpolitik of which they are normally just passive spectators.

- The hostage story reinforced the representation of Saddam Hussein as a 'bully' and the West, more generally, as innocent victim.

- It provided the opportunity to stress traditional 'family values' and, by association, helped in the representation of Britain and the United States as families under threat. A similar stress on the family occurred during the Falklands/Malvinas conflict, as Taylor identifies (1991). In the absence of any photographs, the press had the problem of keeping up the interest. Thus, 'they anchored their coverage to the home front, telling the story of the Task Force, as if it were the story of a family' (ibid: 97).

- Moreover, there were strong emotive connotations of the word 'hostages' (given Western media coverage of the Beirut hostages and particularly in America associations with the hostages held in the US embassy in Tehran after the fall of the Shah in 1979). Significantly, the Iraqis attempted to counter the ideological force of the word 'hostages' by calling them 'guests'.

- Allegations of sexual assault on some women hostages provided the press with titillating 'sex/sensational' angles.

Thus hardly a day went by from early August 1990 until December without a hostage story being given enormous prominence in the press. After a while they acquired a certain repetitive, ritualistic, theatrical dimension. Jostein Gripsrud (1992) locates the sensationalism and personalisation of the popular press in the melodrama of the 19th century stage.

> Melodrama was didactic drama designed to teach the audience a lesson. Today's popular press also teaches the audience a lesson every day. It says that what the world is really about is emotions, fundamental and strong: love, hate, grief, joy, lust and disgust. Such emotions are shared by all human beings, regardless of social positions and so is 'general morality': crime does not pay... (ibid: 87).

Gripsrud argues that the melodramatic imperative of the popular press indicates a popular resistance to abstract, theoretical ways of understanding society and history. Yet 'it is deeply problematic, not least because it is deeply ahistorical' (ibid: 88). Gripsrud goes on to develop the ideas of Jurgen Habermas over the 'classic public sphere' by suggesting the media emphasis on so-called personalities and private lives of public figures may be said to contribute to an erosion of the public sphere. 'It is part of a tendency to distract the public from matters of principle by offering voyeuristic pseudo insights into individual matters' (ibid: 90).

In relation to the hostages story, the melodramatic imperative of the press meant they focused whenever possible on the most vulnerable, the most horrific – thus children, babes and mums take centre stage. The *Mirror* front page headlined on 20 August: 'I'll keep your kids until I win: Butcher's new threat.' Underneath, the report ran: 'The babes of British families held in Kuwait were made prisoners of war last night. Evil Saddam Hussein vowed to keep the several hundred British children trapped in the Gulf until he gets his way. ... There was no hint of compassion from the Iraqi dictator who has threatened to let babies starve and use hostages as human shields.' On page seven of the same issue, the *Mirror* reported: 'Our babes in the grip of the crazed butcher.' Underneath the copy ran: 'Even unborn babies are at the mercy of Saddam.' Next day it was reporting: 'Iraq last night threatened to eat any British or American pilots shot down over their territory. The astonishing warning came from a Baghdad government official as Saddam Hussein seized more Western hostages for use as human shields.'

All this is crude anti-Iraqi propaganda, preparing the public to support a war in a far-away country they knew little about. As if to articulate the *Mirror*'s own response, a man is quoted as saying: 'It's frightening but I think it's time to send the multi-national force into Iraq.'

WHEN BAD DAD MEETS HOSTAGES IN BAGHDAD

The demonisation of Saddam Hussein, the heroism of the hostages, the melodramatic imperative of the press and the mediacentrism of new militarism all came together in the coverage of Saddam Hussein's meeting with a group of British hostages. On 23 August, the Iraqis released film of their president meeting a group of British hostages. Saddam was dressed in civilian clothes. He appeared relaxed and friendly. Here, then, were images which totally contradicted the demonising propaganda of the Western media.

The meaning of images is never naturally given. Someone appears to be crying: are they overjoyed, afraid, sad, or maybe they just have a fly in their eye? Maybe they are not even crying. Interpretations will differ and contradict each other. Post-modernist theorists such as Baudrillard (1988) argue that it is no longer possible to identify a concrete objectivity according to which the reality as represented in the media can be assessed. Opposing this view, John Fiske (1992: 49) argues that the 'powerless' in society seek to subvert the dominant values by revelling in stories that expose the hypocrisies, secrets and lies of the powerful, the great and the good.

He writes of the popular press: 'One of the most characteristic tones of voice is that of sceptical laughter which offers the pleasures of disbelief, the pleasures of not being taken in. This popular pleasure of "seeing through them" (whoever constitutes the powerful "them" of the moment) is the historical result of centuries of subordination which the people have not allowed to develop into subjection.' But James Curran and Colin Sparks (1991) oppose this view of polysemy (in which a multiplicity of meanings is possible) by prioritising the notion of 'preferred reading'. In relation to the coverage of the hostages' meeting with Saddam Hussein, the press's preferred meaning was totally unambiguous. 'The Great Pretender: Butcher uses British kids in sick TV stunt' headlined the *Mirror* on 24 August. The kind daddy of the image was transformed into a supremely evil, monstrous bad dad.

Central to the demonisation of Saddam Hussein was the representation of the Iraqi leader as a cunning propagandist to which the Western vulnerable state could easily fall victim. As *The Sunday Times* of 26 August commented: 'The White House realises it is engaged in an all-out propaganda war with Saddam and Bush's political advisers are considering ways to counter his media offensive as the battle for support in the Arab world intensifies.' In a way, this contradicted the other dominant theme of the coverage which was to stress his madness and unpredictability. Such an unstable man could not command a propaganda machine of global reach. But still the evil propagandist theme was to persist through the massacres. Even when his army was being massacred the press could still represent the Iraqi leader as a credible threat – by virtue of his 'grotesque' propaganda powers.

Such a representation also pictured the anti-Iraq coalition as vulnerable and on the defensive (the myths of vulnerability and defence being essential to the new militarist, strong state). Notice how in *The Sunday Times* comment (above) the US elite with its highly sophisticated, massively financed, global-reaching propaganda machine is represented as caught unawares by Saddam and left 'considering ways of countering' Saddam's offensive. According to Norton (1991), the press coverage of the meeting showed Saddam Hussein as a 'figure of phallic danger'. The press transformed the meeting into an archetypal confrontation between good (little British boys, described as 'terrified' and 'squirming') and evil (the 'cynical', 'sickening', 'utterly repulsive' Saddam Hussein). The ultimate achievement of a secretive society is to expose the secret wiles of 'an enemy'. Hence the media focus on Saddam Hussein's stunt when 'he tried to mask his brutality behind the guise of a kindly uncle' (according to the *Mirror*).

The event provided the media with an opportunity to represent the children (Elliott Pilkington and Stuart Lockwood) as acting out some of the David and Goliath fantasies of warfare/confrontation with the 'evil tyrant': 'A plucky boy of four aimed a punch at Saddam Hussein as the tyrant tried to shake hands with him in a sickening TV charade. Elliott Pilkington put his tiny fist up in rebellion expressing the only way he knew the rage of Britain's helpless hostages.' In typical press fashion, an 'expert' (anonymous, of course, so perhaps merely an invention of the newspaper) is drawn in to support the bias of the coverage. 'Last night a psychologist examining the video said: "You could see little Stuart was terrified by the attention he got from Saddam simply through the way he was holding himself."'

One of the boys featured in a widely-distributed photograph of the event, Stuart Lockwood, was given star billing when he arrived back in Britain on 2 September. 'I was brave in Baghdad', headlined the *Mirror*, seemingly putting words into the young man's mouth. But without any hint of self-parody, the newspaper proceeded to destroy its previously carefully constructed story by quoting his mum: 'Glenda said she was not frightened when an army officer turned Stuart's head around and forced him to look at Saddam during the TV interview. She said: "There were times when we were frightened but that wasn't one of them. Stuart is only five years old. I really don't think he was aware of the situation."' Stuart Lockwood also featured in a *Guardian* Weekend supplement 'That's me in the picture' feature on 6 June 2015. He commented on his famous meeting with Saddam Hussein: 'We thought it was a publicity stunt – that he really wanted to show the world how well we were treated. And to be fair, we were – the Iraqi soldiers were very nice and welcoming. They made a cake for a child's birthday and we had a party.' Bruce Cumings summed up the event in this way (1992: 113):

> Meanwhile Saddam Hussein exhibited his paleolithic grasp of television style. Eager to show the world that he wasn't maltreating the women and children he had seized as hostages, he sat himself in front of the camera, simulated an avuncular grin, and patted terrified little boys on the back, or put his guests at ease by telling them that when they are posted at military targets to ward off bombing, they 'will all be heroes of peace'. A villain from Hollywood central casting, he never knew what hit him.

In some ways, the coverage of the hostages meeting can be seen as a metaphor for much of the press handling of the crisis and massacres – the reality shrouded in patriotic-inspired, sensationalist stereotyping, blatant mystifications, distortion and exaggeration.

NOTES

[1] Daphne Parish, a nurse who was arrested with Bazoft, gives her version of the events in (1992) *Prisoner in Baghdad*, London: Chapman Publishers

[2] Edward Herman (1992: 50) links the 'Hitler' coverage of Saddam Hussein to that of Cambodia's Pol Pot from 1975-1980 'when the US establishment was first trying to overcome the Vietnam syndrome'. He then 'suddenly became a shadowy figure when the US quietly began supporting him and the Khmer Rouge after their ouster by Vietnam in 1979. It would not have been helpful to the US policy of bleeding Vietnam for the Free Press to have called attention to the US support for a man furiously assailed as a mass murderer a few years back; always accommodating, the Free Press remained silent'

[3] King Hussein told Heikal (Ali 2003: 88): 'Numerous meetings were held between the Ba'ath party and American intelligence, the more important in Kuwait. Do you know that on 8 February a secret radio beamed to Iraq was supplying the men who pulled the coup with the names and addresses of the communists there so that they could be arrested and executed.' Ali adds: 'The repression of Iraqi communists was systematic and brutal, prefiguring the massacres in Indonesia which came two years later'

[4] As Christopher Hitchens comments on Jimmy Carter (2003: 81): 'As President, he encouraged Saddam Hussein to invade Iran in 1979 and assured him that the Khomeini regime would crumble swiftly. The long resulting war took at least a million and a half lives, setting what is perhaps a record for Baptist-based foreign policy and severely testing Carter's proclaimed view that war is the last resort'

[5] See The long history of the *Daily Mail* campaigning against the interests of working people, by John Simkin. Available online at http://spartacus-educational.com/spartacus-blogURL53.htm, accessed on 10 December 2015

Chapter Six

Silencing the history of the Middle East

MISSING: THE WHY FACTOR

Every student journalist leans the basic five 'w's (who, what, where, when and why) and the one 'h' (how) of hard news first paragraphs (known as intros). Yet journalists feel most at home with the who, what, when and how of events coverage. And they usually see these elements unproblematically.[1] This was very much the case over the Kuwait invasion of August 1990. Very little space was given to the reasons for the invasion. Most of the coverage dealt with the 'here and now' of the invasion itself (the who, what, when and how): the advance of the Iraqi troops, the flight of the Kuwaiti leadership, the response of the international elites, the build-up of allied troops in Saudi Arabia.

Some background coverage focused on the oil dispute between Iraq and Kuwait. This might be considered an important immediate cause of the invasion but the many underlying causes, or the 'profound' causes as defined by Paul Kennedy (1986), largely ignored by the press, were far more significant. Keith Nelson and Spencer Olin (1979) highlight the political and ideological foundations for assumptions about causes of wars. Liberals, they suggest, tend to emphasise the role of individual personalities and the psychological stresses on major decision-makers. Radicals, in contrast, argue that the real causes of international conflict lie in long-term factors such as economic competition, imperialism, nationalism and racism. Thus, underlying the press's focus on the Saddam factor were specific ideological assumptions. The taboo on linkage in defence of US strategic and political interests was almost a metaphysical denial of the complexities of Middle Eastern politics. As Edward Said commented (1992: 2):

> Linkage means not that there is but that there is no connection. Things that belong together by common association, sense, geography, history are sundered, left apart for convenience sake and for the benefit of US

imperial strategies. … The Middle East is linked by all sorts of ties, that is irrelevant. That Arabs might see a connection between Saddam Hussein in Kuwait and Israel in Lebanon, that too is futile. That US policy is itself the linkage, that is the forbidden topic to broach.

THE MYTH OF THE OVERRIDING OIL FACTOR

On 3 August 1990, the *Express* presented its 17-day countdown to the crisis. All blame is directed at Saddam. On 17 July, he accuses Kuwait and the United Arab Emirates of flooding the oil market and driving down oil prices. Next day he accuses Kuwaitis of stealing oil from wells on the disputed border. On 24 July, tension escalates when the US announces a (defensive) warship and aircraft staging exercise in the Gulf. On 25 July, Saddam summons the US ambassador in Baghdad for a 'dressing down'. Next day, Kuwait and UAE pledge to abide by a new quota agreement. 31 July: diplomats say Iraq has massed 1,000,000 troops on Kuwait's borders.

Thus the vast and complex history of the world's dependency on Middle East oil is shrunk to just 17 days.[2] Since 1901 when the British first obtained concessions to search for oil in Persia, the development of Middle East oil fields had grown to the extent that by the late 1980s they supplied 71 per cent of Japan's consumption, 67 per cent of Italy's, 47 per cent of France's, 38 per cent of Germany's, 28 per cent of the UK's and just 17 per cent of the United States' (Reich 1987). The Middle East and the Gulf possessed at least 66.3 per cent of global oil reserves. In comparison, the US had only 4 per cent; Saudi Arabia had estimated reserves of 252,000m. barrels compared to the US's 35,000m. (Abrahams 1994: 22).

In 1979, President Carter's own doctrine stressed America's commitment to protecting the flow of oil (and petro-dollars so crucial for funding US imperialist adventures) in the face of an 'enemy' (Soviet) advance (Tanzer 1992). Moreover, President Bush and his son with many members of his administration had personal financial interests in Gulf oil which were largely ignored by the mainstream press.[3] Bush's own Zapata Offshore Oil Company had drilled the first well off Kuwait some 30 years earlier (Yant 1991: 87). Friedman reports how six days after the Kuwait invasion, Bush signed 'conflict of interest' waiver documents on behalf of secretary of state James Baker and ten other cabinet officers and officials allowing them to participate in 'current United States policy-making discussions, decisions and actions in response to the Iraqi invasion of Kuwait' (Friedman 1993: 170). Moreover, secret Saudi monies helped bolster Western elites – helping to fund, for instance, the Marshall plan and the Nicaraguan Contra terrorists (Laurens 1992). Abrahams comments:

> Saudi Arabia willingly does imperialism's dirty work. It was responsible
> for financing the Afghan counter-revolutionaries to the tune of billions of
> pounds: it was a conduit of money and arms to the Contras in Nicaragua

and it is the main financier of reactionary Muslim fundamentalist movements devoted to the eradication of communism and socialism in the Arab world (op cit: 23).

Other oil-rich Gulf states are closely linked to the West through investments and high-tech military orders. Private investors from Saudi Arabia, Kuwait and the United Arab Emirates had holdings at the end of the 1980s in the US worth $150 billion. In addition, government-funded agencies of Saudi Arabia, Kuwait, Qatar, Oman and Bahrain held an estimated $200 billion in overseas investments (Schiller 1992: 39).

Yet, contrary to press reports that warned of a new oil crisis, there was, in fact, never any danger of Iraq's invasion of Kuwait disturbing the global oil economy. As Philip Agee argued (1991: 22), access to Middle East oil for the industrialised countries was never threatened. 'The producers, including Iraq, have to sell to sustain their own economic and development projects. They get no benefits from either withholding oil or forcing the price too high. On the contrary, in doing so they hurt themselves.' The global industrial community had learned the lessons from two previous crises – of 1973, when Gulf OPEC ministers raised the price of oil by around 140 per cent, and 1978-1979, when the Iranian revolution cut supplies (Glavanis 1991).

Iraqi and Kuwaiti oil combined accounted for only 9 per cent of US imports (Stone and Kuznick 2013: 477). Moreover, the principal importers of oil diversified their energy consumption reducing their reliance on oil, enormous stocks were built to deal with any emergencies while prices were kept relatively low with the market falling away from OPEC to the industrialised consumer countries (Stork 1986, Roberts 1995: 198-199). Despite the oil embargo on Iraq and the firing of the Kuwait oil fields; despite the media whipping up fears of a major crisis in the Gulf, it can be argued there was never any danger of an oil shock in 1991.[4] As Van Evera comments (1991: 13):

> The price of oil was not at stake in the Gulf. Thus Iraq's seizure of the Gulf would have posed little direct threat to American sovereignty or prosperity. An expanded Iraq would have been a dominant regional power but would have remained a minor world power with little influence beyond the Middle East. It could not have threatened the security of the US or its Western industrial allies. Nor would its expansion have injured democracy since the Gulf states are not democratic. … The containment of Iraq serves American interests if the US intends to sustain its security guarantee to Israel.

Had Iraq retained Kuwait it would still have controlled fewer net resources than Saudi Arabia. In 1986, Iraq plus Kuwait GNP was $62.3 billion; Saudi $77.1 billion. The enlarged Iraq would still have been a minor world power, producing only 1 per cent of Gross World Product. In contrast, the US produced 27 per cent of GWP while Nato states together produced 50 per cent of GWP. 'With this small economic base even an enlargened Iraq could not have built a military machine that could match the militaries of the industrial West' (ibid: 12). It could also be argued that Iraqi complaints about Kuwait's over-production and capture of the Rumaila oil field – in southern Iraq close to the Kuwaiti border – were legitimate. But this view was never heard in the UK (or US) press. Stork and Lesch comment (1990: 12): 'Iraq's complaints in 1990 about Kuwait's over-production sound all too plausible in a region where people have an acute memory of the manipulative role of Western companies and governments usually with the eager compliance of the local beneficiary regime.'

THE MYTH OF SADDAM HUSSEIN'S THREAT TO SAUDI ARABIA

The notion promoted relentlessly in the mainstream UK (and US) press of President Saddam Hussein as the threat to the global economy is entirely dependent on the myth of the unique awfulness of the Iraqi invasion of Kuwait and the marginalisation of many other – equally unacceptable – invasions during the Cold War period. The Indonesian invasion of East Timor (1975), the Soviet invasion of Hungary (1956) and Czechoslovakia (1968), Morocco's seizure of the Western Sahara in 1975, the US invasion of Panama (1989); even the Syrian invasion of Lebanon (which was to follow in October 1990) are just a few obvious cases. But there were many others. For instance, in November 1971, the Shah of Iran with US backing sent his troops to occupy three islands belonging to the United Arab Emirates.

The Saddam threat is also based on the supposed danger the Iraqi army posed to taking control of Saudi Arabia's massive oil fields, containing a quarter of the globe's reserves. *The Sunday Times*, of 5 August, was typical. In debating the possible Iraqi invasion of Saudi Arabia, it reported that the weather was exceptionally hot 'but this should prove no obstacle to the Iraqis many of whom are battle-hardened by eight years' conflict with neighbouring Iran'. Its editorial envisaged the Saudi takeover, leaving Iraq 'the unchallenged regional superpower capable of dictating oil policy for the entire Gulf repository of 65 per cent of the world's oil reserves'. It continued: 'That is the Western nightmare writ large; an evil, anti-Western despot with a stranglehold on the main sources of the West's lifeblood.'

A strong 'balancing' case can be made out to suggest no danger ever existed. But this was never heard in the press. CIA officials, in any case, have since conceded that at 'no time was there any evidence Saddam contemplated such a move' (Cockburn and Cockburn 1992: 354). And according to Stephen Dorril, an MI6 survey of friendly intelligence services in the Gulf found a consensus believing that Iraq did not intend to invade Saudi Arabia (Dorril 1993: 408). Darwish and Alexander (1991: 286) argue that 'once Kuwait had been secured Iraqi deployments were entirely defensive and the much-cited move towards the Saudi border was merely the extending of front lines and the fortifying of defensive positions. … Not only did the Iraqis have no intention of attacking Saudi Arabia, they also avoided the sort of provocative actions that may have precipitated a war'.

Moreover, the ironies of the US defending the profoundly repressive regimes of the Gulf were rarely highlighted in the press. For instance, *The Sunday Times* of 13 January 1991 gave this totally uncritical picture: 'Pre-invasion Kuwait was an immaculately clean desert kingdom. Traditional Islamic values survived while billion pound oil riches sustained one of the best health systems in the world, the first modern university in the Gulf and a centre of international finance.'

The representation of the Kuwait invasion as a sudden 'naked act of aggression' was profoundly anti-historical. Iraq's border dispute with Kuwait, its claims on the islands of Warbah and Bubiyan and for an access to the Gulf were, in fact, all long-standing. An unsuccessful attempt to annex Kuwait had been made in 1932, just after independence and in 1961, just after Kuwait gained independence. In 1938, the Kuwait emir's advisory council recommended union with Iraq – but was prevented from doing so by the British. By the late 1980s, Iraq was keen to develop close relations with Saudi Arabia. A friendship agreement had been signed and, after the invasion of Kuwait, Iraq was at pains to stress its friendship with Saudi Arabia. King Hussein of Jordan always insisted that Iraq had no intention to invade the kingdom. King Fahd was quoted on 7 August 1990 as feeling confident there was no threat. Salinger and Laurent (1991: viii) argue that the Arab world desperately tried to resolve the crisis on the basis of Iraq's non-intervention in Saudi Arabia only to find their efforts undermined by pressure from the United States government (ibid).

Cockburn and Cohen (1991: 21) report that sources close to King Hussein of Jordan and Yasser Arafat, PLO chairman, were claiming that Saddam Hussein had agreed to withdraw as long as the Arab summit of 3-4 August held back from criticising Iraq. 'According to this version of accounts, Mubarak [President of Egypt] agreed to the deal but changed his mind and denounced Iraq when the USA offered to write off billions of dollars of Egypt's debts' (ibid). On 5 August, Saddam Hussein summoned Joe Wilson, the USA *chargé d'affaires* in Baghdad, to say Iraq had no intention of invading Saudi Arabia. This message was relayed to the state department but then on 6 August a prominent story in the *Washington Post* had the Iraqi leader claiming he would invade if the Iraqi pipeline was cut. Cockburn and Cohen comment:

> In other words, within moments of the invasion, a faction within US policy-making circles, determined to press forward to war and to the destruction of Iraq as a regional power, was already manipulating the record with diligence and success. There are also accounts that, in his first trip to persuade King Fahd to accept US troops, US defense secretary Dick

Cheney used satellite photographs selected to demonstrate an Iraq poised for invasion, whereas subsequent photographs refuted such claims (ibid: 21-22; see also Salinger and Laurent op cit: 137-138, and Aburish 1994: 175-178).

The scenario of diplomatic openings from Baghdad being dismissed by the US/UK and marginalised or ignored by their mainstream media was to be repeated on a number of occasions. Heikal (1992: 249) reveals that on 8 August, a prominent Palestinian businessman sent a message by fax to Washington indicating Baghdad's willingness to withdraw from Kuwait, to allow the restoration of the Sabah family. In addition it sought an Iraqi presence on Bubiyan island, a settlement of Iraqi debts and compensation. It was completely ignored. Heikal adds: 'In President Carter's day this would probably have been seen as an opening bid leading the secret talks but Bush had decided there was nothing to discuss' (ibid).

Other offers came from Iraq on 9 August, 19 August, 21 August, 23 August and 2 January 1991; on 24 September (from French President Mitterrand at the UN), on 21 October (by the Saudi defence minister). King Hussein of Jordan, Russian President Gorbachev, the Algerian government and the PLO all made concerted efforts to promote a diplomatic solution – all of them rejected by the Bush administration and marginalised by the press (Cockburn 1991a; Niva 1992). In any case, the US military later generally admitted that Iraq was without the logistical support facilities to invade and occupy Saudi Arabia.

Jean Edward Smith (1992) even argues that President Bush committed himself to using force against Iraq the day before Cheney's meeting with King Fahd of Saudi Arabia. The Saudi Arabian joint forces commander, General Khaled Bin Sultan (1995: 313), provided some authoritative support for this view when, in his memoir of the conflict, he revealed that from the moment Iraq invaded Kuwait, America was planning an offensive strategy.

THE MYTH OF THE KUWAITI SURPRISE

Considerable evidence suggests that the US fully expected an Iraqi invasion of Kuwait in early August 1990. Some even argue that the US encouraged the invasion (Yousif 1991). Yet the dominant view represented 'the world' as vulnerable and being taken by surprise. Peter Pringle, for instance, in the *Independent on Sunday* of 2 December 1990, wrote: 'Considering that the Pentagon had no contingency plan for opposing Saddam, President Bush responded to the invasion of Kuwait with a strikingly grand commitment.'

The border row with Kuwait had been intensifying over a decade, coming to a head in the years following the 1988 ceasefire in the Iraq/Iran Gulf War. US satellites over the Gulf would have provided evidence of troop build-ups. On 25 July, Col. Said Matar, who was based at the Kuwaiti consulate in Basra for 14 months before the invasion, told his government that an Iraqi invasion was planned for 2 August. Following the ending of the 1980-1988 Iran/Iraq war, Iraq replaced Iran as the major Middle East threat in the eyes of American military strategists (Sultan op cit: 313). Just before the invasion, Gen. Schwarzkopf, who was to the lead the coalition forces, was playing computer war games (codenamed 'Internal Look') in which the scenario was an Iraqi invasion of Saudi Arabia through Kuwait (Pilger 1991b; Atkinson 1994: 107). Nigel Gillies, command public information officer at headquarters, United Kingdom Land Forces, also revealed that US Centcom (the re-named Rapid Deployment Force) at Tampa in Florida had carried out an exercise using the scenario of a Kuwait invasion. He continued: 'This exercise validated the requirement for two major centres – one in the Saudi capital at Riyadh, and the other much nearer the scene of action at Dhahran' (Gillies 1991: 12).

THE SECRET ANTI-HUSSEIN STRATEGY

Heikal (op cit: 173-174) suggests that a CIA unit had been working closely with the Kuwait government since 1984 and that they had encouraged Kuwait's provocation of Iraq over the oil dispute. At a meeting between top Kuwaitis and William Webster, CIA chief, in November 1989, it was decided 'to exploit the deteriorating economic situation in Iraq so that we can press its government to accept designation of our frontiers with them' (ibid). Continuing its covert support for Iran, the meeting agreed that Kuwait should re-programme its relations with Iran and reinforce its alliance with Syria.

THE GLASPIE SCAPEGOAT

The *Express*, in its backgrounder on the invasion, had described the American ambassador, April Glaspie, as having been given a 'dressing down' by Saddam Hussein on 25 July 1990. The opposite had occurred. It was a very friendly meeting, in fact. In early September, the Iraqis released an English translation of the session, the accuracy of which was never denied by the Americans (and carried in full in Salinger and Laurent op cit: 47-62). Saddam Hussein is quoted as claiming that economic war was being waged against his country and that $25 was not a high price for a barrel of oil. Glaspie replied: 'We have many Americans who would like to see the price go above $25 because they come from oil-producing states.' She then said that the US had 'no opinion on the Arab-Arab conflicts, like your border disagreement with Kuwait'.

On 28 July, President Bush sent a note of friendship to Saddam Hussein. On 31 July, John Kelly, assistant secretary of state, told the Middle East sub-committee of the house of representatives that if Iraq invaded Kuwait 'we have no treaty, no commitment which would oblige us to use American forces'. On 1 August, a day before the invasion, the Bush administration approved the sale of $695m. of advanced data transmission devices to Iraq. Glaspie was later allowed to be scapegoated by the administration, being blamed for not indicating clearly to Saddam US warnings over any invasion plans. She was quoted as saying: 'Obviously I don't think – and nobody else did – that the Iraqis were going to take all of Kuwait.' This suggests that people might have expected the Iraqis to take some part of Kuwait.

This does not imply that the Iraqi invasion of the whole of Kuwait was expected by a significant section of the US secret state. They probably expected a seizure of the northern oil fields and islands. Once the whole of Kuwait was taken the Americans quickly saw the military opportunities – and took them. The mythology of the surprise is partly based on allegations (quite commonly voiced in the press) that the CIA and British secret service had committed appalling blunders in not halting the Iraqi advance. But if the advance was seen as potentially beneficial to the US then these allegations are spurious.

SILENCING THE IRAQI DIMENSION

Immediately following the invasion the focus for the causes of the ensuing crisis was directed by the press entirely on Iraq. America/Britain/France were nowhere part of the problematic. In fact, this was the consensual perspective maintained throughout the British media. Yet the press coverage of Iraq was totally overshadowed by the demonisation of Saddam Hussein. Saddam became Iraq. As *The Sunday Times*'s profile commented on 29 July 1990 (just before the Kuwait invasion): 'Today Saddam Hussein is Iraq.' Such a focus remained consistent throughout the press during the crisis and massacres.

It thus rendered invisible the complexity of the rich social, political, cultural history of Iraq and its people, the Iraqi regime's diplomatic manoeuvrings during the 1970s and 1980s and its attempts to assert Arab nationalism, particularly in the period following the Israeli/Egyptian Camp David accords of 1978. Iraqi coverage was all too one-dimensional. As Matthew Rendell indicated, the military strategy adopted by the US-led coalition presupposed the existence of 'a monolithic entity called the Iraqi nation which could then be represented by single voices'. He continued: 'The relationship between journalists and the military might hinge on the need of the military to think in terms of monoliths. After all, if an army is not fighting on behalf of a stable, unquestionable entity, then what is it doing?'[5]

Only after the massacres ended on 28 February 1991 did an image of Iraq emerge which was not a monolithic unity but one which had been falling apart for years. Members of the groups who had been opposing the regime, drawn from the rich variety of ethnic and religious communities in the country – Kurds, Shi'as as well as Arabs, Turkomans, Persians, Sunnis and Chaldean Christians – had been slaughtered.

SILENCING THE ROLE OF BRITISH IMPERIALISM

Missing from most of the coverage was a sense of the extraordinary impact Western imperialism had (and continued to have) on the country and the resentments that flowed from it. The dominant new militarist ideological consensus, in fact, eliminated the very notion of imperialism from the mainstream discourse. Clearly the carve-up of the Middle East and the Gulf by the imperial powers after the First Wold War contained the roots of the crisis. The region's nations had been born through secret diplomacy – and their fates continued to be profoundly affected by the imperial powers' overt and covert activities.

During the 1914-1918 war, the Arabs had been promised independence in exchange for support against the Turks. But secretly the 1916 Sykes-Picot agreement between Britain, France and Czarist Russia divided the Arab world between Britain and France (Anderson and Rashidian 1991: 3-8).[6] Iraq was created by joining the Ottoman provinces of Mosul, Baghdad and Basra. Its borders with Kuwait and Nejd, the territorial core of what was to become Saudi Arabia, were fixed in arbitrary fashion by Sir Percy Cox, British high commissioner for Iraq, in November 1922. Kuwait was given a 310-mile coastline with several deep water ports. Iraq was given a mere 36 miles of coastline and just one deep water port which it had to share with Iran.

A monarchical structure was imposed on Iraq by the British in 1922 with the installation of Sherif Hussein's son, Faisal, as King (with his son Abdullah becoming King of Transjordan). Though the country technically gained its independence in 1932, it was still effectively under the rigid control of the British. And the British ruled the territory, considered of strategic significance in relation to India, with an iron hand. It also proved a useful training ground for the RAF which was to provide relatively cheap and effective methods of maintaining security in the southern marshes and northern mountains – allegedly even using chemical weapons during an Iraqi revolt in 1920 (an imperial policy little mentioned in background articles in the press during the build-up to the massacres) (see Simons 1994: 179-181). As minister of the air, Winston Churchill is recorded in a minute of the War Office of 1919 as saying:

> I do not understand this squeamishness about the use of gas. We have definitely adopted the position at the Peace Conference of arguing in favour of the retention of gas as a permanent method of warfare. It is sheer affectation to lacerate a man with the poisonous fragment of a bursting shell and to boggle at making his eyes water by means of lachrymatory gas. I am strongly in favour of using poisoned gas against uncivilised tribes. The moral effect should be so good that the loss of life should be reduced to a minimum. It is not necessary to use only the most deadly gasses: gasses can be used which cause great inconvenience and would spread a lively terror and yet would leave no serious permanent effects on most of those affected (Gilbert 1976).[7]

The leading academic historians of Iraq, Marion Farouk-Slugett and Peter Slugett (1990: 42-45) describe the rule of Salih Jabr on behalf of the British as 'one of the most repressive regimes to come to power in the Middle East in the first half of the century'. Under the premiership of Nuri al-Said (1930-1932), all political parties were banned, leading communists were executed in public, the press was heavily censored, terrible poverty gripped the mass of the population. More liberal forms of government were never considered. The overall concern was internal stability and stronger government.

Indeed, an awareness of the legacy of British imperialism in Iraq was almost totally missing from the press coverage. After all, as Mark Curtis stressed (2010: 174), Britain was leaping to the defence of its ally and the Kuwaiti regime of Jaber al-Sabah, 'whose family had ruled the emirate, under British protection, since the mid-eighteenth century. Al-Sabah was one of Whitehall's closest allies in the region, presiding over an oil-rich state investing billions of its revenue in the British economy'. One clear exception was the reporting of Robert Fisk in the *Independent*. For instance, under the headline 'History haunts new Crusader', he commented on 9 August 1990: 'The European powers who have taken the place of the Turks brought only pain to the Arabs, ignoring earlier promises of independence and dividing up the Arab lands into competing tribes. ... Since the end of the Second World War, Arabs have struggled to shake off the humiliation of their history.' And one of the very rare acknowledgements of the role of Western imperialism in the crisis was made by columnist Robert Harris in *The Sunday Times* of 12 August 1990. But he did so in a feature supporting the build-up of coalition troops: 'Most of us, if we gave the matter thought, will probably agree, however reluctantly, that we have no other course. We should be clear, however, how costly this policy may prove and we should give it its proper name – imperialism.'

THE SECRET OMANI CONFLICT

In a rare analysis of one of Britain's secret wars in the Middle East, Fred Halliday (1987) shows how Fleet Street operated during the Omani war merely as the propaganda arm of the government. The military historian Frank Barnaby (1984: 177) says of the conflict: 'Perhaps the most important military campaign that Britain has fought since 1945, far more vital than the battle for the Falklands was the long guerrilla war between 1968 and 1977 in Oman – a war to keep a pro-Western ruler in charge of the country which dominates the Straits of Hormuz.' Cobain (2016) highlights the crucial roles the SAS and RAF played in crushing an earlier insurgency: 'Between July and December 1958, for example, the RAF flew 1,635 sorties, dropping 1,094 tons of bombs and firing 900 rockets at the insurgents, their mountain-top villages and irrigation works. This was more than twice the weight of bombs that the Luftwaffe dropped on Coventry in November 1940.'

In 1966 another rebellion broke out. The Labour government of Harold Wilson, in power since 1964, had every reason to keep the conflict secret. Cobain continues:

> In their determination to put down a popular rebellion against the cruelty and neglect of a despot who was propped up and financed by Britain, British-led forces poisoned wells, torched villages, destroyed crops and shot livestock. During the interrogation of rebels they developed their torture techniques, experimenting with noise. Areas populated by civilians were turned into free-fire zones. Little wonder that Britain wanted to fight this war in total secrecy (ibid).

Journalists were kept out of the country; politicians just kept quiet about it. Indeed, Halliday (op cit) shows how Fleet Street's coverage (from the 1970 MI6-managed coup which overthrew Sultan Said bin Taimur and installed his 29-year-old son Qabus bin Said – just after the Conservative Edward Heath moved into Downing Street) involved a strange mix of government-inspired disinformation, censorship and information suppression. He concludes: 'Here it is not so much a question of the failings of individual journalists as a whole ideology of news reporting, a set of practices, constraints, values and expectation which combined to make the press so compliant.'

Later, in 1980, MI6 organised a destabilisation exercise in the Soviet-backed Marxist state of South Yemen, training rebels to blow up bridges and other installations (Norton-Taylor 1990: 99).

SILENCING THE ROLE OF AMERICAN IMPERIALISM AND ITS COVERT WARS

The complex, offensive role played by America historically in the Middle East was hardly ever identified in the press. The dominant ideological frame eliminated this perspective – America was seen primarily as the vulnerable defender of the New World Order, resisting the 'naked aggression' of a brutal dictator. As the historian Richard W. van Alstyne comments (1974: 6): 'In the United States it is almost heresy to describe the nation as an empire.' It might be useful to highlight just a few of America's covert and less covert imperial activities marginalised or eliminated by the dominant consensus of the new militarist state.

THE 1952 COUP IN EGYPT

Founded in 1947, the CIA, according to Phillip Knightley, rapidly became a state within a state (Knightley 1986). Between 1947 and 1953 its activities expanded six-fold largely in the covert operations section. Knightley suggests it had been licensed, effectively, to conduct 'a secret Third World War' (ibid: 248). J. K. Galbraith described this as 'the licence for immorality' (Galbraith 1977: 242). CIA activities had global reach – but the Middle East was always a crucial theatre of operations. In 1952, according to Miles Copeland, one of the CIA's earliest officers, the CIA paid $3m. (£50m. today) into Swiss bank accounts to persuade General Mohammed Naguib to organise a coup on 22 July 1952 to oust King Farouk of Egypt (Copeland 1989: 142-171). But William Blum discounts the Copeland account (Blum 2004: 234). Naguib proved to be merely a front man for Col. Gamel Nasser who took over in February 1954 and who for a while was courted and heavily financed by the CIA (Freemantle 1983: 34-35; 103) and backed by the British. But he rapidly turned firmly anti-Western and became the target of a number of CIA and SIS (British secret service) assassination attempts (ibid: 168; Bower 1995: 190; Wright 1987: 202).[8] In October 1956, Britain, in a secret alliance with France and Israel, invaded Egypt in an attempt to dislodge Nasser – but they were stopped largely following the US refusal to back the intervention (Curtis 2010: 63-64).

CIA/MI6 COUP OF 1953: IRAN

In 1951, Dr Mohammed Mossadeq, Prime Minister of Iran, nationalised the Anglo-Iranian Oil Company, introduced parliamentary elections and sought to reduce British influence in the country. Richard J. Aldrich and Rory Cormac (2016: 156) suggest that Mossadeq's rise was, in part, sponsored by the CIA 'because American oil interests, which already dominated Saudi Arabia, were circling like vultures hoping to take British assets'. But when Mossadeq nationalised the enormous British refinery owned by the Anglo-Iranian Oil Company, 'London decided that he was not a man with whom it could do business' (ibid). In their seminal analysis of US press coverage of Iran, Dorman and Farhang (1987) showed how the dominant representation of Mossadeq shifted from that of a quaint nationalist to that of a lunatic and communist dupe. In 1953, the CIA (through Operation Ajax) and British intelligence (through Operation Boot) helped plan a coup which ousted Mossadeq and restored the Shah, who had been the chief partisan of Nazi interests in Persia during the Second World War (Fisk 1997). On the British side, the coup plan had originally been proposed by foreign secretary Herbert Morrison – who advocated gunboat diplomacy to resolve the crisis. But President Truman ruled this out. So Prime Minister Atlee pursued the covert route 'developing a secret plot to overthrow Mossadeq alongside a small circle of his most senior ministerial colleagues' (Aldrich and Cormac op cit: 156).

Significantly, Aldrich and Cormac (ibid: 176) record how Prime Minister Winston Churchill managed to persuade the BBC World Service to alter its usual signal in its Persian-language broadcast. 'Instead of "It is now midnight", the announcer stated: "It is now [pause] exactly midnight." The subtle change served as secret information that Britain was on board and the Shah finally agreed to sack Mossadeq and replace him with [General Fazlollah] Zahedi [an anti-Mossadeq army commander].'

The top CIA operative in Iran was Kermit Roosevelt, a grandson of President Theodore Roosevelt, who revealed the agency's role in his book *Countercoup: The struggle for the control of Iran* (New York: McGraw Hall, 1979).[9] He was assisted by General H. Norman Schwarzkopf, father of the 1991 Gulf conflict general. Key Iranians were bribed, a massive propaganda campaign frightened people about a Soviet takeover, anti-Mossadeq factions in the army were supplied with American equipment. According to Mark Frankland (1999: 88), the 1953 Iran coup was 'the greatest triumph' of the newly-created Special Political Action group of British intelligence, led by Alexis Foster. Bloch and Fitzgerald report (1983: 112): 'The Shah expressed his gratitude to the CIA, and in Britain the papers carried the headlines: "Situation restored, as you were in Iran". The total cost of the exercise was around $10m.' But Dan De Luce, the *Guardian*'s correspondent in Tehran in 2003, commented on the Iran coup (2003): 'While it may be reaching too far to link Mossadeq's overthrow with al-Qaida's terrorism, it certainly helped unleash a wave of Islamic extremism and assisted to power the anti-American clerical leadership that still rules Iran. It is difficult to imagine a worse outcome to an expedient action.'

Thereafter, the Shah proceeded to develop one of the most savage and oppressive regimes of the 20th century (Chomsky 1988: 176). With Britain withdrawing from the Gulf and the American elite still smarting from the Vietnam disaster, President Richard Nixon and his security adviser Henry Kissinger made Iran the focal point of their Middle East strategy, agreeing to sell virtually any conventional arms the Shah wanted. By the time of the 1979 revolution, the $20bn American sales to the Shah had made him the biggest arms customer in history. Britain also established close ties with SAVAK, the ruthless Iranian intelligence service. In exchange for information on Arab countries, SAVAK was given a free hand in intelligence-gathering inside the UK. Bloch and Fitzgerald report (1983: 113):

> While most of the targets were politically active students, they also included Labour MPs who campaigned against the brutality of the Shah's regime. SAS personnel 'on loan' to the Iranian military trained their special forces for operations against Kurdish guerrillas in the north of the country. Another SAS unit was entrusted with the protection of the GCHQ monitoring station near Mashad, close to the Soviet border; four of them were captured and executed by Fedayeen guerrillas in 1972.

CIA AND THE BA'ATHIST COUPS OF 1963 AND 1968

The CIA played significant roles in the coup of 1963 which brought the Ba'athists (and ultimately Saddam Hussein) to power in Iraq (Bulloch and Morris 1991: 55-56; Cockburn 1997; Keegan 2005: 40). Said Aburish (1997) records how the CIA also helped prepare the death lists of up to 5,000 people who were to be eliminated after the coup by Ba'athist squads. They included many doctors, lawyers, teachers and professors who formed the educated elite of Iraq. 'The American agent who produced the longest list was William McHale, who operated under the cover of a news correspondent for the Beirut bureau of *Time* [magazine].' Bulloch and Morris also report that the 1968 coup which returned the Ba'athists to power was also done 'in the interests of the CIA' (1991: 56). America's responsibility for helping create the repressive conditions which ultimately led to the Iranian revolution of 1978-1979 and then the Iran-Iraq war of 1980-1988 was hardly ever acknowledged in the press. Equally, Iraq began its 'tilt' towards the West in 1975 with its first purchases of arms from France. In 1979, it condemned the Soviet invasion of Afghanistan while its invasion of Iran on 22 September 1980 'had at least tacit American support as well as the active backing of some of the Shah's former generals', according to Bulloch and Morris (ibid: 75). The conflict was to cost at least 1 million lives.

Brian Crozier (1994: 162-163) records President Sadat of Egypt saying in an interview with him on 10 November 1980: 'I knew in advance of Saddam Hussein's intention to attack Iran. He went to Saudi Arabia to seek the advice of King Khaled, who gave him the green light. Khaled told the Americans who also gave Saddam the green light.' America's (and Britain's) massive covert support to Iraq between 1980 and 1990 was seriously underplayed in the press after August 1990. It clearly could not be totally ignored. But it was generally passed over as a mistake – one which the global community had to learn from. Thus the *Express* editorial of 3 August commented: 'In large part Saddam is the West's own Frankenstein monster. We have armed and encouraged him. Now he is rampaging free, a danger to all. If there is to be any chance of maintaining some semblance of international order the West will have to be prepared to rattle its own sabre. And be further prepared to use it.'

In 1980, President Jimmy Carter outlined what became known as the 'Carter doctrine': that Gulf oil was vital to American national interests and that the US would use 'any means necessary, including military force' to sustain access to it. The CIA began passing sensitive data to the Iraqi regime through King Hussein (on the CIA books for the previous 20 years) before Iraqi-US diplomatic relations were formally restored in 1984 (Yousif 1991: 62). Friedman reports how America, Britain and France all provided military advice to the Iraqis in the battlefield (op cit: 38). As Norm Dixon reports (2004): 'Not only did Ronald Reagan's Washington turn a blind-eye to the Hussein regime's repeated use of chemical weapons against Iranian soldiers and Iraq's Kurdish minority, but the US helped Iraq develop its chemical, biological and nuclear weapons program.'

From 1987, the CIA engaged in secret bombing missions against Iranian sites (ibid: 42; see also Woodward, Bob 1987: 439). Between 1985 and 1990, the Reagan and Bush administrations approved $1.5bn sales of advanced products to Iraq. By the end of 1980s, Washington had approved a total of $5bn in loan guarantees for Iraq, making it one of the biggest recipients of US largess (Friedman op cit: 104). On 17 May 1987, two Exocet missiles fired by an Iraqi jet hit USS *Stark*, an American frigate, about 85 miles north-east of Bahrain, killing 37 crew (Hiro 1992: 41). Then, on 3 July 1988, the USS *Vincennes* shot down a commercial airline, IranAir 655, killing all 290 on board.

Even more significantly, US arms trading to Iraq continued after August 1990. President Bush and secretary of state James Baker ignored Jordan's violations of the UN embargo after the Kuwait invasion. 'Between 2 August and 4 October 1990, the State Department approved twelve new military equipment orders worth five million dollars, including items such as spare parts and components for TOW missiles, helicopter components for the AH-1S Cobra, 105-mm cartridges for artillery shells and conversion kits for the M-16 rifle' (ibid: 172). But the scandal of covert support to Iraq (Saddamgate/Iraqgate) had to wait two years before emerging (somewhat tamely – since it was election year, after all).

Also during the 1980s, the CIA (in Operation Cyclone) secretly backed the Islamic mujahideen in Afghanistan in their war with the Soviets at an estimated cost to the American taxpayers of more than $3 billion (Kleveman 2003: 246). CIA backing for Islamic radicals in Afghanistan had actually started as early as 1973-1974.[10] Cyclone was one of the longest and most costly CIA operations ever, with the level of arms and equipment shipments peaking at 60,000 tonnes per year by the later 1980s (Todd, Bloch and Fitzgerald 2009: 13).[11] MI6 also secretly supplied weapons, including hand-held Blowpipe missile launchers, to the Afghan rebels (Norton-Taylor 1990: 99). US funding continued even after 1989 as the mujahideen battled the forces of the People's Democratic Party of Afghanistan (PDPA) led by Mohammad Najibullah during the civil war (1989-1992). According to FBI whistleblower Sibel Edmonds, the CIA and Pentagon ran a series of covert operations supporting Islamist militant networks tied to Osama bin Laden – not only in Central Asia, but the Balkans and the Caucasus (Ahmed 2003). Significantly, a report in *The Sunday Times* revealing these ties was 'spiked', allegedly following US state department pressure (ibid). By 1995, backed by Pakistani and US intelligence and Saudi money, the Taliban had secured power in Afghanistan (Neale 2003: 135-137).

RDF: THE GUN WAITING TO BE FIRED?

Nothing more exposes the myth of the 'defensive' United States than the creation of the Rapid Deployment Force. Indeed, it could be argued that by 1990 so much doctrinal theory and financial investment had been directed at this force and to the Middle East strategic region in general that, with the decline of the Soviet Union, the US military was desperate to find an 'enemy' to give it a 'piece of the action' and provide it with some legitimacy. Originally conceived as a small, flexible, quick strike force to protect US interests in the Gulf and elsewhere following the

Iranian revolution of 1979, it rapidly expanded into an enormous fighting force ready for action. It was renamed CENTCOM in January 1983 with responsibility for preserving/promoting US interests from the Horn of Africa and the Arabian peninsula to Pakistan with more than 200,000 US military personnel at its disposal.

The command did not establish new fighting units; rather, forces earmarked for other theatres could be called upon. Special bases were built up: the UK island of Diego Garcia, for instance, was depopulated to make way for the military installations.[12] Up to $1.1bn was spent on improving posts and airfields in Oman, Somalia, Kenya, Egypt, Morocco and Portugal for RDF purposes. British forces were also closely integrated into RDF exercises. But all this developed without any public/media debate in either the US or UK. As Stephen Goose commented (1989: 98): 'The United States is spending billions of dollars to restructure and equip its armed forces so they can intervene more effectively in the Third World, and yet there has been little debate about the implications of those actions.' By August 1990, it could be argued, the RDF was like a 'loaded gun' waiting to be fired.

SILENCING THE ISRAELI LINK

The Israeli link in the Middle Eastern crisis was subtly silenced by the dominant ideological consensus. Since the 1950 the bedrock of US policy in the region has been its devoted support to Israel. Democratic senator Robert Byrd, of West Virginia, on 1 April 1992, indicated for the first time the level of financial backing: some $53bn between 1949 and 1991 – equivalent to 13 per cent of all US military and economic aid over the period (Neff 1992a; 1992b). It became the crucial link country in the US's secret war strategies with the CIA providing it with large subsidies to penetrate Africa in the 1960s in the US interest and later in Asia and Latin America (Hersh 1991: 5). Israel was the crucial power whose roles were to contain the Soviet's supposed aggressive designs on its southern flank during the Cold War years, to contain Arab nationalism and to oversee the West's control over the oil supplies. Cultural and political ties cemented the alliance.

Israel, it has been argued, rates as one of the most terroristic of states (Rose, John 1986).Yet it is rarely defined as such in the Western media. It refuses to withdraw from the occupied territories as demanded by the United Nations; it conducted a brutal war against the Palestinian intifada; it has regularly committed attacks against 'enemy' states. In 1981, for instance, it bombed the Iraqi nuclear plant in Osiraq, near Baghdad. It was the world's first air strike against a nuclear plant.[13] No outrage was expressed on Fleet Street. In 1982, its invasion of Lebanon ended in disaster and with thousands killed.

In 1985, in 'Operation Wooden Leg', it bombed the Tunisian headquarters of the PLO, killing scores of people.[14] The UN Security Council condemned the raid as an act of armed aggression, the US alone abstaining. Mossad, the Israeli secret service, and the Abu Nidal organisation, which, some commentators argue, it has largely infiltrated, had over the years eliminated through assassination three of the four founding fathers of the Fatah wing of the PLO.[15] There is enough evidence to demonise the state of Israel if the media ever wanted – but it never does. In contrast, 'Arab terrorism' up until 2001 and thereafter 'Muslim terrorism' were constant reference points in the Western media.

Just as Saddam Hussein was concerned to link the Iraqi invasion of Kuwait with the Israeli invasion of the West Bank, Golan Heights and Gaza in his negotiating position of 12 August 1990, so the US was equally determined to deny any linkage (Abu-Lughood 1992). Such a policy was seen as compromising with the aggressor. But Fred Halliday argues that for Iraq the promotion of the Palestinian cause was far from a cynical move since it continued a policy established well before the formation of the Ba'ath state in 1968 (Halliday 1991: 223-224). The PLO had set up its HQ in Baghdad after being bombed out of Tunis and saw advantages in an alliance with the growing major Arab power (Jahanpour 1991). For Iraq, support for the PLO could be associated with Saddam Hussein's mounting anti-imperialist rhetoric and advocacy of the cause of the Arab masses against their Western-backed, corrupt and over-wealthy rules. Yet the media followed the Bush agenda, demonising Saddam Hussein and representing Israel as the innocent, 'vulnerable' nation.

Iraq's ambition to gain strategic parity with Israel lay behind much of the political dynamics of the 1988-1990 period. Since 1960, Israel had developed a nuclear weapons programme, first with French assistance, then with covert South African aid.[16] Following revelations to *The Sunday Times* (on 5 and 12 October 1986) by Mordechai Vanunu, a former employee of the Dimona nuclear research centre, it was by the late 1980s estimated to have at least 100 nuclear weapons, making it one of the largest nuclear powers in the world.[17]

The Vanunu revelations came after a report in the *Observer* (of 2 February 1986) that Israel, with financial backing from Iran, had developed a missile capable of carrying nuclear weapons. Yet Israeli politicians have only very rarely admitted to the existence of their nuclear arsenal. They cannot be open about it: America is prevented by law from aiding nations developing nuclear weapons. To admit their existence would render all those billions of dollars of aid illegal. So the Great Lie is maintained.[18] Throughout the demonisation of Saddam Hussein as a nuclear threat in the run-up to the Gulf massacres, the press never chose to 'balance' their coverage with reference to the Israeli arsenal (Kaku 1992). In effect, one of the most important factors in Middle East politics was silenced out of existence. Moreover, Turkey could have been represented as a nuclear state, being home to a vast Nato arsenal including 430 nuclear-capable artillery, 90 surface-to-air missiles and 36 short range ballistic missiles. Turkey was never represented as a nuclear 'threat' in the press. It was a friend to the West, after all (Ehteshami 1987: 149).

NOTES

[1] Morrison, David (1992: 77) *Television and the Gulf War*, Luton: John Libbey and Co. He concludes: '…what is interesting is that the news was more likely to feature the objectives of the war than reasons for the war. In other words, the news tended to adopt a political/militaristic perspective rather than a political/causation perspective.' The reasons supplied on television largely reproduced the government's agenda: to liberate Kuwait – 54 per cent; to uphold international law – 15 per cent; fears of Hussein's expansion capacity – 6 per cent; to ensure world-wide oil supply – 4 per cent; failure of diplomatic means – 7 per cent; other – 14 per cent. Curtis, Liz (1984: 107) *Ireland the propaganda war*, London: Pluto also highlights the absence of relevant contextualising in much of the British media coverage – in this case, Ireland. 'The British media's emphasis on "factual" reporting of incidents, concentrating on "who what where when" and leaving out the background and significance, appears to be objective and straightforward but is, in fact, very misleading. This type of reporting provides the audience with details of age, sex, occupation, type of incident, injuries, location and time of the day. But such information says nothing about the causes of the incident making violence appear as random as a natural disaster or accident.' Lederman, Jim (1992) *Battle lines: The American media and the Intifada*, New York: Henry Holt and Company stresses a more practical factor: 'A newspaper reporter tied to a six hundred word slot on the foreign news page and the radio reporter limited to thirty five seconds have little opportunity to explain complicated issues that may lie behind the event.' Liebes, Tamar (1992) Our war/Their war: Comparing the Intifada and the Gulf War on US and Israeli television, *Critical Studies in Mass Communication*, Vol. 9, No. 1 pp 44-55. Stresses the lack of contextualisation in the media coverage. 'Even the occupation of Kuwait and Saddam Hussein's human rights violations receded as the dynamics of the conflict and the ultimatum, the mobilisation, the logistics, the diplomacy, the preparations for the land war took centre stage' (pp 53-54). The same could be said of the press coverage

[2] Bromley, Simon (1991) Crisis in the Gulf, *Capital and Class*, summer pp 7-14 highlights the oil factor from a leftist position

[3] Landers, Laurie (1992) Restricting reality: Media mindgames and the war, Bennis, Phyllis and Moushabeck, Michel (eds) *Beyond the Storm: A Gulf crisis reader*, Edinburgh: Canongate pp 160-172 highlights involvement of President Bush's policy advisor Brent Scowcroft with the Kuwait Petroleum Corporation p. 168. See also Colhoun, Jack (1992) The family that preys together, *Covert Action Information Bulletin*, Summer pp 50-59. And Dexter, Fred (1991) Ménage à trois: Oil, money, BCCI and the CIA, *Covert Action Information Bulletin*, Winter. Shows that, as the Irangate hearings revealed, Saudi Arabia was to become one of Washington's favourite sources of vast unvouchered money for secret operations during the Reagan years pp 46-48. See also Tisdall, Simon (1992) Bush gave Baker waiver over Iraq, *Guardian*, 19 May

[4] Chomsky, Noam (1992) After the Cold War: US Middle East policy, Bennis, Phyllis and Moushabeck, Michel (eds) *Beyond the Storm: A Gulf crisis reader*, Edinburgh: Canongate pp 75-87 argues that the US and UK are not necessarily opposed to high oil prices. The sharp escalation in 1973 was in many ways beneficial to their economies – the trade balance with oil production rose and the US and UK began to profit from their own high-priced oil in Alaska and the North Sea. Chomsky suggests (ibid: 79-80): 'The US would follow essentially the same policy if it were 100 per cent in solar energy, just as it followed the same policies pre-1970 when it had little need for Middle East oil.' See also Shelley, Toby (1991) Bury the oil demon, Bresheeth, Haim and Yuval-Davis, Nira (eds) *The Gulf War and the new world order*, London: Zed Press pp 166-176

[5] Matthew P. Rendell participated in the discussion with Stewart Purvis, ITN editor, at the Royal Society of Arts, London, on 12 June 1991, on the theme 'The media and the Gulf War'. He is quoted on page 742 of the *RSA Journal*, November 1991, No. 5423

[6] The Bolsheviks, committed to withdrawing from the imperialist war after the November 1917 revolution, discovered the papers relating to the agreement in the Russian archives – and revealed them to the world in *Pravda* and *Izvestia* of 23 November

[7] Ray Douglas, associate professor at Colgate University, New York State, argued in 2009 that claims that the British had used chemical weapons in the early 1920 to quell an Arab rebellion were based on false evidence (see British gas attack on Iraqis a myth, claims historian, by *Daily Telegraph* reporter, 22 October 2009)

[8] According to Aldrich and Cormac, Prime Minister Anthony Eden encouraged numerous assassination plots against Nasser (2016: 198-203). They came to light after Miles Copeland, a CIA officer based in London, revealed them to a US senate committee in January 1977 (ibid: 202) – just a year before Eden's death

[9] The CIA officially only admitted its role in the removal of Mossadeq in 2013 – in a declassified document, titled *The battle for Iran*, obtained and published by the National Security Archive research institute at George Washington University in Washington, DC (Walker, Tim 2013)

[10] See https://verbena19.wordpress.com/2007/06/26/tomgram-roger-morris-the-cia-and-the-gates-legacy/, accessed on 22 August 2016

[11] Todd, Bloch and Fitzgerald (2009: 13) add: 'Of equal significance was the massive provision of military training. Although some Afghani fighters were taken directly to US Special Forces establishments such as Fort Bragg, most training took place in border areas of Pakistan, where a large programme was run under the direction of the (US-trained) Pakistan Inter-Services Intelligence (ISI) with help from China, Israel and Britain's MI6'

[12] The Chagos Islanders, after many years of campaigning, lost their attempt in the Supreme Court to return to their homeland in June 2016. See https://www.theguardian.com/world/2016/jun/29/chagos-islanders-lose-supreme-court-bid-to-return-to-homeland, accessed on 26 July 2016. See also http://www.theguardian.com/politics/2004/oct/02/foreignpolicy.comment, accessed on 26 July 2016

[13] See http://news.bbc.co.uk/onthisday/hi/dates/stories/june/7/newsid_3014000/3014623.stm, accessed on 26 July 2016

[14] See http://www.liveleak.com/view?i=cd0_1400961370, accessed on 26 July 2016.

[15] Seale, Patrick (1992) *Abu Nidal: The world's most notorious terrorist*, London: Arrow Books. He writes: 'Of the four founding fathers of Fatah only Arafat remains. Muhummad Yusif al-Najjar was killed by an Israeli assassination squad in Beirut in 1973; Khalil al-Wazir (Abu Jihad) was killed by Israeli commandos in Tunis in 1988.' He suggests that Abu Iyad, Arafat's No. 2, was killed by Abu Nidal, presumably on the orders of the Israelis, in January 1991, on the eve of the Gulf massacres. Seale argues strongly throughout the book that Abu Nidal is an Israeli agent – though the evidence, he admits, can never be conclusive p. 324

[16] See https://www.wsws.org/en/articles/2000/02/isra-f12.html, accessed on 27 July 2016

[17] After making his revelations, Vanunu befriended a glamorous woman 'Cindy'. This turned out to be Mossad agent Cheryl Bentov. On a 'romantic' trip to Rome, Vanunu was drugged and taken to Israel where he was convicted of treason and espionage and sentenced to 18 years in prison (11 years of it spent in solitary confinement). In May 2010, he was jailed again for speaking to the foreign media. In July 2016, he was tried again for allegedly revealing classified information in an interview with Israel Channel 2 television and for meeting two foreigners three years earlier (see http://www.agreenroadjournal.com/2015/06/mordechai-vanunu-israels-nuclear.html, accessed on 27 July 2016)

[18] See http://www.theatlantic.com/international/archive/2014/09/israel-nuclear-weapons-secret-united-states/380237/, accessed on 27 July 2016

Chapter Seven

New militarism and the making of the military option

I mmediately following the Iraqi invasion of Kuwait on 2 August 1990 virtually all the London-based national press opted for a military response. The new militarist consensus emerged blazing verbal guns. Even the government of the US and US at the time played a dual role, calling for diplomacy but warning of military retaliation. Most of the press had no time for talk – they wanted war and right now. From 3 August, Fleet Street was on a virtual war footing.

Ideological framing was perfectly simple and consistently maintained. Immediately diplomacy and sanctions were downplayed (or identified with 'appeasement'); the Saddam 'monster' threat was emphasised and the military option prioritised. The language was always fighting and fiercely patriotic. On 3 August in the *Mail*, columnist Paul Johnson wrote (under the headline: 'Force – the only answer to this despot'): 'One thing is certain – half measures are not going to be enough. Threats of economic sanctions and fiddling about at the UN will simply confirm Hussein's judgment that he has got away with it.' He continued: 'All the requisite forces – air, land and sea – should be promptly despatched to the area, a task force created, a commander appointed and instructions clearly given to meet any further act of aggression by Iraq with force. ... Force or the convincing threat of force is the only language he has ever understood.' By August 4, the *Mail* was highlighting the war option this way:

> Two military moves would force Hussein out of Kuwait, say defence experts. They are a frontal attack across the Saudi Arabian desert and a massive bombing assault on nuclear and chemical weapons factories around Baghdad. The Gulf nations would need help from the US and European troops in an operation backed by precision bombing techniques developed principally by the US and Britain.

The *Mirror* argued: 'President Bush and Gorbachev supported by Mrs Thatcher and President Mitterrand should meet immediately to agree a unified plan of action against him. The lesson of history is that appeasement never brings peace or security but means only a harder and bloodier fight later on.' Under the headline: 'What can the world do now?' the newspaper wrote: 'If Saddam refused to withdraw Bush could order selective strikes against Iraqi targets like military and oil installations.'

On 4 August, the *Mirror's* page one headline ran: 'Stay put or it's war' with the focus on the military logistical build-up. On 6 August, it commented: 'The military option seemed more likely as it was reported that defense secretary Dick Cheney was heading to Saudi Arabia.' By 8 August, war was almost breaking out: 'Battle stations' was the headline. 'The allied fleet dwarfs Iraq's navy of five missile frigates and 38 patrol craft. But President Saddam Hussein can call up 450 combat planes for air strikes.' On 9 August (almost intoxicated by war fever), it declared: 'US on brink of war with Iraq.' And its editorial commented sternly: 'Saddam Hussein was given his last chance to "pull back from the brink". If he refuses it will mean war. .... If war comes we shall pray it will be won quickly and decisively.'

The Sunday Times of 5 August began its page one lead: 'The threat of large-scale war in the Middle East increased dramatically last night as America prepared to despatch B52 bombers to the region in an effort to deter Iraq from invading Saudi Arabia.' Saudi and Turkish preferences for an Arab solution were described as 'a problem'. Its editorial ruled out a military operation 'at least for now'. 'The logistics of mounting it against a ruthless ruler prepared to use chemical weapons, with almost 1m. battle-hardened troops and more tanks than Rommel, Eisenhower and Montgomery combined had in North Africa, are just too formidable.' The implications being that when the logistical problems were sorted out, then was the time to attack. Just one week later, *The Sunday Times* was backing all-out war. Its editorial commented:

> There will be no real purpose to the American expedition until Mr Bush faces up to the harsh fact that President Saddam will have to be removed, sadly but inevitably, by force. ... The reason why we will shortly have to go to war with Iraq is not to free Kuwait though that is to be desired or to defend Saudi Arabia, though that is important. It is because President Saddam is a menace to the vital interests in the Gulf – above all the free flow of oil at market prices which is essential to the West's prosperity.

For *The Sunday Times*, Britain's biggest-selling Sunday 'quality', the backing for military action to topple 'madman Saddam' became the obsessive, simple theme of all its Gulf editorials from early August onwards.

THE *INDEPENDENT*: NOT INDEPENDENT?

The *Guardian* and the *Independent*, however, stood out against this warmongering campaign. The first (while following the dominant consensus in prioritising the military build-up in its news coverage) was to maintain editorially a sceptical eye towards the Bush/Thatcher/Major agenda, backing the negotiations/sanctions option until the outbreak of hostilities. As principal feature writer Martin Woollocott explained in an interview with the author: 'We were somewhat divided at editorial meetings. Some saw war as inevitable; some saw ways out and for them diplomacy was of major interest. The *Guardian* is traditionally anti-imperialist and we tend to take a hard look at the motives of the major powers.'

The *Independent*'s approach was different. Until 17 August 1990 it backed the negotiations option with a series of editorials stressing the diplomatic route. For instance, on 13 August it responded positively to Iraq's 'encouraging' negotiating offer in which it linked Israel's occupation of the West Bank and Gaza with the Iraqi intervention in Kuwait. 'For the West to overthrow Saddam Hussein by force would be to emulate his behaviour in Kuwait.'[1] On 15 August, it was critical of US acting aggressively in imposing a blockade of Iraq. On the following day it saw Iraq's treaty with Iran as increasing the danger of war. 'It is therefore more necessary than ever to move carefully and to give mediation a chance.' On 17 August, it concluded: 'It is in the UN's long-term interests to seek a negotiated settlement.'

Everything suddenly changed on 20 August. Then the *Independent* joined what Edward Pierce of the *Guardian* dubbed the Editors for War group. Saddam had to be stopped now, it pronounced. Next day it commented: 'Stability will not return to the region while Saddam Hussein remains in power and the only argument he understands is force.' On 22 August, its earlier commitment to negotiations was dumped. 'Iraq offers to negotiate should be treated with the utmost scepticism. Deeds not words are required from them.' On 24 August, it declared: 'The logic of the American and British line in the Gulf leads to war sooner rather than later.' Harvey Morris, in charge of the *Independent*'s Gulf desk during the crisis and massacres, suggested in an interview with the author that the sudden change came about after the editor fully examined the implications of the Iraqi invasion. He denied there was any pressure on the newspaper to shift its editorial stance.

IRAQ: THE NECESSARY GLOBAL THREAT

Running through all the coverage (in fact, on both sides of the Atlantic) was the representation of Saddam Hussein personally as a global threat: the world was threatened and the world (united) was reacting in defence. In order to legitimise the massive build-up of troops the threat of the 'enemy' clearly had to be exaggerated. As Associated Press veteran Mort Rosenblum later admitted (1993: 117): 'From the beginning all of us bought the myth that a nearly naked emperor was clad in triple-ply armor.' There was constant reference to 'Saddam' possessing a '1 million-strong army of battle-hardened soldiers', the fourth largest in the world. This was blatant disinformation which ran through the whole of the UK (and US) corporate press.

In this way, new militarist societies (dependent on relatively small armies and increasingly on small/covert forces and very expensive, low-manpower, high-technology weapons) were subtly able to represent much weaker and less sophisticated militarist societies – such as Iraq – as more powerful than they really were. In fact, the bigger the size of the army, the less effective it was in combat with a professional First World force. Morale amongst conscripts is often low to non-existent as both the Argentinians (in the Falklands/Malvinas conflict in 1982) and later the Iraqis in 1991 were to prove. Moreover, Iraqi troops were known to have performed badly in the 1980-1988 war with Iran when thousands had deserted (al-Jabbar 1992: 5-6). Rather than 'battle-hardened', a more apt description for the Iraqi army in 1990 would have been 'battle-weary'. But it was never applied (see Abbas 1986: 220-222).[2]

Saddam's potential as a global threat was linked to his 'terroristic' ambitions and stressed in the propaganda campaign to actualise the growing possibilities of conflict to the public who may otherwise have felt completely uninterested in a military adventure in a far-away, unknown part of the world. Thus, *The Sunday Times*, of 5 August, on Saddam:

> From his massive command bunker outside Baghdad he put into operation what could be the first stage of a plan to reshape the Middle East and create potential mayhem from the world's economic and political order. … Iraqis in their dark green uniforms are known by their fellow Arabs as the Prussians of the Middle East. The army is the biggest in the region and is reckoned to be a match for Nato's powers such as Britain, let alone the Kuwaiti police guard.

Its editorial warned: 'Iraq could be the unchallenged regional superpower capable of dictating oil plans for the entire Gulf repository of 65 per cent of the world's oil reserves. That is the Western nightmare write large, an evil, anti-Western despot with a stranglehold over the main source of the Western lifeblood.' On 3 August, the *Mirror* asked: 'What can the world do now?' The Iraqi leader was described as militarily 'very strong'. 'He has a well-trained army of a million men who fought an eight-year-long war against Iran. He has thousands of tanks, and artillery pieces, some MIG fighter bombers and ground-to-ground missiles. And chemical weapons that he has used before.' The myth of the global threat was accompanied by the myth of the global response to the invasion. As President Bush said at a news conference on 22 August 1990: 'This is not a matter between Iraq and the USA. It is between Iraq and the entire world community, Arabs and non-Arabs, all nations lined-up to oppose aggression.'

In fact, the world was deeply divided and confused over the attack. America, through a mixture of ruthless diplomacy and bribery, won over sufficient support in the UN to create the appearance of 'world support'. But in the end only 26 countries (out of 160) joined the coalition (many of them with tiny, token forces) with only 11 taking part in the offensive action in Kuwait. News of the massive opposition globally to the build-up to war was marginalised throughout the UK (and US) press. Massive nationwide anti-war demonstrations and sit-ins were largely ignored by the press.[3]

HYPING THE INEVITABILITY OF WAR

Most of Fleet Street represented war in the Gulf as inevitable – from the beginning of the crisis up to the launch of Desert Storm. Many prominent journalists genuinely believed in the war's inevitability from the early days of the crisis. Martin Woollacott, of the *Guardian*, for instance, commented in an interview with the author: 'War was inevitable from September. Neither side could make the necessary concessions because the purposes of the two sides were too radically opposed. A Middle Eastern leader had taken unilateral action to challenge the West's authority. And the prestige gained had to be wiped out.'

But the constant repetition of the inevitability of the conflict, it could be argued, served the ideological and political purpose of rendering opposition marginal and doomed to defeat. It amounted to a sophisticated means of disempowering anti-war voices. From 3 August, the press concentrated on the military build-up in the Gulf – the implication behind virtually all the coverage being that it would shortly be put to use in war. Thus, the *Sun*, on 7 August, under a headline: 'Yanks on warpath', began its report: 'America's mighty war machine was gearing up last night for a military strike as patience in the West finally ran out.' The focus was reinforced with a 'You the Jury' feature which gave a *Sun* poll result of 22,991 to 177 in favour of military action. By 9 August, it summoned up World War Two imagery in this way: 'President Bush spoke with Churchill-like gravity to the American people in a TV address that virtually prepares the world for war.' Next day, it reported the allies and Iraq standing 'ready to do battle today'.

The Sunday Times identified in an editorial on 12 August the reasons why 'we will shortly have to go to war with Iraq'. The following week it headlined: 'US on brink of war with Iraq: Saddam to starve hostage babies' (Hiro 1991: 145). On 6 November, the *Daily Star* carried what it claimed was a 'world exclusive'. 'War this week: Iraq raid go ahead'. The front page of the London *Evening Standard* of 30 November maintained: 'Iraq may strike at any moment' (Keeble 1991). The *Mirror* constantly prioritised the military option and kept up war fever by forever representing the 'world' as on the brink of battle. The Iraqi offer of 12 August, linking withdrawal from Kuwait with other occupations in the Middle East, was ignored by the newspaper. But on 15 August it was writing: 'It is not yet known if Saddam is prepared to negotiate with the West over his invasion of Kuwait.' On the same day it suggested Turkey's army had been put on a war alert after Saddam Hussein's jets had blitzed Turkish villages just inside Iraq.

The *Mirror*'s Ramsey Smith on board HMS York on 16 August was already quoting soldiers as being ready to fight. With those same phrases that were to be repeated time after time over the following months, Petty Officer Mike Lough was quoted: 'I would much rather just get the hell out of here and go home. But we are under no illusion. If the job has to be done then we will have to do it. It is simple as that.' Professional duty was eliminating all moral, political dilemmas for the soldier – just as was happening for so many journalists. On 22 August, the paper headlined: 'War is inevitable warns Mitterrand: French expect air strike in 28 hours.' Three days later it was headlining: 'Countdown to war.' Saddam Hussein was said to be set 'to plunge the Gulf into all-out war within hours'. It quoted an interview with Gen. Ariel Sharon, a leading member of the Israeli cabinet, in another of proprietor Robert Maxwell's newspapers, the *European* (so using news as a publicity stunt), to the effect that the West would have to go to war 'without delay' to curb Saddam.

Consistent with the Bush agenda to promote occasionally peace and yet prepare for war, the *Mirror*, suddenly on 28 August, carried an editorial: 'Give peace a chance.' War, it said, was not inevitable. Mrs Thatcher should give peace a chance. Such views accompanied a story on President Bush supposedly backing a UN peace bid. They didn't last long. The next day it was keeping up the war fever with the report: 'Tyrant Saddam Hussein was warned yesterday that half a million Iraqis could die if he sparked off a war with further military action.'

On 17 September, under the headline: 'Let's blitz Saddam', it reported: 'If war starts, the American air force wants to decapitate Iraq by bombing President Saddam Hussein, his family, his senior commanders, his palace guard and even his mistress.' Such reports fed the demonisation of Saddam Hussein, but in military terms were highly questionable: these were just the people who were to escape once the massacres began, protected in their secret bunkers. Those to die, rather, were the thousands of conscripts (Glasgow University Media Group 1991: 2). By 12 October, it was saying: 'Hurd paves the way for war in the Gulf.' On 31 October, the paper was suggesting Saddam Hussein had put his army on alert for an invasion within the next few days. On 1 November, war was said to be 'imminent'. On 22 November, it highlighted 'Rambo' star Sylvester Stallone calling for a pull-out of US troops and a nuclear attack on 'Saddam Hussein': 'In that way no American would get hurt.'

Roy Greenslade, editor of the *Mirror* at the time, has revealed that not only was a *Mirror* journalist assigned by the newspaper's proprietor Robert Maxwell to sell encyclopaedias published by one of his companies in Saudi Arabia (and threatened with the sack when he refused) but that all the paper's leaders were being written by Maxwell himself (Greenslade 1992: 208). From early August they kept up a constant cry for war. Accompanying a near hysterical support for Israel, 'the West's only real friend and trustworthy ally in the Middle East', and criticism of President Bush for 'playing footsie with Syria's President Assad' (26 November) was a profound contempt for Saddam Hussein.

On 25 October, for instance, under the headline: 'The way to win', the editorial commented: 'Saddam Hussein is clever as well as ruthless. Mrs Thatcher should be strongly supported in her determination to bring him to book by military means. ... An overwhelming pre-emptive strike at night against planes on the ground, arsenals and headquarters would save hundreds of thousands of lives.' The same line was repeated on 27 November. It was blaming the ministry of defence for appeasement on 13 December for supposedly banning 'Christmas carols for our boys in the Gulf'.

On 8 January, it criticised the Labour Party for preferring sanctions to war. 'Too late to chicken out,' it claimed. 'Giving Saddam another breathing space would mean more deaths and terrible injuries among our forces.' The Mirror Group was at the time the only one on Fleet Street providing any consistent support to the Labour Party – not from any kind of principled stand but, it could be argued, out of a simple, capitalist desire to exploit a gap in the market. Now, on an issue as crucial as the Middle East crisis, the *Mirror* turned against Labour.

Roy Greenslade has since argued (in an interview with the author) that, in pushing the 'war is inevitable' line, he had hoped that the British press might have impressed on the Iraqis the allied commitment to action and thus encouraged them to retreat from their invasion of Kuwait. He said it was certainly easier for the *Mirror* to back the war option once Mrs Thatcher was replaced as Conservative leader by the less jingoistic John Major, on 22 November 1990.[4]

SILENCING THE ANTI-WAR VOICES: *DAILY MIRROR* CASE STUDY

Along with the prioritising of the military option went the virtual exclusion of anti-war voices. Hallin (1986) has identified the historic 19th century compromise established between press and government in the US and UK according to which the press abstained from radical criticism of the state in exchange for access to government sources. Journalists are, effectively, agents of the state, reproducing the dominant ideological values, defining the limits of acceptable discourse and marginalising/delegitimising/eliminating radically critical voices. Kellner (1990: 98-99), along with the Italian political theorist Antonio Gransci, modifies this view arguing that the media serve to negotiate and mediate significant democratic tensions in the interests of elite hegemony.

Nowhere was the press's propaganda role more apparent than in the coverage of the crisis and massacres. Voices objecting to the sending of troops to the Gulf were virtually non-existent. And those who advocated using the troops as an offensive force (sooner or later) were privileged far above those who saw them merely as supporting the sanctions policy (Flanders 1992: 160-172). For instance, over the first six days of the crisis the *Mirror* used 67 quotes but only two of them were opposed to the military option. One was from the anxious husband of an air hostess stranded in Kuwait at the time of the Iraqi invasion (7 August); the other was from the stepfather of a stewardess caught in the invasion. In both cases, an assumption could be drawn that both men were speaking out of selfish (though understandable) concern for the fate of their relatives. Once that danger was removed an implication could be that they might support the war. None of these anti-war voices came from a principled, articulate political voice of opposition to the military build-up.

The extraordinary complexity of the Arab responses to the crisis was almost completely ignored by the press (Azzam 1991). Arab views were almost totally excluded. More generally, they were represented stereotypically as hysterical, violent supporters of Saddam Hussein. On 17 August, the *Mirror* carried a profile of Maryam Rajavi, who was supposedly Iraq's youngest general. 'And like the highly trained, battle-hardened women under her command she is a total fanatic.' Running counter to this overall approach was a report on 22 August focusing on British wives of Jordanian men calling for a diplomatic solution to the crisis. Yet the newspaper still managed to headline the report: 'Arab wives on warpath' transforming a call for peace into a war cry and at the same time perpetuating the stereotype of the violent, fanatical Arab (in fact, they were British wives). 'The women, who have made their homes in Jordan, accused the Prime Minister and President Bush of threatening world safety because of greed for oil.' Just four women were quoted.

Given the sexist bias of the newspaper, a picture accompanying the report featuring some attractive women must have helped in its selection. Significantly, the picture was repeated when five days later the newspaper used the letters page to articulate what amounted to its own criticism of the diplomatic option. Under the headline: 'Wailing women', a reader wrote: 'How ridiculous of the British women who married wealthy Arabs to voice their strident uninformed attacks on this country at a carefully rehearsed press conference in Jordan. And their talk of starving Iraqi kids sounded like crocodile tears in view of their obvious prosperity.' People calling for peace are, thus, identified with 'stridency' and ignorance: the implication is that they are ruthless propagandists and wealthy hypocrites. The *Mirror* is, at the same time, delegitimising a view it strongly opposes. Those politicians such as Tony Benn and Edward Heath, who were identified with the peace movement, were vilified. On 7 September, for instance, the newspaper attacked Benn in this way:

> Tony Benn belongs in the mausoleum, ex-Prime Minister Jim Callaghan said yesterday. He launched a broadside against his old colleague who is leading the campaign for a Commons vote against action in the Gulf. 'As far as my friend Mr Tony Benn is concerned I am sure that one day a statue will be erected to him in that mausoleum for people whose self-righteousness exceeds their intellectual ability.'

The implications are clear: Benn is ignorant and self-righteous; those who support the war are presumably intelligent and genuine. There is no pretence at balance: a counter quotation from Benn himself, say. Given the failures of the Labour Party (and Democratic Party in the US) to promote the diplomatic option with any conviction (Rogers 1992: 275), the peace movement in Britain (and the US) lacked any strong institutional base and this, in part, accounted for the marginalisation of peace voices.

NAKED PROPAGANDA

Just before the launch of Desert Storm a man and woman streaked naked at a Tottenham Hotspur football match in protest. Here was a perfect story for the *Mirror*. Of course they carried a picture of the two (discreetly) starkers but then, given their sexist bias, only focused on the woman involved. A whole page was given over to her 'naked truth about her nude New Year sprint' but – apart from the short quotation: 'I decided to do it as a way of drawing attention to the crazy war that could soon break out' – she was given no space to articulate her views. Instead, the story concentrated entirely on the event, how a woman Pc. handled her, what her brother, father, grandfather *felt*. The human interest bias of the press is seen here demonstrating one of its prime ideological functions – to depoliticise the profoundly political.

THE MYTH OF POPULAR SUPPORT: POLLS AND THE MANUFACTURE OF PUBLIC OPINION

Opinion polls play a crucial role in society serving largely to create rather than reflect public opinion on crucial issues. The Middle East crisis of 1990-1991 provides a perfect case study. The central myth of the massacres is that up to 80 per cent of the British public supported the war option. In the forward to his collection of journalism articles on the massacres, Brian MacArthur (1991: 10), of *The Sunday Times*, articulates the dominant view, reproducing this figure to suggest that the British press, in their unanimous support for the war, were once again reflecting the wishes of the public.

Not only does this view discount the views of those 20 per cent who, even according to his reading of the polls, did not support the war and thus were unrepresented (20 per cent reflected in electoral support being quite substantial). It also ignores the fact that Labour, the party leading in the polls at the time, was pressing the case for sanctions when Desert Storm was launched. More significantly still, the MacArthur view obscures the complexities of polling results. Ultimately, it is based on a partial reading of polls which were heavily manipulated towards promoting the war option (Cockburn 1991b). As Fouad Moughrabi argues (1993: 40):

> Opinion surveys presume that people have access to information which informs their attitudes. In reality, of course, the majority of the public has only the information that the media provide, especially about foreign policy issues. In the case of the Middle East, information is often selected and interpreted so that it reinforces existing stereotypes and creates new ones.

He suggests that polls provide major private and public institutions 'a powerful tool to shape, domesticate and manage public opinion'.

People's views are very often confused; they contain ambivalences, contradictions; they can change quickly; they are based, often, on ignorance and prejudice. Sometimes people may be afraid to give their true feelings/thoughts to a questioner; they may even want to make fun of the whole process. People lie. They have learned to imitate the state's secrecy and so keep their true feelings secret. In pre-internet days, views were often influenced by the way and tone in which the question was put, by the personality of the questioner. During the early 1980s, for instance, 80 per cent of Britons polled said they supported Nato. But when asked to spell out Nato and explain what it was only 40 per cent could (Berrington 1989: 18-36). Ask people if they supported the 'independent nuclear deterrent' and a majority would say 'Yes'. Ask them if they supported a nuclear deterrent which, if ever used, would lead to the deaths of thousands and possible global holocaust, only a minority would support it. Similarly, views can be manipulated by restricting the range of questions. This was particularly the case during the Middle East crisis. Journalists often interpret polls unproblematically. And they are drawn to them because they appear to provide 'objective' statistics (Dionne 1992: 154-156). Moreover, when polls can be interpreted in the interests of the elite (or a prominent section of it) then journalists highlight them; when they produce results embarrassing for the elite then the results are often twisted or they are quickly forgotten.[5]

HOW THE POLLS SILENCED THE PEACE OPTION

In August 1990, following the Iraqi invasion of Kuwait, Gallup asked a series of questions on the crisis (Wybrow 1991). The views expressed were extremely contradictory. Some 85 per cent were said to approve of President Bush's action 'to prevent an Iraqi invasion of Saudi Arabia'. Note: they did not support an offensive war against Iraq. Moreover, when asked: 'Do you think the present crisis in the Middle East will be over quite soon or do you think it will go on for a long time?' 72 per cent they thought it would go on for a long time. Only 20 per cent thought it would be over quite soon. At this time the vast majority of the British press were calling for an all-out war against Iraq. But most people opposed this view. They supported the defence of Saudi Arabia if attacked (the attack, of course, never came). They thought the crisis would last a long time (thus ignoring

174

the arguments of Fleet Street editors who were calling for war now) and were presumably preparing to hold on while a diplomatic solution was worked out. When asked about the outcome of the crisis, in fact, the majority, 58 per cent, thought there would be no war.

Most significant of all, none of the Gallup questions invited people to ponder the various aspects of the diplomatic/sanctions option. All the questions were about military and military-related issues. In this way, it could be argued, the polls reinforced the military option so vigorously promoted by the media. No questions were asked about the possibilities of a compromise solution. How many people supported the Iraqi attempt to link withdrawal from Kuwait with Israeli withdrawal from the Occupied Territories? What if Iraq was to be offered the northern Kuwaiti oilfields and UN forces were placed on the border? What about a Middle East peace conference being set up to negotiate all the region's controversies? And so on. These possibilities were hardly ever envisaged by the pollsters. The bias of the public debate on the crisis, it could be argued, was manipulated subtly to promote the war option.

Worse still, the polls introduced into the public domain a debate about the totally unacceptable. People were not asked their views about a Middle East conference, they were asked if the use of nuclear weapons was legitimate (some 26 per cent were in favour). In this way, the polls subtly introduced the possibility of nuclear holocaust into the public domain. Throughout the crisis Gallup asked if people preferred a military assault or a blockade 'that might have to last for a very long time'. The majority was always in favour of the blockade: 63 per cent in September to 55 per cent in December. In the last Gallup poll before the launch of Desert Storm only 31 per cent supported a military assault.

Adding to the complexities, throughout the crisis people voted roughly 60 per cent in favour of military action if the economic blockade alone was found to be failing. But this was never established. The last CIA assessment before the launch of Desert Storm indicated exactly the opposite – that the sanctions were having a crippling effect on the Iraqi economy. But the American elite just could not wait to 'kick Saddam's arse' (as they so often declared). In December, Mori asked five questions for *The Sunday Times*.[6] All of them involved debates around the military option. The majority were in favour of war.[7] But the peace option was nowhere explored. In this way, the limits of legitimate debate are set by the polling organisations and the media they serve.

PRESS MANIPULATION OF PUBLIC OPINION

On 24 August 1990, the *Independent* published an NOP poll on the crisis. Out of 13 question categories, seven were based on the presumption of the inevitability of war. None of the questions explored the possibilities of the diplomatic option. Again the poll raised the possibility of the use of nuclear weapons. But this time, the

Independent raised a new and, it could be argued, equally unacceptable question: it asked if people would support an undercover team to be sent to Iraq to assassinate Saddam Hussein.

This was clearly built on the massive demonisation campaign against the Iraqi leader that was being pursued in the British media and the accompanying glorification of the role of the SAS. Some 61 per cent of people supported this suggestion. Most crucially, the question failed to point out that such an act would break international law.[8] But such questioning pointed to an important element of new militarist societies. During the 1950 and 1960s the CIA indulged in many coups, assassinations, mass killings. And they were largely secret. In the context of the democratic façade of the new militarist state, the secret state was able to thrive in a political climate which could tolerate the open debate over what was once hidden action. Assassination of heads of government became a legitimate, unproblematic political option – but only when a friendly state called for it.

Soon after the Iraqi invasion of Kuwait, the British press reported uncritically President Bush authorising the CIA to assassinate Saddam Hussein. None of the reports pointed out that such action was unlawful. But when the Iranian Ayatollah issues a fatwa and calls for the death of one British writer (Salman Rushdie in 1989) (which is equally unacceptable) the outrage expressed reaches fever pitch. In his coverage of the NOP poll, the *Independent* journalist Peter Kellner merely reinforces the military option. The parallels he draws are all with previous wars – the Falklands, Suez, World War Two. At this stage in late August 1990 the launch of Desert Storm is months away. But for Kellner and the *Independent* (and the British press in general) war was inevitable. Once again the Hitler Hussein line is promoted (though no specific Hitler question was asked): 'There is a widespread belief that Britain faces a modern version of Hitler but that any resort to military force should have the backing of the UN.'

He goes on to discuss the dilemmas posed if PM Thatcher and President Bush attacked without UN blessing. No such pondering over the possibilities of a negotiated settlement. And he concludes: 'A reasonable guess is that a quick, decisive war in the Gulf would attract public acclaim – almost whatever methods were used short of nuclear retaliation.' In other words, the scene was being set early in August for the conflict. In the poll, some 87 per cent supported the blockade to persuade Iraq to withdraw; some 66 per cent supported military action but only if the blockade failed to end the occupation. The failure of sanctions to move Iraqi troops was never established. In fact, the poll could easily be interpreted to promote the need for diplomacy to avert the need for military action. The *Independent*, and the press in general, was committed to a completely different agenda.

THE ART OF IGNORING POLLS

On 16 January 1991, on the eve of Desert Storm, the *Guardian* published an ICM poll. Only 54 per cent of people backed the use of force. Some 32 per cent favoured all action short of the use of force; as many as 13 per cent said Britain should not get involved. In other words, here was a major polling body on the eve of the massacres revealing that only a slim majority backed the military option.

ICM, unusually, asked a question about the peace option. Some 31 per cent said there should be a link between a general conference on the Middle East (including the Palestinian question) and any settlement of the Gulf crisis. So on the most controversial aspect of the Iraqi strategy on the Gulf crisis, the poll found a sizeable minority in support. But perhaps more significantly, the poll found a high percentage (24) were unable to express an opinion. Not surprising since the possibility of a Middle East conference had been virtually ruled out by the press.

THE ART OF DISTORTING POLLS

On 22 October, the *Mirror* carried a rare article on the US peace movement which it described as 'ominous': 'Yanks come home American protesters tell Bush.' But in the opening the report the newspaper said that 86 per cent of people in Britain 'believe our boys should launch a military strike against the Iraqi tyrant'. No poll at that time was producing such a result. It was an invention. But it became an accepted truth. Such was the potency of the press in new militarist societies.

NOTES

[1] For the content of Iraq's 12 August 1990 peace initiative, see Hiro 1992: 146

[2] See also Cook, Nick (1990) Iraqi air power, *Jane's Soviet Intelligence Report*, October. On the poor performance of the Iraqi pilots in the war, he comments: 'Air combat in the eight-year conflict was almost non-existent.' And Friedman, Norman (1991: 112-113) *Desert victory: The war for Kuwait*, Annapolis, Maryland: Naval Institute Press, comments: 'It may be that the Western powers, having backed Saddam during the Iran-Iraq war, could not admit that his forces had been less than competent, even in their triumph in 1988. The evidence was certainly there, in more than a decade of military disaster: against the Israelis, against the Kurds, against the Iranians during much of the war. All of these cases had been well-documented.' While the press represented the allies, in contrast, as relatively inexperienced in battle compared to the Iraqis, Friedman argues the opposite. The US army had made enormous investment in the national training centre in the Mojave Desert where its troops could fight mock battles. New technology, in the form of lasers whose hits could be immediately scored and tabulated, made these battles realistic. 'Thus, in enormous contrast to previous wars, the US Army which came to Saudi Arabia in 1990-1991 was already somewhat battle-hardened and battle-wise' p. 121

[3] This was a profoundly American war. But even in the United States there were deep divisions, the final votes for military action only clearing the senate on 22 January by 53 to 47 and in the house of representatives by 250 to 183 – hardly evidence of a national consensus for war which the media were intent on representing

[4] See http://historylists.org/events/10-key-events-that-led-to-margaret-thatchers-resignation.html, accessed on 3 August 2016. Greenslade also cited the underlying thesis of *Secret state, silent press* in his analysis of Fleet Street coverage leading up to the 2003 invasion in They've lost the battle, will they support the war? *Guardian*, 17 March. He wrote: 'In the aftermath of the 1991 Gulf war – well, so-called war – a media academic analysed the reasons behind the overwhelming Fleet Street support for the desert stormtroopers. Richard Keeble urged us not to see the newspapers' gung-ho

backing for the governments of the United States and Britain as part of a conspiracy between the press and political elite but as a result of a conjunction of profound political, historical, cultural and ideological forces. I don't intend to rehearse Keeble's sophisticated thesis here but he did make a number of telling points about the media's myth-making which had ensured popular endorsement for the war'

[5] Glasgow University Media Group (1985: 19) devote important sections of their study into television coverage of the Falklands/Malvinas conflict to opinion polls. They conclude that television completely distorted poll findings in the interests of government strategy. 'The polls showed attitudes were very complex. Until well into the crisis a majority thought that the issues did not merit losing British life.' A poll, just before the landings, also showed that 76 per cent of the population wished the United Nations to administer the islands pending a diplomatic solution. 'Little of this appeared on ITN.' See also pp 136-143; 305-308 on the theoretical issues raised by opinion polls

[6] *British Public Opinion*: newsletter of Market and Opinion Research International, London, December 1990 p. 5

[7] A similar bias was evident in US polls. A *Washington Post*/ABC News poll taken on 30 November to 2 December asked: 'If Iraq does not withdraw from Kuwait should the United States go to war with Iraq to force it out of Kuwait at some point after 15 January or not?' Some 63 per cent responded yes to war, 32 per cent responded no and 15 per cent expressed no opinion

[8] In the United States, a number of television shows asked similar questions of their audience with similar results

The apparatus of silence in the Gulf 1990-1991: The symbolic significance of the censorship regime

The 1991 Gulf conflict was accompanied by what many commentators identified as unprecedented levels of government censorship and control. John Pilger, for instance, commented: 'During many years reporting wars and coping with propaganda I have never known such manipulation in a self-proclaimed free society' (Pilger 1991d). Journalists were the real prisoners of war, trapped behind the barbed wire of reporting curbs, according to William Boot (1991: 24). Alex Thomson, ITN Channel Four News reporter during the conflict, used the same image: 'The pools were a prison' (1992: 82). Leaders of the International Federation of Journalists (IFJ), representing journalists from 50 countries, met in Brussels during the conflict and endorsed a tough statement criticising the levels of secrecy in Gulf coverage. It warned that 'media controls being applied by the allies are in danger of descending to levels of censorship which have become routine in Iraq'.[1]

Very few journalists were allowed to travel with the troops; very little actual combat was observed; most journalists were confined to hotels in Saudi Arabia. Those journalists who tried to evade these constraints were harassed by the authorities – and sometimes even by colleagues. Yet the importance of these overt, interventionist strategies by the state should be placed in context. Journalists have tended to exaggerate their importance. They help promote the myth of the adversary press. Governments tend to emphasise their censorship moves because they are felt to be in accordance with 'the public mood'. But, in reality, censorship operates on far more subtle levels.

Even where a journalist – such as Robert Fisk of the *Independent* (with considerable experience of covering Beirut and the Lebanon war) – was opposed to many aspects of the war and worked with other colleagues outside the official media structures as so-called 'unilaterals' their impact on the overall coverage in their newspaper was small. Godfrey Hodgson, foreign editor, said that over a six-week period, with an average of more than four pages given over to the crisis each day, the paper used pool copy on fewer than half a dozen occasions – from a correspondent attached to an American group (Hodgson 1991: 14). The *Independent* was firmly behind the US-led coalition's strategies over the massacres so that Fisk, together with other colleagues who worked as unilaterals, could have little impact on the crucial ideological bias of their newspaper. Thus it shared with all the other newspapers the massacres agenda – which was largely set by the military.

As Don McKay, who reported from Bahrain for the *Mirror*, told the author: 'One had one major fear: the commander of the air base could have us kicked off the island at any time. We were just there door-stepping. We could have been bounced anytime.' According to John Macarthur (1993: 95): '

> ... many journalists simply thrill to the excitement of military conflict and are easily swept up by the martial spirit of the moment. Others see war as an opportunity for self-promotion. For most part, the anchors, editors, bureau chiefs and reporters who expressed themselves publicly during the Gulf crisis seemed to be apolitical, respectful of power and careerist to a fault.

New York Times correspondent Chris Hedges summed up journalists' backing for the war in this way (2002: 143): 'The notion that the press was used in the war is incorrect. The press wanted to be used. It saw itself as part of the war effort. ... For we not only believe the myth of war and feed recklessly off the drug but also embrace the cause. We may do it with skepticism. We certainly expose more lies and misconceptions. But we believe. We all believe.'

CONSTRUCTING THE 'THEATRE OF WAR'

Paradoxically, while the essential elements of the fighting were shrouded in secrecy certain features of the strategy were exposed perhaps as never before. Kate Adie reports how Gen. Rupert Smith, head of the British troops, distributed the full battle plan to pool journalists just before the launch of Desert Storm (2002: 331): 'Astutely, the general had decided that journalists entrusted with enormous amounts of confidential information are far less likely to squeal than journalists denied any information at all, who pounce on snippets and rush to divulge them.' Thus the press before the launch of Desert Storm were able to detail the action plan: first the air strikes, then the ground campaign sweeping round the west flank of the Iraqis to encircle them. All this was to be quite quick (contradictions with the 'monstrous, global, Saddam' theme were not explored). In other words, there was an element of theatre/film about the US-led coalition's censorship regime. New militarism had conjured up not a war but the illusion/Hollywood show of a 'war'. So the coalition forces acted each day as if according to a pre-arranged script. This is exactly how Fuad Nahdi, one of three *Los Angeles Times* reporters in

Riyadh, described it to the author. 'The first press conference of the day would be at 7.30 am. From then on you knew exactly what the line for the day was going to be. The script had been written beforehand and I felt like the reviewer of a good play or film.'

Given the absence of any credible enemy, the controllers of the coalition's war effort sought to manipulate the conflict and the public response to it. Today the theme (or, in the American jargon, the 'spin') will be 'victory in sight'. The next day the theme will be: 'Let's not get too confident, there is still a long way to go.' After Iraq broadcast images of captured POWs, the message became: 'Saddam must be punished for his war crimes.' And so on. Each day, representatives of the White House, Pentagon, state department and CIA met to plan the 'spin' for the day. White House spokesman Marlin Fitzwater would test the message at the late morning briefing where no cameras were allowed. The message could then be fine-tuned for the later state department and Pentagon briefings which were both filmed and likely to make the evening news (McDaniel and Fineman 1991: 154). According to Stewart Purvis (1991: 737), British journalists were deliberately fed misinformation by the ministry of defence. He continued:

> ... correspondents have noted, with hindsight, that the military build-up last August was not as big as we were led to believe. Nik Gowing, of ITN's Channel Four News, believes the technology and logistics tail was far slower than the impressive television images of equipment suggested. But the deception worked. It stopped the Iraqi drive into Saudi Arabia (ibid).

SYMBOLIC PURPOSE OF THE CENSORSHIP REGIME

Yet the censorship regime served essentially ideological, symbolic purposes – it was an expression of the arbitrary, monopoly power of the military over the conduct of the war. The military, according to the myth, went into the Vietnam War with their hands tied behind their backs (by traitorous media and peaceniks). Now, after the trial engagements in Grenada, Libya and Panama, the military wanted to show they were in control. Censorship was used not so much to preserve military security but to promote a positive image of the massacres.

In many respects the press went on a war footing immediately after 2 August 1990. No particularly draconian censorship was needed once hostilities began – the press had already proved themselves meek and pliable to the secret state's media manipulation techniques as during normal times of 'peace'. As Michael Traber and Ann Davies (1991: 8) comment: 'It is clear that the military manipulated the media in a way similar to the way government authorities manipulate the media all the year round.' The pro-war consensus was quickly established in August 1990; hostilities were always represented as inevitable sometime in the near future. The US-led coalition forces were glorified, Saddam was demonised. The crucial ideological, patriotic frame was set.

SETTING UP THE CENSORSHIP REGIME

Despite the recommendations of the Hoffman and Sidle reports in the United States (and the *Fog of War* report in the UK)[2] stressing the importance of setting up temporary pooling arrangements upon the start of any major crisis, US defense secretary Dick Cheney first refused to allow any journalists to accompany the troops on 8 August. On 13 August, a 17-member press pool was formed by the US government drawing representatives from each news medium – seven from television, five from news agencies, two from the press, two from magazines and one from radio. And within 12 days of the Iraqi invasion Navy Captain Ron Wildemuth, Gen Norman Schwarzkopf's chief of public relations, had produced a 10-page document, codenamed Annex Foxtrot, in which he wrote: 'News media representatives will be escorted at all times. Repeat: at all times.'

Bowing to the inevitable, Margaret Thatcher's government allowed in a press pool of 16 to accompany the military later in the month. The three nationals were chosen by the director of the Newspaper Proprietors' Association, John Page, drawing their names from a hat. Four of these pools visited Saudi Arabia up to mid-September when, the MoD said, interest fell off. The pool was reactivated in October though more interest was shown by regional media at this time. Hamish Lumsden, chief press officer at the Ministry of Defence, told the author that, by December 1990, 40 British journalists were 'in theatre' in the Gulf getting bored and wanting to get home by Christmas.[3] According to Steve Anderson (1990), fear of being booted out of Saudi Arabia obsessed reporters in the lead-up to Christmas 1990. 'Saudi Arabia isn't known for its hospitality towards foreign journalists and only allows 20 to enter a year. At the moment they are host to more than 800 predominantly American and British and most with entry visas that are valid for one month only. These have either expired or are about to and there are concerns that too much rocking the boat could lead to expulsion with no defence from the military minders.' Boredom was the other major problem. 'No drink, no women and no story.'

British plans for reporting during the hostilities were devised by a team at the MoD including Brig. Bryon Dutton, director of army relations, Capt. Mike Sant, Hamish Lumsden and Mike Barnes, the final guidelines being officially launched at the MoD by Hugh Colver, chief public relations officer, on 14 January. They had, in fact, been drawn up by the Media Advisory Service (attached to the cabinet office) for use in times of national crisis. While the MoD claimed the country was not 'in crisis' the guidelines were brought in all the same. Amongst the Americans a series of meetings was held between 13 media representatives and defense department officials to plan restrictions in the war zone but they failed to come to any consensus and the guidelines went through four draft stages. On 14 December, the assistant secretary of defense for public affairs, Pete Williams, issued a memo to the media saying that 'pool material' would be subject to 'security review at source'. There was also introduced a new concept of 'Phase Three'. This would begin 'when open coverage is possible and would provide for unilateral coverage of activities. The pools would be disbanded and all media would operate independently, although under US central command escort'.

US guidelines were finally released on 7 January 1991 and following criticisms by American editors a reduced version was issued a week later.[4] As in Britain, the establishment of 'voluntary' guidelines in the United States was a subtle move by the authorities. Most importantly they avoided potential legal problems of prior restraint (as emerged during the 1971 case when the court upheld *The New York Times*'s first amendment right to publish the *Pentagon Papers* during the Vietnam War: see Kleinwachter 1991: 6). In theory, they allowed the press freedom to publish at their own discretion – yet in reality the numerous pressures were there to make them conform.

The ground rules identified 12 categories of information not to be reported. Most related to force levels or operational security but they did include the category of 'embargoed information until expiry of embargo' which effectively allowed any information to be restricted, without explanation, simply by declaring it embargoed. In the end overt censorship of copy was to provide only a few niggling problems for journalists. Only five dispatches among 1,300 filed during the war were referred to the Pentagon and only one, which referred to allied intelligence activities, was ultimately suppressed, according to Rick Atkinson (1994: 160).

POOLING THE PRESS PACK

Some 800 journalists (reporters, editors, photographers, technicians) were in the international press corps in Saudi Arabia by December 1990. On 17 January, a US Air Force C-141 cargo plane left Andrew Air Force base with 127 news media personnel on board. And by the start of Desert Storm, the total number of journalists in Saudi Arabia had reached around 1,400. Given that 2,000 normally attend the conventions of the major political parties in the United States this is a relatively small number to cover an event of such global significance. A third of them were based in Riyadh, the capital, where the Allied Joint Information Bureau was situated in the Hyatt Hotel, most of the remainder at the International Hotel in Dharhan – described by Robert Fisk (2006: 736) as a 'grotesquely decorated ballroom of dreams and expectations'. A few were based in Muharaq in Bahrain while Riyadh journalists were occasionally taken to the air base at Tabuk. Eighteen were with the Marines in amphibious ships; seven were with the US Air Force combat pool based at Al-Kharj; 19 were covering the navy at sea while eight were with the medical corps.

The French observed their typical independence, established in the Novotel Hotel three miles away in Riyadh. Only 11 journalists were allowed into their group – which they dubbed the 'Fuck the Pool' pool (McLaughlin 2002: 90). Each day they were flown by SIPRA (*Service d'information de l'armée francaise*) to somewhere near the front line. As reporter Jean-Luc Mano commented on the pooling arrangement: 'It was like a mini Club Mediterranean – with a visit to the pottery on Monday, water ski-ing on Tuesday etc' (Giroud 1991, *translation by the author*). The journey to the front lines would take two hours, they would stay for half an hour under military escort at all times and then fly back for two hours. Not surprisingly the journalists did not like this arrangement.

The highest contingents in the press corps were from Britain (150 in Saudi Arabia – just 60 journalists and 90 technicians, sound crew and producers) and the US (700 plus). Out of these, British and American journalists were assigned places in the pools accompanying the military, the US and UK thus symbolising their power over the global communications networks (Boyd-Barrett and Thussu 1992). The Pentagon gave priority to 'hometowners' – local news reporters who tended to concentrate on 'human interest' features. As Robin Andersen comments (2006: 161): 'The emphasis on local news promoted coverage far more likely to be soft and morale boosting, sending words and pictures of the boys in the field to the folks back home.' Only three places in the pools went to reporters from countries other than the US or UK. Only 43 were with the ground units at the start of Desert Storm, rising to 132 with the army and Marines at the launch of the 'ground offensive'. The British contingent was formed into six media response teams (two attached to British armoured brigades, two with RAF bases, one with the Royal Navy, another at Muharaq). In addition, there was a 13-person Forward Transmission Unit (including Kate Adie of the BBC, Keith Dovkants of the London *Evening Standard*, Stephen Sackur of BBC Radio, Robert Moore of ITN, and Gordon Airs of the *Glasgow Record*) to oversee the sending of copy and film by fax and satellite to London.

But after a while the FTU members, according to Keith Dovkants talking to the author, 'got tired of seeing the war at second hand'. He added: 'We all started pressing to get in on the action and so we converted ourselves into an MRT. We were camped in a berm [sand defence] at Wadi al Batin but we did get to go on a couple of artillery raids. And that turned into something quite good and pretty exciting.' All the FTU members were given pills in case of Iraqi attacks. Keith Dovkants commented: 'I just didn't take them. I don't like taking pills anyway. I thought if worse comes to worst I'll just take a deep breath.'

Kate Adie was, in fact, the only woman in the British pools. Fidelma Cook, senior reporter for the Glasgow *Sunday Mail*, had a visa request rejected because 'there are no facilities for ladies on board ship' (Sebba 1994: 276). In contrast, according to Edie Lederer, of AP and based with the US Air Force, in a telephone interview with the author, there were 'tons' of women in the US pool. It was one of the most impressive aspects of the Gulf reporting for her, confirming the high status gained by women in the US media. The *Washington Post, Los Angeles Times, Philadelphia Enquirer* and *Newsday* were among those newspapers with women representatives in Saudi Arabia.

Non-pool reporters were supposed to remain permanently in their hotels for the duration of the war, dealing with the pooled copy and producing other reports based on press conferences by the military (Fialka 1992). But as Greg McLaughlin commented (2002: 93): 'While the pooling system kept journalists away from the real action, the briefings kept real information away from journalists.' Aidan White, IFJ general secretary, expressed concern over how so many reporters were left sitting in cocktail bars watching wall-to-wall coverage on the US television networks. 'If there is glamour in the work of war reporting, there is precious little of it today in the Gulf,' he said. As James Meek, of the *Scotsman*, recorded: 'They had little to do but eat in lavish restaurants – sometimes over-eating to compensate for lack of alcohol – pore over bland military briefings, watch CNN and pester the military for more access.' McLaughlin is highly critical (op cit: 940):

> The most damning indictment of these journalists must surely be that they did not ask the right questions at the right time and recognise that the briefers were military officers with a war to sell, not messengers from heaven speaking the gospel truth. As in all wars, there were honourable exceptions but not enough to make a real difference. … Like entertaining a party of children, the briefers kept the journalists occupied and out of harm's way. The children for their part got their ringside seat at the circus and wanted to keep it.

On 12 February, the Pentagon, in response to complaints over exclusion, announced the formation of five more seven-member press pools. Of the previous 15 US pools only two were assigned to ground forces, the rest covered ships or airbases (Thomson op cit: 67). On 23 February, Dick Cheney announced the suspension of all press briefings and pool reports as the so-called ground offensive was launched – again more a symbolic, theatrical act demonstrating the power of the military and administration over the media rather than one determined by operational security considerations. It was virtually unprecedented: there had been no equivalent blackout during the Korean War and only two very brief blackouts during the Vietnam War. Predictably, the blackout was quickly broken by Cheney himself after just 12 hours and the first reports of the new offensive came some ten hours after they were filed.

In creating the pools the military knew they were tapping into an essential feature of the journalists' culture where privileged access to sources is an everyday element of professional practice. Yet seen from another perspective the special accreditation that pooling involved was fiercely opposed by the Americans and British in the UNESCO controversy of the 1970s and 1980s over the New World Information Order. Developing World plans for such accreditation had been a significant cause for the two countries eventually to quit the organisation in the mid-1980s.

THE PURPOSE OF THE POOLS

The pooling system was used by the military not to provide access to the front but to keep journalists away. Steve Anderson commented (op cit: 12): 'Those who had schemed and scrapped their way on to the MRTs had been promised a grandstand view of the allied annihilation of Iraq. In the end, all they got to see was a few bombed-out tanks.' And US pool reporter Christopher Hanson (1991: 128) said: 'Most of us never saw a battle and few of us even saw a dead Iraqi soldier but at least we got to be part of a big adventure.' Robert Fisk, of the *Independent*, spoke of the relationship between journalist and soldier becoming 'almost fatally blurred' leading to the 'unquestioning nature of coverage'.[5] Journalists were not forced to wear uniforms (with epaulettes saying 'War correspondent'), according to the MoD's Hamish Lumsden, but happily did so.

Thomson (op cit: 21) saw journalists 'locked into the military system' – 'the honorary rank [of major] was more than a quirk left over from a different age, it was part of the assimilation process'. For Robert Fisk (2006: 738): 'The reporters in uniform and the soldiers with journalism in their veins suggest a symbiotic, even osmotic relationship. Half the reporters in Saudi Arabia, it seems, want to be soldiers. Half the soldiers want to be in the news business.' But according to Kate Adie: 'By deciding to be alongside the army in uniform we had at least signalled to viewers that we had in some way "done a deal" and changed position from that of completely independent reporters to that of Official War Correspondents' (2002: 332). In any case, she experienced only two instances of censorship: once a new American ground-to-air missile fired one night was omitted from her report due to American insistence that its capabilities should not be identified by the Iraqis. And all mention of Christmas was banned so as not to offend Saudi sensibilities.

The pooling system was also used by the military to manipulate coverage by enforcing delays in the transmission of news. Five of the six pool journalists in a survey, *Reporting the war*, by the International Press Institute, complained of delays. Paul Majendie, of Reuters, with the Americans, commented: 'At best the copy took 72 hours to get back to the pool. At worst it just vanished.' He added: 'To send 17 despatches, risk all and then see virtually nothing on the wire is not my idea of a rewarding experience.' According to AP's Edie Lederer: 'For veterans of the Vietnam War like myself, it appeared that the US military deliberately adopted a policy to do as little as possible to facilitate the delivery of pool products.' Almost 80 per cent of the pool reports filed during the 'ground offensive' took more than 12 hours to reach Dhahran, by which time the news was often out-of-date. Some 10 per cent of reports took more than three days which, as Rick Atkinson comments, was 'far longer than the time needed for dispatches to reach New York from the battle of Bull Run in 1861' (op cit: 160).

Resentment about exclusion from the pools was inevitable. Rodney Pinder, of Reuters, comments on how contempt was widespread for a representative of the US women's magazine *Mirabella* whose main quest appeared 'to determine whether female soldiers took their vibrators to the front'. All this meant that journalist was divided against journalist and thus a united press front against military censorship was never a possibility. In any case, journalists' culture gives low priority to long-term planning. Brian McNair (1995: 183) blames journalists' acceptance of the military's management and control of their newsgathering on 'straightforward commercial criteria'. 'Media organisations accepted the pool system in the Gulf, and the restrictions which it entailed, in the knowledge that the alternative was exclusion.' However, the chair of the joint chiefs of staff, Colin Powell (1995a: 528), not surprisingly, disputed these claims. He stressed:

> Of the 2,500 accredited journalists overall, 1,400 crowded the theatre of operations at the peak. Compare this figure with twenty-seven reporters going ashore with the first wave at Normandy on D-Day. Desert Storm correspondents totalled nearly four times the number covering Vietnam during the war's height. And, for the record, Ernie Pyle and his fellow World War 2 reporters were strictly censored. In the Gulf War, sorties were reviewed by the military for security purposes. Of 1,350 print stories submitted by press pool reporters, only one was changed to protect intelligence procedures.

EMERGENCE OF THE MAVERICKS

A few journalists decided to have nothing to do with the official arrangements and so became 'unilaterals' (the military called them 'rovers' or 'mavericks'; in France they were called *chats sauvages*). They shared a mixed fate. They were tolerated (they could clearly have been kicked out at any time) but they were closely watched and heavily intimidated. In mid-February 1991, new military guidelines placed a ban on non-pool reporters from wearing NBC (nuclear, biological, chemical protection) suits. And a memorandum from the military just before the close of the massacres put still further pressure on the unilaterals, stating that any who went within 63 miles of the Saudi-Kuwait border without a military minder risked being shot. As David Beresford, of the *Guardian*, told the IPI survey (p. 4), the unilaterals were left bribing or begging ground troops for equipment as basic as helmets, flak jackets and chemical gear. Some even stole military uniforms, acquired standard four-wheel drive Jeeps and had military style haircuts.

Amongst the unilaterals were Bob Simon (a former Vietnam correspondent with considerable experience reporting from the Middle East) and the other three members of his Columbia Broadcasting System (CBS) team – Peter Bluff, producer, Roberto Alvarez, cameraman, and Juan Caldera, soundman. They went missing on 21 January, were captured by the Iraqis, beaten and released on 2 March. Then there was CBS's Bob McKeown (who achieved world fame for being the first journalist into 'liberated' Kuwait City) and ABC's Forrest Sawyer, the Frenchman Patrice Dutertre, and AP reporter Mort Rosenblum (detained for three hours for operating without military escort). Rosenblum later remarked: 'In 25 years of covering wars around the world, the first time I was held prisoner was by the Americans' (op cit: 122).

Peter Sharp, of ITN, broke the Gulf oil slick story but had his press pack removed for his pains. Sandy Gall, also of ITN, independently joined the Saudi advance into Kuwait and claimed a 'world scoop'. Gall later told the IPI survey (p. 21) the media controls were 'inoperable and so should be scrapped forthwith'. In his autobiography, Gall (1994: 255) relates how during the 'ground war', *The Times* had invited him to write a 1,000-word article on the invasion. He declined because of pressures of time.

> Unbeknown to me, however, someone at ITN in London wrote instead under my name which I thought was a questionable practice although perhaps understandable in the circumstances. But his version was completely inaccurate on one point. My ghost writers had me saying it was the most nerve-racking experience of my life. On the contrary it was a piece of cake.

A wire service photographer was held for six hours by Marines who threatened to shoot him if he left his car. An officer told him: 'We have orders from above to make the pool system work.' *Time* photographer Wesley Bocxe was seized by a Saudi and handed over to the Alabama National Guard who held him overnight, blindfolded and driven to a base 60 miles away where he was lectured by a public affairs officer before being released. Robert Fisk described how he had been driven into the desert to avoid checkpoints specifically set up to prevent journalists travelling. On one occasion an American NBC pool reporter, Brad Willis, ordered him away from the scene during the massacre at Khafji in late January. He commented: 'For the US reporter, the privileges of the pool and the military rules attached to it were more important than the right of the journalist to do his job.'[6] Veteran Italian journalist Oriana Fallaci tried to cover the Khafji slaughter but was prevented by the military. She likened it to her experience in North Vietnam when officials restricted her travel and vetted her interviews. 'It was more than censorship. It's like a cancer' (McGregor and Hooper 2006). Eric Schmitt, John Kifner and Chris Hedges, all of *The New York Times*, were detained by the military. When Hedges went to pick up his credentials, one of the officials at the information bureau, Major Williams Fellows, told him: 'You have an attitude problem' (Apple 1991). British reporter Jon Swain had a completely different experience (2003):

> Three of us formed what we laughingly called LRPG – the Long Range Picnic Group. Sharing a Land Rover kitted out with camouflage netting, entrenching tools and other military-style paraphernalia, and uniformed with sandy-coloured SAS-style berets on our heads, we roamed the Saudi desert south of the Kuwaiti border more or less at will, bluffing our way through checkpoints guarded by Royal Military Police.

BREAKDOWN OF THE POOLS

On 18 February, non-pool journalists threatened to storm the combat zone *en masse*. 'We are claiming our right to free information,' said Perry Kretz, correspondent for Germany's *Stern* magazine.[7] By the time the 'ground offensive' was officially launched on 24 February, journalists' frustration at being denied access to the 'war zone' and getting their patriotic pieces over the wires was at bursting point. On 18 February, after TF1 broadcast an unauthorised interview with French troops in Saudi Arabia critical of the 'war', news crews were banned from the front by the ministry of defence (Badsey 1992: 239). In protest, the French correspondents took the extreme step of agreeing to boycott coverage. But immediately afterwards, the 'ground offensive' was launched and the boycott was abandoned (see Marnham 1991). Colin Bickler, a veteran Reuters correspondent with experience covering conflicts in Malaysia, Cyprus, the Philippines and Pakistan, explained the journalists' reactions this way in an interview with the author:

> You can't blame the correspondents on the ground. Faced with military controls, either they ask to come home and who knows how the editors are going to take this. Or they end up very frustrated. But the most committed are always trying to push the parameters. At the end of the day, they have to go with what they can get.

He was surprised the American news organisations did not do more to get the rules relaxed during the 'war'. 'The British were not in a position to do much. This was essentially a US/Saudi control system.' Inevitably more and more journalists, locked away in hotels in Riyadh and Dharhan, broke free and joined the ranks of the unilaterals. So in the end it was they who first covered the entry into Kuwait City and thus went away with all the major Gulf scoops. As Hodgson (op cit: 18) comments:

> If the war had gone on longer, if the coalition had sustained heavy casualties, if the morale of the Arab members of the coalition had ever been shaken (as many predicted it would be) it is plain that relations between the generals and the journalists would have deteriorated to a point where Vietnam would have seemed a love feast.

CONTROLLING THE IMAGE

'The Gulf war is an important one in the history of censorship. It marks a deliberate attempt by the authorities to alter public perception of the nature of war itself, particularly the fact that civilians die in war.' These are the words of Phillip Knightley (1991: 5), author of the seminal history of war correspondents, *The first casualty: The war correspondent as hero and myth-maker from the Crimea to Kosovo* (2003a [1975]). The war was above all a media spectacle and thus the control over the visual image was of supreme importance to the authorities. As for print journalists, the pools functioned for photographers and broadcast crews to keep them away from the action. The invisible was always far more important than the visible.

Pictures of coalition dead were banned outright. Journalists were denied access to hospitals which further prevented coverage of casualties. Severe controls were placed on photographs of Iraqi dead. Only one photographer went to the front with a pool team (Mike Moore, of *Today*) and the Saudis granted visas to photographers from only three British papers, the *Mirror, Sun* and *Today* (though by the time the 'ground offensive' was launched there were 35 photographers in the American pools) (Article 19 1991). Darkrooms were set up in hotels miles away from the main media centre which further delayed transmission times. And if photographers were not censored by the authorities, journalists did this work for them. A similar process of self-censorship had been at work during the Falklands war (Morrison and Tumber 1988: 97).

The US military also cleverly manipulated coverage by feeding the media shots from attacking aircraft or missile warheads. The head of the defense department information in the Gulf was, significantly, Michael Sherman, formerly responsible for *Top Gun* – a dominant reference point through media coverage of the massacres – *Hunt for red October* and *Flight of the intruder*. Videos supplied by Sherman (such as the one of a missile hitting the ministry of defence in Baghdad) were repeated time after time on television and reproduced in the popular press, providing some of the dominant images of the 'war'. Such images were new and fascinating to the media which, hyped up on their patriotic crusades, handled them unproblematically. Some film reports were used by the military for PR purposes before being released for media use (Levinson 1991).

THE SUBTLE USE OF PRESS CONFERENCES

The agenda-setting role for the massacres was monopolised by the military. One of the subtlest ways in which they did this was to promote the use of live press conferences. Despite evidence of considerable chaos behind the scenes, journalists in Riyadh and Dharhan welcomed these conferences. There was little else to cover, after all. Fuad Nahdi, of the *Los Angeles Times*, stressed how 'professional' the press releases provided by the US military were. They were full of the 'hard facts' (numbers of sorties flown, for instance) and quotable superlatives ('biggest raid in history', for instance) that journalists found irresistible. 'I sent 5,000 words every day. I would just need to change the first and last pars of the press releases, they were so good,' Nahdi commented. But in this way, too, the military were dictating the agenda over the heads of the journalists to the global community. They were building on precedents set by Reagan and Thatcher who used live television performances to promote the image of populist leadership over and above the heads even of representatives in the commons and senate.

In Washington, the Pentagon held daily hour-long televised press briefings at 3pm EST, preceded at 10 am EST (6 pm in Saudi Arabia) by a half-hour briefing from Riyadh, usually given by Brig. Gen. Richard ('Butch') Neal and Gen. Norman Schwarzkopf. It was at these press conferences where Gen. Schwarzkopf, leader of the coalition forces, acquired his enormous prestige during the massacres, and so too Britain's Group Captain Niall Irving, though to a lesser extent. Schwarzkopf's performances were above all theatrical, straight out of the Hollywood tradition. And the 'Stormin' Norman Show' was perfectly suited to the largely male-dominated, chauvinist environment of the press conferences. He helped make the massacres a merry affair for the media corps. He was straight talking, witty and the press clearly liked him. He was a man perfect for the media spectacle war.[8]

For Hodgson, the most abiding image of the 'war' was a photograph of Gen. Schwarzkopf at a briefing. 'This is the conqueror in his late 20th century glory, not dominating a mettlesome horse, like Napoleon or Wellington, not poring over his maps and his order of battle like a Moltke or an Eisenhower but caught by the cameras is the quintessential of the modern commander' (op cit: 20). Yet, even Gen Schwarzkopf's body weight was declared a military secret (Heibert 1995). Intriguingly, in his account of the conflict, Colin Powell (1995: 529) confirms the Hollywoodisation of the Pentagon spin machine:

> We picked the Joint Staff operations chief, Lt General Tom Kelly, as our briefer because Kelly was not only deeply knowledgeable but came across like Norm in the sitcom *Cheers*, a regular guy whom people could relate to and trust. Kelly's partner for the press briefing, Rear Admiral Mike McConnell, was the perfect foil, playing the bookish authority to Kelly's neighbourhood sage...

CENSORS' PEN NOT THE REAL ISSUE

All this meant that, having set the ground rules, the military did not impose overt censorship very often. There were a few cases but since most of the journalists identified with the army and its aims the censors had not a great deal to do. Robert Fisk reported (2006: 766-767) that on the carrier *Kennedy*, news agency 'pool' reporters wrote how US pilots watched pornographic videos to relax, or to become aroused, before their bombing missions – but this was struck from their copy. Keith Dovkants, of the British FTU, told the author in an interview that he had faced only 'odd quibbles' over copy from the two censors attached to his unit, Lt Col. John King and Lt. Chris Sexton. 'We had no sinister arguments. I certainly saw no attempt to manipulate media coverage.' And as Bahrain-based Don McKay, of the *Mirror*, told me: 'Some RAF academy lecturer looked at copy but he became superfluous because of all the "bonding" between reporters and pilots that was going on.' He continued:

We were always conscious we would never say anything that would annoy families back home. I did a couple of stories about Rapier missile batteries downing Scuds with a Bahrain by-line. I did not say the batteries were based in Bahrain but the implication was there. That was enough to annoy the Bahrain government who were aware that the re-opening of the base closed in the 1960s was a highly sensitive one. The commander of the base told me there would be severe trouble if I repeated the story.

During the crisis and massacres, D Notices (a voluntary censorship system arranged between editors and the British government) were activated only once after the lap-top computer with the allied plans was stolen from a car in London. The *Irish Times*, not covered by the notices, subsequently mentioned the theft and so the embargo had to be lifted for all other newspapers. Most of the censorship incidents were cases of media theatre turned farce – none of them involving sensitive operational intelligence. For instance, the MoD imposed a security blackout on weather reports and forecasts from the Gulf – even though Cable News Network continued providing them so making them accessible to the Iraqis (presuming they wanted such information, anyway). The official war artist, John Keane, was refused permission to write a diary for the *Guardian* (see Lawson 1995: 61-76 Article 19 1991: 4).

RESPONSE OF JOURNALISTS TO THE CENSORSHIP REGIME

Many elite journalists were remarkably supportive of the government/military imposed censorship ground rules. Some were positively enthusiastic. An editorial in the *Economist* of 19 January commended opposition politicians for suspending 'the normal play of democratic argument'. 'The truth about the Gulf war, no details expunged, must await the end of the fighting.' Ron Spark, chief *Sun* leader writer, said journalists had a responsibility to support the cause uncritically. 'Newspapers are in the business of telling news and freedom of information is a precious part of our democracy. Yet when we are fighting men and women are in peril, we have no choice but to accept some limitations.' Both he and Sir Peregrine Worsthorne, of the *Sunday Telegraph*, re-invented the archetypal 'vulnerable state' scenario with images of hordes of anti-war voices taking over the press.[9]

Max Hastings, in the *Telegraph* of 5 February 1991, remained 'unconvinced of the case for objectivity as between the US-led coalition forces and Saddam, when even the most moral assessment … suggests he is an exceptionally evil man'. *The Times* said on 23 January 199: 'The media should be able to cover the war without offering gratuitous oxygen in the relentless repetition of horrific images.' The *Independent*, on 8 January, while broadly sympathetic over the government-imposed constraints, was critical of the pooling arrangements: 'Justifying these restrictions, officials cite the demands of the Saudi government. That sounds too convenient an explanation to be wholly credible. Coverage by experienced reporters is in the interests of the public and those in the front line alike.'

Views differed on the value of the London briefings. Peter Almond, of the *Telegraph*, told the author in an interview that they were often better than those in Saudi Arabia, with defence intelligence providing some of the 'deepest' backgrounds. Michael Evans, defence correspondent of *The Times*, said in an interview that he considered the unattributable, off-the-record briefings he attended in London throughout the 'war' 'incredibly good' and 'right on the ball'. Every day, he compiled an 800-word analytical commentary piece and found being based in London crucial for gaining the necessary overview. He was able to cross-check information with contacts in Israel, France and the Pentagon. 'It was not a scoopy kind of event for me. That was more for the chaps in Saudi Arabia. I was being told a hell of a lot of information on an unattributable basis. My time was taken up analysing and writing it up.' Did he feel, in retrospect, he was fed any misinformation? 'It would be highly likely in a war.' Harvey Morris, of the *Independent*, told me in an interview that the censorship regime was not worth opposing since his newspaper had easily worked around it.

Yet a group of dissident journalists did form Media Workers Against the War (MWAW) which proved to be one of the most articulate groups to campaign against the massacres. Packed-out meetings were held in London venues such as Westminster Hall, newsletters were published, branches were formed throughout the country, and Fleet Street journalists such as Victoria Brittain and Edward Pierce, of the *Guardian*, John Pilger and Paul Foot, of the *Mirror*, spoke from campaigning platforms. A lively website www.mwaw.org was set up – helping to publicise its activities across the country (Crouch 2004: 275). But the campaign was almost totally ignored by the mainstream press. The National Union of Journalists, representing some 75 per cent of working journalists, also voted against supporting the war. On 16 January, its executive issued an eight-point *Principles and guidelines for reporting the Gulf War* to counter censorship and government manipulation of information. Point No. 3 stressed: 'Journalists including editors should not succumb to self-censorship and suppress information or comment that might be embarrassing to military or political leaders.'

Journalists in the US were also mixed in their responses to the massacres coverage. In a survey published in the authoritative *Columbia Journalism Review* (March/April 1991) nine of the eleven were deeply critical of the media's performance. William Broyles, former editor-in-chief of *Newsweek*, summed up their views: 'The sense of war as the massing of means of death and destruction and its application against an enemy is, I think, completely lacking.' A number of US journalists also quit the Gulf in protest at the restrictions, eight were arrested (Cumings 1992: 111). According to Dilip Hiro (1992: 5), a total of 24 reporters were detained by US field commanders. But most elite journalists backed the Pentagon. Two major law suits challenged the legitimacy of the censorship regime. On 10 January 1991, the Center for Constitutional Rights, on behalf of a group of news organisations, journalists and writers (*Harpers*, *Mother Jones*, *In These Times*, *Los Angeles Weekly*, the *Progressive*, *Texas Observer*, the *Guardian*, the *Nation*, *Village Voice*, Pacifica Radio, Pacific News Service, E. Doctorow, William Styron, Michael Klare, Scott Armstrong and Sydney Schanberg) claimed the censorship regulations were in violation of the First and Fifth Amendments.

The suit also accused the Pentagon of favouring 'hometowners' (local media crews). Agence France Presse filed a companion suit at the same time in protest at being excluded from the pools. Most of the mainstream press kept well clear of the case, claiming the suit was irresponsible since it could end up enshrining dangerous precedent in law. The case was finally thrown out of court after the end of the massacres with Federal District Judge Leonard Sand declining to issue a sweeping declaratory judgment against future use of the pools. The case was almost totally ignored by the mainstream press in Britain and the US. According to Knightley (2003a [1975]: 490): 'No major media organisation joined the action, although invited to, because they feared that the Pentagon might retaliate and kick them out of its pools, or that if they lost it would set a dangerous precedent.' On 22 February, the American Civil Liberties Union filed a complaint on behalf of several photographers, news media representatives, veteran groups and military family support groups over the banning of the public and press from Dover Air Force Base. No verdict had been given before the ending of the massacres. This was also largely ignored by the mainstream press in both countries.

MIXED FATE OF THE BAGHDAD CORPS

A number of journalists bravely stayed on in Baghdad to report the conflict. Alexander Cockburn (1991b: 14) reported that the US attaché in Baghdad instructed all Americans to leave the capital just before the bombings began while John Simpson revealed in his history of the conflict (1991a: 277): 'President Bush himself telephoned various American editors to urge them to evacuate their teams. That frightened a lot of people.' In the end, the Baghdad-based journalists shared a mixed fate. Certainly the early reports from Peter Arnett of CNN, John Simpson of the BBC, and Brent Sadler of ITN played an important role in defining the 'war' as a sanitised, surreal video game. As Knightley comments (2003a [1975]: 492):

> It was their vivid film of night skies alight with explosions and the exhaust flames of missiles, on a soundtrack of explosions and anti-aircraft fire, interspersed with breathless commentary – 'a Tomahawk missile just went past my hotel window and turned right at the end of the street' [as Simpson reported] – that gripped Western viewers.

But all three journalists were also criticised for reporting from the Iraqi side. Arnett, who had won a Pulitzer Prize for his Vietnam reporting, was accused of being an Iraqi sympathiser while a letter to CNN, signed by 21 members of the house of representatives, claimed his reports gave 'the demented dictator a propaganda mouthpiece to over one hundred nations'. In Britain, the head of the

MoD's press office, Hugh Colver, said some of his colleagues thought they were Iraqi tools and so should leave. And in the *Sunday Telegraph*, Peregrine Worsthorne said journalists based in Baghdad would inevitably become pawns of the Iraqi dictatorship (see Keeble 2009: 238).

NOTES

[1] Appears in Journalists in the firing line, an article for publication issued by Aidan White, general secretary of the Brussels-based IFJ, on 26 February 1991

[2] Mercer, Derrick (1987: 375-386). See also Steeden, Richard: T*he reporting of war in the British press: Does the public have a right to know?* Unpublished MA thesis, University of Sheffield Department of Librarianship, September 1991. Highlights the failure of MoD guidelines to follow the most significant recommendations of the *Fog of war*

[3] Lumsden was interviewed in September 1992 at the MoD HQ in London. He said that the MoD had consulted with the Saudi authorities and had managed to persuade them, with some difficulty, to increase the number of accredited journalists to 60 – with 90 technicians. But to what extent were the MoD using the Saudi's media shyness/repressiveness as an excuse to limit the number of accredited journalists?

[4] *Ground rules and guidelines for Desert Shield* appear in Smith, Hendrick (ed.) (1991: 4-12). Intriguingly, the guidelines were accompanied by this note: 'The following information should not be reported because its publication or broadcast could jeopardise operations and endanger lives'

[5] Robert Fisk, the *Independent*, 6 February 1991. The establishment loves its mavericks and Fisk was rightly much applauded for his reporting. A profile of him by Steve Clarke, In a class of his own, appeared in the *UK Press Gazette*, 4 March 1991 p. 10. Fisk also won a journalism award from City University London, for his Gulf reports

[6] The *Independent*, 6 February 1991

[7] See Reuters: Journalists threaten to storm front, *Guardian*, 19 February 1991

[8] Intriguingly, away from the cameras, Schwarzkopf was known to be far from cool: he was even nicknamed 'the Screamer' (see Hersh 2000)

[9] See the views of Spark, Worsthorne (and Peter Preston, editor of the *Guardian*) in The role of the press at war, *UK Press Gazette*, 18 February 1991 pp 2-3

Chapter Nine

The myth of the clean war, massacrespeak – and the language of silence

THE PERSONAL AND THE POLITICAL

I've always been interested in silence. The first pamphlet I ever wrote was for the Peace Pledge Union back in May 1983 and I called it 'A language of silence'. I looked at the way in which our culture, individual thought processes and language were dominated by militarism. Militarism had become a core defining reality of our society. And our language, in preparing us for the possibility of the ultimate horror – the destruction of the globe in a nuclear confrontation – was moving in a process of self destruction towards silence. Or so I argued.

Significantly, I called my book on the coverage of the 1991 Gulf conflict in the US and UK press *Secret state, silent press: New militarism, the Gulf and the modern image of warfare* (1997). Why silent press? I liked the alliteration with secret state to be frank. But my essential thesis was that the mainstream press had silenced what in reality was a series of US-led massacres beneath the fiction of heroic warfare. Colin Powell (1995), in his account of the conflict, estimated that 250,000 Iraqi soldiers had perished. The reality of that horrific explosion of hi-tech barbarism was silenced in the British and American press which represented the conflict as largely bloodless: a triumph of clean, precise, surgical weaponry.

NEWSPEAK AND THE DESTRUCTION OF LANGUAGE

George Orwell was preoccupied with the potential shift of language towards silence. In his novel *Nineteen Eighty-Four* (1976 [1949]), Orwell described a Big Brother state in which the authorities controlled thought and language by inventing a new one – newspeak. In the Appendix titled 'The principles of newspeak' he wrote: 'The purpose of newspeak was not only to provide a medium of expression for the world-view and mental habits proper to the devotees of Ingsoc but to make all other modes of thought impossible' (ibid: 917). In other words the dominant

197

language served above all to silence all dissident modes of thought. And newspeak was inherently moving towards silence. Syme, Winston Smith's colleague, admonishes him like this: 'You don't grasp the beauty of the destruction of words. Do you know that Newspeak is the only language in the world whose vocabulary gets smaller every year?' (ibid: 773).

NEWSPEAK'S CLONE: NUKESPEAK

During the Cold War, Paul Chilton (1983) coined the term nukespeak. The seminal text (of 1985) he edited was titled *Language and the nuclear arms debate: Nukespeak today*. He had earlier provided a chapter 'Nukespeak: Nuclear language and propaganda' to a text *Nukespeak: The media and the bomb* (Aubrey 1982). In coining the term nukespeak, Chilton was making three main claims. Firstly, there existed a specialised vocabulary for talking about nuclear weapons together with habitual metaphors. Secondly, that this variety of English was neither neutral nor purely descriptive but ideologically loaded in favour of the nuclear culture. And finally, that nukespeak was massively important since it affected how people thought about the subject and largely determined the ideas they exchanged about it (ibid: 95).

But there was no massive conspiracy to inject this vocabulary into the culture: there were no Orwellian grammarians munching their sandwiches at the Ministry of Truth and rewriting the English language. The atomic bombs which fell on Hiroshima and Nagasaki in August 1945 were, indeed, weapons of mass destruction. Their deployment represented, according to Chilton, a revolutionary jump in military strategy. And inevitably it heralded a new order of experience in science, politics and the everyday. Chilton commented: 'The language used to talk about the new weapons of mass extermination was partly an attempt to slot the new reality into the old paradigms of our culture. It was also no doubt a language that served the purpose of those who were concerned to perpetuate nuclear weapons development and deployment' (ibid).

Nukespeak then, as a specific linguistic register, drew on deep patterns of symbolic thought, on myths, religious beliefs, symbols, stereotypes and metaphors which we use to organise and normalise our everyday experiences. In August 1945, politicians together with the mainstream press spoke of the bomb mainly in terms of religious awe. For instance, while Truman was meeting Churchill and Stalin at Potsdam, an official report on the Hiroshima explosion was rushed to him. It said: 'It was the beauty the great poets dream about. … Then came the strong, sustained, awesome roar which warned of doomsday and made us feel that we puny things were blasphemous to dare to tamper with the forces heretofore reserved to the Almighty' (ibid: 97). *The Times* reported eye-witnesses: 'The whole thing was tremendous and awe-inspiring,' said a Captain Parsons of the US Navy. The names given to these horrific bombs are also very telling. They are strangely humanised. They become familiar parts of our normal everyday lives. The Hiroshima bomb was called 'Little Boy', the plutonium bomb dropped on Nagasaki 'Fat Man'. Edward Teller is known as the 'father' of the H-Bomb.

Brian Easlea, in his seminal, feminist history *Fathering the unthinkable* (1983), highlights the creation of nuclear weapons in the context of the masculinity of science. He sees the development of science as a process of domination over both nature and women. According to Easlea, men create science and weapons to compensate for their lack of the 'magical power' of mothering. In other words, the distorted psyche at the heart of masculinity and the 'technical, phallic rationality' it promotes gives birth not to life but death. Easlea quotes a note slipped to Truman at the Potsdam conference on 17 July 1945 after a successful test of the plutonium bomb that said simply: 'Babies successfully born.' And the President knew precisely what it meant (ibid: 103). Significantly, in an exultant profile of the B52 bombers during the Gulf conflict of 1991 in the *Sun* of 24 January, a Major Cole is quoted as saying: 'The devastation underneath these babies is incredible.' In other words, the mass deaths to be inflicted by these bombers is to be a source of celebration, wonder even. Men again have given birth to massacres. A major general is quoted: 'The B52 has a mystique about it. Because of its destructive power it has a sense of awesomeness.'

Following Hiroshima and Nagasaki, later generations (note that word) of nuclear weapons were given military status and a patriotic role. They were called 'Corporal' and 'Sergeant'. 'Honest John' appeared later in the European theatre (another nukespeak term). The devastating 'Minuteman' missile drew on the name of the heroic militiamen of the American revolutionary war who were trained to turn out at a minute's notice. So in this way the missile takes its proud place in national folklore. Or they have been given names of classical gods: such as Polaris, Skybolt, Jupiter, Titan, Poseidon, Trident (Chilton 1982: 104-105). In these various ways weapons of mass destruction have been assimilated into our culture to appear 'natural' and 'civilised'.

HIDING THE HORROR OF WAR

With the later emergence of new militarism, the essential function of the mainstream media was no longer to naturalise and humanise the possibility of nuclear holocaust as during the Cold War but to acclimatise the public to the acceptability of mass slaughters of the nameless 'enemy'. In place of nukespeak there is massacrespeak (Keeble 2005). As *New York Times* reporter Chris Hedges writes (2002): 'War is made palatable. It is sanitised. We are allowed to taste war's perverse thrill but usually spared from seeing its consequences. The wounded and dead are swiftly carted offstage. The maimed are carefully hidden in the wings while the band plays the majestic march.' Robert Fisk (2006: 737) described how a reporter asking about the body bags arriving at Dhahran was quietly told his question was 'morbid'. Fisk added: 'For this was war without risks, war made acceptable. It was clean war – not war as hell, but war without responsibility, in which the tide of information stopped abruptly at the moment of impact.' Journalists too often became part of the war. 'Immaturity, inexperience, upbringing: you can choose any excuse you want. But they created war without death. They lied' (ibid: 767).[1] Central to the manufacture of the myth of warfare has been the constant propaganda focus on precise, clean weapons. War is a civilised, humanitarian business – that's the essential message. As Edward Herman comments (1992: 67): '

> Doing terrible things in an organised and systematic way rests on 'normalisation'. This is the process whereby ugly, degrading, murderous and unspeakable acts become routine and are accepted as 'the way things are done'. ... It is the function of the defense intellectuals and other experts and the mainstream media to normalise the unthinkable for the general public.

And people don't die in new militarist 'wars', massacres never happen – unless through mistakes or through the fault of the 'enemy'. During the 1991 massacres descriptions applied to the weapons of the US-led forces were always positive: sophisticated, super, spectacular, awesome, stunning, brilliant, smart, precise, accurate, amazing, incredible.

New militarism was premised on the notion of 'modern' violence as being of a totally different kind from the 'primitive' form of Iraqi violence. It was smart violence in defence of global order – which actually saved civilian lives. In contrast, Iraqi violence was indiscriminate and anarchic (Aksoy and Robins 1991). Their weapons were dirty and crude (the Iraqi supergun was an exception – but that was being constructed by British firms). Yet the myths on which the clean war can be fought are highly vulnerable. How long can the reality of slaughter be hidden? The new militarist elite know that the myths and constructs on which they base their military adventures, even given the pliant media, cannot be sustained for long – hence the need for quickie wars.

Before the end of Desert Storm it had become a cliché to talk of the video game, micro-chip war. Yet behind the media blitz, appalling secret atrocities were being inflicted. As Robins and Levidow argue (1991: 324): 'The remote technology served to portray as heroic "combat" what was mainly a series of massacres.' Media consumers during the massacres saw warfare more closely than ever before. Shots from video cameras on missiles heading towards their targets (shown on television and reproduced in the press) meant that spectators actually 'became' the weapons. These images, constantly repeated, came to dominate representations of the conflict. Yet, paradoxically, the media spectacle, while offering such openness, in fact, kept secret the reality.

On a basic level such stress on 'pinpoint' weaponry eliminated the existence of non-precision, though utterly devastating bombs. After the conflict it was reported by the US Air Force that 'smart bombs' had constituted only 7 per cent of all US explosive dropped on Iraq and Kuwait but accounted for 84 per cent of the cost of the munitions of the war (Weiner 1996). Moreover, 70 per cent of the 85,500 tons of bombs dropped on the two countries during the massacres had missed their targets. Such figures, in fact, represent a military disaster. In 1993, the armed service committee of congress reported that the US military command had estimated that 388 of the 846 tanks of the Iraqi Republican Guard divisions were destroyed from the air. In fact, only 166 were destroyed. Moreover, during the early 1980s massive peace movements had grown in Europe and North America against the deployment of cruise and Tomohawk. The glorification of those same incredibly expensive weapons during the massacres sought to eliminate the popular protests from the historical record as well as any debate over the redistribution of weapons expenditure (at a time of mass poverty in Africa, South America and Eastern Europe) to more socially useful purposes. But on a deeper level such representation providing hyper-real proximity between killer and victim desensitised the media consumer. As Robins and Levidow comment (op cit: 325):

> It was the ultimate voyeurism: to see the target hit from the vantage point of the weapon. An inhumane perspective. Yet this remote-intimate kind of watching could sustain the moral detachment of earlier military technologies. Seeing was split off from feeling; the visible was separated from the sense of pain and death. Through the long lens the enemy remained the faceless alien.

Similarly Zygmunt Bauman (1990) and Kovel (1983) have pointed to the dehumanising tendencies of technocratic societies. And George Steiner (1971: 478) identified the inhumanity at the root of modern culture and 'civilisation'. The press did not show close-up pictures of Iraqi soldiers being blown to bits as they fled the onslaught with an accompanying commentary condemning them as morally outrageous. Instead, there was Gen. Schwarzkopf drawing laughs from attendant journalists with the quip: 'I am going to show you the luckiest man in Iraq on this particular day' as an Iraqi vehicle was videoed passing through the crosshairs of a bomb site just before the bomb 'took out' a bridge.

THE POST-HEROISM OF NEW MILITARISM

Modern war-fighting strategies have virtually eliminated the possibilities of heroic action. Technology has taken the place of men. Men now largely press buttons and watch the consequences on a video. Electronics and space-based technologies are all important. Luckham comments (1984: 2): 'We are now entering a stage in which the manufacture of warfare is overtaking man and expropriating his culture. Automated warfare and the nuclear bomb have deprived man of this capacity to strive for glory, recognition or safety through combat.'

Alvin and Heidi Toffler (1993: 116) quote Col. Alan Campen, former director of command and control policy at the Pentagon, to the effect that the 1991 Gulf war was 'the first instance where combat forces largely were deployed, sustained, commanded and controlled through satellite communications'. In all, the coalition was said to have used some 60 satellites (such as the KH-11s and Lacrosse satellites). The Tofflers report on how robotic weapons (such as Pioneer RPVs – small, pilotless planes under the control of teleoperators sitting at computer consoles miles away) were secretly used in the conflict (ibid: 133).

The 1991 massacres represented a desperate attempt to resolve the contradictions posed by the destruction of a distinctly masculine heroism in the new militarist, post-heroic age. Hostages became instant media heroes. British Tornado fighter pilots were constantly dubbed 'Top Gun' heroes in the patriotic pops. Don McKay, based in Bahrain for the *Mirror*, in an interview with the author explained the use of the reference this way: 'They were "Top Gun" heroes. They were high echelon pilots. It's a generic term, a form of shorthand. It's not implying they were gung-ho. They were not fools. They were not cowboys. It's like in the First World War they were called "Biggles". It's a suggestion of bravery.'

Yet in sending thousands of soldiers to the Gulf, there was an attempt to revive the heroic images of the Second World War. From a military standpoint many soldiers were largely irrelevant, massively outnumbering their enemy. For the symbolic assertion of the heroic possibilities of warfare, they were essential. Yet, on the other hand, the 'fire and forget' technologies as Zygmunt Bauman (op cit: 30) has argued, 'eliminated face-to-face contact between the actors and the objects of their actions, and with that neutralised their morally constraining impact'. The press made constant efforts to revive the image of major hand-to-hand heroic combat (through cartoon representations and photographs of troops in training); but it was never to come.

THE CELEBRATION OF THE TECHNICALITIES OF WARFARE: HOW WARRIORS WERE REPRESENTED AS PACIFISTS AT HEART

The emphasis on the technicalities of warfare was a feature running through all the media through the crisis to Desert Storm and built on the basic ideological frames and consensual attitudes towards the military established in times of 'peace'. This served to marginalise the broader political, moral and historical factors (such as the responsibility of the major powers in supplying Iraq with such arms) and the horrible death-dealing potentials of such weapons. Harvey Morris, of the *Independent*, in an interview with the author, conceded that his newspaper's coverage of the military hardware was 'too gung-ho'. But his editor and deputy editor were committed to it and he had accepted that.

DEFENDING CIVILISATION

The representations of the military hardware were built around deeply-entrenched frames which all the media reproduced. For instance, there was the rhetorical assertion that the allies were defending civilisation and fighting a just cause. As the

News of the World editorial of 20 January 1991 commented: 'If Saddam has to be stopped by a bullet from his own side, the civilised world will be grateful.' Allied warriors were, in fact, portrayed as pacifists at heart. Kovel comments astutely (op cit: 149): 'There is a tendency for technocracy to stay clear of gross violence and even to appear as the antithesis of violence.' According to Robin Andersen (2006: 164), the celebration of the modern technology of war gave the bombing a kind of moral justification. 'The smart bombs were so accurate and there was no intention of targeting civilians and so these worries were easily set aside.'

One of the reports that fitted this stereotype in the run-up to the massacres was of Iraqi soldiers grabbing babies from incubators at a Kuwaiti hospital. First reported by the *Daily Telegraph* on 5 September 1990, two days later the *Los Angeles Times* published a Reuters account reproducing the atrocity story. In fact, the Citizens for a Free Kuwait (95 per cent of its funding coming directly from the Kuwaiti government in exile) hired the public relations firm, Hill and Knowlton (HK), at a cost of £10.8 million to promote its image and campaign for military intervention. HK arranged for a 15-year-old girl, identified as 'Nayirah', to reproduce the babies horror story at a meeting of the human rights caucus of congress in October. It later emerged that 'Nayirah' was the daughter of Saud al-Sabah, Kuwait's ambassador to the United States. President Bush referred to the dead babies story first on 15 October and then five more times in the following five weeks. It was even reproduced in an Amnesty International report on human rights violations in occupied Kuwait, published on 19 December 1990. But after the massacres, it emerged that the atrocity story had been fabricated (Macarthur 1993: 51-77).

The Sunday Times, of 13 January 1991, highlighted the story, quoting a 'Dr Ali Al-Huwail, 36, a Kuwaiti traced to a secret address in the United Arab Emirates' who 'said he could vouch for only 92 deaths'. A large drawing accompanying the story reinforced the message showing 'devilish'-looking Iraqis seizing the babies from the incubators. But the report ended with quotes from a 'Franco-Jordanian doctor' who was sceptical of the baby atrocity stories. Macarthur claims the dead babies story was a defining moment in the disinformation campaign to prepare the American public for the need to go to war. Garth Jowett and Victoria O'Donnell comment: '…in the senate debate on whether to approve military action, seven senators specifically focused on the story. The final margin of victory in favor of military intervention was five votes' (Jowett and O'Donnell 1992: 262).

ALLIES RATIONAL: ENEMY IRRATIONAL

The allies were rational, cool and modern: the enemy were irrational, fanatical, mad, out of touch with reality. An editorial in the *Independent* of 2 February 1991 said that President Saddam's actions had proved one of Israel's central contentions, namely 'the failure of its Arab neighbours to come to term with the reality of the modern world'. And Martin Woollacott wrote in the *Guardian* of 4 March 1991 that Iraq was 'simply a case of Arab sickness'.

ALLIES CHRISTIAN: IRAQIS ISLAMIC AND BACKWARD

The allies were most commonly identified with Christianity. A lot of editorials, for instance, ended with a prayer for the allies or 'our boys'. The Pope's fervent opposition to the military option was significantly marginalised by the press. In contrast, the Iraqis were identified with Islam which was portrayed negatively as backward, primitive, sick and irrational. Saddam was often identified in copy and in cartoons as the devil.

ON THE PROGRESSIVE MOVEMENT OF SCIENCE

An underlying frame tapped into the belief running deep in Western culture that the movement of science was a progressive one. As history moved, science advanced and thus high technology, as the product of advancing science, could only be good. Luckham comments (op cit: 5): '…weapons more than almost any other human product, embody scientific progress. Like modern culture, they are the fruit of the Enlightenment (albeit in misshapen form) and they are readily legitimised by it.' Modern military science could be seen as people-friendly and politically uncontroversial. Thus, allied weapons (such as the positive sounding Patriot) saved lives; enemy weapons (such as the ugly sounding Scud) were indiscriminate.

COALITION FORCES HUMAN: ENEMY MORE LIKE ANIMALS

The coalition forces were always human with human feelings; the enemy were reduced to the level of animals – to be slaughtered. They became non-human targets. Much of this discourse reproduced the traditional rhetoric of Victorian imperialism in which the enemy were dismissed as 'savages' in need of suppression by the 'civilising hand' of the British (Featherstone 1993a and 1993b). This basic frame had a crucial moral foundation: the US-led coalition were always good, they were not to blame: all fault lay with 'Saddam'. Along with technological supremacy went moral superiority.

According to Aksoy and Robins (op cit: 28): 'The Gulf War demonstrated that the power and the dominance of the technological order had become so well secured that it is now the criterion of what is moral.' In this way the massacres (a definition which is ultimately grounded in a moral response of outrage at the perpetrator and compassion for the victim) were silenced – just as the barbarism civilisation carries was hidden. The dominant ideological frames simply excluded such a perspective. John Bulloch, of the *Independent*, told the author after the massacres that a lot of reporters were 'happy to go along' with their military briefers on the advanced technology of warfare since they were largely unfamiliar with the esoteric and complex subject.

THE PRECISION MYTH

Central to the representation of the massacres was the myth of the 'precision' weapons. The media never lost its commitment to this kind of representation – even when the evidence was conspiring to contradict it. It was almost an article of faith. Yet an assessment by the US house of representatives committee on armed services reported in August 1993: 'The body count given by General Schwarzkopf on Iraqi tanks destroyed during the air campaign was, in all likelihood, exaggerated. A careful analysis of 22 per cent of claimed kills shows an over-estimation of tanks killed by 100 per cent and perhaps by as much as 134 per cent' (Adams 1994: 50).

Allied onslaughts tended to inspire superlatives – such as the 'greatest aerial bombardment in history' – behind which all the terrible human suffering was hidden, silenced. Throughout the Iraqi crisis from the invasion of Kuwait in August 1990 until the formal start of Desert Storm onslaught on January 17 the military monopolised the agenda and the language in which it was articulated – the glorification of military technology was the inevitable consequence (Keeble 1997: 139-159). Let's take an example from the *Sun* of 18 January 1991:

> The Allied blitz on Baghdad and other Iraqi targets – the biggest air raid in history – was also a victory for the state-of-the-art technology packed into the Tornados and American F15E bombers. The cruisers aimed at Saddam Hussein's key installations are believed to have landed exactly where intended. Again sophisticated technology gave the missiles their fantastic precision.

Notice how that word 'Allied' nostalgically draws on Second World War rhetoric. 'Targets' is that impersonal word behind which hides the deaths and suffering and trauma of how many people? With the 'enemy' depersonalised in this way the perpetrators of the atrocities manage to avoid any moral responsibility or feelings of guilt. Soldiers kept on telling the press they were simply doing their job. 'The biggest raid in history' manages to extract a soundbite superlative from the horror of the massacres all the more horrific since there was never any credible enemy. 'Blitz on Baghdad' reduces the slaughter to a game of alliteration, while 'state of the art technology' symbolises the glorification of military hardware that became such a prominent feature of the coverage. New militarist wars were essentially manufactured to provide narratives in which armies could win 'victories'. Hence the necessary stress here on 'victory'. Tornado, like Desert Storm, evokes the inevitable onrush and power of nature while that F15E acronym is so typical of militaryspeak – it's a fetishistic celebration of jargon that shifts from the language of myths and metaphors into the amoral landscape of numbers and letters. Death delivering cruise missiles are here referred to as 'cruisers' – an intimate sounding nickname while the reference to Saddam Hussein continues the hyper-personalisation which was such a central feature of all the coverage (Keeble 1998).

And notice the celebration of the 'fantastic precision' of the weapons. They landed exactly where intended. People are spared in this 'surgical', new non-war; only buildings, installations are destroyed in humanitarian wars. Edward Herman, drawing on Orwell's concept of 'newspeak', highlights the use of 'warspeak' during the 1991 attacks on Iraq (op cit: 62-63). 'The aim is to soften language that might suggest unpleasant happenings and to lend support to our claims of benevolence and decency.' He continues:

> The concept of a surgical strike was developed during the Vietnam War to assert that we were aiming accurately at military targets, and implying that we were able to avoid killing civilians. In reality, massive firepower was used to reduce US casualties. … Vast numbers of Indochinese peasants were killed in 'surgical strikes'.

According to Hugh Gusterson (1991, cited in Petley 2004: 165), media coverage of the 1991 conflict showed 'the power of a system of representation which marginalises the presence of the body in war, fetishes machines and personalises international conflicts while depersonalising the people who die in them'.

THE STEALTH MYTH

One of the military 'stars' of the conflict was the F117 Stealth fighter jet which reportedly had an 80 per cent rate on bombing runs. For instance, on 19 January, US Flight leader Col. Al Whitley was quoted in the *Sun* as saying the Stealth was so accurate and sophisticated 'you could choose to take out the men's room or the ladies' room'. US Air Force commanders were 'delighted' with the 'pinpoint accuracy of the raids'. Mad dog Saddam's palace was shattered after a 'pinpoint blitz' by allied missiles. The paper's resident 'military expert' said the 'amazing accuracy of the allies' air power held the key to victory'. But in July 1996, a report from the congressional general accounting office concluded that the success rate was closer to 40 per cent (Weiner op cit). Furthermore, the much-touted laser technology had done little to liberate pilots from age-old weather problems. The multi-million-dollar sensor system failed to 'see' through fog, rain, clouds, smoke or humidity, the report concluded (Robinson, Stephen 1996). Roy Greenslade, editor of the *Mirror* at the time of the Gulf crisis, admitted to me:

> I was not at all sceptical of the American claims over the success of the 'smart' bombs. We treated the war in a comic-book style: how 'we' shot down 'their' Scud with 'our' Patriot. I was not aware the Americans were lying. I was never aware of the toll of human life in Iraq.

He added: 'If I had an excuse it would be that I was a prisoner of the job. I just didn't think enough about it all.' He said he was in an extremely difficult situation. 'I forbade the use of the phrase "our boys" and tried not to be jingoistic. But then I had a Jewish proprietor [Robert Maxwell] who was exceedingly anti-Arab. You had to work round him.'

After the Second World War the effects of the fire bombing of thousands of civilians in Dresden by the allies was kept secret for years. Only then was the military forced to respond to allegations of 'indiscriminate bombing' (Best 1980). Such a phrase was totally missing from the Gulf coverage. High technology had supposedly cleansed warfare strategies. As the Falklands War leader Marshall Lord Bramall commented in the *Express* on 18 January 1991: 'In the Second World War we indulged in massive area bombing because we could not make the planes more accurate. But now they can locate targets with infra-red which allows you to get your weapon right on target.' He said such 'pin-point accuracy' was vital to 'allow the allies to keep the high moral ground'. On 19 January, the *Express* carried photographs across two pages showing a bomb hitting its target, thus complementing the television coverage of the same event. Under the headline 'Bombing so precise even experts gasped', the copy ran:

> The spectacular surgical precision of allied bombing against Iraq was displayed to the world yesterday. The first combat video of the war showed laser-controlled smart missiles blowing the airforce headquarters in Baghdad to smithereens. …The display had even defence experts gasping in amazement.

An RAF chief is quoted: 'It is amazing. In this case, hi-tech weapons are real war winners.'

INDISCRIMINATE: PRECISELY

The stress on precision warfare served to detract attention not only from the majority of bombs which missed their targets but also from the most commonly used bombs which were the opposite of precise. They were part of the secret war. As Paul Rogers argued (1991: 26): 'Alongside the "precision war" of laser-guided bombs and pinpoint missiles, there was a second type of war. It was fought with munitions specifically designed to kill and injure people on the widest possible scale. …Their use was largely censored during the war – sometimes by and sometimes from the media.' Like napalm and the early cluster bombs, modern area impact munitions (as they are called) are intended to devastate a wide area rather than confine their destruction to a precise target. They do this by creating a mist or cloud of explosives which is then detonated such as the fuel air explosive, or by sending out a large number of bomblets, as with the cluster bomb. The most commonly used area impact bombs were cluster bombs and multiple-launch rocket systems. The death and destruction they caused was colossal.

One of the main purposes of the massacres was to vindicate the enormous expenditure placed on such weaponry in the previous decades. Yet a report by the American human rights group, Middle East Watch, *Needless deaths in the Gulf War* (1991: 120-121), criticised the use of enormous numbers of 'dumb weapons' with 25 per cent accuracy in built-up areas in total contravention of Article 57 of the First Protocol of the Geneva Convention. The report commented:

Public statements by Bush administration and Pentagon officials during the war suggested that the choice of weaponry took into account the need to minimize civilian casualties. But this claim is yet to be squared with the Pentagon's public admission that less than 9 per cent of the total tonnage of ordnance dropped during the air war was precision-guided bombs.

THE PATRIOTIC MYTH

No weapon achieved more fame during the massacres than the Patriots which were quickly deployed in Israel after Iraq launched Scud missiles on Tel Aviv. As Bruce Cumings commented (1992: 124-125): 'The Patriot missile, of course, was the star of the show. ... We all lined up to watch a game called the Patriots vs the Scuds, as if two teams had been added to the National Football league.' Gen. Schwarzkopf told reporters that 'the Patriot's success, of course, is known to everyone. It's 100 per cent'. After the ceasefire, President Bush went in person to the Raytheon plant where they were made to congratulate the company whose orders suddenly soared. The *Sun* on 28 February 1991 described it as 'the most famous weapon in the world'. As late as 10 September 1992, the *Independent* reported: 'Patriot missiles, as every American schoolboy knows, were the ones that shot down Iraqi Scuds in the Gulf war.' Robin Andersen comments on the Patriots (2006: 178): 'In news narratives, they were treated as the superior white knights countering the attacks of the dark forces of Saddam's blunt instruments, the Scud missiles.'

But evidence released subsequently suggests the media were pushing yet another myth, reproducing military/government lies. On 18 January 1991, the Patriot appeared to achieve a historic 'knockout' – being the first defensive missile to destroy an offensive weapon. As Sherwood commented (1992), that first shot 'remains a defining moment embedded in the country's consciousness'. Yet that famous first shot hit at nothing. Satellite information suggested the target had come from two improbably places – the Gulf or Iran. The army ruled out these possibilities. Sherwood concluded: 'Most probably, the "Scud" was a Patriot computer glitch.'

Further evidence debunked the Patriot myth. A US armed services committee report, quoted in the *Guardian* of 17 August 1993, concluded: 'A post-war review of photographs cannot produce a single confirmed kill of a Scud missile.' And on 22 November 1993, the *Guardian* reported Moshe Arens, Israeli chief of staff at the time, and Haim Asa, a member of an Israeli technical team dealing with Patriot missiles, saying that Patriots intercepted just one, or possibly none of the Scuds. According to Alexander Cockburn (1991c):

> 158 Patriots were fired at 47 Scuds within Patriot coverage. Very few of the successfully intercepted Scud warheads were prevented from hitting either a structure or the ground and exploding. Moreover, large numbers of Patriots, some fired at real Scuds and some at radar false alarms, came

down and exploded themselves, contributing substantially to the casualties and damage.

Marc Miller reports (1991) that before Patriots were used 13 Scuds damaged 2,698 apartments and injured 115 people. With Patriots in use 11 Scud attacks damaged 7,778 apartments, wounded 168 people and killed at least one person (see also Andersen 2006: 179). During the 'war', US military briefers claimed 81 Scud launchers had been destroyed. But afterwards former Marine Corps analyst Scott Ritter (later to become well-known as a maverick arms inspector) claimed no mobile Scud launchers had been destroyed with only 12 of the 28 fixed launchers eliminated (Macarthur 1993: 250).[2]

Intriguingly, one of the men deploying the Patriot missiles to protect Israelis against Iraqi Scuds in 1991 was Jay Garner. He went on to the become president of the defence contractor SY Coleman, which specialised in the missile systems including the Patriot, and later director of the Pentagon's short-lived office of reconstruction and humanitarian assistance for Iraq after the 2003 invasion. As Paul Vallely (2003) pointed out in a profile in the *Independent*, Garner's firm supplied the military technology 'responsible for demolishing the country he is to set about rebuilding'.

SILENCING THE HORROR: THE CASUALTIES COVER-UP

The ideological frame in which the necessary new militarist adventure in the Middle East was presented in the dominant media remained remarkably consistent throughout the August 1990 to March 1991 period – and at root was extremely simple. Hence its strength and seductive qualities. Saddam was the monster threatening the world; the allies were fighting a clean war for a just cause. Integral to this frame was the denial of the reality of the horror in the fog of war. As Claude le Borgne argues, the war was, in fact, a series of 'discreet massacres' (le Borgne 1992). The new militarist media machine attempted to revolutionise the image of war. This was to be, essentially, a non-war war. A war with all the blood and butchery and death drained out of it. It had to be quick, cool, clean and victorious. A harmless, heroic spectacle. So it had to be a war fought in secret. Journalists were kept away from virtually all the slaughter. Out of sight – out of mind. Most newspapers carried only one picture of a dead Iraqi – following the massacres at Khafji at the end of February 1991. In contrast, coverage constantly focused on the image of the dead cormorant, a victim, supposedly, of Saddam the 'eco terrorist' who had caused the oil slick disaster in the Gulf. Yet it became known afterwards that the images had been drawn from another Gulf oil slick disaster and that some of the firing of Kuwaiti oil wells resulted from allied bombing (Seager 1992: 25).

Gen Schwarzkopf constantly refused to be drawn on the issue of casualties. This was nothing new. The military had been reticent over casualty figures (defined in militaryspeak as 'collateral damage') during the slaughters of new militarist adventures in Grenada and Panama. Schwarzkopf tried to legitimise the strategy, describing talk of the dead as the 'pornography' of war. The US military were determined to have no repeat of Vietnam when they had tried to explain the complex conflict in the simple language of body counts, BDAs (bomb damage assessments) and KIA (killed in action). The Vietnam conflict appeared to have no clear beginning or end, no clearly marked goals. The 'body counts', it could be argued, were an attempt to bring order to the chaos, to establish a quantifiable assessment of the military's performance. Susan Jeffords comments (1989: 7): 'That false numbers were reported, that anything counted as a body – an arm, leg or torso – and that non-enemy bodies were included in the count confirm the extent to which the technology of performance became ascendant.'

By the time of the Gulf conflict, the propaganda rhetoric had changed. On 5 February, the *Mirror* reported Gen. Schwarzkopf as saying the allies were at pains to avoid hitting innocent people: 'We are not, not, not, not, not deliberately targeting civilian casualties and we never will. We are a moral, ethical people.'

HOW BARBARISM BECOMES A BIG JOKE

Another way in which the press hid the horror of the massacres was to hype them into a fun event. Barbarism became a big joke. With the absence of any credible enemy and the dull repetitiveness of the US-led air attacks, the war rapidly became boring to Fleet Street. This was all the more paradoxical since war reporting traditionally represents the summit achievement for the reporter. As Don McKay of the *Mirror* told me: 'It's every reporter's wish to cover a war. It's the ultimate news story.' But reporting from Bahrain, McKay summed up the problem of Gulf war boredom in this way: '

> With the loss of the Tornados in the early days of the conflict there were ten days of the 'wonderful stuff'. After that even the war became a doorstep. I kept sending over copy – a couple of marriages, a murder scoop even. But little of it was used. It became exceedingly boring. On the launch of the ground war I returned to London hoping to go to Kuwait to cover the attack. But it was over so quickly. So I was left thinking: how dare you finish this war when I'm back in London feeling a mixture of jealousy and frustration.

Not everyone felt the same. Michael Evans, London-based defence correspondent of *The Times*, told the author: 'I never once found it boring. I was zinging from the beginning to the end.' Yet Martin Woollacott, who filed reports from Baghdad, Amman, Syria and Kurdistan during the crisis, massacres and aftermath for the *Guardian*, told me how the war became 'deeply boring'. 'During the air war there were meaningless daily packages of statistics telling us nothing about anything in military or human terms.'

So the patriotic pops solved the problem of the dull war by concentrating on celebrities (the royals, pop stars and television personalities) and human interest angles, making it all a bit of a giggle. Roy Greenslade, editor of the *Mirror* at the time and now professor of journalism at City University London, told me that the war after a while became boring and so his paper was obliged to mix it up with 'razzamatazz and entertainment'. He explained:

> Tabloids are both a contributing factor and a response to the alienation of the working class from political life, social relationships and their old traditions of solidarity. In fact, tabloid newspapers have had on their agenda since the early 1970s the debunking and lampooning of the political process. Trade unionists have helped in this process. People have turned their backs on the political system and industrial organisation and sought a kind of leisure. Thus a serious subject if it is not to lose their attention has to be covered in a way to feed their diet of fun. This even includes war (Keeble 1997: 152).

One of the longest running stories in the paper was archetypally mediacentric – being over a leader in *The Sunday Times* which criticised the performance of the royals during the 'war'. 'Kilroy in telly punch up' (13 February, page one); 'What a right royal fuss' (Anne Robinson comment, 14 February); 'You can't take her anywhere' (on Sarah Ferguson, then wife of Prince Andrew and known commonly in the tabloids as 'Fergie', 16 February) and 'Fergie father in jibe fury' (19 February) were among the follow-up stories. Hardly any other story received such treatment.

The *Sun* tried to encourage its women readers to 'Flash your knickers for our brave boys. Go give 'em a frill', accompanying the story with a picture of a woman bending over and showing her knickers. 'Who bares wins' the paper added. Pushing puns to the limit, it said: 'Our boys know all about military briefings but if you look racy in lacies we want you to give em a cheeky low-down briefing of your own.' Later the paper reported: 'Wives say knickers to Iraq.' Lovesick army wives were supposedly bombarding fellas with their favourite lingerie. And when Harlow Council supposedly ordered workers to tear down a Union Jack 'backing our Gulf heroes', the *Sun* (reporters and Page Three lovelies etc), continuing its well-established strategy of attacking 'loony left authorities', staged its own mock invasion of the town hall in protest. Thus on 31 January, it gave more coverage to its story '*Sun* sends Patriots into Harlow' than to the massacre at Khafji. 'The *Sun*'s Patriots stormed into the shamed town of Harlow yesterday to give the town hall lefties a rocket. ... We flew the Union Jack, the size of a bus, cheered on by citizens who are disgusted at the council's ban on flags supporting Our Boys in the Gulf.'

On 29 January, the *Sun* carried Gulf war jokes under the headline 'Giggle at the Gulf'. For example, Iraqi soldiers are changing their socks every day – because they smell de-feet. On 2 February, the paper invited its readers to learn the 'hilarious new slang used by US troops in the Saudi desert'. For instance, BAM (Big Assed

Marine: women officers); BMD (Black Moving Object: Iraqi woman dressed in Arabic robes). Even the military hardware was transformed into a merry massacring machine. A 'profile' of the B52 bombers (famed for their 'carpet bombing' of Iraqi conscripts) described them as 'Jolly Green Giants'.

BEHIND THE MERRY MYTHS: THE MASSACRES

John Simpson says of the 1991 conflict (2010: 515): '…it was merely a well-planned, well-executed operation by some of the best military machines in the world against a smaller, weaker and utterly demoralised Third World army. The correspondents of a century before would scarcely have recognized it as a battle for them, it would merely have been organized slaughter.' Moreover, following the 42-day round-the-clock bombardment of Iraq by 'the greatest power ever assembled', the devastation caused what a March 1991 UN survey described as a 'near apocalyptic' tragedy. The survey warned that it threatened to reduce a 'highly urbanised and mechanised society to a pre-industrial age'. Saeed Khanum spoke of the 'post nuclear holocaust' landscape of Basra during the January/February period (Khanum 1991; see also Cainkar 1991). Edwards and Cromwell report (2009: 16):

> All of Iraq's eleven major electrical plants as well as 119 substations were destroyed – 90 per cent of electricity generation was out of service within hours; within days all power generation in the country had ceased. Eight multi-purpose dams were repeatedly hit and destroyed – this wrecked flood control, municipal and industrial water storage, irrigation and hydroelectric power. … Twenty-eight civilian hospitals and 52 community health centres were hit.

On 10 February, in the middle of the bombardment, the *Independent on Sunday* was able to comment: 'War is never pleasant. There are certain actions that a civilised society can never contemplate. This carpet bombing is undeniably terrible. But that does not make it wrong' (cited in Pilger 2002: 99).

In September 1992, an international team of researchers from Harvard estimated that 46,900 children under five died in Iraq between January and August 1991 as an indirect result of the bombing, civilian uprisings and UN economic embargo. Those suffering the most were Kurds, the very people the coalition sought support in their conflict with the Iraqi regime. The *Independent* of 24 September 1992 carried these details under the headline: 'War tripled child deaths in Iraq.' The report was worth only ten lines and was buried in an inside page. Focusing just on civilians and soldiers still minimises the enormity of the tragedy. The conflict, it could be argued, involved the deliberate destruction of the Iraqi social and economic infrastructure. Louise Cainkar (1991) commented: 'The decimation of the infrastructure of Iraq was the aim of coalition bombing, a goal achievable only with good intelligence and highly sophisticated technology and weaponry. It naturally follows that most of the civilian casualties of this war would result from this destruction and not from direct hits on civilian areas.'

The massacres created 1.8 million refugees, of whom 30,000 were estimated to have died. Moreover, the Overseas Development Institute estimated that at least 40 low and low-middle income countries faced the economic equivalent of a natural disaster as a result of the massacres (Pilger 1991b and 1991c). In 1990, there was full employment in Iraq while an extra one million Egyptians worked in the country. Two years later, unemployment had risen to more than 50 per cent of the work force (Cockburn 2008: 105).

Many ancient and valuable archaeological sites in cities such as Nineveh and Babylon (the cradle of civilisation) were bombed. No one will ever know how many Iraqis were killed. To the elites of both sides they were irrelevant. Such silence is represented as 'inevitable'. And yet casualties in less well-observed conflicts have been known more precisely. Moreover, while little attempt was made to count bodies considerable precision was applied to estimating Iraqi military equipment losses.

BULLDOZED AND BURNT OUT OF EXISTENCE

Many Iraqis were bulldozed both dead and alive into mass graves (Rosenfeld 1991). News of this activity only emerged after the end of the massacres. Three Labour MEPs, Ken Coates, Peter Crampton and Henry McCubbin, pointed out in a letter to the *Guardian* on 12 March 1991, that such mass burials were contrary to Articles 16 and 17 of the Geneva Convention 1945. But this view is strongly challenged by US journalist Rick Atkinson. He expresses surprise at the 'hue and cry' which arose over the strategy 'as if burying the enemy was less humane than eviscerating them with tank fire or eleven thousand artillery rounds' (Atkinson 1994: 397). He concludes:

> In truth, similar tactics had been used since the advent of armored warfare in World War 1; against the Japanese, beginning with the bloody fight for Tulagi in the South Pacific, US Marines had buried the enemy in their caves and bunkers whenever possible rather than dig them out. The tactic had been reviewed by a United Nations conference on conventional weaponry during the late 1970s and left unregulated as a 'common, longstanding tactic entirely consistent with the law of war'.

Many Iraqi victims were also burnt to ashes making identification more difficult. Robert Fox, of the *Daily Telegraph*, who spent two days after the massacres travelling 235 kilometres along the front line, commented: 'They were consumed in the most terrible way: there is so much fire, there is so much fissile capacity in these weapons now, I don't mean to be disgusting but they are just incinerated. ... A terrifying, novel aspect of this campaign is that even the bones remain' (Keeble 1997: 154).

ELIMINATING 250,000 IRAQIS

We will never know precisely how many Iraqis died as a result of Desert Storm. Julie Flint, in the *Observer* of 3 March, said 100,000 were killed and injured. According to Dilip Hiro (1992: 396), some 80,000 Iraqi soldiers had been taken prisoner. By mid-March the casualty figures were being revised upwards with the *Christian Science Monitor* reporting estimates of 100,000 to 200,000 while on 20 March the *Independent* reported that up to 190,000 Iraqi soldiers had not been accounted for. Gen. Colin L. Powell, chairman of the US Joint Chiefs of Staff, suggests in his personal account of the conflict (1995: 525-526) that half of Iraq's 1 million-strong army were based in the Kuwait theatre and that half of them were eliminated during the conflict. At the end of 1991, the Medical Educational Trust in London also reported that a quarter of a million men, women and children were killed or died as a result of the US attack on Iraq (Pilger 1998: 53).

Three months after the slaughter the US defense department estimated that 100,000 Iraqi troops had been killed (Cohen and Gotti 1991: 270). Dr Sa'adoun Hammadi, deputy prime minister of Iraq, said that 22,000 civilians had been killed in air raids on Baghdad alone (Heikal 1992: 316). Christopher Lee, a defence analyst at Emmanuel College, Cambridge, who acted as the BBC Radio 4's military expert through the Gulf 'war', monitored all the allied briefings and was convinced journalists had failed to press the military hard enough over the casualties issue. Their relationship with the military was far 'too cosy'. 'They gave the impression of just re-writing what the spokesmen said and they didn't publicly press home questions day after day. For example, what are Iraqi casualties even if they knew what the answer was going to be so that they could say to people at home we are asking on your behalf.'[3] Mark Laity, of the BBC, in contrast, argued that journalists should not get involved in the 'morality of war': 'I think a lot of criticism comes from people who seem to think that the only story was whether bombs killed people. Well, of course they do. The big story was were the allies going to win the war.'[4]

THE SILENCING ROLE OF MASSACRESPEAK

Central to the dominant new militarist ideological frame was the denial of the humanity of the Iraqi conscripts. This draws on a tradition of war propaganda. Phillip Knightley has recorded the racist way in which the German enemy in the two world wars and Vietnamese were similarly dehumanised (Knightley 2003a [1975]). During the massacres, the Iraqis were constantly described as 'animals', 'beasts'. The military called them 'turkeys', 'rats', 'ducks', 'ants', 'fish'. The military destroyed 'targets' not people. Kuwait was described as a 'target-rich environment'. Indeed, Luckham (op cit: 18) has identified how strategic discourse borrows 'heavily from the rhetoric of theatre, organised sport and the capitalist market place'. Thus, the slaughter never once drew any outrage from any of the press.

The Iraqi conscripts were, in any case, always enveloped and eliminated in the demonisation of Saddam Hussein. The military were never slaughtering thousands, they were, instead, 'kicking Saddam's arse'. As Paul Johnson described the Americans in the *Mail* of 19 January 1991: 'They are giving Saddam hell and they love it. It's as much as they can do to stop themselves telling you they are bombing Iraq back into the Stone Age.' But that's alright. God's on our side. 'A markedly high proportion of British pilots are regular church-goers,' Johnson continued.

When civilian casualties were reported more widely the dominant view focused on the inevitability of such horrors. Joe Haines, writing in the *Mirror* of 9 February, summed up this view: 'I don't want to appear unfeeling but the constant harping on civilian deaths in Iraq verges on hysteria. Those who support the war but turn every civilian death into an occasion for breast beating are refusing to face up to the reality of what they have chosen to do. Civilians get killed in wars. They always did and always will.' Another strategy, implicit in all the coverage but often stated overtly, was to place all blame on Saddam. Or the focus was shifted almost exclusively to the 'atrocities' committed by the Iraqis in Kuwait, Israel or Saudi Arabia. There was also the suspicion always that casualty figures were part of Saddam's propaganda project.

POST-WAR PERCEPTIONS

Two years after the end of the massacres a new version of the 'precision, clean war' myth emerged to reinforce the original one. The *Independent* reported on its front page of 10 March 1993, a former analyst in the US defense intelligence agency, John Heiderich, as saying that as few as 1,500 Iraqi soldiers may have been killed by allied forces. Christopher Bellamy, defence correspondent, reported: 'Mr Heiderich calculates an absolute maximum of 6,500 dead and 19,500 wounded but only if all Iraqi vehicles struck had full crews. In fact, they did not and the number of Iraqi dead is estimated at 0.5 per cent of those in the theatre, or 1,500.'

David Fairhall, who covered the 'war' from Riyadh for the *Guardian*, said in an interview with the author that journalists had tried very hard to secure more information on casualty figures but they had generally met 'a brick wall'. He continued: 'We assumed very high numbers of casualties, basing that on worst case intelligence assessments. In fact, a lot of Iraqis were never there. They had left before it all started.' He did not believe that talk of the Iraqi army as being the fourth largest in the world by his intelligence sources involved a deliberate attempt to deceive. 'People usually do make errors in wars. They tend to look at wars through very prejudiced lenses and everyone tends to exaggerate the situation.' He also expected more allied casualties. 'If the Iraqis had met experienced Western troops in a straightforward ground battle they would have given a good account of themselves. British military chiefs warned people back home that we should realise we could be taking heavy casualties. That was my conditioning.'

COALITION CONTRASTS

In contrast to the silence over the Iraqi casualties the press predictably gave massive coverage to the relatively few allied deaths. But it remained unclear after the massacres exactly how many allied soldiers were killed in and out of combat and by 'friendly fire'. Arab countries in the coalition failed to provide casualty figures; Palestinians were often counted as non-persons. Indeed, Chris Buckland, in his report in the *Express* of 7 March 1991, throws into doubt the figures of war dead. He wrote: 'Saudi Arabia claimed only one person in Riyadh was killed by Scuds. Hospital staff however say 54 were killed in one attack but as 53 were Third World workers they didn't count.' The 'miraculously low' allied figures, may, in fact, be not so low. Official ministry of defence figures issued after the war gave 23 Britons killed between 23 August 1990 and January 16 and 24 killed during the 'war' (plus four special forces soldiers). Certainly, fewer British soldiers died in the Gulf than during normal peacetime periods.

During the blitz of Iraq the focus was directed at their potential threat to captured allied airmen; Iraqi civilians were completely ignored. Thus, the *Mirror* headlined on 29 January: 'Allied blitz "hits captive air crews."' When the British Tornados were lost or the crews were missing there was enormous coverage. Relations, pen pals, were interviewed; brave mums of hero pilots said their patriotic pieces: 'If he has died I hope he has done so to make a better world for our children' (*Mirror*, 22 January). Fellow pilots were shown weeping for their comrades. Death always occurred during heroic battle.

On 23 February, the *Mirror* reported the first British soldier lost in action, a 'heroic squaddie lost during a fierce gun battle'. He was involved in a 'fearsome battle' against 'overwhelming odds'. But alongside the one British death the report buries the fact that 'scores of Iraqis were believed killed or wounded' in the 'battle'. Great emphasis was given in the run-up to the massacres on the capabilities of the RAF Tornados' JP233 'runway denial system'. But, in fact, the Americans had pulled out of the programme early on because of justifiable fears that it would cause unnecessary casualties forcing pilots to fly extremely low. According to Michael Spaven, the RAF was flying to win its political battles in Whitehall. It needed to justify 20 years of concentrated effort on low-level bombing at its specialised 'offensive counterair' role in attacking enemy airfields. Such coverage during the 'war' would have questioned the patriotic endeavour of 'our' brave pilots – and so rarely appeared (Spaven 1991a and 1991b).

ISRAEL AND THE MYTH OF VULNERABILITY

When Israel came under attack from Scud missiles coverage reached hysterical levels. Only one person was to die from these attacks yet constant reports focused on the enormity of the threat facing the country. As so often happens in media coverage, elite fears are translated in the heat of the moment into reality. Thus, when a Scud missile first hit Tel Aviv on 17 January 1991, it was reported on the midnight news on Channel 4. By 1.38 am the BBC was reporting falsely that Israel was retaliating; soon afterwards Channel 4 reported that the missiles had chemical warheads. The *Mirror* of 18 January reported falsely in its front page lead: 'Pentagon sources were reported as saying Israel is poised to make a "massive retaliatory strike" and the Israelis immediately launched an air counter attack.'

Next day, the newspaper was saying, wrongly again, that the Israelis would defiantly launch revenge attacks on Iraq. Such falsehoods were willed on by accompanying comment. For instance, the editorial of the *Mirror* of 19 January was rhetoric of the kind never directed at the allied bombardments: 'The Iraqi missile onslaught on Israel was an act of barbarous treachery. In its half century of life this brave little country has always followed the Biblical precept of an eye for an eye. If the Israelis now strike back at Saddam, who under God's heaven can blame them?' *Mirror* editor Roy Greenslade has since revealed in an interview with the author that all editorials at the time were compiled by the newspaper's proprietor Robert Maxwell, a fervent supporter of Israel. 'I was prepared to go along with this. It left me free to run the rest of the editorial operation as I wanted.'

Iraq's attacks were certainly designed to spread terror among civilians and thus contrary to Article 51 of the Geneva Conventions. But they were symbolic rather than militarily significant, attempting to actualise the claimed linkage between the Israeli occupation of the West Bank, Golan Heights and Gaza with the invasion of Kuwait. Thus it was important for the media to deny this link and responsibility for any ensuing casualties. Richard Littlejohn, in the *Sun* of 19 January, was on hand to comment:

> Israel seized the West Bank, Gaza and the Golan Heights in a pre-emptive strike in self-defence against hostile armies massing on her borders. Iraq's invasion was straightforward theft motivated by the greed and megalomania of a deranged dictator. ... The crisis has been provoked by one man. He must not live to fight another day.

Accompanying these accounts were dramatic photographs of Israelis (usually women and children) injured in the attacks with captions highlighting the horror. The *News of the World* commented on 20 January: 'We badly need Israel to continue displaying the superhuman self-restraint it has exercised for two days in the face of outrageous provocation from Saddam's Scud missile terrorism.'

John Bulloch, Middle East expert of the *Independent*, remarked in an interview with the author on how Israel was constantly represented as if it were facing Armageddon. This was 'total rubbish', he said. 'The Israelis received huge kudos for doing nothing in response to the Scud attacks. But what else could they do?' He believed the Jewish lobby was extremely powerful and that the 'whole pervading atmosphere in dominant circles' meant that the 'Israelis were seen as the good guys, the Arabs the bad guys'. And Stephen Badsey (1992: 230) suggests that Israel manipulated the international media with its 'customary sophistication' to secure a major military and political victory without firing a shot. 'Like Saudi Arabia, Israel blocked direct coverage of Scud attacks and accurate reporting of target locations after 23 January but thereafter played brilliantly on the major media weaknesses by personalising the event. The world's press was allowed within hours of a Scud attack to interview survivors in the wreckage of their homes.'

FRIENDLY FIRE STORMS

Despite all media attempts to represent the conflict as 'heroic warfare' the facts conspired against this. Very few allied deaths occurred as a result of actual combat; while the massacres were going on the greatest threat to coalition forces was posed by allied soldiers and pilots themselves. Out of those 353 allied deaths, Lt Gen. John Yeosock, commander of all troops, said that only 46 were killed in active service. And of those 24 (52 per cent) were caused by so-called 'friendly fire' (military jargon that slipped effortlessly into the lexicon of the massacres) (Sloyan 1991). Macarthur reports that of the 467 US troops injured, 72 were injured by their own side (op cit: 148). Some 144 US service men and six women died during Operation Desert Storm compared with 108 deaths from early August 1990 to 16 January 1991 (Allen, Berry and Polmar 1991: 220).

Of the British deaths, nine were from so-called friendly-fire and only one of those killed by incoming fire. The rest died as a result of 'malfunctioning equipment' (Sackur 1991). A number of deaths originally said by the military to be the result of enemy fire were later found to be 'friendly fire' deaths. Those British 'friendly fire' casualties became the focus of massive publicity in Britain in 1992 after relatives tried, unsuccessfully, to force the pilots responsible to attend a coroner's inquiry.

NOTES

[1] A study of the pictorial representation of the conflict in the US magazines, *Time, Newsweek, US News* and *World Report* found only 3 per cent showed events occurring in combat zones. Only 2 per cent showed any signs of wounded or killed soldiers (Griffin 2010: 26-27)

[2] According to Dilip Hiro (1992: 378), 36 Iraqi Scuds aimed at Saudi Arabia killed one and wounded 30 whilst 37 fired at Israel killed four and injured 305

[3] Lee, Christopher quoted in a transcript of BBC Radio 4 'File on Four' programme 9 April 1991 pp 11-12

[4] Laity, Mark, quoted in a transcript of BBC Radio 4 'File on Four' programme 9 April 1991 pp 12-13. Laity was later appointed chief of strategic communications at Supreme Headquarters Allied Powers Europe

Chapter Ten

Mediating massacres: Manufacturing the illusion of war

THE MYTH OF THE KHAFJI BATTLE

The battle of Khafji, 12 miles inside Saudi Arabia, at the end of January 1991 came at a crucial time for both sides. The massacres were continuing. Allied forces had complete control over the air and space. As Lambakis (1995: 418) wrote: 'The battle over the control and use of space in the Persian Gulf War was as impressively one-sided on paper as it was in the theatre – simply no contest.' And according to Patrick Cockburn (2008: 72): 'When round-the-clock bombing of the Iraqi army in Kuwait started on 19 January, the soldiers, mostly Shi'a and Kurdish conscripts, knew the war could have only one outcome. They deserted in droves.' Kuwait became a 'target-rich environment'. So far there had been no evidence of anything more than token resistance from the Iraqis – supposedly the fourth largest army in the world and a threat to the new global order.

Then, in the midst of the fog of war, the 'battle' of Khafji, when the Iraqis allegedly held a deserted town (though Gen. Schwarzkopf persisted in calling it a 'village') for 36 hours, provided both sides with 'ammunition' in the propaganda war. Iraq could claim a victory. Eleven Marines were killed, according to Gen. Thomas Kelly at a 30 January Pentagon briefing in Washington. But it later emerged they had been killed through 'friendly fire' along with 18 Saudis – not at Khafji but 150 miles to the west (Thomson 1992: 199). Equally it was in the interest of the US-led coalition commanders to represent Iraq as a credible threat at this stage – and the Khafji confrontation provided just that scenario.

In particular, in order to legitimise the participation of the coalition's ground assault on Kuwait of the Arab forces, an attack was necessary. In September 1990, King Faud of Saudi Arabia had stressed at the Cairo summit that Arab forces would never join in an attack unless attacked themselves (Heikal 1992: 232). The Khafji 'battle' provided them with just the excuse they needed. Indeed, allied commanders stressed (for PR purposes) the role of Saudi and Qatari troops in the 'battle' though it later emerged that US Marines and, for the Arabs, Pakistanis played far more significant roles.

For the allied military there were two competing imperatives: to stress 'victory in battle' against a credible enemy and at the same time their role as victims of a dangerous, ruthless enemy poised for mass attack. Prime Minister John Major was so keen to stress the 'victory' that he did so too early – on 31 January (Hiro 1992: 344). Moreover, press representations dutifully helped the military in their propaganda war. In fact, the reporting, tightly controlled by the US military, served to hide the reality of massacres both at Khafji and to the west. Despite all the chaos and confusion, Thomson concludes: 'In most cases the reporting of Khafji, as the allied command wanted, simply mirrored the information being put out by the briefers in Riyadh and around the world' (op cit: 205). *Independent* maverick reporter Robert Fisk recounted afterwards how pool reporters came to do the military work of controlling the media. As he headed to the town, an NBC reporter shouted at him: 'You asshole, you'll prevent us from working. You're not allowed here. Get out. Go back to fucking Dhahran.' He then betrayed Fisk to a US Marine 'public affairs' officer who told him: 'You're not allowed to talk to US Marines and they're not allowed to talk to you' (Fisk 2006: 766).

ORIGINS OF THE KHAFJI 'BATTLE' SHROUDED IN THE FOG OF WAR

The main source for the origins of the massacre was Marine Major Craig Huddleston whose words were uncritically reported by virtually all the press in Britain. Apparently, on the night of 29-30 January an Iraqi column of about 80 armoured vehicles advanced on Khafji, their turrets reversed to indicate they wanted to defect. But then, according to the official line, they suddenly turned on the Saudi forces and 'battle' commenced. Gen. Sir Peter de la Billière (1995: 250), commander of the British forces in the Gulf, in his best-selling personal account of the massacres, added a new twist to this angle saying the Iraqis produced white flags before firing on Saudi troops.

Huddleston's comments were certainly useful in putting the blame for the massacre on the Iraqis. The *Mirror* headlined the story 'Cowards' but the editor, Roy Greenslade, later regretted using that headline. He told me in an interview: 'I believe that was a wrong assessment of the situation. The one thing they were not was cowardly. It was what I was trying to avoid ... labelling the other side as the worthless, no-good enemy.' There was no military sense to the Iraqi attack – as all the papers were keen to stress. Without any air cover, it was simply a suicide mission. In such a situation, the entry by the Iraqis into the deserted town of Khafji was a desperate defensive action to seek the cover of the buildings more than an attack as it was represented in the British press. Most likely, the Iraqis drifted into no-man's land along the Kuwait/Saudi border (deliberately left deserted by the allies and recently cleared of journalists) without any communication link-ups with their military headquarters. By accident they ended up heading for Khafji where they planned to surrender. (Or, according to the *Sun*, they 'sneaked over the Saudi border'.) They could do nothing else.

As Gen. de la Billière recounted: 'It was exactly what we had expected and hoped for, as it brought enemy vehicles, weapons and men out of their prepared positions and into the open where our pilots were able to see them and pick them off' (ibid: 250). And reporting from Hafar al-Batin, to the west of Khafji, Richard Dowden, of the *Independent* (31 January), spoke of the 'first major engagement of ground forces in this area, an artillery duel started shortly after dusk'. He added: 'It appeared to have been started by the Americans. The US troops appeared to be trying to provoke the Iraqis into giving away their positions in preparation for a full-scale frontal attack.'

Most of the British press, determined to report the massacres in the traditional language of warfare, represented Khafji as the launch of Iraq's 'ground war' (*Guardian*, 31 January). The *Sun*, of 2 February, spoke of an 'enemy attempt to invade Saudi Arabia'. The *Star*, of 31 January, headlined their report: 'Battle for a ghost town'; a number of papers spoke of 'fierce fighting', of a 'bloody battle'. Martin Woollacott, in the *Guardian* of 31 January, commented: 'The Iraqis have struck their first blow in the ground war, that mother of all battles which Saddam Hussein professes he can win.' The following day, the *Guardian*'s front page headlined: 'Iraqis mass for surge south' and the editorial commented: 'Khafji demonstrates again what every infantryman knows. Fighting with tanks and air supremacy in open country is one thing. Street fighting in towns is bloody, quite another thing. There man, not machines, count.' The *Sunday Times*, of 3 February, reported: 'The Iraqis fought much harder than expected' and this had 'led to a fundamental reassessment of the morale of Iraqi troops by the Pentagon'.

Little mention of the slaughter of terrified conscripts. Moreover, there was an ambivalence about the overall coverage. It was necessary to show the Iraqis to be a 'better fighting force than expected'. At the same time it was impossible to deny the fact they faced impossible odds against the coalition forces. *The Sunday Times* summed up this ambivalence on 3 February, reporting that while the soldiers were preparing for the 'greatest land battle since the Second World War, they knew they faced a demoralised, starving and lice-ridden army reduced to scavenging for food among the ruins of Kuwait'. The Kuwaiti 'battlefield' was now left open for 'the biggest turkey shoot of all time'.

MASSACRESPEAK SHROUDS THE HORROR

The popular press openly spoke of massacres. 'Iraqis are massacred in bloody battle of Khafji' headlined the *Express*. 'Massacre in the desert' was the *Sun* headline of 2 February. But there was no moral condemnation involved in this definition – rather it was a dramatic, emotive word to denote merely the massive casualties suffered by the enemy. From the beginning to the end, the agenda and language of the conflict were set by the military. Thus the Iraqis became non-people, animals, mere cannon-fodder. The *Guardian* of 31 January quoted a Marine: 'It felt really good. We kicked their asses.' The *Star* of the same day quoted US Captain Bill Wainright: 'It is a joint operation and it is working like clockwork. It feels good. We're kicking their asses.' The *Express* headlined with the words of Gen. Schwarzkopf: 'We are in the business of shooting them, not counting them.'

The *Sun* of 31 January reported 'hundreds of Iraqis frying in their tanks'. As the massacre to the west of Khafji continued with 'up to 60,000 men trapped in a 15-mile convoy of carnage', on 2 February the paper quoted a US pilot: 'They were virtually defenceless, sitting right on their tails waiting to be hit.' A US spokesman in Dharhan is quoted: 'Our pilots are telling us there is absolute carnage down there and that the Iraqis are sitting ducks.' On 1 February, the *Independent* and *Star* quoted Col. Dick White as saying there were almost too many targets to choose from. 'It's almost like you flipped on the light in the kitchen and the cockroaches start scurrying and we're killing them.' The *Mail on Sunday* quoted a 'delighted Marine': 'They are all over the place like headless chickens.'

The editorial in the *Star* of 31 January showed the extent to which the press had been sucked into the new militarist mindset. 'Saddam Hussein hopes that people in allied countries will be sickened by a long, bloody war. But he should not delude himself. This is a war we are going to win. We are going to kick his ass so hard he's going to scream for mercy. We won't give him any.' There is no humanity in that language.

At the official level there was complete confusion over the casualty figures. First the Americans claimed no Marines were involved: this was a Saudi, Qatari 'defensive' action. But non-pool journalists on the scene saw US Marines in action and the Americans eventually admitted they were present. The British first said 300 Iraqis had died. This was then amended to 30 (perhaps the first sounded too much like a massacre). According to *The Sunday Times* of 3 February, the extra 0 had been added by a typing clerk. Confusions over casualty figures continued well after the massacres. In his account, Gen. de la Billière said the Iraqis suffered 800 casualties (op cit: 250). But Rick Atkinson, in his semi-official report of the massacres, concluded (1994: 211-212): '...thirty Iraqis had been killed and 466 captured, thirty seven wounded among them. Nineteen Saudis and Qataris had died and thirty six were wounded; an uncertain number of these had fallen to friendly fire. American losses, including those in the fighting out west were twenty five dead, nearly half from fratricide.' Robin Andersen (2006: 157) focuses on a press conference given by Gen. Schwarzkopf:

> For 23 minutes the general focused on spectacular videotape of smart bombs obliterating their targets and described Iraqi losses as 'rather sensational'. Only toward the end did he announce that the Marines had eleven 'KIAs [Killed in Action]'. The media followed his lead, and the high-tech video became the emphasis.

INVENTING THE VICTIM SYNDROME

While the coalition forces were inflicting a series of massacres, it was still important to represent them as victims – how else could the representation of the Iraqis as a credible enemy be maintained? Here the mediacentrism of new militarism served a unique role for the elite. For when all was crumbing around the Iraqi leadership, Saddam Hussein could still be represented as having won a propaganda coup. John Cassidy, in *The Sunday Times* of 3 February, spoke of a propaganda victory for Saddam, despite heavy losses. The *Sun* of 1 February wrote under the headline 'Stormin' mad': 'Stormin' Norman is seething over the Iraqi propaganda coup' after 'cheeky Iraqis caught the Yanks with their pants down'.

It also used the case of a woman soldier (Army specialist Melissa Rathbun-Nealy, of the 233rd Transportation Company), captured by the Iraqis along with another soldier, David Lockett, to further demonise Saddam Hussein and tar all Iraqi men with a racist slur. Under the headline 'At the mercy of the beast', the newspaper wrote: 'A US girl Marine was at the mercy of brutish Iraqi troops last night after being captured in the Battle of Khafji.' It continued: 'Allied military chiefs think the Iraqis, who treat their own women appallingly, might abuse or even rape their captive.' Ms Rathbun-Nealy was, in fact, released after 33 days unharmed after the end of the massacres. She was told by her captors that she was a hero, as brave as Sylvester Stallone, and as beautiful as Brooke Shields (Walsh 1991). Her greatest fear was not of Iraqi rapists but, ironically, of allied bombers hitting the place where she was being held (Johnston, Anne 1993: 205).[1] Rape was to feature prominently in the demonisation of Saddam Hussein and the Iraqis in general. Yet, in fact, as became known after the end of the massacres, rapes were running at epidemic levels in the US army. These were never reported at the time. A senate report estimated that 60,000 women had been sexually assaulted or raped while serving in the US armed forces. Senator Dennis DeConcini commented: 'American women serving in the Gulf were in greater danger of being assaulted by our own troops than by the enemy.'[2]

Kate Muir (1992: 156-160) reports that on just one American ship during the conflict 36 women became pregnant but the US navy said no fraternisation had taken place on board. She quotes a Pentagon survey of 1990 which found that two-thirds of women in the forces claimed they had been sexually harassed. There was a 55 per cent rise in reported rapes and sexual assaults over the three years 1987-1990. The US navy secretary was forced to resign in 1992 over reports of sexual harassment of women in the navy. There were no equivalent statistics for the British army but Muir said sexual harassment was a 'growing problem'. Significantly the British media's obsession with the rape angle at Khafji meant that they missed a far more interesting point. Ms Rathbun-Nealy was the first US woman soldier captured in action, as *The New York Times* of 1 February pointed out.

223

MEDIATING A MASSACRE: HOW THE PRESS COVERED THE BOMBING OF THE AMERIYYA SHELTER

On 13 March 1991, the *Sun* reported, *en passant*, that a bunker in Kuwait City, housing 400 Iraqis had been blown to smithereens by one-ton shells from USS *Missouri* in the Gulf. No Western journalists or camera crews were on hand so this outrage went unreported during the massacres. How many such incidents occurred during the biggest bombardment in history? We will never know.

However, on 13 February, two 2,000lb, laser-guided bombs dropped from a Stealth jet (which had become a technological 'star' of the massacres) on to a shelter in the Ameriyya district of Baghdad killing as many as 1,600 people – mainly women and children.[3] According to Dilip Hiro (1992: 362), the bombing was part of an attempt to assassinate Saddam Hussein.

Television shots of appalling carnage were distributed around the world, though journalists at the BBC and ITN censored the worst on grounds of taste (Glasgow University Media Group 1991: 9).[4] All the same, Hoskins (2004: 86-87) argues that the images in the media of bodies and survivors suffering burn wounds 'were the first images of the war to re-connect graphically the notion of bombing with bodily violence, a connection previously obscured through effective media management and coalition censoring'. Yet 'the death of hundreds of innocent civilians and the undermining of the previously dominant language of precision warfare were overwhelmed by a profusion of analysis and counter-analysis'.

The allied military first claimed it was a military bunker: the people had been put there by Saddam Hussein so that he could gain a propaganda victory if they were hit.

In a wide-ranging report published after the massacres, Middle East Watch (1991: 7) accused the US of breaking the rules of law in times of war in attacking the shelter without adequate warning. But in Britain and the United States, the ideological frame established so firmly in August 1990 provided all the tools necessary for the crisis to be resolved in the interests of the elite. Mediacentricism was exploited to deflect away the main moral dimension of the atrocity; most of the emotion provoked by the outrage was redirected away from the allies and on to either the demonic figure of Saddam Hussein or (fuelled by the myth of the 'adversary media') British television. As Steve Platt (1991) observed, the only occasion on which Fleet Street expressed 'outrage' during the massacres was over BBC coverage of the shelter disaster. 'Outrage over BBC bias' headlined one edition of the *Express*. The response of the military and political elite was prioritised; the views of the victims of the bombing and anti-war voices were either marginalised or non-existent.

The bombing came after a considerable campaign by certain sections of the British press to damn the BBC and those organisations with correspondents based in Baghdad. Woodrow Wyatt, in the *News of the World* of 20 January, had even taken exception to a *Panorama* programme which, he claimed, 'was an unbalanced and prolonged onslaught against fighting against Saddam'. The BBC was full of 'left-wing, trendy programme-makers and commentators'. The shelter bombing seemed to confirm all the worst fears of those who opposed the Baghdad press pack.

The overall coverage of the bombing by television predictably prioritised the elite's response. But Jeremy Bowen, of the BBC, looked distinctly distressed as he consistently refused to be drawn by anchorman Michael Buerk to say the shelter appeared to have a dual military purpose. In his later account of the conflict, Bowen commented (2006: 85):

> The aggressive tone of some of the BBC anchormen surprised me. I was being treated like an Iraqi spokesman. In London they must have been feeling the pressure. The idea that the war was a grown-up version of an arcade game, which had been so carefully nurtured by American and British spokesmen with their talk of precision bombing, had taken a big knock and the spin-doctors were counter-attacking by making false claims about the shelter.[5]

Brent Sadler, on ITN, gave a similar version: 'Ameriyya is a middle class residential area. I could see no military or strategic targets in the vicinity.'

Such eye-witness reporting could only provoke the anger of gung-ho editors safe in their Fleet Street bunkers. *Today*, of 15 February, said broadcasters were 'a disgrace to their country'. The headline in the *Mail* over their report of the atrocity ran: 'Outrage as TV's bunker bomb bulletins "show bias to Saddam"' while the *Mail on Sunday* said the coverage, not the bombing, was 'truly disgusting' and 'deplorable'. The *Express* (following up the bombing with two reports on the media controversy) criticised the broadcasters' 'insistence that they are right to report from the enemy' which demonstrated 'the degree to which they have lost touch with the very people they purport to serve'. The BBC was dubbed the 'Baghdad Broadcasting Corporation' by Conservative critics while Brent Sadler was accused of being manipulated by Iraqi propaganda (Shaw 1996: 76). But *The Sunday Times* backed the journalists and said their critics should stop 'carpet bombing' them.

TRANSFORM THE PERPETRATORS OF THE ATROCITY INTO A VICTIM OF A PROPAGANDA COUP

Here the mediacentrism of the new militarist 'vulnerable' state was exploited to mediate the massacres in the interests of the allied elite. Thus *Today*, of 14 February, spoke of Saddam's 'propaganda coup'. 'With sickening haste he ordered TV crews and journalists to the scene. As bodies were still being removed Saddam had his pictures.' The editorial commented on Saddam's 'sick but skilful propaganda armoury'. According to the *Star* of the same day, Saddam stage-managed a TV circus to convince the world there had been an allied atrocity.

The *Mail* highlighted the response of the White House's press secretary, Martin Fitzwater, who accused Saddam of killing civilians intentionally. 'Time and again he has shown a willingness to sacrifice civilian lives and property that has furthered his war aims,' Fitzwater said.

The *Sun*, under the headline '10 facts to damn Saddam', made a number of extraordinary claims: that Saddam's men had started fires after the initial blast and before TV crews arrived on the scene; that the civilian casualties may have been military dead, stripped of their uniforms and dumped at the scene. Saddam was a 'master of propaganda' and so would realise that 'scenes of devastation and reports of hundreds of civilian deaths could damage the allied coalition and give ammunition to anti-war campaigners'. *The Sunday Times*, of 17 February, said it was a 'propaganda victory for Saddam'.

MEEKLY FOLLOW THE MILITARY LINE

Virtually all the press followed the military/elite line. The *Express* headlined an editorial of 14 February: 'It WAS a military bunker.' Hence the precision myth remains intact. Marlin Fitzwater, the US spokeman, is quoted: 'This was a military bunker which fed instructions directly into the Iraqi war machine, painted and camouflaged to avoid detection. We did not know civilians were in it.' Similarly, the *Telegraph* headlined its report: 'Military HQ was in bombed bunker, says Washington' while *The Times*'s main headline ran: 'Hundreds of Iraqis killed in a shelter' with a subordinate line: 'Allied leaders claim bombed bunker was a legitimate military target.' The *Independent* headlined: 'Shelter "a military target"' and began: 'At least 400 civilians died in an attack on a Baghdad bunker described by the allies as a command and control centre.' The *Star* quoted a US spokesman in Riyadh: 'We felt comfortable that the attack was a legitimate target.' *Today* said innocent had died 'in the same camouflaged bunker in which the Iraqi military directed operations'.

In contrast, the *Mirror* led with a photograph of a victim accompanied by the headline: 'Whose fault? Slaughter, says Iraq. Military target, says US.' But Shaw (op cit: 102) points out that the *Mirror* failed to follow-up the story in any way; nor did columnist Paul Foot, strongly opposed to the war, deal with it. The *Guardian* also challenged the military line on the atrocity though it significantly highlighted the propaganda 'disaster' for the US administration.

BLAME SADDAM

The demonisation of Saddam, begun in earnest on 3 August 1990, had always sought, on an ideological level, to deflect any responsibility for the crisis and later massacres away from the allies. They were morally pure. It was all so seductively simple. Whatever happened – from massacre to possible nuclear holocaust – was the fault of one man: Saddam. Thus over the Ameriyya atrocity, most of the press followed the line taken by US spokesman Marlin Fitzwater and blamed Saddam – in hysterical terms. The *Star* under the headline 'Sacrificed: Saddam herds his people to die in military bunker' wrote:

> Saddam Hussein pulled the cruellest con trick of the Gulf War yesterday. He let his own innocent people die in a military bunker. … Women and children went into the Baghdad bunker because he told them it was an air-raid shelter. But he knew the bunker was a top priority military target and due to be hit by American Stealth bombers.

Today wrote under the headline 'Entombed by Saddam': 'Once again the evil tyrant has set up a human shield to protect a key military site – only this time the victims were his own people.' On 15 February, the *Independent* refocused attention on the crimes of Saddam Hussein. Its editorial argued that 'horrible and tragic though the deaths in the shelter at Ameriyya were, they should not obscure untelevised horrors of murder, mutilation and torture that President Saddam inflicted on Kurds and Kuwaitis'.

The Sunday Times of 17 February quoted a *Washington Post*/ABC poll which showed 81 per cent of Americans believed the shelter was a legitimate target while 79 per cent blamed Saddam for the deaths. The *Express* said: 'Saddam Hussein was last night accused of deliberately sacrificing hundreds of women and children in a military bunker he knew was a target for allied bombers.' Woodrow Wyatt, writing in the *News of the World* on 17 February, said it was all Saddam's fault. An editorial in the *Mirror* of 15 February commented: 'If there were innocent victims we grieve for them. But the real guilt belongs to Saddam Hussein.'

STRESS THE INEVITABILITY

Until the Ameriyya atrocity, the media image of the massacres had been dominated by the emphasis on precision bombing, high-tech, clean warfare. Ameriyya represented the first serious threat to that imagery. The US elite resolved the dilemma by ignoring it. The bombing had merely reinforced the precision image. As the *Sun* commented: 'Allied pilots shows that the bombs were delivered with pin-point accuracy and entered the building through a ventilator shaft.' The *Express* editorialised: 'Alas, the awesome precision of the allied bombing cannot guarantee that all escape.'

Another way in which the allies absolved themselves of guilt was to stress the inevitability of the carnage. First the war was clean, then it became, inevitably, dirty. Guilt implies some measure of human responsibility; inevitability, on the other hand, implies humans are victims of forces beyond their control and so not entirely to blame. Yet the atrocities could have been stopped had the will been there: they were not 'inevitable'. According to the *Guardian* of 14 February, it was 'absolutely inevitable' that civilians would be killed along the way. Such a stress on inevitability helped the newspaper rationalise its lack of emotional outrage. 'Yesterday in Baghdad may be horrifying but it is not shocking because utterly predictable.' Columnist Robert Harris wrote in *The Sunday Times* of 17 February that most people 'reluctantly accept that dead children, burning homes and dying soldiers are a fact of war'. In the *Telegraph* of 14 February, editor Max Hastings took a similar line: 'The tragic truth is that it is probably impossible to bring this war to a reasonably swift conclusion, at a terrible cost in both allied and Iraqi lives, without accepting such episodes as that which took place in Baghdad yesterday as part of the price.' And Patrick Cockburn wrote in the *Independent*: 'The development of the allied air offensive over Iraq in the past three weeks made an incident like the bombing of the Baghdad shelter almost inevitable.'

ADMIT IT WAS A 'MISTAKE'

A number of reports immediately after the atrocity implied or admitted it was a 'mistake'. On 15 February, Robert Fisk, in the *Independent*, quoted a somewhat ambivalent anonymous US military source. On the one hand the source was prepared to say the raid was a serious error. 'There's not a soul who believes it was a command and control bunker.' But at the same time, the source managed to blame the Iraqi President for it. 'Saddam Hussein does put civilians in military bunkers and he is to blame for this irresponsibility. But we were wrong too.' By 17 February even the gung-ho *Sunday Times* was ready to admit it was a mistake. And on 27 February, the US national security adviser Brent Scowcroft told foreign secretary Douglas Hurd (who had added his voice to the criticisms of the broadcasters over their coverage of the bombing) that US intelligence had been at fault over the bombing. But a mistake is morally neutral. It focuses attention on the technology of warfare and on the failure of military intelligence. Everyone makes mistakes – even heroic soldiers. There is nothing morally condemnatory about that. The bombing sparked no outrage in Fleet Street – the ideological consensus held firm in the crisis.

SHOW LITTLE REGRET FOR THE LOSS OF LIFE

Most striking about the coverage in both Fleet Street and in the United States was a lack of concern for the victims of the attack. The *Guardian* did carry a moving 'Eyewitness' account under the headline: 'Bodies shrunk by heat of fire' by Alfonso Roj, of the Spanish daily *El Mundo*, who, with Peter Arnett of CNN, was one of only two Western journalists in the Iraqi capital throughout the coalition air attacks. Occasionally tokenistic regret was expressed; usually there was nothing. An editorial in the *Mirror* of 15 February even sought to question the existence of any casualties. Iraqi civilians were only 'alleged' to have died in the bombing. Most papers followed up the atrocity with the news that opinion polls suggested the public still backed the bombing campaign. *The Sunday Times* was pleased to report that television images 'filmed under official Iraqi guidance' of burned babies had had little effect on their continuing support for the 'war'.

NOT GIVING PEACE A CHANCE

The prioritising of the military option from 2 August 1990 was accompanied by the marginalisation of the diplomatic track; anti-war voices were marginalised, eliminated or demonised; peace moves were similarly marginalised or silenced. The corporate media in Britain represented war as inevitable; during the massacres the surge to the 'greatest land battle since 1945' was represented as a sort of natural force (rather like a desert storm, in fact) flowing to an inevitable conclusion.

DEMONISATION OF ANTI-WAR VOICES

Attacks on anti-war voices during the massacres reached vitriolic levels. Every possible form of abuse and stereotypical denigration was levelled at those who called for a halt to the massacres – they were 'mad', 'nutty', 'devils', 'hypocrites', 'animals', 'violent', 'traitors', 'ranters', 'unpatriotic', 'friends of terrorists', 'apologists for Saddam Hussein', 'barbarians' and so on. Virtually all the prominent Fleet Street columnists added their gunshots to the volley of invective.

Richard Littlejohn, in the *Sun* of 17 January, dismissed opponents of the massacres as 'pathetic posturing' protestors. 'They drive Citroen 2CVs to the wine warehouse but take their Volvos to the Dordogne in France every summer. Most of them have never done a proper day's work in their lives.' Their hero was 'Nelson Mandela, a convicted terrorist' (though a few years later, he was to become the globally acclaimed, first black president of South Africa). Similarly, Woodrow Wyatt (dubbed 'The voice of reason') commented in his 20 January column in the *News of the World* on peace protestors: 'They're the heirs of the appeasers of Hitler. They're the people who protest and demonstrate at the drop of a hat. … In our democratic society we have a fixed proportion of nutters. They just love demonstrating and protesting.'

A typical device of the press is to label people who voice views beyond the narrow limits of consensual acceptability as mad. Of anti-war campaigner Tony Benn, MP, the *Sun* on 18 January said he did not need a psychiatrist, he needed 'a hospital full of shrinks'. They called him 'batty Benn'. Columnist Robert Kilroy-Silk, in the *Express* of 11 February, asked if former Conservative Prime Minister Ted Heath, who opposed the war, was 'unhinged or something'. After pop singer Sinead O'Connor objected to the massacres, the *Sun* on 15 February dubbed her a 'she devil' and dragged in their resident 'top psychologist' (a typical *Sun* ploy) who suggested 'her warped outbursts betray a tortured, troubled background'. Labour MPs who opposed or abstained on a motion backing the use of force were called 'treacherous misfits' who 'shame the whole nation' in the *Star* of 22 January. Brian Hitchen, in his *Star* column of the same day, did not mince his words in attacking the peace demonstration in London the previous Saturday. He said they were the 'usual treacherous misfits trying to knife our boys in the back' and were 'mainly made up of assorted rat-droppings, together with misguided contingents from the clergy and fringe show business'.

In a similar vein, the *Sun* reported on 23 January that 'Leftie Labour MPs who voted against Our Boys in the Gulf were blasted by *Sun* readers yesterday. Our switchboard was jammed by hundreds who said the 34 were traitors'. The *Star* returned to the same emotive theme on 1 February when under the headline 'Traitors', it editorialised: 'How childish of Islington Council to ban kids from playing soldiers in the school yard. Whose side are these traitors on? If they feel so strongly about Saddam and his butchers they can go and join him in Baghdad.' This echoes Cold War rhetoric when peace campaigners were alleged to be 'commie backers' and told to go to Moscow.

After some Labour MPs protested over the bombing of the Ameriyya shelter, the *Mirror* directed its anger, not at the Stealth fighter planes, but at the 'enemy within'. Its editorial of 15 February thundered: 'We cannot allow ourselves to be deflected by misguided, twisted individuals always eager to comfort and support any country but their own. They are a danger to us all – the enemy within.' In a similar vein, the *News of the World* of 20 January reported under the headline 'Commie hijack march': 'Extreme left-wing supporters of Saddam Hussein tried to hijack an anti-war march in London yesterday.' And the *Sunday Telegraph* of 24 February claimed criticism of the war was being led by communist-controlled front organisations.

NAILING ROGUE NATIONS: THE ENEMY ABROAD

Anyone or any group/nation which the press felt did not support the massacres with sufficient vigour were similarly tainted. As Traber and Davies comment (1991: 9): 'The media denounced countries as virtual enemies. This was particularly the case of Jordan and the Palestinian leadership whose efforts for peace were hardly acknowledged.' Thus Jordan's King Hussein, whose public stance was to appeal constantly for peace, was accused by Kilroy-Silk in the *Express* of 11 February of lining up with the barbarians – the supporters of terrorists, the hostage-takers, the women and child murderers, the practitioners of chemical warfare. Richard Littlejohn in the *Sun* of 14 February attacked 'curiously named' Queen Nor, wife of the 'odious little weasel, King Hussein' for expressing concern for the casualties in Iraq. In fact, King Hussein was playing a typically ambivalent game (missed by the mass-selling media which represented the conflict in simple black-and-white terms). While his public rhetoric was in support of Iraq, the large Palestinian majority in his country perhaps forcing him in this direction, in secret he was continuing the role he developed in the early 1980s of covertly allowing Western arms to be moved through his country to Iraq. Friedman (1993: 172) reports:

…despite the assurance of congress that military aid to Jordan had been cut off, the flow of weapons from the US, in fact, continued. Bush and Baker's policy on Jordan was cynical enough to ignore even Jordan's violations of the UN embargo after the invasion of Kuwait. Between 2 August and 4 October 1991, the State Department approved 12 new military equipment orders worth five million dollars, including items such as spare parts and components for TOW missiles, helicopter components for AH-1S Cobra, 105-mm cartridges for artillery shells and conversion kits for the M-16 rifle.

On 31 August, Premier Margaret Thatcher met King Hussein at Downing Street for what was described as 'very frosty' talks. The *Mirror* of 1 September spoke of Mrs Thatcher giving the king an 'ear bashing'. 'Furious Premier Margaret Thatcher gave Jordan's King Hussein a dressing down yesterday. Mrs Thatcher is angry with the King for proposing deals which would reward the aggressor.' But Friedman suggests that on 14 September 1990, the department of trade was still continuing its normal approach to Jordan, approving the sale of large quantities of British artillery shells. 'These were shells, the British knew, that were liable to be diverted to Iraq' (ibid).

HOW PEACE BECAME THE 'NIGHTMARE SCENARIO'

Philip Taylor highlights the way in which, following the Ameriyya shelter bombing 'more and more stories about the treatment of Kuwaitis by the Iraqi occupiers began to emerge from various coalition forces' (1992: 227). There were clearly atrocities committed by the Iraqis in Kuwait but as ITN journalist Alex Thomson, who travelled with the soldiers, commented: 'We had been told of the killing grounds, the mass hangings and executions, we had been assured that the city's ice-rink (the ice long-since gone along with the electricity) was full of bodies. Most of the horror stories were either nonsense (like the ice rink) or exaggerated' (op cit: 253). But the outrage over the invented atrocities took attention away from the massacres being inflicted by the allies.

Reports of the Kuwait 'atrocities' also served a powerful political and ideological purpose of further marginalising the crucially important diplomatic dimension of the conflict (on-going since August 1990). The logic was clear – how could the allies talk to such barbarians? The press were in any case hyped up on the inevitability of the ground war – nothing could stop them getting it. Even the *Guardian*, most sceptical of all, was caught up in this mood. It editorialised on 31 January: 'As the ground war approaches we must expect more intensive attacks upon Iraq's infrastructure and inevitably higher casualties.' The logic of battle had taken over. The military and political leaders (supported by an all-party consensus in parliament) thought similarly.

Peace always was the 'nightmare scenario' for the coalition. Thus, when on 31 January, Fleet Street reported the peace moves by American secretary of state James Baker and Soviet foreign minister Alexander Bessmertnykh (according to which hostilities would end if Iraq made an unequivocal commitment to pull out of Kuwait and make immediate steps to comply with all 12 UN resolutions) the focus was directed at the impact it had on the White House: 'Baker's peace offer rattles the White House' said the *Guardian*. 'Disarray in Washington follows offer of ceasefire' was the *Independent* angle. 'Red faces at White House over Baker peace blunder' said the *Express*. Talk of peace, according to Derrick Hall, was 'shabby', 'worrying' and 'bizarre'. The following day the paper suggested 'fears were growing that France was planning another underhand peace initiative'. Its leader that day welcomed as 'reasonable' Prime Minister Mr Major's 'unequivocal opposition to a pause in the hostilities'. When later in February both Iran and the Soviet Union made strenuous efforts to negotiate a ceasefire the negative responses of the US and UK elites were similarly always prioritised. On 5 February, for instance, the *Mirror* devoted two paragraphs to a report on an Iranian initiative headlined: 'Bush cool over peace bid.'

On 15 February, following the intervention of Soviet envoy Yevgeny Primakov, the Iraqis offered to withdraw from Kuwait (though attached a number of conditions) but President Bush quickly dismissed it as a hoax and this view dominated newspaper coverage. In fact, the peace move was seen as an invitation to step up the 'war' effort. The *Sun* of 16 February headlined its report: 'Saddam the sham' and editorialised: 'No amount of twisting and turning, lying and stalling can alter the fact that his latest statement shows he is a beaten man. ... So unfortunately the bombing must go on. It must continue until he finally recognises the futility of his war.' The *Mirror* of the same day followed the predictable line: 'Cruel hoax' was its headline. *The Times* linked its response to the mad Hussein angle: 'Saddam must be truly divorced from reality if he believed these terms would be accepted.' *The Sunday Times* of 17 February dismissed Saddam's display of 'crude political deceit and preposterous diplomatic dissembling'.

Prominent in some of the responses to the Soviet peace initiative were echoes of Cold War fears and stereotypes. Recent violence by Soviet troops in the Baltic states merely added fuel to these fears and *The Sunday Times* of 17 February expressed concern that a 'second Cold War' was about to begin. The offer was, however, welcomed in a number of places: King Hassan, of Morocco, a coalition member, described the Iraqi move as a 'positive step along the path to peace in the region' while Tunisian, Algerian, Iranian and Jordanian leaders also responded positively (Hiro 1992: 366). But these views were either ignored or marginalised. On 16 February, the *Mirror* ran a report on the President of the Council of Mosques in Bradford welcoming the offer – but it covered only two paragraphs.

Moreover, President Bush coupled his denunciation of the offer with a call to the Iraqi military and the Iraqi people to take matters in their own hands and overthrow Saddam Hussein. Not only had the President responded swiftly and unilaterally without consulting coalition members but this call represented a blatant attempt to interfere in the affairs of a foreign country – and thus, in theory, contrary to international law. Debates over these issues were virtually non-existent.

MAKING THE SOVIET DEAL A 'NON-EVENT'

Following the failure of the 15 February offer, the Soviets renewed their efforts to bring a ceasefire. But irrespective of the contents of any such deal, Fleet Street was busy preparing its readers for the 'inevitable' ground war, with only the *Guardian* giving any support to the Russian peace moves. On 18 February, the *Mirror* reported that 'no one in London or Riyadh believes Gorbachev can deliver the peace'. Prominence was given to a statement by French foreign minister Roland Dumas (not usually given such a billing) that the land offensive would start 'within 48 hours'. That's exactly what the press wanted to hear.

The eight-point peace plan agreed between Moscow and Baghdad was finally rejected by President Bush on 22 February. Frantic new negotiations were held so that next day Iraq pledged to withdraw 'immediately and unconditionally from Kuwait'. Even so, the ground offensive was officially launched. Over this period a massive disinformation campaign was launched to accompany the rejection of the peace moves and further demonise the Iraqis. The *Mirror* of 22 February reported: 'American intelligence sources said they suspected Iraq had already launched chemical weapons at allied positions.' It continued: 'Reconnaissance teams spotted tell-tale puffs of grey smoke from exploding grenades on Saudi Arabia's border with Kuwait. US commanders are convinced Saddam will order a full-scale gas attack within the first hour of the ground war.' Such reporting also drew attention away from the coalition's secret decision to use napalm (notorious since its widespread use in Vietnam) against Iraqi positions. This was confirmed by the Earl of Arran, for the government in the house of lords, on 26 February 1991.[6]

Brian MacArthur (1991: 114-115) describes the gloom that descended on *The Sunday Times*'s editorial staff before the launch of the ground war. 'There was no land war, no statement from Bush – merely some opaque discussion in the UN about the Gorbachev plan. It was a depressed group that trouped off to Orso's that night.' But once the land war began at 1 am the excitement returned. In contrast, the *Guardian* said Mr Gorbachev had 'performed a service' removing the need for a land war, while the next day the newspaper criticised Bush's speech as 'an ultimatum, not a reply to the Moscow plan'.

BLOODFEST ON THE ROAD TO BASRA: SILENCING THE SLAUGHTER

By early February 1991, details of the supposedly massive defences erected by the Iraqis were being featured prominently in the mainstream media. The *Mirror*, for instance, on 1 February, carried an illustration of this defensive system – including sand walls, anti-tank ditches, razor wire, anti-tank minefields, camouflaged tanks, artillery batteries, missiles (all inventions, of course, of the coalition's disinformation specialists). Richard Kay (1992: 128), who covered the massacres for the *Mail* and later wrote a short account of his experiences, blamed faulty intelligence:

> Minefields meant to be 2,000 yards deep turned out to be only 140 yards. Oil and napalm-filled tranches, talked of as huge reservoirs, were only a couple of yards wide. The sand berms were pathetic and underground bunkers miserable holes in the ground, lined with corrugated plastic and a few sandbags, inadequate to prevent any explosion while the Iraqi soldiers themselves did not measure up to the menacing warriors they had been built up to be.

Elsewhere Kay describes the Iraqi army as 'closer to a rabble' while much of its equipment was 'useless and old' (ibid: 107). Michael Kelly (1993: 156), who covered the massacres for two American magazines and a newspaper, described the Iraqi bunkers as 'hardly better than the slit-trench works of the First World War'.

But while the massacres were going and starving Iraqi conscripts were deserting in droves, it was still necessary to maintain the myth of the credible threat. Thus the *Mirror* showed the coalition with 605,000 troops, 3,650 armoured personnel carriers, 1,000 artillery pieces, 3,800 tanks facing a credible enemy with supposedly 545,000 troops, 2,800 armoured personnel carriers, 160 helicopters, 3,100 artillery pieces and 4,200 tanks. The only conclusion to be drawn from such figures is that the coalition forces would win – but they would be given a good fight. Press coverage of the massacres, then, was always ambivalent. By 6 February, the *Mirror* was reporting starving Iraqi soldiers begging for food and 'pinpoint' bombing by the allies shattering the Iraqi oil industry. Yet on the same day it was stressing the coalition commanders believing Saddam Hussein's crack Republican Guard to be still 'a formidable fighting force'. 'These men are being kept well fed so they are fit to strike back at the allies when the land war begins.' By 21 February, the *Mirror* was headlining: 'Mass surrender by 500 battered Iraqis.' Mark Dowdney, in London, wrote: 'Four US Apache helicopters pounded the underground bunkers with laser-guided rockets and Hellfire missiles. And not a shot was fired in reply.' A pilot is quoted: 'They made no attempt to defend themselves but fell on their knees facing Mecca and began to pray.'

Troops began advancing in earnest on 24 February for what was billed as 'the largest land battle since 1945'. A three-day news blackout was unilaterally broken by the US government hours later. There was simply no enemy in sight – just conscripts desperate to give themselves up. As the Iraqis withdrew the merciless killing went on. Just 100 hours later a stop was called to the slaughter. Throughout this period the press desperately sought to maintain the fiction that the 'real battle' the elite had wanted all along was just round the corner. Christopher Bellamy, in the *Independent* of 25 February, suggested the Gulf war was 'the biggest armoured battle since the Battle of Kurst in 1943 when the Russians halted the German advance into the Soviet Union'. Next day, the newspaper reported: 'Pentagon officials emphasised real battle has not yet occurred.' Robert Fisk reported a brigadier saying the 'real battle' lay ahead. An article on the Republican Guard quoted an intelligence 'expert': 'These are very capable troops. They have never known what it is to be beaten.'

Military 'expert' Lawrence Freedman was on hand to add to the 'war' myth. He commented on the same day that the allies were going to find it difficult to cope with the 'heavily armoured Republican Guard' which was planning to counter attack for the 'decisive battle'. Yet Richard Dowden with the troops in Kuwait was reporting that one crucial element was missing from the 'mother of battles' – enemy fire. 'Mother of surrenders' was the headline in the *Mirror* accompanying the report from Ramsey Smith in Kuwait telling of coalition forces being overwhelmed by prisoners. But this time the war myth was given an added patriotic touch: 'British Challenger tanks are in the forefront of the battle and will come up against the Iraqis' powerful Russian-made T-72s.' Next day the same reporter profiled a 'bedraggled' Iraqi prisoner without any shoes or socks and desperately pleased to have survived. But he went on: 'Don't let anyone kid you that Saddam's battered army has already given up the fight.' Next day, the newspaper reported the Desert Rats' victory in an 'epic desert battle'; they now expected to 'polish off with relative ease' the remaining Iraqis before they met their final trophy, the Republican Guard.

Alex Thomson reported the experiences of American pool correspondents John Kifner and Rick Davis who flew on two low-level helicopter missions in Iraq: '... not only did they encounter no incoming fire but, astonishingly, they saw little sign at all of the supposedly colossal Iraqi force which Western commanders insisted had been dug in for months along this region' (op cit: 249). And Keith Dovkants, who was travelling with the UK pool Forward Transmission Unit behind British troops as they advanced into Iraq, told the author in an interview: 'There was no action at all; just surrendering all the time. This was not what a lot of people had hoped for.' AP veteran war correspondent Mort Rosenblum (1993: 117) later described how, together with a Reuters colleague, he slipped away from the pack and sped up from Khafji to Kuwait City as the Iraqi defences were collapsing. 'Almost without noticing it, we passed the dreaded Saddam Line, the belt of steel and inflammable oil we had described to our nervous readers time and time again.' He concluded: 'For its own purposes, the government exaggerated the threat. And rather than providing question marks, we [the press] chose exclamation points.'

ELIMINATING THE ANIMALS – THROUGH MINDLESS MASSACRESPEAK

The whole of the 'ground assault' (dubbed Operation Desert Sabre) was mediated through the mindless massacrespeak of the US military. On 1 February 1991, Alan Hall, in the *Sun*, under the headline 'I've just flown a reamer in the KZ' provided an 'A-Z of Gulf warspeak'. Such military jargon, he said, was 'set to come tripping off everyone's tongue'. In this way, the euphemisms, acronyms and crudities of massacrespeak enter and corrupt the popular culture. ITN journalist Alex Thomson commented: 'The urge to look like a soldier rather than whatever a journalist is supposed to look like was a little unnerving. Things became outright spooky when such people began to speak like soldiers.' Significantly, Richard Kay, of the *Daily Mail*, titled his account as a frontline reporter *Desert warrior*.

Accompanying the use of massacrespeak was a contempt for human life. Thus the *Independent* editorialised on 27 February, while thousands of Iraqis were being slaughtered: 'It has been a famous victory with astonishing light casualties.' While the *Star*, on 25 February, expressed the relief of the 'civilised world' at the 'extremely light casualties' – amongst coalition forces, of course. On 1 March reporter Martin Woollacott descended into massacrespeak in the *Guardian* commenting: 'The Iraqi army resembled nothing so much in its last days as a worm which is chopped by a spade – the segments wriggle but the creature is already dead.'

CELEBRATING THE SLAUGHTER

The *Independent* sought to dignify the carnage with superlatives. Christopher Bellamy claimed on 25 February that 'this most cerebral of campaigns' was the result of a 'concentrated programme of intellectual self-improvement throughout the 1980s' in the US army. Bellamy, on 27 February, described the massacres as a 'perfect victory'. The battle for Kuwait was 'awe-inspiring and brilliant'. This is exactly what the military wanted to hear. But there was no battle – it was a merciless walkover. Bellamy was not having any of this. The battle for Kuwait, he argued, combined classical 'geometrical simplicity of conception' with a 'complexity of execution'. The newspaper's editorial of 27 February dismissed the Kremlin's 'ill-considered calls for a ceasefire' and praised the 'brilliant allied strategy'. Air power was the key to the 'spectacular two-day collapse of the fourth largest army in the world'. The *Star*, of 25 February, described the British soldiers as the 'finest fighting force in the world'. Next day, the newspaper was celebrating the technology of slaughter. 'The power of America's £6.3m. Apache helicopters was impossible to fight off. It is the most sophisticated killer copter in the world.'

HIGHWAY TO HELL AND THE ULTIMATE MYTH OF BATTLE

The contradictions in the press coverage – maintaining to the very end the necessary new militarist myth of the credible enemy while reporting evidence of mass, unopposed slaughter – were most clearly evident over the massacres on the 'Highway to Hell'.[7] Gen Colin Powell told journalists just before the launch of the ground assault: 'We're going to cut it off and kill it.' At Mutla Ridge, that is precisely what the coalition forces did. On 25 February hundreds of Iraqi men with their families and some Kuwaiti prisoners began fleeing north from Kuwait City. Encircled by coalition forces, trucks, cars, ambulances and a few tanks ended up jammed on three roads. For 40 hours the area became a 'kill zone' for the coalition forces. B-52s, FA-18 jets, Apache helicopters flying off the deck of USS *Ranger* (as the ship's PA system blasted out the *Lone Ranger* theme) unleashed wave after wave of bombs. Virtually everything that moved was wiped out. Christopher Hitchens (2005: 458) recalled: 'They bombed the front of the convoy to prevent it going any further, and they bombed the rear of it to prevent it from retreating. And then they bombed it some more.' Planes queued to drop their bombs on the 'targets' below. Army sources later estimated that 25,000 people were slaughtered on the highway (Arkin, Durrant and Cherni 1991: 108). A woman and two children were among those who somehow survived. The US lost just one man, hit by a sniper. According to the report of the Commission of Inquiry for the International War Crimes Tribunal:

> US forces left open only two roads out of Kuwait City. All retreating soldiers were forced onto these roads and it was made known that soldiers moving north would not be attacked. Later, the US military feigned ignorance of the troops' intentions and floated the possibility that they sought to reinforce the Republican Guards just over the border in Iraq. Thus, the Pentagon argued, the possibility of a serious threat from this retreating force left the coalition no choice but to attack its adversary. However, the coalition did not merely attack its foe; it massacred them (Clark et al. 1992: 50).

Even so, the *Independent* reported on 27 February that Iraqis fleeing north presented a 'bounty of targets'. Next day it reported: 'The biggest armoured battle of the war developed further north near Basra. Iraqi forces were said to be offering determined resistance.' The *Star* of 27 February described the Iraqis as 'easy prey'. A pilot was quoted: 'We toasted them, we hit here and hit there and circled round and hit here again.' But other pilots are quoted as saying the Iraqis could 'simply be re-grouping for an attack'. There was, in fact, very little evidence of resistance by the Iraqis. Thomson, who visited the site of the carnage, said: 'In the wreckage by Mutla Ridge, tanks, artillery or armoured vehicles were conspicuous by their absence' (op cit: 256). Keith Dovkants, of the London *Evening Standard*, who arrived at the scene with the British pool, told the author during an interview:

> I saw a pretty horrific scene of what looked like deliberate carnage, a massacre. I sent in a piece on the awful scene which would have been the first British account. But then the paper suddenly got a report that Saddam Hussein had fled to Mauritania and my piece didn't make it. The Mauritania piece turned out to be wrong. I spoke to a military chap as the Americans were going after the retreating troops and he said: 'This is not a war as I understand it – bombing the hell out of van drivers and conscripted bank clerks.'

Yet still the 'war' myth survived. Philip Taylor, describing it as a 'battle' (op cit: 256) relies totally on a comment of Major Bob Williams: 'They fought harder than we have seen before.' Later Stephen Sakur, of BBC Radio, spoke to Williams again. He could find no military justification for the carnage. This time, Williams changed his story saying they were slaughtered simply because they were thieves: 'As you look at the vehicles down there you'll find they are filled with booty. ... these were thieves, not professional soldiers ... our cause was just' (Sakur 1991: 266). The military focus on the stolen goods amongst the debris of slaughter was also picked up by the press. As Taylor comments:

> The whole framing of the story by all the news organisations became such that any sympathy which reporters may have felt for the massacred army evoked by the shocking scenes they had witnessed was more than counterbalanced by the sheer scale of the plundering which the Iraqis had clearly undertaken. To consolidate this impression still further came the footage of the burning oil wells which Saddam's escaping army had set ablaze (op cit: 256).

The *Mail*, for instance, on 2 March headlined a report on the slaughter by focusing on the looting in this way: 'On the highway to horror: a bottleneck of carnage as looters fled into ambush.'

OUTRAGE AT THE IRAQIS

Reports about Iraqi atrocities in Kuwait had been gathering for a number of weeks before the final coalition onslaught. Then they reached crescendo point. *Independent* reporter Robert Fisk (1991), who had written consistently against the 'war', wrote on 28 February, under the headline 'Something evil has visited Kuwait City' about the tortures during the Iraqi 'reign of terror'. On 2 March, Fisk wrote that the scenes witnessed by journalists when they arrived in Kuwait made them lose any sympathy they may have had for the Iraqis. But, at the same time, the press used these reports of Iraqi atrocities to deflect attention away from the slaughters being committed by the coalition and, in part, to legitimise them. For example, the *Mirror* of 27 February said the Iraqis were 'brutes' for having seized Kuwaitis, Syrians and Egyptians. 'It was the last act of a brutal occupying force which left behind it a legacy of murder, torture and rape.' Thus, they deserved all they got. The 'rag-tag army' was 'being cut to pieces by allied jets'. But there was no outrage at that. 'A-6 Intruders and overhead jets swooped overhead picking off the Iraqis with cluster bombs. Giant B-52s were plastering the highway with 1,000lb bombs. A US pilot said: "They were like sitting ducks. It was like the road to Dayton beach on a holiday just bumper to bumper."'

The *Express* on 1 March managed to invert the responsibility for the slaughter. Under the headline 'Slaughter of the innocents: Victims litter valley of death', it reported: 'Iraqi troops slaughtered civilians in a last act of wanton destruction as they scurried from Kuwait. Horrific evidence of their atrocities lies along the main route from Kuwait to Iraq where the destruction and human cost of war can be seen at its most shocking.' The *Guardian* came nearest to blaming both sides for the atrocity. On 2 March it commented: 'A combination of allied cluster bombing and Iraqi attacks has turned the main road between Kuwait City and the Iraqi city of Basra into a slaughterhouse.' A retrospective on the slaughter in *The Times* of 27 March by Michael Evans was carried under the headline: 'The final turkey shoot.' But Evans never chose to condemn the slaughter.

Pictures of the carnage appeared on television only on 1 March, significantly after the end of the massacres. Very few bodies, if any, were shown – just lots of burnt out vehicles. Kate Adie, for the BBC, reported that the Iraqis had 'decided to make a fight of it'. The scene was both 'devastating and pathetic'. Christopher Morris, of Sky television, described the scene as 'like a nightmare from Dante's Inferno'. Freelance photographer Kenneth Jarecke was in an American pool and his picture taken on 28 February 1991 of a burnt-out head of an Iraqi soldier slumped over a truck was one of the most appalling images of the war.[8] It appeared once in the UK – in the *Observer* on 3 March. It was re-printed the following day in the *Observer*'s sister paper, the *Guardian*, with its picture editor, Eamonn McCabe, writing a piece (under the headline 'Dilemma of the grisly and the gratuitous') justifying its use. The *Observer* later received several hundred protest letters. Yet Hoskins (op cit: 80) argues: 'The carbonized face of the Iraqi soldier in the Jarecke photograph, despite some of the horrific detail of its features, partly dehumanises the body, and thus reduces rather than increase its impact.'

Only the *Chicago Tribune* in the corporate press in the United States carried it. It was laid out in a double-page spread at *Life* magazine, approved by the picture editor and overall editor – but then was pulled at the last minute after intervention by top management (Hoskins 2004: 79). Five years later, the BBC showed a picture of that same horrific, burnt out head during a four-part series commemorating the 'war'. Predictably, voices from the massive global movement opposed to the conflict were nowhere heard in the series.

NOTES

[1] Ms Rathbun-Nealy later told a website: 'I still have migraines. I have knee problems, post-traumatic stress disorder and I have thyroid problems. My disabilities make it so I can't be employed.' She was experiencing great difficulties securing disability funds from the department of veteran affairs. See http://www.jessica-lynch.com/forums/index.php?showtopic=2425, accessed 14 October 2008

[2] See http://www.nytimes.com/1992/07/01/us/military-women-report-pattern-of-sexual-abuse-by-servicemen.html, accessed on 27 September 2016

[3] Most reports said there were hundreds of casualties. The *Guardian* (14 February) reported 'hundreds of civilian corpses', the *Independent* (14 February) said: 'At least 400 civilians' died in the attack; the *Sun* said: 'Hundreds of women and children died' but that the figure of 400 was 'plucked out of the air' by the Iraqis; the *Star* said: 'While the Iraqis claimed that 500 women,

children and old men had died in the bunker fewer than 40 bodies were seen being removed on stretchers.' But Cainker, Lousie (1992) Desert sin: A post war journey through Iraq, *Beyond the Storm: A Gulf crisis reader*, Bennis, Phyllis and Moushabeck, Michel (eds), Edinburgh: Canongate, suggests that these figures grossly underestimate the casualty figures. Her on-the-spot survey immediately after the massacres showed that men had been excluded from the shelter by the time of the bombing. Local residents said the shelter could take in 2,000 when it was bombed. There were few survivors

[4] Jordanian TV (JTV) did show far more graphic footage, obtained from unedited CNN feeds and Baghdad's World Television News. But even JTV withheld the most obscene images (see Hoskins 2004: 88)

[5] Bowen's two-way interview with Peter Sissons is reproduced verbatim in McLaughlin (2002: 96). McLaughlin comments that Sissons left no doubt that he believed the Pentagon account – rather than Bowen's

[6] See http://hansard.millbanksystems.com/written_answers/1991/feb/26/the-gulf-war-availability-of-napalm, accessed 14 October 2008

[7] According to William Blum (2004: 342) those Iraqis who had earlier tried to flee to Jordan were subjected to relentless air attacks: 'Buses, taxis and private cars were repeatedly assaulted, literally without mercy, by rockets, cluster bombs and machine guns, usually in broad daylight, the targets clearly civilian, with luggage piled on top, with no military vehicles or structures anywhere to be seen … busloads of passengers incinerated, and when people left the vehicles and fled for their lives, planes often swooped down upon them firing away'

[8] See (along with a terrible image showing burnt out bodies piled on a truck) http://www.krysstal.com/democracy_iraq_1991ts.html, accessed on 14 October 2008. A large image of the Mutla Ridge 'rout' is in Stanwood, Frederick, Allen, Patrick and Peacock, Lindsay (1991) *Gulf War: A BBC World Service day-by-day chronicle*, London: Reed International Books (no page numbers but under Day 43 section)

Chapter Eleven

The press and the manufacture of humanitarian warfare: Iraq and Somalia in the 1990s and the war against Yugoslavia 1999

The attempt to resolve the contradictions of new militarism with a quickie, spectacular, manufactured war in the Gulf in 1991 was inevitably represented in the mainstream media as a triumph. *The Times* hailed a 'brief and brilliant military campaign'. *Today*, of 1 March 1991, said the liberation of Kuwait heralded 'a victory for the freedom of all mankind'.

The centrality of sexual politics to the manufacture of the Gulf 'war' became evident in many of the press comments on the victory. The *Sun* (1 March) went so far as to describe President Bush as 'Superman' and credit him with not one but three victories. Under the headline 'By George you're great', the paper pronounced:

America last night finally admitted to President Bush – you're no wimp – you're Superman. Three stunning victories have ensured that the lanky leader will go down in history as one of the greats. Wham! He gave the go-ahead for the most successful military campaign since World War Two. Bam! His stand against naked aggression and Soviet meddling proved him to be the toughest leader since President Roosevelt. Thank you, man. He has handed back America's pride after decades of being haunted by its worst defeat in Vietnam.

And significantly for the *Sun*, the 'war' had helped the President prove his virility: 'Today, Bush's countrymen agree with his wife, Barbara, who said: "I could never understand why people called George a wimp. He's all man – believe me."'

The theme of 'war' as man's sport is continued in the main headline describing Stormin' Norman and spanning pages four and five: 'Man of the match'. (The *Star* had 'Man of the shootin' match'.) New militarist 'warfare' is transmuted into Hollywood-style glitter: Schwarzkopf is described as 'superstar Norman of Arabia. Soon there will be Norman the book followed by Norman the movie...' The 'Images of War' centre-spread carries nine pictures supposedly summing up the conflict – none shows any dead.

A typical follow-up in the press was to taunt those who predicted a long, drawn-out conflict. The *Mail*'s 'Phoney prophets of doom' feature of 1 March was typical. Denis Healey, former Labour minister, Marjorie Thompson, CND chair, Edward Heath, former Prime Minister, 'Anthony Wedgwood Benn' (as it persisted in calling Tony Benn, former Labour minister turned left-wing radical activist), Bruce Kent, former CND chair, Senator Edward Kennedy were among those said to end up 'with egg on their faces'. The *Star* predictably personalised the victory. 'We've kicked his arsenal,' it headlined (1 March). And Saddam Hussein, whose head so much of the Western elite and media had supposedly sought since early August 1990, survived.

THE WANING OF THE HITLER SADDAM HYPE

In many respects, Saddam Hussein's survival in the years immediately following the Gulf crisis of 1991 was useful for the US/UK elite:

- With the collapse of the Soviet Union, the Iraqi President served as a useful 'enemy' to help legitimise the new militarist elite's political, economic, cultural privileges. Following the massacres, Pentagon strategists confirmed moves planning for wars with Third World enemies. The *Guardian* reported (18 February 1992) that leaked classified documents suggested that military chiefs had been told by the Pentagon to request forces 'sufficient to fight large regional wars against Iraq and North Korea, or against both at the same time'.

- It legitimised the Western elites' continuing sales of weapons to the Middle East after the massacres even though publicly calls were made to cut down the arms trade to the region. President Bush created a Center for Defense Trade to stimulate arms sales while offering government guarantees of up to $1 billion in loans for the purchase of US weapons. Arms sales rose from $12 billion in 1989 to almost $40 billion in 1991 (Chomsky 1993: 104-105). Stork (1995: 16) records how the Middle East accounted for more than 72 per cent of the total US arms transfers to the Third World between 1990 and 1993 – up from 61 per cent over the previous four years.

- For the US elite, Saddam Hussein's Iraq served as a useful buffer against the expansion of Iranian power. Asked why the US did not back the Shi'ite rebels after the 1991 massacres, Brent Scowcroft, President Bush's national security adviser, summed up the policy in a word: 'geopolitics' (Gordon and Trainor 2007: 13). Or as Zalmay Khalilzad, then-director of planning at the state department, commented: 'The partitioning of Iraq will not serve our long-term interests. Iraqi disintegration will improve prospects for Iranian domination of the Gulf and remove a restraint on Syria' (Cockburn 2008: 82).

- Iraq also proved to be a focus for the US elite's attempts to make the United Nations an instrument for the implementation of its imperial policies.

But Saddam Hussein's survival also represented, on one level, a serious embarrassment for the US-led coalition. The new militarist strategy was built on the demonisation of Saddam Hussein – to simplify the conflict and make it more credible and acceptable to the doubting masses. Yet, despite all the public rhetoric, the Kurds and the Shi'ites were not favoured as potential leaders of Iraq. Prominent sections of the Western elite even wanted Saddam Hussein to survive immediately after the 1991 massacres. And so the Hitler hype waned.

THE MYTH OF THE END OF THE WAR: THE SECRET WAR CONTINUES

The US secret war against the people of Iraq entered a new phase after the massacres. As Phyllis Bennis (1992: 124) argued, the ceasefire (called for in United Nations resolution 687) was a non-ceasefire, drawn up after typical US 'diplomacy' in the UN against sceptical countries: 'unspecified yet classic threats to Ecuador and irresistible offers of cheap oil to impoverished Zimbabwe'. Bennis concludes: 'The pressure worked. The resolution passed.' The maintenance of crippling sanctions on Iraq was a continuation of 'warfare' by other means. In 1995, a UN Food and Agriculture Organisation (FAO) report estimated that 567,000 Iraqi children under the age of five had died as a result of the sanctions.

Significantly when Lesley Stahl, on CBS's *60 Minutes* on 5 December 1996, asked US secretary of state Madeleine Albright this question on US sanctions against Iraq: 'We have heard that a half million children have died. I mean, that's more children than died in Hiroshima. And, you know, is the price worth it?' Albright replied: 'I think this is a very hard choice, but the price – we think the price is worth it' (Mahajan 2001; Andersen 2006: 183; Chomsky 2001: 73). There were further elements of hypocrisy about this sanctions policy, largely ignored in the press: sanctions had been considered inadequate to dislodge the Iraqi President in 1990. Yet they were felt a suitable 'weapon' after March 1991.

THE GREAT MEDIA MYTHS: HALTING THE HORROR

From the soil of new militarist secrecy, important media myths and fictions can flower. One myth that came to dominate coverage immediately after the halting of the massacres focused on the mediacentrism of the conflict: the President had halted the slaughter because of fears that pictures of scenes such as on the Basra Highway of Hell would turn people against the 'war'. This was most forcibly argued by Nik Gowing, diplomatic editor of ITN. He wrote (1991: 8):

> Fearful of a 'second Vietnam' deep in Iraq and live on television, Bush halted the allied advance into Iraq. It made political not military sense. Fear of what television might witness meant that a significant proportion of Saddam Hussein's army in Kuwait escaped and re-grouped to fight another day – against the Kurds and Shi'as.

243

In fact, photographs of the highway slaughter only appeared days after the ceasefire. They could not have influenced the Bush administration. But the media myth served to promote a notion of 'democratic accountability' to both the press and political elite. Accordingly, the press, acting as the mouthpiece of the 'public will', independent of the state and mirror of an unproblematic reality, articulates the widespread concerns over the slaughter and pressurises the elite to change its policy. Nothing like this occurred. The reasons for the halting of the US-led coalition forces' advance remains obscure – but democratic concerns could not interfere with the elite's Desert Storm script.

THE GREAT MEDIA MYTHS – PART TWO: CARING FOR THE KURDS

The coverage surrounding the Kurds after the halting of the massacres constructed one of the greatest media myths – to compare, for instance, with the great William Howard Russell and Watergate media myths.[1] During the massacres the press had become the overt propaganda arm of the state. The vast majority of journalists accepted the compromises and constraints involved. But the press bases much of its activities on the myth of 'freedom', of autonomy from the state. And so it became vital in the aftermath of the massacres to reassert the traditional role of the media as independent watchdogs on the state. The Kurdish rebellion provided the ideal opportunity for the resurrection of this crucial myth. The press represented itself as acting on behalf of a caring nation, even global community in defence of the 'tragically fated' Kurds and in the face of intransigent and uncaring leadership. The mediacentrism of new militarist society was here serving (not through any great conspiracy but through the workings of complex ideological, political, economic processes) to mask the ruthless thrust of the imperial state. Gowing wrote (op cit: 9):

> [Six weeks after the end of the war] television further forced the hands of Western politicians. Governments could not ignore the horror of the Kurdish catastrophe which unfolded hourly on their TV screens. The pictures were politically uncomfortable and strategically inconvenient. But no government could dare avoid them. Led by John Major, the British government had to jettison policy papers drawn up in the bureaucratic comfort of Whitehall. On an RAF jet flying to Luxembourg Britain's Prime Minister was forced to sketch out – on the back of an envelope – a concept for 'humanitarian enclaves'. As television showed the deepening catastrophe, George Bush had no option but to follow the British initiative. The US troops which he promised he would never send back into Iraq's civil war, were sent back (op cit: 9).

Here then is an extraordinarily clear exposition of the myth. TV (and Gowing could have included the corporate press who were following the same agenda), voicing the views of the compassionate, global community, was forcing governments to change policy and move towards more humanitarian ends. Martin Woollacott, for instance, in the *Guardian* of 20 August 1992, reported that the creation of the Kurdish safe havens was a 'job of which the whole world approved'. Martin Shaw (1996: 122) also argues that the media forced the government's hand on Kurdistan. He writes:

> With the exception of the broadsheets, the press jumped on television's bandwagon at a late stage. Its advocacy was nevertheless important to the campaign's political impact: its chorus was the final straw, the signal to Major that it could not be ignored. ... Since Major's *volte-face* played an important part in Bush's, not only British television and broadsheets but even some tabloids can be said to have made a significant contribution to the change in Western policy on Kurdistan.

In the United States, the same myth was constantly drawn. Daniel Schorr (1991: 22) commented: 'Within a two-week period the President had been forced, under the impact of what Americans were seeing on television, to reconsider his hasty withdrawal of troops from Iraq. ...'

THE ORIGINAL MYSTIFICATION

The Bush administration's policy on the overthrow of Saddam Hussein was ambivalent. Publicly, on 15 February, shortly after the bombing of the Ameriyya shelter, President Bush encouraged the Iraqi people to remove the tyrant. This call, it could be argued, amounted to a gross interference in the internal affairs of a sovereign state – but the dominant view represented it as heralding the revolts in Kurdistan in northern Iraq and amongst the Shi'as in the southern marshes around Basra. Yet the evidence suggests that the Bush administration had no intention to remove the Iraqi dictator: rather after the end of the massacres it did all it could to help him remain in power. John Simpson reported (1991a) that a group of Iraqi generals had approached the US with plans for a coup – but they had been rejected. Moreover, the US made no objections after Iraq used attack helicopters to destroy the revolts in the north and south (Gordon and Trainor 1995: 446-456). Brent Scowcroft, security adviser for the Bush administration, confirmed in an interview in 2001 that it was never the US's goal in 1991 'to get rid of Saddam'.[2]

In March 1991, a number of cities fell to the rebels – Basra in the south and Kirkuk and Sulaymaniyah in Kurdistan, northern Iraq. But by 3 April, Iraqi forces were reported to have forced back the rebels, the regime having preserved its forces (with the backing of the US: see Hitchens 2005: 459; Pilger 2002: 79) to use against its internal threats. An estimated 20,000 Shi'ites died in the aborted rising (Ricks 2006: 5). In the north, once the flight of an estimated 700,000 Kurds towards Turkey and Iran began, the Western media gave the retreat blanket coverage.

The press suggested the original Kurdish rebellion was a sudden resurgence of the revolt which had been going on, with varying degrees of intensity, since the formation of the Iraqi state, in the early 1920s. President Bush's 15 February call along with the disarray in the Iraqi army supposedly gave the Kurds (and the Shi'as in the south) just the chance they had been waiting for. Following the defeat the masses fled. Kamron Dilsoz, of the British Kurdish media bureau, in an interview with the author, hotly disputed this analysis of the origins of the Kurdish revolt and subsequent flight. He argued that Bush's call had little impact on the Kurdish revolt – this had been intensifying since 1988 and hardly needed outside interference to spark it off. And the mass flight began after a rebel strategy badly misfired. In the March/April period rebel leaders showed films of the 1988 Halabja bombings to mass meetings in Kurdish villages in an attempt to rouse up new hatred of the regime. Instead, the films caused an epidemic of panic and so the surge for the safety of the hills started. Bulloch and Morris (1992: 144) support this view. They write:

> Those who watched [the films] were stunned into silence or wept uncontrollably. Afterwards the nationalists asked themselves whether it had been right to show the film to Kurdish civilians at such a time and whether the shock of seeing for themselves the events at Halabja contributed to the subsequent panic-stricken flight into the mountains in the face of the Iraqi counter-offensive.'

In the lead-up to the massacres the Kurdish issue was marginalised in the press. Saddam Hussein was Iraq, after all, and so the dominant frame took little account of the ethnic complexity of the country. Indeed, paradoxically, most of the Iraqis the allies slaughtered were probably Shi'as and Kurds – the very groups whose revolts the allies later attempted to exploit (Pilger 1991a). The romantic presentation of the Kurdish plight (which fitted so neatly into the dominant, one-dimensional goodie versus baddie representational frames) shrouded the CIA's covert involvement in the Kurds' history which was always marginalised in the press.[3] As Heikal (1992: 320) commented on the Kurds and Shi'as: 'If the two uprisings had been truly motivated by the desire for radical changes in the structure of Iraq, they might have succeeded; as it was, many of those involved were merely trying to exploit a chaotic situation for reasons of greed and revenge.'

Moreover, while the media represented Prime Minister John Major (rather quaintly) as dreaming up the enclave idea on the spur of the moment different political pressures probably had far more impact. In particular, the Turkish leadership feared the mass of Kurds fleeing over their borders would add support to the growing revolt of Turkish Kurds spearheaded by the Marxist-oriented Partia Karkaris Kurdistan (PKK), coverage of this group either non-existent or marginalised in the press. In fact, Turkish President Turgut Ozal first suggested the haven for Kurds in northern Iraq on 7 April (Abrahams 1994: 40). Major's proposal came only on the following day. Moreover, Andrew Natsios, director of the US office of foreign disaster assistance, commented (Lynch and McGoldrick 2005: 214-215):

> Major geopolitical considerations drove policy at the time. ... The first was concern for Turkey, one of Washington's closest Muslim allies.... Turkey, with its own Kurdish 'problem', had no desire to take in hundreds of thousands of destitute refugees. ... Even if the cameras had not been there, the Bush administration would have made the same decision.

In the south, Saudi concern over Iranian, Shi'ite advances into Iraq probably doomed that revolt to defeat (ibid: 318).

In contrast to the press's representation of the allied intervention as altruistic and in the interests of the global community, the reality was far different. As Bill Frelick (1992: 27) commented: 'Far from being a breakthrough for human rights and humanitarian assistance to displaced persons, the allied intervention on behalf of the Kurds of Iraq instead affirmed the power politics and hypocrisies that have long characterised the actions of states with respect to refugees and other powerless victims of official terror.' The allied intervention in northern Iraq, dubbed Operation Provide Comfort, mobilised some 23,000 troops from the US, Britain, France, Italy, Spain and the Netherlands, under the command of US General John Shalikashvili. It served as a significant precedent for intervention by the US and UK elites (cynically exploiting the UN behind the idealistic rhetoric of 'humanitarian intervention' and the 'new world order') into the affairs of foreign enemy states.

Ricks comments (op cit: 8): 'It was the US military's first humanitarian relief operation after the Cold War, and it brought home the point that with Soviet rivalry gone, it would be far easier to use US forces overseas, even in sensitive areas on or near former Eastern Bloc territory.' It employed unmanned aerial vehicles to gather intelligence. 'But most significantly, it was the first major long-term US military operation on Iraqi soil.'

In April 1991, a no-fly zone was unilaterally declared over Kurdistan; 16 months later, as the low intensity war continued against Iraq, America (with British and French support) imposed a similar enclave (though it was defined as an 'exclusion zone') in the south – with warplanes flying out of Saudi Arabia and from carriers in the Gulf to attack 'targets' in Iraq. These 'no-fly' zones had no UN legitimacy, nor were they ever discussed or approved by the UN. But, according to *Independent* war reporter, Robert Fisk (2006: 885) 'they were to become the excuse for a continuing air war against Iraq, undeclared and largely unreported by journalists who were so keen to focus on Saddam's own provocations'. The overall cost of the two 'no-fly' zones was about $1 billion a year. France later withdrew from the operation – which continued right up to the 2003 invasion (Gittings 2011: 228). Gittings comments:

The connection with the protection of the two minorities became more tenuous, particularly after the allied pilots' rules of engagement were 'enlarged' in 1999, allowing air strikes on a variety of targets and leading to increased numbers of civilian casualties. In a foretaste of the legal arguments used to justify going to war in 2003, the USA claimed that the enforcement of the zones was consistent with a Security Council resolution in April 1991 calling on Iraq to end repression of its civilian population. However, the Council at no stage gave the necessary authorization for the USA-UK action, required under chapter VII of the Charter (ibid).

SOMALIA 1992: NEW MILITARISM AND HUMANITARIAN INTERVENTION

US intervention in Somalia was an attempt to legitimise new militarism and its moves to overturn the principles of the sovereign equality of states and non-interference (the basis of international law since the Treaty of Westphalia of 1648, reaffirmed in the United Nations Charter of 1945[4]) under the guise of 'peacekeeping' and 'humanitarianism'. During the Cold War, the authoritarian regime of Mohamed Siad Barre was a close ally of the United States and the military facility at Berbera became a significant base for America's Rapid Deployment Force. From the late 1970s until early 1991, the US spent more than $509 million annually supplying arms to Somalia in return for the use of its military bases (Andersen 2006: 221). Almost two-thirds of the country was allocated to the American oil giants Conoco, Amoco, Chevron and Phillips in the final years before Barre was overthrown. 'There is also evidence that the oil company Conoco closely co-operated with the US forces in their "humanitarian effort" and even leased one of its properties in Mogadishu to serve as a temporary US embassy' (McLaughlin 2002: 148).

In addition, Somalia became a dumping ground for excess food produced by US farmers which ended up undermining the domestic economy, encouraging political corruption and intensifying clan divisions. Once the Barre dictatorship collapsed in January 1991, chaos and famine inevitably followed, at least according to dominant voices in the Western media. And in December 1992, with only weeks left in his term as President, George Bush ordered 25,000 troops into Somalia as part of Operation Restore Hope to ensure food aid reached the famine victims.

When US Navy Seals (Sea, Air and Land units) arrived on the beach in Mogadishu on 9 December 1992 they were met by about 600 members of the international press corps. Indeed, as Carruthers (2000: 221) argues, the Somalia intervention 'was conceived in many respects as a public relations stunt'.

Yet Philip Hammond's detailed quantitative analysis of coverage by the *Guardian, Independent, Times* and *Mail* (2007: 21-50) shows that the famine had peaked in August 1992 and was actually waning when the Marines were sent in November. As Ibrahim Seaga Shaw argues (2012: 129), the 'key driver of the US-led intervention in Somalia' was politics, not any genuine humanitarianism.

A detailed, qualitative analysis of the coverage of the Somali conflict by the *Guardian, Independent, New York Times* and *Washington Post* found a preponderance of 'bellicose and jingoistic' perspectives (Workneh 2011). Most press articles lacked historical background and context: relatively few addressed the history of foreign involvement in the country despite its relevance to the crisis, few explored the complex economic (rather than clan-based) factors behind the internal conflicts within Somalia (see de Waal 2003). The most frequently cited sources were US officials and military personnel, appearing in 42.7 per cent of coverage.

For instance, *The Times*, in its 1 December editorial headline 'Shoot to feed', acknowledged that the mission represented a 'radical departure in international law' but continued: 'If only force will save Somali lives, force should be used.' On the same day, the *Independent*'s editorial, titled 'A benign imperium', argued that the intervention would have to be prolonged and 'on a scale grand enough to signal that a fundamental change in international attitudes and law has occurred'. The *Guardian*, in contrast, was more cautious describing it as a 'complex mission' deserving 'a qualified welcome'.

The debate over the supposed power of the mainstream media to influence the direction of foreign/military policy (which became known as the 'CNN effect') revived during the Somali mission (see Robinson 2002). It became particularly prominent after 4 October 1993 when 18 US soldiers were killed in a day-long battle with the militia of a rebel warlord, General Mohamed Farrar Aidid, head of the United Somali Congress. Some US soldiers were even dragged through the streets of the capital Mogadishu under the glare of the international media.[5] Paul Watson, of the *Toronto Star*, happened to be on the scene with his 35mm pocket camera and his pictures of the Rangers' abuse went on to help him win a Pulitzer Prize. Other images came from a Somali stringer and driver Mohammad Hassan – allegedly linked to Aidid (Rid 2007: 92). According to Rid (ibid: 93): 'Images of the naked corpse of a US soldier and the battered face and frightened voice of another captured soldier sent shockwaves through the American body politic.'

Three days later President Clinton announced that all US troops would leave Somalia by March 1994 while the hunt for Aidid was abandoned. According to Hammond (op cit: 23), the images of the dead US troops are best seen as 'speeding up the decision [to quit Somalia] rather than causing it'. *The Times*, on 4 October, stressed that President Clinton had 'already begun to make clear that he intended to withdraw' while on 5 October 1993, the *Independent* reported that he was 'already under intense pressure to pull American troops out'.

By this time US forces were unable to guarantee the safety of those few journalists who remained. In July, three Western journalists had been beaten to death after a US helicopter attack on an Aidid stronghold led to the deaths of 60 Somalis. And the US military even attacked journalists: in September 1993, soldiers lobbed stun grenades at three photographers and reporters in an attempt to keep them away from a military operation (Carruthers 2000: 223).

The US intervention in Somalia (1992-1994) is best seen as a defining moment for the post Cold War international order and the attempts to redefine new militarism as an ethical project. Yet these aspects significantly received virtually no critical discussion in the mainstream press. Moreover, following the US invasion, as the international corporate media moved its gaze away from Somalia, the country became an important centre for radical Islamist jihadists. And these began channelling arms to Somali insurgents in south-eastern Ethiopia who were fighting under the banner of the Ogaden National Liberation. Philip Hammond concludes (2007: 49):

> If Western governments had little strategic interest in Somalia, news editors surely had none. But in a sense they too were trying to find a role for themselves in the new post-Cold War landscape: as professional mediators charged with the task of explaining the world to their audiences, journalists were also responding to the crisis of meaning. In all cases .... the overall approach to international intervention was essentially narcissistic. The sudden interest in 'rescuing' Somalia had less to do with the country's actual problems than with the opportunities it seemed to offer for Western societies.

SADDAM TRANSFORMED FROM 'GLOBAL THREAT' TO 'NAUGHTY SCHOOLBOY'

During the final days of the Bush administration and the start of the Clinton term, the US resumed bombing of Iraq. On 13 January 1993, more than 100 aircraft attacked targets in southern Iraq. Then, in June 1993, US planes again attacked targets in Baghdad after reports emerged in the corporate media (fed by US intelligence and thus impossible to verify at the time) that Iraq had plotted to assassinate former US President Bush during a trip to Kuwait in April. Both these attacks were rapid, risk-free interventions from the air. They were archetypally new militarist: more symbolic than strategically necessary. They served to maintain Saddam Hussein as the necessary bogeyman for the Western military/industrial elites though now he was transformed from 'global threat' to a kind of naughty schoolboy deserving a 'spanking' and a 'lesson' (Keeble 1994).

The *Sun* headline of 14 January ran 'Spank you and goodnight', while the story began: 'More than 100 allied jets … gave tyrant Saddam Hussein a spanking.' Norman Fairclough (1995: 95) comments: 'This is a metaphysical application of an authoritarian discourse of family discipline which is a prominent element in representations of the attack – Saddam as the naughty child punished by exasperated parents.' The *Guardian* editorial, headlined 'More than a smack than a strike', described the attack as 'an act of punishment against a very bad boy who thumbed his nose several times too often'. But in its editorial the *Sun* echoed many of the expressions which were so dominant in the propaganda during the 1990-

1991 crisis. Under the headline 'Wipe out the mad menace', it commented: 'At long last, allied warplanes have bombed the hell out of Saddam Hussein. The Iraqi madman has pushed the West too far. He played a dangerous game and now he must pay the price.' The reference to the 'West' is blatantly propagandistic since the West, in fact, was deeply divided over the attack. And while the USA, Britain and France were claiming to be enforcing a United Nations resolution, neither the 'no-fly' zone they were imposing on southern Iraq nor the attack in the north had been endorsed by the UN. The *Sun* editorial ended in typical gung-ho style: 'The tragedy is that we did not finish him off last time. Go get him boys!' yet for those sections of the Western elites who still backed Hussein, such attacks hardly did his regime any damage. If anything, they achieved the opposite.

'PUNISHING SADDAM' AGAIN – IN 1996 AND 1998

By 5 July 1996, Patrick Cockburn, in the *Independent*, was reporting that 'Saddam has missiles and will use them'. The report was based on the (somewhat dubious) evidence provided by General Wafiq al-Sammara'i, former head of Iraqi military intelligence, who had just escaped from Baghdad, becoming 'one of the highest-ranking officers ever to defect from the Iraqi regime' (Cockburn 1996).

Then, in September 1996, another typical 'Saddam scare' erupted after Iraqi troops were reported to have invaded Kurdistan in support of the KDP Kurdish faction headed by Massoud Barzani against the Iranian-backed PUK faction headed by Jalal al-Talabani. Targets in southern Iraq were attacked by US missiles, supposedly to 'punish Saddam' (as the press stressed) for 'his' advance in the north. In the following month, the PUK faction regained its lost strongholds and the crisis suddenly disappeared from the media. Behind all the simplistic, hyper-personalised anti-Saddam rhetoric, US strategists were following a well-established policy: promoting a divided Kurdistan. Significantly, this remained also the favoured policy of US ally Turkey – always anxious to hinder moves towards Kurdish unity on its doorstep – and the Iraqi elite. Moreover, shortly after the Baghdad-backed assault on Sulaymaniyah in Iraqi Kurdistan, news of a disastrous attempt by the CIA to build an indigenous Kurdish force to overthrow Saddam received prominent coverage in the US and UK press. Reports suggested that President Clinton had authorised $20m. for the covert action. Was this a CIA faction leaking the details to embarrass the weaker anti-Saddam faction within the agency?

On 26 January 1998, Clinton received a letter calling for the removal of Saddam Hussein by leading members of the right-wing think tank, the Project for the New American Century including many who were to hold important positions in the George W. Bush administration: Donald Rumsfeld (defense secretary), Paul Wolfowitz (Rumsfeld's deputy), Richard Perle, Richard Armitage and John Bolton (Newton 2003: 4).

Then, only an 11th hour intervention by UN secretary general Kofi Annan prevented US military strikes on Iraq after a media-hyped crisis exploded in January-February 1998. Soon afterwards, the Republican-led congress approved the Iraq Liberation Act giving the executive branch the authority to dispense up to $97 million worth of military equipment and weapons to an insurgent army (Gordon and Trainor op cit: 14). Then, in December of the same year, US jets attacked targets (including air defence systems, weapons depots, command centres of the Republican Guard and Presidential palaces) in Iraq during a rapid, risk-free action code-named Operation Desert Fox (supposedly because it aimed to 'outfox' Saddam Hussein just hours after the withdrawal of the UN arms inspector).[6]

In August 1998, Baghdad had suspended all co-operation with the United Nations' weapons inspection teams, UNSCOM, claiming – rightly, as it later became known – that it was being used by US intelligence agencies as part of a plot to oust Saddam Hussein (Ritter 2005a). As Scott Ritter revealed: 'The only problem was that this coup, supposedly planned in great secrecy, was well known to the Iraqi government. Many of the defectors being used by the CIA were actually Mukhabarat [Iraqi secret service] double agents' (ibid).

As Edwards and Cromwell argue (2009: 35), the US 'manufactured a conflict in December 1998' with Iraq. Yet most of the corporate press promoted the myth that Iraq had ruthlessly booted out the inspectors well before the launch of Desert Fox.[7] Edwards and Cromwell continue (ibid: 41):

> In 2002, the words 'Iraq and inspectors' were mentioned in 736 *Guardian/Observer* articles. We managed to find some half a dozen articles confirming that arms inspectors had been infiltrated by CIA spies in 1998. These generally make brief mention of the presence of spies, or report spies merely 'passed on secrets' to the US and Israel, omitting to mention that the information was used to launch a major military strike against Iraq.

But, in December 1998, President Clinton, and the Western media, claimed 'Saddam' had defied the UN Security Council – and so battle commenced. During the four-day attacks, 415 cruise missiles (more than the 317 fired during the entire 1991 Desert Storm operation) were launched while US and British jets dropped more than 600 bombs, killing an estimated 1,400 members of the Iraqi Republican Guard. Gordon and Trainor describe this as a 'quiet little war' (op cit). Even so, an estimated 62 Iraqi soldiers and 82 civilians were killed (Fisk 2006: 887).[8] According to Tom Bower (2016: 126), PM Tony Blair told parliament that the RAF had hit their 'targets', even though General Charles Guthrie, chief of the defence staffs, had reported that 'the Tornadoes had missed most of theirs'.

In early January 1999, UNICEF and the World Food Programme reported that the attack had destroyed an agricultural school, damaged schools and hospitals and cut off water supplies for 300,000 people in Baghdad. The attacks occurred just three days after President Clinton was facing an impeachment inquiry over the

Monica Lewinsky sex scandal. As Fisk (ibid: 889) comments: 'No wonder some of the UN inspectors called this "the War of Monica's Skirt".' The Iraqi media dubbed it 'Operation Monica' (McLaughlin 2002: 104).

Also on 20 August 1998, US jets destroyed the Al-Shifa pharmaceutical plant in Sudan which the Clinton administration claimed was being used for the processing of VX nerve agent while its owners had ties to al-Qaeda. American officials later admitted these claims had been based on false information. According to Noam Chomsky, tens of thousands of people, many of them children suffered and died from malaria, tuberculosis and other treatable diseases as a result of the destruction of the plant (Chomsky 2001: 48). But there was no major outpouring of outrage in the British corporate media. McLaughlin (op cit: 104) claimed that reporters 'lapsed into unreflective "wow" journalism and continued to treat the bombing raids as militarily justifiable. They fed contentedly on the usual statistics about numbers of bombing missions and their success rates, or the types of planes and weapons used…'

Anthony Arnove records (2000: 9) that between 1991 and 1999, US and UK forces flew more than 6,000 sorties, dropped more than 1,000 bombs and hit more than 450 targets in Iraq. 'The Pentagon alone spent more than $1 billion to maintain its force of 200 airplanes, nineteen warships and 22,000 troops who are part of the operation.' The Iraq war had become 'the longest sustained US air operation since the Vietnam War'.

By 2001 attacks on Iraq by US and UK jets had become institutionalised gaining hardly a mention in the mainstream media. In February 2001, for instance, after just a month in office, the Bush administration launched air strikes against five sites in the Iraqi anti-aircraft network (Ricks op cit: 26). This was secret warfare *par excellence*! Bob Woodward, in his semi-official account of the 2003 invasion, *Plan of attack* (2004: 10), records how, as part of Operation Southern Watch, US pilots patrolled the southern part of Iraq up to the Baghdad suburbs, flying an 'incredible' 150,000 times between 1991 and 2001. Woodward adds: 'In hundreds of attacks not a single US pilot had been lost.'

THE SECRET 'HUMANITARIAN' WAR AGAINST YUGOSLAVIA 1999

The US/UK-led attacks on Yugoslavia between 24 March and 10 June 1999 (codenamed Operation 'Allied Force') 'turned out to be the most secret campaign in living memory', according to historian Alistair Horne (see Knightley 2003a [1975]: 501).[9] They were risk-free and conducted mainly from the air (as were Nato's earlier strikes against Bosnian Serbs in 1995). There were major ground actions by special forces (SAS, the al-Qaida-linked and CIA-backed Kosovo Liberation Army, BND, the German secret service) but these were largely away from the media glare (Curtis 2010: 241-247). And like other new militarist adventures, it was expected to be over quickly. As Andrew Rawnsley reported (2000: 258), the foreign office leant toward the view of the American state department that Milošević would crack after a few nights of what the Americans termed 'representational' bombing. But Rawnsley continued (ibid: 288), the war that was supposed to last seventy-two hours, in the end took seventy-eight days, 'not least because of military errors and political miscalculations by Nato'.

On coming to power in May 1997, the new foreign secretary, Robin Cook, had pronounced: 'Britain will once again be a force for good in the world. Our foreign policy must have an ethical dimension and must support the demands of other people for democratic rights on which we insist for ourselves.'[10] Celebrated as 'humanitarian' and 'precise', the 1999 attacks on Yugoslavia were seen as crucial manifestations of New Labour's 'ethical' foreign policy. As Prime Minister Tony Blair asserted: 'This is no longer just a military conflict. It is a battle between good and evil; between civilisation and barbarity' (Rawnsley 2000: 263). Later, in a speech to the Chicago Economic Club on 22 April 1999, he spelled out the 'Blair doctrine of the international community': this was a 'just war' based not on any territorial ambitions but on halting or preventing humanitarian disasters such as genocide or ethnic cleansing.[11] Andrew Marr, in the *Observer*, was on hand to praise the Great Leader: the headline over his feature on 4 April 1999 read: 'Brave, bold, visionary: Whatever became of Blair the ultra-cautious cynic?'; on 16 May, the headline ran: 'Hail to the chief: Sorry, Bill, but this time we're talking about Tony' (cited in Edwards and Cromwell 2009: 96).

In fact, the Kosovo conflict is best interpreted as part of a desperate attempt by a newly-enlarged, 19-member Nato alliance to celebrate its 50 years' anniversary with a symbolic victory in a manufactured 'war' (Keeble 1999a: 16). As Prime Minister Tony Blair stressed, failure to bomb 'would have dealt a devastating blow to the credibility of Nato'.[12] Yet the use of Nato by the US (since it failed to gain UN approval for the Serbian attacks) was also opportunistic. As Alex Callinicos comments (2002: 10), for its invasion of Afghanistan two years later, the US treated 'with contempt' Nato, its 'preferred instrument for intervention in the Balkans' and ruthlessly implemented unilateral action.

Nato had been created by the Western powers in 1949 as a defensive alliance to protect the leading democracies against Soviet expansionism. Yet, as Thussu points out (2000: 6): 'In Kosovo, the Western alliance was violating both its own charter and international law by militarily intervening in the internal affairs of a country that was not threatening any of its member states and was outside Nato's area of deployment.' And following the conflict, Natassja Smiljanic commented (1999):

> Another forgotten casualty of Nato's war against Yugoslavia is respect for the principles of international law. ... Nato's justification for taking this action was to safeguard 'human rights', yet its blatant disregard for international law will mean that illegal acts can be justified if taken for 'humanitarian' reasons.

The Kosovo theatre of war was largely a no-go area for the international media. The state systems of Serbia and the US/UK both found it in their interests to deny media access to the front line – though a few brave journalists such as Eve-Ann Prentice (2000), of *The Times*, did file reports from Kosovo. She narrowly escaped death when Nato jets attacked her party of journalists just outside Prizren, in south west Kosovo. Nebojsa Radojevic, 38, a driver, was killed (Prentice 1999a). In all, 25 journalists and media workers lost their lives covering the conflict. They included three Chinese journalists (Shao Yunhuan, of Xinhua news agency, and Xu Xinhu and Zhu Ying, husband and wife, of the *Guangming Daily*) who were killed when Nato bombed the Chinese embassy in Belgrade on 7 May. Slavko Curuvijia, editor and publisher of *Dnevni Telegraph* and *Evropljanin*, was assassinated outside his apartment while two journalists from the German weekly *Stern*, Volker Krämer and Gabriel Grüner, were killed by snipers on 13 June. Goff comments (1999: 26): 'Aside from fearing for their lives, journalists and media workers were regularly harassed, questioned, threatened, accused of being spies, detained, beaten and expelled.'

THE SILENCING FUNCTION OF THE MEDIA CONSENSUS: CREATING THE MYTH OF WARFARE

In keeping with the trend in military strategies since the 1980s, this was no war as commonly defined. There was no credible enemy. According to Phillip Knightley (op cit: 514), following the 79-day bombardments, Belgrade lost 600 soldiers and police and 2,600 civilians.[13] Nato bombers hit 33 hospitals and 340 schools. According to John Pilger (2002: 143), a list of civilian targets in Yugoslavia was published on the internet – but no newspaper carried it. 'Code-named "Stage Three", these targets included public transport, non-military factories, telephone exchanges, food processing plants, fertiliser depots, hospitals, schools, museums, churches, heritage-listed monasteries and farms' (ibid). That only 2 per cent of Nato's precision-guided missiles hit military targets was only 'fleeting news' (ibid).

In all, the attacks caused $60 billion of damage. Moreover, thousands suffered traumas following the relentless bombing of the country, thousands lost their jobs and were thrown into poverty; the bombing of petro-chemical factories sparked an environmental catastrophe in the region; water supplies were threatened for millions while the bombing of bridges over the Danube seriously crippled trade in the region. Serbia was transformed into the poorest country of Europe. Following the conflict, the cost of reconstructing the Balkans was put at more than £20 billion (Rawnsley 2000: 289).

According to Thomas and Mikulan (2006: 49), 730 USAF and 325 other Nato aircraft flew 10,084 strike missions against the Yugoslav Army (VJ) and internal security forces (MPUP). VJ suffered heavily losing 26 tanks, 389 artillery pieces and about 5,000 dead. General Wesley K. Clark, supreme allied commander Europe, later testified at the armed forces committee that Nato had destroyed

110 Serb tanks, 210 armoured personnel carriers and 449 guns and mortars (Der Derian 2009: 199). The BBC's John Simpson gives different figures (2010: 539). He suggests that, while Nato claimed to have eliminated 40 per cent of Serbia's 280 tanks in its 40,000 bombing sorties, in fact it became clear when Nato troops entered Kosovo that just 13 Serbian tanks had been destroyed. Simpson adds: 'It would have been cheaper to have offered Milošević $10 million for each of them, and saved a great many innocent lives.'

Fulfilling the dream of all new militarist strategists, the 'war' concluded with no loss of life on the Nato side – though the Serbs claimed to have shot down 10 Nato jets and three helicopters, while the bodies of 19 American special rescue forces were transported to Greece in body bags to be shipped home (Marshall 1999). In addition, Nato admitted that two US pilots died in an Apache helicopter training accident (Norton-Taylor 2000a).

This was slaughter from the air. Largely unreported was Nato's use of depleted uranium missiles (for instance, the BL755 'multi-purpose' cluster bomb), tested in southern Iraq where leukaemia among children and birth deformities had grown to match the levels following the Hiroshima nuclear bombing of August 1945 (Pilger 1999). As Nato shifted its strategy to take in the deliberate targeting of civilians, in flagrant breach of international law, innocent people became mere 'targets' of the high-flying jets. Just before the ending of the bombings, over 900 aircraft and 35 ships were in operation – more than triple the number at the start of the conflict. In January 2000, Human Rights Watch, a New York-based organisation, accused Nato of deliberately bombing Serbia's civil infrastructure in breach of international law – and condemned its use of cluster bombs (Norton-Taylor 2000b). Amnesty International (unsuccessfully) appealed to the international criminal tribunal to rule that the US air campaign had violated the laws of warfare (Der Derian 2009: 199).

Even media outlets became the targets of Nato's intensified bombing strategy. On 21 April, Nato jets destroyed the headquarters of the Serbian Socialist Party in Belgrade destroying four television stations and four radio stations. On 23 April, as the celebrations for Nato's 50th anniversary began in Brussels (with President Clinton proclaiming: 'When we fight, we fight to prevail') Nato jets attacked the Radio Televizija Srbije (RTS) building in Belgrade killing an estimated 16 Serb media workers and injuring dozens more. Another television building in Novi Sad was bombed on 3 May. According to Chris Paterson (2014: 64):

> The US anti-war campaigning organisation the International Action Center reported that 'between 24 March and 10 June 1999' US/Nato bombs destroyed more than ten private radio and television stations and 36 transmitters. The Pink and Kosava commercial radio and television stations in Belgrade were bombed, apparently without civilian casualties.

PM Blair publicly described the attacks as 'entirely justified'. But, in fact, following advice from government lawyers that the attack could be considered a breach of the Geneva Conventions (on the rules of war), Blair had not allowed British aircraft to be involved in the strikes (Rawnsley 2000: 273). Predictably, on 24 April, the *Mirror's* 'military adviser' Lt General Sir Roderick Cordey-Simpson, under the headline: 'Ordinary folk were hurt too' described the TV station as 'a perfectly legitimate target because it was churning out state propaganda'. But Cordey-Simpson failed to mention any of the ensuing deaths and injuries. People were 'hurt', he claimed because they were being denied their dose of TV entertainment and soaps! Two months after the end of the bombings, the BBC 'revealed' the attack on the RTS building was part of Nato's plans to widen its target list to non-military sites. But Philip Hammond (2000a) argued: 'The only reason the BBC could present old news as an "untold story" was that at the time journalists obediently stuck to Nato's line that they only hit "legitimate military targets" and were careful to avoid "collateral damage".' According to Eve-Ann Prentice (1999b: 463), there was dual culpability in the bombing of the RTS building.

> First of all, it didn't stop the Serb propaganda machine. Military strategists should have known the Yugoslavs were bound to have back-up facilities. On the other hand, it is widely understood that senior Serb officials bullied a number of journalists and media workers to keep manning the building even though they knew it was high on the target list.

In a report on 7 June 2000, Amnesty International described the bombing of the TV station as 'a deliberate attack on a civilian object' which, therefore, constituted a war crime (Edwards and Cromwell 2009: 97).

MAKING THE ALBANIAN KOSOVARS 'WORTHY VICTIMS'

Nato's 'humanitarian' intervention in the Yugoslav war was based on the notion that the sufferings of the Albanian Kosovars in the face of Serbian aggression were exceptionally harsh – and thus required exceptional remedies. The British government, for instance, claimed on 17 June 1999 that Serbs had killed 10,000 ethnic Albanians in Kosovo in more than 100 massacres. Corporate media coverage tended to reproduce such claims uncritically, focusing on the appalling ordeals of the refugees and rape victims, stressing the legitimacy of Nato's military intervention and downplaying the obvious fact that the refugees were fleeing Nato's bombs as much as the Serbian forces. Suddenly, the Albanian Kosovars, ignored for so long by the Western media, were transformed into victims worthy of our compassion and grief.

David Clark, Europe adviser at the foreign office 1997-2001, argued that the speed and extent of Serbia's mobilisation suggested a preconceived plan, not a spontaneous reaction to Nato's bombing (Clark 2009). Some 10,000 people were murdered by Serbian forces. 'These atrocities may not have passed the legal test of genocide, but the reality was awful enough. The Serbian state carried out a crime against humanity – a ruthlessly executed plan to change the ethnic composition of Kosovo through expulsion and mass murder' (ibid). Yet it could be argued that the focus by the Western corporate media on the Albanian Kosovars was essentially for propaganda purposes.

As Noam Chomsky (1999: 48-54) stressed, at the time of the Serbian crisis, in Colombia, Church and human rights groups were estimating that the civil war had created more than one million internal refugees who were fleeing the violence. In Turkey, the number of Kurdish refugees was put at more than two million. Yet since Turkey and Colombia were backed by the leading Nato powers, both these human disasters were ignored by the media. They were victims not worthy of our compassion. Even within Yugoslavia, many of the victims of the Nato attacks were ignored by the media. For instance, 60 per cent of Kosovo's Serbs and Montenegrins – 100,000 people – fled during the 78-day conflict. According to Philip Hammond (2000b: 22-23): 'This did not matter, however, since these refugees were systematically ignored by Western journalists in line with Nato's claim that "humanitarian" bombing could not possibly cause anyone to flee.'

Moreover, research conducted since the end of the Nato bombing suggests that the reports of mass killings by Yugoslavian security forces and paramilitaries were grossly exaggerated for propaganda purposes. The international criminal tribunal for the Former Yugoslavia reported the discovery of 2,108 bodies (though this figure did not distinguish between combatants and civilians nor between Albanians and Serbs) while one team of Spanish pathologists sent by the European Union to investigate the 'killing fields' discovered 187 civilian corpses and not the thousands reported (ibid: 23). And less than 2,500 had died during the Serbian-KLA conflict between 1997 and 1999 (Southwell 2005: 33). In June 1999, the FBI arrived in Kosovo in the hunt for mass graves. Several weeks later, having found none, they went home (Pilger 2002: 144).

PUTTING ALL THE BLAME ON MILOŠEVIĆ

Just as the deployment of ground troops during the Gulf massacres of 1991 was needed for the manufacture of the 'Big War' (to help finally kick the 'Vietnam syndrome') so the demonisation of the Serbs and, in particular, President Milošević as the 'evil new Hitler' helped legitimise the excessive use of force against defenceless targets and manufacture a 'credible' enemy. One of the Western media's propaganda coups came over the coverage of the Rambouillet meeting just before Nato began its bombing of Belgrade.

The breakdown of the talks was universally represented as being the fault of Milošević. Yet, swearing reporters to deep-background confidentiality at the

Rambouillet talks, a senior US state department official had bragged that the United States 'deliberately set the bar higher than the Serbs could accept'. The Serbs needed, according to the official, a little bombing to see reason (Kenny 1999). In his evidence to the defence select committee inquiry into the conflict, the former MP John Gilbert (and later Lord Gilbert) commented:

> I think certain people were spoiling for a fight in Nato at that time. ... If you ask my personal view, I think the terms put to Milošević at Rambouillet were absolutely intolerable; how could he possibly accept them. It was quite deliberate. That does not excuse an awful lot of other things, but we were at a point when some people felt that something had to be done, so you just provoked a fight.[14]

Moroever, US secretary of state Madeleine Albright admitted on Allan Little's BBC2 documentary *Moral combat: Nato at war*, on 12 March 2000 (which marked the first anniversary of the start of the bombings) the talks were manipulated to make it impossible for the Serbs to agree.[15] Any close examination of the final Rambouillet documentation would have discovered this strategy.

In the first instance, the 'accord' provided for Nato's military occupation of the whole of Yugoslavia, not just Kosovo. According to Chapter 7, Article X, Nato gained the right to shoot down any military aircraft over Kosovo and 25 km from the border with Serbia. The accord would also have given Nato unprecedented levels of access in and out of the entire country while Nato forces would have been able to act above and beyond the law. Nato personnel were to be exempt from sales taxes, customs inspections and regulations – and have the right to import and export whatever they deemed necessary. Nato was to take control of the telecommunications services and the accord added: 'The economy of Kosovo shall function in accordance with free market principles.' In fact, it was a deal the Serbs (not their Russian backers) could hardly be expected to accept: as the Western powers realised only too well.[16]

No newspaper carried the Rambouillet documentation in full (though the *Guardian*, for instance, made it available on its website) – yet earlier the broadsheets had carried almost verbatim accounts of the Starr report into President Clinton's affair with Monica Lewinsky.[17] One journalist to highlight critically Western strategies over Rambouillet was John Pilger in his *Guardian* columns – and then he was accused of being a 'traitor' by the government in parliament and denounced by journalist colleagues.

When in mid-April 1999 American F-16s bombed a convoy of refugees on the Prizren-Djakovica road and killed up to 70 innocents, blame throughout the press for the atrocity was redirected towards Milošević. So the *Sun* of 15 April carried the front page headline: 'Our bombs: his fault.' 'Whatever happened,' commented the *Daily Telegraph*, 'it is Slobodan Milošević who is entirely responsible for creating the circumstances that led to their death.' Or as Jamie Shea, Nato's spokesman, put it: 'The evil is not our mistake. The evil here is Milošević' (Knightley 2003a [1975]: 513). Similarly, columnist Rosemary Righter argued in the *The Times* of 2 April: 'The touch-paper of the Balkan conflagration was lit in Kosovo by the inflammatory rhetoric of one man, Slobadan Milošević.' This line, which grossly over-simplified an extraordinarily complex political, economic and ethnic/cultural history through its hyper-personalisation, was reproduced in editorials. For instance, *The Times*, of 28 May, argued that it was a war 'started by a man suspected of atrocities'; the *Independent*, of 10 June, accused Milošević of being 'the architect of a decade of misery in the Balkans' while the *Guardian* of 11 June dubbed the President 'the architect of this historic calamity'.

In this way, the newspapers were merely echoing the rhetoric of the politicians. US President Bill Clinton dubbed Milošević 'a dictator who has done nothing but start new wars'; British Prime Minister Tony Blair called him 'a man who has brought much death and barbarism to the Balkans' while Nato secretary general George Robertson said he was 'hell bent on war'. On 14 July 2000, when tensions rose between Serbia and Montenegro, the *Guardian* continued its demononisation of Milošević: Its editorial commented bluntly:

> The man who more than any other has re-Balkanised the Balkans is well on the way to completing the task of dismembering Yugoslavia that he began a decade ago. … The main reason why Montenegro, too, has not already gone on its own way is a justified fear that the Belgrade bruiser could react by launching yet another war.

AMBIVALENCE – AND THE MANUFACTURE OF SUPER-SLOBBA, THE CREDIBLE ENEMY

As in the case of Iraqi President Saddam Hussein, the necessary demonisation of Milošević often involved a close focus on his alleged personal history and psychology. Dubbed 'Slobba' by the patriotic pops, he was variously described as 'monstrous', 'mad', 'a vile and wicked man', an 'unquestionable villain', 'a walking argument for the existence of hell', 'suicidal, on a mission to destroy everything he touches', 'faintly absurd', 'a liar and a cheat', 'a genius of evil', 'Balkan butcher' (echoing the 'Baghdad/Balkans butcher' jibes at Saddam Hussein) (Hammond 2007: 130-131). The *Sun* urged the West to 'Clobba Slobba' and 'Bomb, Bomb, Bomb' (cited in Edwards and Cromwell 2009: 96).

But just as previously with Saddam Hussein, the coverage was also determined to represent Milošević as a 'credible' leader worth confronting so his political skills were stressed: thus he was variously described as a 'tough and cunning operator', 'a master tactician', 'shrewd and manipulative leader'. Some commentators intervened to critique this widespread demonisation process. David Aaronovitch, in the *Independent* of 8 April, suggested that 'the legend of Super-Slobba, the Belgrade Machiavelli' was one of the 'great myths of the Kosovan war' while the

Guardian's editorial of 12 April warned the government about over-demonising the Serbian leader since his role would be crucial in any future negotiations. But, on the other hand, the *Independent*'s editorial of 3 April stressed: 'The invention of the monster "Slobba" is a justified use of tabloid techniques to portray a tyrant in vivid colours.'

The demonisation of 'Slobba' was often extended to the Serbs as a people. Just as the President was described as the 'new Hitler', so the Serbs were often linked in the mainstream press to the Nazis on many occasions. In this way, the media were echoing again the rhetoric of Nato leaders who constantly used Nazi-associated terms such as 'genocide' and 'genocidal' in their press briefings. Thus, the *Guardian*'s front page report of 1 April described 'scenes reminiscent of the treatment of the Jews in the second world war' while in the *Independent*, Emma Daly and Marcus Tanner's report was headlined 'Serbs try for "final solution"' and in the *Daily Mail* David Williams commented on the 'haunting similarities' between the ethnic cleansing actions of the Serbian forces and those of the Nazis.

Intriguingly, in 2009, it was revealed that Milošević's intelligence chief, Jovica Stanisic, later tried at the international criminal court and the Hague, was, in fact, a CIA agent from 1990-1998 (Fitsanakis 2009, Miller 2009, *Eye Spy* 2009). This news received very little coverage in the UK corporate media.

SILENCING THE ROLE OF US/UK IMPERIALISM IN PROVOKING THE CONFLICT

The United States had been determined since the mid-1980s to push Yugoslavia towards capitalism. As early as March 1984, a secret National Security Decision Directive (No. 133), declassified in 1990, identified the US policy towards Yugoslavia as encouraging its transformation towards capitalism. As Gervasi comments: 'The mechanisms included most favoured nation status, credit policy, IMF stewardship, debt-rescheduling, cultural and educational exchanges, information programmes, high-level visits and restrictions on diplomatic and consular personnel.'[18] The abundant natural resources in Kosovo, with the richest mineral resources in all of Europe west of Russia (including gold, silver, pure lead, zinc, coal and oil) enhanced its importance to Western capitalism. According to John Pilger, the US attack on Yugoslavia began in 1989 with the imposition of 'market reforms' by the International Monetary Fund and the World Bank.

> Millions of jobs were eliminated: in 1989 alone 600,000 workers, almost a quarter of the workforce, were sacked without severance pay. But the most critical 'reform' was the ending of economic support to the six constituent republics and their re-colonisation by Western capitalism. Germany led the way, supporting the breakaway of Croatia, its new economic colony, with the European Community giving silent approval. The torch of fratricide had been lit and the rise of an opportunist like Milošević was inevitable (1999).

From 1990 onwards, as the Czech Republic, Poland and Hungary raced to embrace Nato, Yugoslavia stood out against the alliance's expansionist moves. It had to pay the price. Indeed, the 1999 Nato assault on Serbia might best be viewed as a continuation of Western attempts to take over the country rather than a 'humanitarian' intervention on behalf of the Albanian Kosovars as part of a grand design to encircle Russia (Blackburn 1999: 111).

MARGINALISING THE OPPOSITION TO THE WAR

Significantly, the Fleet Street new militarist consensus held firm over the conflict with virtually all the mainstream media in both the UK and US supporting the action. In Britain, only the *Independent on Sunday* dared to stand outside the consensus. And within weeks of the ending of the air strikes, its editor, Kim Fletcher, was removed. The *Guardian*, traditionally associated with the liberal left and often critical of UK/UK militarism, was a fervent member of the pro-war camp. On the eve of the attacks on Belgrade, it editorialised: 'The only honourable course for Europe and America is to use military force' (see McDonald 2007: 24).

Yet there were important shifts in the consensus. During the Gulf conflict not only did all the editors, safe in their Fleet Street bunkers, loyally bang the drums of war, virtually all the columnists backed it with jingoistic fervour. In many respects in 1991, the editors were reproducing in knee-jerk fashion the consensual frameworks of the Cold War but applying them, just months after the collapse of the Berlin Wall, to the new conditions of the Middle East conflict. By 1999, the Cold War consensus could not be sustained and divisions emerged amongst the elite over the manufactured crisis in the Balkans. Out of 63 prominent Fleet Street commentators, two thirds backed the war (either giving full support to the air campaign or calling for troops to be sent in) while one third (including Richard Gott and Seumas Milne, of the *Guardian*, Richard Littlejohn, of the *Sun* and Matthew Parris and Simon Jenkins, of *The Times*) opposed it (Keeble 2000b, 2004 and 2007b).

As in 1991, editorial commitment to the war meant that opposition to Nato's assault, both within Britain and globally, was marginalised. In Greece, for example, polls suggested that more than 90 per cent of the population were opposed to the attacks – even though it was a Nato country. As John Pilger commented (1999): 'Thousands in Greece and Germany, protests taking place every night in colleges and town halls across Britain. Almost none of this is reported.' Newspapers were too busy reproducing the politicians' rhetoric about the war being waged by a 'united, 'civilised' West against the 'evil Milošević'.

According to Noam Chomsky (2001: 75): 'Nato bombing of Serbia was undertaken by the "international community" according to consistent Western rhetoric, although those who did not have their heads buried in the sand knew that it was opposed by most of the world, often quite vocally.' And in the end, the conflict was halted not through military means (as advocated by most of Fleet Street) but diplomacy. As Seldon (2005: 405) comments: 'In the end, the crucial factor [in facing down Milošević] was diplomacy between the US and Russia which left Milošević isolated.'

NOTES

[1] Knightley, Phillip (2003a [1975]) provides an excellent critical examination of the Russell myth. Says that Russell chronicled the failings of the army in the Crimea but failed to expose and understand the causes. While he criticised the lot of the ordinary soldier he never attacked the officers 'to whose social class he belonged himself'. And Knightley continues (p. 16): 'Above all, Russell made the mistake, common to many a war correspondent, of considering himself part of the military establishment.' Indeed, when he returned from the Crimea, Russell was embraced by the establishment as one of them. He dined with the Queen. But the Russell reports came at a crucial time in the evolution of the press in Britain. The campaign against press taxes had just won its crucial victory and the way was set for the destruction of the radical press and the emergence of elitist newspapers in the 'free' marketplace of opinion (see Curran and Seaton 2003 [1991]: 10-37; Conboy 2002: 66-86). Around Russell's reports in *The Times*, critical of Lord Raglan and the war effort, could emerge the myth of the fourth estate, separate from and critical of the state. *The Times* played only a minor role in the fall of the government. It was one small factor amongst many others. An important section of the British elite was determined on Aberdeen's fall, irrespective of any views expressed in *The Times* (see Barker 2000). But the myth emerged of the adversary press constantly in conflict with the state and the military (see Snoddy 1992: 43-6, de Burgh 2000: 33-4 and Randall 2005: 17-31). Schudson (1992) exposes persuasively the many media myths surrounding Watergate. In particular he argues that the press was just one small factor in bringing down President Nixon amongst many others – the FBI investigators, federal prosecutors, grand jury and congressional committees. The press as a whole did not uncover the scandal; moreover, the scandal did not lead to any great surge of investigative reporting. 'By the Reagan years the investigative binge seemed over' (see de Burgh op cit: 78-79)

[2] See http://www.representativepress.org/evenafter.html, accessed on 14 October 2008

[3] See Agee, Phil (1976) *Covert Action: What next?* Agee/Hosenball Defence Committee, London. Details CIA support for the Kurds 1972-1975 along with the Iranian Shah in their war with Iraq. Once the Shah arranged a deal with Iraq over a crucial border dispute, the CIA support immediately collapsed p. 8. CIA support for the Kurds in 1991 is detailed in Bulloch and Morris (1992) p. 31. See also Blum, William (1986) *The CIA: A forgotten history – US interventions since World War Two*, London: Zed Books p. 278

[4] See http://www.un.org/aboutun/charter/

[5] See http://novaonline.nvcc.edu/eli/evans/his135/Events/Somalia93/Somalia93.html, accessed on 14 October 2008. The US intervention in Somalia and the battle against Aidid's militia became the subject of Ridley Scott's Hollywood blockbuster *Black Hawk Down*. See Andersen (2006: 212-226) for a detailed, critical analysis of the film

[6] See http://www.defenselink.mil/specials/desert_fox/, accessed on 14 October 2008. Robert Fisk (2006: 887) comments that Operation Desert Fox was the nickname of Hitler's General Erwin Rommel 'though that, apparently, did not occur to US military planners'

[7] On Fleet Street's coverage see Keeble 1999a and 1999b

[8] In Seldon's hagiography of Blair (2005: 391), he reports on Operation Desert Fox: 'Clinton and Blair called off the attacks on 20 December, after some 650 sorties on 250 targets had been launched.' There is no mention of any casualties

[9] Earlier, in August 1995, the US had backed Croatia's ethnic cleansing of Serbs with military strikes. As Dragan Playsic (2003: 177) writes: 'In August 1995, [Franjo] Tudgman [President of Croatia] launched Operation Storm, a mass offensive against the Krajina, ethnically cleansing 150,000 Serbs from their homes within a few days. US naval aircraft bombed Krajina Serb missile positions. … The complicity of the US in this act of mass ethnic cleansing received relatively little attention from the Western media'

[10] Moreover, in 1998, British forces had been 'quietly reconfigured from an ostensibly defensive role to an overtly offensive one, with a new focus on "expeditionary warfare" and "power projection" overseas' (Curtis 2010: 249)

[11] Seldon (2005: 398-399) reports that Blair's Chicago speech had been largely drawn up by Lawrence Freedman, 'the doyen professor of defence studies'. While most of Fleet Street was delighted with the speech, 'the Foreign Office most definitely were not: they had received no prior notice of the content and were highly concerned about where it left international law and the position of the United Nations. Washington too was not pleased. Some … were unhappy with the notion of producing a humanitarian rationale to legitimise intervention, believing that the strongest argument for intervention in Kosovo rested on the security implications of Milošević's actions'

[12] See http://news.bbc.co.uk/hi/english/static/events/panorama/transcripts/transcript_12_03_00.txt, accessed on 11 December 2015. Misha Glenny, BBC Central European correspondent in the early 1990s and author of a major history of the Balkans, argued that the Americans were not eager for intervention – but were driven by Blair. He commented: '… with Kosovo, there is this idea that the Americans were trying to consolidate their control of Nato and their presence in Europe. But I was talking regularly with all the US diplomats in the two years prior to the bombing campaign and I can say categorically that they were trying to find anything that did not involve the use of force. They wanted to get out of the Balkans because it is such a liability for the Clinton regime. Their whole aim was to get out of Bosnia. The people who pushed for the bombing of Kosovo were the Blair government'

[13] Though Human Rights Watch said Nato attacks caused around 500 deaths the *Guardian*'s editorial of 20 March 2000 commented: 'Although this toll will rise because of Nato's unjustifiable reluctance to defuse its own unexploded cluster bombs, the record is not so horrendous as some imply'

[14] See Ramsay, Robin (2000) Nato and Kosovo, *Lobster*, Vol 40 pp 22-23

[15] See http://news.bbc.co.uk/hi/english/static/events/panorama/transcripts/transcript_12_03_00.txt, accessed on 11 December 2015

[16] For full text of Rambouillet see http://www.commondreams.org/kosovo/rambouillet.htm, accessed 14 October 2009

[17] *Kosovo: The text of the Rambouillet Agreement*, was published as a pamphlet by *Problems of Capitalism & Socialism*, Belfast BT12 4GQ, in May 1999

[18] See https://www.tmcrew.org/news/nato/germany_usa.htm, accessed on 28 September 2016

Chapter Twelve

The myth of Gulf War 2

There was no war in the Gulf in 2003. Rather, a myth of heroic, spectacular warfare was manufactured, in large part, as a desperate measure to help provide a *raison d'être* for the (increasingly out-of-control) military-industrial complexes in the US and UK – and to hide the reality of a rout of a hopelessly overwhelmed 'enemy' army.[1] The links between mainstream journalists and the intelligence services are crucial factors in the manufacture of the myth. But it is not essentially a massive elite conspiracy. Rather, the myth's origins lie deep within complex military, historical, ideological and political forces which it is crucial to identify.

The US/UK military and political elite anticipated a rapid, new militarist-style victory against a largely manufactured enemy. The policy had been spelled out bluntly in the 1998 strategic defence review: 'Go first, go fast and go home' (Bower 2016: 311). Lord Guthrie, a former chief of defence staff, said US leaders had made it clear to him they intended to 'go in with overwhelming force and then leave': hence their failure to prepare for the consequences (Norton-Taylor 2009). As Paul Rogers commented (2006: 1): 'When the war started in March 2003, there was a high expectation that the "shock and awe" bombing tactics and a sense of liberation from most ordinary Iraqis would lead to a very rapid collapse of the regime followed by an early transition to peace and stability.' It was not to be. The disintegration of new militarism had begun.

The US/UK invasion was supposedly over Iraq's weapons of mass destruction – yet none were ever found. US/UK jets had been bombing Iraqi targets regularly since the end of the 1991 conflict (Pilger 2001). Even between 9/11 and the start of the 2003 invasion, the US dropped 606 bombs on 391 targets including a major airfield in western Iraq. So there was no clear start to the conflict. And with the president of the defeated state melting away into thin air there was no clear end. Casualties on both sides mounted as hostilities continued after the end of the so-called war. Thus the 'shock and awe' bombings of Baghdad on 20 March 2003 became the manufactured 'start' of the 'war' narrative.[2] And there were two, highly staged endings: the symbolic toppling of the Saddam statue in Firdos Square, Baghdad, before the world's media on 9 April (see Griffin 2010: 32-33) and the statement by President Bush before a gathering of US troops on the deck of USS *Abraham Lincoln*,[3] at sea just off the coast of San Diego, on 1 May, that the 'major combat operations' were over (Cottle 2006: 156). While secrecy dominated the planning and execution of the invasion, these major symbolic events were strikingly spectacular in their visibility.[4]

The 'greatest battles since World War Two' were predicted and celebrated in the press, just as during the 1991 Gulf conflict. In the *Guardian*, of 16 November 2002, Toby Dodge, an Iraq expert at Warwick University, predicted a 'long and bloody' conflict – against 375,000 Iraqi troops and 2,200 tanks (Dodge 2002). But in the event there was no real warfare: no credible enemy. In a matter of days the world's mightiest military power[5] inevitably crushed a ragtag army of conscripts and no-hopers. As defence expert John Keegan commented in the *Daily Telegraph* of 8 April 2003: 'In truth, there has been almost no check to the unimpeded onrush of the coalition, particularly the dramatic American advance to Baghdad: nor have there been any major battles. This has been a collapse, not a war.'[6] Similarly John Simpson, of the BBC, commented (2004: 307):

> It was a pushover, with no serious hitches. Often as in the first Gulf war the main danger was the Americans themselves who seemed to find it hard to distinguish between their friends and their enemies. ... Coalition forces had total command of the air. Their forces matched the Iraqis in terms of numbers, and every piece of equipment they had, from assault rifles to tanks was better designed, better maintained and more effective. The years of sanctions, the persistent air attacks, the controls on the import of weapons, had reduced Iraq's armed forces to the level of scarecrows.

AFP photographer Cris Reeves, with the US Marines, saw hardly any action at all. 'It was like two weeks of camping for me with 20-year-old Marines. I was 48 so I was exhausted' (Guillot 2003). Thomas Rid (2007: 159-160) suggested that much of the military advance on Baghdad was kept secret from journalists. For instance, attacks by Iraqi Fedayeen using pick-up trucks (known as 'technicals') on American columns led to 'one-sided slaughter' – at least from the US vantage point.

> But the embedded journalists – inexperienced in combat and unable to put the technicals' assaults into perspective – tended to report the attacks as a serious threat for the advancing US forces. What the journalists did not know was that intelligence gathering drones were able to locate the

regional headquarters of the Ba'ath Party and the Mukhabarat [Iraqi military intelligence service] based on the routes of the returning Toyota vehicles. The UAVs then provided target data to the Air Force enabling its pilots to bomb the enemy at headquarters (ibid).

According to Mark Urban, US, UK and Australian special forces crucially took over in the early part of the conflict large tracts of Iraq – as much as one-third of the country – bordering Saudi Arabia, Jordan, Syria and Turkey as part of Operation ROW. But this was all conducted in total secrecy (Urban 2011: 8-9).

On the sixth day of the advance on Baghdad a massive cloud of red and brown dust gathered over Iraq's desert and 170,000 coalition troops. The embedded reporters represented this as a grave threat to the US-led forces. In fact, the US Air Force was able to locate the Iraqis underneath the thick layer of sand using state-of-the-art satellite and reconnaissance technology and for more than 24 hours B52s, B1s and an entire range of fighter bombers slaughtered the largely defenceless Iraqis (ibid).

War is about killing. We know precisely how many Americans and British soldiers died. Some 115 US troops were killed in combat and 23 in accidents and so-called friendly-fire incidents; 19 British troops died in combat with 25 killed in 'non-hostile situations' (Beaumont and Graham 2003). The US dead included a woman, 23-year-old Army PFC Lori Ann Piestewa (Keegan 2005: 204). All of these casualties were profiled and listed in 'rolls of honour' in the mainstream press (Epstein 2003). According to John Pilger (2003), as many as 10,000 largely nameless Iraqi civilians were killed during the invasion – with up to 300,000 more injured.[7] Some US generals estimated that as many as 60,000 Iraqi soldiers had been killed (Woodward 2004: 408). But the precise figure of how many thousands of Iraqis perished, were maimed or psychologically damaged (in the lead-up to the invasion, during the invasion and the aftermath) we will never know.[8] So silence shrouds the essential horror.

Significantly, a Sky News 'exclusive' about a cruise missile launch from a Royal Navy submarine proved to be a hoax.[9] The outrageous victory claims of the Iraqi minister of information, Mohammed Saeed al-Sahhaf, (dubbed 'Comical Ali' by the Western media) as US troops captured Baghdad airport were only matched, given the scale of the slaughter, by the US/UK's fantastic claims over their supposedly precise weapons.[10] Following a March 22 grenade attack at Camp Pennsylvania in Kuwait, Reuters (along with Fox News, Associated Press and the *Washington Post*) claimed terrorists had infiltrated the camp. But later an American soldier was arrested and charged with two counts of murder and 17 counts of attempted murder.

The controversial comment of the French postmodern theorist, Jean Baudrillard (1991), about the 1991 Gulf conflict 'There was no war', appears equally relevant to the 2003 conflict. The mainstream media, in effect, manufactured the myth of war. Jack Lule (2002: 277) argues that myth is best understood as 'a societal story that expresses prevailing ideas, ideologies, values and belief'. Accordingly, a tidy narrative of quick and relatively easy 'warfare' (built around myths of national glory, macho heroism, monstrous villainy and 'precision weaponry') was manufactured in the British mainstream press while the reality was an illegal, unnecessary assertion of brute force (Mailer 2003).

THE MANUFACTURE OF THE IRAQI THREAT

The assault on Iraq was a long-term plan of the US right and Blair government. But it was only the attack of 9/11 that provided the circumstances to put the plan into action.[11] Just a few months after the atrocity, the all-party parliamentary defence committee repeated the call for a strategy of 'pre-emptive military action' with the UK 'free to deploy significant forces overseas rapidly' (Curtis 2010: 250). Curtis argues that 'the objective case for bombing Saudi Arabia and Pakistan' after 9/11 was 'incomparably greater than targeting Baghdad' (ibid: 250). He continues:

> 9/11 was to a large extent a product of long-standing Saudi and Pakistani sponsorship of radical Islamist groups. Saudi Arabia had, for nearly three decades since 1973, bankrolled a range of Islamist groups, including bin Laden, during the whole of which period Riyadh enjoyed the constant favour of London and Washington. Pakistan, meanwhile, was the creator of the Taliban-controlled Afghanistan, which produced the 9/11 attacks and other atrocities… (ibid: 251).

And Kleveman comments (2003: 7): 'In its efforts to stave off political turmoil, the corrupt regime in Riyadh funds the powerful radical Wahhabi sect that backed the Afghan Taliban and foments terror against American around the world.' Saudi Arabia's direct involvement in 9/11 remains a tightly guarded secret.[12]

But even as early as December 1998, Jonathan Powell, chief of staff to the Blair government (1997-2007), was stating in a private conversation with journalists at the *Guardian* that the government was contemplating the removal of Saddam Hussein and his henchmen. In the notes jotted down by Hugo Young, chief columnist until his death in 2003, following the meeting (and reproduced in the *Guardian* on 17 November 2008), Powell is quoted: 'The regime consists of 100 people, the inner people round Saddam who impose his terror. If you got rid of them, not saying you would have a democracy – but perhaps a process that produced a more benign reality.' In their official history of the military planning of the 2003 invasion, Gordon and Trainor show how the Bush administration were drawing up strategy documents just days after 9/11 (2007: 17-52).

In effect, the plans for an invasion of Iraq were in response to the complete failure of the strategy to remove the Saddam Hussein regime by covert means, a factor laregely ignored in the corporate media's coverage. Significantly, it was only in

December 2015 when Michael Morell, acting director of the CIA until retiring in 2013, admitted that the agency had completely failed to secure any sources inside Iraq's upper echelons before the 2003 invasion.[13]

Following the Gulf massacres of 1991, President George H. W. Bush authorised the CIA to topple Saddam Hussein. In 1996, some 120 CIA-backed former Iraqi officers were executed after the Iraqi secret service penetrated a CIA team. Two years later, congress refused to back another CIA covert plan and instead agreed $97 million in overt assistance to Iraqi opposition groups (Woodward 2004: 70). Then, as Curtis reports (2010: 234):

> In January 1999, the US designated seven Iraqi opposition groups as eligible to receive training and weapons – including SCIRI [the Supreme Council for the Islamic Revolution in Iraq], which, however, refused to accept such US assistance, presumably out of fear of collaborating too actively with Washington. The US funding would support 'a campaign of guerilla warfare' put forward by the INC [Iraqi National Council] to destabilise Saddam's regime, with SAS soldiers expected to instruct the Iraqi exiles: a further example of British forces acting as a *de facto* covert arm of the US government.

In power since 1979, Saddam Hussein by 2003 had erected a massive security apparatus (including the Iraq Special Security Organisation and the Special Republican Guard) to protect him from a coup. Only massive military action by the US could unseat him. Yet, by 2003, the Iraqi economy and society were collapsing under the weight of UN sanctions imposed following the invasion of Kuwait in 1990. As Patrick Cockburn reports (2008: 103):

> Millions of Iraqis saw their lives ruined. … The severity of the sanctions and their devastating impact on ordinary Iraqis were never understood by the outside world. They were not like past sanctions, such as those imposed on South Africa or Rhodesia as a sign of international disapproval, but were more akin to a medieval siege, a siege furthermore that lasted thirteen years. They were supposedly aimed at denying the Iraqi government access to its oil revenues, but in reality it was the mass of the population and not the political elite who were hit hardest.

Here was hardly a credible enemy.

SECRET PLANNING FOR THE IRAQ INVASION – AWAY FROM THE MEDIA GLARE

Formal Pentagon planning for the invasion of Iraq by the Pentagon, led by Army Gen. Tommy R. Franks, head of Central Command, began in November 2001, just after the fall of Kabul, Afghanistan (Ricks 2006: 32).[14] Then, in February 2002, President Bush signed a directive authorising the CIA, already running covert operations in 60 countries, to take every step to overthrow Saddam Hussein. As Bob Woodward reports (2004: 109): 'The cost was set at $200 million a year for two years. The leaders of the senate and house intelligence committees were informed secretly. After some disputes in congress the budget was cut to $189 million for the first year.'

Moreover, James Risen (2006: 70) revealed that Donald Rumsfeld, US defense secretary, had set up his own secret military units (known as 'operational support elements') which functioned beyond presidential authorisation and congressional notification:

> In fact, the Defense Department didn't seem to believe its special teams needed to tell anyone else in government what they were doing, let alone co-ordinate their activities with American ambassadors and CIA station chiefs in the countries in which they were planning to operate. Rumsfeld was creating his own private spy service, buried deep within the Pentagon's vast black budget, with little or no accountability (ibid).

Another counter-terrorism group set up secretly by Rumsfeld was the Proactive Preemptive Operations Group (P2OG) 'responsible for secret missions designed to target terrorist leaders as well as "stimulate reactions" among terrorist groups, provoking them into committing violent acts which would then expose them to "counter-attack" by US forces' (Project Censored 2003: 13).

Then, on 10 April 2002, Tony Blair told the house of commons: 'There is no doubt at all that the development of weapons of mass destruction by Saddam Hussein poses a severe threat not just to the region, but to the wider world' and, later that day, he claimed Saddam Hussein was 'a threat to his own people and to the region and, if allowed to develop these weapons, a threat to us also'.

On 3 September 2002, at a press conference in his Sedgefield constituency, he said: 'Iraq poses a real and a unique threat to the security of the region and the rest of the world.' And in his Foreword to the dossier of 24 September 2002 outlining the Saddam threat and case for military action, he described Iraq armed with weapons of mass destruction as a 'current and serious threat to the UK national interest'. He continued: 'I am in no doubt that the threat is serious and current, that he has made progress on WMD, and that he has to be stopped' (see Morrison 2005).

But while the public rhetoric of the government highlighted the supposed WMD threat, memos of private meetings suggested that the government was determined on military action – irrespective of any response by the Iraqi regime to weapons inspections. The diary entry of Blair's director of communications, Alastair Campbell, for 1 April 2002, reads: 'We discussed whether the central aim was WMD or regime change. ... TB [Tony Blair] felt it was regime change in part because of WMD but more broadly because of the threat to the region and the world' (cited in Baker 2007: 142-143).

Moreover, a memo of a meeting of Blair's inner cabal dating from 23 July 2002 (published, safely, well after the invasion in *The Sunday Times* on 1 May 2005[15]), showed the Prime Minister determined to support the US in its plans to attack Iraq. Foreign secretary Jack Straw also expressed complete faith in President Bush's war planning. He said the US would not take the momentous step of invading and occupying Iraq unless it was assured of winning (Gordon and Trainor 2007: 62). Another leak by *The Sunday Times* on 12 June 2005 quoted from a briefing paper, entitled *Iraq: Conditions for military action*, prepared by the foreign office for the meeting. This stated clearly: 'When the prime minister discussed Iraq with President Bush at Crawford in April he said that the UK would support military action to bring about regime change.' And the reported conclusion of the 23 July 2002 meeting was: 'We should work on the assumption that the UK would take part in any [US] military action.'

Those present at the meeting included the foreign secretary, Jack Straw, the defence secretary, Geoff Hoon, the attorney general, Lord Goldsmith, the chairman of the joint intelligence committee (JIC), John Scarlett, the head of MI6, Sir Richard Dearlove (aka 'C') and the chief of the defence staff, Admiral Boyce. The Prime Minister's closest political advisers, Alastair Campbell, Jonathan Powell and Sally Morgan, were also present.

The minutes of the meeting also reveal that the government did not even consider Iraq a credible military threat. The foreign secretary was quoted: 'It seemed clear that Bush had made up his mind to take military action, even if the timing was not yet decided. But the case was thin. Saddam was not threatening his neighbours, and his WMD capability was less than that of Libya, North Korea or Iran' (ibid).

The former weapons inspector, Scott Ritter, who tried constantly in the lead-up to the 2003 Iraq invasion to highlight the lies about WMD, is damning. He concludes (2005b: 91):

> We know that both the US and the UK intelligence services had, by July 2002, agreed to 'fix the intelligence around the policy'. But the fact remains that, as least as far as the CIA is concerned, the issue of 'fixing the intelligence around policy' predates July 2002, reaching as far back as 1992 when the decision was made to doctor the intelligence about Iraqi Scud missile accounting, asserting the existence of missiles in the face of UNSCOM inspection results which demonstrate that there were none.

Sir Jeremy Greenstock, British special representative at the UN from 1998 to 2003, even said that it was clear at the UN that both America and the UK knew Iraq had no weapons of mass destruction as early as 1998 (McVeigh 2016). Tyler Drumheller, head of the CIA Europe division, revealed in April 2006, that Naji Sabri, Iraq's foreign minister, had even offered to reveal Iraq's military secrets. But when policy-makers heard what he had to say – that there were no WMDs – 'they stopped being interested' (cited in Aldrich and Cormac 2016: 431). Carne Ross, a diplomat at Britain's UN mission in New York during the run-up to the Iraq invasion, also commented, in 2006, that the government never believed Saddam Hussein posed a credible threat. Ross's views were contained in secret evidence to Lord Butler's committee on the abuse of intelligence over Iraq (Norton-Taylor 2006).[16]

HOW THE PRESS HYPED THE LIES ABOUT SADDAM'S WMD

According to the dossier released by the government on 24 September 2002, the Iraqi regime could deploy WMD within just 45 minutes. Since then it has become clear that the government, with the collusion of the heads of the intelligence services, inserted this claim with the deliberate intention of hyping up the Iraqi threat and ultimately legitimising the planned invasion. Sir Richard Dearlove, then head of MI6, told the Hutton inquiry into the death of Dr David Kelly, who in conversation with the journalist Andrew Gilligan (at 6.07 am on the BBC Radio Four *Today* programme on 29 May 2003), had accused the government of 'sexing up' the WMD threat, that the 45-minute claim had come from a single Iraqi source. In July 2003, the government withdrew the claim. Margaret Beckett, who in 2003 was environment secretary, said in December 2006 that ministers had realised before the 2003 invasion that the 45-minute claim was probably wrong (Baker 2007: 112). The propaganda role of the press in promoting the 45-minute lie is significant.

On 19 September 2002, just before the dossier was published, Jonathan Powell, Blair's chief of staff, sent an email to Alastair Campbell and John Scarlett, chair of the joint intelligence chiefs, containing this sentence (ibid: 117): 'Alistair – what will be the headline in the *Standard* on the day of publication? What do we want it to be?' In the event, the front page headline in London *Evening Standard*'s second edition that day, screamed: '45 minutes from attack – dossier reveals Saddam is ready to launch chemical war strikes.' Its first paragraph read: 'Saddam Hussein's armoury of chemical weapons is on standby for use within 45 minutes, the government's dossier on Iraq revealed today. He is developing missiles that could reach British military bases in Cyprus.'[17] The *Sun*, the next day, headlined: 'Brits 45 mins from doom.' While the *Star*'s headline read: 'Mad Saddam ready to attack: 45 minutes from a chemical war.'[18] Lance Price (2010: 364-365) records the response of the press to the September dossier in his study of the relations between Prime Ministers and the media over the last century:

> Alastair Campbell had every reason to be pleased with the initial reaction of the media. With the exception of the *Mirror* and the *Independent*, which would remain the only papers to oppose the war, the rest of the press was supportive. *The Times* and the *Guardian* went beyond anything in the dossier to claim that Saddam's agents were scouring Africa in search of uranium to build a nuclear bomb. It is unlikely that either paper did so without first putting in a call to Downing Street.

Significantly, in July 2011, in secret evidence to the Chilcot inquiry into the events leading to the UK's involvement in the 2003 invasion of Iraq, a senior MI6 officer (code name SIS2) accused Alastair Campbell of being like an 'unguided missile' in his leaking of dubious information to the gullible media. 'From the outset we had concerns. I think he suffered from his propensity to have rushes of blood to the head and pass various stories and information to journalists without appropriate prior consultation' (Brown and Edwards 2011).

In January 2003, the government produced another dossier: *Iraq: Its infrasture of concealment, deception and intimidation*. Once again it received largely favourable coverage. But this was not to last. Within a week of its publication, Channel Four News, basing its report on research by Cambridge University lecturer Dr Glen Rangwala, revealed that much of it had been lifted from a 12-year-old postgraduate dissertation on the internet – and it was dubbed the 'dodgy dossier' (Todd, Bloch and Fitzgerald 2009: 63).[19]

Following Dr Kelly's death in mysterious circumstances in July 2003, journalists were again used by the government to smear him. The Prime Minister's press spokesman, Tom Kelly (no relation), at an unattributable briefing with a small group of journalists, described him as a Walter Mitty character who may have contributed to his own downfall. Most of the journalists present obliged – though the *Independent's* Paul Waugh broke away from the pack and revealed the source (Baker 2007: 185).

Moreover, after Tony Blair made his final appeal in parliament for military action against Iraq on 18 March 2003, Campbell was able to boast: 'This got the best press he had had for ages.' Even the *Independent*, up until then the most critical of the rush to war, argued that 'it was the most persuasive call yet made by the man who has emerged as the most formidable persuader for war on either side of the Atlantic' (Price op cit: 367).[20]

Critics of the WMD claims, such as Scott Ritter and Rolf Ekeus, UNSCOM's executive chairman, were marginalised in the press. Edwards and Cromwell report (2004: 213) that on the *Guardian/Observer* website, Iraq was mentioned in 7,118 articles between 1 January and 6 June 2003 with 961 articles mentioning 'Iraq and weapons of mass destruction'.

> Out of these, Scott Ritter has received twelve mentions and Rof Ekeus two. The *Independent's* website records 5,872 articles mentioning Iraq, with 931 mentions of 'Iraq and weapons of mass destruction'. Ritter records 24 mentions. Ekeus four (ibid).

HOW DUBIOUS INTELLIGENCE SOURCES HYPED UP TERRORIST THREATS

Even before 9/11, the mainstream press were full of intelligence-based reports, hyping up the 'terrorist' threat. For instance, on 30 July 2000, Christina Lamb, in the *Sunday Telegraph*, had a front page report which claimed that Iraqi President

Saddam Hussein had sent belly dancing assassins to London to murder his opponents there. Lamb sourced her report to 'a Foreign Office official'.[21]

But then, following the 11 September atrocities in the United States, the London-based mainstream media were awash with intelligence-inspired leaks stressing the dangers of terrorist attacks in Britain.

Even the *Independent,* most critical of the US/UK rush to military action, gave credibility to dubious 'intelligence' sources. On 16 September 2001, for instance, Paul Lashmar and Chris Blackhurst reported that at least three terrorist cells linked to Osama bin Laden were at large in Britain. An 'intelligence source' was quoted as saying: 'There is no reason why what happened in America couldn't happen in Britain or any European country.' But how much is fiction? (Bright 2002). On 14 October 2001, the *Observer*'s front page carried this headline: 'US hawks accuse Iraq over anthrax.' It was all disinformation, fed to the newspaper by US intelligence (Pilger 2002: 146). In a later feature headlined: 'The Iraqi connection', the *Observer* used unnamed 'intelligence sources' to link Iraq with 9/11. Again, all lies (ibid).

Similarly, in September 2002 the *Daily Express* was awash in intelligence-inspired scare stories. 'Nuclear attack in just months' it thundered on 9 September; 'Anthrax threat on our streets: Britain on alert for Saddam suicide squads' it reported the next day. A climate of fear is manufactured allowing the apparatus of the national security state (surveillance cameras, email snooping, arrest without trials, demonisation of asylum seekers) to expand. On 15 September 2002, drawing on intelligence disinformation linking Iraq to nuclear weapons, the *Sunday Express* editorialised: 'War brings evil but we believe the country must not be frightened from doing what we pray will save the world from the greater evil of nuclear bombs. We see no alternative but to help demolish the Iraqi regime.'

The most significant 'evidence' linking Iraq to 9/11 was the alleged meeting between Mohamed Atta, the terrorists' leader, and an Iraqi intelligence agent in the Czech republic. John Pilger (2002: 148) comments: 'In the British press, the intelligence agent was promoted from being "low level" (the *Guardian*) to "mid-ranking" (*Independent*) to "senior" (*Financial Times*) to the "head of Baghdad's intelligence services" (*Times*). Only the *FT* questioned whether the "meeting" took place at all, or had anything to do with the destruction of the Twin Towers.'

On 18 March 2003, before the major air assault on Baghdad began, the *Sun* typically reported: 'According to intelligence reports Republican Guard units have been equipped with chemical warfare shells to make a desperate last stand south of Baghdad. A source said: "They clearly have given some chemical capability to some forces."' On 2 April, the *Sun* 'revealed' that Saddam Hussein had issued a coded chemical attack on US/UK troops. Coalition intelligence chiefs, it reported, interpreted a reference to 'catching breath' in a speech by Saddam Hussein 'as a signal for lethal chemicals or nerve gas to be unleashed against US forces massing south west of Baghdad'. There were similar reports throughout the mainstream press.

THE CRUCIAL ROLE OF EMBEDDED JOURNALISTS IN THE MANUFACTURE OF THE 'WAR' MYTH

Most of US/UK imperialism advances essentially in secret. Both countries have deployed forces virtually every year since 1945 – most of them away from the glare of the media (Peak 1992). But at various moments the US/UK chose to fight overt, manufactured 'wars'. We, the viewers and readers, have to see the spectacle. It has to appear 'real'. During the first Gulf 'war', the pooling system was used to keep correspondents away from the action (McLaughlin 2002: 88-93). And since most of the action was conducted over the 42 days from the air, with journalists denied access to planes, the reality of the horror was kept secret.

In contrast, during the 2003 conflict, journalists were given remarkable access to the 'frontlines'. And those frontline images and reports from journalists who were clearly risking their lives, aimed to seduce the viewer/reader with their facticity; the correspondents were amazed at their 'objectivity'. Yet beyond the view of the camera and the journalist's eye-witness, with the war unproblematised, the essential simulated, mythical nature of the conflict lay all the more subtly and effectively hidden. Moreover, military censorship regimes always serve essentially symbolic purposes – expressing the arbitrary power of the army over the conduct and representation of 'war'.

Significantly, defence minister Geoff Hoon claimed: 'I think the coverage … is more graphic, more real than any other coverage we have ever seen of a conflict' (Keeble 2003b). The chairman of the joint chiefs, Air Force General Richard Myers, commented that the embedding system 'may over time get us away from some of the cynicism that has developed' in terms of how the news media view the military (Seib 2004: 70). Andrew Hoskins (2004: 60) highlights the way in which the embeds themselves became heroes of the war 'movie':

> There was a real sense of purpose and destination conveyed in these literally rolling live broadcasts, somewhat reminiscent of road movies, with the adventure and camaraderie of travel on the open highway. Moreover, it was the occasional plume of smoke or passing twisted wreckage that offered mere diversions, as the central characters in the movie were the embeds themselves. It was their journey and their story.

Hoskins argues that many of the embeds' reports were 'excessively cinematic' in their descriptions, evoking Hollywood and the Wild West 'and constantly contributed little to the understanding of the broader war' (ibid: 64). War often blurred travel writing and news reporting into what John Urry (2002) has defined as the 'tourist gaze'. Moreover, this transformation of war reporting into touristic entertainment serves to silence the real horror of the conflict.

Most of the critical mainstream coverage highlighted the information overload. But, as David Miller (2003) commented: 'It is certainly true to say that it is new to see footage of war so up-close but it is a key part of the propaganda war to claim that this makes it "real".'

Both US and UK governments attempted to pressurise journalists into quitting Baghdad before the invasion. As a result, the four main US TV networks – CBS, NBC, ABC and Fox – all pulled out. Tim Gopsill reports (2004: 253): 'The Cable News Network (CNN), which had built its reputation on Peter Arnett's dramatic reports from Baghdad in 1991, stayed on but was soon kicked out by the Iraqis.' Of the UK media, only *The Times* and *Daily Telegraph* withdrew (ibid). In the end, some 128 UK journalists, including journalists from the *Western Daily Press*, *Scotsman*, *Manchester Evening News*, *Ipswich Evening Star* and *Eastern Daily Press*, and one from the music network MTV, were 'embedded' with military units. According to Phillip Knightley (2003c):

> The idea was copied from the British system in World War 1 when six correspondents embedded with the army on the Western front produced the worst reporting of just about any war and were all knighted for their services. One of them, Sir Philip Gibbs, had the honesty, when the war was over, to write: 'We identified ourselves absolutely with the armies in the field.' The modern embeds, too, soon lost all distinction between warrior and correspondent and wrote and talked about 'we' with boring repetition.

For instance, Jamie Wilson, reporting from HMS *Marlborough*, pointed out: 'It is undoubtedly much harder for journalists to be impartial when they are living with and have grown to like the people they are writing about. They treated me well and I guess that was always in the back of my mind when I was writing about them' (cited in Hoskins op cit: 51).

US military strategy divided the task into four 'fronts' – political, military, intelligence and media. Thus, according to Danny Schechter (2004: 26): 'The Fourth Estate was thus seen as the Fourth Front.' He continued: 'The war itself was treated as a product to be launched and rolled out. A compliant media constantly briefed, selectively leaked to and [given] pre-developed messages known as the "line of the day".' According to Phillip Knightley, 'more than any other conflict in history', the current war against terrorism 'is a war for information and its suppression' (2003b: 254). On the Pentagon's growing fondness for military discipline called 'Information Operations', Knightley continued:

> Ten groups together function to cover areas ranging from public affairs (PA) to military deception and psychological operations (psyops). In practice, what this means is that those military people whose job traditionally has been to talk to the media and divulge what they are able to say about conflicts now work hand in glove with those whose job it is to support battlefield operations with misinformation. In short, the media risks becoming an unknowing pawn in military strategy (ibid).

The Times media commentator, Brian MacArthur, reported (2003a): 'Embeds inevitably became adjuncts to the forces.' As Chris Ayres, in his humorous debunking of the myth of the super-macho war journalist, said, he suddenly realised one day while embedded with the Marines 'the true genius of the scheme' (2005: 242): '…it had turned me into a Marine. I was thinking like a fighter, not a reporter. And yet I wasn't a fighter. I was an idiot in a blue flak jacket. The Marines didn't even want me there. Being an embed, it seemed, was the loneliest job on earth.'

An analysis commissioned by the ministry of defence of newspaper content produced by embeds found that 90 per cent of their reports were 'either positive or neutral' (Miller 2004). Lewis et al. (2006: 184-194) argue that embedding was particularly useful in the coalition's media management strategy since it meant reporting was more focused on the 'war' and its day-to-day progress than otherwise would have been the case. Audrey Gillan, with the Household Cavalry for the *Guardian*, was one of the few to accuse the military of censorship. She reported that soldiers complained of being like mushrooms – kept in the dark with you know what shovelled on top of them – but she could not use this phrase for fear of upsetting the brigade HQ. Later, Gillan told Roy Greenslade: 'It was irritating but I still saw it as a positive experience. I got good access and I did discover what it's like being a soldier – the boredom, the fear, the awful conditions' (Greenslade 2003).[22]

According to Philip Seib (2004: 53), there were 775 embedded journalists (though 900 places were offered): 70 per cent were from US national media;[23] 10 per cent with US local media, 20 per cent were international; including the 128 British journalists; 85 (11 per cent) were women. By 2 May, one day after President Bush's 'victory' speech, the number of embeds had dwindled to just 108 (Rid 2007: 171). Only 19 per cent of the embeds had previously served in the military (ibid: 150). In all, 153 reporters were embedded with UK forces.[24] Amongst the wire services Reuters, Associated Press and Agence France Presse were given the largest number of slots while Knight Ridder and United Press International were given fewer. The highest number of journalists with the troops at any one time was 600 from 250 news organisations. The invitations, sent out on 11 February 2003, incorporated army 352 slots; 214 Marines 214; 124 navy; 71 air force 71; and 15 special operations.

In total, some 5,000 journalists were in the Gulf region to cover the hostilities. Two thousand were in Kuwait and on ships with the US and UK naval task forces in the Arabian Gulf; 290 were in Baghdad; 900 in Northern Iraq with Kurdish fighters: the rest were in Jordan, Iran, Bahrain and at the Allied Central Command in Doha, Qatar (Milmo 2003). Here there was little consistent challenge to the dominant military agenda. As Phillip Knightley commented (2003a [1975]: 536): 'Stories were floated, picked up, exaggerated, confirmed and then turned out to be wrong.' An uprising was reported in Basra though it never happened. Then it was secured – though this only happened 17 days later. Saddam Hussein had been killed, Tariq Aziz, Iraq's foreign minister, had defected: both reports were untrue.

On one occasion *New York* magazine writer Michael Wolff (2003) dared to break ranks and ask the provocative question: 'Why are we here? Why should we stay? What's the value of what we're learning at this million-dollar press center?' He was soon to pay the price for his daring. Fox TV attacked him for lacking patriotism and after right-wing commentator Rush Limbaugh gave out his email address, one day Wolff received 3,000 hate messages.

The secretary to the defence advisory committee reported that 'despite the hundreds of embedded journalists and unilaterals in theatre there had not been a single breach of security by any part of the UK media. The system and the advice in the five standing DA-Notices had proved entirely adequate and as able to fulfil their role in such operations as in other conflicts and in peace'.[25]

The access to the frontline afforded the embeds meant that reports on the 'fighting' dominated coverage – in both the press and television. Robinson, Goddard, Parry, Murray with Taylor (2010: 82-84) found that almost half of the conflict reports focused on 'battle'. This meant that relatively little coverage was given to other important aspects of the war. 'For example, subjects such as protest, the rationale for war and public opinion, each of which might have generated critical coverage, were significant elements in fewer that one in twenty stories in either medium' (ibid: 83). Based on the analysis of a massive newspaper database, the research team concluded that 'the process of embedding helped to shape reporting of the war in favour of the coalition' (ibid: 99).

Phillip Knightley commented (2003a [1975]: 532): 'I was able to find only two instances of embedded correspondents who reported critically on the behaviour of US troops they were embedded with and which went against the official account of what had occurred.' On 31 March, US soldiers opened fire on a civilian van which had failed to stop at a checkpoint and killed seven women and children. US officials said the driver of the car failed to stop after warning shots and that troops had fired at the car 'as a last resort'. That version was challenged by William Branigin in the *Washington Post* and Mark Franchetti in *The Sunday Times*, London.

But support for the embeds came from Bob Schieffer, a reporter for *Forth Worth Star-Telegram* and later CBS news chief Washington correspondent. He said (Sylvester and Huffman 2005: 23): 'I think putting reporters with the military gave the reporters a better chance of coming to know the military and I dare say it gave the military a chance to have a better understanding of what the press does. So I think it was good for both sides.' And Douglas Kellner (2004) had some praise for the embeds: they 'provided documentation of the more raw and brutal aspects of war and likewise gave telling accounts that often put into question official version of events, namely bringing to light propaganda and military spin'. But he concluded: '...on the whole, embedded journalists were largely propagandists who often outdid the Pentagon and Bush administration in spinning the message of the moment'.[26]

Many non-embedded journalists covered the conflict from the US, high-tech communications headquarters in Qatar (significantly designed by a Hollywood art director who had previously worked with David Blaine, the illusionist). As Graham Spencer (2005: 158-159) comments:

> This carefully controlled and choreographed environment produced round-the-clock information which effectively minimised any oppositional reports emerging and was used to restrict the scope for journalistic interpretations which departed from military lines. By filling airtime with propaganda, the Bush administration and the military succeeded in keeping Iraqi reports from infiltrating coverage and thus helped to maintain the illusion that the war was progressing in much the same way as a Hollywood cinematic experience, with America fulfilling its mythic role as a civilizing force bringing freedom to those subject to barbarism.

EMBEDS SO CRUCIAL IN THE 'INFORMATION BATTLE'

Operation Iraqi Freedom's information campaign was designed in the Pentagon, with 2m. employees worldwide, the world's largest employer (Wal Mart coming second with 1.3m. employees). The strategic picture of the conflict was presented to the international press at briefings in the Pentagon and White House, the operational briefings were held at Central Command's HQ in Doha, Qatar, while the frontline view was provided by reporters embedded with the troops (Rid op cit: 151-152).

According to Jamie Shea, Nato's spokesman during the Kosovo conflict and later director of policy planning for Nato's secretary general, the military had learned important lessons from their mistakes in 1999 (Jones 2009). A story line was constructed which aimed to keep journalists 'as busy as possible'. Keeping journalists occupied was the priority; feeding them constant briefings 'so they don't have much time to go off and find out information for themselves'. Media handlers realised that embedded journalists liked to put on battle fatigues suggesting they were 'part of the action'. Regular press tours to theatre coupled with access to privileged interviews were other priorities. But the military had to make sure the journalists were 'flown home before they have time to look around' for themselves in operations such as Iraq.

In the new media environment – with global television networks, mobile devices, email, online newspapers and blogs – reporters became essential partners with the military in the assault on Iraq. As Thomas Rid (op cit: 181) argues:

> From the military's perspective, the news media could now be used to get better coverage for one's service at home, potentially shield the soldiers against political criticism, to counter enemy disinformation, and even to put psychological pressure on the adversary. From the media's view, the military had finally allowed front-line access and abolished censorship.

279

The commander's objective, winning the war, and the reporter's objective, winning the Pulitzer Prize, ceased to be irreconcilable – at least temporarily and on a tactical level.

Independent reporter Patrick Cockburn is also critical of 'embedding'. He argues that it leads reporters to see conflicts 'primarily in military terms, while the most important developments are political or, if they are military, may have little to do with foreign forces' (Cockburn 2010).

TARGETING JOURNALISTS

Unprecedented access to the 'front lines' was the carrot, but the stick was always on hand. Fifteen non-Iraqi journalists were killed, two went missing and many unilateral non-embeds were intimidated by the military.[27] Had there been the same death rate for journalists during the Vietnam war, there would have been 3,000 killed.[28] As John Donvan (2003) argued, 'coalition forces saw unilaterals as having no business on their battlefield'. Significantly, those embedded with US troops were asked to sign a document which specified that journalists, their relatives and their employers could not hold the government responsible for injury or loss of life, and that the government 'may terminate the embedding process at any time and for any reason, as the government determines appropriate in its sole discretion'. Michael Massing (2003), in the war zone to monitor the fighting for the Committee to Protect Journalists, said 'the US military believed that only reporters who were officially embedded had the right to protection. Everyone else was at risk – and expendable'.

Translator Kamaran Abdurrazak Mohammed travelling with the BBC's John Simpson in Kurdistan was killed in a US attack. Simpson later commented: 'The independent journalists are upholding a great journalistic tradition but, my goodness, they're taking a hammering. The system that allows this to happen, even encourages this to happen, is stupid and despicable' (cited in Gopsill 2014: 256). Unilateral Terry Lloyd, of ITN, was killed by Marines who fired at his car; French cameraman Fred Nerac and Lebanese translator Hussein Osman were also believed to have been caught in the crossfire but their remains were never found. Stewart Purvis, former chief executive of ITN, told an Oxford inquest in October 2006 that the military had been obstructive when investigations into Lloyd's death began. No official reports had been made available to Lloyd's side.[29] Ukrainian Reuters camera operator Tara Protsyuk and Jose Couso, a cameraman for the Spanish TV channel Telecino, died after an American tank fired at the 15th floor of the Palestine Hotel in Baghdad while Tayek Ayyoub, a cameraman for al-Jazeera, died after a US jet bombed the channel's Baghdad office. In February 2003, al-Jazeera had given the Pentagon the actual co-ordinates of its office in an attempt to avoid being targeted by the US military following the November 2001 attack on its Kabul office. But the network was still hit again.

Investigations into the attack on the Palestine Hotel, Baghdad, were complicated after the Spanish government made an official statement about the death of Jose Couso. The defence minister, Frederico Trillo, announced that the coalition had actually declared the hotel a military objective 48 hours before it was attacked and that the correspondetns should have left. But a 2003 report by Committee to Protect Journalists, *Permission to fire*, blamed the US army for a breakdown in communication with the media and claimed the attack on the Palestine Hotel could have been avoided. And an investigation by the US military, released in November 2004, failed to explain why troops were not made aware the hotel was widely used by journalists (Tomlin 2008).

Two journalists working for RTP Portuguese television, Luis Castro and Victor Silva, were held for four days, had their equipment, vehicle and video tapes confiscated and were then escorted out of Iraq by the 101st Airborne Division. Castro told *Arab News*: 'I have covered 10 wars in the past six years – in Angola, Afghanistan, Zaire, and East Timor. I have been arrested three times in Africa, but have never been subjected to such treatment or been physically beaten before.'[30] Fox News' star reporter Geraldo Rivera failed to get into northern Iraq; was eventually embedded with American forces in the south but was thrown out for revealing the position of the forces he was with. In all, during the war, 35 members of the news media, about a dozen of whom were embedded, were asked to leave or were escorted out of the war zone by US authorities (Seib 2004: 52).

According to John Simpson (2004), however, British forces were not to blame for any serious attacks on journalists. A cameraman from al-Jazeera TV, Akil Abdul-Amir, came under fire from British artillery while they were filming the shelling of food warehouses west of Basra. Simpson added (ibid: 359): 'This is, however, the only incident I have come across where British forces attacked journalists.' How many Iraqi journalists perished in the slaughters we will never know. For the most of the Western mainstream media they are non-people.[31]

On 26 March, the seventh day of the conflict, a joint US/UK bombing mission did, indeed, attack the Iraqi television station maintaining that it was part of a 'commandand control centre'. The television centre was in a residential area and several civilians were killed. The International Press Institute declared the attack was a violation of the Geneva Convention and Universal Declaration of Human Rights; Amnesty questioned whether it constituted a war crime (ibid: 324).

Both sides engaged in considerable further harassment of journalists. According to a survey by the International Federation of Journalists, at least 19 journalists were detained, some also beaten, by the Iraqi authorities and seven were expelled (Gospill 2004: 258).

> At least ten were shot at or otherwise attacked by Iraqi forces or irregulars, and several were beaten and robbed in Baghdad and other cities. As for the coalition, British officers three times banned al Jazeera from reporting

from Basra, and US forces detained and badly mistreated two journalists –
one Portuguese and one Israeli – accusing them of spying (ibid).

THE NATURE OF THE FLEET STREET CONSENSUS

For the 1991 conflict all Fleet Street newspapers backed the military response
together with 95 per cent of columnists. For the 1993 and 1998 attacks on Iraq
the consensus fractured with the *Guardian, Independent* and *Express* coming out
against the attacks. Then for the Nato attacks on Serbia in 1999 virtually all of
Fleet Street backed the action, even calling for the deployment of ground troops
(which not even the generals dared adopt as policy). There was one exception – the
Independent on Sunday – and its editor, Kim Fletcher, left the paper just weeks after
the end of the conflict. But there was far more debate amongst columnists. A survey
I conducted showed 33 out of 99 prominent columnists opposed military action
against Serbia. For the attacks on Afghanistan and the toppling of the Taliban, the
whole of Fleet Street backed the action – but again there was a wide-ranging debate
amongst columnists and letter writers (Keeble 2001b).

In 2003, with significant opposition to the rush to war being expressed by
politicians, lawyers, intelligence agents, celebrities, religious leaders, charities and
human rights campaigners – together with massive street protests – both nationally
and internationally,[32] the breakdown in Fleet Street's consensus was inevitable. As
Tom Bower (2016: 295) reports on the PM's on the eve of the conflict: 'Blair's
position was unprecedented. No other British prime minister had planned to
start a war while distrusting his chief of defence, the permanent secretary at the
MoD, the cabinet secretary, the foreign minister, the defence secretary and most
of his cabinet ministers.'[33] Significantly an International Gallup Poll in December
2002 found virtually no support for Washington's announced plans for war in Iraq
carried out 'unilaterally' by America and its allies (in effect, the Anglo-American
coalition) (Ismael and Ismael 2004: 7). Yet still for the invasion of Iraq, the vast
bulk of Fleet Street backed the action (though columnists and letter writers were
divided). The *Independents*, carrying prominently the dissident views of foreign
correspondent Robert Fisk, were the most hostile. Following the massive global
street protests on 15 February, the *Independent on Sunday* editorialised: 'Millions
show this is a war that mustn't happen.'

The *Guardian* did not criticise military action on principle but opposed the US/
UK rush to war and promoted a wide range of critical opinions. The *Mirrors* were
also 'anti' in the run-up to the conflict (perhaps more for marketing reasons since
the Murdoch press was always going to be firmly for the invasion) with the veteran
dissident campaigning journalists John Pilger and Paul Foot given prominent
coverage. As early as 20 December 2002, the *Mirror's* front page headlined: 'There
is a lunatic with weapons of mass destruction "ramping up" for a war that will
imperil the whole world: Stop Him' accompanied by a photograph of President

Bush. On 18 March, the *Mirror*'s front page headline thundered: 'Unlawful, Unethical, Unstoppable' (though it stressed it continued to 'back our forces') while on 20 March 2003, it editorialised: 'Now is not the time to dwell on the insanity of it all. The *Daily Mirror*'s view of this conflict could not be clearer – we believe it is wrong, wrong, wrong.' Four days later, its front page carried a photograph of an Iraqi child with horrific burns and of a captured American soldier being paraded on Iraqi TV – and the striking headline: 'Still anti-war? Yes, bloody right we are.' On 22 March, it went so far as to headline on its front page (above a stark image of the Iraqi capital ablaze): 'Shocking and awful: America's shameful "Shock and Awe" attack on Baghdad last night.' Inside, the editorial commented bluntly: 'The live TV footage of the bombardment of Baghdad last night was sickening to watch and hear. For those who are opposed to this war, it was hideous confirmation of our worst fears.'

But then, after editor in chief Piers Morgan claimed his paper's stance attracted thousands of protesting letters from readers, their opposition softened. And the *Mail*s managed to stand on the fence mixing both criticism of the rush to military action with fervent patriotic support for the troops during the conflict. In his detailed analysis of the *Mirror*'s coverage of the Iraq conflict, Des Freedman concluded astutely (2003: 107):

> Although the *Mirror* was initially keen to express the overwhelming anti-war sentiment in the UK, when military action started and opinion polls revealed a more ambivalent attitude towards the war amongst both its own readers and the general public, the *Mirror* was less willing to be identified with what it saw as minority views. Constrained by a 'responsibility' towards the bottom line, the paper was unable to maintain a consistent opposition towards the war and was forced to 'ameliorate' its coverage. Such is the logic of the newspaper business.

THE DEMONISATION OF 'SADDAM'

The media's focus on the 'monstrous', 'evil', global power of Saddam Hussein had since 1990 been an essential ingredient of the propaganda strategy to manufacture the credible enemy. The Iraqi President has clearly been an appalling dictator – as critics have been stressing since the 1970s (though the CIA played significant roles in the two coups that brought Hussein's Ba'athists to power in 1963 and 1968). But in the 1980s, when Iraq was closely allied to the West during its eight-year war with Iran, Fleet Street's coverage of Hussein was rare and generally positive. Even the reporting of the chemical bombing of Kurds in Halabja on 16 March 1988 was notable for its restraint. And the Iranians, not 'Saddam', were blamed.

The demonisation of 'new Hitler', 'madman', 'monster' Saddam, the 'butcher of Baghdad' only began in earnest following the Iraqi invasion of Kuwait in August 1990. And this hyper-personalisation of the conflict became a constant feature of the press coverage – even in newspapers critical of the US attacks of 1993, 1996, 1998 and 2003. It served to simplify an enormously complex history and direct all blame at one man (Keeble 1998; 2000a).

By 2003, Iraq was a completely dysfunctional state, destroyed following more than a decade of UN sanctions and constant weekly bombings by US/UK – hardly covered in the mainstream media – and with a profoundly unpopular regime. Thus, the focus on the demonised personality of 'Saddam' throughout the media was all the more important in the creation of the war myth. On 19 March, as Iraqis prepared to defend Baghdad, the *Sun* reported on Saddam Hussein: 'Fiend to unleash poisons.' Another report described him as a 'monster'. On the same day, in the London *Evening Standard*, a profile of Saddam Hussein by Said Aburish (2003) highlighted his alleged madness, 'uncontrolled behaviour' and 'belief in his own divinity'. The following day the *Sun* reported Lt Tim Collins calling for 'Our Boys to "rock the world" of Saddam's evil diehards'. Saddam was planning to poison Iraq's water system 'as a last act of savagery'. On 25 March, the *Sun's* front page headline ran: 'Saddam's last stand: 450 tanks, 60,000 men, one target.' In the *Daily Star* of 28 March, the Iraqi President was described as 'an evil dictator', a 'brutal tyrant' while an unnamed military source is quoted as saying: 'There appear no depths to which Hussein will not stoop.'

As the US troops approached Baghdad, on 4 April, the *Mirror* framed its coverage entirely around the personality of 'tyrant' Saddam. 'What will he do?' asked its front page headline. 'As US troops reach Baghdad, the world waits for Saddam to play his final, despotic card.' Significantly, the *Mail's* logo for its coverage of the conflict was 'War on Saddam'. On 30 March, the *Sunday Telegraph* editorialised, highlighting his unique barbarism: 'Saddam's record means that the coalition forces must be ready for anything. This, after all, is a dictator who planned during the last Gulf War to chain American PoWs to the front of his tanks; a murderer who – uniquely in the history of depravity – has turned chemical weapons on his own people.'

On 20 March, Julian Borger, in the *Guardian*, grappled with the contradictions. On the one hand, he reported: 'In terms of technology and sheer might, this coming conflict is likely to be one of the most unequal in history.' Yet, to reaffirm the myth of war, there is always the Saddam demonisation card to play. So Borger continued: 'But the Iraqi leader's proven readiness to embrace desperate and unconventional measures makes him potentially a far more dangerous foe than any the Pentagon has taken on in recent years.'

Significantly, the *Observer*, in outlining its support for military action in its leader of 19 January, framed its entire argument around the demonised personality of 'Saddam'. Firstly, it referred to the 'nature of Saddam Hussein's regime and the call by many Iraqi exiles and dissidents for him to be overthrown'. The war was not about oil. 'For the second motive for displacing Saddam is the danger he poses to the wider world.' And it concluded: '…if Saddam does not yield military action may eventually be the least awful necessity for Iraq.' Significantly, the *Observer* rejected reports by Ed Vulliamy on seven occasions up to March 2003 based on the comments of CIA analysts that the Iraqi regime did not have any weapons of mass destruction (Hewitt and Lucas 2009: 111).

Accompanying the demonisation of 'Saddam' was the representation of Iraqi soldiers as 'monsters', 'savages' etc. For instance, on 24 March 2003, the *Sun* carried the front page headline 'At mercy of savages' over a report of 'terrified US troops captured and paraded on TV by cruel Iraqis'. Inside, the editorial (headlined 'Monstrous, obscene, barbaric, horrific') took the opportunity to compare the savagery of the Iraqis with the humanity of the allied troops:

> The dead and captured were not even front-line fighting troops but reservists ambushed as they delivered water and supplies. Contrast this barbarism with the way the allies treat injured and captured soldiers. We have provided first-aid on the battlefield and flown casualties to our own hospital ships for treatment. … Our troops are under the clearest orders to treat all Iraqis with human consideration.[34]

Even after the toppling of Saddam, the media were used by the intelligence services to spread reports linking the Iraqi regime to the 9/11 attacks. For example, a fraudulent letter, allegedly created by the CIA at the behest of the Bush administration, pushing these lies, was presented as a legitimate document in a report for the *Daily Telegraph*, on 13 December 2003.[35]

THE MANUFACTURE OF THE PRECISE, CLEAN, HUMANITARIAN WAR

Central to the manufacture of the war myth is its representation as clean, precise and humanitarian. All of the US/UK overt major military interventions since Vietnam up until 2003 had been largely risk-free, taking less than 1,000 US troops' lives. All resulted in appalling casualties amongst 'enemy' civilians and soldiers. Yet the propaganda – in Orwellian/doublethink style – constantly stressed the precision of the weapons and claimed the raids were for peaceful purposes: to introduce democracy and freedom. Casualty figures were always covered up (or dubbed in the militaryspeak 'collateral damage').

During the 2003 invasion of Iraq, the press constantly reaffirmed this same propaganda stress on precision, yet reached new heights of exaggeration. As John Pilger (2004b) reported, according to the non-governmental organisation Medact, between 21,700 and 55,000 Iraqis died between 20 March and 20 October 2003. Deaths and injury from unexploded cluster bombs were put at 1,000 a month. And Pilger added: 'These are conservative estimates: the ripples of trauma throughout the society cannot be imagined.' The conflict also created massive unemployment, a health crisis in the country – with one in 25 Iraqis displaced from their homes.[36]

But as the *Sun* of 20 March reported beneath the headline: 'The first "clean" war': 'A senior defence source said last night: "Great attention to precision-guided weapons means we could have a war with zero casualties. We are a lot closer towards that ideal. We may be entering an era where it is possible to prosecute a humanitarian war."' In effect, could not the military's rhetoric about precision and smart weapons have betrayed its ultimate ambition – to destroy war itself?

Even the *Guardian*, one of the most critical of the US/UK rush to invade Iraq, reported on 19 March: 'The last Gulf war may have marked the introduction of space age weapons – from laser-guided bombs to cruise missiles smart enough to know which set of Baghdad traffic lights to turn left at – but as collateral damage figures later proved, the technologies were still largely in their infancy.' Owen Boycott had earlier reported for the same newspaper on 15 March 2003 (Bowcott 2003):

> Last time round RAF munitions were 10 per cent laser-guided 'smart' bombs and 90 per cent conventional devices. This time it will be the other way round: 90 per cent smart and 10 per cent dumb. Since Kosovo, when bad weather prevented air sorties from dropping their payloads, the RAF has invested in satellite-guided systems which can in effect see through clouds.

Following the Ameriyya shelter bombing by an American Stealth jet during the Gulf massacres of 1991 (when hundreds of Iraqi women and children perished) most of Fleet Street blamed 'Saddam', described it as a propaganda coup for the Iraqi leader or claimed it was inevitable (Keeble 1997: 166-172). All of this was part of a strategy to deflect blame for the atrocity away from its perpetrators. Similar strategies appeared during the 2003 invasion. For instance, after a bomb fell on a Baghdad market on 26 March most of Fleet Street followed the military agenda and questioned whether the Iraqis (incredibly) had fired the missile. In the *Mail* of 27 March, the headline focused on 'the propaganda coup Saddam had hoped for' while correspondent Ross Benton reported: 'It was the first major incident of "collateral damage" since the war began but allied officials said they could not confirm that the bombs were dropped by US or British warplanes.' The *Sun* on the same day headlined 'Who's to blame?' and reported: '... if the market blasts were caused by off-target Allied bombs, it will be a propaganda gift to Saddam.' The *Guardian*, alongside a moving eye-witness account by reporter Suzanne Goldenberg of the aftermath of the bombings, highlighted US 'confusion over blame for raid'. But the *Mirror*, fiercely anti-war at the time, discounted US denials and condemned it as 'the worst civilian outrage since the war began a week ago'. No paper listed nor profiled the 14 Iraqis reported killed: they were the nameless victims of the carnage.

Even in those newspapers critical of the US/UK invasion, the dominant images reflected the military agenda of marginalising the reality of the slaughter. For instance, a special issue of the *Independent Review* of 9 April 2003 was devoted to images from the conflict. But out of 14 photographs, just three focused on Iraqi casualties while another showed blurred images of bodies on a road after a 'friendly fire' attack on a convoy of US and Kurdish forces. The pro-Blair *Times'* Section 2 issue of 10 April carried 49 images: out of these just five showed casualties (but pictures of 24 British soldiers killed and the coffins of another six were also carried). Similarly the *Sun's* '24-page souvenir' of 15 April displayed 43 images – all of them predictably celebrating US/UK military heroics, with no casualties shown and Iraqis almost invisible. Again pictures of 'the brave men who died for freedom' were carried. The *Observer* of 13 April carried an eight-page 'war in pictures' supplement: out of 50 images, just six focused on casualties. The dead unnamed are always Iraqi.[37]

Official lying also helped perpetuate the image of 'clean' warfare. In 2005, it was revealed that American officials had lied to British ministers over the use of napalm-type firebombs during the conflict – and the ministers had then reported this misinformation to parliament (Brown 2005).

THE MANUFACTURE OF HEROISM IN A POST-HEROIC AGE

Modern war-fighting strategies have virtually eliminated the possibilities of heroic action. Technology has taken the place of men (and the occasional woman). Soldiers now largely press buttons and watch the consequences on a video. Electronics and space-based technologies are all-important. Luckham commented (1984: 2): 'We are now entering a stage in which the manufacture of warfare is overtaking man and expropriating his culture. Automated warfare and the nuclear bomb have deprived man of his capacity to strive for glory, recognition or safety through combat.'

Slaughtering thousands of conscripts, soldiers and civilians in appalling massacres is hardly heroic. Yet society desperately needs its heroes. And so the spectacular 'war' provides the perfect theatre for the manufacture of heroism. Thus, the patriotic pops are full of celebrations of 'Our Boys' and their heroic deeds. Typically, the *Sun's* leader of 21 March highlighted Prime Minister Tony Blair's 'somber and emotive' broadcast hailing the 'heroism of Our Boys and Girls'. On 24 March, it listed the 31 US and British soldiers killed under the headline: 'How the tragic heroes perished.' In a centre spread on 27 March, the *Sun* had one of three near naked 'Page 3 girls' (or, as they dubbed them, 'phwaor babes') pronouncing: 'We've nothing to hide from the troops. They are our heroes.' On 30 March, the *Mirror* carried images of the coffins of killed soldiers being carried from an RAF plane at Brize Norton and alongside the headline 'The loved and lost' were the photographs of 10 of Britain's 'first fallen'. Under the massive headline 'Brave and victorious', on 7 April, the *Sun* reported: 'An overjoyed Iraqi civilian passed a heartrending note to a British commander yesterday – thanking Our Boys for liberating the city.' By 12 April, the same tabloid was campaigning for a 'victory/liberation parade' for the return of the 'world's best troops': 'Let us cheer our heroes!'

During the 1991 Gulf massacres there was virtually no hand-to-hand combat, and so in an attempt to revive the heroic images of the Second World War, the press constantly used cartoon representations and photographs of troops in training. In 2003, no such devices were necessary. The 'frontline' shots were enough to promote the myth of 'real' battle.

The most blatant manufacture of heroism surrounded the exploits of Private Jessica Lynch which gripped the world's media on 3 April 2003. Lynch had been seriously injured when the Humvee in which she was travelling in Nasiriyah was hit by a rocket-propelled grenade on 23 March 2003. With her was Lori Piestewa who became the first Native American women in the US armed forces to die in combat. Lynch was rushed to the local hospital where the doctors and nurses did their best to treat her.[38]

Then on 3 April 2003, under the strapline, 'An incredible story of heroism as teenage PoW snatched back', the *Sun* reported on the 'daring midnight raid'. 'Army supply clerk Jessica, 19, was plucked to safety by US special forces from a hospital used as a base by Saddam Hussein's death squads.' And it went on to quote Brig. General Vince Brooks: 'America doesn't leave its heroes behind. Never has, never will.' Along with the rest of the mainstream media, the *Guardian* framed its coverage around the title of the 1998 Hollywood blockbuster *Saving Private Ryan*. Under the headline 'Saving Private Lynch: How special forces rescued captured colleague', Rory McCarthy based in Camp as-Sayliya, Qatar, reported on the 'daring midnight raid' (McCarthy 2003). The *Guardian*'s sister Sunday newspaper, the *Observer*, reported on 6 April (Donegan 2003):

> Cable TV's army of retired generals, normally reliable cheerleaders for Central Command, were striking a critical note, while the tame Pentagon press corps had begun to ask the occasional tough question. Even the stock market had decided that the patriotic bull market was bust.

> The Nasiriyah rescue, with its simple yet powerful narrative of American redemption, changed all of that. As the *Washington Post*'s media specialist Howard Kurtz, commenting on the transformation of the national mood, said: 'Goodbye quagmire.'

In a story headlined 'She was fighting to the death', the *Washington Post* reported that when Lynch's unit was originally ambushed in Nasiriyah in central Iraq on March 23, she 'fought fiercely and shot several enemy soldiers ... firing her weapons until she ran out of ammunition'. She 'continued firing at the Iraqis even after she sustained multiple gunshot wounds and watched several other soldiers in her unit die around her'. Deeper in the story ran the disclaimer 'Several officials cautioned that the precise sequence of events is still being determined...' (Seib 2004: 74-77). The next day the commander of the army hospital in Germany where Lynch was being treated said there was no evidence of gunshot wounds and a *Post* story the following day had Lynch's father agreeing with that.

In the end, then, all was found to be fiction. There was no gun battle, simply because there were no Iraqi soldiers in the hospital at the time, as Kampfner (2003) revealed in the *Guardian*. He wrote that the rescue 'will go down as one of the most stunning pieces of news management yet conceived. It provides a remarkable insight into the real influence of Hollywood producers on the Pentagon's media managers'. And Robinson, Goddard, Parry, Murray with Taylor (2010: 140) comment:

> ... the case of 'saving Private Lynch' represents an 'ideal type' example of media management. By carefully directing a flow of news information (with some level of embellishment along the way) that could dovetail with journalistic values of drama, human interest and patriotism, media briefers and news organisations, between them, created a news event that served the interests of each perfectly. In these circumstances, journalistic skepticism and detachment evaporated.

But this kind of analysis perhaps exaggerates the influence of the Pentagon's media management. Hollywood-style journalism now emerges unprompted by the Pentagon, it has become such an integral part of journalists' framing devices.

Given the prominence of media hype in current conflicts it is inevitable that a few critical journalists will deconstruct certain events and expose their manufactured dimension. Even the *Sun*, on 15 April, exposed the story of the heroic 'Stay Lucky' soldier pictured wearing a helmet riddled with bullet holes as a prank. But focusing on individual hoaxes is very different from highlighting the whole 'war' as a construct, a myth.

NOTES

[1] Michael Moore was then right when he bravely shouted out at the 2003 Oscars ceremony (Simpson 2004: 315): 'We like non-fiction and we live in fictitious times. We live in a time where we have fictitious election results that elect a fictitious president. We live in a time where we have a man sending us to war for fictitious reasons...'

[2] Typically, the *News of the World* of 6 April 2003 dubbed it 'Shock and Phwoarr' as it reported 'exclusively': 'The Desert Rats are rolling towards victory in Iraq equipped with the ultimate secret weapon – Nell McAndrew's pink knickers'

[3] The USS *Abraham Lincoln* victory speech was written by Michael Gerson. The Iraq war had been a 'noble cause' and a 'great moral advance' that he linked to Normandy and Iwo Jima, Franklin Roosevelt's Four Freedoms, the Truman Doctrine, Reagan's challenge to the evil empire and the 'war on terror' (Woodward 2004: 412)

[4] Griffin (2010: 32-33) says that the toppling of the Saddam Hussein statue was closely managed by a US colonel and a PSYOP (Psychological Operations) team who cordoned off the square, permitted a small group of Iraqi émigrés to gather around the statue – and then used amoured vhicles and steel cables to pull down the statue in front of the cheering crowd

[5] According to Woodward, Bob (2004: 401) on 20 March 2003, 241,516 military personnel were in the region, joined by 41,000 from the UK, 2,000 from Australia and 200 from Poland. The ground force numbered 183,000. By 2 April, the numbers of soldiers in theatre increased to 310,000

[6] Later, in his book-legth account of the conflict, Keegan (2005: 2) described it as a 'mysterious war': 'Mystery surrounded the progress of the operations. Iraq fielded an army of 400,000 soldiers, equipped with thousands of tanks, armoured vehicles and artillery pieces. Against the advance of an invading force only half its size, the Iraqi army faded away. It did not fight at the frontier, it did not fight at the obvious geographical obstacles, it scarcely fought in the cities, it did not mount a last-ditch defence of the capital, where much of the world media predicted Saddam would stage his Stalingrad'

[7] Significantly, the BBC's chief political correspondent Andrew Marr at the fall of Baghdad told viewers that Blair had said 'they would take Baghdad without a bloodbath and at the end the Iraqis would be celebrating and on both these points he has been proved conclusively right'. According to Gordon Thomas (2009: 363), the numbers of Iraqis killed and injured was 'between 65,000 and 650,000'. On 20 March 20016, the *Independent* published (under the title 'The forgotten victims') the names of 3,000 people known to have died in the Iraq conflict 'just one tenth of the most conservative estimates'

[8] On 29 March, the *Sun* reported 1,500 Iraqi soldiers dying in a 'one-sided gun battle' at Najaf, with only three American deaths. The Iraqi 'fanatical fighters' were 'wiped out in Ambush Alley'

[9] James Furlong invented a story about cruise missiles fired from HMS *Splendid* 'beneath the waters of the Persian Gulf'. In fact, the images were library footage. Furlong resigned from *Sky News* after it was revealed on BBC documentary *Fighting the war*, July 2003 (see 'Will one man's error cost our viewers too much?', by Jake Lynch, *UK Press Gazette*, 25 July 2003 p. 13). He later went on to tragically commit suicide

[10] On 9 April, the *Sun* described al-Sahhaf as heading the 'Ministry of Silly Talks'. They quoted a leading psychologist, Jane Firbank, of the European Therapy Studies Institute, saying that al-Sahhaf 'was showing all the signs of a man out of touch with reality because of stress'. By 17 April, the same tabloid was spreading the false rumour that he had committed suicide (see Lea 2003). In fact, he survived the conflict. On 7 November 2014, the Swedish newspaper *Expressen* posted a video on its website showing al-Sahhaf in a hospital bed in the United Arab Republic

[11] Sixty-seven British citizens died in the 9/11 attacks (Hennessey and Thomas 2009: 601)

[12] See http://whowhatwhy.org/2016/08/14/russ-baker-saudi-911-coverup/, accessed on 19 August 2016. David Swanson comments: 'Saudi Arabia spends three times as much per person as the US does on its military, and it spends the biggest chunk of it buying weapons from US profiteers. An "indefinite waiver" upheld by Presidents George W. Bush and Barack Obama lets Saudi Arabia off the hook in the US State Department for its religious cruelty. Waivers by Bush and Obama also allow the US military to go on training the Saudi military. A waiver created by Secretary of State Hillary Clinton allows US weapons sales. Clinton made that her personal mission after Saudi Arabia put at least $10 million into the Clinton Foundation. As the US State Department was and is well aware, there are no civil liberties in Saudi Arabia. People are jailed, whipped, and killed for speech, and speech is tightly censored. Saudi Arabia didn't even ban slavery until 1962 and maintains a labor system referred to as "a culture of slavery". The "sharia law" that US bigots are constantly fearing will appear in their town actually takes a truly nasty form in Saudi Arabia under a brutal government propped up by US funds and arms.' See http://worldbeyondwar.org/saudi-203-pages/, accessed on 19 August 2016

[13] See We had no asset in Saddam's inner circle, says ex-CIA deputy director, *Intelnews.org*, 29 December 2015, accessed on 29 December 2015

[14] President Bush had decided on 'regime change' in Iraq as early as 20 September 2001, according to Christopher Meyer, the British ambassador to Washington (cited in Adrich and Cormac 2016: 421). Seldon (2005: 569) says that, as early as 12 September, Rumsfeld suggested to his White House colleagues that 9/11 could present an opportunity to attack Iraq while Bush secretly asked Rumsfeld to develop updated invasion plans for Iraq 'as early as 21 November 2001'

[15] See www.timesonline.co.uk/article/0,,2087-1593607,00.html, accessed 14 October 2008. The real news from the memo was not that Blair and Bush had decided as early as April 2002 to go to war with Iraq but to provoke Saddam into providing an excuse for war (see Edwards and Cromwell 2009: 86-95)

[16] Richard J. Aldrich, the official historian of GCHQ, describes the Butler report as 'odd' (2010: 530). It produces the majority of Britain's intelligence but, in the report's 216 pages, it appears only once – and that in a list of abbreviations! Secret to the end…

[17] Bower (2016: 292) reports that Charles Reiss, the *Standard*'s political editor, had been allowed to speed-read the dossier thirty minutes before the deadline for the first issue. 'The newspaper's editor supervised the front-page headline, "45 minutes to attack", above a map showing the rocket's range, which stretched across Israel to British troops in Cyprus'

[18] As Seldon records (2005: 584): 'It transpired that the forty-five-minute claim for Iraq's deployment of WMD came from a single, uncorroborated source, and that it referred only to battlefield biological or chemical weapons, which posed no serious threat to other nations'

[19] See also http://www.globalresearch.ca/plagiarism-british-intelligence-iraq-dossier-relied-on-recycled-academic-articles/513, accessed on 3 September 2016

[20] It should be noted that 139 Labour MPs voted against the motion to go to war (and foreign secretary Robin Cook resigned). Prime Minister Blair only survived because of the support of the Conservative Party

[21] See Ramsay, Robin (2000) A secret service? *Lobster*, Vol. 40 p. 15

[22] *Guardian* editor Alan Rusbridger later claimed that Gillan had so impressed members of the Household Cavalry that they had become *Guardian* readers. See Bates 2003

[23] Among the US embeds in Iraq was former White House aide Col. Oliver North, with the 1st Marine Expeditionary Force. As Hoskins (2004: 62) writes: 'Unsurprisingly, North's reporting resonated with the conversational and decidedly patriotic discourse of Fox'

[24] See *Operations in Iraq: Lessons for the future*, published by the MoD, December 2003, p. 59. Available online at http://www.mod.uk/NR/rdonlyres/734920BA-6ADE-461F-A809-7E5A754990D7/0/opsiniraq_lessons_dec03.pdf, accessed on 14 October 2008. See also Curtis (2004: 105)

[25] See www.dnotice.org.uk/records.htm, accessed 14 October 2008

[26] See https://pages.gseis.ucla.edu/faculty/kellner/papers/mediapropaganda.htm, accessed on 28 September 2016

[27] A full list of the 15 killed journalists appears in the International Press Institute's report *Caught in the crossfire: The Iraq War and the media* of 2003. Available online at www.freemedia.at/IraqReport2003.htm, accessed on 22 March 2004

[28] Christiane Amanpour, chief international correspondent for CNN, quoted in Hodgson, Jessica (2003) Mother of all war journos, the *Observer*, November 2

[29] See http://news.bbc.co.uk/1/hi/uk/6040372.stm, accessed on 7 October 2016

[30] See http://wwww.arabnews.com/Article.asp?ID=24644

[31] At the very end of his chapter on journalist casualties in the conflict, Tim Gopsill (2004: 261) comments: 'There may also have been Iraqi journalists killed but no information is yet available'

[32] International opinion polls showed massive opposition to the invasion: over 90 per cent in Spain, 80 per cent in Italy, 60 per cent in the UK and 40-50 per cent in the US. See Shaw, Martin (2005) *Peace activism and Western wars: Social movements in mass-mediated global politics*, de Jong, Wilma, Shaw, Martin and Stammers, Neil (eds) *Global activism, Global media*, London: Pluto Press p. 135

[33] In the end, parliament was duped by Blair, the final majority for the war being 263 votes on 19 March (Bower 2016: 334)

[34] Significantly, Katy Weitz resigned as a feature writer on the *Sun* – particularly over its coverage of the conflict. She wrote (2003), on seeing th headline 'Show them no pity: they have stains on their souls' as the war began: 'It was sickening. In this illegal invasion of a developing country, whose desperate people have been terrorised and murdered for years, my paper was endorsing the view that they were somehow undeserving of pity. They were less than human, every one in some part guilty for the sins of their leader. My disassociation level hit a dangerous low'

[35] The CIA plot was revealed by Ron Suskind in *The way of the world: A story of truth and hope in an age of extremism*, New York: Harper, 2008

[36] See http://watson.brown.edu/costsofwar/costs/human/refugees/iraqi, accessed on 4 December 2015

[37] Similarly Griffin (2010), in a study of US magazine coverage of the conflict, concluded that photographs of combat were still largely absent from US visual coverage and images of civilian casualties and death remained rare

[38] In an account of the Jessica Lynch story, Pulitzer prize-winner Rick Bragg (2004) claimed she had been raped and sodomised during her capture. But in an interview on the US television network ABC, she denied ever being raped. And Dr Mahdi Khafazji, an orthopaedic surgeon at Nasiriyah's main hospital, who performed surgery on Ms Lynch to repair a fractured femur, said he had found no signs that she was raped or sodomised (Nasiriyah 2003)

Chapter Thirteen

The unmaking of new militarism: Towards disaster militarism

Amidst all the chaos and killing in Afghanistan following the US invasion of 2001, Operation Moshtarak, in 2010, represented a rare attempt to revive the manufacturing of a new militarist victory. It failed. Just as the quickie Nato-led attack on Libya in 2011 achieved its immediate aim of removing President Gaddafi – but it left disaster in its wake. Not surprisingly, the *Asia Times* reporter Pepe Escobar has dubbed US imperialism as the 'Empire of Chaos'.[1]

HOW FLEET STREET COVERED THE 'DODGY DOSSIER' ON AFGHANISTAN

It is easy to forget that the UK's involvement in the 2001 attack on Afghanistan was proceeded by the publication of a 'dodgy dossier' (a more infamous one appearing before the 2003 Iraq intervention). Indeed, after Tony Blair announced to parliament on 3 October 2001 the supposed 'proof' of Osama bin Laden's responsibility for the 9/11 atrocities in the United States even the *Daily Mail* commented: 'Circumstantial it undoubtedly is. A lawyer would have a field day picking holes in it.'[2] Only nine of the document's 70 points focused on the 11 September attacks and provided no evidence that directly linked the Saudi-born dissident to them.[3]

Yet Fleet Street could not allow reason to divert it from standing shoulder-to-shoulder with Prime Minister Tony Blair.[4] So editors over-indulged in Orwellian doublethink pronouncing that the dossier did, indeed, provide all the proof needed to justify military attacks on Afghanistan and the toppling of the Taliban. According to *The Times*, the evidence was 'compelling'. It commented: 'There is no further need for diplomacy or room for negotiation: the choice, as the Prime Minister said, is to defeat the terrorists or be defeated. Action is therefore imminent.' The *Daily Mail* described it as a 'remarkable dossier' that 'was never intended to be picked over by lawyers'.

For the 'liberals' of the *Guardian*, 'it is simply perverse to pretend that anyone other than bin Laden and his group is responsible'. And no independent line was forthcoming from the *Independent*. The dossier, it claimed, was 'more than enough to justify action against al-Qaeda'. The *Express* was worried about the inadequacy of the evidence against the 'prime suspect'. But it continued: 'We have to accept on trust that the vital piece of the jigsaw pointing to bin Laden's guilt is in place.' No such doubts worried the hyper-hawks at the *Daily Telegraph*. 'Even if there had been no evidence at all to link bin Laden with the terrorist attack of September 11 – even if those attacks had not happened – the United States would be wholly justified in tracking him down and killing him,' it commented.

Hardly anyone in the corporate media highlighted the fact that the invasion of Afghanistan was, in fact, completely in contravention of international law (Kent 2009). Having failed to gain a UN Security Council resolution approving military action, President Bush summoned Article 51 of the UN Charter and the right to immediate self defence in the event of armed attack. But Afghanistan did not launch an armed assault on the US on 11 September 2001. All but four of the 19 terrorists were from Saudi Arabia. Significantly, a 2002 UN report on the financing of al-Qaeda said that $16 million was sent to bin Laden's organisation from sources in Saudi Arabia after the 9/11 attacks (Curtis 2010: 313). Britain had about £15 billion worth of investments and joint ventures in Saudi Arabia, which was by far the country's biggest trading partner in the Middle East. All recent British governments have deepened still further the financial interdependence between Britain and Saudi Arabia, aiming to make the City of London the favoured destination for 'Islamic finance' (ibid: 318-319).

AFGHANISTAN AND THE MANUFACTURE OF A 'CREDIBLE ENEMY'

Within this context, it can be seen that the US/UK responses to the 11 September atrocities, with the launch of the endless 'war on terrorism', the assaults on Afghanistan in 2001 and Iraq in 2003 and the threats to the 'rogue' states, Syria, Iran and North Korea, were not distinctly new strategies but accelerating long-standing strategies of military imperial adventurism (Curtis 2003; Boyd-Barrett 2004: 36-38).[5] Al-Qaeda, blamed for the 11 September atrocities and a series of later attacks on Western interests, was in 2001 a particularly shadowy grouping. As Burke comments (2003: 6): '…even when at its most organised in late 2001, it is important to avoid seeing "al-Qaeda" as a coherent and structured terrorist organisation with cells everywhere, or to imagine it had subsumed all other groups within its network.' Certainly against such an elusive threat, traditional war fighting strategies (involving major battle confrontations) were inappropriate.

The attack on Afghanistan in 2001 produced the necessary risk-free 'victory' (with no US soldiers killed in action) against a quickly manufactured 'enemy'. But they remained largely invisible with journalists kept well away from the 'frontlines' as the US proxy forces, the Northern Alliance, advanced on Kabul. More than 800

Afghan civilians were killed in the US airstrikes, though many tens of thousands died through hunger, disease and exposure (ibid: 324). According to Seldon (2005: 508) the Americans made heavy use of 'cluster' and 'daisy cutter' bombs which resulted in 'widespread' civilian casualties. And in the end, al-Qaeda leaders Osama bin Laden and Mullah Omar escaped into the void.[6]

Moreover, following the US assault on Afghanistan, 160,000 refugees had crossed into Pakistan by December 2001 while another 60,000 fled into Iran (Steele 2011: 247). In camps set up by charities for the internally displaced, Jonathan Steele estimated that 1,600 died between September and the end of December 2001 out of a total of around 10,000 who died indirectly because of the US campaign (ibid: 252-253).

With image and entertainment the dominant concerns in new militarist adventures against hopelessly overwhelmed 'enemies', soldiers ended up becoming actors. As Philip Hammond comments (2003: 27): 'The US special forces who went into Kandahar in October 2001 were essentially actors, staging a stunt and videotaping their exploits for the world's media.' The operation was of dubious military value, Hammond argues, since army pathfinders had already gone in beforehand to make sure the area was secure. Hammond (ibid: 23) also sees the 'war on terrorism' primarily as a war of images.

> Just as the September 11 attacks were calculated not simply to wreak terrible destruction but to create a global media spectacle by targeting symbols of American prestige and power, so too the response of the US and UK governments has been highly image-conscious. Particularly in those aspects of the war on terrorism which have involved actual war fighting, producing the right image appears to be at least as important as any tangible results achieved on the ground.

Afghanistan was of no strategic importance to the US; nor did the rag-tag army of the Taliban in any way constitute a credible enemy. The overthrow of the country was achieved in a matter of days by the CIA, with some special forces assistance (the British Special Air Service and Special Boat Service together with soldiers from Australia's Special Air Service regiment, for instance) organising a small Northern Alliance army supported by overwhelming American air power (see Seldon 2005: 510; Neighbour 2011; Newsinger 2015: 148). As Newsinger adds (ibid):

> The Americans installed a gangster warlord regime dominated by drug traffickers ... Indeed, it was if the US had invaded Colombia to install the drug cartels in power. These people only came to power with American support, and clearly would only be able to remain in power with continued American support, but the Bush administration had no interest in the country.

Fleet Street editors predictably largely backed the assault by the most powerful nation on earth on one of the poorest countries in the world. Typically, the *Guardian*, normally seen as the voice of 'liberal' opinion in the UK, editorialised (and eulogised) on a speech by Prime Minister Tony Blair in October 2001:

> The core of the speech – intellectual as well as moral – came when he contrasted the west's commitment to do everything possible to avoid civilian casualties and the terrorists' proven wish to cause as many casualties as possible, a point which Jack Straw followed up in the Commons yesterday. Let them do their worst, we shall do our best, as Churchill put. That is still the key difference (quoted in Edwards and Cromwell 2004: 214).

On 8 October, after the UK and US launched their attacks on Afghanistan, the *Guardian* editorialised: 9/11 was a 'monstrous injustice'. Therefore, at a 'time of such seriousness, it needs to be said as clearly and as unemotively as possible at the outset that the United States was entitled to launch a military response' (Steele 2011: 224). No mention of ruthless revenge there. But in his autobiography published in November 2010, President Bush was blunt about the US response to 9/11: 'My blood was boiling. We were going to find out who did this, and kick their ass' (ibid: 226).

AFGHANISTAN, THE MEDIA AND THE MANUFACTURE OF 'WARFARE'

In such 'operations' as the Afghanistan invasion and subsequent occupation, the essential role of the media embedded with the military and constrained by the enormous risks involved in reporting from such a lawless country, was to manufacture the image of legitimate, heroic so-called 'warfare' against a credible threat. In other words, the conventional language of the military is deployed to describe completely asymmetrical conflict. As Bishop points out (2009: 13):

> Wars with insurgents were always unbalanced. One side had modern conventional weapons. The other fought with what was cheap, portable and easily improvised. But in Afghanistan the scale of the asymmetry at times seemed blackly absurd.

In the process the reality of the conflict, the high-tech violence of the invading forces, the appalling suffering of the Afghan people, was kept secret from the British public. We knew precisely how many coalition troops were killed (all of them, indeed, tragic and unnecessary), their names, their family histories – and how many had been wounded. As James Cogan noted on 23 April (2010): 'Since 2001, the lives of 1,733 US and Nato troops have been squandered in Afghanistan. … At least another 8,000 have been wounded in action, including more than 5,000 Americans. Thousands more have suffered non-battle injuries and illness.' In 2009 alone, there were 1,400 British casualties flown from Afghanistan to the UK, 212 in a critical condition (Willetts 2010).[7] But the Afghan casualties of US/

UK and Taliban attacks remained largely nameless and unknown.[8] Moreover, the so-called Marjah offensive in July 2010[9] had created an estimated 27,000 internal refugees – but these were hardly ever reported in the media (Boone and Norton-Taylor 2010).

Indeed, the Taliban, supported by their al-Qaeda allies, were distinguished largely by their invisibility in the media. Jonathan Steele, who has covered Afghanistan for the *Guardian* for 30 years, describes the Taliban as 'ghosts': 'Heavily equipped high-tech forces try to grapple with a guerrilla enemy that wears civilian clothes and never comes head-on. State-of-the-art night-vision goggles are no use for detecting ghosts' (2011: 14).

They laid booby traps and roadside bombs otherwise known as improvised explosive devices (IEDs: usually home-made from fertiliser[10]), sniped at their enemy – and fled (often on battered motorbikes). In the military jargon, this is known as 'shoot and scoot' (Bishop op cit: 73). Over the six-month period up to June 2010, British soldiers had come across more than 500 IEDs and engaged in more than 1,300 gunfights in central Helmand (Norton-Taylor 2010b). IEDs were accounting for 80 per cent of British injuries and fatalities (Rayment 2010). Many of the guns the Taliban were using dated back to the 1890s (Sengupta 2010a). As Turse and Engelhardt stress (2010):

> Al-Qaeda has no tanks, Humvees, nuclear submarines, or aircraft carriers, no fleets of attack helicopters or fighter jets. … Al-Qaeda specialises in low-budget operations ranging from the incredibly deadly to the incredibly ineffectual. … In the present war on terror, called by whatever name (or, as at present, by no name at all), the two 'sides' might as well be in different worlds. After all, al-Qaeda today isn't even an organisation in the normal sense of the term, no less a fighting bureaucracy. It is a loose collection of ideas and a looser collection of individuals waging open source warfare.

Suicide bomb attacks and assaults on areas suspected of siding with the occupying forces were other Taliban guerrilla tactics. In 2003, there were only two suicide attacks in Afghanistan. In 2006, there were at least 136, six times more than the year before. Eighty were directed at military targets but killed eight times as many civilians as soldiers or policemen. The Taliban also terrorised individuals and communities suspected of siding with the occupation forces. According to Julius Cavendish (2010a), the insurgents executed two civilians whom they suspected of aiding government and international forces every three days during 2009.

Journalists were also targeted. The decapitation of Afghan reporter Ajmal Naqshbandi, in 2007, was filmed and distributed on the internet[11] – but this did not receive the global media attention given to the similar decapitation of the *Wall Street Journal*'s Daniel Pearl, in February 2002.[12] The *Guardian*'s foreign correspondent Ghaith Abdul-Ahad was released along with two other journalists in December 2009 after being held hostage for six days in a remote region of

Afghanistan (Taylor 2009). In January 2010, Rupert Hamer, embedded with US Marines at Nawa in Helmand for the *Sunday Mirror*, became the first UK journalist to be killed in Afghanistan. And this received massive media coverage. The front page of the *Daily Mirror* of 11 January carried a large photograph of Hamer smiling in front of troops with the headline: 'Fine, fearless, dedicated' (Hughes 2010).[13]

The Taliban's basic weapon was an AK-47 rifle of Second World War design, augmented by machine guns and latterly home-made roadside bombs. In addition, the 'legacy mines' left over since the time of the Soviet occupation (1979-1989) posed a durable threat. Facing them, the US-led troops had state-of-the art satellites, spy planes and unmanned drones. Writing in 2009, Patrick Bishop commented in his book celebrating the heroics of 3 Para Battlegroup in Afghanistan (op cit: 12):

> Anti-American rebels had made great use of IEDs and suicide bombs in Iraq but they had been late arriving in Afghanistan [since 2006]. Together they now kept the troops in a constant state of alertness and anxiety. The insurgents' new methods carried less risk to themselves than did their previous confrontational tactics. Even when they suffered losses, though, there seemed to be no shortage of replacements.

With Osama bin Laden and Mullah Omar having mysteriously fled into the unknown following the US invasion of 2001, the Taliban in 2010 had no leader – such as the 'mad dog' Gaddafi, of Libya, or the 'new Hitler, Butcher of Baghdad' Saddam or the 'Butcher of Belgrade', 'Slobo' Milošević – on whom our patriotic editors and the military could direct their venom. The Taliban had no headquarters which US precision-guided missiles could 'take out'.

On 17 February 2010, the media reported American claims that the actual head of the Taliban's military operations had been seized in Karachi: a certain Mullah Abdul Ghani Baradar.[14] But like the rest of the Taliban, Mullah Abdul remained a shadowy, unknown figure. Significantly, no photographs of Taliban's toppled No 2 accompanied the reports.

MOSHTARAK: BILLED AS THE 'BIGGEST US OFFENSIVE SINCE 2001'

Operation Moshtarak, launched on 12 February 2010 in Afghanistan, was billed as 'the biggest US military offensive since the US invasion of 2001' (note how PR-ish superlatives always accompany every new assault by the American military).

The 15,000 coalition forces drawn from the US, the UK, Canada, Denmark, Estonia and most significantly Afghanistan were equipped with a vast arsenal – including Apache, Chinook and Cobra, Black Hawk attack helicopters and unmanned predator aircraft – all of it backed up by ranks of military intelligence operatives and information gathering hi-tech satellites (Keeble 2010 and 2011b). But whom were they 'battling'? Possibly just 400 Taliban, according to some US officers (Lamb 2010). On 7 February, *The Sunday Times* predicted just 1,000

Taliban would be facing the 4,000 crack British troops (Colvin 2010). For the follow-up Kandahar offensive planned for the summer, military intelligence were said to be expecting between just '500 and 1,000' insurgents (Kirkup 2010).

So this was an 'operation': not real warfare. Rather, it was a simulated, mediacentric event providing a symbolic show of US/UK military strength and proof that the new Afghan army was capable of taking over once the occupying forces withdrew. The operation had certainly no credible strategic legitimacy. The target of the US-led assaults was Marjah in Helmand province in the south of the country. But as reporter Anand Gopal told the progressive *Democracy Now!* radio station Marjah was 'a very tiny town'. Gopal continued:

> It's more a show of force by the coalition forces, something they can offer their home audiences of how they've gone into a village and retaken some Taliban. But beyond that, nothing will really change on the ground, regardless of what happens in Marjah. It's just business as usual.[15]

Investigative reporter Gareth Porter (2010: 8) claimed that the picture of Marjah presented by military officials and obediently reported by major news media was 'one of the clearest and most dramatic pieces of misinformation of the entire war, apparently aimed at hyping the offensive as a historic turning point in the conflict'. On 2 February 2010, Associated Press quoted 'Marine commanders' saying they expected 400 to 1,000 insurgents to be 'holed up' in the southern Afghan town of 80,000 people. According to Porter, 'that language evoked an image of house-to-house urban street fighting' (ibid). On 14 February, the second day of the 'offensive', Lt Josh Diddams said the Marines were 'in the majority of the city at this point'. He also used the language that conjured images of urban fighting, claiming the insurgents held some 'neighbourhoods'. Yet, as Porter stressed, Marjah is not a city nor even a real town but either a few clusters of farmers' homes or a large agricultural area covering much of the southern Helmand River Valley.

MAINTAINING THE MYTH OF WARFARE

Predictably the coalition forces were reported as 'storming' Marjah. More superlatives appeared in the press to manufacture the image of credible warfare: the town was suspected of being 'one of the biggest, most dangerous minefields Nato forces had ever faced' (Martin 2010). Brig. Gen. Larry Nicholson, commander of the Marines in southern Afghanistan, was quoted as saying: 'This may be the largest IED threat and largest minefield that Nato has ever faced' while the US military were reported as saying that 'hundreds of beleaguered insurgents could insist to fight until death' (ibid).

On 13 February, Gulab Mangal, governor of Helmand, was reported as saying it was 'the most successful operation we have ever carried out'. Duncan Larcombe (2010), embedded with the Fire Support Company, 1st battalion, the Royal Welsh, in the *Sun* of 15 February trumpeted: 'Our boys are in high spirits after successfully pulling off the largest helicopter assaults in British military history.' Oliver Harvey (2010), embedded with 3 Platoon Queen's Company for the *Sun*, celebrated the flying of the Afghan national flag at the 'Taliban stronghold Marjah' as a 'sign of hope'.

Always the myth of warfare survives: usually as a future danger. So the *Sun* of 11 February reported: 'Fighting ... in Helmand is expected to be ferocious.' In *The Sunday Times* of 14 February, Miles Amoore and Marie Colvin reported (2010): 'Most Taliban appear to have scattered before the onslaught which was strongly signalled in advance. However, military commanders expect them to regroup and attack in the weeks ahead.' And Jon Boone (2010a), in the *Guardian* of 10 March, quoted commanding officer Major Joseph Brannon on the Taliban: 'They know we are making a difference here so we are expecting a pretty strong fight.' But as John Pilger (2010) commented:

> The recent 'liberation of the city of Marja' from the Taliban's 'command and control structure' was pure Hollywood. Marja is not a city – there was no Taliban command and control. The heroic liberators killed the usual civilians, the poorest of the poor. Otherwise it was fake. A war of perception is meant to provide fake news for the folks back home to make a failed colonial adventure seem worthwhile and patriotic.

THE CELEBRITISATION OF 'HEROIC' WARFARE

One way in which the media hide the reality of the horror of warfare is to celebrate the visits of celebrities from the world of politics and entertainment to the troops on the frontlines. The events are pure PR – being usually accompanied by photographs of the smiling visitors shaking hands with equally smiling troops or trying some of the military hardware for the cameras. The language used is always positive and uplifting. Typical, then, was the coverage given to President Barack Obama on 29 March 2010 on his first visit to the war zone since ordering a 'surge' of 30,000 extra US troops in Afghanistan in November 2009. Stephen Foley (2010), in the *Independent*, quoted the President: 'I'm encouraged by the *progress* that's been made. ... One of the main reasons I am here is just to say than you for the *extraordinary efforts* of our troops' (emphasis added).

On 24 May, the *Daily Mail* along with the rest of Fleet Street reported David Beckham, England football 'hero', dropping in on the troops in Camp Bastion, Afghanistan. He told troops of his 'huge admiration' for them.[16]

FLEET STREET BACKS MOSHTARAK OFFENSIVE – DESPITE MASSIVE PUBLIC OPPOSITION

Virtually all the new militarist attacks had won the overall support of Fleet Street editors: Operation Moshtarak, involving 9,500 British troops, was no exception. In 2010, most of Fleet Street was still backing the Nato 'war' in Afghanistan. On

6 December 2009, *The Sunday Times* editorial, titled 'Prepare for the long haul in Afghanistan', welcomed President Obama's 'surge' strategy: 'He took his time, but President Barack Obama reached the right decision with his announcement last week the United States is to send 30,000 more troops and 250 helicopters to Afghanistan.' On 14 February, the same newspaper was hailing, cautiously, Operation Moshtarak: 'Maybe this is the end of the beginning.' According to the *Independent*'s editorial of 9 February 2010, the strategy of General Stanley McChrystal, to put Afghan troops alongside Western troops, had 'logic' and 'should at least be given an opportunity to prove itself'.

On 2 June, the *Daily Telegraph* editorialised: 'The heroic work undertaken by the British forces these past four years has laid the foundations for the new American-led strategy.' The *Guardian*'s editorial on the following day suggested the British government 'could make a bold decision – to withdraw troops from the front, use them to secure Kabul and set themselves the more modest aim of doing things that work'. But by 24 June 2010, the *Guardian* was describing the war as 'dysfunctional' and 'unwinnable'. According to *The Times*' editorial of 10 June 2010, the new Prime Minister, David Cameron, 'to his credit … has chosen to reaffirm the importance of success in Afghanistan and to offer unbridled support to the military'. A follow-up leader the next day concluded, firmly, that 'at a time of austerity, it is imperative that this nation spends more on its defence'. But as during the Nato attacks on Serbia in 1999, the *Independent on Sunday* dared to stand outside the consensus. On Remembrance Sunday, 8 November 2009, its editorial commented:

> It is time, on this solemn day on which we remember the sacrifice of those who gave their lives for our freedom and security, for a change in policy. It is time to say that this war was ill-conceived, unwinnable and counterproductive. It is time to start planning a phased withdrawal of British troops.

Fleet Street's general support for the UK government's Afghan strategy did not match the public mood with polls consistently calling for troops to be withdrawn (Milne 2009). In July 2009, the BBC/*Guardian*, ITN, *The Times* and *Independent* all published polls showing Britons wanted immediate or rapid withdrawal of troops. An ICM study, reported in the *Guardian* on 11 July, found 42 per cent wanted Britain to pull out immediately and 14 per cent by the end of the year. The *Guardian*, however, titled the article 'Public support for Afghanistan is firm, despite deaths'. It stressed that support for the war had increased from 30 per cent in 2006 to 46 per cent but left the call for withdrawal to the last three sentences of the article.

On 11 November 2009, the *Independent* published a vote showing four out of five did not believe the government's main justification – and did not believe that British involvement was keeping the streets of Britain safe from terrorist attacks.

Some 46 per cent felt the war actually increased the threat of attacks by creating anger and resentment among the Muslim population (Sengupta and Morris 2010). Even while Operation Moshtarak was under way, another poll by ComRes for the *Independent* and ITV News showed that almost three-quarters of electors viewed the conflict as unwinnable – and more than half said they did not understand why British troops were still in Afghanistan (Morris 2010). Similar massive public opposition to the war was being recorded in the US. A *Washington Post*/ABC poll released in June 2010 showed 53 per cent of respondents saying the war was 'not worth fighting' – the highest percentage in three years.[17]

Opposition appeared in the mainstream media from a number of prominent columnists – such as Simon Jenkins, Seamus Milne, Peter Preston (all *Guardian*), Andreas Whittam Smith, Johann Hari (*Independent*), Max Hastings and Andrew Alexander (*Daily Mail*), Jeff Randall (*Daily Telegraph*), Peter Beaumont (*Observer*) and Denis McShane MP. But, intriguingly, the loudest protests in the media came largely from those calling for still more investment in the war. The *Sun, Mail, Express* and *Telegraph*, to name but a few of Fleet Street's most hawkish members, criticised loudly the supposed failures of the Gordon Brown New Labour government to equip 'our heroes' properly. Particular attention focused on the alleged failings of the Snatch Land Rover (Sturcke 2008; Bulstrode 2010). The claims of a Catholic bishop at a military funeral that soldiers in Afghanistan urgently needed more helicopters and vehicles in late April 2010 received substantial media coverage (e.g. Bowcott 2010b).

The row promoted an illusion of critical media holding the rulers to account. And yet the controversy was entirely manufactured. By 2010, the US military had spent an estimated one trillion dollars on its post 9/11 wars so far (Stiglitz and Bilmes 2009); it had 1.4 million active duty men and women and another 1.3 million reserve personnel; it employed more than 700,000 civilians in support roles while there were estimated 100,000 members in its civilian intelligence community. Its military budget in 2009 amounted to $661 billion.[18] In June 2010, congress approved an 'emergency' supplemental financing Bill including more than $33 billion, mainly for funding the American military 'surge' in Afghanistan (Astore 2010). Britain had already spent £9.4 billion on its Afghanistan operations by 2010 (Turse and Engelhardt op cit; see also Turse 2008). Its annual military spending was the equivalent of $53.8 billion, the fourth highest in the world (after the US, France and China).[19] So much for under-resourcing.

'Operations' certainly help provide a 'theatre' in which some of these massively expensive weapons and the various branches of the military (army, navy, air force, special forces, satellites, intelligence and so on) can be tested. Significantly, Adam Ingram, a former armed forces minister, suggested that a desire within the army to try out a new range of recently purchased Apache helicopters was a factor in the deployment of British troops to Helmand in 2006 (Haynes 2010). Before the

3,000 British troops arrived, the province had been 'relatively quiet', according to Andrew Krepinevich, who served on the personal staff of three US secretaries of defence, but their arrival 'stirred up a hornet's nest' (Evans 2010).

THE CONTRADICTIONS OF NEW MILITARISM AND THE FAILURE OF OPERATION MOSHTARAK

Central to manufacture of new militarist 'operations' is the celebration of 'victory' to applauding home audiences usually just days after their launch. But since 2001 and the US/UK invasions of Afghanistan and Iraq, the new militarist strategy faced significant setbacks. The occupations of Iraq and Afghanistan attracted massive opposition from local forces and, by 2010, substantial majorities in the UK were calling for the troops to be withdrawn from Afghanistan.

Thus, while the US/UK military remained committed to the launch of media-hyped 'operations', by 2010 they were often no longer achieving their desired results. In the case of Operation Moshtarak, its launch was given predictably massive media coverage yet its conclusion was hardly covered at all. Almost immediately afterwards, the focus shifted to US plans to take over Kandahar, Afghanistan's second city, in the summer. Typical was the report by Julius Cavendish (2010b), in the *Independent* of 21 April 2010. Buried in the coverage of the assassination of the deputy mayor of Kandahar in a mosque was a comment from provincial council member Haji Moqtar Ahmed on Operation Moshtarak: 'My thinking is [there was] no result. It failed. ... If they start without consulting ordinary people, thousands of families will move to Kandahar city. There will be great misery.' Cavendish added:

> Nato's strategy for Kandahar was partly tested in its campaign to restore government control over the town of Marjah in neighbouring Helmand. The campaign, which began in February, has been held up by the Taliban.

The *Morning Star* reported in early May 2010 that resistance forces continued to operate in Marjah and that locals had largely refused to collaborate with occupation troops or Karzai government officials (Mellen 2010). Kim Sengupta (2010b) reported on 28 May 2010 claims by Hajj Mohammad Hassan, a local tribal elder, that there remained no security in Helmand. 'By day there is government. By night it's the Taliban.' The *Guardian*'s editorial of 3 June 2010 commented: 'The Marjah campaign, which was designed as a blueprint for how the Taliban could be rolled back, has become – in Gen. McChrystal's words – a bleeding ulcer of the campaign. There could be bigger wounds yet.' On 9 June 2010, the BBC reported Nato and Afghan official claiming 'success' for the Marjah campaign, but there were reports of continuing violence and Taliban intimidation.[20] And by 17 June, the writer and historian, William Dalrymple (2010), reported:

...it appears that the Taliban have regained control of the opium-growing centre of Marjah in Helmand province, only three months after being driven out by McChrystal's forces amid much gung-ho cheerleading in the US media.

Serious splits over strategy for the planned summer, follow-up 'operation' in Kandahar, amongst military and civilian leaders in both the UK and US, also surfaced prominently in the media (e.g. Helm and Beaumont 2010; Sengupta 2010c).[21] They culminated (amazingly) in the sacking of Gen. McChrystal by President Obama on 23 June 2010 after his outspoken criticisms of the civilian leadership of the US were published in *Rolling Stone* magazine. Moreover, Nato officials were warning that there were no quick, new militarist fixes in Afghanistan with British and foreign troops expected to be engaged in a combat role there for at least three or four more years (Norton-Taylor 2010c).

The performance of local Afghan forces in Operation Moshtarak was also disappointing, according to reports. It was thrown into further disarray with the resignations of two of the 'most internationally respected' members of Karzai's government – interior minister Hanif Atmar and spy chief Amrullah Saleh – after a gathering of 1,600 leaders in Kabul came under Taliban rocket attack (Boone 2010b). Moreover, a survey of 1,994 people in Afghanistan, commissioned by Gen. McChrystal, found that 85 per cent viewed the Taliban as 'our Afghan brothers'. More than two thirds said they viewed Karzai's government as totally corrupt while the occupying forces and Afghan police were considered the greatest threat to personal security by 56 per cent (Cogan op cit).

MISSING FROM THE COVERAGE: THE MASSIVE, GLOBAL OPPOSITION

Largely missing from the Moshtarak coverage was any acknowledgement of the views and protests of the massive anti-war movement in Britain and globally. CND, the Anti-War Coalition, War Resisters International, the Peace Pledge Union, Pax Christi, Campaign Against the Arms Trade, Respect are but a handful of the many groups in the UK largely ignored by the mainstream. On 3 April 2010, for instance, PressTV reported that thousands of peace activists had taken to the streets in 30 towns and cities across Germany demanding an immediate end to the country's unpopular presence in Afghanistan.[22]

BIN LADEN'S KILLING AND THE SOCIETY OF THE SPECTACLE

The assassination of Osama bin Laden on 2 May 2011 confirmed if nothing else that we live in an age of the spectacle – so brilliantly analysed by the post-modern theorists Guy Debord[23] and Jean Baudrillard.[24] Yet, as the French philosopher Christian Salmon stressed,[25] the event also reminded us that, paradoxically, the invisible lies at the heart of our hyper-mediated society.

Take the two iconic images to emerge from the gunning down of bin Laden. There is the extraordinary image of President Barack Obama, supposedly fresh from a game of golf, sitting with members of his national security team in the 'situation room' at the White House. According to Will Dean, the image, taken by White House photographer Pete Souza, 'immediately became as famous as any White House photograph since Stanley Tretick's portrait of John Fitzgerald Kennedy Jr peek-a-booing through his father's Resolute Desk' (Dean 2011). It is a rare peep for people like you and me into the operations and personalities of the secret state. The doors are suddenly thrown open and what do we see? All of them bar one are simply staring at a screen. So we, the media consumers, are left looking at them looking.

But what they are observing remains tantalisingly out of view to us: invisible. Indeed, as invisible as Saddam Hussein's weapons of mass destruction. We are told the national security team are following the shots taken by a camera held by one of the US secret navy Seals engaged in the assault on bin Laden's hideaway home in Abbottobad, Pakistan. That might be true – it might be deliberate misinformation. Yet what is significant is that those inhabitants of the 'situation room' are establishing their status as powerbrokers in the society of the spectacle by claiming the role of privileged voyeurs – in this case, of an assassination mission.

The one whose eyes are fixed elsewhere stares instead at a computer screen. Symbolically it is the military man, Admiral Mike Mullen, chairman of the joint chiefs of staff, who sits closest to the President. So the image confirms both the privileged place of the military in the US – and that its most important activities remain secret, invisible. On a computer keyboard in front of secretary of state Hillary Rodham Clinton lies, tantalisingly, a white sheet where an image has clearly been obscured and pixellated. So once again we voyeurs into the operations of the secret state are reminded of how the invisible and the spectacular necessarily coexist.

According to David Usborne (2001b), had the photograph of the situation room been a little wider, it would have revealed the face of the CIA 'mastermind' 'John' who had made the crucial discovery of the al-Qaeda leader at the Abbottabad compound. The unseen becomes the most important. Of 'John', of course, we know nothing precise: his identity has to remain secret. A profile of him is presented by 'CIA insiders' – but it could all be fiction.

The other iconic image linked to the assassination shows bin Laden apparently in a room in his hideaway. And like those inhabitants of the 'situation room' he is engaged in a simple activity: he is watching a screen. We are told he is looking at footage of himself on television. That might be true or false: we cannot see the image on the TV screen. It has been whitened out: it's invisible. But what is clear is that, within the society of the spectacle, the US propaganda machine deliberately smears their 'Enemy No. One' principally by showing him as a narcissistic voyeur. Even during the hyper-mediated events following the assassination, the invisible remains prominent: the Seals who carried out mission 'Geronimo' are anonymous, the violence of the assault we will never see – nor the image of the slain bin Laden, quickly dumped out of sight into the sea (according to the propaganda).

Even during the hyper-mediated events following the assassination the invisible remains prominent: the Seals (special operations soldiers) who carried out mission 'Geronimo' are anonymous, inhabiting the world of fiction more than 'reality'. Typically, one of the accounts of the raid (full of anonymous quotes and blackened-out faces in the photographs) by Howard E. Wasdin and Stephen Templin (2012) is marketed as fiction: 'As action-packed as a Tom Clancy thriller' says the front cover plug.[26]

The events surrounding the killing also confirm how the banal is such a central ingredient of spectacular. Here is the nation with the most sophisticated surveillance technology at its fingertips (with satellites in the heavens above us supposedly so powerful they can read the number plates on cars) and with one of the most heavily resourced and ruthless intelligence operations in the history of the world. And yet for 10 years bin Laden somehow managed to elude their grasp. And in the end he turns up on the doorstep of a Pakistani military academy close to the country's capital. It is as if the gravitas and righteousness of the 'war on terror' are undermined by the lies on which it is based – and so the rhetoric collapses into banalities.

The 'world's greatest threat', the 'mastermind of a monstrous global terrorist movement' ends up being shown as nothing more than a pathetic old man, huddled beneath a shawl in a scruffy room (looking rather like an untidy, grotty bedsit of your average student) struggling to get his ancient-looking video recorder to work. And so the Hollywoodised myth of the evil recluse plotting the destruction of Western civilisation in his million-dollar mansion is shattered by the banality of the ordinary.

THE 2011 LIBYAN ASSAULT AND DISASTER MILITARISM

Following Libya's decision after the 9/11 US terrorist attacks to build closer ties with the West and renounce all efforts to develop nuclear weapons, UN sanctions against the country were lifted in 2003. To improve the image of Libya in the West, Gaddafi employed the Monitor Group, an American public relations company between 2000 and 2008.[27] The demonisation of Col. Gaddafi predictably declined and members of the political, financial and academic British elite lined up to welcome the Libyan leader back into the 'international community'.[28]

For instance, on 26 March 2004, an editorial in the *Guardian* commented: 'We should congratulate the Foreign Office for its quiet and effective diplomacy. ... Col. Gaddafi should be encouraged, but not at such a forced pace.' An editorial in the *Independent* on the same day described Gaddafi as merely 'the Arab world's most eccentric and unpredictable leader', and, referring to the Lockerbie outrage, added: 'Mr Blair is right to argue that there is real cause for rejoicing in a sinner that repenteth. However distasteful to the families of those murdered, an engagement and reconciliation with Libya that leads to the admission of guilt and compensation is better than continued isolation of the North African country.'[29]

Also during this period, Gaddafi was represented more as an 'eccentric and unpredictable leader' rather than an 'evil dictator'. This picture was reinforced in the coverage of the WikiLeaks revelations on Libya in December 2010. For instance, the cables disclosed that Col. Gaddafi, 68, 'suffered from severe phobias, enjoyed flamenco dancing and horse-racing, acted on his whims and irritated friends and enemies alike'.[30]

Significantly, the demonisation did not intensify even after Abdurahman Alamoudi was jailed after admitting to participating in a Libyan plot to assassinate Prince Abdullah (now King) of Saudi Arabia. According to court records, Gaddafi wanted Abdullah killed after a 2003 Arab League summit where Gaddafi felt he had been insulted. At one point, Abdullah wagged a finger at Gaddafi and said: 'Your lies precede you, while the grave is ahead of you.'[31] But Robert Fisk was keen to emphasise the Blair government's double standards:

> We adore Gaddafi, the crazed dictator of Libya whose werewolves have murdered his opponents abroad, whose plot to murder King Abdullah of Saudi Arabia preceded Tony Blair's recent trip to Tripoli – Colonel Gaddafi, it should be remembered, was called a 'statesman' by Jack Straw for abandoning his non-existent nuclear ambitions – and whose 'democracy' is perfectly acceptable to us because he is on our side in the 'war on terror'.[32]

The 2003-2011 period can, then, be seen as a significant interregnum in the moves by Western governments to eliminate Col. Gaddafi (Keeble 2011a). Both sides in the conflict cynically decided that some kind of 'entente' best served their interests. Gaddafi certainly took the opportunity to secure the lifting of UN sanctions and build up diplomatic and commercial relations with the United States, the European Union and Asian states. The high point of Libya's rapprochement with the West came when Col. Gaddafi addressed the United Nations on 23 September 2009.[33] Yet the WikiLeaks cables revealed that Gaddafi flew into a rage after the US refused to let him pitch his Bedouin-style tent in New York. In return, the Libyan leader refused to allow a 'hot' shipment of highly enriched uranium to be loaded on a transport plane and shipped to Russia as part of his nuclear-dismantling procedure.[34]

But once the uprising against the regime was launched in Tripoli in February 2011, and Nato began its bombing campaign on 19 March (the anniversary of the attack on Iraq in 2003), the 'mad dog', demonisation discourse returned to the media.[35] For instance, on 4 September, *The Sunday Times* headlined a report about the Libyan leader's alleged attempts to escape via the pipes of the $33 billion Great

Man-made River Project: 'Gaddafi and his sons flee like rats up a waterpipe.'[36]

And the Western elites (assisted by a compliant mainstream media) quickly reverted to their previous policy of confrontation with Libya, seizing the new opportunities in their increasingly desperate attempts to eliminate Gaddafi. Immediately after the 25 April attack on Gaddafi, Vladimir Putin, the Russian Prime Minister, accused Nato of aiming to kill the Libyan leader in an attack which completely destroyed his home in Sirte – and going far beyond the remit allowed by the UN resolution 1973 authorising all necessary means 'to protect civilians'. US defence secretary Robert Gates rejected the claim.[37]

The efforts of MI6 and the SAS in assisting the rebels and capturing Gaddafi once his Tripoli compound was raided on 24 August 2011 were reported prominently throughout the conflict.[38] For instance, *The Times* reported on 25 August 2011 that a 30-strong SAS unit had been working with Qatari special forces along the front line with rebel forces. 'The SAS has performed a more discreet role compiling information and co-ordinating with Nato pilots farther back.'[39] The SAS was said to be 'keen to restore its somewhat battered reputation after an abortive early secret mission to Benghazi when six SAS troopers and two MI6 officers were arrested by Libyan farmers'. Reports also emerged of France, Italy and Egypt (in the form of members of Unit 777) sending special forces to support the insurgents.[40]

Indeed, one of the paradoxes of contemporary warfare propaganda is that, at strategic moments such as during the Libyan crisis of 2011, the secret and the invisible are revealed. And on the day Gaddafi's brutal butchering to death (in front of the gaze of the gloating international corporate media) was reported, the *Daily Star*'s headline read: 'Mad dog put down.'[41]

In the wake of the toppling of Gaddafi Libya descended into chaos. As a report by the house of commons foreign affairs committee in September 2016 pointed out, the 2011 rapid intervention had led to political and economic collapse, internecine warfare, a humanitarian crisis and the rise of Islamic State throughout north Africa (Cordon 2016). An intended new militarist, quickie victory had, in fact, turned out a disaster (see Reuter 2016). The then-Prime Minister, David Cameron, was heavily blamed. The role of the corporate media in backing regime change was not highlighted. On the same day, a report from Brown University estimated that Washington had wasted almost $5 trillion since 11 September 2001 on wars launched under the pretext of fighting terrorism (Van Auken 2016).[42]

WESTERN AGGRESSION IN MALI AND THE MEDIA

By January 2013 Britain was at war once again – sending jets to assist the French in quelling a rebellion in the north of Mali. Predictably all the limitations of the corporate media's coverage of warfare and foreign affairs were exposed in Fleet Street's coverage – with all the essential historical, political, economic, military and geo-strategic background missing (Keeble 2013).

The dominant narrative represents the West intervening against a predictable enemy: radical, fundamentalist Islamic groups. The *Guardian*, for instance, on 12 January 2013, reported that French troops were aiming 'to contain Islamist groups which are continuing to clash with the army in a fight for control of the desert north of the west African country'. *The Sunday Times* (on 13 January) reported on French and British joining 'an internationally co-ordinated effort to stop an al-Qaeda-linked rebel alliance from reaching the capital of Mali'. The policy of the French President, François Hollande, they described as 'dynamic'.

Yet most crucially this simple narrative ignores the fact that on many occasions the West has joined with 'Islamic fundamentalists' in overt and covert military activities. Today in Syria, for instance, a complex web of Islamic groupings – backed by the West, Qatar and Saudi Arabia – are competing for prominence in the movement opposing the government of President Bashar al-Assad. Similarly, during the 2011 revolt which toppled Col. Gaddafi in Libya the West relied heavily on the forces of radical Islamic groups. The problems associated with this strategy rebounded on the US when some of those same Islamic fighters stormed the American embassy in Benghazi, in the east of Libya, on 11 September 2012 and assassinated the US ambassador, Christopher Stephens.

This collusion of the West with terrorist groups is nothing new. The historian Mark Curtis reveals in his ground-breaking book *Secret affairs* (2010) that Britain has supported radical Islamic groups in Afghanistan, Iran, Iraq, Libya, the Balkans, Syria, Indonesia and Egypt since the 1940s. Moreover, Curtis shows how British policies of 'divide and rule' exploited Islamic forces to promote imperial interests in India, Palestine, Jordan and Yemen.

Let's consider some of the deeper military/economic factors behind the West's intervention in Mali – largely ignored by the corporate press. At the heart of the conflict is the ongoing rivalry between West and China for access to Africa's rich resources – of oil, diamonds, copper, gold, iron, cobalt, uranium, bauxite, silver, petroleum, woods and tropical fruits.

In 2007, the Pentagon created the African Command (Africom) to spearhead its military advances on the continent and to counter China's growing economic influence (Forte 2012: 187-235, Turse 2015). More than 2,000 Chinese companies have invested in the continent. This is mostly in energy, mining, construction and manufacturing projects though recently tourism, finance, agriculture and aviation have attracted investment from Chinese businesses. It is difficult to know precisely the overall figure, but in mid-2012, China's ambassador to South Africa, Tian Xuejun, said that China's investment in Africa of various kinds exceeded $40 billion. In a rare acknowledgement of the China factor, Joe Glenton, in an *Independent* blog, said they had donated 'hundreds of millions' for development purposes.[43] He went on:

> Some argue that China will sit back and let the French do its work for it by handling the crisis and restoring some kind of stability, with China perhaps

moving back in later. Contrary to that view, it is worth considering that the intervention may be at least partially informed by a need to counter the Chinese, certainly on the part of the US and also on the part of major European countries.

One of the many reasons for Nato's intervention in the Libyan civil war – also ignored by the corporate press – was Gaddafi's refusal to join all the other Maghreb nations in Africom and, instead, develop close economic ties with the Chinese. Significantly, just before the Nato raids began, in March 2011, China hastily withdrew 35,000 of its citizens from the country.

Another consequence of Nato's Libyan intervention was the fleeing of Touareg nationalist militias, who had backed Gaddafi, into northern Mali. Here, the early successes of the National Movement for the Liberation of the Azawad provoked the ousting of President Amadou Toumani Touré in a military coup on 22 March 2012 – and this, in turn, led to the collapse of the Malian army and the continuing successes of Islamists in the north.

Soon afterwards, the US announced the formation of a dedicated 3,500-strong brigade to carry on continuous activities in an estimated 35 countries on the African continent. In November 2012, Hillary Clinton, then-US secretary of state, visited Algeria (just to the north of Mali) to win their support for Western military intervention in Mali. Significantly, this was followed by the first ever US strategic dialogue with the Algerian National Liberation Front government in Washington. In October 2012, *www.wired.com* reported that activities at the US drone base in Djibouti, a tiny French colonial outpost to the north of Somalia, were expanding (Axe 2012). Already the base was hosting eight Predator drones and eight F-15E fighter-bombers plus other warplanes, as well as around 300 Special Operations Forces and more than 2,000 other US troops and civilians.

Another factor behind France's military adventurism, largely ignored by the corporate media, was the importance of West Africa to the country's nuclear industry. The French nuclear company Areva, which provides 78 per cent of the country's electricity, and which is the world's largest developer of nuclear equipment, gets much of its uranium from Mali and neighbouring Niger. Areva draws profits of roughly 3 billion euros every year.

Already French forces had intervened in 2011 in the civil war in the Ivory Coast (with US and UN blessing) to topple President Lauren Gbagbo and install the Western-backed Alassane Quattara. Yet military/foreign policy hardly featured in the 2012 presidential elections in France.

Predictably the West's intervention won the support of the mainstream press. *The Times*, of 14 January, for instance, described it as a 'just mission'. 'France, the former colonial power, has responded with air strikes and Britain is rightly giving logistical support under the terms of a defence treaty signed with France in 2010.'

The *Guardian*, the most 'liberal' of Fleet Street's offerings, backed the intervention in an editorial on 15 January, describing it as 'a calculated gamble' though not without risk. On its website, Gregory Mann was emphatic in his support. 'The intervention was necessary,' he stressed. But it was definitely not a 'neo-colonial offensive'. 'The argument that it is might be comfortable and familiar, but it is bogus and ill-informed.' At the same time, he said, Mali needed 'a diplomatic intervention as urgently as it needed military intervention'. Ian Birrell, in the *Independent* on 14 January, argued that French action was necessary 'to stop the deadly cancer of Islamist extremism spreading further south'.

Media coverage is never monolithic: Owen Jones, author of *Chavs* (2010) (about the demonisation of the working class) and *The establishment: And how they get away with it* (2014), had a piece in the *Independent* of 14 January warning that Britain was 'being led into another war that risks disaster'. The *Daily Mail*, which usually manages to combine undying support for 'our boys on the frontline' in its news reports whenever conflicts erupt, with an editorial scepticism, predictably questioned British involvement in Mali with these words: 'Isn't there a risk we'll be drawn into yet another bloody conflict?'

And yet the views of the global peace movement which consistently opposes military adventurism by the major imperial powers went largely unheard. All the more reason to check out the many alternative websites offering insightful analyses – and challenging the dominant narrative. For instance, *www.wsws.org* was right when it editorialised on 15 January:

> Mali is the fourth country attacked by France in two years, after Libya, the Ivory Coast and Syria. Of these countries, all but Libya were former French colonies. Explanations for this war given by President François Hollande and other French officials – that France aims to defend Mali's 'democracy' from al-Qaeda, and not what Hollande called France's 'fundamental interests' – are cynical lies. French imperialism is setting out to re-establish a dominant position in West Africa, using military force to assert its interests.

Steve Breyman, writing on 15 January in *www.counterpunch.org*, the progressive, investigative site, provided important background and analysis on the Malian conflict, highlighting the response of the US administration:

> The US will collaborate closely with France as the war in Mali escalates. If US participation is limited to drones, there will not be much clamor for invocation of the WPR [War Powers Resolution]. The test will come should the French get bogged down in the vast deserts of northern Mali, and the armed US role expands.

And, finally, Walter Russell Mead, at *The American Interest* (*the-american-interest.com*/), cast a critical eye over President Obama's 'counter-terrorism' policies in North Africa:

> Since Obama took office the US spent almost $600 million to combat Islamic militancy across North Africa. In countries like Mali and Niger US

forces trained local soldiers in counterterrorism skills. Arms and equipment were bought so local governments could protect their territories. This strategy, in theory, would protect North Africa from falling into the hands of Islamist militants – who would impose strict Sharia rule on unwilling locals and use lawless territory to launch attacks on Western targets – without involving a heavy deployment of American troops like in Iraq and Afghanistan. That was the theory. But as heavily armed Islamist militants battle French forces in the Battle for Mali, it's clear Obama's strategy to help weak North African states protect themselves from terrorists has failed catastrophically (Mead 2013).

CHAD: HOW THE PRESS HIDES THE GLOBAL CRIMES OF THE WEST

One of the essential functions of the corporate media is to marginalise or silence acknowledgement of the history – and continuation – of Western imperial aggression. The coverage of the May 2016 sentencing in Senegal of Hissène Habré, the former dictator of Chad, for crimes against humanity, provides a useful case study.[44]

The verdict could well have presented the opportunity for the media to examine in detail the complicity of the US, UK, France and their major allies in the Middle East and North Africa in the appalling genocide Habré inflicted on Chad during his rule – from 1982 to 1990. After all, Habré had seized power via a CIA-backed coup. As William Blum commented in *Rogue State* (2002: 152): 'With US support, Habré went on to rule for eight years during which his secret police reportedly killed tens of thousands, tortured as many of 200,000 and disappeared an indetermined number.'

Indeed, while coverage of Chad has been largely missing from the British corporate media, so too was the massive, secret war waged over these eight years by the United States, France and Britain from bases in Chad against Libyan leader Colonel Gaddafi.[45]

By 1990, with the crisis in the Persian Gulf developing, the French government had tired of Habré's genocidal policies while George Bush senior's administration decided not to frustrate France in exchange for co-operation in its attack on Iraq. And so Habré was secretly toppled and in his place Idriss Déby was installed as the new President of Chad.

Reporting of the Habré sentencing was predictably consistent across all the leading newspapers in the UK and US. Thus the focus was on the jubilant reactions of a few of the victims of Habré's torture and rape, on the comments from some of the human rights organisations involved for many years in the campaign to bring the Chad dictator to justice – and on the fact that it was the first time an African country had prosecuted the former head of another African country for massive human rights abuses. Only a tiny part of the reporting mentioned the West's role in the genocide. None of the reporting placed the Chad events in the broader context of US/Western imperial aggression.

The story in the *Guardian*, by Ruth Maclean, was typical. Some 21 paragraphs were devoted to the report ('After 26-year wait, victims of Chad's former dictator weep tears of joy as he is convicted'[46]). But only in the last one (appearing almost as an after-thought) was there any mention of US complicity: 'The US State department and the CIA propped up Habré, sending him weapons and money in return for fighting their enemy, Mu'ammar Gaddafi.'

In a follow-up editorial on 1 June 2016,[47] the *Guardian* again left mentioning the West's role until the last par: 'Many questions still remain unanswered, including several concerning the responsibility or complicity of Western countries, such as France and the US, which actively supported Habré during the cold war years, turning a blind eye to his methods.'

The *Telegraph* adopted a similar approach. Aislinn Laing, based in Johannesburg, reported briefly: 'Mr Habré, 73, is a former rebel leader who took power by force in Chad in 1982 and was then supported by the US and France to remain at the helm as a bulwark to Muammar Gaddafi in Libya.'[48] Adam Lusher, in the *Independent*, devoted just eight words to contextualising the trial: 'Hissène Habré was once backed by America's Cold War-era CIA.'[49]

In *The New York Times*, buried in par. 24 of a 27-paragraph report by Dionne Searcey are these words: 'Mr. Habré took power during a coup that was covertly aided by the United States, and he received weapons and assistance from France, Israel and the United States to keep Libya, to the north of Chad, and Col. Muammar el-Qaddafi, then the Libyan leader, at bay.'

Similarly, in Paul Schemm's 23-paragraph report in the *Washington Post*, his par. 15 reads: 'Supported by the United States and France in his wars against Libyan leader Moammar Gaddafi, Habré was accused of killing up to 40,000 people and torturing hundreds of thousands.'[50] Neither the *Los Angeles Times*[51] nor the *Belfast Telegraph*[52] could find any space to mention the West's complicity. Intriguingly, the final paragraph in the *Guardian*'s report also included a statement by John Kerry, the US secretary of state, which 'acknowledged his country's complicity': 'As a country committed to the respect for human rights and the pursuit of justice, this is also an opportunity for the United States to reflect on, and learn from, our own connections with past events in Chad.' But how hypocritical is this rhetoric given the fact that the US today is still supporting human rights offenders across the globe – including the current dictator of Chad, Idriss Déby. Moreover, the Western powers, the US and France in particular, are using Chad as a major base for their covert military operations in Africa.[53]

A number of newspapers commented on how the case set an important precedent for holding high-profile human rights abusers to account in Africa. Yet there was little mention of the extraordinary background. For in June 2003, the US actually warned Belgium that it could lose its status as host to Nato's headquarters if the

Habré case went ahead on the basis of a 1993 law, which allowed victims to file complaints in Belgium for atrocities committed abroad. Campaigners determined to bring Habré to justice only then shifted their attention to Africa. William Blum comments in the 'Introduction' to *Killing Hope* (p. 13) on the US's secret wars:

> With a few exceptions, the interventions never made the headlines or the evening TV news. With some, bits and pieces of the stories have popped up here and there, but rarely brought together to form a cohesive and enlightening whole; the fragments usually appear long after the fact, quietly buried within other stories, just as quietly forgotten…

How perfectly this both predicts and explains the corporate media's coverage of the Chad dictator, Hissène Habré!

CONCLUSION: NEW MILITARISM TRANSFORMED INTO DISASTER MILITARISM

Since 2003, Western interventions in the Middle East and Africa have all proven disasters. New militarism (from 1982 to 2003) was built on the manufacture of 'quickie' attacks against puny opposition against whom 'victories' could be rapidly won. The decline and demise of the Soviet Union following the collapse of the Berlin Wall in 1989 meant that US-led forces for a few years indulged in a series of military adventures – with little attention given to the consequences.

From 1976 to January 2004 as few as 900 US service people died overseas due to hostile action, about 38 per cent occurring in Iraq during the ten-month period 19 March to January 2004 (Conetta 2004: 13). Since then US and UK casualties have been mounting. As the years progressed Western forces were dragged into an appalling quagmire in Iraq with local opposition to the occupation mounting – while the war in Afghanistan – which began in 2001 after the US elite, with UK support, sought an immediate target for their anger over the 9/11 atrocity – became one of the longest in US history.

British troops 'handed over security responsibilities to Iraqi authorities' in 2009.[54] And in October 2014, according to official sources, the last UK combat troops left Afghanistan.[55] By the end of 2015, the war in Afghanistan had cost the US an estimated $1 trillion, the war in Iraq $1.7 trillion;[56] in 2013, the Afghan conflict had cost the UK an estimated £37 billion (Norton-Taylor 2013) while the conflict in Iraq £8.4 billion.[57] Some 4,479 US soldiers had died with over 100,000 estimated wounded and 320,000 veterans with brain injuries.[58] In contrast, 179 UK soldiers died.[59] Some 348 journalists had been killed while an estimated 1,455,590 Iraqi deaths were directly due to the Iraq invasion of 2003.[60] Mark Weisbrot went so far as to call this a 'holocaust' (2007). Such a sorry tale, then of unnecessary death and devastation.[61] Massive civilian deaths had also resulted from the US military operations in Yemen that began in 2002 while millions starved following the blockade imposed on the country by Saudi Arabia.

The monstrous expansion of the media/military/industrial complexes in both the UK and US continued to appear out of control.[62] By 2015, US special forces were being deployed in 135 countries – far beyond the gaze of the international corporate media (Turse 2015). US general Joseph Votel, chief of the Special Operations Command, told the senate armed services committee in 2016 that 'on any given day, 10,000 special operators are deployed or forward stationed conducting overseas missions' (*Private Eye* 2016). A freedom of information request in the US had also revealed that UK special forces were involved with American forces in Libya and South Sudan 'in strength' (ibid). From 2007 to 2014, the US even tripled its deployment of special operations forces to Latin America, according to documents obtained via Freedom of Information request by the non-profit Washington Office on Latin America (WOLA) (Hardt 2016).

And US bases were expanding across the globe in an effort to counter mounting opposition to US imperialism (Vine 2016). Afghanistan rapidly deteriorated into a narco-state. As Jane Shallice reports (2009: 15): 'Warlords paid by the coalition to curb opium production instead pocketed the money while yields increased. With the economy in ruins, poppy cultivation became the only reliable source of income for farmers.' In 2007, Afghanistan was producing 8,200 tons of raw opium a year – 93 per cent of total world production (ibid). Many were accusing the US and its allies of committing state crimes over the use of torture, rendition and the disappearing of enemy combatants (Bakir 2016: 2). By 2016 – with Western special forces embroiled in conflicts in Syria and US/UK military strategists increasingly resorting to secret drone attacks in Somalia, Afghanistan, Iraq, Pakistan and Yemen and little reported attacks from the air in Libya and Mali causing countless civilian casualties (Akerman 2014)[63] – new militarism had become disaster militarism.[64, 65]

NOTES

[1] See http://atimes.com/category/empire-of-chaos/

[2] Seldon (2005: 487) reports intriguingly that in September 2001, Blair's inner circle knew little about bin Laden: 'The problem was that bin Laden, al-Qaeda and the Taliban were all virtually unknown to most in the den. Blair had heard of bin Laden but knew little about him. Powell asked for a book to be obtained on the Taliban by Ahmed Rashid, which was later passed around No. 10. One aide admitted: "We thought honestly that al-Qaeda was a bit of an American obsession"'

[3] See http://www.cpbf.org.uk/body.php?id=71&category=freepress&finds=1&string=Richard%20 Keeble, accessed 25 December 2001. The Taliban had actually offered to hand over bin Laden for trial to the Organisation of the Islamic Conference on 15 October. 'But the US never offered the face-saving measures the Taliban needed' (Stone and Kuznick 2013: 507)

[4] As Sheldon reports (2005: 501): '[John] Scarlett [new head of the joint intelligence committee] and his "Assessments Staff" in the JIC took several days to produce the document which contained a mixture of published material and intelligence cleared for publication by SIS. It encountered little dissent in the Commons or from the mainstream press'

[5] Jonathan Steele (2011: 221) points out that on the day before 9/11 the US administration had prepared the way for an attack on Afghanistan: '... national security officials had agreed on a three-phase plan toward the Taliban. They would be presented with a final ultimatum to hand over bin

Laden. Failing that covert military aid would be channelled to anti-Taliban groups. If both those options failed, the US would seek to overthrow the Taliban regime "through more direct action"'

[6] Mystery surrounds Mullah Omar. The BBC carried a report in 2015 suggesting he had died two years previously in a hospital in Pakistan. See http://www.bbc.com/news/world-asia-33703097, accessed on 14 August 2015

[7] Some 23 of the 55 British deaths in Afghanistan from January to June 2010 had taken place around Sangin. Of the total Nato casualties of 1,849 on 21 June 2010 (drawn from the 25 countries of the coalition and including 125 US women), 1,125 were American, 147 Canadian, 44 French and 42 German (see Higginson, John, 'Highest price must be paid', *Metro*, 22 June). Soldiers were also suffering major psychological problems. In June 2010, some 20,000 ex-servicemen were in prison or on probation in Britain – one in ten of the jail population. Since 1982, 264 veterans of the Falklands conflict of that year have committed suicide, compared with 255 who died in action (Newton Dunn 2010)

[8] The Americans, in addition to funding the Afghan police, had directed $1 million on building up private security forces. Yet these companies were operating in a 'culture of impunity' that was encouraging lawlessness and corruption, according to Britain's most senior commander in southern Afghanistan, Major General Nick Carter (Richard Norton-Taylor 2010d). According to investigative reporter Pratap Chatterjee (2010), the US had spent $7 billion on police training since 2003 and had left 'the country of 33 million people with a strikingly ineffective and remarkably corrupt police force. Its terrible habits and reputation have led the inhabitants of many Afghan communities to turn to the Taliban for security'. Fears were also growing that the Taliban had infiltrated the Afghan police (Wintour and Norton-Taylor 2010)

[9] See http://www.stripes.com/news/months-after-marjah-offensive-success-still-elusive-1.110638, accessed on 2 December 2015

[10] According to the *Sun*: 'Evil Taliban improvised bombs are usually packed with filth – they hope those they fail to kill outright die later from infection' (Willetts op cit). A UN Security Council report in June 2010 said that over the previous four months roadside bomb attacks rose by 94 per cent compared with the same period in 2009 while there were three suicide bombings every week. See: http://news.bbc.co.uk/1/hi/world/asia_pacific/10356741.stm

[11] See http://www.democracynow.org/2009/8/17/fixer_the_taking_of_ajmal_naqshbandi, accessed on 1 May 2010

[12] See http://www.truthtube.tv/play.php?vid=2795, accessed on 1 May 2010

[13] Colin Hughes, of the *Daily Mirror*, was later sent death threats after he posted a blog that criticised a charity motorbike ride through Wootton Bassett, through which passed the hearses carrying the bodies of repatriated soldiers (Milmo 2010). After more than 5,000 Facebook members called for a boycott of the *Mirror*, the newspaper apologised for Hughes' posting

[14] Soon after the arrest of Baradar, Pakistan arrested two more senior Taliban figures, Mullah Abdul Salam and Mullah Mir Mohammad. Mystery surrounded the arrests. Some commentators considered that Islamabad was shifting away from its secret support for the Taliban. But as Shah (2010) commented in the *Guardian*: 'A more cynical interpretation suggested that instead of turning its back on the Taliban, Pakistan was simply putting pressure on them to come to the negotiating table'

[15] See http://www.medialens.org/forum/viewtopic.php?t=3070&sid=76d871d7f9209d50c8b991fc9 50f2a5d, accessed on 3 June 2010

[16] See also Patrick Mulchrone's report on Beckham's visit and his praise for the 'fallen heroes' in the *Daily Mirror*. Available online at http://www.mirror.co.uk/celebs/news/2010/05/24/becks-silence-for-the-fallen-115875-22280836/, accessed on I June 2010

[17] See http://www.wsws.org/articles/2010/jun2010/afgh-j19.shtml, accessed on 19 June 2010

[18] See http://www.globalfirepower.com/defense-spending-budget.asp, accessed on 4 June 2010. Britain's figure represented a $3.7 billion increase on the previous year. *Guardian* columnist Simon Jenkins (2010) called for all the £45 billion defence spending 'against fantasy enemies' to be cut

[19] ibid

[20] See http://news.bbc.co.uk/1/hi/world/south_asia/10274262.stm, accessed on 9 June 2010

[21] Nato strategy in Afghanistan was thrown into further disarray with the resignation of the German President, Hörst Kohler, after he had suggested that military deployments were central to the country's economic interests (Connolly 2010)

[22] See inthesetimes.com/2010/04/03/german-easter-rallies-decry-afghanistan-killings, accessed on 4 May 2010

[23] See *Society of the Spectacle*, Rebel Press, 2004

[24] See *Baudrillard Live*, edited by Mike Gane, Routledge, 1993

[25] See Un crime parfait, *le Monde*, 14 May 2011 p. 22

[26] This text is part of an ever-expanding genre of accounts of soldiers' 'heroic' exploits in Afghanistan. Take, for instance Kemp, Col. Richard and Hughes, Chris (2009) *Attack state: Taking the fight to the enemy. The awesome untold story of a landmark tour of duty in Afghanistan*, London: Michael Joseph, and Moore (2003), Scott (2008) and Junger (2010). Geoff Dyer (2010) argues that writing in this non-fiction genre is best able to capture the essence of US-style warfare today: 'Reportage, long-form reporting – call it what you will – has left the novel looking superfluous. The fiction lobby might respond: it's too soon to tell.' He adds: 'We are moving beyond the non-fiction novel to different kinds of narrative art, different forms of cognition. Loaded with moral and political point, narrative has been recalibrated to record, honour and protest the latest, historically specific instance of futility and mess'

[27] Mark Allen, the former MI6 officer, who in September 2011 was at the centre of a row over British intelligence links with Libya, later worked as an advisor to BP and with the Monitor Group. He was also involved in the 2009 release of Abdelbaset al-Megrahi and escorted Gaddafi's son Said al-Islam to meetings in Oxford. See Ian Black, Man in the middle whose WMD triumph may now be overshadowed, *Guardian*, 7 September. Available online at http://www.guardian.co.uk/world/2011/sep/06/libya-mastermind-wmd-triumph-minefield, accessed on 8 September 2011

[28] John Simpson, the BBC's world affairs editor, mentions Gaddafi just once in his overview of the reporting of war over the last century (*Unreliable sources*, London: Macmillan 2010 p. 77), demonising him in the process by linking him with Presidents Ahmadinejad of Iran, Saddam Hussein of Iraq, Robert Mugabe of Zimbabwe, and Idi Amin of Uganda. They all, he said, spoke with 'the half-mocking, half-complaining, self-obsessed tone of a man who has felt himself belittled and now believes he can hit back without any sense of restraint'

[29] Both editorials cited in Noble war in Libya, *Media Lens*, 28 March 2011. Available online at http://www.medialens.org/index.php?option=com_content&view=article&id=611:noble-war-in-libya-part-2&catid=24:alerts-2011&Itemid=68, accessed on 26 August 2011

[30] See http://www.telegraph.co.uk/news/worldnews/wikileaks/8188463/What-WikiLeaks-told-us-about-Colonel-Gaddafi-a-profile-of-an-unpredictable-leader.html, accessed on 26 August 2011

[31] In July 2011, US Federal prosecutors asked a judge to reduce the 23-year prison sentence for Alamoudi. Libya TV commented: 'The documents explaining why prosecutors want to cut Alamoudi's sentence are under seal, and the US Attorney's Office in Alexandria declined to say how many years they are seeking to cut from Alamoudi's term. But such reductions are allowed only when a defendant provides substantial assistance to the government. It is rare for the government to seek a reduction so many years after the initial sentence was imposed.' See http://english.libya.

tv/2011/07/09/prosecutors-ask-to-cut-sentence-of-muslim-activist-in-gaddafis-plot-to-assassinate-saudi-king/, accessed on 18 August 2011

[32] See chapter entitled 'Gold-plated taps' in *The age of the warrior: Selected writings*, by Robert Fisk, London: Fourth Estate 2008 p. 234. Also available online at http://www.independent.co.uk/opinion/commentators/fisk/robert-fisk-welcome-to-palestine-453319.html, accessed on 18 August 2011

[33] See http://www.guardian.co.uk/world/2009/sep/23/gaddafi-un-speech, accessed on 8 September 2011. Significantly the report on the 100-minute speech says Gaddafi 'fully lived up to his reputation for eccentricity, bloody-mindedness and extreme verbiage'. Nowhere is he described as a dictator

[34] See Leigh, David and Harding, Luke (2011) *WikiLeaks: Julian Assange's war on secrecy*, London: Guardian Books p. 143

[35] The attack on Libya, it could be argued, was illegal. As Stone and Kuznick (2013: 568) report: 'Obama defied his own top lawyers, insisting that he did not need congressional approval under the War Powers Resolution to continue military activities in Libya beyond the sixty-day limit inscribed in the resolution. Offering a bizarre, some would say Orwellian, interpretation reminiscent of George W. Bush's definition of "torture" and Bill Clinton's definition of "sex", Obama claimed the US military engagement was outside the legal definition of "hostilities". Even hawkish House Speaker John Boehner was taken aback by Obama's contention that prolonged bombing of Libya as part of an effort to assassinate Muammar Gaddafi and overthrow his regime didn't constitute "hostilities"'

[36] Similar metaphors relating to 'rat in the hole' were used when the former President of Iraq, Saddam Hussein, was captured in December 2003. See, for instance, http://news.bbc.co.uk/1/hi/programmes/breakfast/3319491.stm, accessed on 8 September 2011

[37] See Libya: US rejects Putin's claim that coalition wants to assassinate Gaddafi, Ewen MacAskill and Richard Norton-Taylor, *Guardian*, 26 April 2011. Available online at http://www.wsws.org/articles/2011/apr2011/liby-a27.shtml, accessed on I August 2011. By the end of August 2011, Nato jets had flown 20,000 sorties. For the Nato attempt to assassinate Gaddafi in 2011, see Forte (2012: 122)

[38] See, for instance, http://www.telegraph.co.uk/news/worldnews/africaandindianocean/libya/8716758/Libya-secret-role-played-by-Britain-creating-path-to-the-fall-of-Tripoli.html and http://www.dailymail.co.uk/news/article-2029831/Libya--1m-bounty-Gaddafi-MI6-agents-join-hunt.html, both accessed on 27 August 2011

[39] See Hider, James (2011) Eyes peeled for deluded dictator in woman's garb, says ex-aide, *Times*, 25 August

[40] See *Libya: An uncertain future: Report of a fact-finding mission to assess both sides of Libyan conflict*, Paris, May 2011, published by International Centre for the Study and Research into Terrorism and Assistance to the Victims of Terrorism, French Centre for Intelligence Studies and the Mediterranean Peace Forum. Available online at http://www.cf2r.org/images/stories/news/201106/libya-report.pdf, accessed on 8 September 2011. See also *Libya: The other side of the story*, by Moign Khawaja. Available online at http://outernationalist.net/?p=2559, accessed on 8 September 2011

[41] See https://www.theguardian.com/media/gallery/2011/oct/21/gaddafi-dead-front-pages?CMP=twt_fd#/?picture=380756263&index=15 and for an excellent critique of the coverage of the Gaddafi killing see http://www.medialens.org/index.php/component/acymailing/archive/view/listid-1-alerts-full/mailid-103-killing-gaddafi.html, accessed on 25 August 2016

[42] The author of the report, Professor Neta Crawford, commented: '...a full accounting of any war's burdens cannot be placed in columns on a ledger. From the civilians harmed or displaced by violence, to the soldiers killed and wounded, to the children who play years later on roads and

fields sown with improvised explosive devices and cluster bombs, no set of numbers can convey the human toll of the wars in Iraq and Afghanistan, or how they have spilled into the neighboring states of Syria and Pakistan, and come home to the US and its allies in the form of wounded veterans and contractors.' Almost 7,000 US troops had been killed in Iraq and Afghanistan, with 52,000 listed officially as wounded in action and hundreds of thousands suffering from traumatic brain injuries, PTSD (post-traumatic stress disorder) and other mental health problems. UK and US special forces were still operating in Libya in September 2016 backed by the Royal Navy's Special Purpose Task Force in the southern Mediterranean (see Special Operations: Ask no questions, *Private Eye*, No 1427, 16 September-29 September 2016, p. 37)

[43] See http://www.independent.co.uk/voices/comment/dont-forget-the-critical-role-of-china-in-mali-8452530.html?origin=internalSearch

[44] See http://medialens.org/index.php/alerts/alert-archive/2016/820-how-the-press-hides-the-global-crimes-of-the-west-corporate-media-coverage-of-chad.html, accessed on 1 June 2016. And http://dissidentvoice.org/2016/06/how-the-press-hides-the-global-crimes-of-the-west/; and http://www.shoah.org.uk/2016/06/11/how-the-press-hides-the-global-crimes-of-the-west/

[45] See Targeting Gaddafi: Secret warfare and the media, by Richard Lance Keeble, in *Mirage in the Desert? Reporting the 'Arab Spring'*, edited by John Mair and Richard Lance Keeble, Abramis, Bury St Edmunds, 2011 pp 281-296

[46] See http://www.theguardian.com/world/2016/may/30/chad-hissene-habre-guilty-crimes-against-humanity-senegal

[47] http://www.theguardian.com/commentisfree/2015/jul/21/the-guardian-view-on-hissene-habres-trial-a-major-step-forward-for-justice-in-africa

[48] http://www.telegraph.co.uk/news/2016/05/30/court-to-rule-on-torture-trial-of-hissne-habr-africas-pinochet/

[49] http://www.independent.co.uk/news/world/hissene-habre-chad-former-president-africa-pinochet-found-guilty-of-crimes-against-humanity-a7056186.html

[50] https://www.washingtonpost.com/world/in-landmark-trial-former-chad-dictator-found-guilty-of-crimes-against-humanity/2016/05/30/5572e47a-2661-11e6-8329-6104954928d2_story.html

[51] http://www.latimes.com/world/la-fg-chad-dictator-guilty-20160530-snap-story.html

[52] http://www.belfasttelegraph.co.uk/news/world-news/former-chad-dictator-hissene-habre-given-life-term-for-human-rights-crimes-34757817.html

[53] http://www.tomdispatch.com/blog/176070/tomgram:_nick_turse,_america's_empire_of_african_bases/

[54] See http://www.telegraph.co.uk/news/worldnews/middleeast/iraq/3699368/British-forces-to-withdraw-from-Iraq-timeline-of-our-military-presence.html, accessed on 19 August 2016. The British mainstream media faithfully reported this as 'withdrawal'. 'In reality, the handover was essentially to the Shi'a militias who had long controlled Basra province' (Curtis 2010: 327). A BBC poll conducted in Basra found that only 2 per cent believed the British presence had had a positive impact on the province since 2003 while 86 per cent said the impact had been negative (ibid: 329)

[55] http://www.bbc.co.uk/news/uk-35159951

[56] http://www.counterpunch.org/2016/08/12/catastrophe-in-afghanistan-where-next-for-nato/, accessed on 14 August 2016

[57] http://www.ft.com/cms/s/0/c3e50026-8e99-11de-87d0-00144feabdc0.html#axzz38WKKDSu8

[58] https://antiwar.com/casualties/

[59] http://www.bbc.co.uk/news/uk-10637526

[60] http://www.justforeignpolicy.org/iraq

[61] See http://watson.brown.edu/costsofwar/costs/human/civilians, accessed on 26 October 2016

[62] Under President Barack (Nobel Peace Prize-winning) Obama US defence spending rose to $663.4 billion per year, though if military-related spending by the VA, CIA, Homeland Security, Energy, Justice or State Departments, and interest payments on past military spending are included, this figure rises to $1.3 trillion a year. See http://warisacrime.org/content/record-us-military-budget?link_id=5&can_id=ed31bf4cbc8f991980718b21b49ca26d&source=email-the-unbearable-awesomeness-of-the-us-military&email_referrer=the-unbearable-awesomeness-of-the-us-military&email_subject=the-unbearable-awesomeness-of-the-us-military, accessed on 19 August 2016. By the early years of the 21st century, the US defence establishment, in fact, could be ranked as the world's 17th largest economy. It is the largest oil consumer in the US and 31st in the world. On its books, officially, are listed 725 overseas sites deploying 254,788 personnel in 153 countries (Todd, Bloch and Fitzgerald 2009: 76)

[63] See also https://www.thebureauinvestigates.com/category/projects/drones. A report by Drones Wars UK claimed that the government had spent more than £2 billion on buying and developing military drones over the previous five years. The UK's Reaper drones in Afghanistan flew 11,000 hours and fired over 280 laser-guided Hellfire missiles and bombs at suspected insurgents between May 2011 and May 2012. See https://www.theguardian.com/world/2012/sep/26/drone-spending-britain-tops-2bn, accessed on 22 August 2016. On 10 June 2016, James Dean (2016) reported that the RAF's new artificially intelligent drone would have the ability to attack targets of its own accord. It was being developed under the Unmanned Combat Air System project, an Anglo-French programme costing £1.5 billion – successor to the RAF's Taranis programme and its French equivalent, Neuron

[64] Even as early as July 2004, a survey by Zogby International in six targeted Arab countries showed support for the US in virtual freefall – with those in favour dropping over a two-year period from pre-Iraq figure of 38 per cent to 11 per cent in Morocco, the main supporter of the group (see Todd, Bloch and Fitzgerald 2009: 45)

[65] I would like to thank my son, Gabriel Keeble-Gagnère, for suggesting this phrase for describing the new new militarism. It builds on Naomi Klein's brilliant exposure of disaster capitalism (namely 'the rapid-fire corporate reengineering of societies still reeling from shock') in her *Shock doctrine*, of 2007 (see http://www.naomiklein.org/shock-doctrine)

Bibliography

Abbas, A. (1986) *The Iraqi armed forces, past and present in Saddam's Iraq: Revolution or reaction?*, London: CADRI/Zed Books

Abrahams, Eddie (ed.) (1994) *The new warlords: From the Gulf War to the recolonisation of the Middle East*, London: Larkin Publications

Abu-Lughood, Ibrahim (1992) The politics of linkage: The Arab-Israeli conflict in the Gulf War, Bennis, Phyllis and Moushabeck, Michel (eds) *Beyond the Storm: A Gulf crisis reader*, Edinburgh: Canongate pp 183-190

Aburish, Said K. (1994) *The rise, corruption and coming fall of the House of Saud*, London: Bloomsbury

Aburish, Said K. (1997) *A brutal friendship: The West and the Arab elite*, London: Victor Gollancz

Aburish, Said (2003) Faith in his own divinity means Saddam will never surrender, *Evening Standard*, 19 March

Adair, Gilbert (1991) Saddam meets Dr Stangelove, *Guardian*, 29 January

Adams, James (1987) *Secret armies: The full story of SAS, Delta Force and Spetsnaz*, London: Hutchinson

Adams, James (1994) *The new spies: Exploring the frontiers of espionage*, London: Heinemann

Adams, Valerie (1986) *The media and the Falklands campaign*, London: Macmillan

Adie, Kate (2002) *The kindness of strangers*, London: Headline

Agee, Philip (1991) Gulf War launched 'new world order', *Open Eye*, No. 1 pp 16-23

Ahmed, Nafeez Mossadeq (2003) Why was a *Sunday Times* report on US government ties to al-Qaeda chief spiked?, *Ceasefire*, 17 May. Available online at https://ceasefiremagazine.co.uk/whistleblower-al-qaeda-chief-u-s-asset/, accessed on 15 September 2016

Ahmed, Nafeez Mosaddeq (2005) *The war on truth: 9/11, disinformation and the anatomy of terrorism*, Moreton-in-the-Marsh, Gloucestershire: Arris

Akerman, Spencer (2014) 41 men targeted but 1,147 people killed: US drone strikes – the facts on the ground. Available online at https://www.theguardian.com/us-news/2014/nov/24/-sp-us-drone-strikes-kill-1147, accessed on 14 August 2016

Aksoy, Asu and Robins, Kevin (1991) Exterminating angles: Technology in the Gulf, *Media Development*, October pp 26-29

Aldrich, Richard (1998) *Espionage, security and intelligence in Britain 1945-1970*, Manchester, New York: Manchester University Press

Aldrich, Richard (2009) Regulation by revelation? Intelligence, the media and transparency, Dover, Robert and Goodman, Michael S. (2009) *Spinning intelligence: Why intelligence needs the media. Why the media needs intelligence*, London: Hurst and Company pp 13-35

Aldrich, Richard J. (2010) *GCHQ: The uncensored story of Britain's most secret intelligence agency*, London: Harper Press

Aldrich, Richard J. and Cormac, Rory (2016) *The black door: Spies, secret intelligence and British prime ministers*, London: William Collins

Alexander, Adam (2015) UK surveillance oversight weakest in west, says first UN privacy chief, *Guardian*, 24 August. Available online at https://www.theguardian.com/world/2015/aug/24/we-need-geneva-convention-for-the-internet-says-new-un-privacy-chief, accessed on 13 June 2016

Ali, Tariq (2003) *Bush in Babylon: The recolonisation of Iraq*, London: Verso

Allen, Thomas B., Berry, Clifton F. and Polmar, Norman (1991) *War in the Gulf: From the invasion of Kuwait to the day of victory and beyond*, Atlanta, Georgia: Turner Publishing

Almond, Mark (2003) So how will he be judged? *Guardian*, 15 May

Amoore, Miles and Colvin, Marie (2010) British spearhead allied offensive, *Sunday Times*, 14 February

Andersen, Robin (1992) Oliver North and the news, Dahlgren, Peter and Sparks, Colin (eds) *Journalism and popular culture*, London/Newbury Park/New Delhi: Sage pp 171-189

Andersen, Robin (2006) *A century of media, a century of war*, New York: Peter Lang

Anderson, Ewen W. and Rashidian, Khalil (1991) *Iraq and the continuing Middle East crisis*, London: Pinter Publishers

Anderson, Steve (1990) Who calls the shots?, *Listener*, 22 November

Andrew, Christopher (1995) *For the President's eye only: Secret intelligence and the American presidency from Washington to Bush*, London: HarperCollins

Andrew, Christopher (2009) *The defence of the realm: The authorized history of MI5*, London: Penguin

Apple, R. W. (1991) War in the Gulf: Press, correspondents protest pool system, *New York Times*, 12 February. Available online at http://query.nytimes.com/gst/fullpage.html?res=9D0CE7D81531F931A25751C0A967958260&sec=&spon=&pagewanted=all

Appleyard, Bryan (2016) Under cover: The true story of the spy who saved two coachloads of British children by posing as a tramp, *Sunday Times Magazine*, 2 October pp 19-24

Aris, Ben and Campbell, Duncan (2004) How Bush's grandfather helped Hitler's rise to power, *Guardian*, 25 September. Available online at http://www.theguardian.com/world/2004/sep/25/usa.secondworldwar, accessed on 10 December 2015

Arkin, William, Durrant, Damian and Cherni, Marianne (1991) *On impact: Modern warfare and the environment – a case study of the Gulf War*, Washington DC: Greenpeace

Arnett, Peter (1993) *Live from the battlefield: From Vietnam to Baghdad – 35 years in the world's war zones*, London: Bloomsbury

Arnove, Anthony (2000) (ed.) *Iraq under siege: The deadly impact of sanctions and war*, London: Pluto Press

Arrighi, Giovanni (1994) *The long twentieth century*, London: Viking

Article 19 (1991) *Stop press: The Gulf War and censorship*, Article 19: International Centre on Censorship, No. 1

Ascherson, Neal (2011) Fact and fiction in a cold and secret war, *Observer*, 11 September. Available online at http://www.guardian.co.uk/film/2011/sep/11/neal-ascherson-cold-war-spies, accessed on 14 September 2011

Astore, William, J. (2010) Doubling down in Afghanistan, *tomdispatch.com*, 3 June. Available online at http://www.tomdispatch.com/archive/175256/, accessed on 2 June 2010

Atkinson, Rick (1994) *Crusade: The untold story of the Gulf War*, London: HarperCollins

Aubrey, Crispin (ed.) (1982) *Nukespeak: The media and the bomb*, London: Comedia

Axe, David (2012) US expands secretive drone base for African showdown war, *wired. com*, 26 October. Available online at https://www.wired.com/2012/10/secret-drone-base/, accessed on 6 November 2016

Ayer, A. J. 'Freddie' (1978) *Part of my life*, Oxford/London: Oxford University Press

Ayres, Chris (2005) *War reporting for cowards: Between Iraq and a hard place*, London: John Murray

Azzam, Maha (1991) The Gulf crisis: Perceptions of the Muslim world, *International Affairs*, Vol. 67, No. 3 pp 479-485

Badsey, Stephen (1992) The media war, Pimlott, John and Badsey, Stephen (eds) *The Gulf War assessed*, London: Arms and Armour Press pp 219-245

Badsey, Stephen (1995) Twenty things you thought you knew about the media, *Despatches* (journal of the Territorial Army Pool of Public Information officers), Spring pp 55-61

Baker, Carlos (1972) *Ernest Hemingway: A life story*, Harmondsworth: Penguin

Baker, Chris (1991) The new age of imperialism, *Socialist Action*, Spring pp 3-8

Baker, Norman (2007) *The strange death of David Kelly*, London: Methuen

Baker, Russ (2009) *Family of secrets: The Bush dynasty, America's invisible government, and the hidden history of the last fifty years*, New York: Bloomsbury Press

Bakir, Vian (2016) *Torture, intelligence and sousveillance in the war on terror: Agenda-building struggles*, Abingdon, Oxon: Routledge

Bale, Jeffrey M. (1995) Conspiracy theories and clandestine politics, *Lobster*, June pp 16-22

Barker, Hannah (2000) *Newspapers, politics and public opinion 1700-1850*, London: Longman

Barnaby, Frank (1984) *Future war*, London: Michael Joseph

Barnaby, Frank (1991) Mega bucks and some very big bangs, *Index on Censorship*, Vol. 20, No. 10 pp 9-13

Barnet, Richard (1988) The costs and perils of intervention, Klare, Michael and Kornbluh, Peter (eds) *Low intensity warfare: How the USA fights wars without declaring them*, London: Methuen pp 207-222

Barnett, Anthony (1982) Iron Britannia, *New Left Review*, No. 134 pp 1-59 (occupied whole issue)

Barnett, Anthony (2005) UK arms sales to Africa reach £1 billion mark, *Observer*, 12 June 2005

Bates, Stephen (2003) Bell berates media giants for warmongering words, *Guardian*, 27 May

Baudrillard, Jean (1976) *L'Exchange symbolique et la mort*, Paris: Gallimard

Baudrillard, Jean (1988) *Selected writings*, Cambridge: Polity Press

Baudrillard, Jean (1991) The reality gulf, *Guardian*, 11 January

Baudrillard, Jean (1995) *The Gulf War did not take place*, Bloomington: Indiana University Press

Bauman, Zygmunt (1990) Effacing the surface: On the social management of moral proximity, *Theory, Culture and Society*, No. 7 pp 5-38

Bazalgette, Cary and Paterson, Richard (1981) Real entertainment: The Iranian Embassy siege, *Screen Education*, Winter pp 55-68

Beaumont, Peter (2009) *The secret life of war*, London: Harvill Secker

Beaumont, Peter and Graham, Patrick (2003) Iraq terror spirals out of control as US intelligence loses the plot, *Observer*, 2 November

Beck, Robert (2004) Grenada's echoes in Iraq: International security and international law, *The Long Term View*, Vol. 2, No. 6 pp 73-87

Beckett, Andy (2004) Friends in high places, *Guardian*, 6 November. Available online at https://www.theguardian.com/world/2004/nov/06/usa.politics1, accessed on 17 June 2016

Beckett, Andy (2010) *When the lights went out: What really happened to Britain in the Seventies*, London: Faber and Faber

Beetham, David (2003) The warfare state, *Red Pepper*, June

Belgrano Action Group (1988) *The unnecessary war: Proceedings of the Belgrano enquiry, November 7/8, 1986*, Nottingham: Spokesman

Bell, Martin (1996) *In harm's way: Reflections of a war-zone thug*, London: Penguin Books, second edition

Bennis, Phyllis (1992) False consensus: George Bush's United Nations, Bennis, Phyllis and Moushabeck, Michel (eds) *Beyond the Storm: A Gulf crisis reader*, Edinburgh: Canongate pp 112-128

Berghahn, V. R. (1981) *Militarism: The history of an international debate 1861-1979*, Leamington Spa, Warwickshire: Berg Publishers

Bernstein, Carl (1977) The CIA and the media, *Rolling Stone*, 20 October. Available online at http://www.carlbernstein.com/magazine_cia_and_media.php, accessed on 1 October 2010

Berrington, Hugh (1989) British public opinion and nuclear weapons, March, Catherine and Fraser, Colin (eds) *Public opinion and nuclear weapons*, London: Macmillan

Best, Geoffrey (1980) *Humanity in warfare*, London: Weidenfeld and Nicholson

de la Billière, Sir Peter (1995) *Looking for trouble: SAS to Gulf Command*, London: HarperCollins

Bishop, Patrick (2009) *Ground truth: Back on Afghanistan's frontline – 3 Para's epic new challenge*, London: Harper Press

Blackburn, Robin (1999) Kosovo: The war of Nato expansaion, *New Left Review*, No. 235, May/June pp 107-123

Blakeway, Denis (1992) *Falklands war*, London: Sidgwick and Jackson

Bleifuss, Joel (1990) The first stone, *In These Times*, 26 September

Bloch, Jonathan and Fitzgerald, Patrick (1983) *British intelligence and covert action*, London: Junction Books

Bloom, Clive (2015) *Thatcher's secret war: Subversion, coercion, secrecy and government 1974-90*, Stroud, Gloucestershire: The History Press

Bloxham, Andy (2010) What WikiLeaks told us about President Gaddafi: The profile of an unpredictable leader, *Daily Telegraph*, 8 December. Available online at http://www.telegraph.co.uk/news/worldnews/wikileaks/8188463/What-WikiLeaks-told-us-about-Colonel-Gaddafi-a-profile-of-an-unpredictable-leader.html

Blum, William (2002) *Rogue state: A guide to the world's only superpower*, London: Zed Books

Blum, William (2004) *Killing hope: US military and CIA interventions since World War Two*, London: Zed Books

Blundy, David and Lycett, Andrew (1987) *Qaddafi and the Libyan Revolution*, London: Weidenfeld and Nicolson

Boone, Jon (2010a) Afghanistan: 24-hour patrols in Kandahar to win hearts and find mines, *Guardian*, 10 March

Boone, Jon (2010b) Afghan minister resigns over *jirga* attack, *Guardian*, 7 June

Boone, Jon and Norton-Taylor, Richard (2010) Poppy town that became death trap for British army, *Guardian*, 22 June

Boot, William (1991) The press stands alone, *Columbia Journalism Review*, March/April pp 23-24

Booth, Robert (2013) Failure to warn of Grenada invasion humiliated UK, *Guardian*, 1 August

Borger, Julian (2003) The spies who pushed for war, *Guardian*, 17 July. Available online at http://www.theguardian.com/world/2003/jul/17/iraq.usa, accessed on 6 June 2014

Borger, Julian and Norton-Taylor, Richard (2004) British intelligence still talking to Iraqi source who made false claims, *Guardian*, 14 July

Le Borgne, Claude (1992) *Un discret massacre: L'Orient, la guerre et après*, Paris: François Bourin

Born, Georgina (2005) *Uncertain vision: Birt, Dyke and the reinvention of the BBC*, London: Vintage

Boseley, Sarah (1992) How Margaret Thatcher handbagged Ron's Falklands' truce call, *Guardian*, 9 March

Bowcott, Owen (2003) Tactical lessons that must be learnt, *Guardian*, 15 March

Bowcott, Owen (2010a) 'Licence to kill' proposal for SAS troops invited overseas, *Guardian*, 30 December

Bowcott, Owen (2010b) Army shortages cost lives, bishop warns, *Guardian*, 29 April

Bowcott, Owen (2015) Campaigners say barely debated change in law legalised GCHQ hacking, *Guardian*, 16 May. Available online at https://www.theguardian.com/uk-news/2015/may/15/intelligence-officers-have-immunity-from-hacking-laws-tribunal-told, accessed on 13 June 2016

Bowen, Jeremy (2006) *War stories*, London and New York: Simon and Schuster

Bower, Tom (1995) *The perfect English spy: Sir Dick White and the secret war 1935-1990*, London: William Heinemann

Bower, Tom (1996) *Maxwell: The final verdict*, London: HarperCollins

Bower, Tom (2016) *Broken vows: Tony Blair and the tragedy of power*, London: Faber and Faber

Bowker, Gordon (2003) *George Orwell*, London: Little, Brown

Boyd-Barrett, Oliver (2004) Understanding the second casualty, Allan, Stuart and Zelizer, Barbie (eds) *Reporting War: Journalism in wartime*, London: Routledge pp 25-42

Boyd-Barrett, Oliver and Thussu, Daya (1992) *Contra-flow in global news: International and regional news exchange mechanisms*, London: John Libbey

Braestrup, Peter (1985) *Battle lines: Report of the Twentieth Century Fund Task Force on the military and the media*, New York: Priority Press

Bragg, Rick (2004) *I am a soldier, too: The Jessica Lynch story*, New York: Vintage

Bramley, Corporal Vincent (1991) *Excursion to hell*, London: Bloomsbury

Breyman, Steve (2013) Obama in Africa, *counterpunch.org*, 15 January. Available online at http://www.counterpunch.org/2013/01/15/obama-in-africa/, accessed on 16 January 2013

Bright, Martin (2002) Terror, security and the media, *Observer Online*, 21 July. Available online at http: //observer.guardian.co.uk/libertywatch/story/0,1373,758265,00.html, accessed on 22 July 2002

Broad, William J. (2000) US studied exploding A Bomb on the moon, *International Herald Tribune*, 17 May

Brothers, Caroline (1997) *War and photography*, London: Routledge

Brown, Ben and Shukman, David (1991) *By all necessary means: Inside the Gulf War*, London: BBC Books

Brown, Colin (2005) US lied to Britain over use of napalm in Iraq war, *Independent*, 17 June

Brown, David and Edwards, Ruby (2011) Campbell an 'unguided missile' during build-up to the Iraq war, *Times*, 15 July

Bulloch, John and Morris, Harvey (1991) *Saddam's war*, London: Faber and Faber

Bulloch, John and Morris, Harvey (1992) *No friends but the mountains: The tragic history of the Kurds*, London: Viking

Bulstrode, Mark (2010) Snatch Land Rovers blamed for dozens of deaths, *Independent*, 9 March

Buncombe, Andrew (2005) Global spending on arms tops $1 trillion, *Independent*, 9 June

Burgh, Hugo de (ed.) (2000) *Investigative journalism: Context and practice*, London: Routledge

Burke, Jason (2003) *Al-Qaeda: The true story of radical Islam*, London: Penguin

Cabell, Craig (2008) *Ian Fleming's secret war*, Barnsley, South Yorkshire: Pen and Sword Books

Cainkar, Louise (1991) How Paul Lewis covers post-war Iraq, *Lies of Our Times*, July/August pp 3-5

Callinicos, Alex (2002) The grand strategy of the American empire, *International Socialism*, No. 97, Winter pp 3-38

Campaign Against the Arms Trade (1989) *Death on delivery: The impact of the arms trade on the Third World*, London: CAAT

Campbell, Duncan (1980) Target Britain, *New Statesman*, 31 October pp 6-9

Campbell, Duncan (2011) Whistleblowing: From Xerox machine to WikiLeaks via Ellsberg, Agee and Vanunu, Mair, John and Keeble, Richard Lance (eds) *Investigative journalism: Dead or alive?* Bury St Edmunds: Abramis pp 223-229

Carruthers, Susan L. (2000) *The media at war: Communication and conflict in the twentieth century*, London: Macmillan Press

Caute, David (1986) *The Espionage of the saints: Two essays on silence and the state*, London: Hamish Hamilton

Cavendish, Julius (2010a) Fighters switch back to Taliban after 'broken promises', *Independent*, 23 April

Cavendish, Julius (2010b) Mosque murder leaves Kandahar on edge, *Independent*, 21 April

Chambers, Deborah, Steiner, Linda and Fleming, Carole (eds) (2004) *Women and journalism*, London: Routledge

Chambers, Roland (2009) *The last Englishman: The double life of Arthur Ransome*, London: Faber and Faber

Chatterjee, Pratap (2006) Intelligence in Iraq: L-3 supplies spy support, *Corpwatch*, 9 August. Available online at http://www.corpwatch.org/article.php?id=13993, accessed on 16 September 2016

Chatterjee, Pratap (2010) Policing Afghanistan: How Afghan police training became a train wreck, 21 March. Available online at http://truth-out.org/archive/component/k2/item/88615:policing-afghanistan-how-afghan-police-training-became-a-train-wreck, accessed on 7 October 2016

Chibnall, Steve (1977) *Law and order news*, London: Tavistock

Chilton, Paul (1982) Nuclear language, culture and propaganda, Aubrey, Crispin (ed.) *Nukespeak: The media and the bomb*, London: Comedia pp 94-112

Chilton, Paul (1983) Newspeak: It's the real thing, Aubrey, Crispin and Chilton, Paul (eds) Nineteen Eighty-Four *in 1984: Autonomy, control and communication*, London: Comedia: pp 33-44

Chilton, Paul (ed.) (1985) *Nukespeak today: Language and the nuclear arms debate*, Cambridge: Frances Pinter

Chomsky, Noam (1988) *The culture of terrorism*, London: Pluto Press

Chomsky, Noam (1989) *Necessary illusions: Thought control in democratic societies*, London: Pluto

Chomsky, Noam (1991a) *Deterring democracy*, London: Verso

Chomsky, Noam (1991b) *Pirates and emperors*, Montreal/New York: Black Rose Books

Chomsky, Noam (1993) *Year 501: The conquest continues*, London: Verso

Chomsky, Noam (1999) *Lessons from Kosovo: The new military humanism*, London: Pluto

Chomsky, Noam (2000) *Rogue states: The rule of force in world affairs*, London: Pluto Press

Chomsky, Noam (2001) *9/11*, New York: Seven Stories Press

Chomsky, Noam (2005) *Imperial ambitions: Conversations with Noam Chomsky on the post 9/11 world* (interviews with David Barsamian), London: Penguin

Chomsky, Noam (2007) *What we says goes: Conversations on US power in a changing world: Interviews with David Barsamian*, New York: Metropolitan Books/Henry Holt and Co

Cirino, Robert (1971) *Don't blame the people: How the news media use bias, distortion and censorship to manipulate public opinion*, New York: Vintage Books

Clancy, Tom (2003) *Shadow warriors: Inside the Special Forces*, London: Pan (with General Carl Steiner, Ret. and Tony Koltz)

Clark, David (2009) Kosovo was a just war, not an imperialist dress rehearsal, *Guardian*, 16 April

Clark, Ramsay et al. (1992) *War crimes: A report on United States war crimes against Iraq*, Washington, DC: Maisoneuvre Press

Clarridge, Duane R. (1997) *A spy for all seasons: My life in the CIA*, New York: Scribner

Cobain, Ian (2013) MoD unlawfully conceals files about the Troubles, *Guardian*, 7 October. Available online at http://www.theguardian.com/uk-news/2013/oct/06/ministry-of-defence-files-archive, accessed on 19 January 2016

Cobain, Ian (2014a) Academics consider legal action to force Foreign Office to release public records, *Guardian*, 13 January. Available online at http://www.theguardian.com/politics/2014/jan/13/foreign-office-secret-files-national-archive-historians-legal-action, accessed on 20 January 2016

Cobain, Ian (2014b) Are spooks bugging politicians?, *Guardian*, 15 July. Available online at http://www.theguardian.com/world/2014/jul/14/spies-flouting-wilson-doctrine-bugging-mps, accessed on 15 July 2014

Cobain, Ian (2016) Britain's secret wars, *Guardian*, 8 September

Cockburn, Alexander (1991a) The TV war, *New Statesman and Society*, 8 March p. 14

Cockburn, Alexander (1991b) The greatest story never told, *New Statesman and Society*, 10 January p. 10

Cockburn, Alexander (1991c) Dumb bombs, *New Statesman and Society*, 14 June p. 17

Cockburn, Alexander and Cockburn, Leslie (1992) *Dangerous liaison: The inside story of US-Israeli covert relationship*, London: Bodley Head

Cockburn, Alexander and Cohen, Andrew (1991) The unnecessary war, Brittain, Victoria (ed.) *The Gulf between us: The Gulf War and beyond*, London: Virago Press pp 1-26

Cockburn, Patrick (1996) Saddam has missiles and will use them, *Independent*, 5 July

Cockburn, Patrick (1997) Revealed: How the West set Saddam on the bloody road to power, *Independent*, 28 June

Cockburn, Patrick (2008) *Muqtada al-Sadr and the fall of Iraq*, London: Faber and Faber

Cockburn, Patrick (2010) A distorted view of war, *Independent*, 23 November

Cockett, Richard (1991) *David Astor and the* Observer, London: Deutsch

Cogan, James (2010) Afghanistan: Another massacre as a bloody summer looms in Kandahar, 23 April. Available online at www.wsws.org/articles/2010/apr2010/afgh-a23.shtml, accessed on 24 April 2010

Cohen, Jeff (2006) The myth of the media's role in Vietnam. Available online at http://www.fair.org/index.php?page=2526, accessed on 13 December 2006

Cohen, Julie (1991) Who will unwrap the October surprise?, *Columbia Journalism Review*, September/October pp 32-34

Cohen, Roger and Gotti, Claudio (1991) *In the eye of the Storm: The life of General H. Norman Schwarzkopf*, London: Bloomsbury

Colley, Linda (2007) We fret over Europe, but the real threat to sovereignty has long been the US, *Guardian,* 23 November. Available online at https://www.theguardian.com/commentisfree/2007/nov/23/comment.politics1, accessed on 22 August 2016

Collins, John M. (1991) *Americas small wars*, Washington/London: Brassey's (US)

Colvin, Marie (2010) Special forces assassins infiltrate Taliban strongholds in Afghanistan, *Sunday Times*, 7 February

Combs, James (1993) From the Great War to the Gulf War: Popular entertainment and the legitimation of warfare, Denton, Robert (ed.) *The media and the Persian Gulf war*, Westport, CT: Praeger pp 257-284

Conboy, Martin (2002) *The press and popular culture*, London: Sage

Conetta, Carl (2004) *Disappearing the dead: Iraq, Afghanistan and the idea of 'New Warfare'*, Project on Defense Alternatives Research Monograph 9. Available online at http://www.conw.org/pda/0402rm9.html, accessed on 30 May 2004

Connolly, Kate (2010) German president quits amid accusations of 'gunboat diplomacy' after Afghanistan gaffe, *Guardian*, 1 June

Copeland, Miles (1989) *The game player*, London: Aurum Press

Corbin, Jane (1991) When no publicity is good public relations, *Index on Censorship*, Vol. 20, No. 10 pp 4-5

Corbyn, Jeremy (2003) Rogue states, Monbiot, George et al., *Anti-imperialism: A guide for the movement*, London: Bookmarks pp 33-41

Cordon, Gavin (2016) Cameron takes blames for Libya's collapse into chaos, *Independent*, 14 September

Cottle, Simon (2006) *Mediatized conflict*, Maidenhead: Open University Press

Cottrell, Roger (2008) The Cecil King coup plot as a precursor to Gordon Brown's 'government of all talents', *Lobster*, No. 55, Summer pp 22-28

Crampton, Robert (2008) When the guns fall silent, *Times Magazine*, 13 September

Crick, Bernard (1982) *George Orwell: A life*, Harmondsworth, Middlesex: Penguin Books

Crick, Bernard (1996) Why are the liberal left so eager to give up one of their own, *Independent*, 14 July

Crouch, David (2004) Inside the system: Anti-war activism in the media, Miller, David (ed.) *Tell me lies: Propaganda and media distortion in the attack on Iraq*, London: Pluto pp 269-276

Crozier, Brian (1994) *Free agent: The unseen war 1941-1991*, London: HarperCollins

Cumings, Bruce (1992) *War and television*, London: Verso

Curran, James, Douglas, Angus and Whannel, Garry (1980) The political economy of the human interest story, Smith, Anthony (ed.) *Newspapers and democracy: International essays on a changing medium*, Cambridge, Massachusetts: MIT Press pp 288-316

Curran, James and Seaton, Jean (2003 [1991]) *Power without responsibility: The press, broadcasting and new media in Britain*, London: Routledge, sixth edition

Curran, James and Sparks, Colin (1991) Press and popular culture, *Media, Culture and Society*, Vol. 13, No. 2 pp 224-228

Currey, Cecil (1991) Vietnam: lessons learned, Helling, Phil and Roper, Jon (eds) *America, France and Vietnam: Cultural history and ideas of conflict*, Aldershot: Avebury pp 71-90

Curtis, Mark (2003) *Web of deceit: Britain's real role in the world*, London: Vintage

Curtis, Mark (2004) *Unpeople: Britain's secret human rights abuses*, London: Vintage

Curtis, Mark (2010) *Secret affairs: Britain's collusion with radical Islam*, London: Serpent's Tail

Cushion, Steve (2015) Aerial bombardment in historical perspective, *Socialist History Society Newsletter*, Vol. 4, No. 4 pp 6-7

Dale, Iain (ed.) (2002) *Memories of the Falklands*, London: Politico's

Dalrymple, William (2010) The British army overwhelmed by Afghan warriors. No, not today but in 1842. So can we learn lessons of history before it happens again?, *Dail Mail*, 17 June

Darwish, Adel and Alexander, Gregory (1991) *Unholy Babylon: The secret history of Saddam's war*, London: Victor Gollancz

Davies, Nick (2008) *Flat earth news*, London: Chatto & Windus

Davies, Philip H. J. (2005) *MI6 and the machinery of spying*, London: Frank Cass Publishers

Deacon, Richard (1990) *The French secret service*, London: Grafton Books

Dean, James (2016) RAF drone can attack without human approval, *Times*, 10 June

Dean, Will (2011) Chamber of secrets, *Independent*, 6 May

Debord, Guy (1991) *Comments on the society of the spectacle*, Pirate Press: Sheffield

De Luce, Dan (2003) The spectre of Operation Ajax, *Guardian*, 20 August

Derbyshire, J. Denis and Derbyshire, Ian (1988) *Politics in Britain: From Callaghan to Thatcher*, London: Chambers (orig. 1986: Sandpiper Publishing)

Der Derian, James (2002) Virtuous war: Mapping the media-industrial-entertainment network, *Political Science Quarterly*, Vol. 117, No. 1, 1 April 2002 pp 138-139

Der Derian (2009) *Virtuous war: Mapping the media-industrial-entertainment network*, New York/London: Routledge, second edition

Dickson, Barney (1991) From emperor to policeman: Britain and the Gulf War, Bresheeth, Haim and Yuval-Davis, Nira (eds) *The Gulf War and the New World Order*, London: Zed Books pp 40-48

Dillon, G. M. (1989) *The Falklands, politics and war*, Basingstoke, Hampshire, Macmillan

Dionne, E. J. (1992) The illusion of technique: The impact of polls on reporters and democracy, Mann, Thomas E. and Orren, Gary R. (eds) *Media polls in American politics*, Washington: Brookings Institute pp 150-167

Dixon, Norm (2004) How Reagan armed Saddam with chemical weapons, *CounterPunch*, 17 June. Available online at http://www.counterpunch.org/2004/06/17/how-reagan-armed-saddam-with-chemical-weapons/, accessed on 26 July 2016

Dockrill, Michael (1988) *British defence since 1945*, Oxford: Blackwell

Dodds, Klaus (2005) Contesting war: British media reporting and the 1982 South Atlantic war, Connelly, Mark and Welch, David (eds) *War and the media: Reportage and propaganda 1900-2003*, London: I.B. Tauris pp 218-35

Dodge, Toby (2002) Iraqi army is tougher than US believes, *Guardian*, 16 November

Donaldson, Frances (2005 [1982]) *P. G. Wodehouse: A biography*, London: Carlton Publishing Group

Donegan, Lawrence (2003) How Private Jessica became America's icon, *Observer*, 6 April

Donvan, John (2003) For the unilaterals, no neutral ground, *Columbia Journalism Review*, May/June. Available online at http://www.cjr.org/year/03/3/donvan.asp, accessed on 12 July 2003

Dorman, William and Manzour, Farhang (1987) *The US press and Iran: Foreign policy and the journalism of deference*, Berkeley: University of California Press

Dorril, Stephen (1993) *The silent conspiracy: Inside the intelligence services in the 1990s*, London: Heinemann

Dorril, Stephen (2000) *MI6: Fifty years of special operations*, London: Fourth Estate.

Dorril, Stephen (2003) Spies and lies, *Free Press*, April

Dorril, Stephen (2015) 'Russia accuses Fleet Street': Journalists and M16 during the Cold War, *The International Journal of Press/Politics*, Vol. 20, No. 2 pp 204-227

Dorril, Stephen and Ramsay, Robin (1991) *Smear*, London: Fourth Estate

Drucker, Peter E. (1993) *Post-capitalist society*, Oxford: Butterworth-Heinemann

Dyer, Geoff (2010) The human heart of the matter, *Guardian*, 12 June

Easlea, Brian (1983) *Fathering the unthinkable: Masculinity and the nuclear arms race*, London: Pluto Press

Easthope, Anthony (1986) *What's a man gotta do: The masculine myth in popular culture*, London: Pluto Press

Edmunds, Martin (1988) *Armed services and society*, Leicester: Leicester University Press

Edwards, David and Cromwell, David (2004) Mass deception: How the media helped the government deceive the people, Miller, David (ed.) *Tell me lies: Propaganda and media distortion in the attack on Iraq*, London: Pluto pp 210-221

Edwards, David and Cromwell, David (2009) *Newspeak in the 21st century*, London: Pluto Press

Ehteshami, Anoushiravam (1987) Israel, nuclear weapons and the Middle East, Worsley, Peter and Hadjor, Kofi Buenor (eds) *On the brink: Nuclear proliferation and the Third World*, London: Third World Communications pp 142-158

Engdahl, William (2004) *A century of war: Anglo American oil politics and the New World Order*, London: Pluto, second edition

Epstein, Edward (2003) How many Iraqis died? We may never know, *San Francisco Chronicle*, 3 May

Evans, Harold (1983) *Good times, bad times*, London: Weidenfeld and Nicolson

Evans, Harold (2009a) *My paper chase: True stories of vanished time*, London: Little, Brown

Evans, Harold (2009b) The Cairo riddle, *Sunday Times*, 6 September

Evans, Michael (2003) Blair 'chaired talks on Kelly naming strategy', *Times*, 14 October

Evans, Michael (2009) MI5 compiled dosser on Harold Wilson's KGB links, *Times*, 3 October

Evans, Michael (2010) Complacent British ignored advice that force was too small, say Pentagon offices, *Times*, 10 June

Evans, Peter (2009) *Within the secret state: A disturbing study of the use and misuse of power*, Brighton, Sussex: the Book Guild

Evans, Rob (2003) Briton spied on Orwell in Spain, *Guardian*, 5 May. Available online at http://www.guardian.co.uk/uk/2003/may/05/books.artsandhumanities, accessed on 6 May 2003

Evans, Rob (2016) UK's top policeman challenged over intelligence unit, *Guardian*, 9 January. Available online at http://www.pressreader.com/uk/the-guardian/20160109/281522225076166/TextView, accessed on 11 January 2016

Evans, Rob and Leigh, David (2003) Falklands warships carried nuclear weapons, MoD admits, *Guardian*, 6 December

Eye Spy (2009) CIA's Scorpion: On trial – the Serbian Spymaster and CIA's most senior agent during the traumatic break-up of Yugoslavia, *Eye Spy* intelligence magazine pp 38-39

Fairclough, Norman (1995) *Media discourse*, London: Edward Arnold.

Farago, Ladislas (1967) *The broken seal: The dramatic story of Operation Magic and the Pearl Harbor disaster*, London: Mayflower

Farouk-Slugett, Marion and Slugett, Peter (1990) *Iraq since 1958: From revolution to dictatorship*, London, New York: I. B. Tauris and Co.

Faulks, Sebastian (1997) *The fatal Englishman: Three short lives*, London: Vintage

Featherstone, Donald (1993a) *Victorian colonial warfare: Africa*, London: Blandford

Featherstone, Donald (1993b) *Victorian colonial warfare: India*, London: Blandford

Fenton, Ben (2006) Orwell's comrade in Spain 'was a double agent', *Daily Telegraph*, 30 May

Fialka, John (1992) *The hotel warriors: Covering the Gulf*, Washington: The Media Studies Project/Woodrow Wilson Center

Firmin, Rusty and Pearson, Will (with Stern, Gillian) (2010) *Go! Go! Go!: The definitive inside story of the Iranian Embassy siege*, London: Weidenfeld & Nicolson

Fisk, Robert (1991) Something evil has visited Kuwait City, *Independent*, 28 February

Fisk, Robert (1997) With Sten guns and sovereigns British and US saved Iran's throne for the Shah, *Independent*, 16 March

Fisk, Robert (2006) *The great war for civilisation: The conquest of the Middle East*, London/New York: Harper Perennial

Fisk, Robert (2008) *The age of the warrior: Selected writings*, London: Fourth Estate

Fisk, Robert (2009) Reasons for Alec Collett's death remain buried in Bekaa, *Independent*, 26 November

Fiske, John (1992) Popularity and the politics of information, Dahlgren, Peter and Sparks, Colin (eds) *Journalism and popular culture*, London: Sage pp 45-63

Fitsanakis, Joseph (2009) Former Serb head spy was CIA collaborator, *intelnews.org*, 2 March. Available online at http://intelnews.org/2009/03/02/01-88/, accessed on 13 March 2016

Flanders, Laurie (1992) Reconstructing reality: Media mind games and the war, Bennis, Phyllis and Moushabeck, Michel (eds) *Beyond the Storm: A Gulf crisis reader*, Edinburgh: Canongate pp 160-172

Foley, Stephen (2010) Obama rallies the troops on surprise visit to Afghanistan, *Independent*, 29 March

Fore, William F. (1991) The shadow war in the Gulf, *Media Development*, London, October pp 51-53

Forte, Maximilian (2012) *Slouching towards Sirte: Nato's war on Libya and Africa*, Montreal: Baraka Books

Foster, John Bellamy and McChesney, Robert W. (2014) Surveillance capitalism: Monopoly finance capital, the military-industrial complex and the digital age, *Monthly Review*, Vol. 66, No. 3 pp 1-31

Frankland, Mark (1999) *Child of my time*, London: Chatto & Windus

Freedman, Des (2003) The *Daily Mirror* and the war on Iraq, *Mediactive*, No. 3 pp 95-108

Freedman, Robert (1991) *Middle East from the Iran-Contra affair to the Intifada*, Syracuse: Syracuse University Press

Freemantle, Brian (1983) *CIA: The 'honourable' company*, London: Michael Joseph/Rainbird

Frelick, Bill (1992) The false promise of Operation Provide Comfort: Protecting refugees or protecting state power, *Merip*, May/June pp 22-27

Friedman, Alan (1993) *Spider's web: Bush, Saddam, Thatcher and the decade of deceit*, London: Faber and Faber

Friedman, Norman (1991) *Desert victory*, Annapolis, Maryland: United States Naval Institute

Fukuyama, Francis (1989) The end of history? *National Interest*, Washington, Summer pp 3-18

Fund for Free Expression (1991) Freedom to do as they are told, *Index on Censorship*, Vol. 20, Nos 4/5, April/May p. 37

Galbraith, John Kenneth (1977) *The age of uncertainty*, London: BBC Publications

Gall, Sandy (1994) *News from the frontline: A television reporter's life*, Heinemann: London

Gamble, Andrew (1988) *The free economy and the strong state: The politics of Thatcherism*, Basingstoke, Hampshire: Macmillan Education

Gannett Foundation (1991) *The media at war: The press and the Persian Gulf conflict*, New York City: The Freedom Forum, Columbia University

Garton Ash, Timothy (2003a) Orwell's last secret?, *Guardian Review*, 21 June pp 4-7

Garton Ash, Timothy (2003b) Fight the Matrix, *Guardian*, 5 June

Gearty, Conor (1991) *Terror*, London: Faber

Gellhorn, Martha (1990) The invasion of Panama, *Granta*, Summer pp 205-229

Geraghty, Tony (1980) *Who dares wins: The Story of the SAS 1950-1980*, London: Fontana

Giddens, Anthony (1985) *The nation state and violence*, Cambridge: Polity Press

Gilbert, Martin (1976) *Winston S. Churchill*, London: Heinemann

Gillies, Patrick (1991) Operating Desert Storm media centre, *Despatches* (the journal of the Territorial Army Pool of Public Information Officers) No. 2, Autumn pp 12-16

Giroux, Emmanuel (1991) Journalistes et militaires: Une cohabitation difficile, *Mediapouvoirs*, Paris, July/August/September pp 153-161

Gitlin, Todd (2003 [1980]) *The whole world is watching: Mass media in the making and unmaking of the New Left*, Oakland, California: University of California Press

Gittings, John (2011) *The glorious art of peace: From the Iliad to Iraq*, Oxford: Oxford University Press

Glasgow University Media Group (1985) *War and peace news*, Milton Keynes: Open University Press

Glasgow University Media Group (1991) *The British media and the Gulf War*, research paper, Glasgow

Glavanis, Pandeli M. (1991) Oil and the new helots of Arabia, Bresheeth, Haim and Yuval-Davis, Nira (eds) *The Gulf war and the new world order*, London: Zed Press pp 181-190

Goff, Peter (1999) (ed.) *The Kosovo news and propaganda war*, Vienna: International Press Institute

Goldenberg, Suzanne (2006) Bush to face the ghosts of America's last failed war, *Guardian*, 17 November

Goldman, Francisco (1990) What price Panama: A visit to a barrio destroyed by US forces, *Harpers Magazine*, September pp 71-78

Goodwin, Clayton (2008) How America silenced little Grenada, *New African*, October pp 40-43

Goose, Stephen (1989) Low intensity warfare: The warriors and their weapons, Klare, Michael T. and Kornbluh, Peter (eds) *Low intensity warfare: How the USA fights wars without declaring them*, London: Methuen pp 80-111

Gopsill, Tim (2004) Target the media, Miller, David (ed.) *Tell me lies: Propaganda and media distortion in the attack on Iraq*, London: Pluto pp 251-261

Gordon, Michael R. and Trainor, Gen. Bernard E. (2007) *Cobra II: The inside story of the invasion and occupation of Iraq*, London: Atlantic Books

Gowing, Nik (1991): Dictating the global agenda, *Spectrum*, Independent Television Commission, London, Summer pp 7-9

Greaves, William (1991) The war that almost wasn't fought, *The Times*, 1 January

Greenberg, Andy (2012) *This machine kills secrets: How WikiLeakers, hactivists and cypherpunks aim to free the world's information*, London: Virgin Books

Greenberg, Susan and Smith, Graham (1982) *Rejoice!: Media freedom and the Falklands*, London, Campaign for Press and Broadcasting Freedom

Greenslade, Roy (1992) *Maxwell's fall: The appalling legacy of a corrupt man*, London: Simon and Schuster

Greenslade, Roy (2003) Fighting talk, *Guardian*, 30 June

Gresh, Alain and Vidal, Dominique (1990) *A to Z of the Middle East*, London: Zed Books

Griffin, Michael (2010) Media images of war, *Media, War and Conflict*, Vol. 3, No. 1 pp 7-41

Gripsrud, Jostein (1992) The aesthetics and politics of melodrama, Dahlgren, Peter and Sparks, Colin (eds) *Journalism and popular culture*, London: Sage pp 84-95

Guardian (2005) UK held secret talks to cede sovereignty, 28 June. Available online at https://www.theguardian.com/uk/2005/jun/28/falklands.past, accessed on 16 September 2016

Guillot, Clare (2003) Nassiriya: le soldat Reeves face à la foule en colère, *Le Monde*, 17 April

Gusterson, Hugh (1991) Nuclear war, the Gulf war and the disappearing body, *Journal of Urban and Cultural Studies*, Vol. 2, No. 1 pp 45-55

Guyénot, Laurent (2013) September 11: Inside job or Mossad job? Available online at http://www.voltairenet.org/article179295.html, accessed on 20 July 2013

Hall, Stuart (1995) The whites of their eyes: Racist ideologies and the media, Dines, Gail and Humez, Jean M. (eds) *Gender, race and class: A text reader*, Thousand Oaks/London/New Delhi: Sage pp 18-22

Halliday, Fred (1983) Sources of the New Cold War, Held, David, Anderson, James, Gieben, Bram, Hall, Stuart, Harries, Laurence, Lewis, Paul, Parker, Noel and Turok, Ben (eds) *State and societies*, Oxford: Martin Robertson/Open University pp 540-549

Halliday, Fred (1986) *The making of the Second Cold War*, London: Verso

Halliday, Fred (1987) News management and counter insurgency: The case of Oman, Seaton, Jean and Pimlott, Ben (eds) *The media in British politics*, London: Routledge pp 180-200

Halliday, Fred (1989) *Cold War, Third World: An essay on Soviet American relations*, London: Radius

Halliday, Fred (1991) The Gulf War and its aftermath – first reflections, *International Affairs*, Vol. 67, No. 2 pp 223-234

Hallin, Daniel (1986) *The 'uncensored' war*, Berkeley, CA: University of California Press

Hammond, Philip (2000a) Reporting 'humanitarian' warfare: Propaganda, moralism and Nato's Kosovo war, *Journalism Studies*, Vol. 1, No. 3 pp 365-386. Also available online at http//myweb.lsbu.ac.uk/philip-hammond/2000b.html, accssed on 14 October 2008

Hammond, Philip (2000b) 'Good versus evil' after the Cold War: Kosovo and the moralisation of war reporting, *The Public/Javnost: Journal of the European Institute for Communication and Culture*, Vol. 7, No. 3 pp 19-38

Hammond, Philip (2003) The media war on terrorism, *Journal for Crime, Conflict and Media*, Vol. 1, No. 1 pp 23-36

Hammond, Philip (2007) *Framing post-Cold War conflicts: The media and international intervention*, Manchester: Manchester University Press

Hammond, Philip and Herman, Edward S. (eds) (2000) *Degraded capability: The media and the Kosovo Crisis*, London: Pluto

Hanson, Christopher (Boot, William) (1991) The pool, Smith, Hedrick (ed.) *The media and the Gulf War*, Washington DC: Seven Locks Press pp 128-135

Harclerode, Peter (2000) *Para! Fifty years of the Parachute Regiment*, Leicester: Brockhampton Press

Hardt, Neil (2016) US triples special operations deployment to Latin America, *wsws.org*, 14 September. Available online at http://www.wsws.org/en/articles/2016/09/14/lati-s14.html, accessed on 14 September 2016

Harkins, Hugh (1995) *Tornado: Air defence variant protecting Britain's skies*, Durham: Pentland Press

Harnden, Toby (2014) CIA 'gave Beirut bomber refuge in return for secrets', *Sunday Times*, 25 May

Harper, Tom (2011) *NoW* hacking suspect worked for police as an 'informer', *thisislondon*, 19 July. Available online at http://www.thisislondon.co.uk/standard/article-23971221-hacking-suspect-worked-as-police-informer.do, accessed on 21 July 2011

Harris, Robert (1983) *Gotcha! The media, government and the Falklands crisis*, London: Faber

Harvey, Oliver (2010) The *Sun* goes into Helmand with our brave army medics, *Sun*, 26 February

Hastings, Max (2000) *Going to wars*, London: Macmillan

Haynes, Deborah (2010) The Whitehall brass and mandarins who set up the bloodiest mission since Korea, *Times*, 10 June

Hedges, Chris (2002) *War is a force that gives us meaning*, New York: Public Affairs

Heibert, Ray Eldon (1995) Mass media as weapons of modern warfare, Herbert, Ray Eldon (ed.) *Impact of mass media: Current issues*, New York: Longman US pp 327-334

Heikal, Mohamed (1992) *Illusions of triumph: An Arab view of the Gulf War*, London: HarperCollins

Held, David (1984) Power and legitimacy in contemporary Britain, McLennan, George, Held, David and Hall, Stuart (eds) *State and society in contemporary Britain: A critical introduction*, Cambridge: Polity Press pp 299-369

Hellinger, Daniel and Judd, Dennis (1991) *The democratic façade*, Pacific Grove, California: Cole Publishing Company

Helm, Toby and Beaumont, Peter (2010) Cameron calls Chequers summit as strains grow over coalition's aims in Afghanistan, *Observer*, 30 May

Henderson, Simon (1991) *Instant empire: Saddam Hussein's ambition for Iraq*, San Francisco: Mercury House

Hennessey, Thomas and Thomas, Claire (2009) *Spooks: The unofficial history of MI5*, Stroud, Gloucestershire: Amberley

Hennessy, Peter (2010) *The secret state: Preparing for the worst 1945-2010*, London: Penguin, second edition

Henwood, Doug (1992) The US economy – the enemy within, *Covert Action Information Bulletin*, Summer pp 45-49

Herman, Edward S. (1992) *Beyond hypocrisy*, Boston: South End Press

Hersh, Seymour (1991) *The Sampson option*, London: Faber and Faber

Hersh, Seymour (2000) What happened in the final days of the Gulf War?, *New Yorker*, 22 May pp 49-82

Hertsgaard, Mark (1988) *On bended knee: The press and Reagan presidency*, New York: Farrar Straus Giroux

Hewitt, Steve and Lucas, Scott (2009) All the secrets that are fit to print? The media and US intelligence services before and after 9/11, Dover, Robert and Goodman, Michael S. (2009) *Spinning intelligence: Why intelligence needs the media. Why the media needs intelligence*, London: Hurst and Company pp 105-116

Higgins, Michael and Smith, Angela (2011) Not one of US: Kate Adie's report of the 1986 US bombing of Tripoli and its critical aftermath, *Journalism Studies*, Vol. 12, No. 3 pp 344-358

Hiro, Dilip (1992) *Desert Shield to Desert Storm: The Second Gulf War*, London: Paladin

Hitchens, Christopher (2003) *Regime change*, London: Penguin Books

Hitchens, Christopher (2005) *Love, poverty and war: Journeys and essays*, London: Atlantic Books

Hodgson, Godfrey (1991) *Truth, journalism and the Gulf*, London: City University

Hollingsworth, Mark and Fielding, Nick (1999) *Defending the realm: MI5 and the Shayler Affair*, London: André Deutsch

Hooper, Alan (1982) *The military and the media*, London: Gower

Horowitz, David (1971 [1965]) *From Yalta to Vietnam: American foreign policy in the Cold War*, Harmondsworth, Middlesex: Penguin Books

Horrie, Chris (2004) *Tabloid nation: From the birth of the* Daily Mirror *to the death of the tabloid*, London: Deutsch

Hoskins, Andrew (2004) *Televising war: From Vietnam to Iraq*, London: Continuum International

Hughes, Chris (2010) Fine, fearless, dedicated, *Daily Mirror*, 11 January

Hughes-Wilson, John (2004) *The puppet masters: Spies, traitors and the real forces behind world events*, London: Weidenfeld & Nicolson

Human Rights Watch/Middle East (1995) *Iraq's crime of genocide: The Anfal campaign against the Kurds*, New Haven/London: Yale University Press

Hunter, Jane (1991) Dismantling the war on Libya, *Covert Action Information Bulletin*, Summer pp 47-51

Hunter, Robin (1995) *True stories of the SAS*, London: Virgin

Hussain, Asaf (1988) *Political terrorism and the state in the Middle East*, London/New York: Mansell Publishing

Hutton, Will (1996) *The state we're in*, London: Vintage, second edition

Ingham, Bernard (1991) *Kill the messenger*, London: HarperCollins

'Insight' (1980) *Siege!*, London: Hamlyn

Ismael, Tareq Y. and Ismael, Jacqueline S. (2004) *The Iraqi predicament: People in the quagmire of power and politics*, London: Pluto Press

al-Jabbar, Faleh Abd (1992) Why the uprisings failed, *Merip*, May/June pp 2-14

Jackson, Harold (2006) Jeane Kirkpatrick obituary, *Guardian*, 9 December

Jahanpour, Farhang (1991) A new order for the Middle East?, *The World Today*, May pp 74-77

James, Joy (1990) US policy in Panama, *Race and Class*, Vol. 32 pp 17-32

James, Luke (2015) Spies rigged Shrewsbury pickets trial, 10 December, Campaign for Press and Broadcasting Freedom. Available online at http://www.cpbf.org.uk/body.php?subject=gov&doctype=news&id=3304, accessed on 19 September 2016

Jeffery, Keith (2011) *MI6: The history of the secret intelligence service 1909-1949*, London: Bloomsbury

Jeffords, Susan (1989) *The remasculination of America: Gender and the Vietnam War*, Bloomington and Indianapolis: Indiana University Press

Jenkins, Simon (2010) My once-in-a-generation cut? The armed forces. All of them, *Guardian,* 9 June

Jenkins, Simon (2012) Alfredo Astiz, the man who created the Thatcher legend, *Guardian*, 23 March

Johnson, Paul and MacAskill, Ewen (2016) 'There will be terrorist attacks in the UK. The threat level is severe, that means likely', *Guardian*, 1 November

Johnston, Anne (1993) Media coverage of women in the Gulf War, Denton, Robert (ed.) *The media and the Persian Gulf War*, Westport CT: Praeger pp 197-212

Jones, Nicholas (2009) Nato strategist Jamie Shea gives chilling insight into military's media control at times of war, 1 May. Available online at http://www.spinwatch.org/blogs-mainmenu-29/nicholas-jones-mainmenu-85/5279-nato-strategist-jamie-shea-gives-chilling-insight-into-militarys-media-control-at-times-of-war, accessed on 14 May 2009

Joseph, Sue and Keeble, Richard Lance (eds) (2015) *The profiling handbook*, Bury St Edmunds: Abramis

Joseph, Sue and Keeble, Richard Lance (eds) (2016) *Profile pieces: Journalism and the 'human interest' bias*, Abingdon, Oxon: Routledge

Jowett, Garth and O'Donnell, Victoria (1992) *Propaganda and persuasion*, London: Sage, second edition

Junger, Sebastian (2010) *War*, London: Fourth Estate

Kabani, Rana (1991) The Gulf of misunderstanding, *Independent on Sunday*, 10 February

Kabani, Rana (1994 [1986]) *Imperial fictions: Europe's myths of the Orient*, London: Pandora

Kaku, Michio (1992) Nuclear threats and the New World Order, *Covert Action Information Bulletin*, Summer pp 22-28

Kaldor, Mary (1991) *The imaginary war*, London: Verso

Kampfner, John (2003) The truth about Jessica, *Guardian*, 15 May

Kampfner, John (2010) WikiLeaks shows up our media for their docility at the feet of authority, *Independent*, 29 November 2010. Available online at http://www.independent.co.uk/opinion/commentators/john-kampfner-wikileaks-shows-up-our-media-for-their-docility-at-the-feet-of-authority-2146211.html, accessed on 29 November 2010

Karsh, Efraim and Rautsi, Inari (1991) Why Saddam invaded Kuwait, *Survival*, January/February pp 18-30

Kay, Richard (1992) *Soldier warrior*, London: Penumbra

Keane, John (1991) *The media and democracy*, Cambridge: Polity

Keeble, Richard (1986) Portraying the peace movement, Curran, James et al. (eds) *Bending reality*, London: Pluto pp 47-57

Keeble, Richard (1991) How the media took us to war, *Changes*, 2-15 February p. 7

Keeble, Richard (1994) From butcher to bad boy, Gemini News Service, London, 11 January

Keeble, Richard (1997) *Secret state, silent press: New militarism, the Gulf and the modern image of warfare*, Luton: John Libbey

Keeble, Richard (1998) The myth of Saddam Hussein: New militarism and the propaganda function of the human interest story, Kieran, Matthew (ed.) *Media ethics*, London: Routledge pp 66-81

Keeble, Richard (1999a) A Balkan birthday for Nato, *British Journalism Review*, Vol. 10, No. 2 pp 16-20

Keeble, Richard (1999b) Perennial first casualty, *Tribune*, 22 January p. 6

Keeble, Richard (2000a) New militarism and the manufacture of warfare, Hammond, Philip and Herman, Edward S. (eds) *Degraded capability: The media and the Kosovo Crisis*, London, Pluto Press pp 59-69

Keeble, Richard (2000b) Hiding the horror of 'humanitarian' warfare, *The Public,*Vol. 7, No. 2 pp 87-98

Keeble, Richard (2001a) Orwell as war correspondent: A reassessment, *Journalism Studies*, Vol. 2, No. 3 pp 393-406

Keeble, Richard (2001b) The media's battle cry, *Press Gazette*, October 5

Keeble, Richard (2002) The evil war of the empire; *Tribune*, 15 March

Keeble, Richard (2003a) Spooks are represented on every newspaper, *Press Gazette*, 9 October

Keeble, Richard (2003b) We see more and more of the conflict but we know as little as ever, *Independent on Sunday*, 30 March

Keeble, Richard (2004) Information warfare in an age of hyper-militarism, Allan, Stuart and Zelizer, Barbie (eds) (2004) *Reporting war: Journalism in wartime*, London and New York, Abingdon, Oxon: Routledge pp 43-58

Keeble, Richard (2005) New militarism, massacrespeak and the language of silence, *Ethical Space: The International Journal of Communication Ethics*, Vol. 2, No. 1 pp 39-45

Keeble, Richard (2007a) Media silence over 'crimes against humanity' in Chad, *fifth-estate-online*, 4 December. Available online at www.fifth-estate-online.co.uk/comment/mediasilenceovercrimes.html, accessed on 4 December 2007

Keeble, Richard (2007b) The necessary spectacular 'victories': New militarism, the mainstream media and the manufacture of the two Gulf conflicts 1991 and 2003, Maltby, Sarah and Keeble, Richard (eds) *Communicating war: Memory, media and military*, Bury St Edmunds: Arima pp 200-212

Keeble, Richard and Wheeler, Sharon (2007c) *The journalistic imagination: Literary journalists from Defoe to Capote and Carter*, London: Routledge

Keeble, Richard (2009) *Ethics for journalists*, London: Routledge, second edition

Keeble, Richard Lance (2010) Hacks and spooks – close encounters of a strange kind: A critical history of the links between mainstream journalists and the intelligence services in the UK, Klaehn, Jeffery (ed.) *The political economy of media and power*, New York: Peter Lang pp 87-111

Keeble, Richard Lance (2011a) Targeting Gaddafi: Secret warfare and the media, *Mirage in the desert? Reporting the 'Arab Spring'*, Mair, John and Keeble, Richard Lance (eds) Bury St Edmunds: Arima Publishing pp 281-296

Keeble, Richard Lance (2011b) Operation Moshtarak and the manufacture of credible, 'heroic' warfare, *Global Media and Communication*, Vol 7, No. 3 pp 183-187

Keeble, Richard Lance (2012) Orwell, *Nineteen Eighty-Four* and the spooks, Keeble, Richard Lance (ed.) *Orwell today*, Bury St Edmunds: Abramis pp 151-163

Keeble, Richard Lance (2013) Western aggression in Mali and the media, *the-latest. com*. Available online at http://www.the-latest.com/western-aggression-mali-and-media, accessed on 6 November 2016

Keeble, Richard Lance (2016a) US-led 'Desert Storm' attacks on Iraq remembered, *the-latest.com*, 27 January. Available online at http://the-latest.com/wests-desert-storm-invasion-iraq-remembered, accessed on 28 January 2016

Keeble, Richard Lance (2016b) How the press hides the global crimes of the West, *medialens. org*, 9 June 2016. Available online at http://www.medialens.org/index.php/alerts/alert-archive/2016/820-how-the-press-hides-the-global-crimes-of-the-west-corporate-media-coverage-of-chad.html, accessed on 10 June 2016

Keegan, John (2005) *The Iraq War: The 21-day conflict and its aftermath*, London: Pimlico

Kellner, Douglas (1990) *Television and the crisis of democracy*, Boulder, Colorado: Westview Press

Kelly, Michael (1993) *Martyr's day: Chronicle of a small war*, London: Signet

Kemp, Anthony (1995) *The SAS: Savage wars of peace*, London: Signet

Kennedy, Paul (1986) A. J. P. Taylor and profound forces in history, Wrigley, Chris (ed.) *Warfare, diplomacy and politics: Essays in honour of A. J. P. Taylor*, London: Hamish Hamilton

Kenny, George (1999) Rolling Thunder: The re-run, *Nation*, 27 May. Available online at http://www.thenation.com/doc/19990614/kenney, accessed on 14 October 2008

Kent, Bruce (2009) Afghanistan and the price of an illegal war, (letter) *Times*, 4 August

Kessler, Lauren (1984) *The dissident press: Alternative journalism in American history*, Newbury Park, London: Sage Publications

Khanum, Saeed (1991) Inside Iraq, *New Statesman and Society*, 24 May pp 12-16

Kirkup, James (2010) Kandahar offensive to target 1,000 Taliban, *Daily Telegraph*, 2 June

Klare, Michael T. (1980) Militarism: The issues today, Eide, Asbjorn and Thee, Marek (eds) *Problems in contemporary militarism*, London: Croom Helm pp 36-46

Klare, Michael T. and Kornbluh, Peter (eds) *Low intensity warfare: How the USA fights wars without declaring them*, London: Methuen

Kleinwachter, Wolfgang (1991) National security versus right to know, *Media Development*, October pp 5-6

Kleveman, Lutz (2003) *The new great game: Blood and oil in Central Asia*, New York: Grove Press

Knightley, Phillip (1982) Are we neutral observers? *Journalist*, November pp 8-9

Knightley, Phillip (1986) *The second oldest profession: The spy as bureaucrat, patriot, fantasist and whore*, London: André Deutsch

Knightley, Phillip (1991) Here is the patriotically censored news, *Index on Censorship*, Nos 4/5 pp 4-5

Knightley, Phillip (2003a [1975]) *The first casualty: The war correspondent as hero, propagandist and myth-maker from the Crimea to Iraq*, London: André Deutsch

Knightley, Phillip (2003b) Media, *Anti-imperialism: A guide for the movement*, London: Bookmarks pp 251-256

Knightley, Phillip (2003c) Turning the tanks on the reporters, *Observer*, 15 June

Knightley, Phillip (2006) Journalists and spies: An unhealthy relationship, *Ethical Space: The International Journal of Communication Ethics*, Vol. 3, Nos 2/3 pp 7-11

Koster, R. M. and Bourbon, Guillermo Sanchez (1990) *In the time of tyrants: Panama 1968-98*, London: Secker and Warburg

Kovel, Joel (1983) *Against the state of nuclear terror*, London: Pan

Lamb, Christina (2010) Battle for town is small step on the path to victory, *Sunday Times*, 14 February

Lambakis, Stephen (1995) Space control in Desert Storm and beyond, *Orbis*, Philadelphia, Vol. 39, No. 3, Summer pp 417-437

Landay, Jonathan S. and Wells, Tish (2004) Iraqi group fed false information to news media, 15 March. Available online at http://www.realcities.com/mld/krwashington/8194211. htm, accessed on 16 March

Larcombe, Duncan (2010) Mud 'guts, *Sun*, 15 February

Lashmar, Paul (2013) Urinal or open channel? Institutional flow between the UK intelligence services and news media, *Journalism*, Vol. 14, No. 8 pp 1024-1040

Lashmar, Paul and Day, Peter (1999) Wodehouse secretly in pay of the Nazis, say MI5 files, *Independent*, 17 September

Lashmar, Paul and Oliver, James (1998) *Britain's secret propaganda war 1948-1977*, Stroud: Sutton

Laurens, Henry (1992) Pourquoi Ryad préfère la parapluie américain, *Le Monde Diplomatique*, August pp 8-9

Lawson, Mark (1995) *John Keane: Conflicts of interest*, London/Edinburgh: Mainstream Publishing (in conjunction with Angela Flowers Gallery)

Layne, Christopher (1991) Why the Gulf War was not in the national interest, *Atlantic Monthly*, Boston pp 615-681

Lea, Michael (2003) Comical Ali tops himself, *Sun*, 17 April

Lederman, Jim (1992) *Battle lines: The American media and the Intifada*, New York: Henry Holt and Company

Leigh, David (1980) *The frontiers of secrecy*, London: Junction Books

Leigh, David (1989) *The Wilson plot*, London: Heinemann, second edition

Leigh, David (1998) Libyan exile linked to MI6 and 'plot to murder Gadafy', *Guardian*, 8 August

Leigh, David (2000a) Tinker, tailor, soldier, journalist, *Guardian*, 12 June. Available online at http://www.theguardian.com/media/2000/jun/12/pressandpublishing. mondaymediasection, accessed on 17 February 2016

Leigh, David (2000b) Britain's security services and journalists: The secret story, *British Journalism Review*, Vol. 11, No. 2 pp 21-26

Levinson, Nan (1991) Snappy visuals hard facts and obscured issues, *Index on Censorship*, No. 4/5 pp 27-29

Lewis, Justin et al. (2003) *The role of embedded reporting during the 2003 Gulf War: Summary report*, commissioned by the BBC, Cardiff, Wales: Cardiff University

Lewis, Justin, Brookes, Rod, Mosdell, Nick and Threadgold, Terry (2006) *Shoot first and ask questions later: Media coverage of the 2003 Iraq war*, New York: Peter Lang

Lewis, Peter (1984) *A people's war*, London: Thames Methuen

Livingstone, Ken (1998) A cock-up that reawakens suspicions about our spies, *Independent*, 25 November. Available online at http://www.independent.co.uk/arts-entertainment/a-cockup-that-reawakens-suspicions-about-our-spies-1187129.html, accessed on 1 January 2010

Low, Valentine (2016) Mark Thatcher files stay secret 'to spare blushes on arms deal', *Times*, 21 July

Lucas, Scott (2000) The socialist fallacy, *New Statesman*, 29 May pp 47-50

Lucas, Scott (2003) *Orwell*, London: Haus Publishing

Luckham, Robin (1983) Of arms and culture, *Current Research on Peace and Violence*, IV, Tampere, Finland pp 1-63

Lule, Jack (2002) Myth and terror on the editorial page: *The New York Times* responds to September 1, *Journalism and Mass Communication Quarterly*, Vol. 79, No. 2 pp 275-293

Lule, Jack (2004) War and its metaphors: New language and the prelude to war in Iraq 2003, *Journalism Studies*, Vol. 5, No. 2 pp 179-190

Lycett, Andrew (1995) I study my targets. I find out what makes them tick, *Independent*, 22 June

Lycett, Andrew (1996) *Ian Fleming*, London: Weidenfeld and Nicolson

Lynch, Jake and McGoldrick, Annabel (2005) *Peace journalism*, Stroud, Gloucestershire: Hawthorn Press

MacArthur, Brian (ed.) (1991) *Despatches from the Gulf War*, London: Bloomsbury

MacArthur, Brian (2003) Changing pace of war, *The Times*, 27 June

Macarthur, John R. (1993) *Second front: Censorship and propaganda in the Gulf War*, Berkeley and Los Angeles: University of California Press, second edition

MacAskill, Ewan, Goni, Uki and Balch, Oliver (2006) Argentina ups the ante in new battle over Falklands, *Guardian*, 1 July. Available online at http://www.guardian.co.uk/world/2006/jul/01/argentina.falklands, accessed 14 October 2006

MacAskill, Ewen (2007) Rambo image was based on lie, says US war hero Jessica Lynch, *Guardian*, 25 April. Available online at https://www.theguardian.com/world/2007/apr/25/iraq.usa1, accessed on 13 June 2016

Machon, Annie (2005) *Spies, lies and whistleblowers*, Lewes, East Sussex: the Book Guild

Macintyre, Ben (2014) *A spy among friends: Philby and the great betrayal*, London: Bloomsbury

MacKenzie, John (1984) *Propaganda and Empire: The manipulation of British public opinion 1880-1960*, Manchester: Manchester University Press

Mahajan, Rahul (2001) 'We think the price is worth it': Media uncurious about Iraq policy's effects – there or here, *Extra!* Fairness and Accuracy in Reporting. Available online at http://www.fair.org/index.php?page=1084, accessed on 14 October 2002

Mailer, Norman (2003) We went to war just to boost the white male ego, www.timesonline.co.uk/article/0..482-662789.00.html, accessed on 12 August 2003

Maltby, Sarah and Keeble, Richard (2007) *Communicating war: Memory, media and military*, Bury St Edmunds: Arima

Malvern, Jack (2011) What secret file says about not-so-naïve Wodehouse's ghastly error, *Times*; 26 August

Mann, Michael (1988) *States, wars and capitalism*, Oxford: Blackwell

Marnham, Patrick (1991) Not quite as American as pomme tarte, *Independent*, 26 February

Marr, Andrew (2007) *A history of modern Britain*, London: Pan Macmillan

Marsden, Sam (2013) Thatcher made secret plans to bring in the military during the miners' strike, *Daily Telegraph*, 1 August. Available online at http://www.telegraph.co.uk/news/politics/margaret-thatcher/10213447/Thatcher-made-secret-plans-to-bring-in-the-military-during-the-miners-strike.html, accessed on 28 January 2016

Marshall Cavendish (2007) *The Falklands War 25th anniversary*, London: Marshall Cavendish (no author specified)

Marshall, Jonathan, Scott, Peter Dale and Hunter, Jane (1987) *The Iran-Contra connection*, Boston: South End Press

Marshall, Tim (1999) Belgrade: 'Not everything they show us is false', *Journalist*, May pp 15-16

Martin, David and Walcott, John (1988) *Best laid plans: The inside story of America's war against terrorism*, New York: Harper and Row

Martin, Patrick (2001) US planned war in Afghanistan well before 9/11, *World Socialist Website*, 20 November. Available online at http://www.wsws.org/articles/2001/nov2001/afgh-n20.shtml, accessed on 1 September 2005

Martin, Patrick (2010) US military noose tightens on Afghanistan town, *wsws.org*, 12 February. Available online at http://www.wsws.org/articles/2010/feb2010/afgh-f12.shtml, accessed on 13 February 2010

Mason, Paul (2016) The parallels people draw between Jeremy Corbyn and Michael Foot are almost all false, *Guardian*, 16 August

Massing, Michael (2003) The high price of an unforgiving war, *Columbia Journalism Review*, May/June

Masters, Anthony (1984) *The man who was M: The life of Maxwell Knight*, Oxford: Blackwell

McCarthy, Rory (2003) Saving Private Lynch: How special forces rescued captured colleague, *Guardian*, 3 April. Available online at http://www.theguardian.com/world/2003/apr/03/iraq.rorymccarthy, accessed on 4 December 2015

McConnachie, James and Tudge, Robin (2005) *The rough guide to conspiracy theories*, London: Rough Guides Ltd

McCormick, Thomas J. (1989) *America's half century: United States foreign policy in the Cold War*, Baltimore: Johns Hopkins University Press

McCrum, Robert (2016) How secret dispatches from Moscow cast fresh light on a charming traitor, *Observer*, 29 May

McCrystal, Cal (1999) The sub-secret underworld of the D-Notice business, *British Journalism Review*, Vol. 10, No. 2 pp 26-33

McDaniel, Ann and Fineman, Howard (1991) The President's 'spin' patrol, Smith, Hendrick (ed.) *The media and the Gulf War*, Washington DC: Seven Locks Press pp 154-157

McDonald, Murray (2007) *50,000 editions of the imperialist, warmongering, hate-filled* Guardian *newspaper*, self-published pamphlet: MurrayMcDonald1@googlemail.com

McGarvey, Declan (2010) Falklands veterans march on British embassy to demand return of islands, *Times*, 3 April

McGreal, Chris (2010) US civil rights photographer exposed as FBI informer, *Guardian*, 15 September

343

McGregor, Liz and Hooper, John (2006) Obituary of Oriana Fallaci, *Guardian*, 16 September

McGregor, Peter (1998) *Cultural battles: The meaning of the Vietnam-USA War*, Victoria, Australia: Scam Publications

McLaughlin, Greg (2002) *The war correspondent*, London: Pluto Press

McMahon, Jeff (1984) *Reagan and the world: Imperial policy in the New Cold War*, London: Pluto Press

McManners, Hugh (2008) *Forgotten voices of the Falklands: The real story of the Falklands war*, London: Ebury Press

'McNab, Andy' (pseudonym of SAS member) (1994) *Bravo Two Zero*, London: Corgi

McNair, Brian (1988) *Images of the enemy*, London: Routledge

McNair, Brian (1995) *An introduction to political communication*, London: Routledge

McVeigh, Tracy (2016) The UN security council has lasted through seven turbulent decades, *Observer*, 17 January

Meacher, Michael (2003) The very secret service, *Guardian*, 11 November

Mead, Walter Russell (2013) NYT calls US anti-terror strategy in North Africa a catastrophe, *the-american-interest.com*, 14 January. Available online at http://www.the-american-interest.com/2013/01/14/nyt-calls-us-anti-terror-strategy-in-north-africa-a-catastrophe/, accessed on 15 January 2013

Mercer, Derrick (ed.) *The fog of war*, London: Heinemann

Middle East Watch (1991) *Needless deaths in the Gulf War: Civilian casualties during the air campaign and violations of the laws of war*, New York: Human Rights Watch

Middleton, Neil (ed.) (1973) *The I. F. Stone's Weekly reader*, New York: Simon and Schuster

Miles, Sara (1987) The real wars: Post-Vietnam low intensity conflict, Williams, Reece (ed.) *Unwinding the Vietnam war: From war into peace*, Seattle: the Real Comet Press

Miller, David (2003) Embedding propaganda, *Free Press*, special issue, June

Miller, David (2004) The domination effect, *Guardian*, 8 January

Miller, Greg (2009) Serb spy's trial lifts cloak on his CIA alliance, *Los Angeles Times*, 1 March. Available online at http://articles.latimes.com/2009/mar/01/world/fg-serbia-spy-cia1, accessed on 13 March 2016

Miller, Marc (1991) Patriotic blindness and anti-truth weapons, *Index on Censorship*, No. 10 pp 32-34

Miller, Phil (2014) *Britain's dirty war against the Tamil People 1979-2009*, Bremen: International Human Rights Association

Milmo, Cahal (2003) Reporting for duty, *Independent*, 18 March

Milmo, Cahil (2007) Revealed: How Thatcher handled embassy siege, *Independent*, 24 February

Milmo, Cahil (2010) Forces of Facebook turn on the *Daily Mirror*, *Independent*, 19 March

Mellen, Tom (2010) Afghans 'not ready to fight yet', *Morning Star*, 8-9 May

Milne, Seamus (1995) *The enemy within: The secret war against the miners*, London: Pan

Milne, Seamus (2009) In a war for democracy, why worry about public opinion, *Guardian*, 15 October

Moore, Charles (2013) *Margaret Thatcher: The authorized biography, Vol. 1*, London: Allen Lane

Moore, Robin (2003) *Taskforce Dagger: The hunt for Bin Laden*, New York: Random House

Moran, Chrisopher (2013) *Classified: Secrecy and the state in modern Britain*, Cambridge: Cambridge University Press

Morgan, Kenneth (1990) *The people's peace 1945-1989*, Oxford: Oxford University Press

Morgan, Kenneth O. (2007) *Michael Foot: A life*, London: HarperCollins

Morley, Richard (1991) The lost history of the Falklands War, *Open Eye*, Issue 1, London pp 4-11

Morris, Nigel (2010) Afghan war is unwinnable and we should pull out now, say voters, *Independent*, 21 April

Morrison, David E. (1992) *Television and the Gulf War*, Luton: John Libbey

Morrison, David (2005) Blair's Big Lie. Available online at http://www.spinwatch.org/-articles-by-category-mainmenu-8/51-iraq/160-blairs-big-lie-more, accessed on 14 October 2008

Morrison, David and Tumber, Howard (1988) *Journalists at war: The dynamics of news reporting in the Falklands conflict*, London: Sage

Moughrabi, Fouad (1993) Domesticating the body politic, *Merip*, January-February pp 38-40

Moyers, Bill (1986) *The secret government: The constitution in crisis*, Washington: Seven Locks

Muggeridge, Malcolm (1975) *Chronicles of wasted time, Vol 2: The infernal grove*, London: Fontana

Muir, Kate (1992) *Arms and the woman*, London: Sinclair/Stevenson

Mungham, Geoff (1986) Grenada: News blackout in the Caribbean, Mercer, Derrick (ed.) *The fog of war*, London, Heinemann pp 291-310

Murray, Gary (1993) *Enemies of the state: A sensational exposé of the security services by a former MI5 undercover agent*, New York/London: Pocket Books

Nasiriyah, Scheherezade Faramarzi (2003) Iraqi doctors dismiss claims that Jessica Lynch was raped in hospital, *Independent*, 9 November

Neale, Jonathan (2001) *The American War: Vietnam 1960-75*, London: Bookmarks

Neale, Jonathan (2003) Afghanistan, Monbiot, George et al., *Anti-imperialism: A guide for the movement*, London: Bookmarks pp 131-149

Neff, Donald (1992a) Israel's dependence on the US: The full extent of the special relationship, *Middle East International*, May pp 16-17

Neff, Donald (1992b) America's unconditional hand-outs to Israel, *Middle East International*, 9 October p. 3

Neighbour, Sally (2011) How we lost the war, *The Monthly*, September pp 42-48

Nelson, Keith and Olin, Spencer (1979) *Why war? Ideology, theory and history*, Berkeley: University of California Press

Newsinger, John (1989) A forgotten war: British intervention in Indonesia, *Race and Class*, Vol. 30, No. 4 pp 51-66

Newsinger, John (1995) The myth of the SAS, *Lobster*, No. 30, December pp 32-36

Newsinger, John (1999) The American connection: George Orwell, 'Literary Trotsykism' and the New York intellectuals, *Labour History Review*, Vol. 64, No. 1 pp 23-43

Newsinger, John (2015) Hearts and minds: The myth and reality of British counter-insurgency, *International Socialism*, No. 148 pp 135-160

Newton Dunn, Tom (2010) Troops to get trauma help, *Sun*, 7 June

Newton, Scott (2003) Back to the future: The USA, the UK and Iraq, *Lobster*, Vol. 46 pp 3-9

Newton, Scott (2008/9) Harold Wilson, the Bank of England and the Cecil King 'coup' of May 1968, *Lobster*, Hull, Winter pp 3-8

Niva, Steve (1992) The battle is joined, Bennis, Phyllis and Moushabeck, Michel (eds) *Beyond the Storm: A Gulf crisis reader*, Edinburgh: Canongate pp 55-74

Northmore, David (1990) *Freedom of information handbook*, London: Bloomsbury

Norton, Ann (1991) Gender, sexuality and the Iraq of our imagination, *Merip*, Washington, Vol. 173, No. 21

Norton-Taylor, Richard (1985) *The Ponting affair*, London: Cecil Woolf

Norton-Taylor, Richard (1990) *In defence of the realm? The case for accountable security services*, London: Civil Liberties Trust

Norton-Taylor, Richard (1997) Rank and file caught in cold war paranoia, *Guardian*, 26 August

Norton-Taylor, Richard (2000a) Allies count the cost of war, *Guardian* 20 March

Norton-Taylor, Richard (2000b) Nato under fire for choice of targets in Kosovo, *Guardian*, 7 January

Norton-Taylor, Richard (2006) Britain never thought Saddam was a threat – diplomat, *Guardian*, 16 December

Norton-Taylor, Richard (2009) Ill-equipped, poorly trained, and mired in a 'bloody mess', *Guardian*, 17 April

Norton-Taylor, Richard (2010a) MI5 bugged cabinet room at No. 10, says historian, *Guardian*, 19 April

Norton-Taylor, Richard (2010b) Afghan police failings fuelling Taliban, say UK army chiefs, *Guardian*, 4 June

Norton-Taylor, Richard (2010c) Four more years of Afghan war, warns Nato official, *Guardian*, 30 April

Norton-Taylor, Richard (2010d) Afghan private security firms 'fuelling corruption', *Guardian*, 14 May

Norton-Taylor, Richard (2011) I was not a Nazi collaborator, PG Wodehouse told MI5, *Guardian*, 26 August

Norton-Taylor, Richard (2013) Afghanistan war has cost Britain more than £37bn, new book claims, *Guardian*, 30 May. Available online at https://www.theguardian.com/world/2013/may/30/afghanistan-war-cost-britain-37bn-book, accessed on 14 August 2015

Norton-Taylor, Richard and Bowcott, Owen (2013) Thatcher was 'ready for deal on Falklands', *Guardian Weekly*, 4 January

Norton-Taylor, Richard and Evans, Rob (2005) Goose Green attack was intended to lift morale, *Guardian*, 28 June

Norton-Taylor, Richard and Milne, Seamus (1996) Orwell offered writers' blacklist to anti-Soviet propaganda unit, *Guardian*, 11 July

Nouzille, Vincent (2010) Des armes contre des otages, *Marianne*, Nos 713-714, December pp 135-137

Orwell, George (1976 [1949]) *Nineteen Eighty-Four*, London: Secker and Warburg pp 741-925

Ostertag, Bob (2006) *People's movements, people's press: The journalism of social justice movements*, Boston: Beacon Press

O'Neill, Sean (2016) Police protected Northern Irish terrorists, *Times*, 10 June

Palast, Greg (2006) *Armed madhouse*, London: Allen Lane

Parenti, Michael (1986) *Inventing reality: The politics of the mass media*, New York: St Martin's Press

Parsons, Michael (2000) *The Falklands War*, Stroud, Gloucestershire: Sutton Publishing

Paterson, Chris (2014) *War reporters under threat: The United States and media freedom*, London: Pluto Press

Paxman, Jeremy (1990) *Friends in high places: Who runs Britain?*, London: Michael Joseph

Peak, Steve (1982) Britain's military adventures; *Pacifist*, Vol. 20 p. 10

Pelletiere, Stephen, Johnson, Douglas and Rosenberger, Leif (1990) *Iraqi power and US security in the Middle East*, Strategic Studies Institute: US Army War College (US Government Printing Office)

Pelletiere, Stephen C. (2003) A war crime or an act of war?, *New York Times*, 31 January

Penrose, Barry and Courtiour, Roger (1978) *The Pencourt file*, London: Secker and Warburg

Perry, Mark (1992) *Eclipse: The last days of the CIA*, New York: William Morrow and Company

Peters, E. (1985) *Torture*, Oxford: Blackwell

Petley, Julian (2003) War without death: Responses to distant suffering, *Journal for Crime Conflict and Media*, Vol.1, No. 1 pp 72-85. Available online at www.jc2m.co.uk, accessed on 13 March 2004

Petley, Julian (2004) 'Let the atrocious images haunt us', Miller, David (ed.) *Tell me lies: Propaganda and media distortion in the attack on Iraq*, London: Pluto pp 164-175

Philo, Greg and McLaughlin, Greg (1995) The British media and the Gulf war, Philo, Greg (ed.) *The Glasgow Media Group reader*, Vol. 2, London: Routledge pp 146-156

Phythian, Mark (2003) Arms trade, *Anti-imperialism: A guide for the movement*, London: Bookmarks pp 227-238

Pilger, John (1986) *Heroes*, London: Pan, second edition

Pilger, John (1991a) Who killed the Kurds?, *New Statesman and Society*, 20 March p. 10

Pilger, John (1991b) A one-sided bloodfest, *New Statesman and Society*, 8 March pp 8-9

Pilger, John (1991c) Sins of omission, *New Statesman and Society*, 8 February p. 8

Pilger, John (1991d) The Great British silence: Behind the sanitised media-speak are dead bodies, *Free Press: Journal of the Campaign for Press and Broadcasting Freedom*, January/February p. 1

Pilger, John (1992) Shedding crocodile tears, *New Statesman and Society*, 20 March

Pilger, John (1998) *Hidden agendas*, London: Verso

Pilger, John (1999) Morality? Don't make me laugh, *Guardian*, 20 April

Pilger, John (2001) Britain and America's pilots are blowing the cover on our so-called 'humanitarian' no-fly zones, *New Statesman*, 19 March

Pilger, John (2002) *The new rulers of the world*, London: Verso

Pilger, John (2003) The big lie, *Daily Mirror*, 22 September

Pilger, John (2004a) *Tell me no lies: Investigative journalism and its triumphs*, London: Jonathan Cape

Pilger John (2004b) American terrorist. Available online at www.newstatesman.co.uk, 12 January, accessed on 25 August 2005

Pilger, John (2010) A predatory ideology in denial, *Morning Star*, 27-28 March pp 10-11

Platt, Steve (1991) Casualties of war, *New Statesman and Society*, 22 February pp 12-13

Playsic, Dragam (2003) Balkans, Monbiot, George et al., *Anti-imperialism: A guide for the movement*, London: Bookmarks pp 171-188

Ponsford, Dominic (2015) Former *News of the World* chief reporter reveals 25 years of *Tabloid Secrets* – exclusive book, *Press Gazette*, 15 May. Available online at http://www.pressgazette.co.uk/former-news-world-reporter-neville-thurlbeck-reveals-25-years-tabloid-secrets-exclusive-extracts, accessed on 14 January 2016

Ponting, Clive (1990) *Secrecy in Britain*, Oxford: Blackwell

Ponting, Clive (1994) *Churchill*, London: Sinclair Stevenson

Postman, Neil (1985) *Amusing ourselves to death*, London: William Heinemann

Porter, Gareth (2010) Marja, the city that never was, the *Coldtype Reader* pp 8-9. Available online at http://www.coldtype.net/Assets.10/Pdfs/0410.Reader45.pdf, accessed on 22 May 2010

Powell, Colin (1995) *Soldier's way*, London: Hutchinson (with Joseph E. Persico)

Power, Carla (1991) Writing off Islam, *Index on Censorship*, April/May, London pp 10-11

Prades, John (1986) *President's secret wars: CIA and Pentagon covert operations from World War II through Iranscan*, New York: William Morrow

Prange, Gordon W. (1991) *Pearl Harbor: The verdict of history*, Harmondsworth: Penguin

Prentice, Eve-Ann (1999a) The bomb hit: I thought I was dead, *The Times*, 1 June

Prentice, Eve-Ann (1999b) *The Times*, Goff, Peter (ed.) *The Kosovo news and propaganda war*, Vienna, International Press Institute pp 462-465

Prentice, Eve-Ann (2000) *One woman's war: Life and death on deadline*, London: Duckworth

Preston, Peter (2008) The spooks who ruled the States, *Observer*, 3 February

Preston, Peter (2016) Beware spooks stringing along security reporters, *Observer*, 10 January. Available online at http://www.theguardian.com/world/2016/jan/10/beware-spooks-stringing-along-security-correspondents, accessed on 11 January 2016

Price, Lance (2010) *Where power lies*, London and New York: Simon and Schuster

Prince, Stephen (1993) Celluloid heroes and smart bombs: Hollywood at war in the Middle East, Denton, Robert E. (ed.) *The media and the Persian Gulf war*, New York, Praeger pp 235-256

Project Censored (2003) The most undercovered news in the USA, *Nexus*, December 2003-January 2004 pp 11-18

Private Eye (2016) Nothing special here, No. 1427, 16 September-29 September p. 37

Purvis, Stewart (1991) The media and the Gulf war, *RSA Journal*, Vol. CXXXIX, No. 5423 pp 735-744

Pyle, Richard and Fass, Horst (2003) *Lost over Laos: A true story of tragedy, mystery and friendship*, Cambridge, MA: Da Capo Press

Quigley, John (1992) *The ruses for war: American interventionism since World War Two*, New York: Prometheus

Quinn, Adrian (2011) All roads lead to Assange: WikiLeaks and journalism's duty of care, Mair, John and Keeble, Richard Lance (eds) *Investigative journalism: Dead or alive?*, Bury St Edmunds: Abramis pp 230-243

Rampton, Sheldon and Stauber, John (2003) *Weapons of mass deception: The uses of propaganda in Bush's War on Iraq*, London: Robinson

Ramsay, Robin (2003) A guided democracy, *Lobster*, No. 46 p. 15

Ramsay, Robin (2006 [2000]) *Conspiracy theories*, Harpenden, Herts: Pocket Essentials

Ramsay, Robin (2008) *Politics and paranoia*, Hove: Picnic Publishing

Ramsay, Robin (2009a) Why are we with Uncle Sam?, *Lobster*, No. 57 pp 7-8

Ramsay, Robin (2009b) The miners and the secret state, Williams, Granville (ed.) *Shafted: The media, the miners' strike and the aftermath*, London: Campaign for Press and Broadcasting Freedom pp 73-80

Ramsay, Robin (2016) Oh conspiracy! *Lobster*, Issue 71. Available online at http://www.lobster-magazine.co.uk/free/lobster71/lob71-oh-conspiracy.pdf, accessed on 31 March 2016

Randall, David (2005) *The great reporters*, London: Pluto

Ranelagh, John (1992) *CIA: A history*, London: BBC Books

Rawnsley, Andrew (2000) *Servants of the people: The inside story of New Labour*, London: Hamish Hamilton

Ray, Ellen and Schaap, William H. (1991) Disinformation and covert action, *Covert Action Information Bulletin*, No 37, Summer pp 9-13

Rayment, Sean (2010) The hidden victims of war: 1,000 casualties of the Afghan conflict, *Sunday Telegraph*, 21 February

Reed, Christopher (2014) Ben Bradlee obituary, *Guardian*, 23 October

Reginald, R. and Elliot, Jeffrey M. (1985) *Tempest in a teacup*, San Bernardino, California: Borgo Press

Reich, Bernard (ed.) (1987) *The powers in the Middle East: The ultimate strategic area*, New York: Praeger

Reuter, Christof (2016) Islamic State expands as Libya descends into chaos, *Spiegel Online*, 16 March. Available online at http://www.spiegel.de/international/world/libya-descends-into-chaos-as-islamic-state-expands-a-1081874.html, accessed on 6 November 2016

Reynolds, Charles (1989) *The politics of war: A study of violence in inter-state relations*, London: Harvester Wheatsheaf

Ricks, Thomas E. (2006) *Fiasco: The American military adventure in Iraq*, London: Penguin

Rid, Thomas (2007) *War and media operations: The US military and the press from Vietnam to Iraq*, London and New York: Routledge

Ridley, Yvonne (2001) *In the hands of the Taliban: Her extraordinary story*, London: Robson Books

Rips, Geoffrey (1981) *The campaign against the underground press*, San Francisco: City Lights Books

Risen, James (2006) *State of war*, London: Simon and Schuster

Ritter, Scott (2005a) The coup that wasn't, *Guardian*, 28 September. Available online at https://www.theguardian.com/world/2005/sep/28/iraq.military, accessed on 13 June 2016

Ritter, Scott (2005b) *Iraq confidential: The untold story of America's intelligence conspiracy*, London/New York: I. B. Tauris

Roberts, John (1995) *Visions and mirages: The Middle East in a new era*, Edinburgh, London: Mainstream Publishing

Robins, Kevin and Levidow, Les (1991) The eye of the Storm, *Screen*; London; Vol. 32, No. 3, Autumn pp 324-328

Robinson, Piers (2001) Theorizing the influence of media on world politics: Models of media influence on foreign policy, *European Journal of Communication*, Vol. 16, No. 4 pp 523-544

Robinson, Piers (2002) *The CNN effect: The myth of news, foreign policy and intervention*, London: Routledge

Robinson, Piers (2004) Researching US media-state relations and twenty-first century wars, Allan, Stuart and Zelizer, Barbie (eds) *Reporting war: Journalism in wartime*, London: Routledge pp 96-112

Robinson, Piers, Goddard, Peter, Parry, Katy and Murray, Craig with Taylor, Philip M. (eds) 2010) *Pockets of resistance: British news media, war and theory in the 2003 invasion of Iraq*, Manchester: Manchester University Press

Robinson, Stephen (1996) Gulf War bombs 'were not smart', *Telegraph*, 10 July

Rogers, Ann (1997) *Secrecy and power in the British state: A history of the Official Secrets Act*, London: Pluto Press

Rogers, Ben (1999) *A Life: A .J. Ayer*, London: Chatto & Windus

Rogers, Paul (1991) The myth of the clean war, *Covert Action Information Bulletin*, Washington, No. 37, Summer pp 26-30

Rogers, Paul (1992) Bushbacking: Britain goes to war, Bennis, Phyllis and Moushabeck, Michel (eds) *Beyond the Storm: A Gulf crisis reader*, Edinburgh: Canongate pp 268-279

Rogers, Paul (1994) A note on the British deployment of nuclear weapons in crises with particular reference to the Falklands and Gulf wars and the purpose of Trident, *Lobster*, No. 28 pp 4-6

Rogers, Paul (2006) *A war too far: Iraq, Iran and the New American Century*, London: Pluto Press

Rose, David (2004) Iraqi defectors tricked us with WMD lies, but we must not be fooled again, 30 May, *Observer*. Available online at http://www.guardian.co.uk/media/2004/may/30/Iraqandthemedia.iraq, accessed on 14 October 2006

Rose, David (2007) Spies and their lies, *New Statesman*, 27 September

Rose, John (1986) Israel: The hijack state: America's watchdog in the Middle East, London: Bookmarks

Rose, Stephen (1986) Spend, spend, spend – on military only, *New Statesman*, 3 January pp 11-12

Rose, Steven and Baravi, Abraham (1988) The meaning of Halabja: Chemical warfare in Kurdistan, *Race and Class*, Vol. 30, No. 1 pp 74-77

Roselle, Laura (2006) *Media and the politics of failure: Great powers, Communication strategies and military defeats*, Houndmills, Basingstoke, New York: Palgrave Macmillan

Rosenblum, Mort (1993) *Who stole the news: Why we can't keep up with what happens in the world and what we can do about it*, New York: John Wiley and Sons

Rosenfeld, Nancy Watt (1991) Buried alive, *Lies of Our Time*, October

Rufford, Nicholas (2003) Revealed: How MI6 sold the Iraq war, *Times*, 28 December. Available online at http://www.timesonline.co.uk/tol/news/uk/article839897.ece, accessed on 28 December 2003

Rusbridger, James (1989) *The intelligence game*, London: Bodley Head

Rusbridger, James and Nove, Eric (1991) *Betrayed at Pearl Harbor: How Churchill lured Roosevelt into war*, London: Michael O'Mara

'Ryan, Chris' (pseudonym of SAS member) (1995) *The one that got away*, London: Century

Sabey, Ruth (2002) Disarming the disarmers, Aubrey, Crispin (ed.) *Nukespeak: The media and the bomb*, London: Comedia/Minority Press Group pp 55-63

Sackur, Stephen (1991) The charred bodies at Mutla Ridge, *London Review of Books*, 4 April. Reproduced in MacArthur, Brian (ed.) *Despatches from the Gulf war*, London: Bloomsbury pp 261-267

Sadria, Mojtaba (1992) United States, Japan and the Gulf War, *Monthly Review*, Vol. 43 April pp 1-16

Said, Edward (1981) *Covering Islam: How the media and experts determine how we see the rest of the world*, London: Routledge

Said, Edward (1992) Thoughts on a war: Ignorant armies clash by night, Bennis, Phyllis and Moushabeck, Michel (eds) *Beyond the Storm: A Gulf crisis reader*, Edinburgh: Canongate pp 1-6

Said, Edward (2000) The treason of the intellectuals, Ali, Tariq (ed.) (2000) *Masters of the Universe? Nato's Balkan crusade*, London: Verso

Said, Edward (2003) A window on the world, *Guardian Review*, 2 August

Salinger, Pierre and Laurent, Eric (1991) *Secret dossier: The hidden agenda behind the Gulf War*, Harmondsworth, Middlesex: Penguin

Sampson, Anthony (1992) The anatomy of Britain in 1992, *Independent on Sunday*, 29 March

Sampson, Anthony (2004) *Who runs this place? The anatomy of Britain in the 21st century*, London: John Murray

Sardar, Ziauddin and Davies, Merryl Wynn (2002) *Why do people hate America?*, Cambridge: Icon Books

Saunders, Frances Stonor (1999) *Who paid the piper? The CIA and the cultural cold war*, London: Granta Books

Schechter, Danny (2004) Selling the Iraq War: The media management strategies we never saw, Kamalipour, Yahya R. and Snow, Nancy (eds) *War, media and propaganda: A global perspective*, Oxford: Rowman and Littlefield pp 25-32

Schiller, Herbert I. (1992) Manipulating hearts and minds, Mowlana, Hamid, Gerbner, George and Schiller, Herbert I. (eds) *Triumph of the image: The media's war in the Persian Gulf – a global perspective*, New York: Vintage Books pp 22-29

Schlesinger, Philip (1991) The media politics of siege management, *Media, state and nation: Political violence and collective identities*, London: Sage pp 29-59

Schlesinger, Philip, Murdock, Graham and Elliott, Philip (1983) *Televising terrorism: Political violence in popular culture*, London: Comedia Publishing Group

Schorr, Daniel (1991) Ten days that shook the White House, *Columbia Journalism Review*, July/August pp 21-23

Schostak, John (1993) *Dirty marks: The education of self, media and popular culture*, London: Pluto

Schudson, Michael (1995) *The power of news*, Boston, Mass.: Harvard University Press

Schwarzkopf, General Norman H. (1992) *It doesn't take a hero*, London/New York: Bantam Press

Scott, Jake (2008) *Blood clot: In combat with the Patrols Platoon, 3 Para, Afghanistan, 2006*, Solihull: Helion and Company

Seager, Joni (1992) Torching the earth, *New Internationalist*, October pp 24-26

Searle, Chris (1989) *Your daily dose: Racism and the* Sun, London: Campaign for Press and Broadcasting Freedom

Seaton, Jean (2015) War on the BBC, *Guardian*, 21 February. Available online at https://www.theguardian.com/books/2015/feb/20/bbc-war-margaret-thatcher-life-on-earth-grange-hill-eastenders-falklands, accessed on 13 June 2015

Sebba, Anna (1994) *Battling for news: The rise of the woman reporter*, London: Hodder and Stoughton

Segaller, Stephen (1986) *Invisible armies: Terrorism in the 1990s*, London: Michael Joseph

Seib, Philip (2004) *Beyond the front lines: How the news media cover a world shaped by war*, New York: Palgrave Macmillan

Seldon, Anthony (2005) *Blair*, London: Simon and Schuster

Seldon, Anthony (2007) *Blair unbound*, London: Simon and Schuster

Sengupta, Kim (2010a) Army given new rifles to engage enemies from further away, *Independent*, 7 June

Sengutpa, Kim (2010b) Warning to politicians about early Afghan troop pull-out, *Independent*, 28 May

Sengupta, Kim (2010c) British military split over plans to move troops to Kandahar, *Independent*, 27 April

Sengupta, Kim and Morris, Nigel (2010) Afghan war is bad for security, voters say, *Independent*, 11 November

Serfati, Claude (2003) Militarism and imperialism in the 21st century, *International Viewpoint*, March. Available online at http://www.3bh.org.uk/IV?Issues?2003?IV348%20 0!.htm, accessed on 3 June 2004

Servaes, Jan (1991) Was Grenada a testcase for 'disinformation war'?, *Media Development*, October pp 41-44

Shah, Saeed (2010) Taliban arrest in Pakistan amid talk of policy shift, *Guardian*, 19 February

Shallice, Jane (2009) Afghanistan: A brief history, *Red Pepper*, No. 166, June/July pp 15-16

Shaw, Ibrahim Seaga (2012) *Human rights journalism: Advances in reporting distant humanitarian interventions*, London: Palgrave Macmillan

Shaw, Martin (1987) Rise and fall of the military-democratic state 1940-1985, Shaw, Martin and Creighton, Colin (eds) *The sociology of war and peace*, London: Pluto pp 143-158

Shaw, Martin (1991) *Post military society*, Cambridge: Polity Press

Shaw, Martin (1996) *Civil society and media in global crises: Representing distant violence*, London: Pinter

Shaw, Martin and Carr-Hill, Roy (1991) *Mass media attitudes to the Gulf War in Britain*. Paper presented to EPOP conference, Oxford, 28 September

Shelden, Michael (1991) *Orwell: The authorized biography*, London: Heinemann

Sherwood, Ben (1992) That first Patriot scored a hit – on a cloud, *International Herald Tribune*, 25 September

Shirley, John (2015) Obituary: Admiral Sir Jeremy Black, *Guardian*, 17 December

Simons, Geoff (1992) 'Honest' Perot's Irangate secret, *Socialist*, 17 July

Simons, Geoff (1994) *From Sumer to Saddam*, London, New York: St Martin's Press

Simpson, John (1991a) *From the house of war*, London: Arrow Books

Simpson, John (1991b) Surviving in the ruins, *Spectator*, 10 August pp 8-10

Simpson, John (1998) *Strange places, questionable people*, London: Pan Books

Simpson, John (2004) *The wars against Saddam: Taking the hard road to Baghdad*, London: Pan

Simpson, John (2010) *Unreliable sources*, London: Macmillan

Simpson, Paul (2013) *A brief history of the spy: Modern spying from the Cold War to the War on Terror*, London: Constable and Robinson

Sisman, Adam (2015) *John le Carré: The biography*, London: Bloomsbury

Skey, Michael (2006) 'Undue reverence': Questioning national identities in the media coverage of the 1982 Falklands war. Available online at http://www.falklands-malvinas. com/skey.htm, accessed on 19 November 2006

Sloyan, Patrick (1991) The silver bullet in Desert Storm, *Guardian*, 23 May

Smiljanic, Natassja (1999) A licence to bomb, *Socialist Review*, No. 232, July/August p. 10

Smith, Dan and Smith, Ron (1983) *The economics of militarism*, London: Pluto

Smith, Hendrick (ed.) *The media and the Gulf War*, Washington: Seven Locks

Smith, James (2015) *British writers and MI5 surveillance 1930-1960*, Cambridge: Cambridge University Press

Smith, Jean Edward (1992) *George Bush's war*, New York: Henry Holt

Smith, Jeffery A. (1999) *War and press freedom: The problem of prerogative power*, Oxford and New York: Oxford University Press

Snoddy, Raymond (1992) *The good, the bad and the unacceptable: The hard news about the British press*, London: Faber and Faber

Solomon, Norman (2007) *War made easy: Presidents and pundits keep spinning us to death*, Hoboken, New Jersey: John Wiley and Sons

Southwell, David (2005) *Secrets and lies: Exposing the world of cover-ups and lies*, London: Sevenoaks

Spaven, Malcolm (1991a) A piece of the action: The use of US bases in Britain, Thompson, Edward and Kaldor, Mary (eds) *Mad dogs: The US raids on Libya*, London: Pluto pp 16-34

Spaven, Malcolm (1991b) Too close to the ground, *Guardian*, 27 January

Spencer, Graham (2005) *The media and peace: From Vietnam to the 'war on terror'*, Houndmills, Hampshire: Palgrave Macmillan

Steele, Jonathan (2011) *Ghosts of Afghanistan: Hard truth and foreign myths*, London: Portobello Books

Steiner, George (1971) In Bluebeard's castle, *Listener*, 15 April pp 472-479

Stephen, Andrew (2003) America, *New Statesman*, 4 August

Stephen, Chris and Black, Ian (2014) High ambition of the renegade general who blazed across Libya, *Guardian*, 23 May

Stiglitz, Joseph and Bilmes, Linda (2009) *The three trillion dollar war*, London: Penguin

Stinnett, Robert B. (2000) *Day of deceit: The truth about FDR and Pearl Harbor*, New York: Simon and Schuster

Stockholm International Peace Research Institute (1988) *Iran-Iraq war 1980-1988: Military costs and arms trade*, Stockholm: SIPRI

Stockwell, John (1991) *The Praetorian Guard: The US role in the New World Order*, Boston: South End Press

Stone, Andrew (2004) Casualties of war; London, *Socialist Review,* March pp 11-13

Stone, Oliver and Kuznick, Peter (2013) *The untold history of the United States*, London: Ebury Press

Stork, Joe (1986) Oil, arms and the Gulf War, *Khamsin* pp 19-26

Stork, Joe (1995) The Middle East arms bazaar after the Gulf War, *Middle East Review*, Washington DC, November/December pp 11-18

Stork, Joe and Lesch, Ann (1990) Why war? Background to the crisis, *Merip*, No 167, November/December pp 11-18

Strange, Hannah (2009) We were starved, tortured and killed by our own officers, say Falklands war conscripts, *Times*, 18 June

Sturcke, James (2008) SAS commander quits in Snatch Land Rover row, *Guardian*, 1 November. Available online at http://www.guardian.co.uk/uk/2008/nov/01/sas-commander-quits-afghanistan, accessed on 1 May 2009

Sultan, Khaled Bin (1995) *Desert warrior: A personal view of the Gulf War by the Joint Forces Commander* (with Seale, Patrick), London: HarperCollins

Sutherland, John (2016) *Orwell's nose: A pathological biography*, London: Reaktion Books

Sutton, Anthony C. (1976) *Wall Street and the rise of Hitler*, Sudbury, Suffolk: Bloomfield Books

Swain, Jon (2003) Why the reporter is the last bastion of truth, *Observer*, 16 March; reproduced from the *British Journalism Review*, Vol. 14, No. 1 pp 23-29

Sylvester, Judith and Huffman, Suzanne (2005) *Reporting from the front: The media and the military*, Oxford/New York: Rowman and Littlefield

Tanzer, Michael (1992) Oil and the Gulf crisis, Bennis, Phyllis and Moushabeck, Michel (eds) *Beyond the Storm: A Gulf crisis reader*, Edinburgh: Canongate pp 263-267

Tarock, Adam (1996) US-Iran relations: Heading for confrontation, *Third World Quarterly*, Vol. 17, No. 1 pp 149-167

Taylor, John (1991) *War photography: Realism in the British press*, London: Routledge

Taylor, John (1998) *Body Horror: Photojournalism, catastrophe and war*, Manchester: Manchester University Press

Taylor, Matthew (2009) Kidnapped *Guardian* journalist released, *Guardian*, 17 December

Taylor, Philip (1992) *War and the media: Propaganda and persuasion in the Gulf War*, Manchester: Manchester University Press

Taylor, Robert (1970) The Campaign for Nuclear Disarmament, Bogdanor, Vernon and Skidelsky, Robert (eds) *The age of affluence 1951-1964*, Basingstoke/London: Macmillan pp 221-253

Teimourian, Hazhir (1988) Silence deep as death, *New Statesman and Society*, 16 September pp 20-22

Thee, Marek (1980) Militarism and militarisation in contemporary international relations, Elde, Asbjorn and Thee, Marek (eds) *Problems of contemporary militarism*, London: Croom Held pp 15-35

Thomas, Gordon (2009) *Inside British intelligence: 100 years of MI5 and MI6*, London: JR Books

Thomas, Hugh (1967) *The Suez affair*, London: Weidenfeld and Nicolson

Thomas, Nigel and Mikulan, Krunoslav (2006) *The Yugoslav wars: Bosnia, Kosovo and Macdedonia 1992-2001*, Oxford: Osprey Publishing

Thomas, Rosamund M. (1991) *Espionage and secrecy: The Official Secrets Acts 1911-1989 of the United Kingdom*, London: Routledge

Thompson, Edward P. (1980) *Writing by candlelight*, London: Merlin Press

Thompson, Edward P. (1982) Notes on exterminism: The last stage of civilisation, *Exterminism and the Cold War*, London: Verso pp 151-163

Thomson, Alex (1992) *Smokescreen: The media, censors, the Gulf*, Tunbridge Wells: Laburnum Books

Thursby, Rowena (2004) Operation Rockingham, *globalresearch.ca*, 31 July. Available online at http://www.globalresearch.ca/articles/THU407A.html, accessed on 22 August 2016

Thussu, Daya Kishan (2000) Nato's first war and the transformation of the Western security alliance, *Javnost/The Public: The Journal of the European Institute for Communication and Culture*, Vol 7, No. 3 pp 5-18

Thussu, Daya (2007) *The news as entertainment: The rise of global infotainment*, London: Sage

Thussu, Daya Kishan and Freedman, Des (eds) *War and the media reporting 24/7*, London: Sage

Timmerman, Kenneth R. (1992) *The death lobby: How the West armed Iraq*, London: Fourth Estate

Tisdall, Simon (2010) World briefing: Back in the dock: Why the Americans still fear Noriega, *Guardian*, 29 April

Todd, Paul and Bloch, Jonathan (2003) *Global intelligence: The world's secret services today*, London: Zed Books

Todd, Paul, Bloch, Jonathan and Fitzgerald, Patrick (2009) *Spies, lies and the war on terror*, London and New York: Zed Books

Toffler, Alvin and Toffler, Heidi (1995) *War and anti-war: Making sense of today's global chaos*, London: Warner Books

Tomlin, Julie (2008) US short on answers, *Press Gazette*, 18 April

Traber, Michael and Davies, Ann (1991) Ethics of war reporting, *Media Development*, October pp 7-9

Trainor, Lt Gen. Bernard E. (1991) The military and the media: A troublesome embrace, Smith, Hendrick (ed.) *The media and the Gulf War*, Washington: Seven Locks pp 69-80

Travis, Alan (2005) How Britain averted a Falklands invasion in 1977, *Guardian*, 1 June

Travis, Alan (2008) Revealed: Britain's secret propaganda war against al-Qaida, *Guardian*, 26 August

Trelford, Donald (2009) The spying game, *Independent*, 14 September

Treverton, Gregory F. (1987) *Covert action: The CIA and the limits of American intervention in the post-war world*, London: I.B. Tauris and Co Ltd

TUCND (n.d.) *War on Iraq: Not in our name*, Carlisle: TUCND

Tunander, Ola (2009) Democratic state vs. deep state: Approaching the dual state of the West, Wilson, Eric (ed.) *Government of the shadows: Parapolitcs and criminal sovereignty*, London: Pluto pp 56-72

Turner, Alwyn W. (2010) *Rejoice! Rejoice! Britain in the 1980s*, London: Aurum

Turner, John (2006) Powerful information, Keeble, Richard (ed.) *The newspapers handbook*, Abingdon, Oxon: Routledge, fourth edition pp 164-191

Turse, Nick (2008) The trillion dollar tag sale, 26 October. Available online at http://www.nickturse.com/articles/tom_trillion.html, accessed on 1 May 2009

Turse, Nick (2013) *Kill anything that moves: The real American war in Vietnam*, New York: Picador

Turse, Nick (2015) US Special Ops forces deployed in 135 nations, *tomdispatch.com*, 24 September. Available online at http://mondediplo.com/openpage/u-s-special-ops-forces-deployed-in-135-nations, accessed on 23 August 2016

Turse, Nick and Engelhardt, Tom (2010) Shooting gnats with a machine gun, 14 January. Available online at www.tomdispatch.com/dialogs/print/?id=175191, accessed on 1 December 2015

Undercover (1993) Libya, No. 2, February/March pp 42-48

Urban, Mark (1996) *UK Eyes Alpha: The inside story of British intelligence*, London: Faber

Urban, Mark (2011) *Task Force Black: The explosive true story of the SAS and the secret war in Iraq*, London: Abacus

Urry, John (2002) *Sociology beyond societies: Mobilities for the twenty-first century*, London: Routledge

Usborne, David (2011a) 'Eccentric Gadaffi' leak sees US envoy sent home, *Independent*, 7 January

Usborne, David (2011b) Revealed: The CIA mastermind who cornered bin Laden, *Independent*, 6 July

Vallely, Paul (2003) The US general waiting to replace Saddam, *Independent*, 5 April

Van Alstyne, Richard W. (1974) *The rising American empire*, New York: Norton

Van Auken, Bill (2016) US has spent nearly $5 trillion on wars since 9/11, *wsws.org*, 14 September. Available online at http://www.wsws.org/en/articles/2016/09/14/wars-s14.html, accessed on 14 September 2016

Van Evera, Stephen (1991) American intervention in the Third World, *Security Studies*, London, Vol. 1, No. 1 Autumn pp 1-24

Vaux, Kenneth L. (1992) *Ethics and the Gulf War: Religion, rhetoric and righteousness*, Boulder, San Francisco: Westview Press

Verkaik, Robert (2009) Britain offered Gaddafi £14m to stop supporting the IRA, *Independent*, 5 October

Verkaik, Robert (2016) Why we need an ombudsman for extremism, *Guardian*, 27 January. Available online at http://www.theguardian.com/commentisfree/2016/jan/27/ombudsman-for-extremism-mohammed-emwazi-jihadi-john-mi5-grievances, accessed on 27 January 2016

Vidal, Gore (1991) The national security state, *A view from the diners club*, London: André Deutsch pp 174-180

Vidal, Gore (2002) *Perpetual war for perpetual peace: How we got to be so hated*, New York: Thunder's Mouth Press/Nation Books

Vidal, Gore (2003) *Dreaming war: Blood for oil and the Cheney-Bush junta*, New York: Clairview

Vine, David (2016) Doubling down on a failed strategy: The Pentagon's dangerous new base policy, *tomdispatch.com*, 14 January. Available online at http://www.tomdispatch.com/post/176090/tomgram%3A_david_vine%2C_enduring_bases%2C_enduring_war_in_the_middle_east/#more, accessed on 23 August 2016

Vinen, Richard (2009) *Thatcher's Britain: The politics and social upheaval of the 1980s*, London: Simon and Schuster

Vulliamy, Ed (2016) How a US president and J. P. Morgan created the state of Panama – and turned it into a tax haven, *Observer*, 10 April

Waal, Alex de (2003) The wrong lessons: The vanishing legacy of Operation Restore Hope, *Boston Review*, December/January 2004. Available online at http://bostonreview.net/BR28.6/dewaal.html, accessed on 14 October 2008

Walker, Peter (2013) Questioning of spy agency chiefs 'wouldn't have scared a puppy', *Guardian*, 7 November. Available online at http://www.theguardian.com/world/2013/nov/07/questioning-spy-chiefs-wouldnt-scared-puppy, accessed on 14 January 2016

Walker, Tim (2013) CIA finally comes clean over its agents' role in Iran coup, *i*, 20 August

Walker, Tom and Laverty, Aidan (2000) CIA aided Kosovo guerrilla army, *Sunday Times*, 21 March

Wallace, William (1970) World without tears, Bogdanor, Vernon and Skidelsky, Robert (eds) *The age of affluence 1951-1964*, London: Macmillan pp 192-220

Walsh, Edward (1991) As brave as Stallone....Beautiful as Brooke Shields, *Washington Post*, 6 March

Walton, Calder (2013) *Empire of secrets: British intelligence, the Cold War and the twilight of empire*, London: William Collins

Wasdin, Howard E. and Templin, Stephen (2011) *Seal Team Six: An incredible story of an elite sniper – and the special operations unit that killed Osama bin Laden*, London: Sphere

Watson, Roland (2013) Denis dried wife's tears during darkest hours of conflict, *Times*, 22 April

Weaver, Matthew (2015) How Yvonne Fletcher's killer was allowed to 'go free' for 30 years, *Guardian*, 19 November. Available online at http://www.theguardian.com/uk-news/2015/nov/19/yvonne-fletcher-killer-free-30-years-libya, accessed on 11 January 2013

Webster, Frank (2003) Information warfare in an age of globalization, *War and the media* (eds) Thussu, Daya Kishan and Freeman, Des, London: Sage pp 57-86

Weeks, John and Gunson, Phil (1991) *Panama: Made in the USA*, London: Latin American Bureau

Weiner, Tim (1996) Smart arms in the Gulf War are found overrated, *International Herald Tribune*, 10 July

Weisbrot, Mark (2007) Holocaust denial, American style, *AlterNet*, 21 November

Weitz, Katy (2003) Why I quit the *Sun*, *Guardian*, 31 March

Wells, Donald A. (1967) *The war myth*, New York: Pegasus

West, W. J. (1992) *The larger evils: Nineteen Eighty-Four: The truth behind the satire*, Edinburgh: Canongate

Wheen, Francis (2004) *How mumbo-jumbo conquered the world*, London: Harper Perennial

Whiting, Charles (1999) *Hemingway goes to war*, Stroud: Sutton

Wilford, Hugh (2008) *The mighty Wurlitzer: How the CIA played America*, Cambridge, Massachusetts, London: Harvard University Press

Wilkinson, Nicholas (2009) *Secrecy and the media: The official history of the United Kingdom's D-Notice system*, London: Routledge

Willetts, David (2010) A wing and a prayer, *Sun*, 7 June

Williams, Kevin (1987) Vietnam: The first living-room war, Mercer, Derrick (ed.) *The fog of war*, London: Heinemann pp 213-260

Williams, Kevin (1993) The light at the end of the tunnel: The mass media, public opinion and the Vietnam War, Eldridge, John (ed.) *Getting the message: News, truth and power*, London: Routledge pp 305-328

Williams, Reece (ed.) (1987) *Unwinding the Vietnam War: From war to peace*, for the Washington Project for the Arts, Seattle, WA: The Real Comet Press

Williams, Ryan T. (2011) Dangerous precedent: America's illegal war in Afghanistan. Available online at https://www.law.upenn.edu/journals/jil/articles/volume33/issue2/Williams33U.Pa.J.Int'lL.563(2011).pdf, accessed on 30 November 2015

Wills, Garry (1988) *Reagan's America: Innocents at home*, London: Heinemann

Wilson, Eric (ed.) (2009) *Government of the shadows: Parapolitics and criminal sovereignty*, London: Pluto Press

Wintour, Patrick and Norton-Taylor, Richard (2010) Commanders fear Taliban infiltration as troops hunt assassin, *Guardian*, 11 May

Wolfe, Gregory (1995) *Malcolm Muggeridge: A biography*, London: Hodder and Stoughton

Wolff, Michael (2003) I was only asking, *Guardian*, 14 April

Woodcock, Andrew (2003) Parliament urged to probe 'disinformation operation', *PA*, 21 November

Woodward, Bob (1987) *Veil: The secret wars of the CIA*, London: Simon and Schuster

Woodward, Bob (1991) *The commanders*, New York/London: Simon and Schuster

Woodward, Bob (2004) *Plan of attack*, London: Simon and Schuster/Pocket Books

Woodward, Gary C. (1993) The rules of the game: The military and the press in the Gulf War, Denton, Robert E. (ed.) *The media and the Persian Gulf War*, Westport, CT: Praeger pp 1-26

Woolf, Marie (2004) Shredded! Hundreds of thousands of government documents are destroyed in the great Freedom of Information Act scandal, *Independent*, 23 December. Available online at http://www.independent.co.uk/news/uk/politics/shredded-hundreds-of-thousands-of-government-documents-8004480.html, accessed on 20 September 2016

Worcester, Robert (1991) *British public opinion: A guide to the history and methodology of public opinion polling*, Oxford: Basil Blackwell

Workneh, Tewodros W. (2011) War journalism or peace journalism? A case study of US and British newspapers coverage of the Somali conflict, *Global Media Journal: Mediterranean Edition*, Vol. 6, No. 1 pp 40-49. Available online at http://globalmedia.emu.edu.tr/index.php?option=com_content&view=article&id=91:spring-2011&catid=48:archive&Itemid=60, accessed on 16 September 2016

Wright Mills, C. (1956) *The power elite*, Oxford: Oxford University Press

Wright, Patrick (2000) *Tank: The progress of a monstrous war machine*, London: Faber and Faber

Wright, Peter (1987) *Spycatcher*, New York: Dell Publishing Group. Available online at https://wikispooks.com/w/images/a/a5/Spycatcher.pdf, accessed on 15 June 2016

Wybrow, Robert (1991) *The Gulf crisis: A political perspective*, International Journal of Public Opinion Research, Vol. 3, No. 3 pp 260-276. Available online at https://ijpor.oxfordjournals.org/content/3/3/local/front-matter.pdf, accessed on 21 September 2016

Wynne-Jones, Ros (1996) Orwell's little list leaves the left gasping for more, *Independent*, 14 July

Yallop, David (1994) *To the ends of the earth: The hunt for the Jackal*, London: Corgi

Yant, Martin (1991) *Desert mirage: The true story of the Gulf War*, Buffalo, New York: Prometheus

Yapp, Robin (2013) Britain discussed giving Argentina a Falklands base on eve of conflict, *Times*, 21 February

Young, Hugo (1989) *One of us*, London: Macmillan

Yousif, Sami (1992) The Iraqi US war: A conspiracy theory, Bresheeth, Haim and Yuval-Davis, Nira (eds) *The Gulf war and the new world order*, London: Zed Books pp 51-66

Zollmann, Florian (2009) Is it either or? Professional ideology v. corporate media constraints, *Westminster Papers in Communication and Culture*, Vol. 6, No. 2 pp 97-118

Index

www.ingramcontent.com/pod-product-compliance
Lightning Source LLC
Chambersburg PA
CBHW070544270326
41926CB00013B/2199